Study Guide
to Accompany
McConnell

ECONOMICS

SEVENTH EDITION
Study Guide to Accompany McConnell

ECONOMICS

ROBERT C. BINGHAM
Professor of Economics
Kent State University

McGraw-Hill Book Company
New York St. Louis San Francisco Auckland Bogotá Düsseldorf Johannesburg
London Madrid Mexico Montreal New Delhi Panama Paris São Paulo
Singapore Sydney Tokyo Toronto

Study Guide to Accompany McConnell

ECONOMICS

ISBN   0-07-044915-5

 34567890 BABA 7832109

This book was set in Helvetica by Monotype
Composition Company, Inc. The editors were
J. S. Dietrich, Marjorie Singer, and Edwin Hanson;
the text designer was Merrill Haber; the cover was
designed by Betty Binns; the production supervisor was
Leroy A. Young. New drawings were done by
J & R Services, Inc.
George Banta Company, Inc., was printer and binder.

TO PQK

CONTENTS

THE ECONOMICS OF THE FIRM AND RESOURCE ALLOCATION

CURRENT ECONOMIC PROBLEMS

INTERNATIONAL ECONOMICS AND THE WORLD ECONOMY

HOW TO USE THE STUDY GUIDE TO LEARN ECONOMICS

This *Study Guide* is designed to help you read and understand Campbell R. McConnell's textbook, *Economics: Principles, Problems, and Policies,* Seventh Edition. If used properly, a guide can be a great aid to you in what is probably your first course in economics.

No one pretends that the study of economics is easy, but it can be made easier. Of course a study guide will not do your work for you, and its use is no substitute for reading the text. You must be willing to read the text, spend time on the subject, and work at learning if you wish to understand economics.

Many students do read their text and work hard on their economics course and still fail to learn the subject. This is because principles of economics is a new subject for them, and they have had no previous experience in learning economics. They want to learn but do not know just how to go about it. Here is where the *Study Guide* can come to their assistance. Let us first see what the *Study Guide* contains and then how to use it.

WHAT THE STUDY GUIDE IS

The *Study Guide* contains forty-five chapters—one for each chapter in the text—, an *answer section,* and a *glossary.* Each of the chapters has eight parts.

1. An *introduction* explains what is in the chapter of the text and how its subject matter is related to material in earlier and later chapters. It points out topics to which you should give special attention, and reemphasizes difficult or important principles and facts.
2. A *checklist* tells you the things you should be able to do when you have finished the chapter.
3. A *chapter outline* shows how the chapter is organized and summarizes briefly the essential points made in the chapter.

4. A list of the *important terms and concepts* found in the chapter points out what you must be able to define in order to understand the material in the chapter. A definition of each of these terms and concepts will be found in the glossary at the end of the *Study Guide.*
5. *Fill-in questions* (short-answer and list questions) help you to learn and remember the crucial and important generalizations and facts in the chapter.
6. *Problems and projects* assist you in learning and understanding economic relationships and get you to think about certain economic problems.
7. *Objective questions* (true-false and multiple-choice) can be used to test yourself on the material in the chapter.
8. *Discussion questions* can be used to test yourself, to identify important questions in the chapter, and to prepare for examinations.

HOW TO STUDY AND LEARN WITH THE HELP OF THE STUDY GUIDE

For best results, quickly read the introduction, outline, list of terms and concepts, and checklist in the *Study Guide* before you read the chapter in the text. Then read the chapter in the text slowly, keeping one eye on the outline and the list of terms and concepts. Always read with pencil in hand and use your textbook as if you expected to sell it for wastepaper at the end of the year. The outline in the *Study Guide* contains only the major points in the chapter. Outline the chapter as you read it by identifying the major *and the minor* points and by placing appropriate numbers or letters (such as I or A or 1 or a) in the margins. It is also wise to underline the major and minor points in the chapter and to circle important terms and concepts. When you have completed the chapter, you will have the chapter outlined and your underlining will give you a set of notes on the chapter. It is not necessary to keep a separate notebook for textbook notes or outlines. Be careful to underline only the really important or summary statements.

After you have read the chapter in the text through once, turn again to the introduction, outline, and list of terms and concepts in the *Study Guide.* Reread the introduction and outline. Does everything there make sense? If not, return to the text and reread the topics that you do not remember well or that still confuse you. Look at the outline. Try to recall each of the minor topics or points that were contained in the text under each of the major points in the outline. When you come to the list of terms and concepts, go over them one by one. Define or explain each to yourself and then look for the definition of the term or concept either in the text chapter or in the glossary. Compare your own definition or explanation with that in the text or glossary. The quick way to find the definition of a term or concept in the text is to look in the index of the text for the page or pages on which that term or concept is mentioned. Make any correction or change in your own definition or explanation that is necessary.

When you have done all this, you will have a pretty fair general idea of what is in the text chapter. Now take a look at the short-answer questions, the problems and projects, and the objective questions. Tackle each of these three sections one at a time, using the following procedure. (1) Answer as many questions as you can without looking in the text or in the answer section. (2) Check the text for whatever help you need. It is a good idea to do more than merely look for answers in the text; reread any section for which you were not able to answer questions. (3) Then consult the answer section for the correct answers and reread any section of the text for which you missed questions.

The questions in these three sections are not all of equal difficulty. Do not expect to get them all right the first time. Some are designed to pinpoint things of importance which you will probably miss the first time you read the text and to get you to read about them again. None of the questions is unimportant. Even those that have no definite answers will bring you to grips with many important economic questions and increase your understanding of economic principles and problems.

In answering the discussion questions—for which no answers are given—it is not necessary to write out answers. All you need to do is mentally outline your answer. For the more difficult discussion questions you may want to write out a brief outline of the answer or a full answer. Do not avoid the difficult questions just because they are more work. Answering these questions is often the most valuable work a student can do toward acquiring an understanding of economic relationships and principles.

Before you turn to the next chapter in the text and *Study Guide,* return to the checklist. Note that this is a list which tells you the "very least you should be able to do when you have finished" a chapter. If you cannot honestly check off each of the items in the list, you have not done the *minimum* amount of work needed. If you can do each of the things on the list, you have at least learned the minimum amount expected of you by the author of the text and your course instructor.

SOME FINAL WORDS

Perhaps the method of using the *Study Guide* outlined above seems like a lot of work. It is. Study and learning necessarily entail work on your part. This is a fact you must accept if you are to learn economics.

After you have used the *Study Guide* to study three or four chapters, you will find that some sections are of more value to you than others. Let your own experience determine how you will use it. But do not discontinue use of the *Study Guide* after three or four chapters merely because you are not sure whether it is helping you. Stick with it.

In addition to the material in the *Study Guide,* there are questions at the end of each chapter in the text. Some of these questions are similar to questions in the *Study Guide,* but none is identical. It will be worthwhile for you to examine all the questions at the end of each chapter and to work out or outline answers for them. The student who has trouble with the problems in the *Study Guide* will find the end-of-chapter problems useful in determining whether he has actually mastered his difficulties. All students will find many of the end-of-chapter questions more thought-provoking than the discussion questions in the *Study Guide.*

For those of you who either have trouble with or wish to learn more rapidly the sections of the text containing explanations of economic theory (or principles), let me recommend my *Economic Concepts: A Programmed Approach.* A programmed book is a learning device which speeds and increases comprehension. Its use will greatly expand your understanding of economics.

After six editions it is time that I record in print the names of those who have helped me with this book. In addition to the students who made suggestions for improving the guide (often by pointing out the errors that I had made) and the instructors who gave me their critical (and often warranted) comments, Campbell R. McConnell encouraged me, Fred R. Kucera reviewed my work, and Jerry L. Petr produced the behavioral objectives which are the foundation of the checklists found in this edition of the *Study Guide.*

Robert C. Bingham

Study Guide
to Accompany
McConnell
ECONOMICS

The Nature and Method of Economics

Chapter 1 introduces the reader to the study of economics. Its aim is to explain the subject matter of economics and the methods economists employ in the study of this subject matter.

While this chapter attempts to indicate the value to be derived from the study of economics and the importance of economic questions and problems to every individual, the heart of the chapter is the discussion of economic principles. Economic principles are generalizations based on facts; but, because the subject matter of economics is human behavior and because the economist cannot employ laboratory experiments to test his generalizations, these principles are always imprecise and subject to exceptions. Economics is a science but it is not an exact science.

If the study of economics is to be of any worth to a student, it is necessary to understand from the very beginning that economic principles are simplifications—approximations—of a very complex real world and that both the formulation and application of these principles present many opportunities for the making of serious mistakes. Economic principles are not the answers to economic questions but are tools—intellectual tools—for analyzing economic problems and finding policies to solve these problems. Selection of the economic policies to follow depends not only upon economic principles but also upon the value judgments of society—that is, upon the goals of the economy.

Pages 13 to 18 of the textbook outline a few of the almost innumerable errors of commission and omission of which the beginner in economics ought to beware. The study of economics is difficult enough without compounding the difficulty with emotional, logical, and semantical errors.

■ CHECKLIST

The very least you should be able to do when you have finished this chapter is:

□ Give two (allegedly) good reasons for studying economics.

□ Define descriptive economics.

□ Explain what an economic principle is and how economic principles are obtained.

□ List the two important characteristics of every economic principle and explain each of these characteristics.

□ Accurately construct a graph of two variables based on numerical data presented to you.

□ Identify the three dangers of economic models.

□ Explain what an economic policy is.

□ Explain the two ways in which economic principles are valuable.

□ Identify the six economic goals.

□ State several reasons for dissatisfaction with the accomplishments of economics.

□ Recognize the "pitfalls to straight thinking" when confronted with examples of them.

■ CHAPTER OUTLINE

1. Citizens in a democracy must understand elementary economics in order to understand the present-day problems of their society and to make intelligent decisions when they vote. Economics is an academic rather than a vocational subject, but a knowledge of it is valuable to businessmen, consumers, and workers.

2. Economists gather relevant facts to obtain economic principles that may be used to formulate policies which will solve economic problems.

a. Descriptive economics is the gathering of relevant facts about the production, exchange, and consumption of goods and services.

b. Economic theory is the analysis of the facts and the derivation of economic principles. These principles are generalizations and abstractions (or approximations) of reality.

c. Policy economics is the combination of economic principles and economic values (or goals) to control economic events.

3. Economists in recent decades have rapidly expanded our economic knowledge; but a number of people have, for a variety of reasons, criticized economics.

4. Straight thinking in the study and use of economic principles requires strict application of the rules of logic—rules in which personal emotions are irrelevant, if not detrimental. There are many pitfalls encountered in studying and applying economic principles.

■ IMPORTANT TERMS

Descriptive economics	Economic theory (analysis)
Economic principle (law)	Generalization

Economic model	Emotionally loaded terminology
Abstraction	Dual terminology
"Other things equal" assumption	Social point of view
Directly related	Fallacy of composition
Inversely related	Macroeconomics
Induction	Microeconomics
Deduction	*Post hoc, ergo propter hoc* fallacy
Applied (policy) economics	Correlation
Economy policy	Causation
Value judgment	Intentions vs. realizations
Mutually exclusive goals	Expectations (anticipations)

■ FILL-IN QUESTIONS

1. The study of economics is the study of the ___Prudvction___, ___exchange___, and ___Consumtion___ of goods and services.

2. Economic principles are ___generalizations___ concerning man's economic behavior and as such necessarily involve ___abstractions___ from reality.

3. Economic laws are imprecise and subject to exceptions because ___individuals and institutions act in different ways___

4. Economic principles enable the economist to predict the result of a certain economic act or of certain economic behavior; this ability to predict is valuable because it makes it possible to ___predict and prepare and control events___

5. Six widely accepted economic goals in the United States are ___Economic Growth, Full emp.___ ___Price Stab.___, ___Econ. Feedom___, ___equal distribution of income___ ___Econ. Security___ and ___

6. The three steps involved in the formulation of economic policy are:

a. ___Clear Statement of Goals___

b. _recognize (alternate effects of policy_

c. _evaluate policies and improve_

7. What three dangers are inherent in the construction and application of economic models?

a. _distinguish relevant and irrelevant facts_

b. _too technical_

c. _re ethnic neutrality_

8. The correct economic policy to employ to-day to achieve a given end may be inappropriate for the achievement of the same end tomorrow because _our economy_ _is a dynamic, changing organism_

9. Economists often use "dual terminology." This means that they _use two labels for the same thing_

10. Macroeconomics is concerned with the _total_ output of the economy and the _general_ level of prices, while microeconomics is concerned with output in a(n) _individual industry_ and the price of a(n) _particular product_

■ PROBLEMS AND PROJECTS

1. "In 1975 the Russian demand for wheat in the United States increased and caused the price of wheat throughout the United States to rise." This is a *specific* instance of a more *general* economic principle. Of which economic *generalization* is this a particular example? _____

_____

_____

2. Following is a list of economic and non-ecomomic factors which may or may not be related to the number of automobiles produced in the United States in a year and the average price at which the automobiles are sold. In the space to the right of each factor indicate whether you think the factor is rele-

vant (R) or irrelevant (I) and whether in your opinion the factor is economic (E) or non-economic (N).

a. The cost of living in Detroit _____

b. The price of the rotary engine Mazda _____

c. The attitude of the oil-producing nations toward the foreign policies of the United States _____

d. The average price of stocks on the New York Stock Exchange _____

e. The rate at which corporation profits are taxed _____

f. The extent to which automation has been introduced into the production of auto-mobiles _____

g. The price of gasoline in the United States _____

h. The size of the budget deficit of the United States government ___I N___

i. The percentage of the United States pop-ulation living in rural areas _____

j. Bus fares in Hoboken, New Jersey _____

k. The provisions of the Federal laws re-quiring the installation of antipollution and safety devices in new cars _____

l. The star of a television program spon-sored by the Ford Motor Company _____

m. The chief of the Antitrust Division of the U.S. Department of Justice _____

n. The price of wheat in Kansas City, Mis-souri _____

3. Below are several current economic ques-tions or problems. Indicate in a few words what you believe the answer to the question is or what should be done to solve the problem. You are not really expected to have, at this point in your study of economics, well-thought-out and/or correct answers, but you probably have some opinions or ideas on these questions and problems.

a. How to prevent inflation. _____

_____

b. How to prevent unemployment. _____

_____

c. Whether to impose a ceiling on the price of gasoline in the United States. _____

_____

d. How to reduce poverty in the United States. _____

e. How to help underdeveloped and backward nations to raise their standards of living.

_____

f. Whether the public (national) debt is too large. _____

4. Examine your answers to question 3 and use the following criteria.

a. Is your solution or answer based on what others have told you the solution or answer should be? _____

b. Is your solution or answer practical? Is it politically feasible? _____

c. Are you employing a theory to arrive at a solution or answer? _____

d. Do you need more facts to answer the question? If so, what kind of facts? _____

_____

e. Are you guilty of being an "economic quack," or biased? Have you based your answer on some preconceived notions which might be completely wrong? _____

5. Below are four statements. Each of them is an example of one of the pitfalls frequently encountered in the study of economics. Indicate in the space following each statement the type of pitfall involved.

a. "Thrift (or saving) promotes the welfare of the economy." _____

b. "An unemployed worker can find a job if he looks diligently and conscientiously for employment; therefore, all unemployed workers can find employment if they are diligent and conscientious in looking for a job." _____

_____

c. *Jones:* "Underdeveloped nations are unable to increase their standards of living because they are unable to accumulate capital." *Smith:* "This is not correct. They are unable to increase their standards of living because they are consuming all they produce." _____

d. "The stock market crash of 1929 was followed by and resulted in 10 years of depression." _____

6. Below are three exercises in making graphs. On the graphs plot the economic relationships contained in each exercise. Be sure to label each axis of the graph and to indicate the unit of measurement and scale used on each axis.

a. _____

National income, billions of dollars	Consumption expenditures, billions of dollars
$600	$600
650	645
700	685
750	720
800	750
850	775
900	800

Graph national income on the horizontal axis and consumption expenditures on the vertical axis; connect the seven points and label the curve "Consumption Schedule." The relationship between national income and consumption expenditures is a(n) _____ one and the Consumption Schedule a(n) _____ sloping curve.

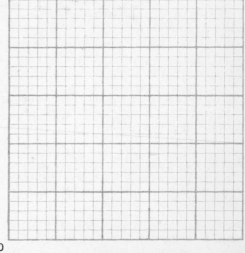

0

b.

Graph investment expenditures on the horizontal axis and the rate of interest on the

Rate of interest, %	Investment expenditures, billions of dollars
8	$15
7	17
6	20
5	24
4	29
3	35
2	42

vertical axis; connect the seven points and label the curve "Investment Schedule." The relationship between the rate of interest and

investment expenditures is a(n) _____ one and the Investment Schedule is a(n)

_____ sloping curve.

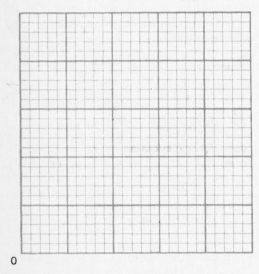

0

c.

Graph average salary on the horizontal axis and whisky consumption on the vertical axis; connect the seven points.

Average salary, American college professors	Annual per capita whisky consumption in the U.S., gal.
$12,000	1.5
13,000	1.6
14,000	1.7
15,000	1.8
16,000	1.9
17,000	2.0
18,000	2.1

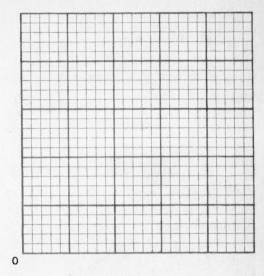

0

(1) The average salary of a college professor and whisky consumption (are, are not)

_____ correlated; and the higher average

salary (is, is not) _____ the cause of the greater consumption of whisky.

(2) The relationship between the two variables may be purely _____;

or, as is more likely, both the higher salaries and the greater consumption of whisky may

be the result of the higher _____ in the American economy.

■ SELF-TEST

Circle the T if the statement is true, the F if it is false.

1. Economics is academic and of little value because it does not teach the student how to earn a living.   T Ⓕ

2. Economic principles are derived from the facts of economic behavior.   Ⓣ F

3. Economics deals with the activities by which man earns a living and improves his standard of living.   Ⓣ F

4. The ability to predict the economic consequences of various acts is important because it enables both businessmen and government officials to formulate policies that will tend to bring about the results they desire.   Ⓣ F

5. The first step in the formulation of an economic policy, the statement of the goal or desired result, may be an occasion for disagreement because different people may have different and conflicting goals.   **T** F

6. Once a single goal or end has been determined as the sole objective of economic policy, there is seldom any question of which policy to adopt to achieve that goal.   **T** **F**

7. If you speak of "capital" to the average person, he understands you to be referring to money. The economist, therefore, is obligated to use the term "capital" to mean money.

T **F**

8. "Business expects to be able to sell 10,000 pairs of shoes this year and so produces 10,000 pairs. They actually sell 12,000 pairs." This illustrates the difference between macroeconomics and microeconomics.   **T** **F**

9. It is relatively easy to distinguish propositions involving economic quackery from those based on scientific economic principles by a careful examination of economic statistics and by testing the propositions in the harsh light of economic reality.   **T** F

10. The Law of Demand is an example of an economic policy.   **T** F

Underscore the letter that corresponds to the best answer.

1. Economics is a practical field of study in several ways. Which one of the following is *not* an element of its practicality? (a) every person affects and is affected by the operation of the economy; (b) every person has to earn a living in some manner, and economics develops skills and trains the student in the art of making a living; (c) every person in a democracy is confronted with its political problems, many of which are economic in nature; (d) every person who understands the overall operation of the economy is in a better position to solve his personal economic problems.

2. One economic principle states that the lower the price of a commodity, the greater will be the quantity of the commodity which consumers will wish to purchase. On the basis of this principle *alone,* it can be concluded that (a) if the price of mink coats falls, more mink coats will be purchased by consumers; (b) if the price of mink coats falls, Mrs. James will purchase two instead of one;

(c) if the price of mink coats falls and there are no important changes in the other factors affecting their demand, the public will probably purchase a greater quantity of mink coats than it did at the higher price; (d) if more mink coats are purchased this month than last month, it is because the price of mink coats has fallen.

3. Knowing that as the price of a commodity rises the quantity of the commodity sold decreases and that the imposition of a tax on a commodity increases its price, the economist concludes that if the government taxes cigarettes, fewer cigarettes will be sold. This is an example of: (a) prediction; (b) control; (c) policy; (d) the fallacy of composition.

4. An economic model is *not:* (a) an ideal type of economy or an economic policy for which we ought to work; (b) a tool which the economist employs to enable him to predict; (c) one or a collection of economic principles; (d) an explanation of how the economy or a part of the economy functions in its essential details.

5. Which of the following is *not* a danger to be encountered in the construction or application of economic models? (a) it may contain irrelevant facts and omit more relevant data; (b) it may come to be accepted as "what ought to be" rather than as "what is"; (c) it may be overly simplified and so be a very poor approximation of the reality it explains; (d) it may result in a conclusion that is unacceptable to the citizens or the government of a nation.

6. Which of the following economic goals is subject to reasonably accurate measurement? (a) economic security; (b) full employment; (c) economic freedom; (d) an equitable distribution of income.

7. To say that two economic goals are mutually exclusive means that: (a) it is not possible to achieve both goals; (b) these goals are not accepted as goals in the U.S.S.R. (c) the achievement of one of the goals results in the achievement of the other; (d) it is possible to quantify both goals.

8. During World War II the United States employed price controls to prevent inflation; this was referred to as "a fascist and arbitrary restriction of economic freedom" by some and as "a necessary and democratic means of preventing ruinous inflation'' by others. Both labels are examples of: (a) economic quackery; (b) the fallacy of composition; (c) the misuse of commonsense definitions; (d) emotionally loaded terminology.

9. The government increases its expenditures for road-construction equipment and the average price of this equipment falls. To reason that the lower price was due to the increase in government expenditures may be an example of: (a) the *post hoc, ergo propter hoc* fallacy; (b) the fallacy of composition; (c) a generalization that is true during a depression but untrue during prosperity; (d) using dual terminology.

10. If an individual determines to save a larger percentage of his income, he will no doubt be able to save more money. To reason, therefore, that if all individuals determine to save a larger percentage of their incomes they will be able to save more money is an example of: (a) the *post hoc, ergo propter hoc* fallacy; (b) the fallacy of composition; (c) a generalization that is true during a depression but untrue during prosperity; (d) using dual terminology.

■ **DISCUSSION QUESTIONS**

1. What are the principal reasons for studying economics?

2. What is the relationship between facts and theory? Can a theory be *proved*? Can a theory be *disproved*?

3. Define and explain the relationships between descriptive economics, economic theory, and applied economics.

4. What is a ''laboratory experiment under controlled conditions''? Does the science of economics have any kind of laboratory? Why do economists employ the ''other things equal'' assumption?

5. What is meant by an ''economic model''? Can you think of any models employed in the other courses you are taking (or have taken)? (Omit from your consideration courses in the Art Department.)

6. Why are economic principles and models necessarily abstract and generalized?

7. In what ways are the construction and application of economic models dangerous?

8. What procedure should be followed in formulating sound economic policies?

9. ''Good economic policy depends upon the development of good economic theories.'' Is this true? Are good economic theories all that is necessary to bring about improved economic conditions?

10. Of the six economic goals listed in the text, which one would you *rank* first, second, third, etc.? Would you add any other goals to this list? If economic goals 2 and 3 were mutually exclusive, which goal would you prefer? Why? If goals 1 and 4 were mutually exclusive, which would you prefer? Why?

11. What evidence is there ''that economics has achieved rapid and significant progress in recent decades''? Despite this progress economics has been the subject of a good deal of criticism. Why?

12. Explain briefly the difference between (a) macroeconomics and microeconomics; (b) deduction and induction; and (c) correlation and causation.

An Introduction to the Economizing Problem

The aim of Chapter 2 is to explain the central problem of economics and the Five Fundamental Questions into which this central problem can be divided.

The central problem of economics is that resources—the ultimate means of satisfying material wants—are scarce *relative* to the insatiable wants of society. Economics as a science is the study of the various aspects of the behavior of society in its effort to allocate the scarce resources—land, labor, capital, and entrepreneurial ability—in order to satisfy as best it can its unlimited desire for consumption. This basic problem becomes, in reality, five problems: what to produce, how to produce it, for whom to produce it, the achievement of full employment of resources, and the maintenance of economic flexibility.

The production possibilities table and curve are used in this chapter to illustrate the meaning of the scarcity of resources and of increasing costs. It is only an illustrative device, but it should help the student to understand the nature of several economic concepts and problems.

Every economy is faced with the problem of scarce resources and has to find answers to the Five Fundamental Questions. But no economy arrives at solutions to its fundamental economic problems in the same way

that another economy does. Between the extremes of pure laissez faire capitalism and communism lie various economic systems; all systems are simply different devices—different methods of organization—for finding answers or systems which are employed to find economic answers; Chapters 3 to 8 explain in greater detail how the American economy is built and operates.

Throughout Chapter 2 of the textbook there are numerous economic definitions and classifications. It would be well for the student to learn these definitions *now*. They will be used later on and it will be necessary for the student to know and understand them if he is to understand what follows.

■ CHECKLIST

The very least you should be able to do when you have finished this chapter is:

□ Write a definition of economics that incorporates the relationship between resources and wants.

□ Identify the economic resources and the type of income associated with each.

□ Construct a production possibilities curve when you are given the appropriate data.

□ Define opportunity cost and utilize a production possibilities curve to explain the concept.

□ Use a production possibilities curve to illustrate economic growth, underemployment of resources, and increasing costs.

□ Identify the Five Fundamental Questions.

□ List the major distinguishing characteristics of pure capitalism, liberal socialism, and authoritarian socialism.

■ **CHAPTER OUTLINE**

1. The bases upon which the study of economics rests are two facts.

a. Society's material wants are unlimited.

b. The economic resources which are the ultimate means of satisfying these wants are scarce in relation to the wants.

2. Economics, then, is the study of how society's scarce resources are used (administered) to obtain the greatest satisfaction of its material wants.

a. To be efficient in the use of its resources an economy must achieve both full employment and full production.

b. The production possibilities table indicates the alternative combinations of goods and services an economy is capable of producing when it has achieved full employment and full production.

c. The data contained in the production possibilities table can be plotted on a graph to obtain a production possibilities curve.

d. Which of these alternative combinations society chooses—which product-mix it selects—depends upon the preferences of that society; and preferences are subjective and nonscientific.

e. Because resources are not completely adaptable to alternative uses, the production of any product is subject to the law of increasing costs.

3. The following modifications make the production possibilities concept more realistic.

a. The failure to achieve full employment and full production reduces the output of the economy.

b. Improvements in technology and increased amounts of resources expand the output the economy is capable of producing.

c. The combination of goods and services an economy chooses to produce today helps

to determine its production possibilities in the future.

4. Faced with unlimited wants and scarce resources, every economy must find answers for the Five Fundamental Economic Questions: what goods and services to produce, how to produce them, how to divide the total output among the members of society, how to bring about the full employment of its resources, and how to assure a flexible economic system.

5. Different economic systems—capitalism, socialism, and communism—are based on different philosophies and institutions and employ different methods to obtain answers to these Five Fundamental Questions.

■ **IMPORTANT TERMS**

The economizing problem	**Consumer goods**
Unlimited wants	**Capital goods**
Scarce resources	**Economic efficiency**
Land, capital, labor, and entrepreneurial ability	**Production possibilities table**
Real capital	**Production possibilities curve**
Money (financial) capital	**Opportunity cost**
Rental income, interest income, wages, and profit	**Law of increasing costs**
Factors of production	**Economic growth**
Economics	**Five Fundamental Economic Questions**
Full employment	**Economic flexibility**
Full production	**Laissez faire capitalism**
Unemployment	**Liberal or democratic socialism**
Underemployment	**Communism or authoritarian socialism**
Disguised unemployment	

■ **FILL-IN QUESTIONS**

1. The two fundamental facts which provide the foundation of economics are:

a. _____

b. _____

2. Complete the following classification of resources:

a. _____

(1) _____

(2) _____

b. _____

(1) _____

(2) _____

3. The incomes of individuals are received from supplying resources. Four types of incomes are _____,

_____,

_____,

and _____

4. Economics can be defined as _____

_____

_____

5. When a production possibilities table or curve is constructed, four assumptions are made. These assumptions are:

a. _____

b. _____

c. _____

d. _____

6. Both consumer goods and capital goods satisfy material wants. However, consumer

goods satisfy human wants _____

while capital goods satisfy human wants _____

_____

7. Below is a production possibilities curve for tractors and suits of clothing.

Tractors

0   Suits of clothing

a. If the economy moves from point *A* to point *B* it will produce (more, fewer) _____ _____ tractors and (more, fewer) _____ suits of clothing.

b. If the economy is producing at point *X*, some of the resources of the economy are

either _____ or _____

c. If the economy moves from point *X* to point *B* (more, fewer) _____ tractors and (more, fewer) _____ suits will be produced.

d. If the economy is to produce at point *Y*, it must either _____

or _____

8. The more an economy consumes of its current production, the (more, less) _____ it will be capable of producing in future years, other things being equal.

9. The cost of producing a commodity tends to increase as more of the commodity is

produced because _____

_____

10. List the Five Fundamental Questions which every economy must attempt to answer.

a. _____

b. _____

c. _____

d. _____

e. _____

11. The quantity of other goods and services an economy must go without in order to produce low-cost housing is the _____ of producing low-cost housing.

12. Economic efficiency requires that there

be both _____

of resources and _____

13. All the combinations of products shown in the production possibilities table (or on the curve) can be achieved only if there are both full employment and full production in the economy; the best combination of products depends upon the _____

of that society and is a _____
matter.

14. Different societies have different output

_____ and employ different economic

_____ and _____
to achieve them. The two extreme systems of
economic organization in the modern, indus-

trially advanced nations are _____

_____ and _____

■ **PROBLEMS AND PROJECTS**

1. Below is a list of resources. Indicate in
the space to the right of each whether the
resource is land, capital (C), labor, entrepreneurial ability (EA), or some combinations of
these.

a. Fishing grounds in the North Atlantic

_____

b. A cash register in a retail store _____

c. Uranium deposits in Canada _____

d. An irrigation ditch in Nebraska _____

e. The work performed by the late Henry
Ford _____

f. The oxygen breathed by human beings

_____

g. The U.S. Steel plant in Gary, Indiana

_____

h. The goods on the shelf of a retail store

_____

i. The work done by a laborer on an as-

sembly line _____

j. The tasks accomplished in perfecting

color television for commercial sales _____

2. A production possibilities table for two
commodities, wheat and automobiles, follows (page 12). The table is constructed employing the usual assumptions. Wheat is
measured in units of 100,000 bushels and
automobiles in units of 100,000.

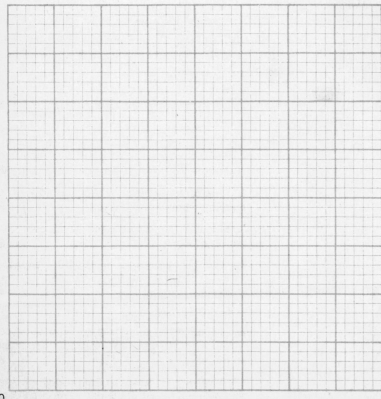

0

Combination	Wheat	Automobiles
A	0	7
B	7	6
C	13	5
D	18	4
E	22	3
F	25	2
G	27	1
H	28	0

a. Following the general rules for making graphs (Chapter 1), plot the data in the table on the graph (page 11) to obtain a production possibilities curve. Place wheat on the vertical axis and automobiles on the horizontal axis.

b. Fill in the table below showing the *opportunity cost per unit* of producing the 1st through the 7th automobile.

Automobiles	Cost of production
1st	_____
2d	_____
3d	_____
4th	_____
5th	_____
6th	_____
7th	_____

3. Below is a production possibilities curve. Draw on this graph:

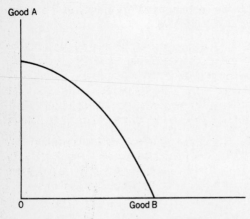

a. A production possibilities curve which indicates greater efficiency in the production of good *A*.

b. A production possibilities curve which indicates greater efficiency in the production of good *B*.

c. A production possibilities curve which indicates an increase in the resources available to the economy.

4. Below is a list of economic goods. Indicate in the space to the right of each whether the good is a consumer good (CON), a capital good (CAP), or whether the answer depends (DEP) upon who is using it and for what purpose.

a. An automobile _____

b. A tractor _____

c. A taxicab _____

d. A house _____

e. A factory building _____

f. An office building _____

g. An ironing board _____

h. A refrigerator _____

i. A telephone _____

j. A quart of Scotch whisky _____

k. A cash register _____

l. A screwdriver _____

■ **SELT-TEST**

Circle the T if the statement is true, the F if it is false.

1. The wants with which economics is concerned include only those wants which can be satisfied by goods and services. **T F**

2. Resources are scarce because society's material wants are unlimited. **T F**

3. Money is a resource and is classified as "capital." **T F**

4. It is not possible for an economy capable of producing just two goods to increase its production of both. **T F**

5. The cost of producing a good tends to increase as more of it is produced because resources less suitable to its production must be employed. **T F**

6. At full employment and full production, the more capital goods an economy produces today, the smaller the amount of consumer goods it will be able to produce today. **T   F**

7. If an economy increases the percentage of the current output it consumes, its production possibilities curve will move to the left. **T   F**

8. The more capital goods an economy produces today, the greater will be the total output of all goods it can produce in the future, other things being equal. **T   F**

9. The opportunity cost of producing anti-pollution devices is the other goods and services the economy is unable to produce because it has decided to produce these devices. **T   F**

10. It is economically desirable to have unemployed resources at the outbreak of a war because resources need not be shifted from consumer-good production in order to produce military goods. **T   F**

Underscore the letter that corresponds to the best answer.

1. An ''innovator'' is defined as an entrepreneur who: (*a*) makes basic policy decisions in a business firm; (*b*) combines factors of production to produce a good or service; (*c*) invents a new product or process for producing a product; (*d*) introduces new products on the market or employs a new method to produce a product.

2. A farmer who produces his crops by inefficient methods is: (*a*) an unemployed worker; (*b*) an underemployed worker; (*c*) a fully employed worker; (*d*) an apparently unemployed worker.

3. At point *A* on the production possibilities curve in the first illustration: (*a*) more wheat than tractors is being produced; (*b*) more tractors than wheat are being produced; (*c*) the economy is employing all its resources; (*d*) the economy is not employing all its resources.

4. If the production possibilities curve on the second graph moves from position *A* to position *B*, then: (*a*) the economy has increased the efficiency with which it produces wheat; (*b*) the economy has increased the efficiency with which it produces tractors; (*c*) the economy has put to work previously idle resources; (*d*) the economy has gone from a full-employment situation to a less-than-full-employment situation.

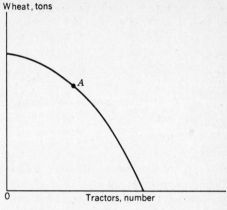

Wheat, tons

0   Tractors, number

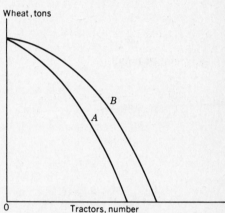

Wheat, tons

0   Tractors, number

5. If there is an increase in the resources available within the economy: (*a*) more goods and services will be produced in the economy; (*b*) the economy will be capable of producing more goods and services; (*c*) the standard of living in the economy will rise; (*d*) the technological efficiency of the economy will improve.

6. Which one of the following is *not* one of the Five Fundamental Economic Questions which every economy must answer? (*a*) determining what is to be produced; (*b*) deciding the level of resource use; (*c*) distributing output; (*d*) enforcing the law of increasing costs.

7. During the Middle Ages the feudal society found answers to the Fundamental Economic Questions through a system of: (*a*) custom and tradition; (*b*) laissez faire capitalism; (*c*) democratic socialism; (*d*) communism.

8. If the economic system of a nation is liberal or democratic socialism, there is: (*a*) public ownership and control of the bulk of industry and agriculture; (*b*) virtually no government planning or control; (c) a mixture of public and private ownership and decision making; (d) reliance on the price system only as a means of implementing central planning.

9. The combination of products in a society's production possibilities table which is its optimum product-mix depends upon that society's: (a) resources; (b) technology; (c) level of employment; (d) values of priorities.

10. An economy is efficient when it has achieved: (a) full employment; (b) full production; (c) either full employment or full production; (d) both full employment and full production.

■ DISCUSSION QUESTIONS

1. Explain what is meant by the "economizing problem." Why are resources scarce?

2. In what sense are wants satiable and in what sense are they insatiable?

3. What are the four economic resources? How is each of these resources defined? What is the income earned by each of them called?

4. When is a society economically efficient? What is meant by "full production" and how does it differ from "full employment"?

5. Why cannot an economist determine which of the combinations in the production possibilities table is "best"? What determines the optimum product-mix?

6. Explain the difference between a "good" and a "service."

7. Why is the production possibilities curve "concave" to the origin? What would such a curve show if it were convex to the origin or a straight line connecting the two axes?

8. What four assumptions are made in drawing a production possibilities curve or schedule? How do technological advance and an increased supply of resources in the economy affect the curve or schedule?

9. What is the important relationship between the *composition* of the economy's current output and the *location* of future production possibilities curves?

10. What is opportunity cost? What is the law of increasing cost? Why do costs increase?

11. What are the Five Fundamental Economic Questions and how are they related to the economizing problem?

12. Laissez faire capitalism, democratic socialism, and communism differ in their underlying assumptions, institutions, and methods for solving their fundamental economic problems. Contrast these economic systems.

CHAPTER

3

Pure Capitalism and the Circular Flow

Chapter 3 has three principal aims: to outline six ideological and institutional character- istics of pure capitalism, to explain three practices found in all modern economics, and to sketch in extremely simple terms the fun- damental operation of a capitalistic economy. A more detailed explanation of the institu- tions, practices, and behavior of the American economy—which is not *purely* capitalistic— is found in the chapters that follow. If the aims of this chapter are accomplished, you can begin to understand the system and methods employed by our economy to find answers to the Five Fundamental Economic Questions discussed in Chapter 2.

The resources of the American economy are owned by its citizens, who are free to use them as they wish in their own self-interest; prices and markets serve to express the self- interests of resource owners, consumers, and business firms; and competition serves to regulate self-interest—to prevent the self- interest of any person or any group from working to the disadvantage of the economy as a whole and to make self-interest work for the benefit of the entire economy.

Based on comparative advantage and spe- cialization, trade is made more convenient by the use of money as a medium of exchange. Trade increases the production possible in an economy with a given quantity of resources.

Trade also increases the interdependence of the members of the economy. The principle of comparative advantage is the basis for all trade between individuals, firms, regions, and nations; and you ought to be sure to under- stand what is meant by comparative advan- tage, how specialization is determined on the basis of comparative advantage, and why trade and specialization tend to increase the total production of the economy.

The circular-flow-of-income model (or dia- gram) is a device which illustrates for a capi- talistic economy the relation between house- holds and businesses, the flow of money and economic goods and services between households and businesses, their dual role as buyers and sellers, and the two basic types of markets essential to the capitalistic process.

Understand these essentials of the eco- nomic skeleton first; then a little flesh—a little more reality, a little more detail—can be added to the bones. Understanding the skele- ton makes it much easier to understand the whole body and its functioning.

■ **CHECKLIST**

The very least you should be able to do when you have finished this chapter is:

□ Identify and explain the six important institutional characteristics of capitalism.

□ Name and explain the three characteristics of all modern economies.

□ Compute the comparative costs of production from production possibilities data.

□ Determine which of two economic units has a comparative advantage and show the gains from trade when you are given cost data for the two units.

□ Indicate the range in which the terms of trade will be found.

□ Draw the circular flow diagram; and correctly label the real and money flows and the two major types of markets.

■ CHAPTER OUTLINE

1. The American economy is not pure capitalism, but it is a close approximation of pure capitalism. Pure capitalism has six important peculiarities that distinguish it from other economic systems.

2. In common with other advanced economies of the world, the American economy has three major characteristics.

 a. It employs complicated and advanced methods of production and vast amounts of capital equipment to produce goods and services.

 b. It is a highly specialized economy; specialization is based on the principle of comparative advantage and increases the productive efficiency of the economy.

 c. It also uses money extensively to facilitate trade and specialization.

3. The circular flow model is a device used to clarify the relationships between households and business firms in a purely capitalistic system, the part that each of them plays in the economy, and their respective roles in the resource and product markets.

■ IMPORTANT TERMS

Private property

Self-interest

Competition

Freedom of choice

Freedom of enterprise

Roundabout production

Specialization

Division of labor

Comparative cost

Comparative advantage

Terms of trade

Money

Medium of exchange

Barter

Coincidence of wants

Circular flow of income

Household

Resource market

Product market

■ FILL-IN QUESTIONS

1. The ownership of the means of production by private individuals and organizations is the institution of _____

2. Two basic freedoms encountered in a capitalistic economy are the freedoms of _____

_____

and _____

3. Self-interest means that each economic unit attempts to _____;
this self-interest might work to the disadvantage of the economy as a whole if it were not regulated and constrained by _____

4. According to the economist, competition is present if two conditions prevail; these two conditions are:

 a. _____

 b. _____

5. If the number of buyers and sellers in a market is large, no single buyer or seller is able to _____

6. In a capitalistic economy no one individual determines the answers to the fundamental questions of what and how to produce and how the product will be distributed. These decisions are made by many individuals and are made effective through a

_____ system in a _____

_____ type of economy.

7. In a capitalistic economy new products and more efficient methods of production are introduced by _____

motivated by the desire for _____

8. The three practices or institutions common to all modern economies are _____

_____ ,

_____ ,

and _____

9. If an economy engages in extensive specialization the individuals living in the economy are extremely _____ ; and if these individuals are to enjoy the benefits of specialization they must _____ among themselves.

10. In modern economies money functions chiefly as a _____

11. Barter between two individuals will take place only if there is a _____

12. In the circular flow model, households are buyers and businesses sellers in the _____

_____

market; and businesses are buyers and households sellers in the _____ market.

13. For an item to be "money," it must be

_____

14. The income of any household depends upon two things: _____

and _____ ; the income of any business also depends upon two things: _____

and _____

_____

15. Modern economies make extensive use of capital goods and engage in roundabout production because it is more_____ than direct production.

■ **PROBLEMS AND PROJECTS**

1. The countries of Lilliput and Brobdingnag have the production possibilities tables for apples and bananas shown below.

  Note that the costs of producing apples and bananas are constant in both countries.

LILLIPUT PRODUCTION POSSIBILITIES TABLE

Product (lbs.)	Production alternatives					
	A	B	C	D	E	F
Apples	40	32	24	16	8	0
Bananas	0	4	8	12	16	20

BROBDINGNAG PRODUCTION POSSIBILITIES TABLE

Product (lbs.)	Production alternatives					
	A	B	C	D	E	F
Apples	75	60	45	30	15	0
Bananas	0	5	10	15	20	25

  _a._ In Lilliput the cost of producing:

  (1) 8 apples is _____ bananas

  (2) 1 apple is _____ bananas
  _b._ In Brobdingnag the cost of producing:

  (1) 15 apples is _____ bananas

  (2) 1 apple is _____ bananas
  _c._ In Lilliput the cost of producing:

  (1) 4 bananas is _____ apples

  (2) 1 banana is _____ apples
  _d._ In Brobdingnag the cost of producing:

  (1) 5 bananas is _____ apples

  (2) 1 banana is _____ apples
  _e._ The cost of producing 1 apple is lower in the country of _____ and the cost of producing 1 banana is lower in the country of _____
  _f._ Lilliput has a comparative advantage in the production of _____ and Brobdingnag has a comparative advantage in the production of _____ _g._ The information in this problem is not sufficient to determine the exact terms of trade; but the terms of trade will be _greater_ than _____ apples for 1 banana and _less_ than _____ apples for 1 banana. Put another way, the terms of trade will be between _____ bananas for 1 apple and _____ bananas for 1 apple.
  _h._ If neither nation could specialize, each would produce production alternative C. The combined production of apples in the two

countries would be _____ apples and the combined production of bananas would be

_____ bananas.

(1) If each nation specializes in producing the fruit for which it has a comparative advantage, their combined production will be

_____ apples and _____ bananas.

(2) Their gain from specialization will be

_____ apples and _____ bananas.

2. Here is another problem to help you understand the principle of comparative advantage and the benefits of specialization. A tailor named Hart has the production possibilities table for trousers and jackets given below. He chooses production alternative D.

HART'S PRODUCTION POSSIBILITIES TABLE

Product	Production alternatives					
	A	B	C	D	E	F
Trousers	75	60	45	30	15	0
Jackets	0	10	20	30	40	50

Another tailor, Schaffner, has the production possibilities table below and produces production alternative E.

SCHAFFNER'S PRODUCTION POSSIBILITIES TABLE

Product	Production alternatives						
	A	B	C	D	E	F	G
Trousers	60	50	40	30	20	10	0
Jackets	0	5	10	15	20	25	30

a. To Hart

(1) the cost of one pair of trousers is _____ jackets

(2) the cost of one jacket is _____ pairs of trousers
b. To Schaffner

(1) the cost of one pair of trousers is _____ jackets

(2) the cost of one jacket is _____ pairs of trousers
c. If Hart and Schaffner were to form a partnership to make suits

(1) _____ should specialize in the making of trousers because he can make

a pair of trousers at the cost of _____ of a

jacket while it costs his partner _____ of a jacket to make a pair of trousers.

(2) _____ should specialize in the making of jackets because he can make a

jacket at the cost of _____ pairs of trousers

while it costs his partner _____ pairs of trousers to make a jacket.
d. Without specialization and between them Hart and Schaffner were able to make 50 pairs of trousers and 50 jackets. If each specializes completely in the item in the production of which he has a comparative advantage, their combined production will be _____

pairs of trousers and _____ jackets. Thus the

gain from specialization is _____

e. When Hart and Schaffner come to divide the income of the partnership between them, the manufacture of a pair of trousers should

be treated as the equivalent of from _____ to

_____ jackets (or a jacket should be treated

as the equivalent of from _____ to _____ pairs of trousers).

3. In the circular flow diagram below, the upper pair of flows (*a* and *b*) represent the product market and the lower pair (*c* and *d*) the resource market.

Supply labels or explanations for each of the four flows:

a. _____

b. _____

c. _____

d. _____

■ SELF-TEST

Circle the T if the statement is ture, the F if it is false.

1. The American economy can correctly be called "pure capitalism."   **T F**

2. There are definite legal limits to the right of private property.   **T F**

3. The consumer is sovereign in a capitalistic economy because it is he who ultimately determines what the economy will produce.

T F

4. Businessmen and resource owners always act only to further their own self-interest.

T F

5. If a person, firm, or region does not have a comparative advantage in the production of a particular commodity, it should not specialize in the production of that commodity.

T F

6. Money is a device for facilitating the exchange of goods and services.   **T F**

7. "Coincidence of wants" means that two persons desire to acquire the same good or service.   **T F**

8. Cigarettes may serve as money if sellers are generally willing to accept them as money.   **T F**

9. In the circular flow of income, the household functions on the demand side of the resource and product markets.   **T F**

10. The price system is not employed in communistic and socialistic economies.   **T F**

Underscore the letter that corresponds to the best answer.

1. Two regions, Slobovia and Utopia, have the production possibilities tables below.

SLOBOVIA PRODUCTION POSSIBILITIES TABLE

Product	Production alternatives					
	A	B	C	D	E	F
Cams	1,500	1,200	900	600	300	0
Widgets	0	100	200	300	400	500

UTOPIA PRODUCTION POSSIBILITIES TABLE

Product	Production alternatives				
	A	B	C	D	E
Cams	4,000	3,000	2,000	1,000	0
Widgets	0	200	400	600	800

In Slobovia the comparative cost: (*a*) of 1 cam of 3 widgets; (*b*) of 1 widget is ⅓ cam; (*c*) of 1 cam is ⅓ widget; (*d*) of 3 widgets is 1 cam.

2. Using the production possibilities tables in the question above, which of the following statements is *not* true? (*a*) Slobovia should specialize in the production of widgets; (*b*) Slobovia has a comparative advantage in the production of widgets; (*c*) Utopia should specialize in the production of widgets; (*d*) Utopia has a comparative advantage in the production of cams.

3. Employing the same information contained in question 1, the terms of trade will be: (*a*) greater than 7 cams for 1 widget; (*b*) between 7 cams for 1 widget and 5 cams for 1 widget; (*c*) between 5 cams for 1 widget and 3 cams for 1 widget; (*d*) less than 3 cams for 1 widget.

4. Still using the schedules in question 1, assume that if Slobovia did not specialize it would produce alternative C and that if Utopia did not specialize it would select alternative B. The gains from specialization are: (*a*) 100 cams and 100 widgets; (*b*) 200 cams and 200 widgets; (*c*) 400 cams and 500 widgets; (*d*) 500 cams and 400 widgets.

5. Which of the following is *not* a necessary consequence of specialization? (*a*) people will use money; (*b*) people will engage in trade; (*c*) people will be dependent upon each other; (*d*) people will produce more of some things than they would produce in the absence of specialization.

6. In an economy in which there are full employment and full production, constant amounts of resources, and unchanging technology: (*a*) to increase the production of capital goods requires an increase in the production of consumer goods; (*b*) to decrease the production of capital goods necessitates a decrease in the production of consumer goods; (*c*) to increase the production of capital goods is impossible; (*d*) to increase the production of capital goods a decrease in the production of consumer goods is needed.

7. Which of the following is *not* a characteristic of competition as the economist sees it? (*a*) the widespread diffusion of economic power; (*b*) a large number of buyers in product markets; (c) at least several sellers of all products; (d) the relatively easy entry to and exit of producers from industries.

■ DISCUSSION QUESTIONS

1. Explain the several elements—institutions and assumptions—embodied in capitalism.

2. What do each of the following seek if they pursue their own self-interest? Consumers, resource owners, and businessmen.

3. Explain what economists mean by competition. Why is it important in an economy whose members are motivated by self-interest?

4. What are the advantages of "indirect" or "roundabout" production?

5. How does an economy benefit from specialization and the division of labor?

6. What disadvantages are there to specialization and the division of labor?

7. Why do specialization and an advanced technology go hand in hand?

8. Explain what is meant by comparative cost and comparative advantage. What determines the terms of trade? What is the gain that results from specialization in the products in the production of which there is a comparative advantage?

9. What are the principal disadvantages of barter?

10. What is money? What important function does it perform? Explain how money performs this function and how it overcomes the disadvantages associated with barter. Why are people willing to accept paper money in exchange for the goods and services which they have to sell?

11. In the circular-flow-of-income model: (a) What two markets are involved? (b) What role do households play in each of these markets? (c) What role do businesses play in each of these markets? (d) What two income flows are pictured in money terms? In real terms? (e) What two expenditure flows are pictured in money terms? In real terms?

12. What are the five shortcomings of the circular-flow-of-income model?

The Mechanics of Individual Prices: Demand and Supply

CHAPTER

Chapter 4 is an introduction to the most fundamental tools of economic analysis: demand and supply. If you are to progress successfully into the later chapters it is essential that you understand what is meant by demand and supply and how to use these powerful tools.

Demand and supply are simply "boxes" or categories into which all the forces and factors that affect the price and the quantity of a good bought and sold in a competitive market can conveniently be placed. It is necessary to see that demand and supply do determine price and quantity exchanged and to see *why* and *how* they do this.

Many students never do understand demand and supply because they never learn to *define* demand and supply *exactly* and because they never learn (1) what is meant by an increase or decrease in demand or supply, (2) the important distinctions between demand and quantity demanded and between supply and quantity supplied, (3) the equally important distinctions between an increase (or decrease) in demand and an increase (or decrease) in quantity demanded and between an increase (or decrease) in supply and an increase (or decrease) in quantity supplied.

Having learned these, however, it is no great trick to comprehend the so-called "law of supply and demand." The equilibrium price—that is, the price which will tend to prevail in the market as long as demand and supply do not change—is simply the price at which quantity demanded and quantity supplied are equal. The quantity bought and sold in the market (the equilibrium quantity) is the quantity demanded and supplied at the equilibrium price. If you can determine the equilibrium price and quantity under one set of demand and supply conditions, you can determine them under any other set and so will be able to analyze for yourself the effect of changes in demand and supply upon equilibrium price and quantity.

The chapter includes a brief examination of the factors that influence demand and supply and of the ways in which changes in these influences will affect and cause changes in demand and supply. A graphic method is employed in this analysis in order to facilitate an understanding of demand and supply, equilibrium price and quantity, changes in demand and supply, and the resulting changes in equilibrium price and quantity. In addition to understanding the definitions of demand and supply *exactly,* it is necessary to understand the two counterparts of demand and supply: the demand *curve* and the supply *curve.* These are simply graphic (or geometric) representations of the same data contained in the schedules of demand and supply.

If you wonder why an entire chapter has been devoted to demand and supply you will find the answer in the last major section of the chapter. Demand and supply have so many applications that they are the most important single tool in economics. You will employ this tool over and over again. It will turn out to be as important to you as jet propulsion is to an astronaut. You can't get off the ground without it.

■ **CHECKLIST**

The very least you should be able to do when you have finished this chapter is:

□ Define demand, quantity demanded, supply, and quantity supplied.

□ Graph demand and supply when you are given demand and supply schedules.

□ State the law of demand and the law of supply.

□ List the major determinants of demand and of supply.

□ Determine when you are given the demand for and the supply of a good what the equilibrium price and the equilibrium quantity will be.

□ Explain why the price of a good and the amount of the good bought and sold in a competitive market will be the equilibrium price and the equilibrium quantity, respectively.

□ Predict the effects of changes in demand and supply on equilibrium price and equilibrium quantity; and on the prices of substitute and complementary goods.

□ Explain the meaning of the rationing function of prices; and the economic effects of legally established prices.

■ **CHAPTER OUTLINE**

1. Demand is a schedule of prices and the quantities which buyers will purchase at each of these prices during some period of time.

a. As price rises buyers will purchase smaller quantities, and as price falls they will purchase larger quantities; this is the law of demand.

b. The demand curve is a graphic representation of demand and the law of demand.

c. Market (or total) demand for a good is a summation of the demands of all individuals in the market for that good.

d. The demand for a good depends upon the tastes, income, and expectations of buyers; the number of buyers in the market; and the prices of related goods.

e. A change (either an increase or a decrease) in demand is caused by a change in any of the factors (in *d*) which determine demand, and means that the demand schedule and demand curve have changed.

(1) If an increase in the income of a consumer increases his demand for a good, the good is a normal one; if it decreases his demand, the good is an inferior one.

(2) If an increase (decrease) in the price of one good causes the demand for another good to increase (decrease), the two goods are substitute goods; if it causes the demand for the other good to decrease (increase), the two goods are complementary; and if it causes no change, the two goods are independent goods.

f. A change in demand and a change in the quantity demanded are *not* the same thing.

2. Supply is a schedule of prices and the quantities which sellers will sell at each of these prices during a given period of time.

a. The law of supply indicates that as the price of the good rises larger quantities will be offered for sale, and that as the price of the good falls smaller quantities will be offered for sale.

b. The supply curve is a graphic representation of supply and the law of supply; the market supply of a good is the sum of the supplies of all sellers of the good.

c. The supply of a good depends upon the prices of the resources used to produce it, the prices of other goods which might be produced, the techniques which are used to produce it, price expectations, the number of sellers of the product, and the extent to which the good is taxed or subsidized.

d. Supply will change when any of the determinants of supply changes; a change in supply is a change in the entire supply schedule or curve.

e. A change in supply must be distinguished from a change in quantity supplied.

3. The market or equilibrium price of a commodity is that price at which quantity demanded and quantity supplied are equal; and the quantity exchanged in the market (the equilibrium quantity) is equal to either the quantity demanded or the quantity supplied.

a. The rationing function of price is the elimination of either a shortage or surplus of the commodity.

b. A change in demand, supply, or both affects both the equilibrium price and quantity in definite ways.

c. In resource markets suppliers are households and demanders are business firms, and in product markets suppliers are business firms and demanders are householders; supply and demand are useful in the analysis of prices and quantities exchanged in both these markets.

d. When demand and supply schedules (or curves) are drawn up it is assumed that all the nonprice determinants of demand and supply remain unchanged.

4. Understanding how demand and supply determine price and quantity in a competitive market is a powerful tool which:

a. has a large number of applications;

b. can be used to predict the effects of legally established price supports and price ceilings;

c. may be employed to solve such problems and pollution and congestion.

■ IMPORTANT TERMS

Demand schedule	Supply schedule
Quantity demanded	Quantity supplied
Law of demand	Law of supply
Demand curve	Supply curve
Individual demand	Nonprice determinant of supply
Total or market demand	Increase (or decrease) in supply
Nonprice determinant of demand	Equilibrium price
Increase (or decrease) in demand	Equilibrium quantity
Normal (superior) good	Rationing function of prices
Inferior good	(Price-increasing (-decreasing) effect
Substitute (competing) goods	Quantity-increasing (-decreasing) effect
Complementary goods	Price support
Independent goods	Price ceiling

■ FILL-IN QUESTIONS

1. In resource markets prices are determined by the demand decisions of _businesses_ and the supply decisions of _households_; in product markets they are determined by _supply decisions of businesses_ and _demand decisions of households_

2. When demand or supply is graphed, price is placed on the _vert._ axis and quantity on the _horz._ axis.

3. The relationship between price and quantity in the demand schedule is a(n) _inverse_ relationship; in the supply schedule the relationship is a(n) _direct_ one.

4. When a consumer demand schedule or curve is drawn up, it is assumed that five factors that determine demand are fixed and constant. These five determinants of consumer demand are:

a. _Taste_

b. _Income_

c. _Related goods_

d. _Number of buyers_

e. _Expectations_

5. A decrease in demand means that consumers will buy (larger, smaller) _smaller_ quantities at every price or will pay (more, less) _less_ for the same quantities.

6. If a consumer's demand for a product decreases when his income increases, the product is a(n) _inferior_ good; if his demand for it increases when his income increases, the product is a(n) _Normal_ good.

7. If a consumer's demand for a product decreases when the price of another product increases, the two products are _Complementary_ goods; if a consumer's demand for a product increases when the price of another product increases, the two products are _Substitutes_ _____ goods.

8. A change in income or in the price of another product will result in a change in the (demand for, quantity demanded of) _____ the given product, while a change in the price of the given product will result in _____

9. The fundamental factors which determine the supply of any commodity in the product market are:

a. _Number of supplies_

b. _Technology_

c. _Prices of other goods_

d. _Natural Resources_

e. _Expectations_

f. _Taxes_

10. An improvement in the technology of producing a product is apt to _increase_ _____ the supply of that product; a(n) (increase, decrease) _decrease_ __in the price of resources used to produce the product will have the same effect.

11. The equilibrium price of a commodity is the price at which _Quality Supplied_ _) equal to the Quantity demanded_

12. If quantity demanded exceeds quantity supplied, price is (above, below) _below_ the equilibrium price; and the (shortage, surplus) _Shortage_ will cause the price to (rise, fall) _rise_

13. In the spaces below each of the following, indicate the effect [*increase* (+), *decrease* (−), *no change* (0), or *indeterminate* (?)] upon equilibrium price *and* equilibrium

quantity of each of these changes in demand and/or supply.

a. Increase in demand, supply constant

_+_   _+_

b. Increase in supply, demand constant

_−_   _+_

c. Decrease in demand, supply constant

_−_   _<_

d. Decrease in supply, demand constant

_−_   _<_

e. Increase in demand, increase in supply

_0_   ____

f. Increase in demand, decrease in supply

_+_   ____

g. Decrease in demand, decrease in supply

_−_   ____

h. Decrease in demand, increase in supply

_−_   ____

14. If supply and demand establish a price for a good such that there is no shortage or surplus of the good, then price is successfully performing its _Market_ _____ function.

15. To assume that all the nonprice determinants of demand and supply do not change is to employ the _____ assumption.

16. The effect of a price support for a good is a (shortage, surplus) _surplus_ _____ of that good; and the effect of a price ceiling is a ____ _Shortage_ ____

■ **PROBLEMS AND PROJECTS**

1. Using the demand schedule below, plot the demand curve on the graph (page 25). Label the axes and indicate for each axis the

Price	Quantity demanded, 1,000 bushels of soybeans
$7.20	10
7.00	15
6.80	20
6.60	25
6.40	30
6.20	35

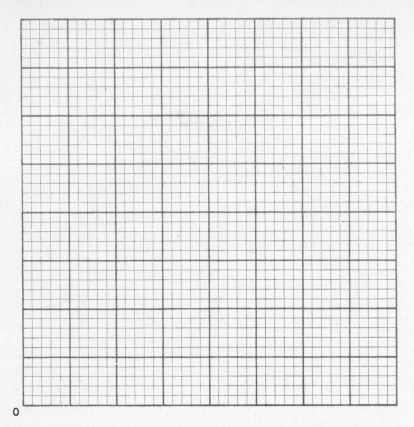

0

units being used to measure price and quantity.

2. The demand schedules of three individuals (Roberts, Charles, and Lynn) for loaves of bread are shown below. Assuming there are only three buyers of bread, draw up the total or market demand schedule for bread.

Price	Quantity demanded, loaves of bread			Total
	Roberts	Charles	Lynn	
$.40	1	4	0	_____
.36	3	5	1	_____
.32	6	6	5	_____
.28	10	7	10	_____
.24	15	8	16	_____

3. Below is a demand schedule for bushels of apples. In columns 3 and 4 supply *any* new figures for quantity which represent in column 3 an increase in demand and in column 4 a decrease in demand.

(1) Price	(2) Quantity demanded	(3) Demand increases	(4) Demand decreases
$6.00	400	_____	_____
5.90	500	_____	_____
5.80	600	_____	_____
5.70	700	_____	_____
5.60	800	_____	_____
5.50	900	_____	_____

4. Assume that O'Rourke has, when his income is $100 a week, the demand schedule for good A shown in columns 1 and 2 of the table on page 26 and the demand schedule for good B shown in columns 4 and 5. Assume that the prices of A and B are $.80 and $5, respectively.

 a. How much A will O'Rourke buy? _____

How much B? _____

 b. Suppose that, as a consequence of a $10 increase in O'Rourke's weekly income, the

Demand for A (per week)			Demand for B (per week)		
(1) Price	(2) Quantity demanded	(3) Quantity demanded	(4) Price	(5) Quantity demanded	(6) Quantity demanded
$.90	10	0	$5.00	4	7
.85	20	10	4.50	5	8
.80	30	20	4.00	6	9
.75	40	30	3.50	7	10
.70	50	40	3.00	8	11
.65	60	50	2.50	9	12
.60	70	60	2.00	10	13

quantities demanded of A become those shown in column 3 and the quantities demanded of B become those shown in column 6.

(1) How much A will he now buy?_____

How much B? _____

(2) What type of good is A? _____

(3) What type of good is B? _____

5. The market demand for good X is shown in columns 1 and 2 of the table below. Assume the price of X to be $2 and constant.

(1) Price	(2) Quantity demanded	(3) Quantity demanded	(4) Quantity demanded
$2.40	1,600	1,500	1,700
2.30	1,650	1,550	1,750
2.20	1,750	1,650	1,850
2.10	1,900	1,800	2,000
2.00	2,100	2,000	2,200
1.90	2,350	2,250	2,450
1.80	2,650	2,550	2,750

a. If as the price of good Y rises from $1.25 to $1.35 the quantities demanded of good X become those shown in column 3, it can be

concluded that X and Y are _____ goods.

b. If as the price of good Y rises from $1.25 to $1.35 the quantities demanded of good X become those shown in column 4, it can be

concluded that X and Y are _____ goods.

6. Plot the supply schedule which follows on the same graph on which you plotted demand in problem 1.

Price	Quantity supplied, 1,000 bushels of soybeans
$7.20	40
7.00	35
6.80	30
6.60	25
6.40	20
6.20	15

a. The equilibrium price of soybeans will be

$_____

b. _____
thousand bushels of soybeans will be exchanged at this price.

c. Indicate clearly on the graph the equilibrium price and quantity by drawing lines from the intersection of the supply and demand curves to the price and quantity axes.

d. If the Federal government supports a price of $7.00 per bushel there will be a

_____ of _____ bushels of soybeans.

7. In a local market for hamburger on a given date, each of 300 sellers of hamburger has the following supply schedule. In column 3 construct the market supply schedule for hamburger.

(1) Price	(2) Quantity supplied— one seller, lb.	(3) Quantity supplied— all sellers, lb.
$1.05	150	_____
1.00	110	_____
0.95	75	_____
0.90	45	_____
0.85	20	_____
0.80	0	_____

8. Below is the market demand schedule for hamburger on the same date and in the same market as that given in problem 7.

Price	Quantity demanded, lb.
$1.05	28,000
1.00	31,000
0.95	36,000
0.90	42,000
0.85	49,000
0.80	57,000

a. The equilibrium price of hamburger will be between $_____ and $_____ a pound.
b. The equilibrium quantity will be between _____ and _____ pounds.
c. If the Federal government sets the ceiling price of hamburger at 90 cents a pound the result will be a _____ of _____ pounds of hamburger in this market.

9. Each of the following events would tend to affect (that is, increase or decrease) either the demand for or the supply of television sets, and thus affect the price of television sets. In the first blank indicate the effect upon demand or supply and in the second the effect (increase or decrease) upon price.
a. It becomes known that a local department store is going to have a sale on television sets three months from now _____;

_____
b. The workers who produce the sets go on strike for over two months _____;

_____
c. The workers in the industry receive a 90-cent-an-hour wage increase. _____;

_____
d. The average price of movie tickets increases. _____; _____
e. The firms producing the sets undertake to produce a large volume of missile components for the Defense Department. _____;

_____
f. Several large areas in the country, previously without television stations, become regions in which programs can be received.

_____; _____

g. Because of the use of mass-production techniques, the amount of labor necessary to produce a set decreases. _____;

_____
h. The price of high-fidelity phonograph sets decreases. _____; _____
i. The average consumer believes that a shortage of sets is developing in the economy. _____; _____
j. The Federal government imposes a $50 per set tax upon the manufacturers of TV sets.

_____; _____

■ **SELF-TEST**

Circle the T if the statement is true, the F if it is false.

1. Demand is the amount of a commodity or service which a buyer will purchase at a particular price.   **T** F

2. The law of demand states that as price increases, the quantity of the product demanded increases.   T **F**

3. In graphing supply and demand schedules, supply is put on the horizontal axis and demand on the vertical axis.   T **F**

4. If price falls, there will be an increase in demand.   T F

5. If the demand curve moves from D_1 to D_2 in the graph below, demand has increased.
T F

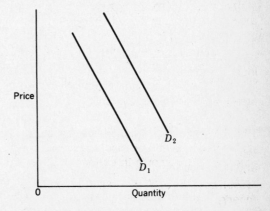

6. A fall in the price of a good will cause the demand for goods which are substitutes for it to increase.   T **F**

7. If two goods are complementary, an increase in the price of one will cause the demand for the other to increase.   **T** **F**

8. If the market price of a commodity is for a time below its equilibrium price, the market price will tend to rise because demand will decrease and supply will increase.
                                   T **F**

9. The equilibrium price of a good is the price at which the demand and the supply of the good are equal.   **T** **F**

10. The rationing function of prices is the elimination of shortages and surpluses.
                                   T **F**

Underscore the letter that corresponds to the best answer.

1. Which of the following can cause a decrease in consumer demand for product X? (*a*) a decrease in consumer income; (*b*) an increase in the prices of goods which are good substitutes for product X; (*c*) an increase in the price which consumers expect will prevail for product X in the future; (*d*) a decrease in the supply of product X.

2. If two goods are substitutes for each other, an increase in the price of one will necessarily: (*a*) decrease the demand for the other; (*b*) increase the demand for the other; (*c*) decrease the quantity demanded of the other; (*d*) increase the quantity demanded of the other.

3. The income of a consumer decreases and he increases his demand for a particular good. It can be concluded that the good is: (*a*) normal; (*b*) inferior, (*c*) a substitute; (*d*) a complement.

4. If the supply curve moves from S_1 to S_2 on the next graph, there has been: (*a*) an increase in supply; (*b*) a decrease in supply; (*c*) an increase in quantity supplied; (*d*) a decrease in quantity supplied.

5. An increase in demand and a decrease in supply will: (*a*) increase price and increase the quantity exchanged; (*b*) decrease price and decrease the quantity exchanged; (*c*) increase price and the effect upon quantity exchanged will be indeterminate; (*d*) decrease price and the effect upon quantity exchanged will be indeterminate.

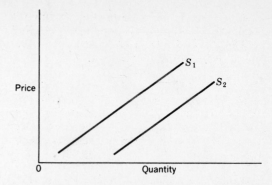

6. An increase in supply and an increase in demand will: (*a*) increase price and increase the quantity exchanged; (*b*) decrease price and increase the quantity exchanged; (*c*) affect price in an indeterminate way and decrease the quantity exchanged; (*d*) affect price in an indeterminate way and increase the quantity exchanged.

7. Which of the following could not cause an increase in the supply of cotton? (*a*) an increase in the price of cotton; (*b*) improvements in the art of producing cotton; (*c*) a decrease in the price of the machinery and tools employed in cotton production; (*d*) a decrease in the price of corn.

8. The law of supply states that as price increases: (*a*) supply increases; (*b*) supply decreases; (*c*) quantity supplied increases; (*d*) quantity supplied decreases.

9. Demand and supply may be employed to explain how price is determined in: (*a*) product markets; (*b*) resource markets; (*c*) markets for foreign currency; (*d*) all of the above markets.

10. When government places a ceiling on the price of a good and that ceiling is below the equilibrium price, the result will be: (*a*) a surplus of the good; (*b*) a shortage of the good; (*c*) an increase in the demand for the good; (*d*) a decrease in the supply of the good.

■ **DISCUSSION QUESTIONS**

1. Carefully define demand and state the law of demand. Now define supply and state the law of supply.

2. Explain the difference between an increase in demand and an increase in quantity demanded, and between a decrease in supply and a decrease in quantity supplied.

3. Neither demand nor supply remain constant for long because the factors which determine demand and supply do not long remain constant. What are these factors? How do changes in them affect demand and supply?

4. How are normal, inferior, substitute, complementary, and independent goods defined, and how can these concepts be used to predict the way in which a change in income or in the price of other goods will affect the demand for a given good?

5. Given the demand for and the supply of a commodity, what price will be the equilibrium price of this commodity? Explain why this price will tend to prevail in the market and why higher (lower) prices, if they do exist temporarily, will tend to fall (rise).

6. Analyze the following quotation and explain the fallacies contained in it. "An increase in demand will cause price to rise; with a rise in price, supply will increase and the increase in supply will push price down. Therefore, an increase in demand results in little change in price because supply will increase also."

7. What is meant by the "rationing function of prices"? How do legally established price supports and price ceilings interfere with the rationing function and what are the effects of these legally established prices?

8. What is the difference between individual and market demand; and what is the relationship between these two types of demand? Does this distinction and relationship also apply to individual and market supply?

9. Suppose homemakers, because of higher meat prices, decide to boycott meat. What effect will the boycott, as long as it lasts, have upon the demand for meat and the price of meat? After the homemakers end their boycott what will happen to the demand for and the price of meat?

10. The supply of beef has decreased (because of the increased costs of producing beef) and the price of beef has started to rise toward its new equilibrium price when the Federal government freezes the price of beef at its original equilibrium price. What will be the effects of the beef-price freeze upon cattle ranchers? Upon the homemaker?

The Five Fundamental Questions and the Price System

In Chapters 2, 3, and 4 we examined the institutions and characteristics of pure capitalism and saw how supply and demand determine equilibrium prices and equilibrium quantities in resource and product markets. Chapter 5 draws these elements together into an explanation of the ways in which the market system finds answers for the first four of the Five Fundamental Economic Questions. This explanation is only an approximation—a simplified version or a model—of the methods actually employed by American capitalism. Yet this simple model, like all good models, contains enough realism to be truthful and is general enough to be understandable.

The model is intentionally and specifically unrealistic because the economic role of government is ignored and because actual competition in American capitalism is probably much less effective than is assumed in Chapter 5. These shortcomings, however, do not weaken the major points made in the chapter about the functioning of the price-market system; and the shortcomings are corrected in later chapters to make the model more realistic.

The section entitled "Operation of the Price System" (beginning on page 87 of the textbook) is both the most important part of this chapter and the part the student will find most difficult. If you will try to understand how the American system of prices and markets finds answers for each of the four basic questions by examining them *individually* and in the order in which they are presented, you will understand more easily how the price system as a whole operates. Actually the price system finds answers for all these questions simultaneously, but it is much simpler to consider them as if they were separate questions.

In addition to explaining how the price system operates, Chapter 5 also takes up the question of *how well* it operates. Here you will find the going much easier. It should be particularly noted, however, that the price-market system is a widely accepted method of allocating scarce resources because it is economically quite efficient in the allocation of resources. But even so, it, like every other economic system devised by man, is not as efficient as it might be. The specific criticisms leveled against the price-market system are well worth noting because, as will be seen in Chapter 6, many of government's functions in the economy are directed toward the correction of the system's faults which have been pointed out by its critics; in fact, one of the reasons for ignoring the role of government in Chapter 5 is to emphasize the shortcomings of pure capitalism in the absence of government.

A few final words of advice to the student.

You should be sure to understand the *importance* and *role* of each of the following in the operation of the price-market system: (1) the rationing and directing functions of prices, (2) substitutability between different products and between different resources, (3) the profit motive of business firms, (4) the entry into and exodus of firms from industries, (5) competition, and (6) consumer sovereignty.

■ **CHECKLIST**

The very least you should be able to do when you have finished this chapter is:

□ Explain how a competitive price system determines what will be produced.

□ Distinguish between normal profit and economic profit.

□ Predict what will happen to the price charged by and the output of a prosperous and an unprosperous industry; and explain why these events will occur.

□ Explain how production is organized in a competitive price system.

□ Find the least-cost combination of resources when you are given the technological data and the prices of the resources.

□ Explain how a competitive price system determines the distribution of total output.

□ Define flexibility; and explain why a competitive price system is both adaptable and conducive to change.

□ Present the case for and the case against the price system.

□ Identify the two basic differences between an ideal price system and the price system found in the United States.

■ **CHAPTER OUTLINE**

1. The price system consists of product and resource markets in which prices and quantities exchanged are determined. In the product markets households demand the products supplied by business firms; and in the resource markets businesses demand the resources supplied by households.

2. Households and business firms as demanders and suppliers are faced with the necessity of making choices.

a. Choices are necessary because resources are scarce.

b. Choices are possible only to the extent that there is substitutability among resources and among products.

c. The actual choices made by households and firms depend upon the prices (or scarcity) of products and resources and upon the amount of substitution possible.

3. The system of prices and markets and the choices of households and business firms furnish the economy with answers to the first four Fundamental Economic Questions.

a. The demands of consumers for products and the desire of business firms to maximize their profits determine what and how much of each product is produced and its price.

b. The desire of business firms to maximize profits by keeping their costs of production as low as possible guide them to employ the most efficient techniques of production and determines their demand for and prices of the various resources; competition forces them to use the most efficient techniques and ensures the most efficient will be able to stay in business.

c. With resource prices determined, the money income of each household is determined; and with product prices determined, the quantity of goods and services which these money incomes will buy is determined.

d. The price-market system communicates changes in consumer tastes, in the availability of resources, and in techniques of production to business firms.

(1) The desire for maximum profits and competition will then result in a new set of answers to the first three Fundamental Economic Questions.

(2) Competition and the desire to increase profits promote both better techniques of production and capital accumulation.

e. Competition in the economy compels firms seeking to promote their own interests to promote (as though led by an "invisible hand") the best interest of society as a whole: an allocation of resources appropriate to consumer wants, production by the most efficient means, and the lowest possible prices.

4. The price system has been praised and damned because it has both merits and faults.

a. The major merits of the system are that it efficiently allocates scarce resources and allows individuals large amounts of personal freedom.

b. The chief faults are the decline in the competitiveness of markets and wasteful and inefficient production.

c. The analysis of the price system found in this chapter is only a rough approximation of how the American economy actually operates because the bigness of some buyers and sellers has often resulted in weak competition and because the economic role of government has been ignored.

■ **IMPORTANT TERMS**

Substitutability	Directing (guiding) function of prices
Economic choice	
Normal profit	Invisible hand
Economic cost	Least-cost technique
Economic profit	Self-limiting adjustment
Expanding (prosperous) industry	
	Market failure
Declining (unprosperous industry)	External (spillover) benefit
Economic efficiency	External (spillover) cost
Consumer sovereignty	

■ **FILL-IN QUESTIONS**

1. The competitive price system is a mechanism for both _____ the decisions of producers and households and _____ these decisions.

2. Given its money income, each household tries to spend its income on that combination of products which _____ _____ _____

3. The economy—producers and households —must make economic choices because ____ _____ ; choices are possible only because different products and different resources are, to some degree, _____ for each other.

4. A normal profit is an economic cost because _____ _____

5. If firms in an industry are earning economic profits, firms will _____ the industry, the price of the industry's product will _____, and the industry will employ a _____ quantity of resources and produce a _____ quantity of output; the industry's economic profits will _____ to _____

6. In determining the distribution of total output in the economy, the price system is involved in two ways, which are:

a. _____

b. _____

7. In deciding whether an economy is flexible, the two questions which must be answered are:

a. _____

b. _____

8. The *opportunity* for technological advance exists in the capitalistic system because there are no _____ to restrict it.

9. The entrepreneur uses money which he obtains either from _____ or from _____ to acquire capital goods.

10. If the price system is competitive, there is an identity of _____ interests and the _____ interest: firms seem to be guided by an _____ to allocate the economy's resources efficiently.

11. The chief economic advantage of the price system, it is said, is that _____ _____ ; its chief noneconomic advantage is that_____

_____

_____

12. Critics of the price system argue that:
a. competition tends to weaken because

_____

and _____
b. the system is inefficient because

(1) the distribution of income is _____
(2) even competitive markets fail to recog-

nize external _____ and _____
and to take into account the demand for

_____ goods;

(3) resources are _____

(4) it does not ensure the _____

_____of resources.

■ **PROBLEMS AND PROJECTS**

1. Assume that a firm can produce either product A, product B, or product C with the resources it currently employs. These re- sources _cost_ the firm a total of $50 per week. Assume, for the purposes of the problem, that the firm's employment of resources cannot be changed. The market prices of and the quan- tities of A, B, and C these resources will pro- duce per week are given below. Compute the firm's profit when it produces A, B, and C; and enter these profits in the table below.

Product	Market price	Output	Economic profit
A	$7.00	8	$_____
B	4.50	10	_____
C	.25	240	_____

a. Which product will the firm produce?____
b. If the price of A rose to $8, the firm

would _____
(_Hint:_ You will have to recompute the firm's profit from the production of A.)
c. If the firm were producing A and selling it at a price of $8, what would tend to happen to the number of firms producing A?

_____

2. Suppose that a firm can produce 100 units of product X by combining labor, land, capi- tal, and entrepreneurial ability in three differ- ent ways. If it can hire labor at $2 per unit, land at $3 per unit, capital at $5 per unit, and entrepreneurship at $10 per unit; and if the amounts of the resources required by the three methods of producing 100 units of product X are indicated in the table, answer the questions below it.

Resource	Method		
	1	2	3
Labor	8	13	10
Land	4	3	3
Capital	4	2	4
Entrepreneurship	1	1	1

a. Which method is the least expensive way

of producing 100 units of X? _____
b. If X sells for 70 cents per unit, what is

the economic profit of the firm? $ _____
c. If the price of labor should rise from $2 to $3 per unit and if the price of X is 70 cents,
(1) The firm's use of:

Labor would change from _____ to _____

Land would change from _____ to _____

Capital would change from _____ to _____

Entrepreneurship would not change.
(2) The firm's economic profit would change

from $_____ to $_____

■ **SELF-TEST**

Circle the T if the statement is true, the F if it is false.

1. Prices are indicators of the relative scarcity of resources and products.   **T F**

2. Industries in which economic profits are earned by the firms in the industry will attract the entry of new firms into the industry.
                                          T F

3. If firms have sufficient time to enter and leave industries, the economic profits of an industry will tend to disappear.   **T F**

4. Resources will tend to be used in those industries capable of earning normal or economic profits. **T F**

5. If the market price of resource A increases, firms will tend to employ smaller quantities of resource A. **T F**

6. Changes in the tastes of consumers are reflected in changes in consumer demand for products. **T F**

7. The incentive which the price system provides to induce technological improvement is the opportunity for economic profits. **T F**

8. Contraction in the size of an industry is always the consequence of improved methods of production in that industry. **T F**

9. In a capitalistic economy it is from the entrepreneur that the demand for capital goods arises. **T F**

10. An increase in the size of the firms in an industry generally leads to a smaller number of firms in the industry. **T F**

Underscore the letter that corresponds to the best answer.

1. The wants of consumers are expressed on: (a) the demand side of the resource market; (b) the demand side of the product market; (c) the supply side of the resource market; (d) the supply side of the product market.

2. Which of the following best defines economic costs? (a) total payments made to workers, landowners, suppliers of capital, and entrepreneurs; (b) only total payments made to workers, landowners, suppliers of capital, and entrepreneurs which must be paid to obtain the services of their resources; (c) total payments made to workers, landowners, suppliers of capital and entrepreneurs *less* normal profits; (d) total payments made to workers, landowners, suppliers of capital, and entrepreneurs *plus* normal profits.

3. If less than normal profits are being earned by the firms in an industry, the consequences will be that: (a) lower-priced resources will be drawn into the industry; (b) firms will leave the industry, causing the price of the industry's product to fall; (c) the price of the industry's product will rise and fewer resources will be employed by the industry; (d) the price of the industry's product will fall and thereby cause the demand for the product to increase.

4. Which of the following would *not* necessarily result, sooner or later, from a decrease in consumer demand for a product? (a) a decrease in the profits of the industry producing the product; (b) a decrease in the output of the industry; (c) a decrease in the supply of the product; (d) an increase in the prices of resources employed by the firms in the industry.

5. If firm A does not employ the most "efficient" or least costly method of production, which of the following will *not* be a consequence? (a) firm A will fail to earn the greatest profit possible; (b) other firms in the industry will be able to sell the product at lower prices; (c) new firms will enter the industry and sell the product at a lower price than that at which firm A now sells it; (d) firm A will be spending less on resources and hiring fewer resources than it otherwise would.

6. Which of the following is *not* a factor in determining the *share* of the total output of the economy received by any household: (a) the prices at which the household sells its resources; (b) the quantities of resources which the household sells; (c) the tastes of the household; (d) the prices which the household must pay to buy products.

7. If an increase in the demand for a product and the resulting rise in the price of the product cause the supply of the product, the size of the industry producing the product, and the amounts of resources devoted to its production to expand, price is successfully performing its: (a) guiding function; (b) rationing function; (c) medium-of-exchange function; (d) standard-of-value function.

8. In a capitalistic economy characterized by competition, if one firm introduces a new and better method of production, other firms will be forced to adopt the improved technique: (a) to avoid less-than-normal profits; (b) to obtain economic profits; (c) to prevent the price of the product from falling; (d) to prevent the price of the product from rising.

9. Which of the following would be an indication that competition does not exist in an industry? (a) less-than-normal profits in the industry; (b) inability of the firms in the industry to expand; (c) inability of firms to enter the industry; (d) wages lower than the average wage in the economy paid to workers in the industry.

10. Economic criticism of the price system is widespread and has pointed out many of the failures of the system. However, the chief economic virtue of the system remains that of: (*a*) allowing extensive personal freedom; (*b*) efficiently allocating resources; (*c*) providing an equitable distribution of income; (*d*) eliminating the need for decision making.

■ **DISCUSSION QUESTIONS**

1. Explain why the substitutability of resources for each other and the substitutability of products for each other are important if an economy is to allocate its resources efficiently and best satisfy human wants.

2. In what way does the desire of entrepreneurs to obtain economic profits and to avoid losses make consumer sovereignty effective?

3. Why is the ability of firms to enter industries which are prosperous important to the effective functioning of competition?

4. Explain *in detail* how an increase in the consumer demand for a product will result in more of the product being produced and in more resources being allocated to its production.

5. Explain the difference between a price system which is adaptable to change and a price system which is conducive to change.

6. To what extent are firms "free" to produce what they wish by methods which they choose? Do resource owners have freedom to use their resources as they wish?

7. What is meant when it is said that competition is the mechanism which "controls" the price-market system? How does competition do this? What do critics of the price system argue tends to happen to this controlling mechanism as time passes, and why do they so argue?

8. What are the two important functions of prices? Explain the difference between these two functions.

9. "An invisible hand operates to identify private and public interests." What are private interests and what is the public interest? What is it that leads the economy to operate as if it were directed by an invisible hand?

10. If the basic economic decisions are not made in a capitalistic economy by a central authority, how are they made?

11. What reasons are advanced to explain why modern technology results in firms which are large both in absolute size and in relation to the size of their markets?

12. What five arguments do critics of the price system advance to refute the contention that the price system allocates resources efficiently?

13. What are the two principal kinds of market failures? Include in your answer definitions of an external cost and an external benefit.

14. To what extent is this chapter unrealistic?

Mixed Capitalism and the Economic Functions of Government

Chapter 6 introduces the student to the five basic functions performed by Federal, state, and local governments in America's mixed capitalistic economy. This is an examination of the actual role of government (the public sector) in an economy which is neither a purely planned nor a purely market-type economy. The discussion points out the degree and the ways in which government causes the American economy to differ from a purely market-type economy. The chapter does not attempt to list all the *specific* ways in which government affects the behavior of the economy. Instead it provides a *general* classification of the tasks performed by government.

Following an explanation of each of the five functions of government in the American economy, the chapter attempts to evaluate the economic role of government in the United States. Here it is pointed out that people generally agree that government should perform these functions. But they disagree on how far government should go in performing them and over whether specific government actions and programs are needed for government to perform these functions. Governments today frequently employ benefit-cost analysis to determine whether they should or should not undertake some specific action—a particular act,

project, or program. This kind of analysis forces government to estimate both the added costs and the additional benefits of the project or program; to expand its activities only where the additional benefits exceed the added costs; and to reduce or eliminate programs and projects when the additional costs exceed the added benefits.

The latter part of Chapter 6 examines two important questions which are related to the economic role of government in the American economy. The first question is whether government fails to solve social problems because the process it uses to make decisions is an inherently inefficient mechanism for allocating resources. The question is whether there has been a public sector failure; and the author presents some of the reasons why the public sector's decision-making process may result in a misallocation of resources in the economy. The second question is whether an increase in the size of government's role in the economy reduces or expands the freedoms of the individual members of the American society. The author presents the case of those who argue that expanded governmental activity reduces personal freedom and the case of those who contend it may actually lead to greater individual freedom.

■ CHECKLIST

The very least you should be able to do when you have finished this chapter is:

□ Explain the basic difference between a market economy and a planned economy; and why the American economy is mixed capitalism.

□ Enumerate the five economic functions of government in the United States; and explain the difference between the purpose of the first two and the purpose of the last three functions.

□ Define monopoly and explain why government wishes to prevent monopoly and to preserve competition in the economy.

□ Explain why government feels it should redistribute income and list the principal policies it employs for this purpose.

□ Define a spillover cost and a spillover benefit; explain why a competitive market fails to allocate resources efficiently when there are spillovers; and list the things government may do to reduce spillovers and improve the allocation of resources.

□ Define a social good and a private good and explain how government goes about reallocating resources from the production of private to the production of social goods.

□ Use benefit-cost analysis to determine the extent to which government should apply resources to a project or activity when you are given the cost and benefit data.

□ Explain what is meant by "public sector failure" and list several possible causes of this alleged failure.

□ Present briefly the case for and the case against the proposition that an expanded public sector reduces personal freedom.

■ CHAPTER OUTLINE

1. The American economy is neither a pure market economy nor a purely planned economy. It is an example of mixed capitalism and predominantly a market economy with some government direction and planning.

2. Government in the American economy performs five economic functions. The first two of these functions are designed to enable the price system to operate more effectively; and the other three functions are designed to eliminate the major shortcomings of a purely market-type economy.

3. The first of these functions is to provide the legal and social framework that makes the effective operation of the price system possible.

4. The second function is the maintenance of competition and the regulation of monopoly.

5. Government performs its third function when it redistributes income to reduce income inequality.

6. When government reallocates resources it performs its fourth function.

a. It reallocates resources to take account of spillover costs and benefits.

b. It must also reallocate resources to provide society with social (public) goods and services; and these are goods and services which are not subject to the exclusion principle and which have large spillover benefits.

c. Government reallocates resources from the production of private to the production of social goods by levying taxes and using the tax revenues to purchase (or produce) the social goods.

7. Its fifth function is stabilization of the price level and the maintenance of full employment.

8. In evaluating government's role in the economy it should be noted that:

a. It is generally agreed that it is desirable for government to perform these five functions; but there is a good deal of controversy about how far it should go in performing them.

b. Benefit-cost analysis may be employed by government to determine whether it should employ resources for a project and to decide upon the total quantity of resources it should devote to a project. Additional resources should be devoted to a project only so long as the marginal benefit to society from using the additional resources for the project exceeds the marginal cost to society of the additional resources.

9. Critics of the governmental or public sector of the economy argue that this sector has failed to find solutions for social problems; and the theory of public choice suggests that the public sector has failed because the process it uses to make decisions is inherently weak and results in an economically inefficient allocation of resources.

a. The weakness of the decision-making process in the public sector and the resulting inefficient allocation of resources is often the result of pressures exerted on Congress and the bureaucracy by special interests.

b. Those seeking election to public office frequently favor (oppose) programs whose benefits (costs) are clear and immediate and whose costs (benefits) are uncertain and deferred even when the benefits are less (greater) than the costs.

c. When the citizen must vote for candidates who represent different but complete programs the voter is unable to select those parts of a program which he or she favors and to reject the other parts of the program.

d. It is argued that the public sector (unlike the private sector) is inefficient because those employed there are offered no incentive to be efficient; and because there is no way to measure efficiency in the public sector.

e. Just as the private or market sector of the economy does not allocate resources perfectly, the public sector does not perform its functions perfectly; and the imperfections of both sectors make it difficult to determine which sector will provide a particular good or service more efficiently.

10. The nature and amount of government activity and the extent of individual freedom may be related to each other.

■ **IMPORTANT TERMS**

Market economy	Private good
Planned economy	Exclusive principle
Mixed capitalism	Quasi-public good
Monopoly	Benefit-cost analysis
Spillover (externality)	Public sector
Spillover cost	Theory of public choice
Spillover benefit	Special-interest effect
Social (public) good	Fallacy of limited decisions

■ **FILL-IN QUESTIONS**

1. All actual economies are "mixed" because they combine elements of a _____ economy and a _____ economy.

2. List the five economic functions of government:

a. _____

b. _____

c. _____

d. _____

e. _____

3. To control monopoly in the United States government has:

a. created commissions to _____ the prices and the services of the _____ monopolies;

b. taken over at the local level the _____ _____ electric and water companies;

c. enacted _____ laws to maintain competition.

4. The price system, because it is an impersonal mechanism, results in _____ in the distribution of income. To redistribute income from the upper to lower income groups the Federal government has:

a. enacted _____programs;

b. engaged in _____ intervention;

c. used the _____ tax to raise much of its revenues.

5. In a competitive market for a product:
a. the marginal benefits to consumers from using the product is shown by the _____ curve for the product;

b. the marginal cost of producing the product is shown by the _____curve;

c. in equilibrium the marginal _____ _____ of the last unit of the product consumed is equal to the marginal _____ _____ of producing that last unit.

6. Competitive markets bring about an optimum allocation of resources only if there are no_____ or _____ in the consumption and production of the good or service.

7. There is a spillover whenever some of the costs of producing a product or some of the benefits from consuming it accrue to_____

_____

8. Whenever in a competitive market there are:
  a. spillover costs the result is an (over-, under-) _____ allocation of resources to the product because units of the product whose marginal _____ exceed their marginal_____ are produced;

  b. spillover benefits the result is an _____

  _____ allocation of resources to the product because units of the product whose

  _____ exceed their _____

  _____ are not produced.

9. What two things can government do to:
  a. Make the market reflect spillover costs?

  (1) _____

  (2) _____
  b. Make the market reflect spillover benefits?

  (1) _____

  (2) _____

10. Social goods tend to be goods which are

not subject to the _____ principle

and which have large _____ benefits.

11. To reallocate resources from the production of private to the production of social goods government reduces the demand for

private goods by _____ consumers and

firms and then _____ social goods.

12. To stabilize the economy, government:
  a. when there is less than full employment

  _____ aggregate demand by

  _____ its expenditures for social goods

and services and by_____
taxes;
  b. when there are inflationary pressures

  _____ aggregate demand by

  _____ its expenditures for social goods

and services and by_____
taxes.

13. Throughout most of its history government in the United States has performed in some degree each of the five functions except

that of _____

14. In applying benefit-cost analysis, government should employ more resources in the public sector if the marginal benefits from the

additional _____
exceed the marginal costs that result from

having fewer _____

15. When government employs benefit-cost analysis it often finds that:

  a. it is difficult to_____
the benefits and the costs of a program;
  b. the program not only reallocates re-

sources but also affects the _____

of the economy and the _____
of income.

16. When governments use resources to solve social problems and the employment of these resources does not result in solutions

to the problems there has been_____

_____

17. Four possible reasons for public sector failure are:

  a. the _____effect;
  b. the fact that the benefits from a program

or project are often _____

and its costs are frequently_____
  c. the inability of individual voters to

  _____ the particular quantities
of each social good and service they wish the public sector to provide;

  d. the weak _____ to be efficient in the public sector and the absence

of any way to _____
the efficiency of the public sector.

18. Those who allege that there are inherent deficiencies in the processes used to make decisions in the public sector and that these deficiencies produce economic inefficiency

are interested in the theory of _____

19. Despite the recognition of inefficiency in the public sector:
  a. it should be recognized that there is also

inefficiency in the _____
of the economy;
  b. the institutions employed in both sectors

to allocate resources are _____
  c. it is, therefore, difficult to determine to which sector the production of a particular

good or service should be _____

20. To reason that increased governmental activity necessarily reduces private economic activity is an example of the fallacy of

_____

■ **PROBLEMS AND PROJECTS**

1. Below is a list of various government activities. Indicate in the space to the right of each into which of the five classes of government functions the activity falls. If the activity falls under more than one of the five functions, indicate this.

  a. Maintaining an army _____
  b. Providing for a system of unemployment

compensation _____

  c. Establishment of the Federal Reserve

Banks _____

  d. Insuring employees of business firms

against industrial accidents _____

  e. Establishment of an Antitrust Division in

the Department of Justice _____

  f. Making it a crime to sell stocks and bonds

under false pretenses _____

  g. Providing low-cost lunches to school

children _____

  h. Taxation of whisky and other spirits ____

_____

  i. Regulation of organized stock, bond, and

commodity markets _____
  j. Setting tax *rates* higher for large incomes

than for smaller ones_____

2. On the graph are the demand and supply curves for a product bought and sold in a competitive market. Assume that there are no spillover benefits or costs.

  a. Were this market to produce an output of Q_1 there would be an underallocation of resources to the production of this product because at output Q_1 the marginal benefit

from the last unit consumed equals _____

and exceeds the marginal _____ cost of producing that last unit.
  b. Were this market to produce Q_2 there would be an overallocation of resources because at Q_2 the marginal cost of producing

the last unit is _____ and exceeds the mar-

ginal benefit of _____ obtained from consuming that last unit.
  c. At the equilibrium output of Q_e there is

an _____ allocation of resources to the production of this product because the marginal cost and the marginal benefit obtained from the last unit of the product

produced both equal _____

3. On two graphs on page 41 are product demand and supply curves that do *not* reflect either the spillover costs of producing the product or the spillover benefits obtained from its consumption.

 a. On the graph below draw in another curve that reflects the inclusion of spillover *costs.*

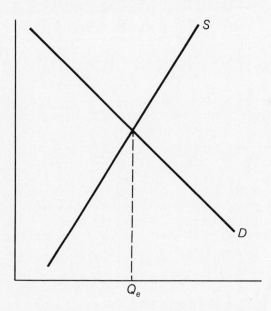

(1) The inclusion of spillover costs in the total cost of producing the product (increases, decreases) _____ the output of the product and _____ its price.

(2) Were the output Q_e produced there would be an overallocation of resources to this product because at Q_e the marginal cost is _____ than the marginal benefit to the economy.

 b. On the next graph draw in another curve that reflects the inclusion of spillover *benefits.*

(1) The inclusion of the spillover benefits in the total benefits obtained from consuming the product (increases, decreases) _____ the output of the product and _____ its price.

(2) Were the output Q_e produced there would be an underallocation of resources to this product because at Q_e the marginal cost is _____ than the marginal benefit to the economy.

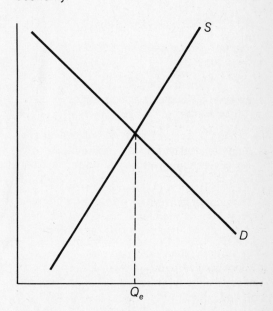

4. Imagine that a state government is considering the construction of a new highway to link its two largest cities. Its estimate of the total costs and the total benefits of building 2, 4, 6, and 8 lane highways between the two cities are shown in the table below. (All figures are in millions of dollars.)

 a. Compute the marginal cost and the marginal benefit of the 2, 4, 6, and 8 lane highways.

 b. Will it benefit the state to allocate resources to construct a highway? _____

 c. If the state builds a highway:

Project	Total cost	Marginal cost	Total benefit	Marginal benefit
No highway	$ 0		$ 0	
2 lane highway	500	$_____	650	$_____
4 lane highway	680	_____	750	_____
6 lane highway	760	_____	800	_____
8 lane highway	860	_____	825	_____

(1) It should be a _____ lane highway.

(2) The total cost will be $_____

(3) The total benefit will be $_____

(4) The *net* benefit to the state will be $___

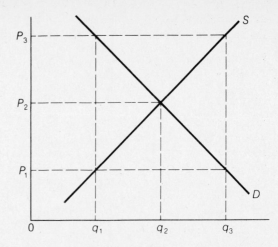

■ SELF-TEST

Circle the T if the statement is true, the F if it is false.

1. The American economy cannot be called "capitalistic" because its operation involves some "planning."   **T   F**

2. When the Federal government provides for a monetary system, it is functioning to provide the economy with social goods and services.   **T   F**

3. An economy in which strong and effective competition is maintained will find no need for programs designed to redistribute income.   **T   F**

4. Competitive product markets ensure an optimal allocation of an economy's resources.   **T   F**

5. In a competitive product market and in the absence of spillover costs, the supply curve or schedule reflects the marginal cost of producing the product.   **T   F**

6. If demand and supply reflected all the benefits and costs of a product, the equilibrium output of a competitive market would be identical with its optimum output.   **T   F**

The graph in the next column should be used to answer true-false question 7 and multiple-choice questions 3 and 4.

7. Assuming there are no spillover costs or benefits, the production of q_1 units of this product would result in an overallocation of resources to the production of the product.   **T   F**

8. The inclusion of the spillover benefits would increase the demand for a product.   **T   F**

9. When there are spillover costs involved in the production of a product, more resources are allocated to the production of that product and more of the product is produced than is optimal or most efficient.   **T   F**

10. Reduced taxation of firms producing goods which provide spillover benefits will usually result in a better allocation of reserves.   **T   F**

11. If the economic role of government in the United States is evaluated objectively, it becomes clear that the scope of the government's activities is too large.   **T   F**

12. Reduced government spending is the same as economy in government.   **T   F**

13. When there is widespread unemployment of labor in the economy the marginal cost to society of putting the unemployed to work producing social goods is, for all practical purposes, equal to zero.   **T   F**

14. In practice it is usually quite simple to estimate the costs and the benefits of a project financed by government.   **T   F**

15. The reallocation of resources from the private to the public sector does not ordinarily affect the distribution of income or the stability of the economy.   **T   F**

16. There is a failure in the public sector whenever a governmental program or activity has been expanded to the level at which the marginal social cost exceeds the marginal social benefit.   **T   F**

17. The special-interests effect, it is argued by those concerned with the theory of public choice, tends to reduce public sector failures because the pressures exerted on government by one special-interest group are offset by the pressures brought to bear by other special-interest groups. **T F**

18. When the costs of programs are hidden and the benefits are clear vote-seeking politicians tend to reject economically justifiable programs. **T F**

19. The nonselectivity of citizens refers to the inability of individual voters to select the precise bundle of social goods and services that best satisfies the citizen's wants when he or she must vote for a candidate and the candidate's entire program. **T F**

20. Both liberals and conservatives agree that the expansion of government's role in the economy has reduced personal freedom in the United States. **T F**

Underscore the letter that corresponds to the best answer.

1. Which of the following is *not* one of the methods utilized by government to control monopoly? (*a*) the imposition of special taxes on monopolists; (*b*) government ownership of monopolies; (*c*) government regulation of monopolies; (*d*) antitrust laws.

2. One of the following is *not* employed by government to redistribute income. Which one? (*a*) the negative income tax; (*b*) direct market intervention; (*c*) income taxes which take a larger part of the incomes of the rich than the poor; (*d*) public assistance programs.

Use the graph on page 42 to answer the following two questions.

3. If there are neither spillover costs nor spillover benefits, the output which results in the optimum allocation of resources to the production of this product is (*a*) q_1; (*b*) q_2; (*c*) q_3; (*d*) none of these outputs.

4. If there are no spillover costs or benefits, the marginal benefit from producing q_3 units of this product is (*a*) p_1; (*b*) p_2; (*c*) p_3; (*d*) none of these.

5. When the production and consumption of a product entail *both* spillover costs and benefits, a competitive product market results in (*a*) an underallocation of resources to the product; (*b*) an overallocation of resources to the product; (*c*) an optimum allocation of resources to the product; (*d*) an allocation of resources that may or may not be optimum.

6. Which of the following is the best example of a good or service providing the economy with spillover benefits? (*a*) an automobile; (*b*) a drill press; (*c*) a high school education; (*d*) an operation for appendicitis.

7. In the American economy the reallocation of resources needed to provide for the production of social goods is accomplished mainly by means of: (*a*) government subsidies to the producers of social goods; (*b*) government purchases of social goods from producers; (*c*) direct control of producers of both private and social goods; (*d*) direct control of producers of social goods only.

8. In asserting the desirability of government performing the five basic economic functions in the United States, there seems to be rather general agreement that: (*a*) the functions ought to be increased in number and government's role in the economy expanded; (*b*) the functions ought to be decreased in number and government's role in the economy reduced to a minimum; (*c*) the functions are those which the government ought to perform, but there is no general agreement as to the extent to which government should go in performing them; (*d*) with the exception of stabilizing the economy, these are legitimate tasks for government to perform as long as government, in performing them, does not interfere with the operation of the economy.

9. Which of the following is characteristic of social goods? (*a*) they have large spillover benefits; (*b*) they are sold in competitive markets; (*c*) they are subject to the exclusion principle; (*d*) they can be produced only if large spillover costs are incurred.

10. Which of the following functions of government most affects the area of macroeconomics: (*a*) maintaining competition; (*b*) redistributing income; (*c*) reallocating resources; (*d*) stabilizing the economy.

11. Assume that a government is considering a new antipollution program and it may choose to include in this program any number of four different projects. The total cost and the total benefits of each of the four projects is given on the next page. What total amount should this government spend on the antipollution program? (*a*) $2 million; (*b*) $7 million; (*c*) $17 million; (*d*) $37 million.

Project	Total cost	Total benefit
#1	$2 million	$5 million
#2	$5 million	$7 million
#3	$10 million	$9 million
#4	$20 million	$15 million

12. Which of the following is *not* one of the reasons for the alleged greater efficiency of the private sector? (*a*) the least efficient workers in the economy gravitate to the public sector; (*b*) strong incentives to be efficient are largely absent in the public sector; (*c*) there is no simple way to measure or test efficiency in the public sector; (*d*) there is a tendency in the public sector to increase the budgets of agencies that have failed to perform efficiently.

■ **DISCUSSION QUESTIONS**

1. Why is it proper to refer to the United States economy as "mixed capitalism"?

2. What are the five economic functions of government in America's mixed capitalistic economy? Explain what the performance of each of these functions requires government to do.

3. Would you like to live in an economy in which government undertook only the first two functions listed in the text? What would be the advantages and disadvantages of living in such an economy?

4. Why does the market system provide some people with lower incomes than it provides others?

5. Explain why, when there are neither spillover costs nor spillover benefits, competitive product markets bring about an optimum allocation of resources to the production of the goods and services bought and sold in these markets. Why do spillover costs and benefits bring about a less than optimum allocation of resources?

6. What is meant by a spillover, a spillover cost, and a spillover benefit? What specific spillover costs and benefits seem to you to be significant in the American economy? How would the inclusion of spillover costs and the inclusion of spillover benefits affect the allocation of the economy's resources?

7. What methods do governments employ to (*a*) redistribute income; (*b*) reallocate resources to take account of spillover costs; (*c*) reallocate resources to take account of spillover benefits?

8. What is meant by the "exclusion principle"? How is this principle related to the distinction made between private and social goods?

9. What basic method does government employ in the United States to reallocate resources away from the production of private goods and toward the production of social goods?

10. Is there agreement on whether government should perform its five economic functions? Why is there criticism of government activity?

11. Explain what benefit-cost analysis is and how it is used. What is the major problem encountered when benefit-cost analysis is utilized by government?

12. Explain what is meant by "public sector failure."

13. The theory of public choice suggests that there are a number of possible causes of public sector failures. What are these causes? Explain how each would tend to result in the inefficient allocations of the economy's resources.

14. It is generally agreed that "national defense must lie in the public sector while wheat production can best be accomplished in the private sector." Why isn't there agreement on where many other goods or services should be produced?

15. Do you think government limits or expands personal freedom by performing its economic functions?

The Facts of American Capitalism: The Private Sector

The American economy has two major parts or sectors. This chapter is concerned with the private sector: the seventy-four million households and the thirteen and one-half million business firms in the economy. The next chapter deals with the public sector of the economy: the more than seventy-eight thousand governments found in the United States. These two chapters aim to acquaint the student with a few of the facts relevant to an understanding of American capitalism.

The first part of Chapter 7 examines the households of the economy, the distribution of income in the United States, and the uses to which the households put their incomes. The distribution of income means the way in which the total income which people receive is divided up (or distributed) among them. Two different ways of viewing the distribution of income are stressed: the way in which it is distributed among people according to the function they perform in the economy and the way in which it is distributed among the different income classes in the economy. Attention should be concentrated on the *general* facts of income distribution (not the exact figures), the conclusions which are drawn from these general facts, and the definitions of the new terms employed. In the examination of the different uses households make of their incomes, several new terms and

concepts are introduced; and figures are employed in the discussion. Again, attention should be paid to the generalizations and to the new terms.

The latter part of the chapter is concerned with the business firms of the United States. It is apparent that what most characterizes American business is the differences existing among firms insofar as their size, legal form, and life-span are concerned, as well as in the products they produce. The student should note the distinction between a proprietorship, a partnership, and a corporation and the advantages and disadvantages of each.

The chapter concludes with an introduction to what many economists consider a serious economic and political problem in the United States today: the large size of a relatively few firms. There is an examination of the degree to which "big business" prevails in the economy, of why and how firms get to be giants, and of the question of whether these giants are good or bad for the economy as a whole.

■ **CHECKLIST**

The very least you should be able to do when you have finished this chapter is:
□ Define and distinguish between a functional and a personal distribution of income.

□ State the relative size of the five shares in the functional distribution.

□ Explain the relationship between the personal distribution and the size and composition of the national output.

□ Explain the determinants of a household's income in a capitalistic economy.

□ List the three uses to which households put their incomes and state the relative size of each.

□ Distinguish among durable goods, nondurable goods, and services.

□ Explain the difference between a plant, a firm, and an industry; and between limited and unlimited liability.

□ State the advantages and disadvantages of the three legal forms of business enterprise.

□ Report the relative importance of each of the legal forms of business enterprise in the American economy.

□ Explain the extent to which bigness is found in the American economy; the means by which bigness has been accomplished and the motives for it; and the possible dangers of bigness.

■ **CHAPTER OUTLINE**

1. Households play a dual role in the economy: They supply the economy with resources, and they purchase the greater share of the goods and services produced by the economy. They obtain their incomes in exchange for the resources they furnish the economy. The way in which the total income of all households is divided among (or shared by) them is called the distribution of income.

a. A functional distribution of income indicates the way in which total income is divided into wages, rent, interest, and profits.

b. A personal distribution of income indicates the way in which total income is divided among households in various income classes and is of particular importance because it affects the total output of the economy and the types of goods and services demanded by consumers. The income of a household depends on its contribution to the total output of the economy.

2. Households use their incomes to purchase consumer goods, to pay taxes, and to accumulate savings.

a. Personal taxes constitute a deduction

from a household's total income; what remains after taxes can be either saved or spent.

b. Saving is what a household does not spend of its after-tax income.

c. Households spend for durable goods, nondurable goods, and services.

d. Consumer protection and the improvement of consumer knowledge results in a better allocation of society's resources.

3. The business population of the American economy consists of many imperfectly defined and overlapping industries; business firms which operate one or more plants and produce one or more products are the components of these industries. Firms vary greatly in size and in the length of time they remain in business.

4. The three principal legal forms of organization of firms are the proprietorship, the partnership, and the corporation; each form has special characteristics, advantages, and disadvantages. The form of organization which any business firm should adopt depends primarily upon the amount of money capital it will require to carry on its business. Although the proprietorship is numerically dominant in the United States, the corporation accounts for the major portion of the economy's output.

5. A relatively large percentage of the total output of and employment in the American economy is generated by the relatively small percentage of firms in the manufacturing sector of the economy.

6. Big business is characteristic of the American economy; the economy and many of its industries are dominated by giant firms which produce a relatively large proportion of the total output.

a. While no simple measure exists to calculate the extent of industrial concentration, statistics do reveal that concentration exists in many industries.

b. Business firms have grown large in order to increase their productive efficiency, their power and prestige, their chances of survival, and their profits by the elimination of competition. This growth has resulted both from the internal expansion of firms and from the combination of firms.

c. Whether big firms should be feared depends upon the answer to this question: Do the advantages associated with large-scale production outweigh the disadvantages associated with a decline in competition?

■ **IMPORTANT TERMS**

Private sector	Horizontal combination
Functional distribution of income	Vertical combination
Personal distribution of income	Conglomerate combination
Personal consumption expenditures	Sole proprietorship
Durable good	Partnership
Nondurable good	Corporation
Personal taxes	Unlimited liability
Personal saving	Limited liability
Plant	Separation ("divorce") of ownership and control
Firm	Internal growth
Industry	Combination

■ **FILL-IN QUESTIONS**

1. The approximately _____ million households in the United States play a dual role in the economy because they _____ and _____

2. The share of national income going for wages and salaries is about _____%.

3. The personal distribution of income is of particular importance because it affects the _____ and the _____ of national income, output, and employment.

4. In a price-market system the money income of a family or person depends roughly upon its _____

5. The total income of households is disposed of in three ways: _____, _____, and _____

6. Households use about _____ % of their total income to pay personal taxes, the greater part of which goes to the _____

government to pay their personal _____ taxes.

7. Based on their durability, consumer spending is classified as spending for _____

_____ ,

_____ ,

and _____

8. Households save primarily in order to obtain _____ and for purposes of _____

9. There are today about _____ business firms in the United States. The legal form of the great majority of these firms is the _____ ; and the legal form that produces over one-half the output of the American economy is the _____

10. The liabilities of a sole proprietor and of partners are _____ where the liabilities of stockholders in a corporation are _____

11. Indicate in the spaces to the right of each of the following whether these business characteristics are associated with the proprietorship (PRO), partnership (PART), corporation (CORP), two of these, or all three of these legal forms.
  a. Much red tape and legal expense in beginning the firm _____

  b. Unlimited liability _____

  c. No specialized management_____
  d. Has a life independent of its owner(s)

_____

  e. Decided tax advantage if its profits are large_____
  f. Greatest ability to acquire funds for the expansion of the firm_____
  g. Permits some but not a great degree of specialized management _____
  h. Possibility of an unresolved disagreement among owners over courses of action

_____

i. Makes it possible for a businessman to avoid responsibility for illegal actions _____

12. In terms of its contribution to the national income and the number of people employed, the largest industry class is

_____

13. The United States is often called a big business economy because a relatively _____

firms produce a relatively _____
part of the output of the economy and of some industries. Big business seems to be

most significant in the _____
industries of the economy and least significant in _____

14. What are the four basic reasons why business firms desire to grow big?

a. _____

b. _____

c. _____

d. _____

15. Small firms become large firms either as

consequence of _____

or _____
or both. Most large firms have depended to a

large degree upon_____

16. In examining the question of whether big business should be feared we find two schools of thought.
  a. One school of thought holds that big business is necessary if firms are to utilize

the best available _____
  b. The other school argues that many businesses are larger than they need to be to be

_____

and that these firms have _____
power.

■ **PROBLEMS AND PROJECTS**

1. The table below shows the functional distribution of income in the United States for the year 1972. In the spaces at the right, place the figures which indicate the percentage shares of income. (Because of rounding, the sum of the shares does not equal the total.)

	Billions of dollars	Percentage share
Wages and salaries	$ 921.4	_____
Proprietors' income	83.3	_____
Corporate profits	100.6	_____
Interest	81.6	_____
Rents	21.1	_____
National income	1208.1	100.0

2. Indicate to the best of your ability what you would call the industries in which the following firms operate:
  a. Sears, Roebuck and Company
  b. The General Electric Company
  c. A used-car dealer in your town
  d. Gimbels department stores
  e. Your local gas or electric company
  f. A new-car dealer
  g. The Mars Candy Company
  h. The Aluminum Company of America
  i. The Anaconda Copper Company
  j The William Wrigley Chewing Gum Company

3. Look at the list of firms in question 2 above.
  a. In which industry *class* would you put each of these firms?
  b. Are any of these firms in industries which Table 29-1 of the text lists as highly concentrated manufacturing industries?

■ **SELF-TEST**

Circle the T if the statement is true, the F if it is false.

1. The personal distribution of income describes the manner in which society's total income is divided among wages, rent, interest, and profit. **T F**

2. Corporate profits over the years have tended to be an unstable percentage of national income. **T F**

3. A distribution of income which is based on the productivity of resources usually results in considerable *in*equality in the size of incomes.   **T   F**

4. In both relative and absolute terms, personal taxes have exceeded personal saving in recent years.   **T   F**

5. A "durable good" is defined as a good which has an expected life of one year or more.   **T   F**

6. The families that receive more than $50,000 a year account for most of the personal savings done in the United States.   **T   F**

7. *Dissaving* means that personal consumption expenditures exceed after-tax income.   **T   F**

8. A plant is defined as a group of firms under a single management.   **T   F**

9. An industry is a group of firms that produce the same or nearly the same products.   **T   F**

10. The corporate form of organization is the least used by firms in the United States.   **T   F**

11. Corporations account for over one-half the total output of the privately owned business firms in the United States.   **T   F**

12. The corporation in the United States today always has a tax advantage over other legal forms of business organization.   **T   F**

13. Whether a business firm should incorporate or not depends chiefly upon the amount of money capital it must have to finance the enterprise.   **T   F**

14. Most giant firms in the United States have grown and become big by internal growth rather than through combination with other firms.   **T   F**

15. Not all economists and observers agree that modern technology requires firms as large as some of those in the United States today.   **T   F**

Underscore the letter that corresponds to the best answer.

1. There are in the United States approximately how many households (families)? (*a*) 65 million; (*b*) 70 million; (*c*) 75 million; (*d*) 80 million.

2. The functional distribution for the United States shows that the largest part of the national income is (*a*) wages and salaries; (*b*) proprietors' income; (*c*) corporate profits; (*d*) interest and rents.

3. When national income declines (as in a recession or depression): (*a*) wages remain constant and the other distributive shares of national income decrease; (*b*) wages decrease and the other distributive shares increase; (*c*) wages increase and other distributive shares decrease; (*d*) wages and the other distributive shares decrease.

4. Which of the following is *not* a factor affecting the amount of money income received by the individual household? (*a*) the quantity of resources the household has available to supply to business firms; (*b*) the amount of saving done by the household; (*c*) the prices paid for the various resources in the market; (*d*) the actual level of employment of the household's resources.

5. The personal distribution of income affects: (*a*) the total output of the economy; (*b*) the number of people who find employment in the economy; (*c*) the composition of the total output of the economy; (*d*) all of the above.

6. Expenditures for *nondurable* goods in recent years have amounted to approximately what percentage of personal consumption expenditures? (*a*) 30%; (*b*) 40%; (*c*) 50%; (*d*) 60%.

7. Which of the following is a true statement? (*a*) The durable goods and service parts of personal consumption expenditures vary more over time than do the expenditures for nondurables; (*b*) expenditures for nondurables vary more than do the expenditures for durable goods and services; (*c*) expenditures for nondurables vary more than the expenditures for services and less than the expenditures for durables; (*d*) expenditures for nondurables vary more than the expenditures for durables and less than the expenditures for services.

8. In recent years personal taxes have been approximately what percentage of total income? (*a*) 14%; (*b*) 18%; (*c*) 24%; (*d*) 30%.

9. If we include self-employed farmers and professional people, there are approximately how many million business firms in the United States? (a) 5; (b) 8; (c) 14; (d) 15.

10. A group of three plants which is owned and operated by a single firm and which consists of a farm growing wheat, a flour milling plant, and a plant which bakes and sells bakery products is an example of: (a) a horizontal combination; (b) a vertical combination; (c) a conglomerate combination; (d) a corporation.

11. Limited liability is associated with: (a) only proprietorships; (b) only partnerships; (c) both proprietorships and partnerships; (d) only corporations.

12. Which of the following forms of business organization can most effectively raise money capital? (a) corporation; (b) partnership; (c) proprietorship; (d) vertical combination.

13. Which of the following industries has the largest number of firms? (a) agriculture, forestry, and fishing; (b) manufacturing; (c) wholesale and retail trade; (d) mining.

14. Which of the following industries produces the largest percentage of the national income? (a) agriculture, forestry, and fishing; (b) manufacturing; (c) wholesale and retail trade; (d) government.

15. The 100 largest manufacturing firms in the United States today own approximately what percentage of the net capital assets of all manufacturing firms? (a) 40%; (b) 45%; (c) 50%; (d) more than 50%.

■ **DISCUSSION QUESTIONS**

1. Explain the difference between a functional and a personal distribution of income. Rank the five items in the functional distribution in the order of their size.

2. The present personal distribution of income affects both the level of resource use and the allocation of resources in the economy. What is the connection between the distribution of income and the employment and allocation of resources?

3. What determines how large a money income an individual household will have? In what way is a household's income related to its productivity? Why does a personal distribution of income based on productivity lead to personal income inequality?

4. Which, in your opinion, would result in greater total saving and less consumption spending out of a national income of a given size: a more or less nearly equal distribution of income?

5. The purchase of what type of consumer goods is largely postponable? Why is this? How is it possible for a family's personal consumption expenditures to exceed its after-tax income?

6. What is meant by "consumer protection"? Why might consumer protection and increased consumer knowledge lead to a better allocation of resources? Are there any problems that might arise as a result of the imposition by government of quality standards for products?

7. What does it mean when it is said that the business population in the United States is both "diverse" and "fluid"?

8. What is the difference between a plant and a firm? Between a firm and an industry? Which of these three concepts is the most difficult to apply in practice? Why? Distinguish between a horizontal, a vertical, and a conglomerate combination.

9. What are the principal advantages and disadvantages of each of the three legal forms of business organization? Which of the disadvantages of the proprietorship and partnership accounts for the employment of the corporate form among the big businesses of the American economy?

10. Explain what "separation of ownership and control" of the modern corporation means. What problems does this separation create for stockholders and the economy?

11. What figures can you cite to show that the typical firm engaged in agriculture is relatively small and that the average firm engaged in manufacturing is relatively large? Are firms engaged in wholesaling and retailing; mining; and finance, insurance, and real estate relatively large or relatively small?

12. Is manufacturing in the United States an industry dominated by big business? What evidence do you use to reach this conclusion?

13. Why do business firms want to grow and become bigger? How do they go about expanding?

14. What are the two opposing views often advanced in answer to the question, "Is big business bad for the economy"?

The Facts of American Capitalism: The Public Sector

The facts of public sector or government finance in the United States presented in Chapter 8 center on two questions: Where do governments get their incomes? On what do they spend these incomes?

The organization of the chapter is relatively simple. First, the trends which taxes collected and expenditures made by all levels of government—Federal, state, and local—have taken since 1929 are examined briefly. Second, a closer look is given to the major items upon which governments spend their incomes, the principal taxes they levy to obtain their incomes, and the relative importance of these taxes. Third, the chapter looks at revenue sharing as a means of reducing the mismatch between the fiscal wants and resources of the Federal government on the one hand, and the wants and resources of state and local government on the other hand. Fourth, the chapter examines the principles applied in levying taxes, the way tax rates vary as personal incomes change, who really pays the taxes levied against various groups in the economy, and how much of their incomes Americans pay to government in the form of taxes.

What should the student get out of this chapter? There are at least six important sets

of facts: (1) the trend which taxes and government expenditures have taken in recent years and why; (2) the relative importance of the principal taxes and the relative importance of the various expenditure items in the budgets of the three levels of government; (3) the nature of the fiscal imbalance between the Federal government and state and local governments, how revenue sharing might remedy this imbalance; (4) the meaning and philosophy of the benefits-received and ability-to-pay principles; (5) the meaning of progressive, regressive, and proportional taxation, the shifting and incidence of taxes, and the incidence of the major types of taxes; and (6) the degree of progressiveness that exists in the taxing systems of Federal, state, and local government; and the percentages of income turned over to government by all households and by families with different incomes.

The student is cautioned again to avoid memorizing statistics. He should look instead for the trends and generalizations which these statistics illuminate. He should spend his time, also, on the terms used, the classifications employed, and the conclusions which are drawn and which embody these terms and classifications.

■ CHECKLIST

The very least you should be able to do when you have finished this chapter is:

□ List the six causes of the expansion of government tax revenues and expenditures during the past five decades.

□ Explain the differences between government purchases and transfer payments; and the effect of each of these two kinds of expenditures on the composition of the national output.

□ Describe the two greatest sources of revenue and the two largest categories of expenditures of the three levels of government.

□ Define and explain the difference between the marginal and the average tax rate.

□ Explain why the Federal government has a revenue sharing program.

□ Distinguish between the ability-to-pay principle and the benefits-received principle.

□ Define and explain the differences among a regressive, proportional, and progressive tax.

□ Describe the regressivity or progressivity of the Federal and of the state and local tax systems; of the combined Federal, state, and local tax system; and of their combined tax-transfer (net tax) system.

■ CHAPTER OUTLINE

1. Government's functions in the economy are felt most directly when it collects revenue by taxation and expends this revenue for goods and services; and there is an important difference between the voluntary transactions in the private and the compulsory transactions in the public sector of the economy.

2. In both absolute and relative terms, government tax collections and spending have increased during the past forty-five or so years.

a. The increased tax collections and spending are the result of hot and cold wars, population increases, urbanization and the greater demand for social goods, pollution of the environment, egalitarianism, and inflation.

b. Government spending consists of purchases of goods and services and transfer payments; and these two types of spending have different effects on the composition of the national output.

3. At the Federal level of government:

a. Over 40% of the total expenditure is for income security and health and about 25% is for national defense (but over 40% is for military preparedness and past wars).

b. The major sources of revenue are personal income, payroll, and corporate income taxes.

c. Tax-exempt securities and capital gains are tax loopholes for some persons and firms.

4. At the other two levels of government:

a. State governments depend largely on sales and excise taxes and use a large part of their revenues for education and highways.

b. Local governments rely heavily upon property taxes and spend the greater part of their revenues for education.

5. Because of an imbalance between the ability of state and local governments to expand their tax collections and the growing desire of these governments to deal with social and economic problems, the Federal government has resorted to revenue sharing to reduce this imbalance.

6. Although the overall level of taxes is important to the economy, the question of who pays the tax bill is equally important.

a. Two philosophies, the benefits-received principle and the ability-to-pay principle, are widely employed to determine how the tax bill should be apportioned among the economy's citizens.

b. Taxes can be classified as progressive, regressive, or proportional according to the way in which the *tax rate* changes as income increases.

c. A tax levied upon one person or group of persons may be shifted partially or completely to another person or group; to the extent that a tax can be shifted or passed on through lower prices paid or higher prices received, its incidence is passed on. The incidence of the four major types of taxes is only probable and is not known for certain.

d. Federal taxes tend to be progressive and state and local taxes regressive; and the tax system as a whole is roughly proportional. But when transfer payments received are deducted from the taxes paid the combined tax-transfer system is, on the whole, progressive.

■ IMPORTANT TERMS

Government transfer payment

Personal income tax

Marginal tax rate

Average tax rate

Payroll tax

Corporation income tax

Double taxation

Sales tax

Excise tax

Capital gain

Property tax

Revenue sharing

Intergovernmental grant

Categorical grant

Unrestricted grant

State and Local Fiscal Assistance Act

Benefits-received principle

Ability-to-pay principle

Progressive tax

Regressive tax

Proportional tax

Tax incidence

Tax shifting

Net taxes

Combined tax-transfer system

■ FILL-IN QUESTIONS

1. It is through the _____ and the _____ of government that the functions of government are most directly felt by the economy.

2. Transactions in the private sector of the economy are _____ while those in the public sector, by and large, are _____

3. Government transfer payments are _____ _____

4. When government raises $20 billion by taxation and uses it to purchase goods it shifts resources from the production of _____ to the production of _____ goods; but when it uses the $20 billion to make transfer payments it changes the _____ of the output of private goods.

5. The most important source of revenue for the Federal government is the _____ tax; next in importance are the _____ taxes. The two largest categories of Federal

expenditures are spending for _____ and for _____

6. Corporation income is said to be "taxed double" because _____ _____

7. State governments rely primarily upon_____ and _____ taxes for their incomes which they spend mostly on _____ and _____

8. At local levels of government the single most important source of revenue is the_____ _____ tax and the single most important expenditure is for _____

9. Two important Federal tax loopholes are _____ and _____

10. To increase the incomes of state and local governments and enable them to expand their efforts to solve serious social and economic problems facing them the Federal government has engaged in _____

11. The two philosophies of apportioning the tax burden which are most evident in the American economy are the_____ principle and the _____ principle.

12. As the income *decreases,* a proportional tax involves a _____ tax rate, a regressive tax, an _____ tax rate, and a progressive tax, a _____ _____ tax rate.

13. Indicate in the space to the right of each of the following taxes whether that tax (as applied in the United States) tends to be regressive (R) or progressive (P).

a. Personal income tax _____

b. Sales tax _____

c. Payroll tax _____

d. Property tax _____

e. Corporation income tax _____

14. What is the probable incidence of each of the following taxes?

a. Personal income tax: _____

b. Sales and excise tax: _____

c. Corporate income tax: _____

d. Property tax: _____

15. In the United States:
a. the tax systems of state and local governments tend to be _____
b. the tax system of the Federal government is _____
c. the tax system for all levels of government combined is roughly _____
d. the tax-transfer system for all levels of government combined is _____

■ **PROBLEMS AND PROJECTS**

1. At the top of the next column are several levels of taxable income and hypothetical marginal tax rates applicable to each $1000 increase in income. Compute for each income level the tax and the average tax rate.

2. In the table below are seven levels of taxable income and the amount that would be paid at each of the seven levels under three tax laws: A, B, and C. Compute for each of the three tax laws the *average* rate of taxation at each of the seven income levels and indicate whether the tax is regressive, proportional, progressive, or some combination thereof.

Taxable income	Marginal tax rate, %	Tax	Average tax rate, %
$1500		$300	20
2500	22	_____	_____
3500	25	_____	_____
4500	29	_____	_____
5500	34	_____	_____
6500	40	_____	_____
7500	47	_____	_____

3. Assume a state government levies a 4 percent sales tax on all consumption expenditures. Consumption expenditures at six income levels are shown in the table below.

Income	Consumption expenditures	Sales tax paid	Average tax rate, %
$ 5,000	$5,000	$_____	_____
6,000	5,800	_____	_____
7,000	6,600	_____	_____
8,000	7,400	_____	_____
9,000	8,200	_____	_____
10,000	9,000	_____	_____

a. Compute the sales tax paid at each income.
b. Compute the average tax rate at each income.
c. Using income as the tax base, the sales tax is a _____ tax.

Income	Tax A		Tax B		Tax C	
	Tax paid	Av. tax rate %	Tax paid	Av. tax rate %	Tax paid	Av. tax rate %
$ 500	$ 15.00	_____%	$ 5.00	_____%	$ 50.00	_____%
1,500	45.00	_____	30.00	_____	135.00	_____
3,000	90.00	_____	90.00	_____	240.00	_____
5,000	150.00	_____	150.00	_____	350.00	_____
7,500	225.00	_____	187.50	_____	450.00	_____
10,000	300.00	_____	200.00	_____	500.00	_____
15,000	450.00	_____	300.00	_____	600.00	_____
Type of tax:	_____		_____		_____	

4. The table below shows the amount of taxes paid and the size of the government transfer payments received at five different levels of income. Taxes are proportional because the average tax rate is 30% at each income level.

Income	Taxes paid	Transfer payments received	Net taxes	Net tax rate
$ 2,000	$ 600	$1,000	$_____	_____%
4,000	1,200	800	_____	_____
10,000	3,000	600	_____	_____
15,000	4,500	300	_____	_____
25,000	7,500	0	_____	_____

a. Compute and enter in the table the net tax at each of the five income levels.

b. Now compute and enter in the table the average *net* tax rate at each income. (*Hint:* Divide the net tax at each income by the income to find the average net tax rate.)

c. The tax-transfer system is (progressive,

regressive, proportional) _____

because the net tax rate _____ as the level of income increases.

■ **SELF-TEST**

Circle the T if the statement is true, the F if it is false.

1. Taxes collected by, and expenditures of, all levels of government in the United States exceed $550 billion per year.   **T F**

2. When a government levies taxes and uses the tax revenue to make transfer payments it shifts resources from the production of private goods to the production of social goods.   **T F**

3. The chief source of revenue for the Federal government is the corporation income tax.
          T F

4. The level of Federal expenditures in 1976 was about $300 million.   **T F**

5. There is a major loophole in the Federal tax system because personal income tax rates are progressive.   **T F**

6. Total taxes collected by the Federal government are approximately equal to the amount of taxes collected by all state and local governments.   **T F**

7. The State and Local Fiscal Assistance Act of 1972 provides for categorical grants to state and local governments.   **T F**

8. The chief difficulty in applying the benefits-received principle of taxation is to determine who receives the benefits of many of the goods and services which government supplies.   **T F**

9. A sales tax generally turns out to be a proportional tax.   **T F**

10. The state and Federal taxes on gasoline are good examples of taxes levied on the benefits-received principle.   **T F**

Underscore the letter that corresponds to the best answer.

1. Today all government expenditures equal approximately what percentage of the American economy's total output? (*a*) 10%; (*b*) 18%; (*c*) 22%; (*d*) 33%.

2. Which of the following would *not* be a government transfer expenditure? (*a*) contributions of employers to support the social security program; (*b*) social security payments to the aged; (*c*) unemployment compensation benefits; (*d*) payments to the widows of war veterans.

3. Past wars and military preparedness account for approximately what percentage of all Federal expenditures? (*a*) 40%; (*b*) 55%; (*c*) 60%; (*d*) 65%.

4. Which of the following accounts for the largest percentage of all Federal expenditures? (*a*) income security and health; (*b*) national defense; (*c*) interest on the public debt; (*d*) veterans' services.

5. Which of the following pairs represents the chief source of income and the most important type of expenditure of *state* governments? (*a*) personal income tax and expenditures for education; (*b*) personal income tax and expenditures for highways; (*c*) sales and excise taxes and expenditures for public welfare; (*d*) sales and excise taxes and expenditures for education.

6. Which of the following pairs represents

the chief source of income and the most important type of expenditure of *local* governments? (*a*) property tax and expenditures for highways; (*b*) property tax and expenditures for education; (*c*) sales and excise taxes and expenditures for public welfare; (*d*) sales and excise taxes and expenditures for police, fire, and general government.

7. Which of the following is *not* true of the ability-to-pay principle as applied in the United States? (*a*) it is more widely applied than the benefits-received principle; (*b*) income is generally taken as the measure of the ability to pay; (*c*) it is more widely applied by state and local than by Federal government; (*d*) as the tax base increases, taxes paid increase both absolutely and relatively.

8. Which of the following tends to be a progressive tax in the United States? (*a*) income tax; (*b*) property tax; (*c*) sales tax; (*d*) payroll tax.

9. Which of the following taxes can be least easily shifted? (*a*) personal income tax; (*b*) corporation income tax; (*c*) sales tax; (*d*) business property tax.

10. Which of the following is roughly proportional? (*a*) The state and local tax system; (*b*) the Federal tax system; (*c*) the American tax system as a whole; (*d*) the American tax-transfer system.

■ DISCUSSION QUESTIONS

1. How do transactions in the public sector differ from those in the private sector of the economy?

2. What have been the causes which have contributed to the absolute and relative increases in government spending over the last forty-five years?

3. Government expenditures fall into two broad classes: expenditures for goods and services, and transfer payments. Explain the difference between these and give examples of expenditures which fall into each of the two classes.

4. Explain the difference between exhaustive and nonexhaustive government spending.

5. When government collects taxes and spends the tax revenues it affects the composition of the total output of the economy. What is the effect on the composition of total output if government uses the tax revenues to purchase goods and services? What is the effect if it uses them to make transfer payments?

6. Explain precisely the difference between the marginal tax rate and the average tax rate.

7. Explain in detail the differences that exist between Federal, state, and local governments in the taxes upon which they primarily rely for their revenues and the major purposes for which they use these revenues.

8. What is a tax "loophole"? What are the two principal loopholes in the Federal tax system? How do these loopholes affect the distribution of income?

9. Why has the Federal government increasingly shared its tax revenues with state and local governments. Explain the difference between a categorical grant and an unrestricted grant; and the major provisions of the State and Local Fiscal Assistance Act of 1972.

10. What are the two basic philosophies for apportioning the tax burden in the United States? Explain each. What are the difficulties encountered in putting these philosophies into practice?

11. Explain the differences among progressive, regressive, and proportional taxes. Which taxes fall into each of these three categories? What can be said about the progressivity or regressivity of Federal taxes, state and local taxes, the overall tax system, and the combined tax-transfer system?

12. Which of the following taxes tends to be shifted? (*a*) personal income tax; (*b*) corporate income tax; (*c*) sales and excise taxes; (*d*) property tax. From whom is the tax shifted and upon whom is the tax incidence?

CHAPTER

National Income Accounting

National income (or social) accounting is the subject matter of Chapter 9. This type of accounting aims to measure or estimate (1) the gross national product, the total output of all final goods and services in the economy during a year; (2) the net national product, the annual output of all final goods and services over and above (in excess of or "net of") the stock of capital goods with which the economy began the year; (3) the national income, the total income or output earned by owners of land and capital and suppliers of labor and entrepreneurial ability during a year; (4) personal income, the total income or output actually received—whether earned or unearned—by these suppliers of resources (or the total income earned and received plus unearned income) before the payment of personal taxes; and (5) disposable income, the total income or output available to resource suppliers after the payment of personal taxes.

This is national income (or social) accounting because it involves estimating output or income for the nation or society as a whole, rather than for an individual business firm or family. Note that the terms "output" and "income" are interchangeable because the nation's output and its income are identical. The value of the nation's output equals the total expenditures for this output, and these

expenditures become the income of those in the nation who have produced this output. Consequently, there are two equally acceptable methods, both discussed in the chapter, for obtaining each of the five income-output measures listed above. These two methods are the expenditures method and the income method.

Accounting is essentially an adding-up process. This chapter explains in detail and lists the items which must be added to obtain by both methods each of the five income-output measures. It is up to you to learn precisely *what* to add, i.e., how to compute GNP, NNP, NI, PI, and DI by both methods. This is a fairly difficult chapter, and the only way to learn the material is simply to sit down and learn it—memorize it if necessary! A careful reading of the chapter, however, will enable you to avoid the necessity of memorizing. You should first try to understand what each of the five income-output measures attempts to measure and the two alternative approaches to these measurements. Remembering the items to be added will then be much simpler.

In addition to explaining the two methods of computing the five income-output measures and each of the items used in the computation process, the chapter discusses the purpose of social accounting; the means by which income-output measures for different years may be adjusted to take account of changes in the price level so that comparisons between years are possible; and the shortcomings and dangers inherent in national income accounting. Chapter 9 is the essential background for Parts Two and Three, which explain the history of and the factors that determine the level of total output and income in the economy. The chapter is important in itself because it presents one of the several means of measuring the well-being of the economy and the individuals comprising the economy in a given year and over the years.

■ CHECKLIST

The very least you should be able to do when you have finished this chapter is:
□ Give the purposes of national income accounting.
□ Adjust the money GNP, when you are given the relevant price index, to find the real GNP.
□ Present five reasons why GNP is not an index of social welfare.
□ Define GNP; and compute it using either the expenditures or the income approach when you are given the necessary data.
□ Explain: the difference between gross and net investment; why changes in inventories are investment; and the relation between net investment and economic growth.
□ Define each of the following; and, when you are given the needed data, compute each by two different methods: NNP, NI, PI, and DI.

■ CHAPTER OUTLINE

1. National income (or social) accounting consists of concepts which enable those who use them to measure the economy's output, to compare it with past outputs, to explain its size and the reasons for changes in its size, and to formulate policies designed to increase it.

2. The gross national product (GNP) is the market value of all final goods and services produced in the economy during a year.
  a. GNP is measured in dollar terms rather than in terms of physical units of output.

b. Because the price level changes over time, it is necessary to adjust dollar GNP figures when comparing GNPs in different years.
  c. To adjust dollar GNP figures for changes in the price level, divide the dollar GNP in any year by the price index for that year.
  d. To avoid double counting, GNP includes only *final* goods and services (goods and services that will not be processed further during the *current* year).
  e. Nonproductive transactions are not included in GNP; purely financial transactions and secondhand sales are, therefore, excluded.
  f. GNP is not, for several reasons, a measure of social welfare.
  g. Measurement of GNP can be accomplished by two methods—the expenditures and the income methods—but the same result is obtained by either method.

3. Computation of GNP by the expenditures method requires the accountant to add the following four types of spending for final goods and services.
  a. Personal consumption expenditures of households.
  b. Government purchases of goods and services.
  c. Gross private domestic investment (business expenditures for machinery, equipment, and tools; construction of buildings; and changes in inventories).
    (1) A change in inventories is included in investment because it is the part of output of the economy which was not sold during the year.
    (2) Investment does not include expenditures for stocks or bonds or for second-hand capital goods.
    (3) Gross investment exceeds net investment by the value of the capital goods worn out during the year.
    (4) An economy in which net investment is positive (zero, negative) is an expanding (a static, a declining) economy.
  d. Net exports (exports minus imports of goods and services).

4. Computation of GNP by the income method requires the accountant to total the nine uses to which the income derived from the production and sale of final goods and services are put. These nine items are:

a. Depreciation (capital consumption allowance).

b. Indirect business taxes.

c. Compensation of employees (the sum of wages and salaries *and* wage and salary supplements).

d. Rents.

e. Interest (only the interest payments made by business firms are included; the interest payments made by government and consumers are excluded).

f. Proprietors' income (the profits or net income of unincorporated firms).

g. Corporate profits which are subdivided into:

(1) Corporate income taxes

(2) Dividends

(3) Undistributed corporate profits

5. In addition to GNP, four other national income measures are important in evaluating the performance of the economy. Each has a distinct definition and can be computed by making additions to or deductions from another measure.

a. NNP is equal to GNP minus depreciation (capital consumption allowance).

b. NI equals NNP less indirect business taxes.

c. PI is found by *adding* transfer payments to and *subtracting* social security contributions, corporate income taxes, and undistributed corporate profits from NI.

d. DI is PI less personal taxes and is also equal to personal consumption expenditures plus personal saving.

e. The relations among the five income-output measures are summarized for you in Table 9-7.

■ IMPORTANT ITEMS

National income (social) accounting

Gross national product

Real gross national product

Inflating

Deflating

Price index

Base year

Given year

Final goods

Intermediate goods

Double counting

Value added

Nonproductive transaction

Nonmarket transaction

Expenditures approach

Income approach

Personal consumption expenditures

Government purchases of goods and services

Gross private domestic investment

Noninvestment transaction

Net private domestic investment

Expanding economy

Static economy

Declining economy

Net exports

Nonincome charges

Capital consumption allowances (depreciation)

Indirect business taxes

Compensation to employees

Wage and salary supplements

Net national product

National income

Personal income

Disposable income

Personal saving

■ FILL-IN QUESTIONS

1. Social accounting is invaluable because it provides a means of keeping track of the ____

_____

and the information necessary to devise and put into effect _____

_____

2. Gross national product is a monetary measure of all final goods and services produced during a year; to measure the value of these goods and services, the goods and services are valued at their _____

3. In order to compare the gross national product in two different years, it is necessary to adjust money GNP because _____

_____

4. In measuring GNP only final goods and services are included; if intermediate goods and services were included, the accountant would be _____

5. A firm buys materials for $200 and produces from them a product which sells for $315. The $115 is the _____ by the firm.

6. The total value added to a product at all

stages of production equals _____

_____

7. Public transfer payments, private transfer payments, and security transactions are all examples of the _____ type of nonproductive transactions.

8. The capital consumption allowance and indirect business taxes, by the income approach, are referred to as _____ charges or allocations.

9. Gross private domestic investment basically includes _____ ,

_____ ,

and _____
Net private domestic investment is less than gross private domestic investment by an amount equal to _____

10. If gross private domestic investment is greater than capital consumption, the economy is _____ ;
and if it equals capital consumption, the economy is _____

11. The compensation of employees in the system of social accounting consists of actual wages and salaries *and* wage and salary _____

_____ which are the payments employers make to

_____

and to _____

12. Corporate profits are disposed of in three ways: _____ ,

_____ ,

and _____ .

13. Gross national product overstates the economy's production in a given year because it fails to _____

14. Net national product equals gross national product minus _____

15. National income equals net national

products minus _____ ;
this deduction is made because national income is income _____
and the subtracted item is not considered to be a payment to a factor of production which contributes to the production of output.

16. *Transfer payments* include the following five items:

a. _____

b. _____

c. _____

d. _____

e. _____

17. Personal income equals national income plus _____

and minus _____ ,

_____ ,

and _____ .

It also equals the sum of _____ ,

_____ ,

and _____

18. Disposable income equals personal income minus _____ ;

disposable income also equals _____

plus _____

19. Personal saving equals disposable income minus _____

20. The *interest* included in the measurement of the GNP (by the income approach) is the interest paid by _____

The interest payments made by _____

and by _____
are not included in this item.

■ **PROBLEMS AND PROJECTS**

1. Price indices, deflating and inflating:
a. Below are hypothetical figures for five different years showing the prices of a typical commodity in each of the five years.

Year	Price	Price index (1967 equals 100)	Price index (1975 equals 100)
1967	$ 9		
1969	11		
1971	6		
1973	7		
1975	8		

(1) Using 1967 as the base year, compute the index of prices in each of the five years.

(2) Using 1975 as the base year, compute the index of prices in each of the five years.

b. Below are hypothetical figures for money or unadjusted gross national product in each of the five years.

Year	Money or unadjusted GNP, billions of dollars	Adjusted GNP in 1967 dollars	Adjusted GNP in 1975 dollars
1967	$ 90	$	$
1969	120		
1971	60		
1973	65		
1975	70		

(1) Compute the real (or adjusted) gross national product measured in 1967 dollars.

(2) Compute the real (or adjusted) gross national product measured in 1975 dollars.

2. You are given the following national income accounting data.

	Billions of dollars
Personal taxes	$ 37
Social security contributions	10
Indirect business taxes	19
Corporate income taxes	38
Transfer payments	17
Gross national product	468
Undistributed corporate profits	34
Gross private domestic investment	74
Personal consumption expenditures	310
Net private domestic investment	51

Compute each of the following:

a. Capital consumption allowance: $_____

b. Net national product: $ _____

c. National income: $ _____

d. Personal income: $_____

e. Disposable income: $ _____

f. Personal saving: $_____

3. Following are hypothetical social accounting figures for the United States.

	Billions of dollars
Exports	$ 12
Dividends	13
Capital consumption allowance	22
Government expenditures for goods and services	71
Rents	9
Indirect business taxes	11
Compensation of employees	238
Gross private domestic investment	56
Personal saving	34
Corporate income taxes	15
Transfer payments	26
Interest	6
Proprietors' income	21
Personal consumption expenditures	217
Imports	7
Social security contributions	7
Undistributed corporate profits	14
Personal taxes	55

Complete the table on pages 63 and 64 in which the five income-output measures are computed by both methods. Identify each of the several amounts which you add (and/or subtract) to compute each of the five measures.

4. Below is a list of items which may or may not be included in the five income-output measures. Indicate in the space to the right of each which of the income-output measures includes this item; it is possible for the item to be included in none, one, two, three, four, or all of the measures. If the item is included in none of the measures, indicate why it is not included.

a. Interest on the national debt _____

b. The sale of a used air conditioner _____

Income method		Expenditures method	
Gross National Product			
(1)	$	(1)	$
(2)		(2)	
(3)		(3)	
(4)		(4)	
(5)		Gross national product	$_____
(6)			
(7)			
(8)			
(9)			
Gross national product	$_____		
Net National Product			
(1)	$	(1)	$
(2)		(2)	
(3)		(3)	
(4)		(4)	
(5)		Net national product	$_____
(6)			
(7)			
(8)			
Net national product	$_____		
National Income			
(1)	$	(1)	$
(2)		(2) Less:	
(3)		National income	$_____
(4)			
(5)			
(6)			
(7)			
National income	$_____		
Personal Income			
(1)	$	(1)	$
(2) Plus:		(2)	
(3) Less:		(3)	
(4) Less:			
(5) Less:		Personal income	$_____
Personal income	$_____		

Income method	Expenditures method

Disposable Income

(1) $ (1) $

(2) Less: (2)

   Disposable income $_____

                               Disposable income $_____

c. The production of shoes which are not sold by the manufacturer _____

d. The income of a bootlegger in a "dry" state _____

e. The purchase of a share of common stock on the New York Stock Exchange _____

f. The interest paid on the bonds of the General Motors Corporation _____

g. The labor performed by a homemaker _____

h. The labor performed by a paid baby-sitter _____

i. The monthly check received by an idler from his rich aunt _____

j. The purchase of a new tractor by a farmer _____

k. The labor performed by an assembly-line worker in repapering his own kitchen _____

l. The services of a lawyer _____

m. The purchase of shoes from their manufacturer by a shoe retailer _____

n. The monthly check received from the government by a student studying on the GI Bill of Rights _____

o. The rent a homeowner would receive if he did not live in his own home _____

■ **SELF-TEST**

Circle the T if the statement is true, the F if it is false.

1. Gross national product measures at their market value the total output of all goods and services produced in the economy during a year. **T F**

2. Comparison of gross national product with the gross national product of an earlier year when the price level has risen between the two years necessitates the "inflation" of the GNP figure in the later year. **T F**

3. To adjust money gross national product for a given year so that a comparison between GNP in that year and in the base year can be made, it is necessary to divide money GNP in the given year by the price index—expressed as a decimal—for that year. **T F**

4. The total value added to a product and the value of the final product are equal. **T F**

5. The two approaches to the measurement of the gross national product yield identical results because one approach measures the total amount spent on the products produced by business firms during a year while the second approach measures the total income of business firms during the year. **T F**

6. In computing gross national product, net national product, and national income by the expenditures approach, transfer payments are excluded because they do not represent payments for currently produced goods and services. **T F**

7. If gross private domestic investment is greater than capital consumption during a given year, the economy has declined during that year. **T F**

The data in the table on page 65 should be used to answer true-false questions 8 through 10 and multiple-choice questions 8 through 10.

8. Gross private domestic investment is equal to $25 billion. **T F**

9. National income equals the net national product minus $8 billion. **T F**

10. Disposable income is equal to $245 billion. **T F**

	Billions of dollars
Net private domestic investment	$ 32
Personal taxes	39
Transfer payments	19
Indirect business taxes	8
Corporation income taxes	11
Personal consumption expenditures	217
Capital consumption allowance	7
United States exports	15
Government purchase of goods and services	51
Undistributed corporate profits	10
Social security contributions	4
United States imports	17

Underscore the letter that corresponds to the best answer.

1. Which of the following is *not* an important use to which social accounting is put? (*a*) provides a basis for the formulation and application of policies designed to improve the economy's performance; (*b*) permits measurement of the economic efficiency of the economy; (*c*) makes possible an estimate of the output of final goods and services in the economy; (*d*) enables the economist to chart the growth or decline of the economy over a period of time.

2. If both money gross national product and the level of prices are rising, it is evident that: (*a*) real GNP is constant; (*b*) real GNP is rising but not as rapidly as prices; (*c*) real GNP is declining; (*d*) no conclusion can be drawn concerning the real GNP of the economy on the basis of this information.

3. To include the value of the parts used in producing the automobiles turned out during a year in gross national product for that year would be an example of: (*a*) including a nonmarket transaction; (*b*) including a nonproductive transaction; (*c*) including a noninvestment transaction; (*d*) double counting.

4. The sale in 1969 of an automobile produced in 1968 would not be included in the gross national product for 1969; doing so would involve: (*a*) including a nonmarket transaction; (*b*) including a nonproductive transaction; (*c*) including a noninvestment transaction; (*d*) double counting.

5. The service a baby-sitter performs when she stays at home with her baby brother while her parents are out and for which she receives no payment is not included in the gross national product because: (*a*) this is a nonmarket transaction; (*b*) this is a nonproductive transaction; (*c*) this is a noninvestment transaction; (*d*) double counting would be involved.

6. Which of the following does *not* represent investment? (*a*) an increase in the quantity of shoes on the shelves of a shoe store; (*b*) the construction of a house which will be occupied by its owner; (*c*) the purchase of newly issued shares of stock in the General Motors Corporation; (*d*) the construction of a factory building using money borrowed from a bank.

7. A refrigerator is produced by its manufacturer in 1968, sold during 1968 to a retailer, and sold by the retailer to a final consumer in 1969. The refrigerator is: (*a*) counted as consumption in 1968; (*b*) counted as investment in 1969; (*c*) counted as investment in 1968 and consumption and disinvestment in 1969; (*d*) not included in the gross national product of 1968.

Questions 8 through 10 use the national income accounting data given in the table in the true-false section.

8. The net national product is equal to: (*a*) $298 billion; (*b*) $302 billion; (*c*) $317 billion; (*d*) $321 billion.

9. National income exceeds personal income by: (*a*) $6 billion; (*b*) $15 billion; (*c*) $21 billion; (*d*) $44 billion.

10. Personal saving is equal to: (*a*) −$28 billion; (*b*) −$8 billion; (*c*) $8 billion; (*d*) $28 billion.

■ **DISCUSSION QUESTIONS**

1. Of what use is national income accounting to the economist and to the policy makers in the economy?

2. Why are GNP, NNP, etc., monetary measures, and why is it necessary that they be monetary measures?

3. Why do economists find it necessary to inflate and deflate GNP when comparing GNP in different years? How do they do this?

4. Why is GNP not a measure of the social welfare of society?

5. Why does GNP exclude nonproductive transactions? What are the two principal types of nonproductive transactions? List some examples of each.

6. Why are there two ways, both of which yield the same answers, of computing GNP, NNP, etc.?

7. What is meant by a nonincome charge or allocation? What are the two principal nonincome charges included in GNP? Why are they excluded from NI?

8. Why are transfer payments excluded from GNP, NNP, and NI?

9. Is residential construction counted as investment or consumption? Why? Why is a change in inventories an investment?

10. How do you define a static, an expanding, and a declining economy? What is the relationship between gross private domestic investment and the capital consumption allowance in these three economies?

11. Why are indirect business taxes "indirect"?

12. Under what conditions can personal saving be negative? How is this possible?

The Business Cycle: Unemployment and Inflation

CHAPTER

10

This chapter begins the explanation of what determines the levels of gross national product, net national product, national income, etc., actually achieved in any year. In the preceding chapter you learned how to compute these income-output measures and what each of them means. In the chapters that follow you should learn what causes income and output to be what they are, what causes them to fluctuate, and how they might be controlled for the welfare of the economy as a whole.

Chapter 10 is concerned with the ups and downs which occur in employment, output, income, and price level over the years. These ups and downs are usually referred to as the business cycle. The chapter is in part historical and descriptive. It examines recent American economic history to see how prices, employment, income, and output have changed; the relationships between changes in these variables; and the immediate causes of these changes. One purpose of the chapter is to give you a few historical facts which will be used in the next three chapters as a basis for generalizations about the determinants of income and output. The chapter is not purely descriptive and historical, how-

ever. Sections of it deal with the reasons the economic variables behave the way they do and why certain relationships exist between them.

Particular attention should be paid to the following: (1) the most important cause of changes in employment, output, income, and the price level; (2) the relationship between the level of employment in the economy and the effect of increased spending upon prices and employment; (3) what full employment means; (4) the relationship between the level of employment in the economy and the effect of increased spending upon the output of durable and nondurable goods; (5) the effect of price inflation upon the real incomes of various groups in the economy; (6) who is hurt by and who benefits from the inflation and deflation; (7) the specific causes of the periods of prosperity, depression, and inflation experienced by the American economy during the last fifty-five years or so; and (8) what seem to be the prospects for economic stability in the future.

The facts, relationships, and explanations in Chapter 10 are too important to be overlooked, and they must be mastered if you are to understand the chapters that follow.

■ **CHECKLIST**

The very least you should be able to do when you have finished this chapter is:

□ Identify the three elements in the macroeconomic trilogy.

□ Explain the effects of an increase in total spending (demand) on output and employment *and* on the rate of increase in the price level in ranges 1, 2, and 3.

□ Distinguish between frictional, structural, and cyclical unemployment; and explain the causes of these three kinds of unemployment.

□ Define full employment.

□ Define inflation and deflation.

□ List three groups that are hurt and two groups that benefit from inflation.

□ Explain what is meant by creeping inflation; and present the chief argument in the case for and the two arguments in the case against creeping inflation.

□ Explain what is meant by the business cycle; and identify the two types of noncyclical fluctuations.

□ Distinguish between the impact of cyclical fluctuations on industries producing capital and consumer durable goods and on those producing consumer nondurable goods; and on high- and low-concentration industries.

□ Explain why the mid-1970s was a "bad scene"; and the forces at work during this period.

□ Make four observations about cyclical fluctuations in the American economy.

□ List five reasons why many economists believe the economy is now less unstable than it was in the past; and the facts which have diminished their confidence in this belief.

■ **CHAPTER OUTLINE**

1. The macroeconomic trilogy is evident in the history of the American economy: economic growth has been interrupted by periods in which prices and employment (and output) were unstable.

2. The levels of employment, output, and prices actually achieved by the economy have depended largely upon the level of total spending or demand in the economy.

a. When the economy is in a severe recession an increase in total demand will usually increase both output and employment and have almost no effect on the price level.

b. As the economy approaches full employment increases in total demand will continue to increase output and employment and will result in premature inflation.

c. If the economy is fully employing all of its resources an increase in total demand will have no effect on output or employment and will bring about pure inflation.

d. At or near full employment decreases in total demand will decrease output and employment, but will not, however, reduce the price level.

3. Full employment does not mean that all workers in the labor force are employed and that there is no unemployment in the economy.

a. There is always some frictional unemployment; and this kind of unemployment is generally desirable.

b. And in addition there is the structural unemployment that is the result of changes in technology and in the types of goods and services consumers wish to buy.

c. Cyclical unemployment is the result of insufficient aggregate demand in the economy.

d. Because some structural and frictional unemployment is unavoidable, full employment means that 96% of the labor force is employed (and 4% is unemployed).

e. The economic cost of unemployment is unproduced output (a GNP gap); and this cost is unequally distributed among different groups in the economy.

f. Unemployment also leads to serious social problems.

4. Inflation and deflation mean increases and decreases, respectively, in the level of prices in the economy.

a. Even if the total output of the economy did not change, inflation and deflation would redistribute real income; and would benefit some groups and hurt other groups in the economy.

b. But inflation and deflation may also affect the total output of the economy.

c. Creeping inflation involves small annual increases in the level of prices and may or may not be desirable for the economy as a whole.

5. The business cycle means alternating periods of prosperity and depression. These recurrent ups and downs in employment, output, and prices are irregular in their occurrence and intensity.

a. Not all changes in employment and output which occur in the economy are cyclical; some are due to seasonal and secular influences.

b. The business cycle affects almost the entire economy, but it does not affect all parts in the same way and to the same degree. In particular, the production of durable and nondurable goods does not fluctuate to the same degree during the cycle.

6. Since 1920 the American economy has witnessed great changes in the levels of employment, output, and prices; these changes can best be understood by reviewing the ways in which total spending changed during this period and the reasons for these changes in total spending.

7. Many economists believe that the economy is more stable today than it was in the past because of changes which have occurred in the economy; but this belief has been shaken by events in the 1970s.

■ **IMPORTANT TERMS**

Macroeconomic trilogy	Deflation
Demand-pull inflation	Money income
Premature inflation	Real income
Pure inflation	Creeping inflation
Frictional unemployment	Hyper-(galloping) inflation
Structural unemployment	Rule of 70
Cyclical unemployment	Inflationary psychosis
Full employment	Business cycle
GNP gap	Seasonal variation
Inflation	Secular trend
	Stagflation

■ **FILL-IN QUESTIONS**

1. The basic determinant of the levels of employment and output and of the price level

is the volume or level of _____ in the economy.

2. Complete the following chain (using such words as more, less, larger, smaller, increase, decrease, etc.). An increase in total spending in the economy will make it profitable for

business to produce a _____

output; to do this it must employ _____

resources and this _____ the incomes received in the economy and

may _____ the price level.

3. Increases in total spending when the economy is at *less* then full employment may result in a rise in the price level; this is

termed _____ inflation. Increases in spending when the economy is at full employment result only in a rise in the price

level; and this is called _____ inflation.

4. Full employment in the American economy

is achieved when approximately _____% of the labor force is employed and there is no

_____

unemployment; but even at full employment

there is always some _____

and _____ unemployment in the economy.

5. The GNP gap is equal to _____

GNP *minus* _____GNP.

6. Inflation means a _____

and deflation a _____

_____

7. A person's *real* income depends upon his

_____

and _____

_____

8. List under the appropriate headings in the table at the top of page 70 as many of those groups as you can who are affected by inflation and deflation.

9. Creeping inflation means an increase in

the level of prices of from about _____

to _____% per year.

Inflation		Deflation	
Hurt	Benefit	Hurt	Benefit
_____	_____	_____	_____
_____	_____	_____	_____
_____	_____	_____	_____
_____	_____	_____	_____
_____	_____	_____	_____

10. If the business cycle is divided into four phases, these phases are often called _____

_____ ,

_____ ,

_____ ,

and _____ ;
if it is divided into two phases, it is common

to call these phases _____

and _____

or _____

and _____

11. In addition to the changes brought about by the operation of the business cycle, changes in output and employment may be

due to _____

and _____

12. Production and employment in the _____

_____ goods industries are affected to a greater degree by depression and expansion than they are in the _____ goods industries; prices vary to a greater ex-

tent in the (low-, high-) _____ concentration industries.

13. During the period of economic expansion that began in early 1961, the *rate* of growth

_____ and *un*employment

_____ .

Until 1965 the price level was _____ ;

but after 1965 the economy experienced _____

_____

14. In the early 1970s the real output of the United States did not grow and:

a. both the rate of _____ and the

_____ rate increased;
b. the macroeconomic condition of the

economy was referred to as _____
c. the Federal government introduced a

_____ Policy which included

a(n) (increase, decrease) _____
in taxes and the imposition of wage and price

_____

15. The five main causes of the rapid inflation which began in 1973 were:

a. _____

b. _____

c. _____

d. _____

e. _____

16. The inflation of the mid-1970s:

a. was accompanied by a severe _____
and was largely the result of forces which

operated on the _____ or _____
side of the market;
b. and when the Federal government restricted demand to fight the inflation the

result was _____

17. From an examination of the business

cycle since 1920 it seems evident that _____
spending is the most variable component of

total spending; that changes in the _____
supply affect the levels of output, employ-

ment, and prices; and that upswings and downswings in economic activity are _____

18. List five reasons why many economists in the late 1960s believed the economy would be more stable.

a. _____

b. _____

c. _____

d. _____

e. _____

■ **PROBLEMS AND PROJECTS**

1. In the table below are statistics* showing the civilian labor force and total employment in the United States during the years 1974, 1975, and 1976. Make the computations necessary to complete the statistics. (Numbers of persons are in thousands.)

a. How is it possible to have *both* employment and unemployment increase? _____

_____

b. In relative terms, if unemployment increases employment will decrease. Why? ____

_____

c. Would you say that these years were years of full employment? _____

d. Why is the task of maintaining full employment over the years more than just a problem of finding jobs for those who happen to be involuntarily idle in any given year? ____

_____

* Board of Governors of the Federal Reserve System, Federal Reserve Bulletin, vol. 63, no. 3, March, 1977, p. A47.

2. In the space below, indicate for each of the following situations the effects of an increase in total spending on *incomes, output, employment,* and the *price level,* respectively, using the following symbols: A, no effect or slight increase; B, increase; and C, sharp increase.

a. Depression and widespread unemployment

____ ____ ____ ____

b. Prosperity, but moderate unemployment

____ ____ ____ ____

c. Prosperity and full employment

____ ____ ____ ____

3. Indicate in the space to the right of each of the following the effect—beneficial (B), detrimental (D), or indeterminate (I)—of inflation and deflation on these persons:

a. A retired schoolteacher living on her savings   ____ ____

b. A retired schoolteacher living on the dividends she receives on the shares of stock she owns   ____ ____

c. A farmer who has mortgaged his farm at the local bank for $20,000, which must be paid off in ten years   ____ ____

d. A pensioner   ____ ____

e. A widow whose income consists entirely of interest received on the corporate bonds she owns   ____ ____

f. A schoolteacher   ____ ____

g. A union member who works in a steel plant   ____ ____

h. A state government employee

____ ____

4. Suppose that in 1984 the economy is at full employment and has a GNP of $2400

	1974	1975	1976
Civilian labor force	91,011	92,613	94,773
Total employment	85,935	84,783	87,485
Total unemployment	____	____	____
Percent of civilian labor force employed	____	____	____
Percent of civilian labor force unemployed	____	____	____

billion. GNP is capable of growing at a rate of 5% per year.

a. Compute the economy's *potential* GNP in 1985 and 1986 and enter them in the table below. (*Hint:* Potential GNP in any year is equal to 105% of the potential GNP in the previous year.)

Year	Potential GNP	Actual GNP	GNP gap
1984	$2400	$2400	$ 0
1985	_____	2472	_____
1986	_____	2572	_____

b. *Actual* GNP in 1985 and 1986 is shown in the table. Complete the table by computing the GNP gap in these two years.

5. Employing "the rule of 70," how many years would it take for the price level to double if the annual increases in the level of prices were:

a. 12%: _____ years

b. 10%: _____ years

c. 7%: _____ years

6. On the two graphs to the right the price *level* is measured along the vertical axis and real *national* output is measured along the horizontal axis. The demand for and the supply of national output are shown by the curves labeled *D* and *S*.

a. Applying the principles of demand and supply which you learned in Chapter 4, the equilibrium price level is the price level at which the national output demanded and the

national output supplied are _____

and the equilibrium national output is _____

_____

b. Draw on the first graph a new demand curve which represents an *increase* in the demand for national output.

(1) The effect of this increase in demand is a rise in the equilibrium price level and a(n)

_____ in the equilibrium national output.

(2) This rise in the price level is an example of _____inflation.

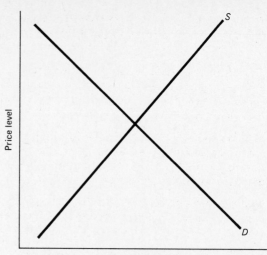

Real national output

c. On the second graph draw a new supply curve which represents a *decrease* in the supply of national output.

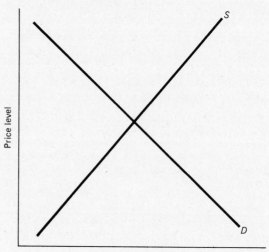

Real national output

(1) The effect of this decrease in supply is a _____ in the equilibrium price level and a _____ in the equilibrium national output.

(2) These effects are an example of _____

■ **SELF-TEST**

Circle the T if the statement is true, the F if it is false.

1. In practical terms, full employment means that 96% of the total work force is employed. **T F**

2. With a moderate amount of unemployment in the economy, an increase in total spending will generally increase both the price level and the output of the economy. **T F**

3. If the economy is operating at full employment a decrease in total spending can be expected to reduce both the price level and employment in the economy. **T F**

4. If the price level increases by 10% each year the price level will double every ten years. **T F**

5. Not all changes which occur in output and employment in the economy are due to the business cycle. **T F**

6. Industries which are highly concentrated show small relative decreases in output and large relative decreases in prices during a downswing of the business cycle. **T F**

7. Inflation tends to work to the advantage of those persons whose income is derived from corporate profits and to the disadvantage of those whose income is derived from interest on corporate bonds. **T F**

8. Economists agree that creeping inflation benefits the economy as a whole. **T F**

9. The economy's GNP gap is measured by deducting its actual GNP from its potential GNP. **T F**

10. Changes in the nation's money supply appear to have little or no effect upon the economy's output, employment, and price levels. **T F**

11. The New Economic Policy included both an increase in taxes and wage and price controls. **T F**

12. The rising prices of the 1970s are a clear case of demand-pull inflation. **T F**

Underscore the letter that corresponds to the best answer.

1. Which of the following is *not* part of the macroeconomic trilogy? (*a*) price stability; (*b*) economic growth; (*c*) full employment; (*d*) full production.

2. If the resources of the economy are fully employed, an increase in total spending will cause: (*a*) output and employment to increase; (*b*) output and prices to increase; (*c*) incomes and prices to increase; (*d*) employment and incomes to increase.

3. If the economy is experiencing a depression with substantial unemployment, an increase in total spending will cause: (*a*) a decrease in the *real* income of the economy; (*b*) little or no increase in the level of prices; (*c*) an increase in the *real* income and a decrease in the *money* income of the economy; (*d*) proportionate increases in the price level, output, and income in the economy.

4. In range 2 there is (*a*) price stability; (*b*) premature inflation; (*c*) stagflation; (*d*) pure inflation.

5. Insufficient total demand results in (*a*) frictional unemployment; (*b*) structural unemployment; (*c*) seasonal unemployment; (*d*) cyclical unemployment.

6. Total employment in December of this year was greater than total employment in December of 1928. This is no doubt due to the effect of: (*a*) seasonal variations; (*b*) secular trend; (*c*) the business cycle; (*d*) the diverse impact of the business cycle.

7. If employment in the agricultural sector of the American economy during last August and September was 112% of what it normally is in those months, this is probably a consequence of: (*a*) seasonal variations; (*b*) secular trend; (*c*) the business cycle; (*d*) both seasonal variations and the business cycle.

8. Production and employment in which of the following industries would be least affected by a depression? (*a*) nondurable consumer goods; (*b*) durable consumer goods; (*c*) capital goods; (*d*) iron and steel.

9. Which of the following would *not* benefit from deflation? (*a*) those living on fixed incomes; (*b*) those who find prices falling faster than their incomes; (*c*) those who have money savings; (*d*) those who became debtors during a period when prices were higher.

10. Which of the following are *not* characteristic of the American economy in the 1960s? (*a*) a decline in the level of consumer prices; (*b*) a decline in the percentage of the labor force that is unemployed; (*c*) an increased rate of economic growth; (*d*) increased spending by Federal, state, and local governments.

11. In the early 1970s (a) the unemployment rate increased; (b) the rate of inflation increased; (c) stagflation occurred; (d) all of the above took place.

12. It seems clear today that (a) the price level and the unemployment rate are inversely related; (b) the economy is stable; (c) restricting demand can prevent inflation; (d) cost increases may produce both inflation and recession.

■ **DISCUSSION QUESTIONS**

1. What is meant by the macroeconomic trilogy?

2. Explain why and how total spending affects output, employment, and income in the economy.

3. Explain what will tend to happen to employment, output, income, and the price level if total spending increases and the resources of the economy are: (a) widely unemployed, (b) moderately unemployed, (c) fully employed. If total spending *decreased* would the effects on employment, output, income, and the price level be just the opposite? Why?

4. Distinguish (a) between premature and pure inflation; and (b) between frictional, structural, and cyclical unemployment.

5. Why will the price level tend to increase as a consequence of an increase in total spending in the economy *before* all the resources of the economy are fully employed?

6. When is there full employment in the American economy? How are the concepts of frictional and structural unemployment related to this definition of full employment?

7. What are inflation and deflation? What groups benefit from and what groups are hurt by inflation and deflation? Why?

8. Why do some economists believe that creeping inflation is beneficial to the economy?

9. What are the two principal arguments against creeping inflation? How can creeping inflation turn into hyperinflation and eventually result in depression and unemployment?

10. The business cycle is only one of three general causes of changes in output, income, and employment in the economy. What are the other influences which affect these variables?

11. Compare the manner in which the business cycle affects output, prices, and incomes in the industries producing capital and durable goods with industries producing nondurable goods and services. What causes these differences?

12. The level of total spending in the economy is an important determinant of the levels of income, output, employment, and prices. What were the fundamental factors affecting total spending during: (a) the 1920s; (b) the 1930s; (c) the 1940s; (d) the 1950s; (e) the 1960s?

13. What was the macroeconomic condition of the economy in the early 1970s? How did the New Economic Policy attempt to deal with this condition?

14. What were the forces that produced the inflation of the mid-1970s in the United States? What was the "remarkable and disconcerting fact" about this inflationary period? How does the cause of the inflation in this period differ from the usual cause of inflation and why were the restrictive fiscal and monetary policies of the Federal government "a serious policy blunder"?

15. After reviewing the upswings and downswings in the American economy during the past fifty-five years, what four observations can be made?

16. What reasons have economists offered to support their belief that the American economy is more stable and less prone to depression that it was in the past? Why are these economists today reappraising their theories, the policies they recommend, and their belief in a depression-proof economy?

The Background and Analytical Tools of Employment Theory

Chapters 11 and 12 are really one chapter which has been divided into two parts and are probably the most important and crucial chapters in the first half of the text. They both concern the critical question of what determines the actual levels of employment and output the economy achieves in a given year.

Most of the material contained in the two chapters deals with the Keynesian theory or modern explanation of how employment and output are determined. This modern explanation is not the only possible explanation, however. It is with an alternative explanation called the classical theory of employment that the first part of Chapter 11 deals. The classical theory is described there for several reasons: to impress upon you the fact that an alternative theory does exist; to examine the assumptions upon which the theory rests; to point out the weaknesses—both in fact and in logic—of the explanation; to provide an understanding of the reasons lying behind the "cures" for depression often advanced both in the past and at the present time; and, finally and most important, to enable you to understand and evaluate the modern theory.

The outstanding thing about the classical theory is its conclusion that the economy will *automatically* function to produce the maxi-

mum output it is capable of producing and to provide employment for all those who are willing and able to work. Compare this with the conclusion drawn by the exponents of the modern theory that the economy functions in no such way, that both depression and inflation can prevail with no automatic tendency to be corrected, and that full employment and maximum output, when achieved, are accidental. Compare also the political philosophies of the proponents of the two theories. Those accepting the classical theory have advocated as little government interference with the economy as possible in the belief that such interference would only prevent the achievement of full employment and maximum output. Adherents of the modern theory have proposed that government action is necessary to eliminate the periods of depression and periods of inflation that can occur.

In studying this part of Chapter 11 you should focus your attention on the following: (1) the three assumptions listed on pages 222 and 223 of the text which are used throughout Chapters 11 and 12 to simplify the explanation, (2) Say's Law, (3) how the classical economists were able to conclude that whatever part of their incomes people choose to save would nevertheless be spent, (4) the part played by flexible prices and flexible wages in ensuring that all workers will be employed and that the economy will produce its maximum output, and (5) why the classical theory is not a good explanation of how the economy actually operates.

The basic proposition contained in the modern theory is that the level of total spending (aggregate demand) in the economy determines the sizes of the economy's output (NNP) and the total amount of employment. The latter part of the chapter analyzes the economic factors which determine two principal components of aggregate demand—consumption demand and investment demand. You should pay particular attention to the relationships called the consumption schedule, the saving schedule, and their characteristics; and to the four propensity concepts as well as to the "nonincome" determinants of consumption and saving.

Investment demand—that is, the purchase of capital goods—depends upon the rate of net profits which business firms expect to earn from an investment and upon the rate of interest they have to pay for the use of money. Because firms are anxious to make profitable investments and to avoid unprofitable ones, they undertake all investments which have an expected rate of net profit greater than (or equal to) the rate of interest and do not undertake an investment when the expected rate of net profit is less than the interest rate. You should see that because business firms behave this way the lower the rate of interest the larger will be the dollar amount invested; and that this relationship between the interest rate and the level of investment spending, called the investment-demand schedule, is an inverse one. But you should not confuse the investment-demand schedule (or curve) with the investment schedule (or curve) which relates investment spending to the NNP and which may show investment is either unrelated to or directly related to the NNP. Five noninterest determinants of investment spending influence the profit expectations of business firms; and these are analyzed. You should learn how changes in these determinants affect investment; and why investment spending is unstable.

In the next chapter the tools and ideas developed and explained in Chapter 11 are put together to form a complete and coherent picture of how aggregate demand determines the level of NNP.

■ CHECKLIST

The very least you should be able to do when you have finished this chapter is:

□ List the three simplifying assumptions made in this and the next chapter and the two implications of these assumptions.

□ State Say's Law and explain how classical economists were able to reason that all saving would be borrowed and spent for capital goods.

□ Explain how classical economists were able to reason that price-wage flexibility would eliminate a recession and unemployment.

□ Present three reasons why the rate of interest may not guarantee the equality of saving and investment; and two reasons why price-wage flexibility may not guarantee full employment.

□ State what determines the amount of goods and services produced and the level of employment in the Keyneian theory.

□ Explain how consumption and saving are related to disposable income.

□ Compute, when you are given the necessary data, the four propensities.

□ Explain what happens to the size of the two average propensities as income increases.

□ List the nonincome determinants of consumption and saving; and explain how a change in each of these determinants will affect the consumption and saving schedules.

□ Explain the difference between a change in the amount consumed (or saved) and a change in the consumption (or saving) schedule.

□ List the two basic determinants of investment; and explain when a firm will and will not invest.

□ Compute, when given the appropriate data, the investment-demand schedule; and explain why the relationship between investment spending and the rate of interest is inverse.

□ List the five noninterest determinants of investment demand; and explain how a change in each of these determinants will affect the investment-demand curve.

□ Explain the two variables found in an investment schedule; and the two kinds of relationships that might be found to exist between these two variables.

▢ List the four factors which explain why investment spending tends to be unstable.

■ **CHAPTER OUTLINE**

1. The classical theory of employment reached the conclusion that the economy would automatically tend to employ its resources fully and produce a full-employment level of output; this conclusion was based on Say's Law and the assumption that prices and wages were flexible.

a. Say's Law stated that the production of goods produced an equal demand for these goods because changes in the rate of interest would ensure that all income not spent (that is, income saved) by consumers would be loaned to investors, who would spend these borrowed funds for capital goods.

b. If there were an excess supply of goods or an excess supply of labor (unemployment), prices and/or wages would fall until the excesses were eliminated and full employment and maximum output again prevailed in the economy.

c. Believing that capitalism would automatically ensure a full-employment level of output, the classical economists saw no need for government interference with the operation of the economy.

2. J. M. Keynes, in *The General Theory of Employment, Interest, and Money,* denied that flexible interest rates, prices, and wages would automatically promote full employment; he set forth the modern theory that there was nothing automatic about full employment and that both depression and inflation might prevail without any tendency existing for them to be self-correcting.

3. Aggregate output and employment are directly related to the level of total spending in the economy; to understand what determines the level of total spending at any time it is necessary to explain the factors that determine the levels of consumption and investment spending.

4. Consumption is the largest component of total spending; and saving is income not spent for consumer goods.

a. Disposable income is the most important determinant of both consumption and saving; the relationships between income and consumption and between income and saving are both direct (positive) ones.

b. The consumption schedule shows the amounts that households will spend for consumer goods at various levels of income.

c. The saving schedule indicates the amounts households will save at different income levels.

d. The average propensities to consume and to save and the marginal propensities to consume and to save can be computed from the consumption and saving schedules.

e. In addition to income, there are several other important determinants of consumption and saving; changes in these nonincome determinants will cause the consumption and saving schedules to change.

f. A change in the amount consumed (or saved) is not the same thing as a change in the consumption (or saving) schedule. If these schedules change they change in opposite directions; but the schedules are very stable.

5. The two important determinants of the level of investment in the economy are the expected rate of net profits from the purchase of additional capital goods and the rate of interest.

a. The expected rate of net profits is directly related to the net profits (revenues less operating costs) that are expected to result from an investment and inversely related to the cost of making the investment (purchasing capital goods).

b. The rate of interest is the price paid for the use of money. When the expected rate of net profits is greater (less) than the rate of interest a business will (will not) invest because the investment will be profitable (unprofitable).

c. For this reason, the lower (higher) the rate of interest, the greater (smaller) will be the level of investment spending in the economy; and the investment-demand curve indicates this inverse relationship between the rate of interest and the level of spending for capital goods.

d. There are at least five noninterest determinants of investment demand; and a change in any of these determinants will shift the investment-demand curve.

e. Investment spending in the economy may also be either independent or directly related to the NNP; and the investment schedule may show that investment either remains constant or increases as NNP increases.

f. Because the five noninterest determinants of investment are subject to sudden changes, investment spending tends to be unstable.

■ **IMPORTANT TERMS**

Classical theory of employment

Say's Law

Rate of interest

Money market

Saving

Investment

Price-wage flexibility

Keynesian economics

Dissaving

Consumption schedule

Saving schedule

Average propensity to consume

Average propensity to save

Marginal propensity to consume

Marginal propensity to save

Nonincome determinants of consumptions and saving

Change in amount consumed (saved)

Change in the consumption (saving) schedule

Expected rate of net profits

Investment-demand schedule (curve)

Noninterest determinants of investment

Investment schedule (curve)

■ **FILL-IN QUESTIONS**

1. Three "simplifying assumptions" used throughout most of the chapter are that the economy is a _____ that all saving is _____ saving, and that the government _____ _____

The implications of these assumptions are:

a. _____ = _____ = _____ = _____

b. aggregate demand = _____ + _____

2. Full employment, in the classical theory, was assured by _____ and _____ _____

3. According to Say's Law, the production of goods and services creates an equal _____ _____

4. Changes in _____, according to the classical economists, ensure that what is not spent on consumer goods is spent on capital goods.

5. In the classical theory, if saving is greater than investment the rate of interest will _____ and if investment is greater than saving it will _____ ; the rate of interest will have a tendency to _____ where saving and investment are equal.

6. According to the classical way of thinking, if the interest rate did not equate saving and investment, and if total output exceeded the level of spending, prices in the output markets would tend to _____ because of competition among business firms; this would make some production unprofitable and temporarily cause _____ in resource markets; but competition among resource suppliers would tend to drive resource prices _____ and _____ employment. This process would continue until _____ _____

7. According to the modern theory of employment, saving and investment are done by _____ and for _____ and the funds to finance investment come not only from current saving but from the _____ _____ of households and from _____

8. Keynes, in attacking the classical theory of employment, contended that price-wage flexibility would not guarantee full employment, first, because _____ and, second, because wage reductions would

simply lead to _____ ,

_____ ,

and _____

9. Reasoning that if a price and wage rate reduction would increase the output and employment of an individual firm, then a general reduction in prices and wages will increase output and employment in the economy as a

whole is an example of the fallacy of _____

10. Keyes argued that:
 a. the national output and employment de-

pend (directly, inversely) _____

upon the level of _____
 b. the most important determinant of consumption and of saving in the economy is the

economy's _____
 c. and that both consumption and saving

are (directly, inversely) _____
related to this determinant.

11. The largest single component of total

spending is _____
spending.

12. As disposable income falls, the average

propensity to consume will _____

and the average propensity to save will _____

_____

13. The most important determinants of consumption spending, other than the level of disposable income, are:

 a. _____

 b. _____

 c. _____

 d. _____

 e. _____

 f. _____

14. A change in the consumption (or saving)

schedule means that _____

_____

while a change in the amount consumed (or

saved) means that _____

_____

15. Investment is defined as spending for

additional _____ ;
and the total amount of investment spending in the economy depends upon:

 a. the _____ rate of net _____

 b. the rate of _____

16. A business firm will invest in more capital if the expected rate of net profits on this in-

vestment is (greater, less) _____
than the rate of interest it must pay for the use of money.

17. The relation between the rate of interest and the total amount of investment in the

economy is (direct, inverse) _____
This means that if the rate of interest:

 a. rises investment will _____

 b. falls investment will _____

18. Five noninterest determinants of investment-demand are:

 a. _____

 b. _____

 c. _____

 d. _____

 e. _____

19. The consumption schedule and the saving schedule tend to be (stable or unstable)

_____

while investment demand tends to be _____

_____

20. The demand for new capital goods tends

to be unstable because of the _____ ;

of capital goods, the _____ of

innovation, and the _____ of actual and expected profits.

■ **PROBLEMS AND PROJECTS**

1. On the next page is a consumption schedule. Assume taxes and transfer payments are zero and that all saving is personal saving.

NNP	C	S	APC, %	APS, %	MPC, %	MPS, %
$350	$351	_____	_____	_____		
360	360	_____	_____	_____	_____	_____
370	369	_____	_____	_____	_____	_____
380	377	_____	_____	_____	_____	_____
390	385	_____	_____	_____	_____	_____
400	392	_____	_____	_____	_____	_____
410	399	_____	_____	_____	_____	_____
420	405	_____	_____	_____	_____	_____

a. Compute saving, the average propensity to consume, and the average propensity to save for each of the eight levels of NNP.

b. Compute the marginal propensity to consume and the marginal propensity to save for each of the seven changes in NNP.

c. Plot the consumption schedule, the saving schedule, and the 45° line on the graph below.

2. Indicate in the space to the right of each of the following events whether the event will tend to increase (+) or decrease (−) the saving schedule.

a. Development of consumer expectations that prices will be higher in the future _____

b. Gradual shrinkage in the stock of durable goods owned by consumers _____

c. Increase in the volume of consumer indebtedness _____

d. Growing belief that disposable income will be lower in the future _____

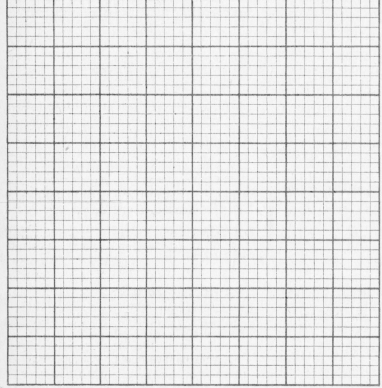

0   NNP

e. Rumors that a current shortage of consumer goods will soon disappear _____

f. Rise in the actual level of disposable income _____

g. A build-up in the dollar size of liquid assets owned by consumers _____

h. Development of a belief by consumers that the Federal government can and will prevent depressions in the future _____

3. The schedule below has nine different rates of net profit and the dollar amounts of investment expected to have each of these net-profit rates.

Rate of net profit	Amount of investment (millions)
10%	$0
9	1
8	2
7	3
6	4
5	5
4	6
3	7
2	8
1	9

a. If the rate of interest in the economy were 10%, business firms would plan to spend $_____ million for investment; but if the interest rate were 9% they would plan to spend $_____ million for investment.

b. Should the interest rate be 8% they would still wish to make the investments they were willing to make at interest rates of 10% and 9%; they would also plan to spend an additional $_____ million for investment; and their total investment would be $_____ million.

c. Were the rate of interest 7% they would make all the investments they had planned to make at higher interest rates plus an additional $_____ million; and their total investment spending would be $_____ million.

d. Complete the next table by computing the amount of planned investment at the six remaining interest rates.

Rate of interest	Amount of investment (millions)
10%	$ 0
9	1
8	3
7	6
6	_____
5	_____
4	_____
3	_____
2	_____
1	_____

e. Graph the schedule you completed above on the graph below. Plot the rate of interest on the vertical axis and the amount of investment planned at each rate of interest on the horizontal axis.

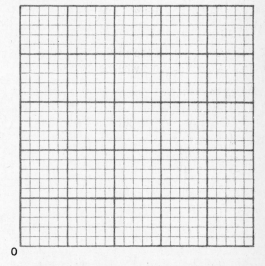

0

f. Both the graph and the table show that the relation between the rate of interest and the amount of investment spending in the economy is _____
This means that when the rate of interest:

(1) increases, investment will _____

(2) decreases, investment will _____

g. It also means that should we wish to:
(1) increase investment, we would need to

_____ the rate of interest
(2) decrease investment, we would have to

_____ the rate of interest

h. This graph (or table) is the _____

_____ curve (or schedule).

4. Indicate in the space to the right of each of the following events whether the event would tend to increase (+) or decrease (−) investment demand.

a. Rising stock market prices _____
b. Development of expectations by businessmen that business taxes will be higher

in the future _____
c. Step-up in the rates at which new products and new production processes are being

introduced _____
d. Business belief that wage rates may be

lower in the future _____

e. A mild recession _____
f. A belief that business is "too good" and the economy is due for a period of "slow"

consumer demand _____
g. Rising costs in the construction industry

_____

h. A rapid increase in the size of the economy's population _____
i. A period of a high level of investment spending which has resulted in productive capacity in excess of the current demand for

goods and services _____

5. Below are two schedules showing several NNPs and the level of investment spending (I) at each NNP. (All figures are in billions of dollars.)

Schedule number 1		Schedule number 2	
NNP	I	NNP	I
$ 850	$90	$ 850	$ 75
900	90	900	80
950	90	950	85
1000	90	1000	90
1050	90	1050	95
1100	90	1100	100
1150	95	1150	105

a. Each of these schedules is an _____ schedule.
b. When such a schedule is drawn up it is

assumed that the rate of interest is _____
c. In schedule:

(1) number 1, NNP and I are _____

(2) number 2, NNP and I are _____ related.

■ **SELF-TEST**

Circle the T if the statement is true, the F if it is false.

1. Say's Law states that demand for goods and services creates an equal supply of goods and services. **T F**

2. In the classical theory, if saving exceeds investment the rate of interest will rise until saving and investment are equal. **T F**

3. According to the classical economists involuntary unemployment is impossible. **T F**

4. The level of saving in the economy depends primarily upon the level of disposable income. **T F**

5. The consumption schedule which is employed as an analytical tool is also a historical record of the relationship of consumption to disposable income. **T F**

6. Statistics show and economists agree that the marginal propensity to consume rises and the marginal propensity to save falls as disposable income rises. **T F**

7. An increase in the taxes paid by consumers will decrease both the amount they spend for consumption and the amount they save. **T F**

8. Both the consumption schedule and the saving schedule tend to be relatively stable over time. **T F**

9. A business firm will purchase additional capital goods if the rate of interest it must pay exceeds the expected rate of net profits from the investment. **T F**

10. An increase in an economy's income may induce an increase in investment spending. **T F**

Underscore the letter that corresponds to the best answer.

1. If government neither taxes nor spends, and all saving done in the economy is personal saving: (*a*) gross national product equals net national product; (b) gross national product equals national income; (c) net national product equals disposable income; (d) disposable income equals personal consumption expenditures.

2. Which of the following could *not* be called a classical economist? (a) John Maynard Keynes; (b) J. B. Say; (c) A. C. Pigou; (d) John Stuart Mill.

3. If the rate of interest did not equate saving and investment and total output was greater than total spending, the classical economists argued, competition would tend to force: (a) product and resource prices down; (b) product prices up and resource prices down; (c) product prices up and resource prices up; (d) product prices down and resource prices up.

4. Which of the following is *not* involved in Keynes's criticism of the classical theory of employment? (a) a reduction in wage rates will lead only to a reduction in total spending, not to an increase in employment; (b) investment spending is not influenced by the rate of interest; (c) prices and wages are simply not flexible downward in modern capitalistic economies; (d) saving in modern economies depends largely upon the level of disposable income and is little influenced by the rate of interest.

5. If consumption spending increases from $358 to $367 billion when disposable income increases from $412 to $427 billion, it can be concluded that the marginal propensity to consume is: (a) 0.4; (b) 0.6; (c) 0.8; (d) 0.9.

6. If when disposable income is $375 billion the average propensity to consume is 0.8, it can be concluded that: (a) the marginal propensity to consume is also 0.8; (b) consumption is $325 billion; (c) saving is $75 billion; (d) the marginal propensity to save is 0.2.

7. When the disposable income of consumers decreases (a) consumption increases and saving decreases; (b) consumption decreases and saving increases; (c) both consumption and saving increase; (d) both consumption and saving decrease.

8. Which of the following would *not* cause the consumption schedule to increase (that is, cause the consumption curve to rise)? (a) a decrease in consumers' stocks of durable goods; (b) an increase in consumers' ownership of liquid assets; (c) a decrease in the amount of consumers' indebtedness; (d) an increase in the income received by consumers.

9. A decrease in the level of investment spending would be a consequence of: (a) a decline in the rate of interest; (b) a decline in the level of wages paid; (c) a decline in business taxes; (d) a decline in stock market prices.

10. Which of the following relationships is an inverse one? (a) The relationship between consumption spending and disposable income; (b) the relationship between investment spending and the rate of interest; (c) the relationship between saving and the rate of interest; (d) the relationship between investment spending and net national product.

■ **DISCUSSION QUESTIONS**

1. According to the classical economists, what level of employment would tend to prevail in the economy? On what two basic assumptions did their analysis of the level of employment rest?

2. What is Say's Law? How were the classical economists able to reason that whatever is saved is spent?

3. In the classical analysis Say's Law made it certain that whatever was produced would be sold. How did flexible prices, flexible wages, and competition drive the economy to full employment and maximum output?

4. On what grounds did J. M. Keynes argue that flexible interest rates would not ensure the operation of Say's Law? What were his reasons for asserting that flexible prices and wages would not ensure full employment?

5. "Savers and investors are largely different groups and are motivated by different factors." Explain in detail who these groups are and what motivates them. Does the rate of interest play any role in determining saving and investment?

6. Explain briefly how the average propensity to consume and the average propensity to save vary as disposable income varies. Why do APC and APS behave this way? What happens to consumption and saving as disposable income varies?

7. Why do the sum of the APC and the APS and the sum of the MPC and the MPS always equal exactly one?

8. Explain briefly and explicitly *how* changes in the six nonincome determinants will affect the consumption schedule and the saving schedule and *why* such changes will affect consumption and saving in the way you have indicated.

9. Explain (*a*) when a business firm will or will not purchase additional capital goods; (*b*) how changes in the five noninterest determinants of the investment spending will affect the investment-demand curve; and (*c*) why investment spending tends to rise when the rate of interest falls.

10. Why does the level of investment spending tend to be highly unstable?

The Equilibrium Levels of Output, Employment, and Income

Chapter 12 explains in simple terms what determines the equilibrium level of NNP—the actual size of the NNP which will tend to be produced in the economy. You *must* understand this chapter if you are to acquire an understanding of what causes NNP to rise and fall; of what causes unemployment, depression, inflation, and prosperity; and of what can be done to prevent recession and inflation and to foster price stability, full employment, and economic growth.

The equilibrium level of NNP is determined by the level of total spending or *aggregate demand* in the economy. In Chapter 11, the two principal components of aggregate demand, consumption demand and investment demand, were analyzed. In this chapter the equilibrium level of NNP is explained with both tables and graphs, first by using the aggregate demand–aggregate supply approach and then by employing the leakages-injections approach. These two approaches are complementary and are simply two different ways of analyzing the same process and of reaching the same conclusions. For each approach it is important for you to know, given the consumption (or saving) schedule and the level of investment demand, *what* NNP will tend to be produced and *why* this will be the NNP which will be produced.

It is also important that you understand the significant distinctions between intended (planned) saving and actual (realized) saving; and between intended (planned) investment and actual (realized) investment. Actual saving is always equal to actual investment because both are defined in exactly the same way: the output of the economy minus its consumption. Intended saving and intended investment are not, however, equal by definition; they are equal only when NNP is at its equilibrium level. When NNP is *not* at its equilibrium level, intended saving and intended investment are *not* equal; but actual saving and investment will, as always, be equal because actual investment includes *un*intended (or *un*planned) investment or disinvestment. Remember: Equilibrium NNP is achieved when *intended* saving and investment—*not actual* saving and investment—are equal.

The consumption (and the saving) schedule and the investment schedule—especially the latter—are subject to change, and when they change equilibrium NNP will also change. The relationship between a change in the investment (or a change in the consumption) schedule and a change in equilibrium NNP is called the multiplier. Three things to note here are: *how* the multiplier is defined, *why* there is a multiplier effect, and upon *what* the size of the multiplier depends. Because of the multiplier, the paradoxical consequence of an attempt by the economy to save more is either no increase or a decrease in the level of saving in the economy. The explanation of this paradox will be evident to you when you understand the equilibrium NNP and the multiplier effect.

The final portion of the chapter emphasizes that equilibrium NNP is not necessarily the NNP at which full employment without inflationary pressures is achieved. Equilibrium NNP may be greater or less than the full-employment noninflationary NNP: if it is greater there is an inflationary gap, and if it is less there exists a recessionary gap. The next chapter deals with the fiscal policies that can be employed by government to eliminate these gaps. Chapter 12 has purposely ignored government and assumed an economy in which government neither taxes nor spends. But Chapter 13 does not ignore the role of government in the economy and discusses fiscal policies and their effects upon equilibrium NNP.

■ CHECKLIST

The very least you should be able to do when you have finished this chapter is:
□ Find the equilibrium NNP, when you are given the necessary tabular or graphical data, by employing either the aggregate demand–aggregate supply or the leakages-injections approach.
□ Explain why the economy will tend to produce its equilibrium NNP rather than some smaller or larger NNP.
□ State the difference between planned (intended) investment and actual (realized) investment; and explain how it is possible for actual saving and investment to be equal when planned saving and investment are not equal.
□ Determine the economy's new equilibrium NNP when there is a change in the consumption (or saving) schedule or in the investment schedule.
□ Find the value of the multiplier when you are given the needed information; and cite the two facts upon which the multiplier effect (a multiplier greater than one) is based.
□ Draw a graph to explain the paradox of thrift.
□ Distinguish between the equilibrium NNP and the full-employment noninflationary level of NNP.
□ Find the recessionary and the inflationary gaps when you are provided the relevant data.

□ Explain why it may not be possible for the economy to have both full employment and stable prices.

■ CHAPTER OUTLINE

1. Two alternative approaches are used to explain what level of NNP the economy will tend to produce (that is, what the equilibrium NNP will be). Both approaches yield the same answer. Employing the aggregate demand–aggregate supply approach, the equilibrium NNP is the NNP at which planned consumption plus planned net investment is equal to planned consumption plus planned saving; and at which unintended investment in inventories is zero.

2. Using the leakages-injections approach, equilibrium NNP is the NNP at which planned saving and planned net investment are equal.

3. The saving and investment schedules indicate what consumers and investors *plan* to do. When planned saving and planned net investment are not equal, either unintended investment or unintended disinvestment in inventories has occurred; and NNP will change until planned saving and net investment are equal and there is no unintended investment or disinvestment. *Realized* saving and net investment are always equal because the latter includes unintended investment or disinvestment.

4. Changes in the net investment schedule or in the consumption and saving schedules will cause the equilibrium level of NNP to change.
a. If net investment changes, NNP will change in the same direction by an amount greater than the change in net investment; this is called the multiplier effect; the value of the simple multiplier is equal to the reciprocal of the marginal propensity to save.
b. The paradox of thrift is that an increase in the saving schedule results in no increase, and may result in a decrease, in saving; the increase in the saving schedule causes a multiple contraction in NNP and at the lower NNP the same amount or even less saving takes place.

5. The equilibrium level of NNP may turn out to be an equilibrium at less than full employment, at full employment, or at full employment with inflation.

a. If the equilibrium NNP is *less* than the NNP consistent with full employment, there exists a recessionary gap; the size of the recessionary gap equals the amount by which aggregate demand must increase to increase *real* equilibrium NNP to the full-employment NNP without creating inflation.

b. If equilibrium NNP is *greater* than the NNP consistent with stable prices there is an inflationary gap. The size of the inflationary gap equals the amount by which aggregate demand must decrease to decrease *money* NNP without reducing *real* NNP or creating unemployment.

c. As aggregate demand increases and moves the economy closer to full employment both the economy's real NNP and its price level tend to rise; and this premature inflation makes it impossible to achieve both full employment and price stability.

■ **IMPORTANT TERMS**

Aggregate demand	Actual (realized) saving
Aggregate supply	
Aggregate quantity demanded	Actual (realized) investment
Aggregate quantity supplied	Equilibrium level of NNP
Aggregate demand—aggregate supply approach	Multiplier effect
	Multiplier
Leakages-injections approach	Complex multiplier
Leakage	Simple multiplier
Injection	Paradox of thrift
Planned (intended) saving	Supermultiplier
Planned (intended) investment	Recessionary gap
	Inflationary gap

■ **FILL-IN QUESTIONS**

1. Two complementary approaches which are employed to explain the equilibrium level of output, employment, and income are the

_____

approach and the _____ approach.

2. In the modern theory of employment, income, employment, and output depend directly upon the level of _____ in the economy.

3. Assuming a governmentless economy, the equilibrium level of NNP is that NNP at which

NNP equals _____

plus _____

4. When the leakages-injections approach is used:

a. in this chapter the only leakage considered is _____ and the only injection considered is _____

b. In later chapters two additional:

(1) leakages considered are _____

and _____

(2) injections considered are _____

and _____

5. If:

a. Aggregate quantity demanded is greater than aggregate quantity supplied, planned saving is _____ than planned investment, there is unintended _____ in inventories, and NNP will _____

b. Aggregate quantity demanded is less than aggregate quantity supplied, planned saving is _____ than planned investment, there is unintended _____ in inventories, and NNP will _____

c. Aggregate quantity demanded is equal to aggregate quantity supplied, planned saving is _____ planned investment, unintended investment in inventories is _____ and the NNP will _____

6. At every level of NNP _____

saving is equal to _____ investment.

a. But if planned investment is greater than planned saving by $10:

(1) there is $10 of unintended _____

(2) the NNP will (rise, fall) _____

by an amount equal to $10 times _____

b. And if planned investment is less than planned saving by $5:

(1) there is $5 of unintended _____

(2) the NNP will _____ by _____

_____

7. When full employment has been achieved, if aggregate quantity demanded is greater than aggregate quantity supplied, planned investment will be _____than

planned saving, prices will tend to _____,

output to _____,

income to _____,

employment to _____,

and the result will be _____

8. The value of the simple multiplier equals

_____

or _____ .
The fact that NNP will increase by more than an increase in investment demand is due to

two facts: _____

and _____

9. If the economy decides to save more (consume less) at every level of NNP, the equilib-

rium NNP will _____

and the equilibrium level of saving in the

economy will either _____

or _____
This consequence of an increased desire to

save is called the _____

10. A recessionary gap exists when equilibrium NNP is (greater, less) _____
than the full-employment NNP; to bring NNP to the full-employment level, aggregate de-

mand must _____ by an amount
equal to the difference between equilibrium

and full-employment NNP divided by _____

_____

11. When equilibrium money NNP is greater than the full-employment NNP at which prices

are stable, there is a(n) _____

_____gap; to eliminate this gap

_____ must decrease by

_____

divided by the multiplier.

12. When the economy is at:
a. full employment and the price level has risen because of an increase in aggregate

demand it is called _____inflation.
b. less than full employment and the price level has risen because of an increase in

aggregate demand it is called _____
inflation.

■ **PROBLEMS AND PROJECTS**

1. The table below shows consumption at various levels of NNP. Assume the economy

NNP	C	S	I	C + I	UI
$300	$290	$____	$____	$____	$____
310	298	____	____	____	____
320	306	____	____	____	____
330	314	____	____	____	____
340	322	____	____	____	____
350	330	____	____	____	____
360	338	____	____	____	____
370	346	____	____	____	____
380	354	____	____	____	____
390	362	____	____	____	____
400	370	____	____	____	____

is closed and government neither taxes nor spends.

a. Complete the saving column in the table.

b. The next table is an investment-demand schedule which shows the amounts investors plan to invest at different rates of interest (*i*). Assume the rate of interest is 6% and complete the investment, the consumption-plus-investment, and the unintended investment (UI) columns—showing unintended investment with a + and unintended disinvestment with a −.

i	*I*
10%	$ 0
9	7
8	13
7	18
6	22
5	25
4	27
3	28

c. The equilibrium level of NNP will be

$_____

d. The marginal propensity to consume is

_____ ,

and the marginal propensity to save is _____

e. The value of the simple multiplier is _____

f. If the rate of interest should fall from 6% to 5%, investment spending would (increase,

decrease) _____ by $_____; and the equilibrium NNP would, as a result (increase,

decrease) _____by $_____.

g. Suppose the rate of interest were to rise from 6% to 7%. Investment spending would

_____ by $_____; and the equilib-

rium NNP would _____by $_____.

h. Assume the rate of interest is 6%. (1) On the graph below, plot *C*, *C + I*, and aggregate supply, and indicate the equilibrium NNP.

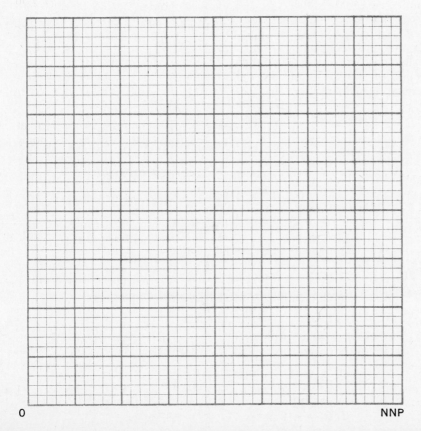

0   NNP

(2) On the graph below, plot S and I and indicate the equilibrium NNP.

0   NNP

2. Assume the marginal propensity to consume is 0.8 and the change in investment spending is $10. Complete the table at the bottom of this page modeled after Table 12–2 in the textbook.

3. In the next column are a saving schedule and two investment schedules—one (I_a) indicating that investment spending is constant and the other (I_i) indicating that the investment schedule is upsloping.

a. Using either investment schedule, the equilibrium NNP is $_____ and saving and investment are both $ _____

b. The marginal propensity to save is_____ and the simple multiplier is _____

c. A $2 rise in the I_a schedule will cause NNP to rise by $_____, while a $2 rise in the level of the I_i schedule will cause NNP to rise by $ _____

d. The value of the supermultiplier in the second case is, therefore _____

e. Use the two investment schedules given in the table and assume a $2 increase in the saving schedule in the table—that is, planned saving at every NNP increases by $2.

(1) If the investment schedule is I_a, equilibrium NNP will _____ to $_____ and at this NNP saving will be $_____

(2) If the investment schedule is I_i, equilibrium NNP will _____ to $_____ and at this NNP saving will be $_____

(3) The effect of the increase in the saving schedule is to _____ equilibrium NNP and either to _____ or to _____ saving; this is called the _____

(4) The amount by which NNP changes depends upon the size of the change in the saving schedule and the size of _____

NNP	S	I_a	I_i
$300	$ 5	$15	$10
310	7	15	11
320	9	15	12
330	11	15	13
340	13	15	14
350	15	15	15
360	17	15	16
370	19	15	17
380	21	15	18
390	23	15	19
400	25	15	20

	Change in income	Change in consumption	Change in saving
Increase in investment of $10	+ 10	_____	_____
Second round	_____	_____	_____
Third round	_____	_____	_____
Fourth round	_____	_____	_____
Fifth round	_____	_____	_____
All other rounds	_____	_____	_____
Totals	_____	_____	_____

4. In the table below are consumption and saving schedules. Assume that the level of NNP at which full employment without inflation is achieved is $590.

NNP	C	S
$550	$520	$30
560	526	34
570	532	38
580	538	42
590	544	46
600	550	50
610	556	54
620	562	58
630	568	62

a. The value of the multiplier is _____
b. If investment demand is $58, equilibrium

NNP is $ _____ and exceeds the full-employment noninflationary NNP by

$_____. There is a(n) _____

gap of $_____
c. If investment demand is $38, equilibrium

NNP is $_____ and is less than

full-employment NNP by $ _____.

There is a(n) _____

gap of $_____

■ **SELF-TEST**

Circle the T if the statement is true, the F if it is false.

The first two questions below are based on the data supplied for multiple-choice questions 1 and 2.

1. If saving at each level of NNP decreased by $5 and if investment demand remained constant at $24, equilibrium NNP would decrease by $16⅔ and saving in the economy would decrease by $5.   **T   F**

2. If consumption spending at each level of NNP increased by $10, the equilibrium level of NNP would tend to rise by $30.   **T   F**

3. Both the saving schedule and the investment schedule are schedules of plans rather than schedules of saving and investment actually realized.   **T   F**

4. Realized saving and realized investment are always equal.   **T   F**

5. Actual saving at any level of NNP equals planned investment plus unintended investment (or minus unintended disinvestment).   **T   F**

6. If NNP were to decline by $40, consumers would probably reduce their consumption expenditures by an amount less than $40.   **T   F**

7. A decrease in the rate of interest will, other things remaining the same, result in a decrease in the equilibrium NNP.   **T   F**

8. The larger the marginal propensity to consume, the larger the size of the multiplier.   **T   F**

9. The existence of a recessionary gap in the economy is characterized by the full employment of labor.   **T   F**

10. The evidence suggests that the American economy is capable of achieving both full employment and stable prices.   **T   F**

Underscore the letter that corresponds to the best answer.

Questions 1 and 2 below, as well as true-false questions 1 and 2, are based on the following consumption schedule.

NNP	C
$200	$200
240	228
280	256
320	284
360	312
400	340
440	368
480	396

1. If planned investment is $60, the equilibrium level of NNP will be: (*a*) $320; (*b*) $360; (*c*) $400; (*d*) $440.

2. If planned investment were to increase by $5, the equilibrium NNP would increase by: (*a*) $5; (*b*) $7¹/₇; (*c*) $15; (*d*) 16⅔.

3. When the economy's actual NNP exceeds its equilibrium NNP: (*a*) there is unintended investment in the economy; (*b*) planned investment exceeds planned saving; (*c*) the aggregate quantity demanded exceeds the aggregate quantity supplied; (d) there is an inflationary gap.

4. If planned saving is greater than planned investment: (a) businesses will be motivated to increase their investments; (b) aggregate quantity demanded will be greater than aggregate quantity supplied; (c) NNP will be greater than planned investment plus planned consumption; (d) realized saving will tend to increase.

5. If NNP is $275 billion, consumption $250 billion, and investment $30 billion, NNP: (a) will tend to remain constant; (b) will tend to increase; (c) will tend to decrease; (d) equals aggregate demand.

6. If the value of the marginal propensity to consume is 0.6 and NNP falls by $25, this was caused by a decrease in aggregate demand of: (a) $10; (b) $15; (c) $16⅔; (d) $20.

7. If the marginal propensity to consume is 0.6⅔ and if both investment demand and the saving schedule increase by $25, NNP will: (a) increase by $75; (b) not change; (c) decrease by $75; (d) increase by $25.

8. The paradox of thrift means that: (a) an increase in saving lowers the level of NNP; (b) an increase in the average propensity to save lowers or leaves unchanged the level of savings; (c) an increase in the marginal propensity to save lowers the value of the multiplier; (d) an increase in NNP increases investment demand.

9. To eliminate an inflationary gap of $50 in an economy in which the marginal propensity to save is 0.1 it will be necessary to: (a) decrease aggregate demand by $50; (b) decrease aggregate demand by $5; (c) increase aggregate demand by $50; (d) increase aggregate demand by $5.

10. If the economy's full-employment noninflationary NNP is $1200 and its equilibrium NNP is $1100 there is a recessionary gap of: (a) $100; (b) $100 divided by the multiplier; (c) $100 multiplied by the multiplier; (d) $100 times the reciprocal of the marginal propensity to consume.

▪ DISCUSSION QUESTIONS

1. Explain why the equilibrium level of NNP is that level of NNP at which NNP equals aggregate demand and at which saving equals investment. What will cause NNP to rise if it is below this level and what will cause it to fall if it is above this level?

2. Explain what is meant by a leakage and by an injection. What are the three major leakages and the three major injections in the flow of income in the American economy? Which leakage and which injection are considered in this chapter? Why is the equilibrium NNP the NNP at which the leakages equal the injections?

3. What is meant by "the distinction between saving and investment plans or intentions and the actual amounts which households manage to save and businesses to invest"? Are the saving schedule and the investment schedule planned or realized saving and investment? What adjustment causes planned and realized saving and investment to become equal?

4. What is the multiplier effect? *Why* does there tend to be a multiplier effect (that is, on what basic economic facts does the multiplier effect depend)? What determines how large the simple multiplier effect will be?

5. What is meant by the paradox of thrift? When would an increase in the saving schedule cause saving (at equilibrium) to decrease?

6. What relationship is there between the equilibrium level of NNP and the level of NNP at which full employment without inflation is achieved?

7. Explain what is meant by a recessionary gap and an inflationary gap. What economic conditions are present in the economy when each of these gaps exists? How is the size of each of these gaps measured?

8. How does premature inflation differ from demand-pull inflation? What are the consequences of premature inflation if two of the economic goals of the United States are full employment and price stability?

Fiscal Policy and the Public Debt

Chapter 13 is really a continuation of the two preceding chapters and is concerned with the chief practical application of the principles discussed in those chapters.

It is worth recalling that principles of economics are generalizations about the way the economy works; and that these principles are studied in order that policies may be devised to solve real problems. Over the past one-hundred or so years the most serious problems encountered by the American economy have been those problems that resulted from the business cycle. Learning what determines the output, employment, and price levels of an economy and what causes them to fluctuate will make it possible to discover ways to bring about full employment, maximum output, and stable prices. Economic principles, in short, suggest the policies that will eliminate both recessionary and inflationary gaps.

Government spending and taxing have a strong influence on the economy's output and employment and its price level. Federal expenditure and taxation policies designed to affect total production and employment and the level of prices are called fiscal policies. (The Federal Reserve Banks are also able to affect these variables by applying monetary policy; but the study of monetary policy must wait until the effect of banks on

the operation of the economy is examined in Chapters 14, 15, and 16.)

Talking about fiscal policies and the amounts the Federal government spends and taxes is really a discussion of the Federal budget. Chapter 13 opens with an examination of three budget philosophies. The brief second section makes it clear that Congress in the Employment Act of 1946 committed the Federal government to using fiscal (and monetary) policy to achieve a trio of economic goals—economic growth, stable prices, and full employment. This act also established the Council of Economic Advisors to advise the President and the Joint Economic Committee to advise Congress on matters pertaining to national economic policy.

The section entitled "Discretionary Fiscal Policy" is the crucial part of Chapter 13. It introduces government taxing and spending into the analysis of equilibrium NNP. It is important to note that government spending for goods and services adds to aggregate demand; and that taxation reduces the disposable income of consumers, and thereby reduces both the amount of consumption and the amount of saving that will take place at any level of NNP. Both "approaches" are again employed, and you are warned that you must know *what* NNP will tend to be produced and *why*. Special attention should be directed to the exact effect taxes have upon the consumption and saving schedules and the multiplier effects of changes in government spending and taxes.

Once you learn how government spending and taxing affect the equilibrium NNP it is fairly easy to understand what fiscal policies will be expansionary and reduce a recessionary gap and what fiscal policies will be contractionary and lessen an inflationary gap. It is at this point that the distinction between discretionary and nondiscretionary fiscal policy becomes significant. Discretionary fiscal policy requires that Congress take action to change tax rates, transfer payment programs, or expenditures for goods and services. Nondiscretionary fiscal policy does not require Congress to take any action; and is a built-in stabilizer of the economy.

Unfortunately, nondiscretionary fiscal policy by itself is not able to eliminate any recessionary or inflationary gap that might develop; and discretionary fiscal policy will be necessary if the economy is to produce its full-employment noninflationary NNP. But the built-in stabilizers make it more difficult to use discretionary fiscal policy to achieve this goal because they produce fiscal drag, and create the illusion that the Federal government's policy is expansionary or contractionary when in fact its policy is just the opposite. Because of the illusions created by the built-in stabilizers, economists developed the full-employment budget to enable them to discover whether Federal fiscal policy was actually expansionary or contractionary and to determine what policy should have been followed to move the economy toward full employment without inflation.

In addition to this, you should be aware (1) that if the government has a budget deficit or surplus there are several ways of financing the deficit or disposing of the surplus, and that the way the deficit or surplus is handled can affect the economy's operation as much as the size of the deficit or surplus; (2) that which taxes and which expenditures government changes when it employs discretionary fiscal determines how effective its fiscal policy will be; and (3) that there are quite a few specific problems connected with the actual application of fiscal policy.

Whenever the Federal government applies fiscal policy and incurs either a budget deficit or surplus, the size of the public (i.e., the national) debt is affected. In the final section of the chapter the public debt is considered. Here you should become aware of how large the debt and interest on the debt are, both absolutely and relatively; why an internally held public debt is a debt to ourselves and a public credit; and how and why the debt has grown. You should understand that the existence of the public debt both causes several economic problems and has its economic advantages—but that the problems are *not* those of bankrupting the government or of shifting the cost of a war (or of other government programs) to future generations.

Overall, it should become apparent that the size of the national debt is not of great importance. Changes in its size are important because they are the result of either deficits or surpluses; and a deficit or a surplus reflects the application of fiscal policy to affect the performance of the economy.

■ CHECKLIST

The very least you should be able to do when you have finished this chapter is:

□ Explain each of the three budget philosophies.

□ State the responsibility imposed on the Federal government by the Employment Act of 1946 and the roles of the CEA and JEC in fulfilling this responsibility.

□ Distinguish between discretionary and nondiscretionary fiscal policy.

□ Find the equilibrium NNP in an economy in which government spends for goods and services and levies net taxes when you are given the necessary data.

□ Determine the effect on the equilibrium NNP of a change in government spending for goods and services and in net taxes.

□ Explain why the balanced-budget multiplier is equal to one.

□ Explain when government should pursue an expansionary and a contractionary fiscal policy; what each of these policies might entail; and the effect of each upon the Federal budget.

□ Indicate how the built-in stabilizers help to eliminate recession and inflationary pressures.

□ Describe the best way to finance a government deficit and to dispose of a surplus.

□ List several of the complications encountered in employing fiscal policy.

□ State the absolute and relative size of
the public debt and of the annual interest
charges on this debt; the principal cause of
the debt; and why it is also a public credit.

□ Lay to rest the two widely held myths
about the public debt.

□ List the real burdens and the advantages
of the public debt.

■ **CHAPTER OUTLINE**

1. Fiscal policy is the manipulation by the
Federal government of its expenditures and
tax receipts in order to affect total spending
in the economy (and thereby to affect output,
employment, and prices).

2. Three budgetary philosophies may be followed by a government; the adoption of any
of these philosophies will affect the employment, the output, and the price level of the
economy.
a. Proponents of an annually balanced
budget would have government expenditures
and tax revenues equal in every year; but
such a budget is pro- rather than countercyclical.
b. Those who advocate a cyclically balanced
budget propose matching surpluses (in years
of prosperity) with deficits (in depression
years) to stabilize the economy; but there is
no assurance that the surpluses will equal the
deficits over the years.
c. Advocates of functional finance contend
that deficits, surpluses, and the size of the
debt are of minor importance; that the goal
of full employment without inflation should
be achieved regardless of the effects of the
necessary fiscal policies upon the budget and
the size of the national debt.

3. The Employment Act of 1946 set the goals
of American fiscal policy and provided for a
Council of Economic Advisors to the President and the Joint Economic Committee.

4. Discretionary fiscal policy involves congressional changes in tax rates and expenditure programs in order to eliminate recessionary and inflationary gaps.
a. Government expenditures for goods and
services add to aggregate demand and increase equilibrium NNP; an increase in these
expenditures has a multiplier effect upon
equilibrium NNP.
b. Taxes decrease planned consumption
and aggregate demand by the amount of the
tax times the MPC; an increase in taxes thus
decreases equilibrium NNP by a multiplier
which is equal to MPC/MPS.
c. If the government both taxes and spends,
the equilibrium NNP will be the NNP at which
(1) Aggregate quantity demanded (planned
consumption + planned investment + government spending for goods and services)
equals aggregate quantity supplied (NNP or
planned consumption + planned saving + net
taxes).
(2) Planned investment + government
spending for goods and services equals
planned saving + net taxes.
d. Equal increases (decreases) in taxes and
in government expenditures increase (decrease) equilibrium NNP by the amount of
the change in taxes (or in expenditures).
e. The elimination of the inflationary (recessionary) gap is accomplished by contractionary (expansionary) fiscal policy and by
increasing (decreasing) taxes, decreasing (increasing) expenditures, and incurring budget
surpluses (deficits).

5. In the American economy net tax revenues
(tax receipts minus government transfer payments) are not a fixed amount or lump sum;
they increase as the NNP rises and decrease
as the NNP falls.
a. This net tax system serves as a built-in
stabilizer of the economy because it reduces
purchasing power during periods of inflation
and expands purchasing power during
periods of recession.
b. But built-in stability:
(1) can only reduce and cannot eliminate
economic fluctuations;
(2) creates fiscal drag and makes it difficult
to reduce unemployment during a recession
and to maintain full employment in a growing
economy;
(3) and requires that the full-employment
budget be used to determine whether the
Federal budget is actually expansionary or
contractionary.

6. For a better understanding of fiscal policy
it is necessary to include two important re-
finements.
a. In addition to the size of the deficit or
surplus, the manner in which the government

finances its deficit or disposes of its surplus affects the level of total spending in the economy.

b. And the types of taxes and the types of expenditures upon which the government relies to operate its fiscal policy help to determine the effectiveness of that fiscal policy in promoting economic stability.

7. Certain other specific complications arise in enacting and applying fiscal policy, and the degree of success achieved in solving these problems determines whether fiscal policy will actually be employed and whether it will be appropriate and effective.

8. Any government surplus or deficit automatically affects the size of the public debt.
a. The public debt has grown substantially since 1929.
(1) This debt is primarily the result of Federal borrowing during wartime; and is only secondarily the consequence of expansionary fiscal policies.
(2) It is almost entirely internally held.
(3) The relative size of the public debt and the interest payments on it have not grown so rapidly as the absolute size of the debt and the interest payments; and it has grown less rapidly than private debt.
b. The contentions that a large debt will eventually bankrupt the government and that borrowing to finance expenditures passes the cost onto future generations are myths.
c. There are, however, a number of real economic problems which a large public debt creates.
d. But, on the other hand, there are several desirable aspects to this debt.

■ **IMPORTANT TERMS**

Fiscal policy	Discretionary fiscal policy
Annually balanced budget	
Cyclically balanced budget	Balanced-budget multiplier
Functional finance	Expansionary fiscal policy
Employment Act of 1946	Contractionary fiscal policy
Council of Economic Advisors	Nondiscretionary fiscal policy
Joint Economic Committee	Net taxes
	Built-in stability

Fiscal drag	Externally held public debt
Full-employment budget	Retiring the public debt
Crowding-out effect	
Public debt	Refinancing the public debt
Internally held public debt	

■ **FILL-IN QUESTIONS**

1. An annually balanced budget is procyclical rather than countercyclical because _____ _____

2. A cyclically balanced budget suggests that to ensure full employment without inflation, the government incur deficits during periods of _____ and surpluses during periods of _____ _____ with the deficits and surpluses equaling each other over the business cycle. The budget over the cycle may not balance, however, because _____ _____

3. Functional finance has as its main goal the achievement of _____ ; and would regard budget _____ and increases in the _____ as of secondary importance.

4. The use of monetary and fiscal policy to reduce inflationary and recessionary gaps became national economic policy in the _____ _____ Act of _____. This act also established the _____ to the President and the _____ in Congress.

5. Taxes tend to reduce consumption demand at each level of NNP by an amount equal to the taxes multiplied by the _____ _____ ; saving will decrease by an amount equal to

the taxes multiplied by the _____
_____

6. In an economy in which government both taxes and spends, the equilibrium level of NNP is the NNP at which:

a. NNP is equal to _____

plus _____

plus _____ ;

b. _____ plus _____

equals _____ plus _____

7. Equal reductions in taxes and government spending will _____

NNP by an amount equal to _____

8. In order to increase real NNP during a period of recession, taxes should be _____

_____ and government expenditures

_____ ; to decrease money NNP during a period of inflation, taxes should be

_____ and

government expenditures _____

9. If fiscal policy is to have a countercyclical

effect, a budget _____
should be incurred during a recession and a

budget _____ during inflation.

10. Net taxes:

a. equal _____ minus _____

b. in the United States will (increase, decrease) _____ as the NNP rises and will

_____ as the NNP falls.

11. When net tax receipts are directly related

to the NNP the economy has some _____
stability because:

a. when the NNP rises, leakages (increase,

decrease) _____ and the budget surplus

will _____ (or the budget deficit

will _____)

b. when the NNP falls, leakages _____

and the budget deficit will _____

(or the budget surplus will _____)

12. The built-in stability of the American net tax system:

a. is not by itself capable of _____

_____ ;

b. results in _____ ;

c. makes it difficult to determine from an examination of the Federal budget whether discretionary fiscal policy has or has not been

_____

13. Fiscal drag means that when net tax receipts vary directly with the NNP and are not a lump sum it is more difficult for discretionary fiscal policy to raise the level of _____

_____ in the short run and to maintain

_____ in the long run.

14. The full-employment budget:

a. indicates what the Federal _____

_____ would have been if the economy

had operated at _____ during
the year;

b. tells us whether the Federal budget was

in fact _____ or _____

15. The two principal means available to the Federal government for financing budget

deficits are _____

and _____ ;

the (former, latter) _____

is least contradictory because _____

_____

16. If the MPS were 0.2, a $1 billion increase in government expenditures for goods and

services would increase NNP by $_____
billion; but a $1 billion increase in transfer

payments would increase by only $_____
billion.

17. Most, though not all, economists would agree that a $10 billion increase in a (pro-

gressive, regressive) _____
tax would be the more contractionary.

18. There is a problem of timing in the use of discretionary fiscal policy because of the

_____ , _____ ,

and _____lags.

19. The public debt of the United States is almost entirely _____ held.

20. Today the public debt is about _____ percent, and interest charges on the debt are approximately _____ percent of GNP in the United States.

21. The cost of World War II was not passed on to future generations because the generation that fought the war had to go without

_____

22. As the full-employment NNP of the economy increases, the amount of saving done at full employment _____ .
To maintain full employment, all this saving must be _____ and

_____

23. If the saving done at full employment is not all borrowed and spent by business and consumers, _____ must borrow and spend the saving. If it:
a. does *not* borrow and spend it, NNP and the rate of economic growth will _____

b. does borrow and spend it, the public debt will _____

24. The existence of a large public debt may dampen _____

in the economy, have a(n) _____

effect on investment, increase _____

and make it difficult to use _____
to control inflation.

25. The existence of a large public debt is desirable to the extent that it provides _____

_____ ,

cushions the impact of _____ ,

and provides a means of applying _____

_____
policies.

■ PROBLEMS AND PROJECTS

1. A consumption function is shown below.
a. Assume the government levies $10 in taxes at all levels of NNP and the marginal propensity to consume remains constant. Compute the new consumption column (*C'*), the saving column (*S'*), and the saving plus taxes column (*S'* + *T*) at each of the 13 levels of NNP.

NNP	C	C'	S'	S' + T	I + G	C' + I + G
$350	$325	____	____	____	____	____
360	334	____	____	____	____	____
370	343	____	____	____	____	____
380	352	____	____	____	____	____
390	361	____	____	____	____	____
400	370	____	____	____	____	____
410	379	____	____	____	____	____
420	388	____	____	____	____	____
430	397	____	____	____	____	____
440	406	____	____	____	____	____
450	415	____	____	____	____	____
460	424	____	____	____	____	____
470	433	____	____	____	____	____

b. Suppose that investment demand is $15 and government spending for goods and services is $20. Complete the investment-plus-government-spending column $(I + G)$ and the consumption-plus-investment-plus-government-spending column $(C' + I + G)$.

c. On the graphs below and on page 100 plot:

(1) C', $I + G$ and $C' + I + G$, and aggregate supply. Show the equilibrium NNP.

(2) $S' + T$ and $I + G$. Show the equilibrium NNP.

d. The equilibrium level of NNP will be

$ _____

(To answer the question below it is not necessary to recompute C, S, $S + T$, and $C + I + G$. Use the multipliers.)

e. If taxes remained at $10 and government expenditures rose by $10, NNP would rise by

$ _____

f. If government expenditures remained at $20 and taxes increased by $10, NNP would

fall by $ _____

g. The effect of a $10 increase in taxes *and* a $10 increase in government spending

is to _____ NNP by $_____

2. In the table on page 100 are nine NNPs and the net tax receipts of government at each NNP.

a. Looking at the two columns on the left of the table, it can be seen that:

(1) when NNP increases by $50, net tax

receipts (increase, decrease) _____

by $_____

0   NNP

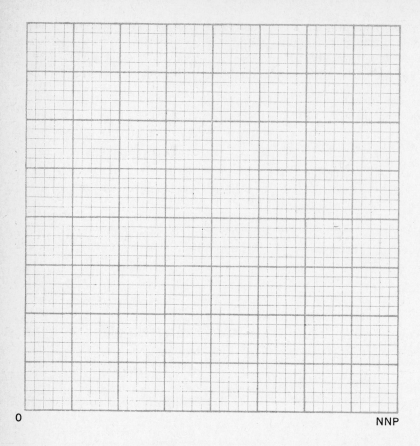

0   NNP

NNP	Net tax receipts	Government expenditures	Government surplus
$ 800	$160	$_____	$_____
850	170	_____	_____
900	180	_____	_____
950	190	_____	_____
1000	200	_____	_____
1050	210	_____	_____
1100	220	_____	_____
1150	230	_____	_____
1200	240	_____	_____

(2) when NNP decreases by $100, net tax receipts _____ by $_____
(3) the relation between NNP and net tax receipts is (direct, inverse) _____
b. Assume the investment multiplier has a value of 10 and that investment spending in the economy decreases by $10.

(1) *If* net tax receipts remained constant, the equilibrium NNP would decrease by $_____
(2) But when NNP decreases, net tax receipts also decrease; and this decrease in net tax receipts will tend to (increase, decrease) _____ the equilibrium NNP.
(3) And, therefore, the decrease in NNP brought about by the $10 decrease in investment spending will be (more, less)_____ than $100.
(4) The direct relationship between net tax receipts and NNP has (lessened, expanded) _____ the impact of the $10 decrease in investment spending on NNP.
c. Suppose the government expenditures multiplier is also 10 and government wishes to increase the equilibrium NNP by $50.
(1) *If* net tax receipts remained constant, government would have to increase its expenditures for goods and services by $_____
(2) But when NNP rises, net tax receipts

also rise; and this rise in net tax receipts will

tend to (increase, decrease) _____ the equilibrium NNP.

(3) The effect, therefore, of the $5 increase in government expenditures will be to increase the equilibrium NNP by (more, less)

_____ than $50.

(4) The direct relation between net tax receipts and NNP has (lessened, expanded)

_____ the effect of the $5 increase in government expenditures; and to raise the equilibrium NNP by $50 government will have to increase its expenditures by (more, less)

_____ than $5.

d. Imagine that the full-employment NNP of the economy is $1150 and that government expenditures for goods and services are $200.

(1) Complete the table on page 100 by entering the government expenditures and by computing the budget surplus at each of the NNPs. (Show a government deficit by placing a minus sign in front of the amount by which expenditures exceed net tax receipts.)

(2) The full-employment surplus equals

$_____

(3) Were the economy in a recession and producing an NNP of $900, the budget would

show a (surplus, deficit) _____of

$_____

(4) This budget deficit or surplus makes it appear that government is pursuing a(n) (ex-

pansionary, contractionary) _____ fiscal policy; but this deficit or surplus is not the result of countercyclical fiscal policy but

the result of the _____

(5) If government did not change its net tax rates it could increase the equilibrium NNP from $900 to the full-employment NNP of $1050 by increasing its expenditures by (approximately) $70. At the full-employment NNP the budget would show a (surplus,

deficit) _____ of $_____

(6) If government did not change its expenditures it could increase the equilibrium NNP from $900 to the full-employment NNP of $1050 by decreasing net tax receipts at all NNPs by a lump sum of (approximately) $80. The full-employment budget would have a

(surplus, deficit) _____ of $_____

3. Indicate in the space to the right of each of the following the effect—increase (+), decrease (−), or no effect (0)—on money NNP, output, and employment.

a. The economy is at less than full employment and:

(1) Government reduces its expenditures

for goods and services _____ _____ _____

(2) Government reduces net taxes

_____ _____ _____

(3) Investment increases

_____ _____ _____

(4) Households plan to save more

_____ _____ _____

(5) Households plan to consume more

_____ _____ _____

b. The economy is operating at full employment and:

(1) Government increases its expenditures

for goods and services _____ _____ _____

(2) Government increases transfer pay-

ments _____ _____ _____

(3) Investment increases

_____ _____ _____

(4) Households plan to save more

_____ _____ _____

(5) Households plan to consume less

_____ _____ _____

■ **SELF-TEST**

Circle the T if the statement is true, the F if it is false.

1. Proponents of functional finance argue that a balanced budget, whether it is balanced annually or over the business cycle, is of minor importance when compared with the objective of full employment without inflation.

T F

2. There is no assurance that a nation can both use fiscal policy to promote full employment and balance its budget cyclically.

T F

3. The Employment Act of 1946 commits the Federal government to using monetary and fiscal policy to achieve economic stability.

T F

4. If the MPS were 0.3 and taxes were levied by the government so that consumers paid $20 in taxes at each level of NNP, comsumption expenditures at each level of NNP would be $14 less. **T F**

5. If taxes only are reduced by $10 at all levels of NNP and the marginal propensity to save is 0.4, equilibrium NNP will rise by $25. **T F**

6. Even a balanced budget can be a weapon in fighting depression and inflation. **T F**

7. A governmental deficit is contractionary. **T F**

8. Built-in stabilizers are not sufficiently strong to prevent recession or inflation, but they can reduce the severity of recession or inflation. **T F**

9. A regressive tax system is more conducive to built-in stability than a progressive one. **T F**

10. The full-employment budget indicates how much government must spend and tax if there is to be full-employment in the economy. **T F**

11. It is generally believed that public works expenditures have a greater expansionary effect than transfer payments and that regressive taxes are more contractionary than progressive taxes. **T F**

12. The fiscal policies of state and local governments have tended to assist and reinforce the efforts of the Federal government to mitigate depression and inflation. **T F**

13. The public debt is about $620 billion. **T F**

14. The primary reason for the large increase in the public debt since 1930 is the deficit spending during the years of the Great Depression. **T F**

15. A nation can experience prosperity and growth in its real output though its national debt is increasing rapidly. **T F**

16. The chief disadvantage of the public debt of the United States is that as the debt becomes payable, the government may be unable to tax or to borrow sufficient money to redeem its securities. **T F**

17. The amount of saving done at full employment increases in a growing economy. **T F**

18. To maintain full employment in a growing economy it is necessary for the total of public and private debt to increase. **T F**

Underscore the letter that corresponds to the best answer.

1. Which of the following would involve reducing government expenditures and increasing tax rates during a depression? (a) an annually balanced budget policy; (b) functional finance; (c) cyclically balanced budget policy; (d) a policy employing built-in stability.

The next four questions are based on the consumption schedule below.

2. If taxes were zero, government expenditures for goods and services $10, and investment $6, equilibrium NNP would be: (a) $310; (b) $320; (c) $330; (d) $340.

NNP	C
$300	$290
310	298
320	306
330	314
340	322
350	330
360	338

3. If taxes were $5, government expenditures for goods and services $10, and investment $6, equilibrium NNP would be: (a) $300; (b) $310; (c) $320; (d) $330.

4. Assume investment is $42, taxes $40, and government spending for goods and services zero. If the full-employment level of NNP is $340, the gap can be eliminated by reducing taxes by: (a) $8; (b) $10; (c) $13; (d) $40.

5. Assume that investment is zero, that taxes are zero, and that government spending for goods and services is $20. If the full-employment-without-inflation level of NNP is $330, the gap can be eliminated by decreasing government expenditures by: (a) $4; (b) $5; (c) $10; (d) $20.

6. Which of the following policies would do the *most* to reduce inflation? (a) increase taxes by $5 billion; (b) reduce government expenditures for goods and services by $5 billion; (c) increase taxes and government expenditures by $5 billion; (d) reduce both taxes and government expenditures by $5 billion.

7. If the government wishes to increase the level of NNP, it might: (a) reduce taxes; (b) reduce its expenditures for goods and services; (c) reduce transfer payments; (d) reduce the size of the budget deficit.

8. If the marginal propensity to consume is 0.6⅔ and both taxes and government expenditures for goods and services increase by $25, NNP will: (a) fall by $25; (b) rise by $25; (c) fall by $75; (d) rise by $75.

9. If the economy is to have built-in stability, when NNP falls: (a) tax receipts and government transfer payments should fall; (b) tax receipts and government transfer payments should rise; (c) tax receipts should fall and government transfer payments should rise; (d) tax receipts should rise and government transfer payments should fall.

10. A direct relation between net tax receipts and NNP (a) automatically produces budget surpluses during a recession; (b) makes it easier for discretionary fiscal policy to move the economy out of a recession and toward full employment; (c) makes it easier to maintain full employment in a growing economy; (d) reduces the effect of a change in investment spending upon the national output and employment.

11. Which of the following by itself is the most expansionary (least contractionary)? (a) redemption of government bonds held by the public; (b) borrowing from the public to finance a budget deficit; (c) a build-up in the size of the government's checking account in the central banks; (d) issuing new money to finance a budget deficit.

12. Which of the following would be the most contractionary? (a) increased personal income taxes, the receipts being used to retire part of the national debt; (b) increased sales and excise taxes, the receipts being used to retire part of the national debt; (c) increased personal income taxes, the receipts being used to increase the cash balance of the government; (d) increased sales and excise taxes, the receipts being used to increase the cash balance of the government.

13. As a percentage of the gross national product, the public debt and interest on the debt are, respectively, about: (a) 50% and 1%; (b) 35% and 2%; (c) 105% and 3%; (d) 125% and 6%.

14. Incurring internal debts to finance a war does not pass the cost of the war on to future generations because: (a) the opportunity cost of the war is borne by the generation that fought it; (b) the government need not pay interest on internally held debts; (c) there is never a need for government to refinance the debt; (d) wartime inflation reduces the relative size of the debt.

15. Which of the following is a consequence of the public debt in the United States? (a) it increases incentives to work and invest; (b) it provides some built-in stability during a recession; (c) it reduces income inequality; (d) it leads to greater saving at the various levels of disposable income.

16. Which of the following would be a consequence of the total retirement of the public debt? (a) a reduction in the nation's productive capacity; (b) a reduction in the nation's standard of living; (c) a redistribution of the nation's wealth among its citizens; (d) an increase in aggregate demand in the economy.

17. Suppose the average propensity to save is constant and equal to 0.2 of NNP. If the full-employment NNP increases from $1200 billion to $1260 billion, saving at full employment will increase by: (a) $3 billion; (b) $6 billion; (c) $9 billion; (d) $12 billion.

18. Suppose the multiplier is 3. Were the amount of saving done at full employment to increase by $20 and were private borrowing to increase by $5, to maintain full employment, public borrowing and the public debt would have to increase by: (a) $5; (b) $15; (c) $45; (d) $60.

■ **DISCUSSION QUESTIONS**

1. What is meant by fiscal policy? What methods can government use to increase NNP? What policies can it follow to reduce NNP?

2. Explain why an annually balanced budget is not "neutral" and how it can intensify, rather than reduce the tendencies for NNP to rise and fall.

3. How does a cyclically balanced budget philosophy differ from the philosophy of functional finance?

4. Why do advocates of functional finance argue that budget deficits and a mounting public debt are of secondary importance?

5. In the Employment Act of 1946, (a) what responsibility was given to the Federal government; (b) what tasks were assigned to the Council of Economic Advisors and the Joint Economic Committee; and (c) what specific kinds of policy were to be used to achieve the goals established by the act?

6. Explain why, with government taxing and spending, the equilibrium NNP is the NNP at which NNP equals consumption plus investment plus government spending for goods and services; and saving plus taxes equals investment plus government spending. What will cause NNP to move to its equilibrium level?

7. What is the exact effect which taxes will have on the consumption schedule? On the saving schedule?

8. If both taxes and government spending increase by equal amounts, NNP will increase by that amount. Why?

9. What is the difference between discretionary and nondiscretionary fiscal policy? How do the built-in stabilizers work to reduce rises and falls in the level of NNP?

10. What kind of tax system works best to promote built-in stability? Why? Which tax system does the least to promote built-in stability? Why?

11. Explain why a tax system in which net tax receipts vary directly with the level of NNP makes it difficult to achieve and to sustain full employment.

12. What is the full-employment budget? What was the problem which the use of the full-employment budget was designed to solve?

13. What are the alternative means of financing deficits and disposing of surpluses available to the Federal government? What is the difference between these methods insofar as their expansionary and contractionary effect is concerned?

14. In what sense has state and local fiscal policy been procyclical rather than countercyclical? What accounts for this fiscal perversity?

15. How big is the national debt of the United States absolutely and relatively? How large are the interest charges on the debt absolutely and relatively? What has happened to the size of the debt and interest charges since 1930? Why?

16. Explain the difference between an internally held and an externally held public debt. If the debt is internally held government borrowing to finance a war does not pass the cost of the war on to future generations. Why?

17. What are the principal advantages and disadvantages of a public debt internally held? Which of its disadvantages seems most important to you at this point in your study of economics?

18. In what ways does the existence of a large public debt contribute to inflation? Why does an increase in the size of the debt abet inflation? Which tends to be more inflationary, the existence of the debt or increases in its size?

19. What tends to happen to the absolute and the relative amounts of saving done at full employment as the full-employment NNP grows?

20. Why, in a growing economy, must borrowing and debt increase in order to maintain full employment and economic growth? What will happen to NNP if private borrowing and private debt do not increase? What must government do to maintain full employment if private borrowers do not increase their borrowings and debt enough to maintain full employment? What will this do to the public debt?

Money and Banking in American Capitalism

By and large, Chapter 14 is descriptive and factual. It contains no explanation of how the banking system affects the operation of the economy. The purpose of this chapter is, however, to prepare you for such an explanation. Of special importance are many terms and definitions which will be new to you. These must be learned if the following two chapters and their analysis of how the banking system affects the performance of the economy are to be clearly understood. Chapter 14 also contains a factual description of the institutions which comprise the American banking system—the Board of Governors of the Federal Reserve System, the Federal Reserve Banks, and the commercial banks—and the functions of these institutions.

You will do well to pay particular attention to the following. (1) What money is and the functions it performs, what types of money exist in the American economy and their relative importance, and what constitutes the money supply; (2) what gives value to or "backs" American money; and (3) the three principal institutions of the American banking system, their functions, and their relationships.

Several points are worth repeating here because so much depends upon their being fully understood. First, money is whatever performs the three functions of money, and in the United States money consists largely of the debts (promises to pay) of the Federal Reserve or of commercial banks. In the United States, this money is "backed" by no more than the goods and services for which its owners can exchange it—not by gold, because no one can redeem dollars for gold at the Treasury or the Federal Reserve Banks.

Second, the central bank in the United States is the twelve Federal Reserve Banks and the Board of Governors of the Federal Reserve System which oversees their operation. These banks, while privately owned by the commercial banks, are operated more or less as an agency of the Federal government —not for profit, but primarily to regulate the nation's money supply in the best interests of the economy as a whole and secondarily to perform other services for the banks, the government, and the economy. They are able to perform their primary function because they are bankers' banks where commercial banks can deposit and borrow money. They do not deal directly with the public.

Third, commercial banks, like many other financial institutions, accept deposits and make loans, but they also—and this distinguishes them from financial intermediaries —are literally able to create money by lending demand deposits. Because they are able to do this, they have a strong influence on the size of the money supply and the value of money. The Federal Reserve Banks exist primarily to regulate the money supply and its value by influencing and controlling the amount of money commercial banks create.

■ CHECKLIST

The very least you should be able to do when you have finished this chapter is:

□ List the three functions of money; and explain the meaning of each function.

□ Define the money supply, M_1.

□ List several near-monies and present four reasons why they are important; and then define M_2.

□ Explain why money in the American economy is debt; and whose debts paper money and demand deposits are.

□ Present three reasons why currency and demand deposits are money and have value.

□ Indicate the precise relationship between the value of money and the price level.

□ Enumerate the two devices employed by government to stabilize the value of money.

□ Describe the structure of the American banking system.

□ Identify the tools used by the Federal Reserve Banks to control the size of the money supply.

□ Explain why the Federal Reserve Banks are central, quasi-public, bankers' banks.

□ List several kinds of financial intermediaries; explain the role played by these intermediaries; and state the critical distinction between a financial intermediary and a commercial bank.

□ Enumerate the six functions of the Federal Reserve System; explain the meaning of each of these functions; and indicate which is the most important.

■ CHAPTER OUTLINE

1. Money is whatever performs the three basic functions of money: a medium of exchange, a standard of value, and a store of value.

2. In the American economy:

a. The narrowly defined money supply is called M_1 and consists of

(1) coins which are token money and the smallest part of the total money supply;

(2) paper money which is primarily Federal Reserve Notes; and

(3) demand deposits which are bank-created money and the largest component of the money supply;

(4) and is not owned by the Federal government or the Federal Reserve or commercial banks.

b. The more broadly defined money supply is called M_2 and is equal to M_1 plus saving and time deposits in commercial banks and in thrift institutions.

3. In the United States:

a. Money is largely the promise of either a commercial or a Federal Reserve bank to pay; but these debts cannot be redeemed for anything tangible.

b. Money has value only because people can exchange it for desirable goods and services.

c. The price of money is inversely related to the price level.

d. Money is "backed" by the confidence which the public has that the value of money will remain stable; and the Federal government can use monetary and fiscal policy to keep the value of money relatively stable.

4. The centralized American banking system consists of thousands of privately owned and operated commercial banks and the twelve Federal Reserve Banks, which are owned by the commercial banks and whose operation is directed by the Board of Governors of the Federal Reserve System.

a. The banking system is centralized because the absence of centralization in the past led to an inflexible supply of money, a multitude of different kinds of money, and a mismanagement of the money supply which caused recurrent financial panics and speculation.

b. In the Federal Reserve System:

(1) The Board of Governors exercises control over the supply of money and the banking system.

(2) The Federal Reserve Banks are central, quasi-public, bankers' banks.

(3) Over 14,000 commercial banks—either state or national banks—perform the two essential functions of holding deposits and making loans.

(4) Financial intermediaries lend funds de-

posited with them and serve only as intermediaries between savers and investors.

(5) Commercial banks also function as financial intermediaries; but, unlike other financial intermediaries, they create and destroy demand deposit money.

c. The Board of Governors and the Federal Reserve Banks perform six functions aimed at providing certain essential services, supervision of the private commercial banks, and the regulation of the supply of money.

■ IMPORTANT TERMS

Medium of exchange	Qualitative (selective) credit controls
Standard of value	
Store of value	Federal Open Market Committee
Money supply	
M_1	Federal Advisory Committee
Token money	Federal Reserve Bank
Intrinsic value	
Face value	Central bank
Paper money	Quasi-public bank
Federal Reserve Note	Bankers' bank
Demand deposit	Commercial bank
Currency	State bank
Near-money	National bank
M_2	Member bank
Fiat money	Financial intermediary
Legal tender	
Board of Governors	Member bank deposits (or reserves)
Quantitative credit controls	Collection of checks

■ FILL-IN QUESTIONS

1. Three functions of money are:

a. _____

b. _____

c. _____

2. The supply of money, M_1, in the United States consists of _____,

_____ ,

and _____

not owned by _____

or _____

3. The most important near-monies in the American economy are _____ and _____ deposits in commercial banks and _____ institutions. Another important near-money is U.S. government _____

4. The money supply, M_2, is equal to the most important near-monies plus _____

5. List four reasons why the discussion of near-monies is important.

a. _____

b. _____

c. _____

d. _____

6. Money in the United States consists largely of the debts of _____

or the debts of _____

7. Money in the United States has value because _____

_____ ;

the value of money varies _____

with changes in the _____

8. What are the three basic quantitative controls employed by the Federal Reserve Banks?

a. _____

b. _____

c. _____

9. Two groups which help the Board of Governors of the Federal Reserve System to formulate its policies are the _____

_____ and the _____

_____ .

10. The three principal characteristics of the Federal Reserve Banks are:

a. _____

b. _____

c. _____

11. If a bank is a bankers' bank it means

that _____

and _____

12. Commercial banks are banks which ____

_____

and _____

and in doing so _____

13. The *other* financial intermediaries:

a. include such institutions as _____

_____ banks, _____

associations, investment banks, and _____

_____ companies;

b. only channel funds from _____

to _____

c. do not either _____ or _____
money.

14. The six major functions of the Federal Reserve Banks are:

a. _____

b. _____

c. _____

d. _____

e. _____

f. _____

The most important of the functions which the Federal Reserve Banks perform is that

of _____

15. When it is said that the Federal Reserve Banks act as a fiscal agent for the Federal government, it is meant that the Federal Reserve Banks _____,

_____ ,

and _____

■ **PROBLEMS AND PROJECTS**

1. From the data in the table below, it can be concluded that on the date to which the figures pertain:
a. The amount of currency owned by the

public is $_____ billion.

b. The money supply, M_1, is $_____
billion.

c. M_2 is equal to $_____ billion.

2. If you were to deposit $500 in currency in your checking account in a commercial bank, the *size* of the supply of money, as a

consequence of your deposit, would have ____

_____

and the *composition* of the money supply

would have _____

3. If the price level:
a. Fell by 20%, the value of money would

_____ by _____%.
b. Rose by 10%, the value of money would

_____ by _____%.

■ **SELF-TEST**

Circle the T if the statement is true, the F if it is false.

	Billions of dollars
Total currency outstanding	88.6
Total savings and time deposits	884.8
Commercial bank reserves at the Federal Reserve Banks	26.2
Demand deposits of the Federal government at the Federal Reserve Banks	13.3
Currency owned by commercial banks	8.3
Demand deposits of the public at commercial banks	225.4
Government bonds owned by the public	294.6
Currency owned by the Federal government	0.5
Demand deposits of the Federal government at commercial banks	10.2
Currency owned by the Federal Reserve Banks	0.8

1. If a coin is "token money," its face value is less than its intrinsic value. **T F**

2. The demand deposits of the Federal government at the Federal Reserve Banks are a component of M_1. **T F**

3. M_2 exceeds M_1 by the amount of savings and time deposits in commercial banks and in various thrift institutions. **T F**

4. The larger the volume of near-monies owned by consumers, the larger will be their average propensity to save. **T F**

5. If money is to have a fairly stable value, its supply must be limited relative to the demand for it. **T F**

6. The Board of Governors of the Federal Reserve System is appointed by the President of the United States and confirmed by the Senate. **T F**

7. The Federal Reserve Banks are owned and operated by the United States government. **T F**

8. Federal Reserve Banks are bankers' banks because they make loans to and accept deposits from commercial banks. **T F**

9. All national banks are members of the Federal Reserve System. **T F**

10. The most important function of the Federal Reserve Banks is the control of the size of the economy's money supply. **T F**

Underscore the letter that corresponds to the best answer.

1. Which of the following constitutes the largest element in the nation's money supply, M_1? (*a*) currency; (*b*) Federal Reserve Notes; (*c*) time deposits; (*d*) demand deposits.

2. Demand deposits are money because they are (*a*) legal tender; (*b*) fiat money; (*c*) a medium of exchange; (*d*) token money.

3. If a person deposits $75 in currency in his checking account at a commercial bank, the supply of money has (*a*) decreased by $75; (*b*) increased by $75; (*c*) not changed in any way; (*d*) not changed in amount, but its composition has changed.

4. The supply of money, M_1, consists almost entirely of the debts of (*a*) the Federal government; (*b*) the Federal Reserve Banks; (*c*) commercial banks; (*d*) the Federal Reserve and commercial banks.

5. Which of the following *best* describes the "backing" of money in the United States? (*a*) the gold bullion stored at Fort Knox, Kentucky; (*b*) the belief of holders of money that it can be exchanged for desirable goods and services; (*c*) the willingness of banks and the government to surrender something of value in exchange for money; (*d*) the faith and confidence of the public in the ability of government to pay its debts.

6. If the price level increases 20%, the value of money decreases: (*a*) $14\frac{1}{7}$%; (*b*) $16\frac{2}{3}$%; (*c*) 20%; (*d*) 25%.

7. Which of the following is *not* a quantitative credit control? (*a*) regulation of consumer credit for purchasing homes; (*b*) open-market operations; (*c*) setting of the reserve requirement; (*d*) setting of the discount rate.

8. Less than one-half of all commercial banks are members of the Federal Reserve System; these member banks have about what percentage of all deposits in commercial banks? (*a*) 20%; (*b*) 40%; (*c*) 60%; (*d*) 80%.

9. Which of the following is *not* a financial intermediary? (*a*) a Federal Reserve Bank; (*b*) a commercial bank; (*c*) a savings and loan association; (*d*) an insurance company.

10. Which of the following functions distinguishes a commercial bank from other financial intermediaries? (*a*) accepts deposits; (*b*) creates and destroys money; (*c*) makes loans; (*d*) deals in debts.

■ **DISCUSSION QUESTIONS**

1. How would you define money? What constitutes the supply of money, M_1, in the United States? Which of these is the largest element in the money supply?

2. What is a near-money? What are the most important near-monies in the American economy? Define M_2.

3. For what reasons are demand deposits included in the money supply?

4. What "backs" the money used in the United States? What determines the value of money? Explain the relationship between the value of money and the price level.

5. What must government do if it is to stabilize the value of money?

6. Why is it necessary to have central banks in the United States?

7. Outline the structure of the Federal Reserve System and the chief functions of each of the three parts of the system.

8. As briefly as possible outline the three characteristics of the Federal Reserve Banks and explain the meaning of these characteristics.

9. How are commercial banks *like* other financial intermediaries? How do commercial banks *differ* from other financial intermediaries?

10. What are the chief functions which the Federal Reserve Banks perform? Explain briefly the meaning of each of these functions. Which function is the most important?

15

How Banks Create Money

Chapter 14 explained the institutional structure of banking in the United States today, the functions which banks and money perform, and the composition of the money supply in the United States. Chapter 15 explains how banks literally create money—checking account money—and the factors which determine and limit the money-creating ability of commercial banks.

The device (and a most convenient and simple device it is) employed to explain commercial banking operations and money creation is the balance sheet. All banking transactions affect this balance sheet, and the first step to understanding how money is created is to understand how various simple and typical transactions affect the commercial bank balance sheet.

In reading this chapter you must analyze for yourself the effect upon the balance sheet of each and every banking transaction discussed. The important items in the balance sheet are demand deposits and reserves, because demand deposits *are* money, and the ability of a bank to create new demand deposits is determined by the amount of reserves the bank has. Expansion of the money supply depends upon the possession by commercial banks of excess reserves. Excess reserves do not appear explicitly in the balance sheet but do appear there implicitly because excess reserves are the difference between the actual reserves and the required reserves of commercial banks.

Two cases—the single commercial bank and the banking system—are presented in order to help you build an understanding of banking and money creation. It is important here to understand that the money-creating potential of a single commercial bank differs in an important way from the money-creating potential of the entire banking system; it is equally important to understand how the money-creating ability of many single commercial banks is *multiplied* and results in the money-creating ability of the banking system as a whole.

Certain assumptions are used throughout most of the chapter to analyze money-creating ability; in certain instances these assumptions may not be completely realistic and may need to be modified. The chapter concludes with a discussion of how the earlier analysis must be modified—but not changed in its essentials—to take account of these slightly unrealistic assumptions.

■ CHECKLIST

The very least you should be able to do when you have finished this chapter is:

□ Explain the effects of the deposit of currency in a checking account on the composition and size of the money supply.

□ Compute a bank's required and excess reserves when you are given the needed balance-sheet figures.

□ Explain why a commercial bank which is a member of the Federal Reserve System is required to maintain a reserve; and why this reserve is not sufficient to protect the depositors from losses.

□ Indicate how the deposit of a check drawn on one commercial bank in a second commercial bank will affect the reserves and excess reserves of the two banks.

□ Show what happens to the money supply when a commercial bank makes a loan (or buys securities); and what happens to the money supply when a loan is repaid (or a bank sells securities).

□ Explain what happens to a commercial bank's reserves and demand deposits after it has made a loan, a check has been written on the newly created demand deposit, deposited in another commercial bank, and cleared; and what happens to the reserves and demand deposits of the commercial bank in which the check was deposited.

□ Describe what would happen to a commercial bank's reserves if it made loans (or bought securities) in an amount that exceeded its excess reserves.

□ State the money-creating potential of a commercial bank (the amount of money a commercial bank can safely create by lending or buying securities).

□ State the money-creating potential of the banking system; and explain how it is possible for the banking system to create an amount of money which is a multiple of its excess reserves when no individual commercial bank ever creates money in an amount greater than its excess reserve.

□ Compute the size of the demand deposit multiplier and the money-creating potential of the banking system when you are provided with the necessary data.

□ List the two leakages which reduce the money-creating potential of the banking system.

■ CHAPTER OUTLINE

1. The balance sheet of the commercial bank is a statement of the assets, liabilities, and net worth of the bank at a specific time.

2. By examining the ways in which the balance sheet of the commercial bank is affected by various transactions, it is possible to un-

derstand how a single commercial bank in a multibank system can create money.

a. Once a commercial bank has been founded,

(1) by selling shares of stock and obtaining cash in return;

(2) and acquired the property and equipment needed to carry on the banking business;

(3) the deposit of cash in the bank does not affect the total money supply; it only changes its composition by substituting demand deposits for currency in circulation;

(4) when it joins the Federal Reserve System, three reserve concepts become vital to an understanding of the money creating potential of a commercial bank:

(a) the *legal reserve deposit* (required reserve) which a member bank *must* maintain at its Federal Reserve Bank (or as vault cash—which can be ignored) equals the reserve ratio multiplied by the deposit liabilities of the commercial bank;

(b) the *actual reserves* of a commercial bank are its deposits at the Federal Reserve bank (plus the vault cash which is ignored);

(c) the *excess reserves* equal the actual reserves less the required reserve;

(5) the writing of a check upon the bank and its deposit in a second bank results in a loss of reserves and deposits for the first and a gain in reserves and deposits for the second bank.

b. When a single commercial bank lends or buys securities it increases its own deposit liabilities and, therefore, the supply of money by the amount of the loan or security purchase. But the bank only lends or buys securities in an amount equal to its excess reserves because it fears the loss of reserves to other commercial banks in the economy.

c. An individual commercial bank balances its desire for profits (which result from the making of loans and the purchase of securities) with its desire for safety (which it achieves by having excess reserves or vault cash).

3. The ability of a banking system composed of many individual commercial banks to lend and to create money is a multiple (greater than one) of its excess reserves; and is equal to the excess reserves of the banking system multiplied by the demand deposit (or monetary) multiplier.

a. The banking system as a whole can do this even though no single commercial bank ever lends an amount greater than its excess reserve because the banking system, unlike a single commercial bank, does not lose reserves.

b. The demand deposit (or monetary) multiplier is equal to the reciprocal of the required reserve ratio.

c. The potential lending ability of the banking system may not be fully achieved if there are

(1) leakages because borrowers choose to have currency or bankers choose to have excess reserves;

(2) or bankers are either not willing or not able to lend;

(3) and if bankers lend as much as they are able during periods of prosperity and less than they are able during recessions they add to the instability of the economy.

■ **IMPORTANT TERMS**

Balance sheet	The lending potential of an individual commercial bank
Vault cash (till money)	
Legal (required) reserve (deposit)	Commercial banking system
Reserve ratio	The lending potential of the banking system
Fractional reserve	
Actual reserve	Demand deposit (monetary) multiplier
Excess reserve	Leakage

■ **FILL-IN QUESTIONS**

1. The balance sheet of a commercial bank is a statement of the bank's _____,

_____

and _____
at some specific point in time.

2. The coins and paper money which a bank has in its possession are called _____

_____

or _____

3. Another name for a checking account is a

_____ ;

a savings account is also called a _____

_____

4. The legal reserve deposit of a commercial bank (ignoring vault cash) must be kept in the

_____

and must equal (at least) its _____

multiplied by the _____

5. The excess reserves of a commercial bank

equal its _____

less its _____

6. If commercial banks are allowed to accept (or create) deposits in excess of their reserves, the banking system is operating under

a system of _____
reserves.

7. When a person deposits cash in a commercial bank and receives a demand deposit in return, the size of the money supply has

(increased, decreased, not changed) _____

_____

8. When a check is drawn upon bank X, deposited in bank Y, and cleared, the reserves of bank X are (increased, decreased, not

changed) _____

and the reserves of bank Y are _____ ;

deposits in bank X are _____

and deposits in bank Y are _____

9. A single commercial bank in a multibank system can safely make loans or buy government securities equal in amount to the

_____

of that commercial bank.

10. When a commercial bank makes a new loan of $10,000, it (increases, decreases)

_____

the supply of money by $ _____

11. When a commercial bank sells a $2000 government bond to a securities dealer the

supply of money (increases, decreases) _____

_____

by $ _____

12. A bank ordinarily pursues two conflicting goals; they are _____

and _____

13. The banking system can make loans (or buy government securities) and create money in an amount equal to its excess reserves multiplied by the _____

Its lending potential per dollar of excess reserves is greater than the lending potential of a single commercial bank because it does not lose _____ to other banks.

14. The greater the reserve ratio is, the (larger, smaller) _____ is the deposit multiplier.

15. If the required reserve ratio is 16⅔ percent, the banking system is $6 million short of reserves and the banking system is unable to increase its reserves, the banking system must _____

the money supply by $ _____

■ **PROBLEM AND PROJECTS**

1. In the next column is a simplified balance sheet for a commercial bank. Assume that the figures given show the balance sheet of the bank *prior* to each of the following transactions. Draw up the balance sheet as it would appear after each of the transactions is completed, and place the balance sheet figures in the appropriate column.

	(1)	(2)	(3)	(4)
Assets:				
Cash	$100	$__	$__	$__	$__
Reserves	200	__	__	__	__
Loans	500	__	__	__	__
Securities	200	__	__	__	__
Liabilities:				
Demand deposits	900	__	__	__	__
Capital stock	100	__	__	__	__

a. A check for $50 is drawn by one of the depositors of the bank, given to a person who deposits it in another bank, and cleared (column 1).

b. A depositor withdraws $50 in cash from the bank, and the bank restores its vault cash by obtaining $50 in additional cash from its Federal Reserve Bank (column 2).

c. A check for $60 drawn on another bank is deposited in this bank and cleared (column 3).

d. The bank sells $100 in government bonds to the Federal Reserve Bank in its district (column 4).

2. Below are five balance sheets for a single commercial bank (columns 1a–5a). The required reserve ratio is 20%.

a. Compute the required reserves (A)—ignoring vault cash; the excess reserves* (B) of the bank, and the amount of new loans it can extend (C).

* If the bank is short of reserves and must reduce its loans or obtain additional reserves, show this by placing a minus sign in front of the amounts by which it is short of reserves.

	(1a)	(2a)	(3a)	(4a)	(5a)
Assets:					
Cash	$ 10	$ 20	$ 20	$ 20	$ 15
Reserves	40	40	25	40	45
Loans	100	100	100	100	150
Securities	50	60	30	70	60
Liabilities:					
Demand deposits	175	200	150	180	220
Capital stock	25	20	25	50	50
A. Required reserve	$__	$__	$__	$__	$__
B. Excess reserve	__	__	__	__	__
C. New loans	__	__	__	__	__

b. Draw up for the individual bank the five balance sheets as they appear after the bank has made the new loans that it is capable of making (columns 1b–5b).

	(1b)	(2b)	(3b)	(4b)	(5b)
Assets:					
Cash	$____	$____	$____	$____	$____
Reserves	____	____	____	____	____
Securities	____	____	____	____	____
Liabilities:					
Demand deposits	____	____	____	____	____
Capital stock	____	____	____	____	____

3. At the right above are several reserve ratios. Compute the deposit multiplier for each of the reserve ratios and enter the figures in column 2. In column 3 show the maximum amount by which a single commercial bank can increase its loans for each dollar's worth of excess reserves it possesses. In column 4 indicate the maximum amount by which the banking system can increase its loans for each dollar's worth of excess reserves in the system.

4. Below is a simplified consolidated balance sheet for all commercial banks in the economy. The reserve ratio is 20%. Assume that this is the balance sheet as it appears *prior* to each of the following three transactions.

	(1)	(2)	(3)	(4)
12½%	____	$____	$____
16⅔%	____	____	____
20%	____	____	____
25%	____	____	____
30%	____	____	____
33⅓%	____	____	____

a. The public deposits $5 in cash in the banks and the banks send the $5 to the Federal Reserve, where it is added to their reserves. Fill in column 1. If the banking system extends the new loans it is capable of extending, show in column 2 the balance sheet as it would then appear.

b. The banking system sells $8 worth of securities to the Federal Reserve. Complete column 3. Assuming the system extends the maximum amount of credit of which it is capable, fill in column 4.

c. The Federal Reserve lends $10 to the commercial banks; complete column 5. Complete column 6 showing the condition of the banks after the maximum amount of new loans which the banks are capable of making is granted.

■ **SELF-TEST**

Circle the T if the statement is true, the F if it is false.

		(1)	(2)	(3)	(4)	(5)	(6)
Assets:							
Cash	$ 50	$____	$____	$____	$____	$____	$____
Reserves	100	____	____	____	____	____	____
Loans	200	____	____	____	____	____	____
Securities	200	____	____	____	____	____	____
Liabilities:							
Demand deposits	500	____	____	____	____	____	____
Capital stock	50	____	____	____	____	____	____
Loans from Federal Reserve	0	____	____	____	____	____	____
Excess reserves		____	____	____	____	____	____
Maximum possible expansion of the money supply		____	____	____	____	____	____

1. The balance sheet of a commercial bank shows the transactions in which the bank has engaged during a given period of time.

        T   F

2. Roberta Lynn, the dancing star, deposits a $30,000 check in a commercial bank and receives a demand deposit in return; an hour later the Manfred Iron and Coal Company borrows $30,000 from the same bank. The money supply has increased $30,000 as a result of the two transactions.   T   F

3. A single commercial bank can safely loan an amount equal to its excess reserves multiplied by the required reserve ratio.   T   F

4. A commercial bank which is a member of the Federal Reserve System may maintain its legal reserve either as a deposit in its Federal Reserve Bank or as government bonds in its own vault.   T   F

5. The legal reserve which a commercial bank maintains must equal at least its own deposit liabilities multiplied by the required reserve ratio.   T   F

6. The actual reserves of a commercial bank equal excess reserves plus required reserved.

        T   F

7. A commercial bank's assets plus its net worth equal the bank's liabilities.   T   F

8. The reserve of a commercial bank in the Federal Reserve Bank is an asset of the Federal Reserve Bank.   T   F

9. A check for $1000 drawn on bank X by a depositor and deposited in bank Y will increase the excess reserves of bank Y by $1000.   T   F

10. To say that a commercial bank seeks *profits* and *liquidity* is an example of dual terminology—using two different words to mean the same thing.   T   F

11. When a borrower repays a loan of $500, either in cash or by check, the supply of money is reduced by $500.   T   F

12. The granting of a $5000 loan and the purchase of a $5000 government bond from a securities dealer by a commercial bank have the same effect on the money supply. T   F

13. If the banking system has $10 million in excess reserves and if the reserve ratio is 25%, it can increase its loans by $40 million.

        T   F

14. While a single commercial bank can increase its loans only by an amount equal to its excess reserves, the entire banking system can increase its loans by an amount equal to its excess reserves multiplied by the reciprocal of the reserve ratio.   T   F

15. When borrowers from a commercial bank wish to have cash rather than demand deposits, the money-creating potential of the banking system is increased.   T   F

Underscore the letter that corresponds to the best answer.

1. A bank has excess reserves of $3000 and deposit liabilities of $30,000; the required reserve ratio is 20%. The actual reserves of the bank are: (*a*) $3000; (*b*) $6000; (*c*) $9000; (*d*) $10,000.

2. A bank has excess reserves of $5000 and deposit liabilities of $50,000 when the required reserve ratio is 20%. If the reserve ratio is raised to 25%, the bank's excess reserves will be: (*a*) $1000; (*b*) $1500; (*c*) $2000; (*d*) $2500.

3. A depositor places $750 in cash in a bank, and the reserve ratio is 33⅓%; the bank sends the $750 to the Federal Reserve Bank. As a result, the *reserves* and the *excess reserves* of the bank have been increased, respectively, by: (*a*) $750 and $250; (*b*) $750 and $500; (*c*) $750 and $750; (*d*) $500 and $500.

4. A bank has deposit liabilities of $100,000, reserves of $37,000, and a required reserve ratio of 25%. The amount by which a *single commercial bank* and the amount by which the *banking system* can increase loans are, respectively: (*a*) $12,000 and $48,000; (*b*) $17,000 and $68,000; (*c*) $12,000 and $60,000; (*d*) $17,000 and $85,000.

5. A bank has no excess reserves, but then a depositor places $600 in cash in the bank, and the bank adds the $600 to its reserves by sending it to the Federal Reserve Bank. The bank then loans $300 to a borrower. As a consequence of these transactions the size of the money supply has: (*a*) not been affected; (*b*) increased by $300; (*c*) increased by $600; (*d*) increased by $900.

6. A bank has excess reserves of $500 and a required reserve ratio of 20%; it grants a loan of $1000 to a borrower. If the borrower writes a check for $1000 which is deposited in another bank, the first bank will be short of reserves, after the check has been cleared, in the amount of: (a) $200; (b) $500; (c) $700; (d) $1000.

7. The banking system has excess reserves of $700 and makes new loans of $2100 and is just meeting its reserve requirements. The required reserve ratio is: (a) 20%; (b) 25%; (c) 30%; (d) 33⅓%.

8. A bank sells a $1000 government security to a securities dealer. The dealer pays for the bond in cash, which the bank adds to its vault cash. The money supply has: (a) not been affected; (b) decreased by $1000; (c) increased by $1000; (d) increased by $1000 multiplied by the reciprocal of the required reserve ratio.

9. The commercial banking system, because of a recent change in the reserve ratio required, finds that it is $50 million short of reserves. Before the change in the reserve ratio, it was loaned up but not short of reserves. It has deposit liabilities of $500 million and reserves of $100 million. The change in the reserve ratio which took place was from 20% to (a) 25%; (b) 30%; (c) 33⅓%; (d) 40%.

10. Only one bank in the commercial banking system has excess reserves, and its excess reserve is $100,000. This bank makes a new loan equal to the maximum amount it can loan. The borrower receives half the loan in the form of a demand deposit and half in cash, which the bank obtains from its Federal Reserve Bank. The required reserve ratio for all banks is 20%, and the cash is *not* redeposited in a bank. The maximum amount that the money supply can be expanded by the banking system as a result of the entire transaction is: (a) $250,000; (b) $300,000; (c) $500,000; (d) $600,000.

■ DISCUSSION QUESTIONS

1. Commercial banks seek both profits and safety. Explain how the balance sheet of the commercial banks reflects the desires of bankers for income and for liquidity.

2. Do the reserves held by commercial banks satisfactorily protect the bank's depositors? Are the reserves of commercial banks needed? Explain your answers.

3. Explain why the granting of a loan by a commercial bank increases the supply of money. Why does the repayment of a loan decrease the supply of money?

4. The owner of a sporting goods store writes a check on his account in a Kent, Ohio, bank and sends it to one of his suppliers who deposits it in his bank in Cleveland, Ohio. How does the Cleveland bank obtain payment from the Kent bank? If the two banks were in Kent and New York City, how would one bank pay the other? How are the excess reserves of the two banks affected?

5. Why is a single commercial bank able to loan safely only an amount equal to its excess reserves?

6. No one commercial bank ever lends an amount greater than its excess reserve, but the banking system as a whole is able to extend loans and expand the money supply by an amount equal to the system's excess reserves multiplied by the reciprocal of the reserve ratio. Explain why this is possible and how the multiple expansion of deposits and money takes place.

7. On the basis of a given amount of excess reserves and a given reserve ratio, a certain expansion of the money supply may be possible. What are two reasons why the potential expansion of the money supply may not be fully achieved?

The Federal Reserve Banks and Monetary Policy

CHAPTER 16

Chapter 16 is the third chapter dealing with money and banking. It explains how the Board of Governors of the Federal Reserve System and the Federal Reserve Banks affect output, income, employment, and the price level of the economy. Central-bank policies designed to affect these variables are called monetary policies, the goal of which is full employment without inflation.

You should have little difficulty with this chapter if you have understood the material in Chapter 15. In Chapter 16 attention should be concentrated on the following: (1) the cause-effect chain between monetary policy; commercial bank reserves and excess reserves; the supply of money; the cost and availability of credit; and investment spending, aggregate demand, output, employment, and the price level; (2) the principal items on the balance sheet of the Federal Reserve Banks; (3) the three major quantitative controls available to the Federal Reserve Banks, and how employment of these controls can affect the reserves, excess reserves, the actual money supply, and the money-creating potential of the banking system; (4) the minor qualitative controls which the Federal Reserve banks use or have used to influence the economy; (5) the actions the Federal Reserve would take if it were pursuing a tight money policy to curb inflation, and the actions it would take if it were pursuing an easy money policy to prevent or eliminate depression; and

(6) the relative effectiveness of the various types of monetary controls and of monetary policy in general in curbing inflation and depression.

In order to acquire a thorough knowledge of the manner in which each of the Federal Reserve transactions affects reserves, excess reserves, the actual money supply, and the potential money supply, you must study very carefully each of the sets of balance sheets which are used to explain these transactions. On these balance sheets the items to watch are again reserves and demand deposits! Be sure that you know why each of the balance-sheet changes is made and are able, *on your own,* to make the appropriate balance-sheet entries to trace through the effects of any transaction.

The last section of Chapter 16 is a summary of Chapters 9 through 16. It will recall for you the main outline of the theory of employment and the principal public policies that may be used to promote full employment without creating inflation. They will help you to see that the various principles discussed in the previous chapters are *not* separate theories but are, in fact, connected parts of the one theory of employment; and that the public policies discussed in earlier chapters are *not* really separate policies but are alternative means of achieving the goal of economic stabilization.

This one theory of employment and the

alternative means of achieving this one goal are summarized for you in Figure 16–2. This is probably the single most important figure in the textbook. But you should be aware that it *is* a summary and that a summary necessarily sacrifices detail and completeness in exchange for generality and briefness. A few of the "Complications and Problems" which are hidden by Figure 16–2 and which are an essential part of a full understanding of the theory of employment and of stabilization policy are examined at the end of the chapter.

▪ CHECKLIST

The very least you should be able to do when you have finished this chapter is:

□ Explain, using the cause-effect chain, the links between a change in the money supply and a change in the equilibrium NNP.

□ List the principal assets and liabilities of the Federal Reserve Banks.

□ Identify the three quantitative controls; and explain how each may be employed by the Federal Reserve to expand and to contract the money supply.

□ Prescribe the three specific monetary policies the Federal Reserve should utilize to reduce unemployment; and the three specific policies it should employ to reduce inflationary pressures in the economy.

□ Identify two selective controls; and explain how each is used to promote economic stability.

□ State which of the three quantitative controls is the most effective.

□ Draw an investment-demand schedule and use it to show the effects of a change in the rate of interest on investment spending; and construct a single leakages-injections graph to show the effects of a change in investment demand on the equilibrium NNP.

□ List five shortcomings and three strengths of monetary policy.

□ Summarize the Keynesian theory of employment and the policies that may be utilized to promote a full-employment noninflationary NNP.

□ Enumerate the four "complexities and problems" found in the Keynesian theory and its application.

▪ CHAPTER OUTLINE

1. The objective of monetary policy is full employment without inflation.

a. The Federal Reserve Banks attempt to accomplish this objective by exercising control over the amount of excess reserves held by commercial banks and thereby influencing the size of the money supply, the rate of interest, and the level of aggregate demand.

b. Decreases (increases) in the rate of interest tend to increase (decrease) investment spending and, therefore, aggregate demand.

2. By examining the consolidated balance sheet and the principal assets and liabilities of the Federal Reserve Banks, an understanding of the ways in which the Federal Reserve can control and influence the reserves of commercial banks and the money supply can be obtained.

a. The principal assets of the Federal Reserve Banks (in order of size) are U.S. government securities, gold certificates, loans to commercial banks, and cash.

b. Their principal liabilities are Federal Reserve Notes, the reserve deposits of commercial banks, and U.S. Treasury deposits.

3. The Federal Reserve Banks employ three quantitative controls to affect the total amount of bank credit and the size of the money supply.

a. The Federal Reserve can change the reserve ratio.

b. It can buy and sell government bonds in the open market.

c. And it can also change the discount rate.

d. Changes in the discount rate and the purchase and sale of government bonds affect the amount of Reserve Bank credit and the amount of commercial bank reserves.

e. A tight (easy) money policy involves increasing (decreasing) the reserve ratio, selling (buying) bonds in the open market, and increasing (decreasing) the discount rate.

4. The Federal Reserve also employs qualitative controls to affect the volume of credit available for and the amount of spending on certain types of goods and securities.

a. These controls consist of setting the margin requirements for the purchase of stocks and the terms of credit available to purchasers of homes and durable consumer goods.

b. In addition, moral suasion is used to influence commercial bank lending.

5. Open-market operations are the most effective device for controlling credit and the money supply.

6. Graphically, when monetary policy decreases (increases) the rate of interest, investment spending increases (decreases) on the downsloping investment-demand curve; and on a leakages-injections graph this moves the investment curve upward (downward) and expands (contracts) the equilibrium NNP.

7. Whether monetary policy is effective in promoting full employment without inflation is a debatable question because monetary policy has both shortcomings and strengths in fighting recession and inflation.

8. The income, employment, output, and prices of an economy are positively related to the level of aggregate demand, which has three principal components.
   a. Consumption spending depends upon the income of the economy and the several factors which affect the location of the consumption schedule.
   b. Investment spending is the more unstable component because it depends upon profit expectations which are themselves highly variable.
   c. Government spending depends partly on what level of spending is necessary to achieve full employment and price stability.
   d. To achieve economic stability, government employs both fiscal and monetary policy.
   e. The use of the theory of employment to achieve economic stability is complicated by several considerations.

■ **IMPORTANT TERMS**

Monetary policy	Open-market operations
Easy money policy	
Tight money policy	Discount rate
Gold certificates	Moral suasion
Quantitative control	Margin requirement
Qualitative control	Velocity of money
Reserve Bank credit	Cost-push inflation

■ **FILL-IN QUESTIONS**

1. The general objective of monetary policy in the United States is _____ ; the _____ is generally responsible for the monetary policies which are put into effect by _____ _____

2. To eliminate inflation the monetary authority should seek to _____ the reserves of commercial banks; this would _____ the supply of money; cause the rate of interest to _____ and investment spending, aggregate demand, and the equilibrium NNP to _____

3. The two largest assets of the Federal Reserve Banks are _____ and _____. Their two largest liabilities are _____and _____

4. The three quantitative (or major) controls employed by the monetary authority are changing _____, charging _____, and _____

5. Changes in the reserve ratio affect the ability of commercial banks to create money in two ways: they affect the _____ _____ and the _____

6. Government securities are bought and sold in the open market by the Federal Reserve Banks in order to _____ and to _____

7. If the Federal Reserve Banks were to sell $10 million in government bonds to the public and the reserve ratio were 25%, the supply of money would immediately be reduced $ _____ ,

the reserves of commercial banks would be reduced $ _____ ,
and the excess reserves of the banks would be reduced $ _____ ;
if these bonds were sold to the commercial banks, the supply of money would immediately be reduced $ _____ ,
the reserves of the banks would be reduced $ _____ ,
and the excess reserves of the banks would be reduced $ _____

8. Reserve Bank credit is the sum of _____

_____

and _____

9. To increase the supply of money, the Federal Reserve Banks should _____ the reserve ratio, _____

the discount rate, and/or _____
government securities in the open market; to decrease the supply of money, it should _____

_____

the reserve ratio, _____

the discount rate, and/or _____
securities in the open market.

10. Indicate in the space to the right of each of the following transactions whether it will increase (+) or decrease (−) commercial bank excess reserves.
  a. Federal Reserve sells bonds in the open market _____
  b. Commercial banks borrow from the Federal Reserve _____
  c. Federal Reserve reduces the reserve ratio

_____

11. The qualitative (or minor) controls are the two selective controls and _____
The two selective controls are changes in

_____

and in _____

12. The most effective quantitative control is

_____

13. The levels of output, employment, income, and prices depend upon the level of

_____ which in turn depends (in a closed economy) upon the amounts of _____ ,

_____ , and _____

14. The theory of employment explains each of the three primary components of aggregate demands as follows:
  a. Consumption depends upon the level of

_____ and the position of the

_____

  b. Net investment depends upon the _____
rate of _____ of business firms and the
rate of _____
  c. Government expenditures for goods and services depend upon _____

_____

15. Government seeks to stabilize the economy by employing _____ and _____
policies.

16. Applying fiscal and monetary policies to achieve continuous full employment without inflation is difficult because there is a trade-off between _____ and _____
because employment and the price level are affected not only by macroeconomic factors

but also by _____ and _____

factors; because we do not know the _____
of the fiscal or monetary change called for;

and because it is necessary to _____
the fiscal and monetary policies employed.

■ **PROBLEMS AND PROJECTS**

1. Below are various items which belong in the balance statement of the Federal Reserve Banks. Place them in their proper place in the blank balance sheet by listing them either on the asset or on the liability side and in the order of their dollar importance.

Member bank reserves	Treasury deposits
Securities	Cash
Loan to member banks	Gold certificates
Federal Reserve Notes	

Assets	Liabilities

2. Assume that the consolidated balance sheet below is for all commercial banks. Assume also that the required reserve ratio is 25%, that cash is *not* a part of the commercial banks' legal reserve, and that the demand schedule below shows the amounts of commercial bank loans from the Federal Reserve that will be outstanding at various rates of interest.

Assets		Liabilities	
Cash	$ 50	Demand deposits	$400
Reserves	100	Loans from Federal	
Loans	150	Reserve	25
Securities	200	Net worth	75
	$500		$500

Discount rate, %	Amounts commercial banks will owe to the Federal Reserve
3.0	$ 0.0
2.5	12.5
2.0	25.0
1.5	37.5
1.0	50.0
0.5	62.5

a. To increase the supply of money by $100, the Federal Reserve Banks could *either:*

(1) _____ the reserve ratio to ____%

(2) _____ securities worth $_____ in the open market

(3) _____ the discount rate to ____%

b. To reduce the supply of money by $50, the Federal Reserve Banks could *either:*

(1) _____ the reserve ratio to ____%

(2) _____ securities worth $_____ in the open market

(3) _____ the discount rate to ____%

3. On page 123 are the consolidated balance sheets of the Federal Reserve and of commercial banks. Assume that the reserve ratio for commercial banks is 25%, that cash is *not* a part of a bank's legal reserve, and that the balance-sheet figures in column 1 prevail at the start of each of the following problems. Place the new balance-sheet figures in the appropriate columns and complete A, B, C, and D. *Do not cumulate your answers!*

a. The Federal Reserve Banks sell $3 in securities to the public which pays by check (column 2).

b. The Federal Reserve Banks buy $4 in securities from the commercial banks (column 3).

c. The Federal Reserve Banks lower the required reserve ratio for commercial banks to 20% (column 4).

d. The U.S. Treasury buys $5 worth of goods from American manufacturers and pays the manufacturers by checks drawn on its accounts at the Federal Reserve Banks (column 5).

e. Because the Federal Reserve Banks have raised the discount rate, commercial banks repay $6 which they owe to the Federal Reserve (column 6).

4. Below is an investment-demand curve which shows the amounts of investment spending at various rates of interest.

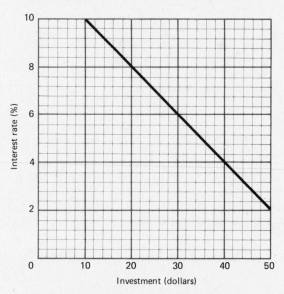

a. On the next graph is the saving curve in an economy in which the only leakage from the NNP is saving. (There are no taxes collected and no imports of goods and services.)

	(1)	(2)	(3)	(4)	(5)	(6)
Federal Reserve Banks						
Assets:						
Gold certificates	$ 25	$___	$___	$___	$___	$___
Securities	30	___	___	___	___	___
Loans to commercial banks	10	___	___	___	___	___
Liabilities:						
Reserves of commercial banks	50	___	___	___	___	___
Treasury deposits	5	___	___	___	___	___
Federal Reserve Notes	10	___	___	___	___	___
Commercial Banks						
Assets:						
Reserves	$ 50	$___	$___	$___	$___	$___
Securities	70	___	___	___	___	___
Loans	90	___	___	___	___	___
Liabilities:						
Demand deposits	200	___	___	___	___	___
Loans from Federal Reserve	10	___	___	___	___	___
A. Required reserves		___	___	___	___	___
B. Excess reserves		___	___	___	___	___
C. Initial change in the money supply		___	___	___	___	___
D. Total potential change in the money supply		___	___	___	___	___

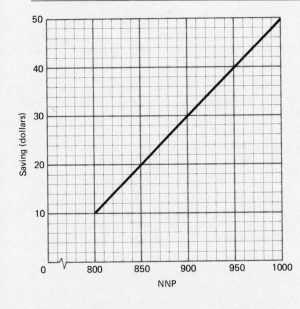

(1) On this graph plot the investment curve for the economy when the rate of interest is 8%.

(2) If the only injection into this economy is investment spending (that is, if there is no government spending for and no exports of goods and services), the equilibrium NNP will be $ _____

b. Assume the rate of interest falls to 6%. On the second graph draw the new investment curve. The equilibrium NNP will now be

$_____.

c. Suppose the full-employment noninflationary NNP in this economy is $875.

(1) At this NNP saving would be $_____
(2) For this NNP to be the equilibrium NNP, investment would have to be equal to $_____
(3) And for investment to be at this level the rate of interest would have to be _____%.

d. In this economy:
(1) the marginal propensity to save is equal to _____ and the multiplier is, therefore, equal to _____;

(2) a one percentage point decrease in the interest rate will _____ investment by $_____ and will, therefore, _____ the equilibrium net national product by $_____

■ **SELF-TEST**

Circle the T if the statement is true, the F if it is false.

1. Consumer spending is more sensitive to changes in the rate of interest than is investment demand. **T F**

2. The securities owned by the Federal Reserve Banks are almost entirely U.S. government bonds. **T F**

3. A change in the reserve ratio will affect the multiple by which the banking system can create money, but it will not affect the actual or excess reserves of member banks. **T F**

4. If the reserve ratio is lowered, some required reserves are turned into excess reserves. **T F**

5. If the Federal Reserve Banks buy $15 in government securities from the public in the open market, the effect will be to increase the excess reserves of commercial banks by $15. **T F**

6. When commercial banks borrow from the Federal Reserve Banks they increase their excess reserves and money creating potential. **T F**

7. Reserve bank credit is equal to the sum of the loans of the Federal Reserve Banks to commercial banks and the securities owned by the Federal Reserve Banks. **T F**

8. If the monetary authority wished to follow a tight money policy, it would seek to reduce the reserves of commercial banks. **T F**

9. The policies of the Federal Reserve Banks during a period of inflation are reinforced by the desire of the United States Treasury to keep interest rates low. **T F**

10. Monetary policy is more effective in fighting recession than it is in curbing inflation. **T F**

11. It is generally agreed that fiscal policy is more effective than monetary policy in controlling the business cycle because fiscal policy is more flexible. **T F**

12. Unlike fiscal policy, monetary policy is an effective means of controlling cost-push inflation. **T F**

Underscore the letter that corresponds to the best answer.

1. The agency directly responsible for monetary policy in the United States is: (*a*) the twelve Federal Reserve Banks; (*b*) the Board of Governors of the Federal Reserve System; (*c*) the Congress of the United States; (*d*) the U.S. Treasury.

2. In the chain of cause and effect between changes in the excess reserves of commercial banks and the resulting changes in output and employment in the economy (*a*) an increase in excess reserves will decrease the money supply; (*b*) a decrease in the money supply will increase the rate of interest; (*c*) an increase in the rate of interest will increase aggregate demand; (*d*) an increase in aggregate demand will decrease output and employment.

3. Which of the following is most likely to be affected by changes in the rate of interest? (*a*) consumer spending; (*b*) investment spending; (*c*) the spending of the Federal government; (*d*) the exports of the economy.

4. The largest single asset in the Federal Reserve Banks' consolidated balance sheet is: (*a*) securities; (*b*) gold certificates; (*c*) cash; (*d*) the reserves of member banks.

5. The largest single liability of the Federal Reserve Banks is: (*a*) the reserves of member banks; (*b*) the deposits of the U.S. Treasury; (*c*) Federal Reserve Notes; (*d*) loans to member banks.

6. Assuming that the Federal Reserve Banks sell $20 million in government securities to member banks and the reserve ratio is 20%, then the effect will be: (*a*) to reduce the actual supply of money by $20 million; (*b*) to reduce the actual supply of money by $4 million; (*c*) to reduce the potential money supply by $20 million; (*d*) to reduce the potential money supply by $100 million.

7. Which of the following acts would *not*

have the same general effect upon the economy as the other three? (a) the Federal Reserve Banks sell bonds in the open market; (b) the Federal Reserve increases the discount rate; (c) the Federal Reserve lowers the down payments required for the purchase of consumer durables; (d) the Federal Reserve raises the reserve ratio.

8. Which of the following is *not* one of the qualitative controls which have been employed by the Federal Reserve? (a) setting tariff rates; (b) moral suasion; (c) setting margin requirements; (d) setting minimum down payments and the maximum periods for repayment for certain consumer durable goods.

9. Which of the following is the most important control used by the Federal Reserve Banks to regulate the money supply? (a) changing the reserve ratio; (b) open-market operations; (c) changing the discount rate; (d) changing the margin requirements.

10. The effectiveness of monetary policy is weak if (a) investment spending is highly sensitive to changes in the interest rate; (b) the velocity of money increases during recessions and decreases during periods of inflation; (c) large monopoly firms do the bulk of the investing; (d) the investment-demand curve moves to the left during periods of inflation and to the right during recessions.

11. Which of the following is *not* one of the difficulties encountered in using monetary and fiscal policy to achieve continuous full employment without inflation? (a) the employment-price level tradeoff; (b) government policies designed to reallocate resources and redistribute income; (c) the inability to determine the size of the needed government deficit or surplus; (d) the relative ineffectiveness of changing the discount rate to change the money supply.

12. Which of the following are coordinated policies? (a) an increase in government expenditures and in the money supply; (b) a decrease in personal tax rates and in the money supply; (c) an increase in transfer payments and a decrease in the money supply; (d) an increase in corporate tax rates and in the money supply.

■ DISCUSSION QUESTIONS

1. Explain how the Board of Governors and the Federal Reserve Banks can influence income, output, employment, and the price level. In your explanation, employ the following concepts: reserves, excess reserves, the supply of money, the availability of bank credit, and the rate of interest.

2. Why are changes in the rate of interest more likely to affect investment spending than consumption and saving?

3. What are the principal assets and liabilities of the Federal Reserve Banks? Which of these items seems most crucial in its effect on the levels of income, output, employment, and prices in the economy?

4. What is Reserve Bank credit? Why is it so called? How is it related to commercial bank reserves and the supply of money?

5. Explain how the quantitative controls of the Federal Reserve Banks would be used to contract the supply of money. How would they be used to expand the supply of money?

6. What is the difference between the effects of the Federal Reserve's buying (selling) government securities in the open market from (to) commercial banks and from (to) the public?

7. How do the qualitative controls differ from general or quantitative controls? What are the principal selective controls? Explain how the Federal Reserve would use these controls in following a tight and an easy money policy.

8. Which of the control devices available to the Federal Reserve is most effective? Why is it more effective than other quantitative controls?

9. Why is monetary policy more effective in controlling inflation than in reducing unemployment?

10. Why did the Federal Reserve and the Treasury disagree in the post-World War II period of inflation over the policy the Federal Reserve should follow with respect to its open-market operations?

11. Looking back at your answer to question 1, explain why monetary policy may be ineffectual in controlling inflation and preventing depression.

12. What are the strengths of monetary policy?

13. Explain as briefly as possible what determines the level of national output in the American economy.

14. Distinguish between fiscal and monetary policy and explain how we may use each of them to achieve reasonably full employment and relatively stable prices.

15. What complications and problems are encountered in using monetary and fiscal policy to eliminate inflationary and recessionary gaps?

Monetarism: An Alternative View

Economics has always been an arena in which conflicting theories and policies opposed each other. This field of intellectual combat, in major engagements, has seen Adam Smith do battle with the defenders of a regulated economy. It witnessed the opposition of Karl Marx to the orthodox economics of his day. In more recent times it saw Keynes in conflict with the classical economists. Around these major engagements have been countless minor skirmishes between opposing viewpoints. Out of these major and minor confrontations have emerged not winners and losers but the advancement of economic theory and the improvement of economic policy.

Monetarism is the latest challenger to enter this intellectual arena. The opponent is the reigning champion, Keynesianism, which bested classical economics in the same arena during the 1940s. The monetarists are often thought of as political conservatives; but they see themselves as liberals who wish to free the economy from the regulations and restraints imposed on it by government. They view the Keynesians as the proponents of the controlled economy in which individual freedoms steadily decline. Such terms as *liberal* and *conservative* are convenient labels for different political ideologies; but you should be sure you understand the differences between the liberal and conservative philosophies as these terms are now employed. You should also be careful, because the terms are emotionally loaded, not to equate liberal with "good" and conservative with "bad."

But this chapter is more than a comparison of the attitudes of monetarists and Keynesians toward individual freedom and the role of government in the economy. And it is more than a comparison of the basic equations of the two schools of thought. The basic equation of the Keynesians and the equation of exchange of the monetarists say pretty much the same thing. The equation of exchange ($MV = PQ$) is another way of saying that the economy will produce the NNP which is equal to the aggregate quantity of goods and services demanded.

The issue is whether the income velocity of money—the V in the equation of exchange—is stable or unstable. If it is stable, as the monetarists contend, then the only kind of policy that can be used to control (to increase or decrease) money NNP is monetary policy; and fiscal policy cannot expand or contract money NNP. But if V is unstable, as the Keynesians argue, then fiscal policy is the only effective means and monetary policy is an ineffective means of controlling money NNP. The issue of whether V is stable or unstable becomes an issue of whether the size of the money supply matters very much or very little. Monetarists argue that the M in the equation of exchange is the only thing that matters and their Keynesian rivals contend that it doesn't matter very much.

The emphasis in Chapter 17 is on monetarism because earlier chapters have emphasized Keynesianism. You are not expected, however, to determine which of the two groups is correct. But you should see that monetarism is an alternative to Keynesianism; that the economic issue is the stability of V; and that the political issue is, therefore, whether monetary or fiscal policy is more effective. Out of the debate between the two groups, as out of the confrontations of the past, will eventually come better economic theory and policy. In the meantime you can adopt an eclectic position: neither the Keynesians nor the monetarists are entirely correct and neither of them is wholly wrong.

■ CHECKLIST

The very least you should be able to do when you have finished this chapter is:

□ State the philosophical and ideological position of the Keynesians and of the monetarists; and compare the two positions.

□ Write the equation of exchange and define each of the four terms in the equation.

□ Show how the basic Keynesian equation is "translated" into the equation of exchange.

□ Explain why the monetarists believe money NNP is directly and predictably linked to M.

□ Present two reasons why Keynesians favor and two reasons why monetarists reject the use of fiscal policy to stabilize the economy.

□ State the monetary rule of the monetarists; and the two reasons why they propose a rule instead of discretionary monetary policy.

□ Contrast the Keynesian and monetarist views on the stability of V and on the relation of PQ (equal to money NNP) to M in the equation of exchange.

□ Compare the monetarist and Keynesian views on the functions of money; on why households and firms demand money; and on what determines the quantity of money demanded.

□ Write a brief scenario which explains what

monetarists believe will happen to change the money NNP when M is increased.

□ Construct a scenario which explains what Keynesians believe will happen if M is increased (or decreased); and another scenario which explains what they believe will happen if government pursues an expansionary (or contractionary) fiscal policy.

■ CHAPTER OUTLINE

1. Monetarism is an alternative to the Keynesian macroeconomic theory and policy recommendations; and monetarists emphasize the importance of the money supply in determining national output, employment, and the price level.

2. Keynesians and monetarists differ philosophically and ideologically.

a. Keynesians tend to be political liberals who believe that the market system has serious shortcomings; that one of these shortcomings is macroeconomic instability; and that fiscal policy should be used to achieve stability.

b. Monetarists tend to be political conservatives who believe that free competitive markets allocate resources efficiently; that the economy would be stable if it were not for government interferences; and that discretionary fiscal and monetary policies have resulted in macroeconomic instability.

3. In the Keynesian model the equilibrium output of the economy is the output at which

$$C + I_n + G = NNP$$

and in the monetarist model the basic equation is the equation of exchange,

$$MV = PQ$$

but because MV (total spending) $= C + I_n + G$ and $PQ = NNP$, the two equations are different ways of stating the same relationship.

a. While Keynesians assign a secondary role to money because they believe the links in the cause-effect chain of the previous chapter are loose ones; monetarists, believing V in the equation of exchange is constant, find that PQ (or NNP) is directly related to M, the money supply.

b. For at least two reasons, Keynesians favor the use of fiscal policy to stabilize the economy; but the monetarists argue that the use of fiscal policy is both harmful and ineffective.

c. Arguing that discretionary changes in *M* have produced monetary mismanagement and macroeconomic instability, the monetarists have proposed the monetary rule that *M* be increased at the same annual rate as the potential annual rate of increase in the real GNP.

4. Whether *V* in the equation of exchange is stable or unstable is a critical question because if it is stable *PQ* is closely linked to *M*; and if it is unstable the link between *PQ* and *M* is loose and uncertain.

a. Empirical evidence confirms neither the contention of the monetarists that *V* is stable nor the contention of the Keynesian that it is variable (or unstable).

b. *V* is inversely related to the size of the money (or liquid) balances which households and firms desire to hold; and is equal to NNP/*M* (and also equal to *PQ*/*M*).

c. Reasoning that money is a medium of exchange and that the demand for money is a transaction demand, monetarists conclude that the quantity of money demanded is a stable percentage of NNP (that NNP/*M* is constant) and that *V* is, therefore, stable in the short run.

d. But Keynesians argue that consumers and business firms also use money as a store of value and that there is, therefore, a speculative demand for money; that this speculative demand is inversely related to the rate of interest; and that *V* (equal to NNP/*M*) is unstable because it changes when the interest rate changes.

e. Looking back at the monetarist and Keynesian views on monetary policy:

(1) the monetarist position is that an increase (a decrease) in *M* will leave firms and households with more (less) money than they wish to have; that they will, therefore, increase (decrease) spending for consumer and capital goods; and that this will cause the NNP and the amount of money they wish to hold for transaction purposes to rise (fall) until their demand for money is equal to *M* and NNP/*M* = *V*.

(2) the Keynesian position is that an increase (a decrease) in *M* will decrease (increase) the interest rate, increase (decrease) the speculative demand for money, lower (raise) *V*, and leave the effect on NNP uncertain.

(3) Keynesians argue that fiscal policy is effective because an expansionary (contractionary) fiscal policy increases (decreases) the demand for money, raises (lowers) the interest rate, reduces (expands) the speculative demand for money, and so increases (decreases) *V* and the NNP (without changing *M*).

f. The debate between Keynesians and monetarists will, for a number of reasons, continue into the future.

■ IMPORTANT TERMS

Keynesianism

Monetarism

Equation of exchange

Crowding-out effect

Monetary rule

Income (circuit) velocity of money

Medium of exchange

Transaction demand for money

Store of value

Speculative demand for money

■ FILL-IN QUESTIONS

1. Keynesians believe that capitalism (or the free-market system) misallocates _____, unequally distributes _____, and has no mechanism to guarantee macroeconomic _____; and favor the use of _____ policy to correct these shortcomings.

2. Monetarists argue that the free-market system allocates resources _____, that government decision making is inefficient and that government interference results in the loss of individual _____ and in macroeconomic _____; and favor the use of _____ policy.

3. The basic equation of the monetarists is

_____ = _____.

a. This equation is called the _____
_____

b. Indicate below what each of the four letters in this equation represents.

(1) *M:* _____

(2) *V:* _____

(3) *P:* _____

(4) *Q:* _____

4. The basic equation of the Keynesians is $C + I_n + G = $ NNP.

a. $C + I_n + G$ is _____
and in the equation of exchange is equal to

_____.

b. Money NNP is equal to _____
in the equation of exchange.

5. Indicate in the spaces provided the effect—increase (+), decrease (−), or no change (0)—upon *P* and *Q* of an increase in *M* under the following conditions. Assume that *V* is constant.

a. The economy is at full employment.

_____ _____

b. The economy is close to but not at full employment. _____ _____

c. The economy is in a severe recession.

_____ _____

6. In the debate on the use of fiscal policy:
a. the Keynesians contend that
(1) for the purpose of stabilization of the economy the more effective tool is _____

_____ policy;

(2) and that it can also be used to _____

resources and _____ income;
b. the monetarists argue that
(1) government borrowing to finance a budget deficit will _____ the rate of

interest and have a _____
effect on investment spending;
(2) and the steps taken to remedy microeconomic shortcomings have adverse effects

on the _____ to work, invest, and bear risks and in the production by government of goods and services which are either

_____ or more cheaply

produced in the _____

_____of the economy.

7. Monetarists would have the supply of money increase at the same annual rate as

the potential rate of growth of _____

and this is a rate of from _____ to _____%.

8. If *V* in the equation of exchange is:
a. stable, there is a direct relationship between _____ and _____.

b. unstable, this relationship is _____

_____

9. If the money NNP is $1000 billion and the demand for money is $200 billion, *V* is

_____ but if money NNP is $1000 billion and the demand for money is $250 billion,

V is _____. The relation between the demand for money and *V* is, therefore, a(n)

_____ one.

10. In the debate on the stability of *V*:
a. monetarists argue that money is used

only as a _____, that

the demand for money is a _____
demand, that this demand is a fixed percentage of _____ and that *V* is,

therefore, _____
b. Keynesians contend that money is also

used as a _____ and

that there is also a _____
demand for money, that this demand is inversely related to the _____,

and that *V* is, therefore, _____.

11. An increase in *M*:
a. to the monetarists' way of thinking will

(1) leave the public with (more, less) _____
money that it wishes to have,
(2) induce the public to (increase, decrease)

_____ its spending for consumer and capital goods,

(3) which will result in a(n) _____
in money NNP.
(4) until the money NNP (or *MV*) is equal to

_____ times _____.
b. to the Keynesians' way of thinking will

(1) result in a(n) _____
in the rate of interest,

(2) which will _____ the demand
for money

(3) and _____ V,

(4) and the effect on money NNP will be ____

_____

12. When government employs an expansionary fiscal policy, Keynesians argue, government borrows to finance its budget deficit; and this:

a. results in a(n) (increased, decreased)
_____ demand for borrowed
funds

b. which (raises, lowers) _____
the interest rate

c. and so (reduces, expands) _____
the speculative demand for money

d. and, thereby, _____ V.

■ **PROBLEMS AND PROJECTS**

1. You must imagine that you are a monetarist in this problem and assume that V in the equation of exchange is constant and equal to 4.

a. In the table below is a schedule which shows Q (the physical output of goods and services which producers will offer for sale) at seven different price levels (P).

P	Q	PQ	MV
$1.00	100	$____	$____
1.00	200	____	____
1.00	300	____	____
1.10	400	____	____
1.25	500	____	____
1.50	600	____	____
1.60	600	____	____

(1) Compute and enter in the table above the seven values of PQ.

(2) On the graph on page 132 use the vertical axis to measure P and the horizontal axis to measure PQ; plot the seven values of PQ; and connect the seven points with a curve.

b. Assume M is $50.

(1) Enter the value of MV on each of the seven lines in the table above.

(2) On the graph use the horizontal axis to measure MV: plot MV at each of the five prices; and connect the five points with a curve.

c. Using either the table or the graph:

(1) The equilibrium money NNP is $_____

(2) The equilibrium price level is $_____

and the equilibrium real NNP is $_____

d. When M increases to $75, MV at each

price level is $_____, the equilibrium

money NNP is $_____, the equilibrium

price level is $_____, and the real NNP

is $_____

e. Should M increase to $225, money NNP

would be $_____, the price level would

be $_____, and real NNP would be

$_____

f. But if M should increase to $240, while

the money NNP would increase to $_____

and the price level would rise to $_____

the real NNP would _____

2. In this problem you are a Keynesian. The table at the left below shows the amounts of money firms and households wish to have for transactions at different levels of money NNP. To the right below is a table which shows the amounts of money they want to have for speculation at different rates of interest.

a. Suppose the money NNP is $500, the interest is 7%, and the supply of money is $125.

Money NNP	Transactions demand	Interest rate	Speculative demand
$ 500	$ 50	7.0%	$ 75
600	60	6.8	80
700	70	6.6	85
800	80	6.4	90
900	90	6.2	95
1000	100	6.0	100

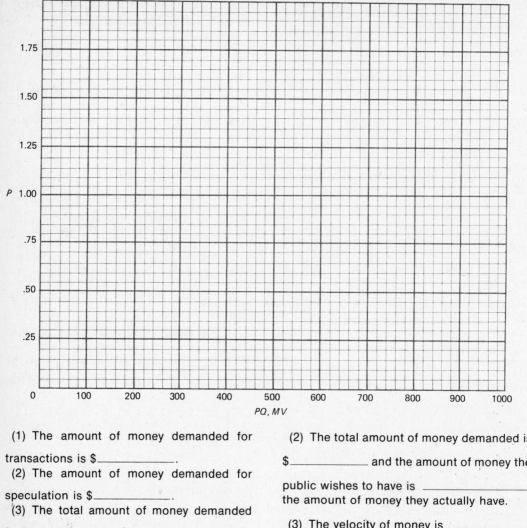

PQ, MV

(1) The amount of money demanded for transactions is $_____.

(2) The amount of money demanded for speculation is $_____.

(3) The total amount of money demanded for both purposes is $_____.

(4) The amount of money firms and households wish to have is (greater than, less than, equal to) _____ the amount of money they actually have.

(5) The velocity of money (equal to money NNP divided by the supply of money) is

_____

b. Assume the Federal Reserve Banks expand the supply of money to $160 by purchasing securities in the open market; and that as a result the rate of interest falls to 6% and the money NNP rises to $600.

(1) The amount of money demanded for transactions is now $_____ and the amount demanded for speculations is now

$_____

(2) The total amount of money demanded is $_____ and the amount of money the public wishes to have is _____ the amount of money they actually have.

(3) The velocity of money is _____

c. Suppose the Federal government pursues an expansionary fiscal policy which raises the money NNP from $600 to $800 and the interest rate from 6% to 6.8%; and the money supply remains at $160.

(1) The transactions demand for money is

$_____, the speculative demand is

$_____ and the total demand is

$_____

(2) The velocity of money is _____

d. The effect of the easy money policy was to (increase, decrease) _____ the velocity of money and the effect of the expansionary fiscal policy was to _____ it.

■ SELF-TEST

Circle the T if the statement is true, the F if it is false.

1. The chief proponent of the monetarist position is Milton Friedman.   **T   F**

2. Monetarists argue that the money supply not only affects the price level but also affects the levels of real output and employment in the economy.   **T   F**

3. The basic equations of the Keynesians and the monetarists are no more than two different ways of stating the same relationship.   **T   F**

4. Keynesians contend that changes in monetary policy will have an uncertain and weak effect on investment spending.   **T   F**

5. Monetarists argue that V in the equation of exchange is stable and that a change in M will bring about a direct and proportional change in P.   **T   F**

6. Keynesians maintain that relatively small changes in the interest rate have relatively large effects on investment spending.   **T   F**

7. Monetarists conclude that discretionary monetary policy has resulted in macroeconomic instability.   **T   F**

8. Keynesians contend that the velocity of money is unstable.   **T   F**

9. Statistical evidence reveals that the income velocity of money has remained almost constant from one year to the next.   **T   F**

10. If money NNP is constant, an increase in the demand for money will increase the velocity of money.   **T   F**

11. From the monetarist viewpoint, the economy is in equilibrium when the amount of money firms and households want to hold is equal to the money supply.   **T   F**

12. In the monetarists' analysis the demand for money is directly related to money NNP.   **T   F**

13. In the Keynesians' analysis the demand for money is directly related to the rate of interest.   **T   F**

14. Keynesians argue that a decrease in the rate of interest will decrease the velocity of money.   **T   F**

15. An expansionary fiscal policy will, the Keynesians contend, decrease the velocity of money.

Underscore the letter that corresponds to the best answer.

1. Keynesians (a) believe the market system allocates resources efficiently; (b) would use fiscal policy to redistribute income; (c) argue against the use of discretionary monetary policy; (d) contend that capitalism should be replaced by socialism.

2. Monetarists (a) believe the market system efficiently allocates resources; (b) would employ both monetary and fiscal policy to stabilize the economy; (c) argue for the use of discretionary monetary policy; (d) contend that government policies have reduced the macroeconomic instability of the economy.

3. Which of the following is *not* true? (a) MV is total spending; (b) PQ is the real NNP; (c) PQ is money NNP; (d) $MV = C + I_n + G$.

4. If V in the equation of exchange is constant, an increase in M will necessarily increase (a) P; (b) Q; (c) both P and Q; (d) P times Q.

5. The crowding-out effect is the effect of borrowing funds to finance a government deficit on (a) imports into the economy; (b) the money supply; (c) investment spending; (d) consumer expenditures.

6. The rule suggested by the monetarists is that the money supply increase at the same rate as (a) the price level; (b) the real output of the economy; (c) the velocity of money; (d) none of the above.

7. If money NNP is $750 billion and the supply of money is $150 billion (a) the velocity of money is 5; (b) the price level is $1.50 and real NNP is $500 billion; (c) the price level is $1.00 and real NNP is $750 billion; (d) the velocity of money is 0.2.

8. Monetarists contend that (a) the only demand for money is the transactions demand; (b) the only demand for money is the speculative demand; (c) there is no transactions demand; (d) there is both a transactions and a speculative demand for money.

9. Keynesians argue that (a) the only demand for money is the speculative demand; (b) the only demand for money is the transactions demand; (c) there is no transactions demand; (d) there is both a transactions and a speculative demand for money.

10. From the monetarist viewpoint, an increase in the supply of money will (a) raise the rate of interest; (b) increase spending for consumer and capital goods; (c) increase the speculative demand for money; (d) increase the demand for government securities.

11. If the Federal Reserve Banks believed the income velocity of money were 3 and constant, to increase the money NNP by $15 billion they should (a) increase M by $45 billion; (b) decrease M by $5 billion; (c) decrease M by $45 billion; (d) increase M by $5 billion.

12. From the Keynesian viewpoint, an increase in supply of money will (a) raise the rate of interest; (b) increase spending for consumer and capital goods; (c) increase the speculative demand for money; (d) increase the demand for government securities.

■ **DISCUSSION QUESTIONS**

1. What, according to the Keynesians, are the shortcomings of capitalism (or the free-market system)? Why do they advocate the use of fiscal policy to remedy these shortcomings?

2. What is the monetarist view on the efficiency and the macroeconomic stability of the free-market system and on government decision making and interference in the economy?

3. What is the basic equation of the Keynesians and the basic equation of the monetarists? Define all terms in both equations and explain how the Keynesian equation can be converted to the monetarist equation.

4. Why do Keynesian believe that monetary policy is an "uncertain, unreliable, and weak stabilization tool as compared to fiscal policy"?

5. Explain how a change in M in the equation of exchange will, to the monetarist way of thinking, affect P and Q during a recession, during a period of prosperity without full employment, and during a period of full employment.

6. Why do the Keynesians advocate and the monetarists reject the use of fiscal policy to stabilize the economy?

7. What is the monetary rule? Why do monetarists suggests this rule to replace discretionary monetary policy?

8. What empirical evidence is there to support the Keynesian contention that V in unstable or the monetarist convention that it is relatively stable?

9. What is meant by the demand for money? Given the economy's money NNP, why must the velocity of money vary inversely with the money supply?

10. Explain the differences between the monetarist and Keynesian views on why firms and households demand money (or liquid balances); on what determines the demand for money; and the stability, therefore, of the income velocity of money.

11. Why, in the Keynesian view, would any one be willing to hold money rather than interest-bearing bonds? Now explain why firms and households will increase (decrease) their demand for money when the interest rate falls (rises) and the effect of changes in the rate of interest on velocity.

12. Suppose firms and households, because of an increase in the money supply, find themselves with more money than they wish to have. What do the monetarists believe they will do with this excess money? What effect will this have on the velocity of money and money NNP?

13. If firms and households find themselves with larger cash balances than they wish to hold, what do the Keynesians believe they will do with their excess liquid balances? What effect will this have on the rate of interest, the velocity of money, and money NNP?

14. Explain the effect from the Keynesian viewpoint of an expansionary fiscal policy on the interest rate, the velocity of money, and the money NNP.

15. Why is the debate between the monetarists and Keynesians apt to continue and why has their debate been "healthy"?

CHAPTER 18

Unemployment and Inflation: New Problems and New Policies

Until a few years ago most economists believed that it was possible for the American economy to have both full employment and stable prices. This belief was based on the assumption that the price level would not rise until the labor force was fully employed. All that was necessary if there was to be full employment without inflation was just the right level of aggregate demand. Fiscal and monetary policy, thought economists, could be used to assure that aggregate demand was adequate but not excessive.

But the assumption which was the basis of the economists' belief that monetary and fiscal policy could guarantee a stable price level and the full employment of the labor force was not at all realistic. The price level rises before full employment is achieved; and the closer the economy moves to full employment the more rapid appears to be the rate at which prices rise. This premature inflation (that is, inflation *before* full employment is reached) seems to be the result of the ability of big unions to raise wage rates, of the power of big business firms to raise prices, and of the fact that some types of labor become fully employed while other kinds of workers have not yet all found jobs. But no matter what the causes of this premature inflation, the economy finds itself on the spot. It can have full employment with inflation or it can have stable prices with unemployment; *but* it can't have both full employment and stable prices.

Is there any way for the economy to avoid this problem? It may be possible for the economy to avoid both horns of this dilemma; but whether the suggested policies for escaping from both inflation and unemployment will work is still quite uncertain. It may turn out that we have no real alternative to putting up with inflation at times and with unemployment at other times.

While this problem and the policy dilemma it created were bad enough, an even worse problem emerged in the United States during the 1970s. This is the problem of stagflation. Rising prices were accompanied not by falling but by rising unemployment rates. This inflation was not the result of excessively high levels of demand and the failure to utilize fiscal and monetary policies to control demand. It was the consequence of increases in the costs of producing goods and services.

Recalling the ordinary demand and supply analysis (which you encountered in Chapter 4), the supply curves for many products have moved upward, equilibrium prices have increased, equilibrium outputs have declined, and—as a direct result—the employment of workers has diminished. For this reason the inflation which accompanies falling output and employment is also called supply-side inflation.

Stagflation has compelled economists to reexamine the Phillips Curve because rising prices *and* rising unemployment are just not consistent with a downsloping Phillips Curve. To make stagflation consistent with this kind of Phillips Curve, an economist must argue that the Phillips Curve of the American economy has been moving to the right; and this is the argument made by Keynesians to explain stagflation. But the monetarists (whom you met in the last chapter and who in this chapter are called "accelerationists") contend that the downsloping Phillips Curve is a figment of Keynesian imagination; that it is actually a vertical line; and that attempts to reduce the unemployment rate below the rate at which this vertical Phillips Curve meets the horizontal axis produces an accelerating rate of inflation. Whether the Keynesians or the accelerations are right is more than a theoretical detail. It is a matter of great practical importance. The selection of the correct policies for controlling inflation and reducing unemployment depends upon whether the Phillips Curve slopes downward and constantly shifts to the right or is vertical. But regardless of which view and set of policies are correct, the macroeconomic events of the past fifteen years in the United States have taught Americans a lot about the problems of unemployment and inflation and of controlling them.

■ **CHECKLIST**

The very least you should be able to do when you have finished this chapter is:

□ State in a few words the demand-pull theory of inflation and use the equation of exchange to explain this theory.

□ Explain what is meant by premature inflation; draw (after properly labeling the two axes) a traditional Phillips Curve; and state the two basic causes of the premature inflation shown in the Phillips Curve.

□ Determine what happens to unit labor cost when the money wage rate rises more and less rapidly that the average productivity of labor.

□ Explain and use the Phillips Curve to illustrate the stabilization policy dilemma.

□ State the two kinds of market policies that might be employed to shift the Phillips Curve to the left.

□ Distinguish between wage-price controls and the wage-price guideposts; state the wage and the price guideposts; explain why adherence to these guideposts would prevent inflation; and outline the cases for and against an income policy based on guideposts.

□ Explain the cause of the inflation in the American economy during the late 1960s and of the failure of the Nixon "game plan"; and enumerate the four economic shocks to the American economy and the causes of stagflation in the early 1970s.

□ State the accelerationist view on the Phillips Curve and explain how they come to this conclusion.

□ State the Keynesian view on the Phillips Curve and the policy implication of their position.

□ Enumerate the four macroeconomic lessons of the 1970s.

■ **CHAPTER OUTLINE**

1. Modern economics often assumes that the price level is stable until the economy achieves full employment; and that excess aggregate demand is the sole cause of inflation.

2. But the experiences of the American and other economies indicate that inflation occurs before aggregate demand becomes excessive and before full employment has been achieved. The Phillips Curve seems to show that the unemployment rate and the rate of inflation are inversely related; and suggests that to reduce unemployment (inflation) the economy must endure greater inflation (unemployment).

a. There are at least two reasons why inflation occurs before the economy reaches full employment.

(1) Scarcities of some kinds of labor develop before the economy's entire labor force is fully employed; and these scarcities increase wage rates, production costs, and prices.

(2) Labor unions and business firms have market power and they raise wage rates and prices as the economy approaches full employment.

b. Only if increases in wage rates exceed the increases in the productivity of labor do labor costs rise and contribute to cost-push inflation.

c. While fiscal and monetary policy can be employed to change aggregate demand and to affect unemployment and the rate of inflation, the nation faces a serious policy dilemma: full employment without inflation and price stability without unemployment appear impossible and a choice must be made between inflation and unemployment.

3. To make possible the achievement of both full employment and price level stability it will be necessary to introduce new policies to supplement fiscal and monetary policy.

a. Market policies would try to eliminate the causes of premature inflation and would include:

(1) manpower policies to reduce the scarcities of particular kinds of labor that occur before the labor force is fully employed;

(2) pro-competition policies to reduce the power of labor unions and business firms to raise wage rates and prices.

b. Wage-price (or income) policies would try to restrict increases in wages and prices by utilizing either guideposts or controls.

(1) Wage-price guideposts are voluntary restraints; would restrict money wage increases in all industries to the rate at which the productivity of labor in the economy has increased; and would allow an industry to increase the price of its product by an amount equal to the increase in its unit labor cost.

(2) Wage-price controls are mandatory (or legal) restraints; and were employed in 1971 as a part of the New Economic Policy designed to eliminate the inflationary recession in the American economy.

(3) Whether to employ wage-price policies to limit inflation has been a vigorously debated issue; and the proponents and opponents have based their arguments on the questions of workability and compliance, allocative efficiency, and economic freedom of choice.

(4) In addition to market and wage-price policies, government might impose an excess wage settlement tax on firms which increase money wage rates by more than the increase in the productivity of labor; or adopt the real wage insurance plan to induce firms and employees to limit price and wage increases.

4. During the past ten or so years economists have come to doubt the existence of a stable Phillips Curve.

a. Beginning with little inflation and above normal unemployment in the early 1960s, a tax cut in 1964 and increases in military expenditures in the following four years resulted in a decline in unemployment and demand-pull inflation.

b. To control this inflation the Nixon administration in the 1969–1971 period used fiscal and monetary policy to reduce aggregate demand; but inflation continued and unemployment rose because it was a cost-push (or supply side) inflation.

c. Then in the early 1970s four events occurred to increase costs and the rate of inflation sharply, to raise the unemployment rate, and to create stagflation.

d. This stagflation seems to be inconsistent with Keynesian economics and the Phillips Curve; and appears to have been the result of the "tax" placed on the economy by OPEC, the rise in corporate and personal tax collections that automatically accompany inflation, and misguided fiscal and monetary policies which tried to control a cost-push inflation by limiting aggregate demand.

5. In reexamining the Phillips Curve, Keynesian economists argue that it has shifted to the right; but accelerationists contend that the traditional Phillips Curve does not exist.

a. In the view of the accelerationists, an increase in aggregate demand sponsored by government which reduces unemployment and increases the price level also reduces the real wages of workers who demand and obtain higher money wages; this expands unemployment to its original level; the process is repeated when government again tries to reduce unemployment; and the rise in the price level accelerates. The traditional downsloping Phillips Curve does not, in short, exist; and the real Phillips Curve is a vertical line.

b. In the view of the Keynesian the downsloping Phillips Curve does exist and has been shifted to the right by the changing composition of the labor force (more women and teenagers) and by the inflationary expectations which induce workers to increase their money wage demands and induce business firms to raise prices.

c. If the traditional Phillips Curve is shifting

to the right, the policy prescriptions of Keynesians will have to be modified to use increases in aggregate demand only to move the economy toward full employment; and to employ wage-price or manpower policies to increase employment when the Phillips Curve shifts and the rate of inflation begins to rise.

6. From the American economic experiences of the last one and one-half decades have emerged:
  a. Four lessons which are that
  (1) macroeconomic instability in the U.S. is related more and more to events outside of the U.S.;
  (2) in selecting economic policies to control inflation it is extremely important to know whether the inflation is the result of demand pull or cost push;
  (3) controlling aggregate demand cannot by itself produce stability; and
  (4) changes in the institutions and structure of the economy may require economists to alter their macroeconomic theory and policy recommendations.
  b. A renewed interest among some economists in central (Federal) economic planning to limit inflation and reduce unemployment; and skepticism and fear of this planning among others.

■ **IMPORTANT TERMS**

Demand-pull inflation

Premature inflation

Phillips Curve

Stagflation

Cost- (wage-, profit-) push inflation

Stabilization policy dilemma

Wage-price (income) policy

Wage-price guideposts

Wage-price controls

Wage guidepost

Price guidepost

New Economic Policy

Excess wage settlement tax

Real wage insurance plan

Accelerationist view

Inflationary expectations

Central economic planning

Humphrey-Hawkins bill

■ **FILL-IN QUESTIONS**

1. In the traditional view of inflation,
  a. prices would not rise until the economy reached _____

  b. inflation was the result of excess _____ _____ and was, therefore, called _____ inflation.

2. Premature inflation:
  a. means that prices rise _____ _____

  b. is the result of the market power of _____ _____ and _____ and of imbalances or bottlenecks in _____ markets.

3. The Phillips Curve:
  a. is the relation between the annual rate of increase in the _____ and the _____ rate;
  b. has a (positive, negative) _____ slope;
  c. shows that the economy is subject to (demand-pull, premature) _____ inflation.

4. The cost-push theory explains inflation as follows: labor unions possessing considerable _____ are able to obtain wage increases from employers who also possess considerable _____ during periods in which there is _____ in the economy; these wage increases plus _____ are passed on to buyers in the form of _____ _____

5. In the equation $L = W/P_L$:
  a. L is _____
  b. W is _____
  c. P_L is _____
  d. If W increases at a rate:
  (1) greater than the rate at which P_L increases, L will (increase, decrease, remain constant) _____
  (2) less than the rate at which P_L increases, L will _____

(3) equal to the rate at which P_L increases, L will _____

6. The policy dilemma faced by the American economy is that to have full employment it must also have _____, and to have stable prices it must tolerate

_____

7. The two categories of policies designed to reduce premature inflation are _____ and _____ policies; and would, if successful, move the Phillips Curve to the _____

_____

8. Market policies to limit inflation include:

a. _____ policies to reduce

_____ in labor markets;

b. and _____ policies to decrease the _____ of business firms and labor unions.

9. Two things that might be done to reduce the market power of:

a. big business firms are to apply the _____

_____ laws more vigorously and to eliminate _____

b. labor unions are to apply the _____ laws to unions and to prohibit labor unions

from _____

10. Wage-price policies:

a. are sometimes called _____ policies because _____
b. involve either:

(1) wage-price _____ which rely upon the _____ cooperation of labor unions and business firms:

(2) or wage-price _____ which have the force of _____ to make them effective.

11. The wage-price guideposts for curbing inflation limit wage increases in an industry to

the overall rate of increase in the _____

of labor and limit price increases in an industry to an amount equal to the increases in

_____ in that industry.

12. Critics of wage-price (or incomes) policies contend that such policies are _____

and difficult to _____, prevent the

efficient _____ of resources, and

limit economic _____.

13. When the maximum legal price that may be charged for a product is set below the price that would be charged in a free and competitive market:

a. there will be a persistent _____

of the product, the likelihood that a _____ market for the product will develop, and the

possibility that government will _____ the product; and

b. an increase in demand (will, will not) _____

_____ result in the increased production of the product and there will be an (over-,

under-) _____ allocation of resources to the industry producing the product.

14. The stagflation of the 1970s led:
a. some economists to believe that the Phillips Curve had _____ to the

_____;
b. others to believe that the economy had

been subjected to _____

events or "_____";
c. still others to conclude that the traditional downsloping Phillips Curve does not

_____

15. During the middle and late 1960s a decrease in _____ and an increase

in _____ expenditures resulted in

a decline in _____ and a rise

in the _____ level.
a. This was clearly a (demand-pull, cost-

push) _____ inflation.
b. The Nixon administration utilized monetary and fiscal policy to reduce _____

demand; but prices continued to rise while employment (rose, fell) _____ because the inflation had become a _____

_____ inflation.

16. List the four cost-push shocks to the American economy after 1972.

a. _____

b. _____

c. _____

d. _____

17. The rising unemployment and sharp inflation—the stagflation—of 1973–1975 period:

a. Was largely the result of the increase in

the price of imported _____, the automatic increases in personal and corporate _____ taxes, and the use of monetary and fiscal policies to (reduce, expand) _____ aggregate demand to control a (demand-pull, cost-push) _____

_____ inflation.

b. Can be understood by employing the equation of exchange, $MV = PQ$.

(1) Cost-push forces increased _____

and, with MV constant, decreased _____.

(2) To prevent P from rising still further, government decreased MV and this brought

on a further decrease in _____.

18. It is the belief of:

a. the Keynesians that the traditional, downsloping Phillips Curve has shifted to the right because of:

(1) a change in the composition of the _____

_____ and

(2) inflationary _____ and that this shift requires government to

put less emphasis on _____ and

_____ policies and more emphasis on

_____ and _____ policies as a means of increasing employment;

b. the accelerationists that:

(1) the traditional downsloping Phillips

Curve _____,

(2) the Phillips Curve is actually a _____

_____ line at an unemployment rate that is (greater, less) _____ than the unemployment rate government would like to achieve, and

(3) attempts by government to reduce the unemployment rate to this level brings about a rate of inflation that (increases, decreases)

_____

19. What four lessons have emerged from American macroeconomic experiences during the last ten to fifteen years?

a. _____

b. _____

c. _____

d. _____

20. Stagflation in the United States had led some economists to conclude that Keynesian economics is no longer relevant and to pro-

pose _____ planning for the American economy. This proposal has resulted in the introduction of

the _____ bill in Congress.

■ **PROBLEMS AND PROJECTS**

1. Below is a traditional Phillips Curve.

a. At full employment (a 4% unemployment rate) the price level would rise by _____% each year.

b. If the price level were stable (increasing by 0% a year) the unemployment rate would be _____%.

c. Which of the combinations along the Phillips Curve would you choose for the economy? _____ Why would you select this combination? _____

_____

2. Assume that the overall rate of increase in the productivity of labor in the economy is 4% per year.

a. The general level of wages in the economy can increase by _____% a year without increasing unit labor costs and inducing cost-push inflation.

b. If the wage rate were increased by this percentage,

(1) In an industry in which the productivity of labor had increased 3%, labor costs per unit would _____; and the price of the product produced by this industry would _____

(2) In an industry in which the productivity of labor had increased 5%, labor costs per unit would _____; and the price of the product would _____

(3) In an industry in which the productivity of labor had increased 4%, labor costs per unit would _____; and the product price would _____

c. Granting all workers in the economy this same percentage increase in wages regardless of the rate of productivity increase in their industry means that

(1) The general level of prices in the economy will _____

(2) Prices in the various industries will ____

_____ , _____ ,

or _____ depending upon whether productivity increases in these industries were less than, greater than, or the same as the economy's rate of productivity increase.

3. The table below describes the way in which accelerationists see the trade-off between the unemployment rate and the rate of inflation.

Line	Annual rate of increase in the price level (%)	Unemployment rate (%)
First	0	6
Second	1	6
Third	2	6
Fourth	3	6
Fifth	4	6

a. Imagine the economy is on the first line in the table. Prices are stable and the unemployment rate is 6%. Government now employs monetary and fiscal policies to reduce the unemployment rate to 4% and the price level increases by 1%.

(1) If money wage rates remain constant, the increase in the price level will (increase, decrease) _____ the profits of business firms and (increase, decrease) _____ the *real* wages and incomes of workers.

(2) Workers now demand and obtain a 1% increase in their money wage rates. This will _____ the real wages of workers but it will _____ business profits; and employers will discharge workers until the unemployment rate rises from 4 to ____%.

(3) The economy is now on the second line in the table. The price level has risen by _____% and the unemployment rate has

_____

b. To reduce unemployment to 4% government uses monetary and fiscal policy and increases the price level by 2%.

(1) With the money wage rate constant, the _____ of business firms will increase and the _____ of workers will decrease.

(2) When workers ask for and obtain a 2% increase in money wages employers reduce the employment level and the unemployment rate will rise to _____%.

(3) The economy is now on the _____ line in the table. The _____ rate has risen to 2% and the _____ rate has remained constant.

c. Should government try once more to decrease the unemployment rate to 4% by utilizing monetary and fiscal policy the price level would rise by _____% and the economy would move to the fourth line of the table; but the unemployment rate would in the long run remain at _____%.

d. Attempts by government to reduce the unemployment rate below 6% result in a rate of inflation that _____

■ SELF-TEST

Circle the T if the statement is true, the F if it is false.

1. In the demand-pull theory of inflation, at less than full employment an increase in MV (in the equation of exchange) results in an increase in both P and Q.   **T   F**

2. As the economy approaches full employment, some types of labor become fully employed before all of the labor force is fully employed.   **T   F**

3. According to the traditional Phillips Curve the rate of inflation increases as the level of unemployment decreases.   **T   F**

4. Stagflation refers to a situation in which the price level is rising and the output of the economy is either falling or constant (and below the full-employment output).   **T   F**

5. When the money wage rate increases at a rate greater than the rate at which the productivity of labor increases, the unit labor cost will rise.   **T   F**

6. Because of the negative slope of the Phillips Curve fiscal and monetary policies cannot be used to increase employment or to reduce the rate of inflation in the economy.   **T   F**

7. Of the new policies that might be employed to deal with inflation, both market and wage-price policies are designed to move the Phillips Curve to the left.   **T   F**

8. Application of the antitrust laws has proved effective in the past in curbing the market power of big business; and so it is a promising technique for fighting premature inflation.   **T   F**

9. Voluntary restraint by business and labor leaders is not apt to be effective in preventing price and wage increases because such restraint requires them to abandon their major goals.   **T   F**

10. The wage-price guideposts for preventing cost-push inflation are to limit wage increases to the overall rate of increase in labor productivity in the economy.   **T   F**

11. The excess wage settlement tax would impose a 3% surtax on the personal incomes of union members who receive inflationary wage increases.   **T   F**

12. The real wage insurance plan would have the Federal government guarantee that no worker would find his or her real income has decreased as a result of a rise in the consumer price index.   **T   F**

13. Unemployment rates and the rates of inflation during the 1950s and 1960s were consistent with the traditional downsloping Phillips Curve.   **T   F**

14. In the late 1960s the Nixon administration was able to reduce the rate of inflation (while increasing the unemployment rate) by restricting aggregate demand.   **T   F**

15. The American system of taxing the incomes of firms and households helps to prevent output and employment from falling during a period of inflation.   **T   F**

16. Accelerationists contend that when the price level rises the traditional downsloping Phillips Curve moves to the left.   **T   F**

17. Keynesians reason that expectations of inflation and the increased participation of women and teenagers in the labor force have moved the Phillips Curve to the right.   **T   F**

18. If inflation and expectations of inflation are encountered and move the Phillips Curve to the right as the economy approaches full employment, any further increase in aggregate demand may increase the rate of inflation without creating more jobs.   **T   F**

19. The full-employment rate of unemployment in the U.S. seems to have increased.

T   F

20. The central economic planning advocated by some American economists in the hope of reducing the rates of inflation and unemployment is similar to the central planning employed is the U.S.S.R.   **T   F**

Underscore the letter that corresponds to the best answer.

1. If inflation is explained solely by the demand-pull theory, then: (*a*) price changes occur only if there is full employment; (*b*) inflation is the result of chronic unemployment; (*c*) inflation is the result of wage increases obtained by labor unions; (*d*) an increase in the level of prices results from the monopoly power of large business firms.

2. Premature inflation is the result of (*a*) excess aggregate demand; (*b*) full employment; (*c*) chronic unemployment; (*d*) market power.

3. The traditional Phillips Curve (*a*) shows the inverse relation between the rate of increase in the price level and the unemployment rate; (*b*) makes it possible for the economy to achieve full employment and stable prices; (*c*) indicates that prices do not rise until full employment has been achieved; (*d*) slopes upward from left to right.

4. If inflation during periods of less than full employment is to be explained by the cost-push theory, it must be assumed that: (*a*) only unions possess considerable market power; (*b*) only employers possess considerable market power; (*c*) both unions and employers possess considerable market power; (*d*) neither unions nor employers possess considerable market power.

5. Labor-market adjustments do not eliminate bottleneck problems when there is less than full employment in the economy. Which of the following is *not* one of the reasons for these labor-market imbalances? (*a*) unemployed workers often lack the skills or training needed for a new occupation; (*b*) the demand for workers in the markets in which there are labor shortages is inadequate; (*c*) there are artificial restrictions which prevent unemployed workers from filling the job openings; (*d*) unemployed workers do not know of the shortages of workers in other labor markets in the economy.

6. The public policy dilemma illustrated by a Phillips Curve is the mutual inconsistency of: (*a*) more employment and price stability; (*b*) a higher unemployment rate and price stability; (*c*) inflation and more employment; (*d*) inflation and a lower unemployment rate.

7. Which of the following is *not* one of the manpower policies that might reduce premature inflation? (*a*) application of anti-monopoly laws to labor unions; (*b*) removal of racial discrimination as an obstacle to employment; (*c*) improvement of the flow of job information between workers without jobs and employers with unfilled positions; (*d*) expansion of job training programs.

8. Which one of the following proposals for fighting inflation is aimed more at demand-pull inflation than at premature inflation? (*a*) restriction of total spending; (*b*) restriction of the market power of labor unions; (*c*) restriction of the market power of business firms; (*d*) restriction by government of price and wage increases.

9. If the wage rate in an industry increases from $6.00 to 6.30 an hour while the hourly productivity of labor increases from 40 to 42, the unit labor cost (*a*) has decreased; (*b*) has not changed; (*c*) has increased; (*d*) cannot be determined from this information.

10. Suppose the overall rate of increase in the productivity of labor in the economy is 4%. If the productivity of labor in a particular industry has increased at a rate of only 3%, the wage-price guideposts would allow this industry (*a*) to increase both the wage rate and the price of its product by 3%; (*b*) to increase the wage rate by 3% and would allow no increase in price; (*c*) to increase the wage rate by 4% and would allow no increase in price; (*d*) to increase the wage rate by 4% and to increase price by about 1%.

11. If the maximum price that may be legally charged for a product is below the price that would prevail in a competitive market (*a*) there will be a surplus of the product; (*b*) there will be an overallocation of resources to the industry producing the product; (*c*) the supply of the product will tend to increase; (*d*) some kind of rationing of the product will be necessary.

12. If the traditional Phillips Curve cannot be moved to the left by the employment of market or wage-price policies it will be necessary for the economy (a) to suffer from continuing inflation; (b) to have less than full employment and to produce less than the maximum output; (c) to experience both a and b; (d) to experience either a or b.

13. The late 1960s and early 1970s demonstrated (a) that the traditional Phillips Curve had shifted to the right; (b) that the economy had been subjected to random "shocks"; (c) that the traditional downsloping Phillips Curve did not exist; (d) either a or b or c.

14. Which of the following was *not* one of the cost-push shocks to the American economy after 1972? (a) the reduction in military expenditures when the Vietnam war ended; (b) poor agricultural harvests in the U.S.S.R. and Asia; (c) devaluation of the dollar; (d) the formation of OPEC.

15. The equation of exchange explains stagflation in the following way: (a) an increase in MV increases P and leaves Q unchanged; (b) an increase in P, MV constant, reduces Q; (c) a decrease in Q reduces MV and P; (d) an increase in MV increases both P and Q.

16. In the view of the accelerationists, the long-run Phillips Curve is (a) horizontal; (b) vertical; (c) downsloping; (d) upsloping.

17. Accelerationists argue that if increases in money wage rates lag behind increases in the price level, when government attempts to reduce unemployment by using fiscal and monetary policies (a) employment and the price level rise in the long run; (b) employment remains constant and the price level rises in the short run; (c) employment rises and the price level remains constant in the short run; (d) employment remains constant and the price level rises in the long run.

18. Which of the following is *not* one of the economic lessons of the 1970s? (a) the distinction between cost-push and demand-pull inflation is of critical importance in devising policies to control inflation; (b) controlling aggregate demand by using fiscal and monetary policies cannot simultaneously reduce unemployment and prevent inflation; (c) American macroeconomic instability can often be traced to events outside of the U.S.; (d) central economic planning is the only

means by which the economy's resources can be efficiently allocated and full employment without inflation achieved.

■ DISCUSSION QUESTIONS

1. What does the traditional demand-pull theory of inflation regard as the cause of inflation? What monetary and fiscal policies will prevent this kind of inflation?

2. Explain what is meant by premature inflation and the two major causes of this variety of inflation. Include in your explanation a definition and explanation of cost-push inflation.

3. What is a Phillips Curve? What is the public policy dilemma illustrated by this curve?

4. When are increases in money wage rates inflationary?

5. What are the two kinds of market policies that might be employed to shift the Phillips Curve to the left? Within each of these two categories, what specific things might be done to reduce the causes of premature inflation?

6. Explain (a) what is meant by wage-price policy; (b) why wage-price policy is often called income policy; and (c) the difference between wage-price guideposts and wage-price controls.

7. What (a) was the wage guidepost; (b) the price guidepost; and (c) were the methods employed by the Federal government to encourage business firms and labor unions to conform to the guideposts?

8. What wages and prices were controlled during the period of the New Economic Policy? Why did it seem necessary to control them?

9. State the cases *for* and *against* the use of wage-price (or incomes) policy to limit inflation. Build each case upon the three points around which the wage-price policy debate has centered.

10. Explain why economists have come to doubt the existence of a stable and downsloping Phillips Curve. Do Keynesians argue that it has been unstable or that it is not downsloping? What do the accelerationists argue?

11. What (a) were the causes of the rising employment and price level in the late 1960s; (b) was the reason for the failure of the Nixon "game plan"; (c) were the four cost-push shocks to the American economy in the early 1970s?

12. What is stagflation and why is it not consistent with Keynesian economics and the Phillips Curve? What were the causes of stag-flation in the U.S. during the 1970s? Use the equation of exchange to explain this stag-flation.

13. What are the views of the accelerationists on (a) the traditional downsloping Phillips Curve; (b) the long-run Phillips Curve; and (c)

the reasons for the third kind of long-run curve?

14. What are the views of Keynesians on (a) what has happened to their Phillips Curve over time; (b) why this has happened; (c) and the modifications in macroeconomic policy this requires?

15. What are the four economic lessons to be found in the macroeconomic events of the past fifteen or so years?

16. Why is there a renewed interest in some form of central economic planning for the American economy? What would be the goal of this planning and how is it proposed to achieve this goal? Why is there a fear of and skepticism toward central economic plan-ning?

The Simple Analytics of Economic Growth

19

This is the first of three chapters dealing with the important and controversial topic of economic growth. Chapter 19 presents the theory of growth; Chapter 20 examines the American economic growth record and the controversy surrounding further growth in the United States; and Chapter 21 explains the special problems which underdeveloped nations encounter in their attempts to grow.

The purpose of Chapter 19 is to explain what makes economic growth possible. After briefly defining and pointing out the significance of growth, the text analyzes the six factors that make growth possible. The four *supply* factors increase the output potential of the economy. Whether the economy actually produces its full potential—that is, whether the economy has both full employment and full production—depends upon two other factors: the level of aggregate demand (the *demand* factor) and the efficiency with which the economy reallocates resources (the *allocative* factor).

The crucial thing to note about the supply factors is that when labor increases more rapidly than natural resources, or capital, or both of these, the economy will be subject to diminishing returns and eventually to decreasing output per person and to a declining standard of living. This will breed the misery and poverty forecast by Malthus over 175 years ago. Diminishing returns can, however,

be offset—and more than offset—by increasing the amount of capital the economy possesses, by technological progress, and by improving the quality of the labor force at a more rapid rate. This is the way to achieve growth, and diminishing returns have been *more* than offset by those nations which have experienced economic growth. The nations which have not experienced growth have found the force of diminishing returns too great for them: their improvements in technology, capital, and labor just barely offset the effect of diminishing returns. And in some nations, these improvements were so weak that diminishing returns were dominant and the standard of living actually fell.

Probably the most important principle or generalization developed in the chapter employs the theory of output and employment already presented in Chapter 12. Here we discover that the maintenance of full employment in an economy whose productive capacity is increasing annually requires that investment increase annually to ensure a sufficient aggregate demand for the expanding full-employment output. And because investment increases an economy's productive capacity, not only must investment increase from year to year, but it must also increase by increasing amounts to assure the production of the full-employment output. You must be sure you understand the "why" of this principle, because it is fundamental to an understanding of full employment without inflation in the growing economy.

Actually, Chapter 19 contains very little that is really new. It uses a few of the ideas, terms, and theories found in earlier chapters to explain what makes an economy capable of growing (that is, what increases the size of its full-employment or capacity output) and what is necessary if it is actually to grow (that is, if it is to produce all which its expanding capacity allows). With careful reading you should have little or no trouble with Chapter 19, providing you have done a good job on the earlier chapters and providing you keep in mind the fundamental distinction between the supply factors and the demand and allocative factors.

■ **CHECKLIST**

The very least you should be able to do when you have finished this chapter is:
□ Distinguish between Keynesian economics and growth economics.
□ Define economic growth in two different ways.
□ Explain why economic growth is important to any economy.
□ Identify the four supply factors in economic growth.
□ State the law of diminishing returns.
□ Compute marginal and average product when you are given the necessary data; and explain the relationship between marginal and average product.
□ State the Malthusian thesis and explain why Malthus reached this conclusion.
□ Explain how the effects of diminishing returns on the standard of living can be offset or forestalled.
□ Contrast the income-creating and capacity-creating effects of net investment.
□ Calculate the full-employment rate of growth when you are supplied with the needed data; and explain why NNP must grow at this rate to maintain full employment.

■ **CHAPTER OUTLINE**

1. While modern employment theory is concerned with the short run and an economy with a fixed productive capacity, growth economics deals with the long run and changes in productive capacity over time.
a. Economic growth means an increase in either the total or the per capita real output of an economy.
b. Economic growth is important because it lessens the burden of scarcity: it provides the means of satisfying existing wants more fully and of fulfilling new wants.
c. One or two percentage point differences in the rate of growth result in substantial differences in annual increases in the economy's output.

2. Whether economic growth *can* occur depends upon four supply factors; and whether it *will* occur depends upon the demand factor and the allocative factor.

3. The amount by which total output can increase depends upon the amount and the proportion in which resources are increased.
a. In an economy where the quantities of land and capital are relatively fixed, the law of diminishing returns operates so that increases in the quantity of labor employed eventually result in declining increases in total output per additional unit of labor.
b. A proportionate increase in all resources moves the production possibilities curve to the right in the same proportion. But a disproportionate increase in resources moves it to the right by a percentage less than the percentage by which the most expanded resource has increased.
c. When diminishing returns set in and the marginal product of labor declines, the average product of labor will eventually decline.
d. The optimum population is the population at which the average product of labor (or real output per capita) is at a maximum.
e. Because of diminishing returns and the tendency for population to increase, Malthus predicted widespread poverty as time passed.
f. But growth can occur and poverty can be avoided if diminishing returns are offset by the increases in the productivity of workers that are brought about by more capital, better methods, and an improved labor force.

4. The amount the actual output of the economy increases depends not only upon the supply factors but also upon the demand factor.
a. To maintain full employment without inflation aggregate demand must grow at the

same rate as the economy's productive capacity.

b. In the simple macroeconomic growth model the full-employment rate of growth equals the average propensity to save divided by the capital-output ratio; and achievement of the full-employment rate of growth requires that net investment grow at the same rate.

5. For economic growth to be possible, the economy must also be capable of reallocating its resources with reasonable speed and completeness.

■ IMPORTANT TERMS

Economic growth	Increasing returns
Supply factor	Optimum population
Demand factor	Income-creating aspect of investment
Allocative factor	
Law of diminishing returns	Capacity-creating aspect of investment
Marginal product	Capital-output ratio
Average product	Full-employment rate of growth

■ FILL-IN QUESTIONS

1. Keynesian (or modern) employment theory assumes the productive capacity of the economy is _____ ; while growth economics is concerned with an economy whose productive capacity _____ _____ over time.

2. Economic growth can mean an increase in either the _____ or the _____ of an economy.

3. An increase in output per capita _____ _____ the standard of living and _____ the burden of scarcity in the economy.

4. Assume an economy has a GNP of $1200 billion. If the growth rate is 5%, GNP will increase by $_____ billion a year; but if the rate of growth is only 3%, the annual in-crease in GNP will be $_____ billion. A two percentage point difference in the growth rate results in a $_____ billion difference in the annual increase in GNP.

5. The four supply factors in economic growth are _____ ,

_____ ,

_____ , and

_____ .

The other two growth factors are the _____

_____ factor and the _____ factor.

6. If there are no diseconomies or economies of scale and if *all* resources expand by 8%, the productive capacity of the economy will increase by _____%.

7. The law of diminishing returns says that when additional equal quantities of one resource are used along with fixed quantities of other resources, total output (beyond some point) will _____ by _____ amounts.

8. Assume an economy employs only two resources. One of these increases by 10% and the other increases by 3%. Technology and the quality of the resources are fixed. If this economy is subject to diminishing returns, its productive capacity will increase by less than _____%.

9. When an economy is subject to diminishing returns and the marginal product of labor decreases, the _____ product of labor will sooner or later _____

10. The population size which results in the maximum output per capita (or the maximum average product of labor) is the _____

_____

11. Malthus predicted that because of diminishing returns and the tendency for the _____ of an economy to in-crease, the standard of living would _____

_____

12. The tendency for the standard of living to fall as the population increases can be lessened or even overcome by increasing the

_____ of workers.

13. In an economy increasing its productive capacity each year it is necessary that _____

_____
increase by the right amount each year if full employment is to be maintained.

14. Expenditures for new capital goods both

increase _____ and add to

the _____ of the economy; the amount by which investment expenditures expand the latter depend upon the volume of investment expenditures and the

_____

15. To have the economic growth which the supply and demand factors make possible, an

economy must also be able to _____ its resources from one use to another.

■ **PROBLEMS AND PROJECTS**

1. The table below shows the total production of an economy as the quantity of labor employed increases. The quantities of all other resources employed are constant.

Units of labor	Total production	Marginal product of labor	Average product of labor
0	0		0
1	80	_____	_____
2	200	_____	_____
3	330	_____	_____
4	400	_____	_____
5	450	_____	_____
6	480	_____	_____
7	490	_____	_____
8	480	_____	_____

   a. Compute the marginal products of the first through the eighth unit of labor and enter them in the table.

b. There are increasing returns to labor from the first through the _____ unit of labor and decreasing returns from the

_____ through the eighth unit.
   c. When total production is increasing, marginal product is (positive, negative) _____

_____ and when total production is decreasing, marginal product is _____

_____

   d. Now compute the average products of the various quantities of labor and enter them in the table.
   e. When the marginal product of labor is greater than the average product, average

product is (increasing, decreasing) _____

_____; and when the marginal product is less than the average product,

average product is _____
   f. The optimum population in this economy would be _____ units of labor, because with

this many units of labor the _____

_____

of labor is _____

2. Column 1 of the table below lists the various quantities of labor an economy might employ. Columns 2 and 3 show total production and the average product of labor for each quantity of labor.

(1) Quantity of labor	(2) Total production	(3) Average product of labor	(4) New total production	(5) New average product of labor
0	0	0	0	0
1	80	80	100	_____
2	200	100	220	_____
3	330	110	360	_____
4	400	100	500	_____
5	450	90	600	_____
6	480	80	660	_____
7	490	70	700	_____
8	480	60	720	_____

a. Assume the economy has and employs 4 units of labor. The average product of labor is

_____

b. Now suppose the total productivity of workers increases from the figures shown in column 2 to those given in column 4. Compute the new average products of labor and enter them in column 5.

c. If the economy continued to employ 4 units of labor, the average productivity of labor would have increased by _____%.

d. This increase in the productivity of workers could be due to more _____

_____, improved _____,

better _____, or any two or three of these.

e. As a result of this increase in productivity the optimum population for this economy has

_____ from 3 to _____ units of labor.

f. If, while the productivity of workers increased, the number of units of labor this economy had, and employed, increased from 4 to:

(1) 5, the average product of labor would have (increased, decreased) _____

from 100 to _____

(2) 7, the average product of labor would

have _____

(3) 8, the average product of labor would

have _____

3. Assume that in an economy in which aggregate demand contains only consumption and net investment components the average propensity to consume is 0.80, that in year 1 the economy's equilibrium output (NNP) is its full-employment of $1000, and that the supply factors make it possible for the full-employment output to increase at a rate of 10% per year.

a. Complete the table below by computing:
(1) the full-employment output in year 2 and in year 3.
(2) the amounts that would be spent for consumption and saved if the economy produced its full-employment output in year 2 and in year 3.
(3) the amounts that would have to be invested and aggregate demand in years 2 and 3 if the equilibrium output of the economy is to equal its full-employment output. (Investment will have to be equal to the saving done when the economy produces a full-employment output; and $C + I$ must equal the full-employment output.)

b. Examination of the table completed above reveals that to maintain full employment in an economy in which the average propensity to save is a constant and in which the full-employment output is growing at the rate of 10% annually:
(1) aggregate demand must grow at a rate

of _____% per year; and
(2) net investment must grow at an annual

rate of _____%.

c. Further examination of the completed table above shows that when the:
(1) average propensity to consume is constant and equal to 0.8, the marginal propen-

sity to consume is equal to _____

and is _____
(2) average propensity to save is constant and equal to 0.2, the marginal propensity to

save is equal to _____ and is

_____

(3) the value of the investment multiplier is

equal to _____

d. Employing your knowledge of the multiplier, had net investment increased by 5% from $200 to $210 between year 1 and year 2, the equilibrium output of the economy

			Full-employment		
Year	Output (NNP)	Consumption	Saving	Investment	Aggregate demand (C + I)
1	$1,000	$800	$200	$200	$1,000
2	_____	_____	_____	_____	_____
3	_____	_____	_____	_____	_____

would have increased from $1000 to $_____

(1) This is a _____% increase in NNP.
(2) The equilibrium NNP is (greater than,

less than, equal to) _____
the full-employment output of the economy.

(3) There is in year 2 _____
in the economy.

e. Still employing the multiplier, if net investment increased by 15% from $200 to $230 between year 1 and year 2, the equilibrium output of the economy would have

tried to increase from $1000 to $ _____

(1) This equilibrium output is (greater than,

less than, equal to) _____
the full-employment output and (can, cannot)

_____ actually be produced.

(2) There will in year 2 be _____
in the economy.

f. Still further examination of the table completed above reveals that for the economy to grow at any given rate—such as 10%—the *amount* that net investment must increase

(increases, decreases, remains constant) ____

_____

4. This problem is much like problem 3 above; but it is a little more difficult because it does not ignore the capacity-creating aspect of investment as problem 3 did.

Assume in an economy in which the only two components of aggregate demand are consumption and saving that the average propensity to consume is 0.7, the capital-output ratio is 3, and in year 1 the economy is producing a full-employment output of $900.

a. In the table below compute the amount of saving that would be done in year 1 if the economy produced its full-employment output and the amount of investment that would be needed if the economy were to produce

an equilibrium output equal to its full-employment output; and enter these two figures in the table.

b. Now compute the increase in full-employment output between year 1 and year 2 that results from the investment undertaken in year 1. (*Hint:* Divide the investment in year 1 by the capital-output ratio.)

c. Add the increase in full-employment output that results from the investment in year 1 to the full-employment output of year 1 to find the full-employment output of year 2; and calculate the amount of saving that would be done at full employment in year 2, the amount of investment needed to bring about full employment, and the increase in the full-employment output between year 2 and year 3.

d. Find the full-employment output and saving in year 3, the necessary amount of investment in year 3, and the increase in full-employment output between year 3 and year 4.

e. This economy's full-employment rate of growth is 10% and:

(1) will be achieved if _____
grows at a rate of 10%
(2) can be calculated by dividing the econ-

omy's _____

by the _____
f. Were the economy's average propensity to save 0.1 and its capital-output ratio 4 its full-employment rate of growth would be

equal to _____%.

■ **SELF-TEST**

Circle the T if the statement is true, the F if it is false.

1. Growth economics is concerned with an economy in which productive capacity is not fixed.   **T F**

	Full-employment			
Year	Output (NNP)	Saving	Investment	Increase in full-employment output
1	$900	$____	$____	$____
2	____	____	____	____
3	____	____	____	____

2. The best of the two definitions of economic growth is an increase in the per capita real output of the economy.　　**T　F**

3. Suppose two economies both have GNPs of $500 billion. If the GNPs grow at annual rates of 3% in the first and 5% in the second economy, the difference in their amounts of growth in one year is $10 billion.　　**T　F**

4. The demand factor in economic growth refers to the ability of the economy to expand its production as the demand for products grows.　　**T　F**

5. The allocative factor in economic growth refers to the ability of the economy to move resources from one use to another as the productive capacity of the economy grows. **T　F**

6. Diminishing returns for a resource are the eventual result of increasing the employment of that resource by larger percentages than the employment of other resources is increased.　　**T　F**

7. The effect of diminishing returns to labor upon the standard of living is overcome whenever the average productivity of labor is increased.　　**T　F**

8. When average product is falling, marginal product is greater than average product.　　**T　F**

9. When marginal product is negative, total production (or output) is decreasing. **T　F**

10. If the volume of investment expands more rapidly than is necessary to keep the full-employment output of the economy expanding at the rate which the supply factors allow, the result will be unemployment. **T　F**

11. Other things being constant, the productive capacity of an economy will increase by an amount equal to net investment multiplied by the capital-output ratio.　　**T　F**

12. One of the requirements for allocative efficiency is the reasonably rapid and complete employment of the new workers in the labor force.　　**T　F**

Underscore the letter that corresponds to the best answer.

1. Which of the following is *not* one of the benefits of economic growth to a society? (a) everyone enjoys a greater real income; (b) the standard of living in that society in-

creases; (c) the burden of scarcity decreases; (d) the society is better able to satisfy new wants.

2. Suppose an economy has a GNP of $700 billion and an annual growth rate of 5%. Over a *two*-year period GNP will increase by: (a) $14 billion; (b) $35 billion; (c) $70 billion; (d) $71¾ billion.

3. If the production possibilities curve of an economy moves from *AB* to *CD* on the graph below, and the economy changes the combination of goods it produces from *X* to *Y*, there has been: (a) improvement in both the supply and the other growth factors; (b) an improvement in only the supply factor; (c) an improvement in only the demand and allocative growth factors; (d) an improvement in the level of total employment in the economy.

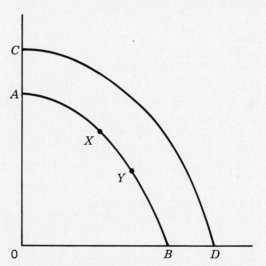

4. Which of the following is *not* a supply factor in economic growth? (a) an expansion in purchasing power; (b) an increase in the economy's stock of capital goods; (c) more natural resources; (d) technological improvements.

Units of labor	Total production
0	0
1	50
2	110
3	160
4	200
5	230
6	250
7	260
8	265

For questions 5 and 6 use the data given in the table on page 152.

5. The marginal product of the fifth unit of labor is: (a) 40) (b) 30; (c) 20; (d) 10.

6. The average product of 4 units of labor is: (a) 70; (b) 60; (c) 50; (d) 40.

7. The law of diminishing returns says that as increased quantities of one resource are added to fixed quantities of other resources, there will eventually be a decrease in: (a) total production; (b) marginal product; (c) average product; (d) the optimum population.

8. The "optimum population" of an economy is: (a) the largest population the resources of that economy are capable of supporting; (b) the level of population which enables the economy to produce the largest possible output; (c) the level of population which enables the economy to produce the largest possible per capita output; (d) the level of population which results in the greatest amount of natural resources and capital equipment per capita in the economy.

9. Which of the following will *not* usually increase the average product of labor? (a) technological improvements; (b) an expanded labor force; (c) an increase in the amount of capital per worker; (d) better-educated workers.

10. If an economy is to maintain a constant *rate* of economic growth, assuming that the average propensity to consume is constant: (a) the volume of investment spending must increase at a more rapid rate; (b) the volume of investment spending must increase at the same rate; (c) the volume of investment spending need only remain constant; (d) the volume of investment spending must increase by the same amount that the output of the economy increases.

■ **DISCUSSION QUESTIONS**

1. What is meant by economic growth? Why should the citizens of the United States be concerned with economic growth?

2. How does growth economics differ from the theory of employment (or the theory of national income determination)?

3. What are the six basic ingredients of economic growth? What is the essential difference between the supply factors and the other two factors? Is there any relationship between the strength of the supply factor and the strength of the demand factor?

4. State the law of diminishing returns. What is the cause of diminishing returns?

5. What does an expansion in the quantity of resources employed do to the production possibilities curve if: (a) all resources expand proportionally and (b) all resources do not expand proportionally?

6. Define the marginal and the average product of labor. If marginal product at first increases and then decreases as more labor is employed, what will happen to the average product? Why will average product behave this way?

7. What is an optimum population? Why is this concept important?

8. What predictions did Malthus make for the economic future of mankind? On what bases did he make this prediction?

9. What can be done to offset or overcome the tendency for the average product of labor and the standard of living to decline as the employment of labor and the population increase?

10. Explain why an increasing level of aggregate demand is necessary in an economy whose productive capacity is increasing if full employment is to be maintained. Why does the maintenance of full employment in a growing economy in which the average propensity to save is constant require that investment increase at the same rate as the full-employment output?

11. What determines (a) how much the investment of one year will increase the full-employment output of the economy; (b) the full-employment rate of growth in an economy? What two events would bring about an increase in the full-employment rate of growth?

12. What is meant by allocative efficiency? Why is this kind of efficiency important if there is to be economic growth?

Economic Growth: Fact and Controversy

Chapter 20 is the second of the three chapters concerned with economic growth. It is concerned primarily with economic growth in the United States.

Using the two definitions of growth found in Chapter 19, Chapter 20 begins by describing how much and how fast the American economy has grown. That it has grown rapidly is fairly obvious. The net result of this rapid growth is that Americans now enjoy one of the highest standards of living in the world.

Why has the United States grown economically? Because the six growth factors explained in Chapter 19 have made growth possible. The four supply factors in economic growth have increased the productive capacity of the economy more rapidly than the population has expanded. More capital, a larger and better labor force, additional natural resources, and technological advance all have contributed to increased productive capabilities. In addition, aggregate demand has expanded sufficiently to bring about most of the actual growth that the supply factors made possible. And the economy has been able to reallocate its resources with enough speed and completeness to realize the better part of the growth which the supply and demand factors gave the economy power to achieve.

The latter part of Chapter 20 asks two important questions. Whether further economic growth is *desirable* in the already affluent American economy is the first of these questions. The controversy over whether growth should be a social goal with a high priority in the United States has, of course, two sides to it. The case for and the case against growth are both considered. You will have to decide for yourself which case is the stronger and whether the social benefits from growth are worth the costs.

The second question is whether further economic growth in the world is *possible.* Here the author looks at the dismal predictions of the Club of Rome. The Club of Rome is an informal group of all kinds of people from all over the world who first met in that city in 1968 and later commissioned a team of professors from the Massachusetts Institute of Technology to prepare a report on the "Predicament of Mankind." Their report, a book entitled *The Limits to Growth,* aroused a storm of controversy throughout the world. Their prediction is that the way things are going throughout the world today, not only will world growth end within the next 100 years but population and the standard of living will also suddenly decline or collapse. In addition to noting the trends or assumptions upon which such a pessimistic forecast is made, you should also take note of the policies which the Club of Rome believes are necessary if Doomsday is to be avoided. More optimistically, the critics of the Doomsday model, in the last section of the chapter, point out that there are good reasons to be suspicious of these dismal predictions. The end of the world may not be at hand.

■ CHECKLIST

The very least you should be able to do when you have finished this chapter is:

□ Describe the growth record of the American economy in the twentieth century.

□ Explain how each of the four supply factors has contributed to the economic growth of the United States.

□ Explain why the rate of growth in the United States has been unstable.

□ List the two requirements which the social environment of a society must meet if there is to be economic growth; the ways in which the American social environment has been conducive to growth; explain the role of the price system in the reallocation of resources which growth requires; and enumerate several of the impediments to resource reallocation.

□ List the two fundamental ways by which an economy can increase its real output; and explain the relative importance of these two methods in the growth of the American economy since World War II.

□ Present the case against further economic growth in the United States.

□ Defend further economic growth.

□ Outline the assumptions and conclusions of the Doomsday models; and state the policies advocated by those who defend these models.

□ Criticize the assumptions of the Doomsday models and explain how the feedback mechanisms might work to prevent the collapse of the economy.

■ CHAPTER OUTLINE

1. Over the last seventy or so years the growth record of the American economy has been impressive; but American growth in recent years has been slower than in many of the developed nations.

2. The six growth factors are the source of the impressive growth of the American economy.

a. Natural resources have been generally abundant.

b. The human resources of the economy have increased in quantity and improved in quality.

c. Technological progress has increased the efficiency with which natural, human, and capital resources are employed.

d. Investment has expanded the American economy's stock of capital goods and thereby provided the American worker with more tools, equipment, and machinery with which to work.

e. Variations in the rate of economic growth and a growth rate less than what the supply factors made possible were largely the result of insufficient increases in aggregate demand.

f. The social, political, and cultural environment surrounding the economy has been conducive to economic change. It has encouraged new products, new production processes, and new capital equipment; and the economy has been sufficiently flexible to provide for the reallocation of resources required by these changes.

g. In recent years increases in the quantities of labor and capital accounted for about 45% and improvements in technology, the quality of the labor force, and resource allocation accounted for about 55% of the increases in the total output of the American economy.

3. Americans today debate whether economic growth is or is not desirable.

a. Those opposed to rapid economic growth contend that it pollutes the environment; it is not needed to resolve domestic problems; it makes people more anxious and insecure; and, while providing more goods and services, it does not result in a better life.

b. Those in favor of growth argue that the benefits from growth—a higher standard of living—outweigh the costs of growth; that growth is not the cause of pollution; that growth is the easiest way to bring about a more equitable distribution of income; and that ending or slowing growth will not improve the quality of life.

4. The Doomsday models not only forecast an end to economic growth but also predict sudden collapses in the world's population and its capacity to produce goods and services; and to avoid collapse the Doomsday forecasters advocate policies to reduce the current rates of economic and population growth to zero.

5. Critics of the Doomsday models argue that the forecasters have:
  a. made unrealistic assumptions;
  b. underestimated future technological progress; and
  c. made inadequate allowances for such feedback mechanisms as the price system and changes in human behavioral patterns.

■ **IMPORTANT TERMS**

R and D	ZEG
Club of Rome	ZPG
Doomsday model	Feedback mechanism

■ **FILL-IN QUESTIONS**

1. In the United States:
  a. during this century the real GNP has increased about _____ fold.
  b. since 1940 real per capita GNP has increased more than _____ fold.

2. Since 1870 the rates of growth in real GNP and per capita real GNP have, on the average, been _____% and _____%, respectively.

3. Figures showing the real GNP and the per capita real GNP of the United States over the last seventy years fail to take account of improvements in the _____ of the products produced, increases in the amount of _____ Americans have, deterioration in the _____ of the United States, or a possible decline in the quality of _____

4. One of the supply factors explaining past American economic growth is the relatively fixed but generous quantity and quality of the _____ with which the economy was endowed.

5. The size of the nation's labor force depends basically upon the _____ while the quality of the labor force seems to depend upon such factors as its _____

_____ ,

_____ ,

and _____

6. Technological progress means that we learn how to employ given quantities of resources to obtain greater _____ ; and, more often than not, this progress requires _____ in new machinery and equipment.

7. The average American worker today has about $_____ worth of capital equipment with which to work; and about _____ times as much capital per worker-hour of labor is employed today as was employed at the end of the nineteenth century.

8. When aggregate demand does not increase as much as the productive capacity of the economy increases, the result is a _____ _____ gap and a _____ rate of growth.

9. The social environment of a society must meet two requirements if there is to be economic growth in that society; these requirements are that _____ and _____ ; reallocation in the United States has been accomplished by the _____

10. Since 1948 about _____% of American economic growth has been due to increases in the quantities of capital and labor; the remainder has been due to _____

_____ ,

_____ ,

and _____

11. Influential economists arguing against the need for growth in the United States believe that growth _____

the environment, does not lead to the solution of _____,
breeds _____ and
_____, and does not result
in the _____

12. Those who favor growth for the American

economy argue that the _____

from growth exceed the _____
of this growth, the economic growth does not

necessarily result in _____,
that growth is the only practical way of ob-

taining a more _____

distribution of _____,
and that limiting growth will not bring about

_____

13. The Doomsday models:
  a. are based on current and projected

trends in world _____,

_____, _____,

_____, and _____

  b. predict that within the next _____
years there will be a sudden collapse in the

world's _____ and _____

14. To avoid the collapse predicted by the
Doomsday models it is necessary, the fore-

casters say, to have _____

and _____

15. The criticisms of the Doomsday models

are that the models employ _____

assumptions, underestimate future _____

_____,

and make inadequate allowance for _____
mechanisms.

■ **PROBLEMS AND PROJECTS**

1. Suppose the real GNP and the population of an economy in seven different years
were those shown in the table below.

Year	Population, millions	Real GNP, billions of dollars	Per capita real GNP
1	30	$ 9	$_____
2	60	24	_____
3	90	45	_____
4	120	66	_____
5	150	90	_____
6	180	99	_____
7	210	105	_____

  a. How large would the real per capita GNP
of the economy be in each of the seven years?
Put your figures in the above table.
  b. What would have been the size of the

optimum population of this economy? _____
  c. What was the *amount* of growth in:
  (1) Real GNP between year 1 and year 2?

$_____
  (2) Real GNP per capita between year 2

and year 3? $_____
  d. What was the *rate* of growth in:
  (1) Real GNP between year 3 and year 4?

_____%
  (2) Real GNP per capita between year 4

and year 5? _____%

2. Column 2 of the table below gives the
productive capacities of an economy *in constant dollars* during the four different years
shown in column 1. Productive capacity is
growing at a constant rate of 10%.

(1) Year	(2) Productive capacity	(3) Aggregate demand	(4) Output of economy
1	$200.0	$200.0	$_____
2	220.0	210.0	_____
3	242.0	265.0	_____
4	266.2	266.2	_____

  a. Aggregate demand, also *in constant dollars,* during these four years is shown in column 3. Given that an economy will produce
an output equal to the level of aggregate demand up to the limits of the productive capa-

city of the economy, what were the *actual outputs* of this economy *in constant dollars* in each of the four years? Place these outputs in column 4.

b. Between year 1 and year 2 the rate of growth in output was _____%. This rate of growth was (more, less) _____ than the rate of growth of productive capacity, because _____

_____

c. In year 2:

(1) The economy had an unused productive capacity of _____ constant dollars.

(2) About _____% of its productive capacity was idle.

d. Between years 2 and 3:

(1) The economy had an increase in productive capacity equal to _____ constant dollars.

(2) Aggregate demand increased by _____ constant dollars.

(3) The increase in aggregate demand was (more, less) _____ than the combined increase in productive capacity and the idle productive capacity in year 2.

(4) The actual rate of growth in output was about _____%.

(5) The price level would tend to _____ because _____

_____

(6) How could output increase by more than the increase in productive capacity? _____

_____

_____

e. In year 4:

(1) Aggregate demand was _____ than in year 3 and was _____ the productive capacity of the economy.

(2) The price level would tend to _____

_____

(3) There (would, would not) _____ be full employment and the absence of unused productive capacity.

3. To understand the predictions of Doomsday made by the Club of Rome models, look at Figure 20–4 on page 427 of the text.

a. From 1900 until the present the world's:

(1) population, pollution, food output per capita, and industrial output per capita have all (increased, decreased) _____ by (increasing, decreasing, constant) _____ _____ amounts.

(2) natural resources have _____ by _____ amounts.

b. If these trends continue, the models predict that somewhere between the year 2000 and the year 2100:

(1) population and food and industrial output per capita will begin to _____

(2) as a result _____ will begin to _____

(3) while _____ continue to decrease.

c. To limit increases in pollution and decreases in natural resources between now and the future and to prevent the eventual collapse of per capita food and industrial production and of population predicted by the models requires that steps be taken now to end all further increases in the world's

_____ and in per capita _____

■ **SELF-TEST**

Circle the T if the statement is true, the F if it is false.

1. Real GNP has tended to increase more rapidly than per capita GNP in the United States. **T F**

2. Growth and rates of growth estimates generally attempt to take account of changes in the quality of goods produced and in the amount of leisure members of the economy enjoy. **T F**

3. The quantity and quality of the natural resources with which the United States was endowed can accurately be described as generous. **T F**

4. The population of the United States has increased by 300% since 1900. **T F**

5. More often than not technological progress requires the economy to invest in new machinery and equipment.   **T   F**

6. The American economy has a stock of capital with a value which exceeds $20 trillion.   **T   F**

7. Changes in the supply factors do not cause changes in the demand factor, and vice versa.   **T   F**

8. The American social, cultural, and political environment has, in general, worked to slow the economic growth of the United States.   **T   F**

9. The most important single source of the growth of the total output of the American economy since 1948 has been the improved training and education of its labor force.   **T   F**

10. Since 1948 improved technology has accounted for nearly 35% of the growth of total real output in the United States.   **T   F**

11. The Club of Rome model predicts that if present trends continue the world's population and its per capita outputs of industrial products and food will decline before the year 2100.   **T   F**

12. To prevent the collapse predicted by the Doomesday models from coming about the Club of Rome recommends that the current rate of growth of the economy be increased and that there be no increase in the world's population.   **T   F**

Underscore the letter that corresponds to the best answer.

1. During the twentieth century real GNP in the United States has increased about (*a*) fivefold; (*b*) sevenfold; (*c*) ninefold; (*d*) elevenfold.

2. Since about 1870 the total output of the American economy has increased at an average *annual* rate of about: (*a*) ½ of 1%; (*b*) 2%; (*c*) 3½%; (*d*) 5%.

3. Total output per capita in the United States since 1870 has increased at an average annual rate of about: (*a*) 1%; (*b*) 2%; (*c*) 3%; (*d*) 4%.

4. The supply of which of the following is the most nearly fixed? (*a*) natural resources; (*b*) labor; (*c*) capital; (*d*) money.

5. There are in the American labor force approximately how many million workers? (*a*) 75; (*b*) 85; (*c*) 95; (*d*) 205.

6. Approximately what percentages of the labor force have completed high school and four years of college? (*a*) 45% and 8%; (*b*) 44% and 13%; (*c*) 60% and 8%; (*d*) 69% and 15%.

7. The United States currently spends about what percentage of its gross national product on research and development? (*a*) 2%; (*b*) 2.3%; (*c*) 2.8%; (*d*) 5%.

8. Which of the following is *not* one of the consequences when aggregate demand increases by less than the productive capacity of the economy? (*a*) inflation; (*b*) a GNP gap; (*c*) a slower rate of economic growth; (*d*) unemployed labor.

9. Which of the following is *not* an artificial impediment to economic growth? (*a*) labor union restrictions on the size of their membership; (*b*) the failure of a firm to employ a newly developed productive technique because it would make its capital facilities obsolete; (*c*) the reluctance of workers to move to new communities and to take new jobs; (*d*) unfair competition by firms in an industry to prevent the entry of new firms into the industry.

10. About what percentage of the increase in the total output of the American economy since 1948 was due to increases in the quantities of capital and labor employed? (*a*) 20%; (*b*) 23%; (*c*) 30%; (*d*) 45%.

11. Which of the following is *not* a part of the case against economic growth? (*a*) Growth produces pollution; (*b*) growth impedes the increased production of consumer goods; (*c*) growth prevents the attainment of a better life; (*d*) growth is not needed to provide us with the means of solving domestic social problems.

12. Which of the following is *not* a part of the case in defense of economic growth? (*a*) Growth lessens the unlimited wants-scarce resources problem; (*b*) growth lessens the extent of anxiety and insecurity; (*c*) growth need not be accompanied by the pollution of the environment; (*d*) growth is the only practical way to reduce poverty.

■ **DISCUSSION QUESTIONS**

1. What has been the growth record of the American economy in the twentieth century and since 1870? Compare recent American growth rates with those in other nations.

2. Some economists contend that the natural resources of the United States explain much of its past economic growth *and* they will limit its economic growth in the future. Explain how natural resources made past growth possible and may slow future growth.

3. What long-run changes have occurred in the size of the American population and labor force? What qualitative changes have occurred?

4. Why are technological advance and capital formation closely related processes?

5. What are the economic consequences if aggregate demand increases more than the productive capacity of the economy in-creases? If aggregate demand increases less than productive capacity increases?

6. In what ways has the American social environment been conducive to economic growth?

7. What role does the price-market system play in promoting the reallocation of scarce resources? What impediments are there in the United States to the reallocation of resources which must occur if there is to be economic growth?

8. What have been the sources of the economic growth which the United States has experienced since 1948?

9. What arguments can be presented on both sides of the question of whether growth in the United States is desirable?

10. What are the assumptions and conclusions of the Club of Rome models? What policies do they suggest to avoid the Doomsday which the models predict? What have the critics had to say about the models and their predictions?

CHAPTER 21

Growth and the Underdeveloped Nations

Chapter 21 is the third of the three chapters concerned with economic growth. Chapter 19 dealt with the theory of growth; and Chapter 20 examined the record and problems of economic growth in the United States.

This chapter looks at the problem of raising the standard of living faced by the underdeveloped nations of the world. Economic growth both in these underdeveloped nations and in the developed or the advanced nations requires that the nation's resources and technological knowledge be expanded. Application of this principle in the underdeveloped nations, however, faces a set of obstacles quite different from those that limit economic growth in the United States. The emphasis in this chapter is on the obstacles to economic growth in the poor and underdeveloped nations of the world. You should concentrate your attention on these obstacles. You will then understand why increasing the quantity and quality of resources and improving technology is especially difficult in the world's underdeveloped nations.

The existence of these special obstacles does not mean that increases in the living standards of the underdeveloped nations are impossible. What it does mean is that the underdeveloped nations are going to have to do things that did not need to be done in the United States (or in the other developed nations) in order to grow. Governments of the poor countries will have to take an active role in promoting growth. Population increases are going to have to be limited. And dramatic changes in social practices and institutions will be required. If these things are not done it will not be possible to eliminate or reduce the obstacles to growth.

No matter how successful the underdeveloped nations are in eliminating these obstacles they probably will still not be able to grow very rapidly without the help of the developed nations. There seem to be at least two reasons why the developed nations will offer the less developed ones some amount of assistance. The citizens of the more advanced nations feel some moral obligation to aid the less fortunate peoples of the world; and they may feel it is in their own self-interest to aid the poor of the world. (It is just this motive for extending aid—the self-interest of those extending the aid—that leads some of the underdeveloped nations to fear foreign aid, and to argue that foreign aid is nothing more than a new form of colonialism designed to return the underdeveloped nations to an inferior status.)

The question that always remains to be answered is the one posed in the final section of this chapter. Will the poor nations increase their standards of living by substantial amounts in the future? What appears to be the best available answer—no one can really see into the future—is well expressed by the term "cautious optimism." Many of the underdeveloped nations will raise their living standards substantially *if* they do the many things that have to be done. The terrible *if!* Will these things be done?

On this note of uncertainty we conclude the topic of economic growth and end our study of marcoeconomics. An examination of microeconomic principles, problems, and policies begins in the next chapter.

■ **CHECKLIST**

The very least you should be able to do when you have finished this chapter is:

□ Distinguish between developed, semideveloped, and undeveloped nations; and locate the former and latter nations geographically.

□ Identify the Third World nations; and describe the output, population, and rate of growth of the Third World.

□ Enumerate the human implications of the poverty in the underdeveloped nations.

□ Identify the four factors which make growth in real GNP possible.

□ Identify the three specific problems related to human resources that plague the underdeveloped nations.

□ Explain the obstacle to saving and the two obstacles to capital accumulation in the poor nations of the world.

□ Provide an explanation of the relationship among investment, the capital-output ratio, the rate of growth in real GNP, in population, and in the standard of living.

□ Enumerate several of the sociocultural and institutional factors which inhibit growth in the underdeveloped nations.

□ Explain why poverty in the poor nations is a vicious circle.

□ List several reasons why governments in the underdeveloped nations will have to play a crucial role if the vicious circle is to be broken.

□ Identify the three ways in which the developed nations may help the underdeveloped nations to grow economically.

□ Explain why the Third World feels that the relationship between it and the indus-

trially advanced nations can be called neo-colonialism.

□ Write three scenarios describing the future of the Third World.

■ **CHAPTER OUTLINE**

1. The underdeveloped nations of the world comprise two-thirds of the world's population.

a. Most of the countries of Asia, Africa, and South America are underdeveloped, and all of them have one common characteristic—poverty (that is, a low per capita income or standard of living).

b. The world's nations can be divided into the industrially advanced market economies, the centrally planned economies, and the Third World countries; and it is the latter which are underdeveloped (or semideveloped), contain one-half the world's population, produce only one-eighth of the world's output, and increase their standards of living more slowly.

c. Compared with the developed nations, the underdeveloped or Third World nations have lower life expectancies, more disease, less food per person and more malnutrition, less schooling and literacy, smaller amounts of cloth per capita, and fewer nonhuman sources of energy.

d. Because of an increasing disparity between the standards of living in the developed and the underdeveloped nations, and because many of the underdeveloped nations became politically independent only after World War II, these nations are discontented and determined to raise their standards of living.

e. The economic and social environment of the underdeveloped nations is vastly different from that in which the United States found itself when it began its development; consequently, the underdeveloped nations cannot develop merely by following the examples of the United States and other advanced nations.

2. Economic development requires that the quantity and quality of economic resources be increased and that technological knowledge be expanded; but there are many special obstacles to such a program in the underdeveloped nations.

a. Many (but not all) underdeveloped nations possess inadequate natural resources and this limits their ability to develop.

b. The typical underdeveloped nation is overpopulated, is plagued by unemployment, and has a poor quality labor force.

c. Usually very short of capital goods, underdeveloped nations find it difficult to accumulate capital because of their low saving potentials and the absence of investors and incentives to invest.

d. Technological knowledge is primitive in underdeveloped nations; and they might adopt the technologies employed in the advanced nations if obstacles to technological advance did not exist.

e. In addition, a nation must have a strong will to develop and alter its own social and institutional environment to grow economically.

3. In summary, underdeveloped nations save little and, therefore, invest little in real and human capital because they are poor; and because they do not invest, their output per capita remains low and they remain poor. Even if this vicious circle were to be broken, a rapid increase in population would leave the standard of living unchanged.

4. It is probable that the governments of these nations will have to play a major role by sponsoring and directing many of the early development plans if the obstacles to growth are to be overcome.

5. The advanced nations of the world can in a number of ways help the poor nations to develop.

a. They can lower the barriers which prevent the underdeveloped nations from selling their products in the developed nations.

b. The flow of private capital from the advanced nations helps the underdeveloped nations increase their productive capacities and per capita outputs.

c. Loans and grants from governments and international organizations also enable the underdeveloped nations to accumulate capital.

6. Many in the Third World believe that the help extended by industrially advanced nations is designed to exploit the underdeveloped nations and to preserve neocolonialism.

7. No one can now predict whether the Third World nations will in the future grow or stagnate; but at least three scenarios can be written to forecast the course of events during the next thirty or so years.

■ **IMPORTANT TERMS**

Underdeveloped nation

Third World

Investment in human capital

Domestic capital formation

Nonfinancial investment

Basic social capital

Capital-saving technological advance

Capital-using technological advance

The "will to develop"

World Bank

Neocolonialism

Green revolution

■ **FILL-IN QUESTIONS**

1. The common characteristic of underdeveloped nations is _____

2. The underdeveloped nations are found chiefly in the following areas of the world:

_____ ,

_____ ,

and _____ ;

and they account for approximately _____

_____

of the world's population.

3. The nations of the world can be divided into the industrially advanced countries with either market or centrally planned economies

and the _____ countries. In these latter countries are found

_____% of the world's population but

only _____% of the world output of goods and services; and the annual rate of

growth of output per capita is _____%.

4. To grow, every economy must increase

its _____ ,

_____ ,

and _____

and improve its _____

5. Which resource is *least* easily increased in the typical underdeveloped nation? _____

_____

6. Three characteristics of the human resources in underdeveloped nations are:

a. _____

b. _____

c. _____

7. The per capita standard of living = _____

_____

and social unrest = _____

minus _____

8. If the process of capital accumulation is "cumulative," this means that _____

_____

9. Domestic capital accumulation requires that a nation _____

and _____.
The former is difficult in underdeveloped nations because of a _____
and the latter is difficult because of a lack of

_____

and _____

10. Nonfinancial investment involves the transfer of surplus labor from _____

to _____

or _____

11. Technological advance in an underdeveloped nation does not ordinarily require an expensive program of research and development because _____

_____

12. If technological advances make it possible to replace a worn-out plow, costing $10 when new, with a new $5 plow, the technological advance is _____

13. The "will to develop" in underdeveloped nations involves a willingness to change the

_____
of the nation.

14. In the typical underdeveloped nation saving is small because the _____ per capita is small. Because saving is small,

_____ in real and human capital is also small. And for this reason the _____

_____ of labor and the _____
per capita remain small.

15. List six reasons why the role of government in fostering economic development will need to be large in the underdeveloped nations, especially during the early stages of development:

a. _____

b. _____

c. _____

d. _____

e. _____

f. _____

16. The three major ways in which the United States can assist economic development in the underdeveloped nations are _____

_____,

_____,

and _____

17. Among the Third World nations there is a feeling that the business firms and governments of North America and Europe wish to

_____ them and to keep them

_____ upon the richer nations; and they feel there exists an economically

based _____

18. No one can forecast the future course of events in the Third World nations; but at least three senarios can be written.
a. In the most optimistic scenario real GNP grows at a rate of 5 to 6% a year; and there is

little or no growth in the _____

and an improved _____
b. In a second scenario groups of under-

developed nations form _____

to raise the prices of _____
  c. And in the third scenario the poor nations

acquire _____ capabilities and en-

gage in wars of _____
with the rich nations.

■ **PROBLEMS AND PROJECTS**

1. While economic conditions are not identical in all underdeveloped nations, there are
certain conditions common to or typical of
all. In the spaces after each of the following
characteristics, indicate briefly the nature of
this characteristic in the typical underdeveloped nation.
  a. Standard of living (per capita income).

_____

  b. Average life expectancy. _____

  c. Extent of unemployment. _____

  d. Literacy. _____

  e. Technology. _____
  f. Percentage of the population engaged in

agriculture. _____
  g. Size of the population relative to the land

and capital available. _____

  h. The birth and death rates. _____

  i. Quality of the labor force. _____
  j. Amount of capital equipment relative to

the labor force. _____

  k. Level of saving. _____

  l. Incentive to invest. _____

  m. Amount of basic social capital. _____

  n. Extent of industrialization. _____
  o. Size and quality of the entrepreneurial

class and the supervisory class. _____

_____

  p. Per capita public expenditures for educa-

tion and per capita energy consumption. _____

_____

  q. Per capita consumption of food and

cloth. _____

  r. Disease and malnutrition. _____

2. Suppose that it takes a minimum of 5
units of food to keep a person alive for a
year, that the population can double itself
every 10 years, and that the food supply can
increase every 10 years by an amount equal
to what it was in the beginning.

Year	Food supply	Population
0	200	20
10	_____	_____
20	_____	_____
30	_____	_____
40	_____	_____
50	_____	_____
60	_____	_____

  a. Assume that both the population and the
food supply grow at these rates. Complete the
table by computing the size of the population
and the food supply in years 10 through 60.
  b. What happens to the relationship between the food supply and the population in

the 30th year? _____
  c. What would actually prevent the population from growing at this rate following the

30th year? _____
  d. Assuming that the actual population
growth in the years following the 30th does
not outrun the food supply, what would be the
size of the population in:

  (1) Year 40: _____

  (2) Year 50: _____

  (3) Year 60: _____
  e. Explain why the standard of living failed
to increase in the years following the 30th
even though the food supply increased by

75% between years 30 and 60. _____

_____

■ **SELF-TEST**

*Circle the T if the statement is true, the F if it
is false.*

1. Among the nations of the world with populations greater than one million persons the United States had the highest per capita income in 1973. **T F**

2. The difference between the per capita incomes in the underdeveloped nations and the per capita incomes in the developed nations has been decreasing over the past years. **T F**

3. It is impossible to achieve a high standard of living with a small supply of natural resources. **T F**

4. Nations with large populations are overpopulated. **T F**

5. The chief factor preventing the elimination of underemployment in the agricultural sector of underdeveloped nations is the small number of job openings available in industry. **T F**

6. The marginal propensity to consume of the mass of the people in underdeveloped nations is less than 1.0. **T F**

7. Before private investment can be increased in underdeveloped nations it is necessary to reduce the amount of investment in basic social capital. **T F**

8. The policies of the governments of underdeveloped nations have often tended to reduce the incentives of foreigners to invest in the underdeveloped nations. **T F**

9. Underdeveloped nations will not need foreign aid if the developed nations will reduce tariffs and import quotas on the goods which the underdeveloped nations export. **T F**

10. An increase in the output and employment of the United States works to the advantage of the underdeveloped nations because it provides the underdeveloped nations with larger markets for their exports. **T F**

11. Foreign aid from the United States to the underdeveloped nations has consistently exceeded 1% of its GNP. **T F**

12. Many in the Third World nations believe that the public and private aid extended by the developed to the underdeveloped nations is designed to increase profits in the former and to exploit the latter nations. **T F**

Underscore the letter that corresponds to the best answer.

1. Which of the following is the most underdeveloped nation? (*a*) U.S.S.R.; (*b*) Israel; (*c*) Canada; (*d*) India.

2. Which of the following is the most serious obstacle to economic growth in underdeveloped nations? (*a*) the supply of natural resources; (*b*) the size and quality of the labor force; (*c*) the supply of capital equipment; (*d*) technological knowledge.

3. An increase in the total output of consumer goods in an underdeveloped nation may not increase the average standard of living because; (*a*) of diminishing returns; (*b*) it may provoke an increase in the population; (*c*) of disguised unemployment; (*d*) the quality of the labor force is so poor.

4. Which of the following best describes the unemployment found in the underdeveloped nations? (*a*) the result of cyclical fluctuations in aggregate demand; (*b*) the agricultural workers whose marginal product is zero or less than zero; (*c*) the workers in excess of the optimum population; (*c*) workers whose productivity is subject to diminishing returns.

5. Which of the following is *not* a reason for placing special emphasis on capital accumulation in underdeveloped nations? (*a*) the inflexible supply of arable land; (*b*) the low productivity of workers; (*c*) the low marginal productivity of capital equipment; (*d*) the possibility that capital accumulation will be "cumulative."

6. Which of the following is *not* a factor limiting saving in underdeveloped nations? (*a*) the incomes of the mass of people are too low to allow saving; (*b*) those who are able to save are unwilling to save; (*c*) the highly unequal distribution of income; (*d*) the low marginal productivity of capital equipment.

7. Which of the following is an example of basic social capital? (*a*) a steel plant; (*b*) an electric power plant; (*c*) a farm; (*d*) a demand deposit in a commercial bank.

8. Which of the following seem to be the *most* needed and widespread institutional change required of underdeveloped nations? (*a*) adoption of birth control; (*b*) development of strong labor unions; (*c*) increase in the nation's basic social capital; (*d*) land reform.

9. Suppose the average propensity to save in

an underdeveloped nation is .09 and that the capital-output ratio is 3. At what rate can total real output increase? (a) 2.7%; (b) 3.0%; (c) 3.3%; (d) 3.9%.

10. Assume the total real output of an underdeveloped economy increases from 100 billion to $115.5 billion while its population expands from 200 million to 210 million people. Real income per capita has, as a result, increased by (a) $50; (b) $100; (c) $150; (d) $200.

11. The role of government in the early stages of economic development will probably be a major one for several reasons. Which one of the following is not one of these reasons? (a) only government can provide a large amount of the needed basic social capital; (b) the absence of private entrepreneurs to accumulate capital and take risks; (c) the necessity of creating new money to finance capital accumulation; (d) the slowness and uncertainty of the price system in fostering development.

12. Which of the following is a Third World nation? (a) the People's Republic of China; (b) Canada; (c) Belgium; (d) Egypt.

■ DISCUSSION QUESTIONS

1. What nations of the world can be called "developed"? Which can be classified as "semideveloped"? Where are the "underdeveloped" nations of the world found?

2. Compare the incomes (per capita) and rates of growth in the developed and Third World nations. What are the "human implications" of the poverty found in the latter nations? (Use the socioeconomic indicators found in Table 21–1 of the text to contrast the quality of life in the developed and underdeveloped nations.)

3. What recent events have increased the desire of the underdeveloped nations to improve their standard of living? Why should social unrest increase in the underdeveloped nations even though their standards of living have been increasing?

4. Why is advice to the underdeveloped nations to follow the example of the United States inappropriate and unrealistic?

5. What must any nation, developed or underdeveloped, do if it is to increase its standard of living? Answer in terms of the production possibilities curve concept.

6. What obstacles do the human resources of underdeveloped nations place in the path of economic development? Why is it difficult to eliminate unemployment in underdeveloped nations?

7. What reasons exist for placing special emphasis on capital accumulation as a means of promoting economic growth in underdeveloped nations?

8. Why is domestic capital accumulation difficult in underdeveloped nations? Answer in terms of both the saving side and the investment side of capital accumulation. How does a lack of basic social capital inhibit investment in underdeveloped nations?

9. In addition to the obstacles which limit domestic investment, what other obstacles tend to limit the flow of foreign capital into underdeveloped nations?

10. Why is it possible for underdeveloped nations to improve their technology without engaging in slow and expensive research?

11. What is meant by the "will to develop"? How is it related to social and institutional change in underdeveloped nations?

12. Explain the "vicious circle" of poverty found in the underdeveloped nations. How does population growth make an escape from this vicious circle difficult?

13. Why is the role of government expected to be a major one in the early phases of development in underdeveloped nations?

14. How can the United States help underdeveloped nations? What types of aid can be offered?

15. Discuss the World Bank in terms of its purposes, characteristics, sources of funds, promotion of private capital flows, and success. What are its affiliates and their purposes?

16. How is it possible for the United States to assist underdeveloped nations without spending a penny on "foreign aid"? Is this type of aid sufficient to ensure rapid and sub-

stantial development in the underdeveloped nations?

17. Explain what the Third World nations mean by neocolonialism; and why they believe both private capital flows and foreign aid lead to neocolonialism.

18. Write the three scenarios which might plausibly forecast the future of the Third World nations.

The Market Structures of American Capitalism

CHAPTER

22

In this chapter the text shifts from the study of macroeconomics to the study of microeconomics; from an analysis of national output and the price level to an analysis of the output and prices of firms and industries; and from an examination of the economy as a whole to an examination of the parts of the economy. In addition, the central question to be answered is no longer what will be the level of resource employment, but how are resources allocated among different products, by whom and by what methods will these products be produced, and how will the income generated in their production be distributed among the owners of various resources.

It has been pointed out in earlier chapters that the price system is the particular device which American capitalism employs to answer these questions; and we have seen that in competitive product markets price depends upon the supply of and the demand for the product. If we are to understand the operation of the economy and the method by which it answers the basic economic questions it is necessary to discover what determines supply and demand in competitive markets; and we will find that supply in a competitive market depends upon the cost of producing the product.

Not all product markets, however, are perfectly competitive. Most are imperfectly competitive. But even in these markets the cost of producing the product (along with demand) will determine the price of the product and the amount of the product produced and sold. The way in which the costs of production and demand together determine price and output depends upon the characteristics of the market in which the product is sold —upon the amount of competition in that market.

Chapter 22 focuses attention upon the different characteristics or structures of markets in which products are sold. Because demand is also influenced by the characteristics of the market in which goods and services are purchased, some attention is paid to the relationship between demand and the character of the market.

Chapter 22's first major section describes four market structures from the point of view of sellers. Although these are no more than generalized categories into which almost all real market situations can be placed, you should concentrate your attention upon the five major characteristics of each of the four market situations. Most of the analysis in later chapters is based on an understanding of these categories and their characteristics. To facilitate the learning process, a table—Table 22–1—is provided in the summary at the end of the chapter.

The second section of the chapter describes

four market situations from the buyers' side of the market. Each of these situations is defined solely in terms of the number of buyers —one, few, fairly many, or very many—and they are, therefore, quite easy to learn and remember.

The third section of the chapter points out that the amount of competitiveness in a market depends not only upon the five characteristics of each market category but also upon the geographic size of the market, how much competition there is between firms and products in *different* industries, the extent of nonprice competition, and how much competition there is *over time* from new products, processes, and firms. In evaluating the competitiveness of any market you should keep these four factors in mind.

The final topic with which the chapter is concerned is the reasons why any industry or market becomes the type of market or industry it is. Four general factors are suggested as causes for the actual development of a market into one of the four categories.

■ CHECKLIST

The very least you should be able to do when you have finished this chapter is:

□ Name the four basic market models on the sellers' side of the market and list the *five* characteristics of *each*.

□ Name the four market models on the buyers' side of the market and define each in terms of its single characteristic.

□ Identify four additional factors which affect the competitiveness of a market and explain how each of them affects competition.

□ List the four major determinants of market structure and describe how each of them influences the structure of a market.

■ CHAPTER OUTLINE

1. On the sellers' side of the market, markets fall into one of four categories: pure competition, pure monopoly, monopolistic competition, and oligopoly. The distinction between market categories depends upon the number of sellers, the type of product, the degree of control which one seller has over price, the ease of entry into the market, and the extent of nonprice competition.

2. On the buyers' side of the market, markets also fall into one of four categories: pure competition, pure monopsony, monopsonistic competition, and oligopsony; the distinction among these market categories depends solely upon the number of buyers.

3. How competitive these markets are depends upon four additional elements: the geographic extent of the market and the amount of interindustry, nonprice, and technological competition.

4. The type of market which develops for the exchange of any good or service depends upon such things as the government's laws, regulations, and policies; the practices and behavior of the firms in the market; the technology employed in producing the product; and the institutions of the capitalistic economy.

■ IMPORTANT TERMS

Pure competition	**Monopsony**
Pure monopoly	**Monopsonistic competition**
Monopolistic competition	
	Oligopsony
Oligopoly	**Bilateral monopoly**
Standardized product	**Quality competition**
Nonprice competition	**Imperfect competition**
Product differentiation	**Interindustry competition**
Price-taker	
Price-maker	

■ FILL-IN QUESTIONS

1. The efficient management of economic resources requires that the resources be both

_____

and _____ ;
the present chapter begins the study of the

(latter, former) _____
aspect of the efficient use of resources.

2. List the five characteristics of pure competition:

a. _____

b. _____

c. _____

d. _____

e. _____

3. Oligopoly is a market model viewed from

the _____

side of the market and monopsonistic compe-

tition is a model viewed from the _____

_____

side.

4. The products produced by purely competi-

tive firms are _____

while those produced by monopolistically

competitive firms are _____ ;

the product produced by the pure monopolist

has no _____

5. A pure monopolist has no close rivals or

competitors because _____

_____

6. The advertising done by a pure monop-

olist tends to be of a _____

or _____

nature.

7. Monopolistic competition is like pure com-

petition because _____

and _____ ,

but like pure monopoly because _____

_____

8. List the five characteristics of pure mo-

nopoly:

a. _____

b. _____

c. _____

d. _____

e. _____

9. In order for the number of firms in a

monopolistically competitive industry to be

considered "large," it is necessary that _____

_____

10. List the five characteristics of monopolis-

tic competition:

a. _____

b. _____

c. _____

d. _____

e. _____

11. Pure competition and monopolistic com-

petition differ chiefly because _____

_____

12. The product produced by the firms in

an oligopoly may be either _____

or _____

13. Oligopolistic firms which produce a

standardized product are typically found in

those industries which produce either _____

_____

or _____

14. The number of firms in an oligopoly is

_____

and each firm supplies _____
of the total market supply.

15. The degree of control which an oligopo-

listic firm possesses over the price of its

product depends upon two factors: _____

_____

and _____

16. In column (1) of the table below, list the
four market models viewed from the buyers'
side of the market. In column (2) opposite
each of the four market models, list their
distinguishing characteristic.

(1) Market model	(2) Distinguishing characteristic
_____	_____
_____	_____
_____	_____
_____	_____

17. In addition to the type of product, the number of sellers, the ease of entry, and the degree of control over price, the competitiveness or noncompetitiveness of a market depends upon _____,

_____,

_____,

and _____

18. The four factors that have been important determinants of market structures in the United States are:

a. _____

b. _____

c. _____

d. _____

■ **PROBLEMS AND PROJECTS**

1. Employing the following set of terms, complete the table below by inserting the appropriate letter or letters in the blanks.

a. one   h. considerable
b. few   i. very easy
c. many   j. blocked
d. a very large number   k. fairly easy
e. standardized   l. fairly difficult
f. differentiated   m. none
g. some

2. Listed below are several firms or types of firms. In the blanks, indicate (1) into what market type—from the sellers' side of the market—this firm falls and (2) the chief reason(s) for placing it in this classification.

a. A local dry-cleaning firm _____

_____

b. A manufacturer of toothpaste _____

_____

c. A farmer raising pigs _____

_____

d. The Ford Motor Company _____

_____

e. A used-car dealer _____

_____

f. A steel producer _____

3. Indicate for each of the following industries whether its firms compete in any significant way with firms in other industries and what the competing industries are.

a. Airlines _____

b. Silk _____

c. Plastics _____

d. Television sets _____

e. Copper _____

■ **SELF-TEST**

Circle the T if the statement is true, the F if it is false.

1. Every industry in the American economy falls clearly into one of four market models.
        T   F

2. The definition of competition is one of the very few economic concepts upon which the layman and the economist find it easy to agree.   **T   F**

Market characteristics	Market situation			
	Pure competition	Pure monopoly	Monopolistic competition	Oligopoly
Number of firms	_____	_____	_____	_____
Type of product	_____	_____	_____	_____
Control over price	_____	_____	_____	_____
Entry	_____	_____	_____	_____
Nonprice competition	_____	_____	_____	_____

3. Although no individual purely competitive firm is able to influence the market price of the product which it produces, all the firms in a purely competitive industry can influence the market price.　　　　**T　F**

4. A large number of sellers does not necessarily mean that the industry is purely competitive.　　　　**T　F**

5. Only in a purely competitive industry do individual firms have no control over the price of their product.　　　　**T　F**

6. Because he is the sole supplier of a product, the pure monopolist cannot affect the market price of his product.　　　　**T　F**

7. Insofar as pure monopoly is concerned, the industry and the firm are one and the same.　　　　**T　F**

8. There are no substitutes for the product produced by the pure monopolist.　　**T　F**

9. The monopolistic competitor has only a limited amount of control over the price of his product.　　　　**T　F**

10. Entry into the monopolistically competitive industry is usually quite difficult.　**T　F**

11. The greater the degree of product differentiation in an oligopoly, the larger will be the amount of control a firm has over the price of its product.　　　　**T　F**

12. If an oligopolistic firm is producing a differentiated product, it is more likely to engage in advertising and sales promotion than a firm producing a standardized product.
　　　　T　F

13. The existence of just two sellers in a market is called "bilateral monopoly."　　**T　F**

14. The policies of the Federal government have been consistently directed at preventing or eliminating monopoly and at encouraging competition.　　　　**T　F**

15. The economics of mass production and the role of research in the development of new products and techniques of production generally lead to an increase in the number of firms in an industry and a decrease in the size of these firms.　　　　**T　F**

Underscore the letter that corresponds to the best answer.

1. Which of the following is *not* one of the four market models as viewed from the seller's side of the market? (*a*) pure competition; (*b*) monopoly; (*c*) monopolistic competition; (*d*) oligopsony.

2. Which of the following is characteristic of monopolistic competition? (*a*) standardized product; (*b*) very few firms; (*c*) entry is fairly easy; (*d*) very little nonprice competition.

3. Which of the following is *not* characteristic of pure competition? (*a*) large number of sellers; (*b*) differentiated product; (*c*) easy entry; (*d*) no advertising.

4. If the product produced by an industry is standardized, the market structure can be: (*a*) pure competition or monopolistic competition; (*b*) pure competition or oligopoly; (*c*) monopolistic competition or oligopoly; (*d*) pure competition, monopolistic competition, or oligopoly.

5. Into which of the following industries is entry least difficult? (*a*) pure competition; (*b*) pure monopoly; (*c*) monopolistic competition; (*d*) oligopoly.

6. Which of the following industries comes *closest* to being purely competitive? (*a*) wheat; (*b*) shoes; (*c*) retailing; (*d*) farm implements.

7. Which of the following is the *best* example of a pure monopoly? (*a*) the local telegraph company; (*b*) the local water company; (*c*) the Aluminum Company of America; (*d*) the United States Steel Corporation.

8. With respect to which of the following characteristics are purely competitive industries and monopolistically competitive industries most similar? (*a*) type of product; (*b*) number of firms; (*c*) difficulty of entry; (*d*) extent of nonprice competition.

9. Which of the following industry classifications encompasses the greatest number of actual market situations in the American economy? (*a*) pure competition; (*b*) pure monopoly; (*c*) monopolistic competition; (*d*) oligopoly.

10. Which of the following is an example of an oligopoly producing a differentiated product? (*a*) automobiles; (*b*) steel; (*c*) shoes; (*d*) women's dresses.

11. From the buyers' side of the market, the market for automobile workers in Detroit would be: (a) purely competitive; (b) monop-sonistic; (c) monopsonistically competitive; (d) oligopsonistic.

12. Under which of the following pairs of conditions would the oligopolistic firm have the greatest degree of control over the price of its product? (a) no collusion between firms in the industry and a standardized product; (b) no collusion between firms in the industry and a differentiated product; (c) collusion between firms in the industry and a standardized product; (d) collusion between firms in the industry and a differentiated product.

■ **DISCUSSION QUESTIONS**

1. What does it mean when it is said that "the purely competitive firm is at the mercy of the market"? In your answer explain the difference between a price-taker and a price-maker; and why firms outside of purely competitive industries are not at the complete mercy of the market.

2. Why do purely competitive firms do little advertising? Why do monopolistically competitive firms do so much?

3. Explain in what sense the monopolistically competitive firm is competitive and in what sense it is monopolistic.

4. What seems to be the most important factor in preventing rivals from developing to compete with pure monopolists?

5. What limits the ability of a monopolistically competitive firm to control the price of its product?

6. Why is entry into a monopolistically competitive industry more difficult than into a purely competitive industry?

7. "Clear-cut mutual interdependence" is one of the characteristics peculiar to oligopoly. What does this mean?

8. What are the barriers to entry typically found in oligopolistic markets?

9. What determines whether an oligopolist will engage in extensive advertising and other forms of sales promotion?

10. Why might an industry which at first glance seems to be purely competitive or monopolistically competitive because of its large number of firms at second glance turn out to be monopolistic or oligopolistic?

11. What are the four market models as seen from the buyers' side of the market and their distinguishing characteristics?

12. In assessing the competitiveness or non-competitiveness of a market, what factors should be considered?

13. How does competition over *time* differ from competition at a *point in time*?

14. What factors are important in determining the type of market or industry a particular group of firms will become?

15. How has the Federal government contributed to the formation of monopolies? In what ways has it attempted to limit their formation or to regulate them?

16. Why is it dangerous to employ just four market models—from the sellers' side of the market—in classifying and analyzing American industries?

Demand, Supply, and Elasticity: Some Applications

Before you begin to read Chapter 23, you are urged (you would be commanded if this were possible) to read and study Chapter 4 again. It is absolutely necessary that you have mastered Chapter 4 if the new material of this chapter is to be understood and digested.

As might be guessed, Chapter 23 is, in a sense, a continuation of Chapter 4. In the earlier part of the book it was necessary for you to have only an elementary knowledge of supply and demand. Now the economic principles, problems, and policies to be studied require a more detailed examination and analysis of supply and demand principles. Of particular importance and value in studying much of the material found in the remainder of the text is the concept of elasticity, to which the major portion of Chapter 23 is devoted.

With respect to the concept of elasticity of demand, it is essential for you to understand (1) what elasticity measures; (2) how the price-elasticity formula is applied to measure the elasticity of demand; (3) the difference between elastic, inelastic, and unitary elasticity of demand; (4) how total revenue varies in each of these three cases; and (5) the meaning of perfect elasticity and perfect inelasticity.

When you have become thoroughly acquainted with the elasticity of demand concept, you will find you have very little trouble understanding the elasticity of *supply* and that the transition requires no more than the substitution of the words "quantity supplied" for the words "quantity demanded." Here attention should be concentrated upon the meaning of elasticity of supply, its measurement, and its principal determinant.

In the final section of the chapter three topics are discussed. The first of these topics is price ceilings and supports. The student should note that these ceilings and supports prevent supply and demand from determining the equilibrium price of a commodity and from determining the quantity of the commodity which will be bought and sold in the market. The consequences will be shortages or surpluses of the commodity.

The incidence of a sales or excise tax is the second topic. Incidence means "who ends up paying the tax." The most important thing you will learn is that the elasticities of demand *and* of supply determine how much of the tax will be paid by buyers and how much of it will be paid by sellers. You should be especially careful to learn and to understand how the two elasticities affect the incidence of a tax.

The third topic introduces the student to several important new revenue concepts. These concepts are a necessary part of the analysis of the behavior of the business firm under the four sets of market conditions discussed in Chapters 26 through 29, and you should master them now if you are to understand what follows. Here it is important to distinguish between the way in which the individual pure competitor sees the demand for his product and the way in which the imperfect competitor sees the demand for the product of his firm. After this distinction is understood, the further distinction between the nature of the demand, total-revenue, average-revenue, and marginal-revenue schedules confronting the pure competitor and those confronting the imperfect competitor needs to be made. First learn the revenue concepts, and then learn the difference between the ways in which the pure and the imperfect competitor see them.

■ CHECKLIST

The very least you should be able to do when you have finished this chapter is:
□ Define demand and state the *law of demand*.
□ Define supply and state the *law of supply*.
□ Determine the equilibrium price and the equilibrium quantity.
□ Predict the effect of changes in demand and/or supply on the equilibrium price and quantity.
□ Explain the economic consequences of price supports and price ceilings.
□ Define the elasticity of demand and compute the coefficient of elasticity when you are given the demand data.
□ Explain the meaning of elastic, inelastic, and unitary elastic demand; and apply the total-revenue test to determine whether demand is elastic, inelastic, or unitary elastic.
□ List the major determinants of the elasticity of demand; and explain how each of these will affect elasticity.
□ Define the elasticity of supply; compute the coefficient of the elasticity of supply from data; and explain how time affects the elasticity of supply.
□ State the relationship between the elasticities of demand and supply and the incidence of an excise tax.
□ Define total revenue, average revenue, and marginal revenue; and compute each when you are given demand data.

□ Explain the difference between the way in which a purely competitive and an imperfectly competitive firm sees the demand for its product and the marginal revenue from the sale of an additional unit of its product.

■ CHAPTER OUTLINE

1. It is necessary to review the analysis of supply and demand and the concepts found in Chapter 4 before studying this chapter.

2. Price elasticity of demand is a measure of the sensitivity of quantity demanded to changes in the price of the product.
  a. The exact degree of elasticity can be measured by using a formula to compute the elasticity coefficient. Demand is either elastic, inelastic, or of unitary elasticity.
  b. The way in which total revenue changes (increases, decreases, or remains constant) when price changes is a test of the elasticity of demand for a product.
  c. The elasticity of demand for a product depends upon the number of good substitutes the product has, its relative importance in the consumer's budget, whether it is a necessity or a luxury, and the period of time under consideration.
  d. Elasticity of demand is of great practical importance in matters of public policy and in the setting of prices by the individual business firm.
  e. Price elasticity of supply is a measure of the sensitivity of quantity supplied to changes in the price of the product; while there is no total-revenue test, the formula used to measure elasticity of demand can also be used to measure elasticity of supply. The elasticity of supply depends upon the amount of time sellers have to adjust to a price change.

3. Supply and demand analysis and the elasticity concepts have many important applications.
  a. Legal price ceilings and price supports prevent price from performing its rationing function.
  (1) A price ceiling results in a shortage of the commodity; may bring about formal rationing by government and a black market; and causes a misallocation of resources.
  (2) A price support creates a surplus of the commodity; and may induce government to undertake measures either to increase the

demand for or to decrease the supply of the commodity.

b. The imposition of a sales or excise tax on a commodity decreases the supply of the commodity and increases its price. The amount of the price increase is the portion of the tax paid by the buyer; the seller pays the rest.

(1) The more elastic (inelastic) the demand for the commodity, the greater (smaller) is the portion paid by the seller.

(2) The more elastic (inelastic) the supply of the commodity, the greater (smaller) is the portion paid by the buyer.

c. The way in which the individual firm sees the demand for its product depends upon whether the firm is a pure competitor or an imperfect competitor.

(1) Under conditions of pure competition, it sees demand as perfectly elastic, average revenue and marginal revenue as equal and constant at the fixed market price, and total revenue as constantly increasing as the firm's output increases.

(2) Under conditions of imperfect competition, it sees demand as less than perfectly elastic, marginal revenue as less than average revenue, both decreasing as the firm's output increases, and total revenue as increasing at first but then decreasing as its output increases.

■ IMPORTANT TERMS

Review

Demand	Rationing function of prices
Supply	
Law of demand	Change in demand
Law of supply	Change in supply
Equilibrium price	Change in quantity demanded
Equilibrium quantity	Change in quantity supplied
Competition (competitive market)	

New

Price elasticity of demand	Perfect inelasticity of demand
Elastic demand	Perfect elasticity of demand
Inelastic demand	
Total-revenue test	Price elasticity of supply
Elasticity coefficient	
Elasticity formula	Elastic supply
Unitary elasticity	Inelastic supply

Market period	Tax incidence
Short run	Total revenue
Long run	Average revenue
Price ceiling	Marginal revenue
Price support	

Note: Before answering the Fill-in, Self-test, and Discussion questions and working out the Problems and Projects, you should return to Chapter 4 in this study guide and review the terms and concepts, answer the questions, and rework the problems.

■ FILL-IN QUESTIONS

1. If a relatively large change in price results in a relatively small change in quantity demanded, demand is _____ ; if a relatively small change in price results in a relatively large change in quantity demanded, demand is _____

2. When demand is elastic, buyers are relatively (sensitive, insensitive) _____ to change in the price of the product; when demand is inelastic, they are relatively _____

_____ to changes in price.

3. If demand is elastic, price and total revenue are _____ related; if demand is inelastic, they are _____

_____ related.

4. Complete the summary table.

If demand is	The elasticity coefficient is	If price rises, total revenue will	If price falls, total revenue will
Elastic	_____	_____	_____
Inelastic	_____	_____	_____
Of unitary elasticity	_____	_____	_____

5. If a change in price causes no change in quantity demanded, demand is _____

_____ ;

if an extremely small change in price results in an extremely large change in quantity demanded, demand is _____

_____.
When the former is graphed, the demand

curve is _____ ;

a graph of the latter demand curve is _____

_____

6. If the price of a commodity declines,
  a. When demand is inelastic the loss of

revenue due to the lower price is _____

_____ the gain in revenue due to the
greater quantity demanded.
  b. When demand is elastic the loss of reve-

nue due to the lower price is _____

_____ the gain in revenue due to the
greater quantity demanded.
  c. When demand is of unitary elasticity the

loss of revenue due to the lower price is _____

_____ the gain in revenue due to
the greater quantity demanded.

7. List four determinants of the elasticity of demand:

  a. _____

  b. _____

  c. _____

  d. _____

8. The most important factor affecting the

elasticity of supply is _____

9. If the demand and supply schedules for a certain product are those given in the table, answer the following questions.

Quantity demanded	Price	Quantity supplied
12,000	$10	18,000
13,000	9	17,000
14,000	8	16,000
15,000	7	15,000
16,000	6	14,000
17,000	5	13,000
18,000	4	12,000

  a. The equilibrium price of the product is

$_____ and the equilibrium

quantity is _____
  b. If the government imposes a price ceiling of $5 on this product, there would be a

_____

of _____
units.
  c. If the government supports a price of $8,

there would be a _____

of _____
units.

10. Price ceilings imposed by the United States government have usually occurred

during _____

periods, result in _____
of the commodities, and require that the gov-

ernment institute _____

11. Price ceilings and price supports prevent

prices from performing their _____
function.

12. The two most common examples of government-imposed minimum prices are _____

_____

and _____

13. A minimum price imposed by the government on a commodity causes a _____
of the commodity and requires that the gov-

ernment either _____

or _____
to eliminate this.

14. When a sales or excise tax is levied on a commodity, the amount of the tax borne by

buyers of the commodity is equal to _____

_____.
The incidence of such a tax depends on the elasticity of demand and of supply.
  a. The buyer's portion of the tax is larger

the (more, less) _____elastic

the demand and the _____
elastic the supply.

b. The seller's portion of the tax is larger the _____ elastic the demand and the _____ elastic the supply.

15. An individual firm which is purely competitive finds that as it increases its output, the price it must charge to sell this output ___

_____ ,

while the imperfectly competitive firm finds that the price it must charge to sell a larger

output _____ ;
for this reason the purely competitive firm

finds that margin revenue is _____
average revenue, and the imperfectly competitive firm finds that marginal revenue is

_____

average revenue.

16. On the demand schedule which is less than perfectly elastic, the elasticity of demand typically varies with price. Demand tends to

be _____

in the upper range of prices, _____
in the lower range, and of unitary elasticity at a price between the two ranges.

■ **PROBLEMS AND PROJECTS**

1. In the following table, using the demand data given, complete the table by computing total revenue at each of the seven prices and the six elasticity coefficients between each of the seven prices, and indicate whether demand is elastic, inelastic, or of unitary elasticity between each of the seven prices.

Price	Quantity de- manded	Total revenue	Elasticity coeffi- cient	Character of demand
$1.00	300	$_____		
.90	400	_____	_____	_____
.80	500	_____	_____	_____
.70	600	_____	_____	_____
.60	700	_____	_____	_____
.50	800	_____	_____	_____
.40	900	_____		

2. Using the supply data in the schedule below, complete the table by computing the six elasticity-of-supply coefficients between each of the seven prices, and indicate whether supply is elastic, inelastic, or of unitary elasticity.

Price	Quantity supplied	Elasticity coefficient	Character of supply
$1.00	800		
.90	700	_____	_____
.80	600	_____	_____
.70	500	_____	_____
.60	400	_____	_____
.50	300	_____	_____
.40	200	_____	_____

3. On the graph below are three different supply curves (S_1, S_2, and S_3) for a product bought and sold in a competitive market.

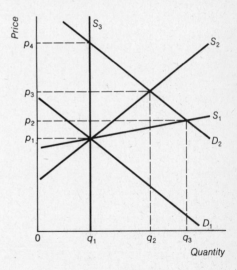

a. The supply curve for the:

(1) market period is the one labeled _____

(2) short run is the one labeled _____

(3) long run is the one labeled _____
b. No matter what the period of time under consideration, if the demand for the product were D_1, the equilibrium price of the product

would be _____ and the equilibrium quantity

would be _____ .

c. Were demand to increase from D_1 to D_2:
(1) in the market period the equilibrium price would increase to _____ and the equilibrium quantity would _____
(2) in the short run the price of the product would increase to _____ and the quantity would increase to _____
(3) in the long run the price of the product would be _____ and the quantity would be _____

d. The longer the period of time allowed to sellers to adjust their outputs the (more, less) _____ elastic is the supply of the product.

e. The more elastic the supply of a product, the (greater, less) _____ is the effect on equilibrium price and the _____ is the effect on equilibrium quantity of an increase in demand.

4. In the table below are the demand and supply schedules for copra in the New Hebrides Islands.

a. Before a tax is imposed on copra, its equilibrium price is $ _____

b. The government of the New Hebrides now imposes an excise tax of $.60 per pound on copra. Complete the after-tax supply schedule in the right-hand column of the table below.

c. After the imposition of the tax, the equilibrium price of copra is $ _____

d. Of the $.60 tax, the amount borne by

(1) the buyer is $_____ or _____%

(2) the seller is $_____ or _____%

5. Two graphs follow.

a. On the graph below draw a perfectly elastic demand curve and a normal upsloping supply curve for a commodity.

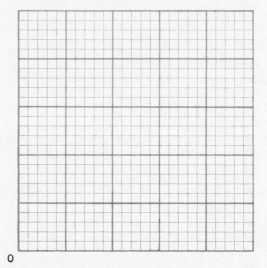

(1) Now impose an excise tax on the commodity, and draw the new supply curve that would result.

Quantity demanded (pounds)	Price (per pound)	Before-tax quantity supplied (pounds)	After-tax quantity supplied (pounds)
150	$4.60	900	_____
200	4.40	800	_____
250	4.20	700	_____
300	4.00	600	_____
350	3.80	500	_____
400	3.60	400	_____
450	3.40	300	0
500	3.20	200	0
550	3.00	100	0

(2) As a consequence of the tax, the price of the commodity has _____

(3) It can be concluded that when demand is perfectly elastic, the buyer bears _____ of the tax and the seller bears _____ of the tax.

(4) Thus the *more* elastic the demand, the _____ is the portion of the tax borne by the buyer and the _____ is the portion borne by the seller.

(5) But the *less* elastic the demand, the _____ is the portion borne by the buyer and the _____ is the portion borne by the seller.

b. On the next graph draw a perfectly elastic supply curve and a normal down-sloping demand curve.

(1) Again impose an excise tax on the commodity and draw the new supply curve.

(2) As a result of the tax, the price of the commodity has _____

(3) From this it can be concluded that when supply is perfectly elastic, the buyer bears _____ of the tax and the seller bears _____ of the tax.

(4) Thus the *more* elastic the supply, the _____ is the portion of the tax borne by the buyer and the _____ is the portion borne by the seller.

(5) But the *less* elastic the supply, the _____ is the portion borne by the buyer and the _____ is the portion borne by the seller.

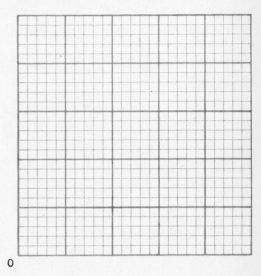

0

6. If the demand schedule confronting an individual firm is as shown in the table below, complete the following questions.

a. Complete the table by computing average revenue, total revenue, marginal revenue, and the coefficient of the price elasticity of demand.

b. Is this firm operating in a market which is purely or imperfectly competitive? _____

How can you tell? _____

Price	Quantity demanded	Average revenue	Total revenue	Marginal revenue	Elasticity coefficient
$11	0	$_____	$_____		
				$_____	_____
10	1	_____	_____		
				_____	_____
9	2	_____	_____		
				_____	_____
8	3	_____	_____		
				_____	_____
7	4	_____	_____		
				_____	_____
6	5	_____	_____		
				_____	_____
5	6	_____	_____		
				_____	_____
4	7	_____	_____		
				_____	_____
3	8	_____	_____		
				_____	_____
2	9	_____	_____		

c. On the graph below plot the demand schedule, average revenue, total revenue, and marginal revenue; label each of these curves. (*Note:* Plot marginal revenue at ½, 1½, 2½, etc., units of output rather than at 1, 2, 3, etc.)

d. By examination of the total-revenue, marginal-revenue, and price elasticity of demand coefficients, it can be seen that:

(1) Where total revenue is increasing as

price falls, demand is _____

and marginal revenue is _____

(2) Where total revenue is decreasing as

price falls, demand is _____

and marginal revenue is _____

(3) Where total revenue is constant as price

falls, demand is _____

and marginal revenue is _____

e. Using the tables above, explain why marginal revenue is less than average revenue.

_____

_____

7. Below is another demand schedule for an individual firm.

Price	Quantity demanded	Average revenue	Total revenue	Marginal revenue
$10	0	$_____	$_____	$_____
10	1	_____	_____	
10	2	_____	_____	_____
10	3	_____	_____	_____
10	4	_____	_____	_____
10	5	_____	_____	_____
10	6	_____	_____	_____

a. Complete the table by computing average revenue, total revenue, and marginal revenue.

b. Is this firm operating in a market which

is purely or imperfectly competitive? _____

How can you tell? _____

c. On the next graph plot the demand schedule, average revenue, total revenue, and

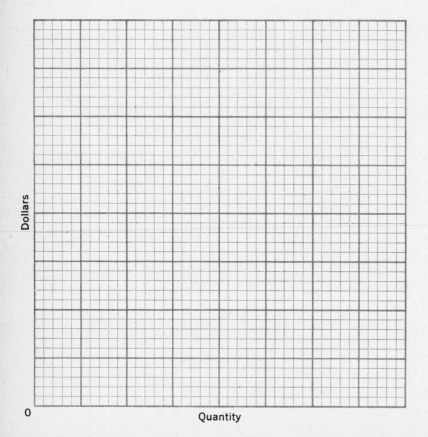

Dollars

0

Quantity

marginal revenue; label each of these curves. (*Note:* Plot marginal revenue at ½, 1½, 2½, etc., units of output rather than 1, 2, 3, etc.)

d. The coefficient of the price elasticity of demand is the same between every pair of quantities demanded. How much is it? _____

e. What relationship exists between average revenue and marginal revenue? _____

■ SELF-TEST

Circle the T if the statement is true, the F if it is false.

1. Demand tends to be inelastic at high prices and elastic at low prices. **T   F**

2. Total revenue will not change if the elasticity of demand is unitary. **T   F**

3. If the relative change in price is greater than the relative change in quantity demanded, the elasticity coefficient is greater than one. **T   F**

4. Elasticity of demand and the slope of the demand curve are two different things. **T   F**

5. The demand for most agricultural products is inelastic. Consequently, an increase in supply will reduce the total income of producers of agricultural products. **T   F**

6. If an increase in product price results in no change in the quantity supplied, supply is perfectly elastic. **T   F**

7. If the government imposes a price ceiling above what would be the free-market price of a commodity, a shortage of the commodity will develop. **T   F**

8. The purely competitive firm views an average-revenue schedule which is identical to its marginal-revenue schedule. **T   F**

9. As an imperfectly competitive firm increases its output, it finds that its total revenue at first decreases, and that after some output level is reached, its total revenue begins to increase. **T   F**

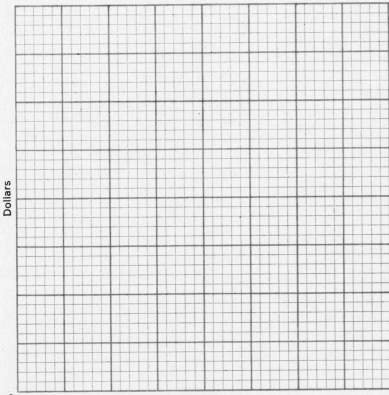

0   Quantity

10. In the range of prices in which demand is inelastic, marginal revenue is a negative amount. **T F**

11. When an excise tax is placed on a product bought and sold in a competitive market, the portion of the tax borne by the seller equals the amount of the tax less the rise in the price of the product due to the tax. **T F**

12. The more elastic the demand for a good, the greater will be the portion of an excise tax on the good borne by the seller. **T F**

Underscore the letter that corresponds to the best answer.

1. If when the price of a product rises from $1.50 to $2, the quantity demanded of the product decreases from 900 to 1000, the elasticity of demand coefficient is: (*a*) 3.00; (*b*) 2.71; (*c*) 0.37; (*d*) 0.33.

2. If a 1% fall in the price of a commodity causes the quantity demanded of the commodity to increase 2%, demand is: (*a*) inelastic; (*b*) elastic; (*c*) of unitary elasticity; (*d*) perfectly elastic.

3. Which of the following is *not* characteristic of a commodity the demand for which is elastic? (*a*) the elasticity coefficient is less than unity; (*b*) total revenue decreases if price rises; (*c*) buyers are relatively sensitive to price changes; (*d*) the relative change in quantity is greater than the relative change in price.

4. Which of the following is *not* characteristic of a good the demand for which is inelastic? (*a*) there are a large number of good substitutes for the good; (*b*) the buyers spends a small percentage of his total income on the good; (*c*) the good is regarded by consumers as a necessity; (*d*) the period of time for which demand is given is very short.

5. If a 5% fall in the price of a commodity causes quantity supplied to decrease by 8%, supply is: (*a*) inelastic; (*b*) of unitary elasticity; (*c*) elastic; (*d*) perfectly inelastic.

6. If supply is inelastic and demand decreases, the total revenue of sellers will: (*a*) increase; (*b*) decrease; (*c*) decrease only if demand is elastic; (*d*) increase only if demand is inelastic.

7. If the government sets a minimum price for a commodity and this minimum price is less than the equilibrium price of the commodity, the result will be: (*a*) a shortage of the commodity; (*b*) a surplus of the commodity; (*c*) neither a shortage nor a surplus of the commodity; (*d*) an increase in total receipts from the sale of the commodity if demand is inelastic.

8. The demand schedule or curve confronted by the individual purely competitive firm is: (*a*) perfectly inelastic; (*b*) inelastic but not perfectly inelastic; (*c*) perfectly elastic; (*d*) elastic but not perfectly elastic.

9. The imperfectly competitive firm finds that marginal revenue is: (*a*) less than average revenue; (*b*) greater than average revenue; (*c*) equal to average revenue; (*d*) sometimes greater and sometimes less than average revenue.

10. The chief determinant of the elasticity of supply of a product is: (*a*) the number of good substitutes the product has; (*b*) the length of time producers have to adjust to a change in price; (*c*) whether the product is a luxury or a necessity; (*d*) whether the product is a durable or a nondurable good.

11. In a competitive market the portion of an excise tax borne by a buyer is equal to: (*a*) the amount the price of the product rises as a result of the tax; (*b*) the amount of the tax; (*c*) the amount of the tax less the amount the price of the product rises as a result of the tax; (*d*) the amount of the tax plus the amount the price of the product rises as a result of the tax.

12. Which of the following statements is correct? (*a*) the more elastic the supply, the greater the portion of an excise tax borne by the seller; (*b*) the more elastic the demand, the greater the portion of an excise tax borne by the seller; (*c*) the more inelastic the supply, the greater the portion of an excise tax borne by the buyer; (*d*) the more inelastic the demand, the greater the portion of an excise tax borne by the seller.

■ **DISCUSSION QUESTIONS**

1. Define and explain the elasticity of demand concept in terms of each of the following: (*a*) the relative sensitiveness of quantity demanded to changes in price; (*b*) the behavior of total revenue when price changes;

(c) the elasticity coefficient; (d) the relationship between the relative (percentage) change in quantity demanded and the relative (percentage) change in price.

2. In computing the elasticity coefficient, it usually makes a considerable difference whether the higher price and lower quantity or the lower price and higher quantity are used as a point of reference. What have economists done to eliminate the confusion which would arise if the elasticity of demand coefficient varied and depended upon whether a price rise or fall were being considered?

3. What is meant by perfectly elastic demand? By perfectly inelastic demand? What does the demand curve look like when demand is perfectly elastic and when it is perfectly inelastic?

4. When the price of a commodity declines, the quantity demanded of it increases. When demand is elastic, total revenue is greater at the lower price; but when demand is inelastic, total revenue is smaller. Explain why total revenue will sometimes increase and why it will sometimes decrease.

5. What are the factors which affect the elasticity of demand for a product?

6. Of what practical importance is the concept of elasticity of demand?

7. Explain what determines the elasticity of supply of an economic good or service.

8. Why does the government from time to time impose price ceilings and minimum prices on certain goods and services? What are the consequences of these ceilings and minimums if they are not set at the price which would prevail in the free market?

9. Explain the effect which the imposition of an excise tax has upon the supply of a commodity bought and sold in a competitive market. How do you find what part of the tax is passed on to the buyer and what part is borne by the seller? What determines the division of the tax between buyer and seller?

10. What is the relationship between the elasticity of demand for a commodity and the portion of an excise tax on a commodity borne by the buyer and by the seller? What is the relationship between the elasticity of supply and the incidence of the tax?

11. Explain the basic difference between the way in which purely competitive and imperfectly competitive individual firms see the demand for their products in terms of (a) price elasticity of demand; (b) the relation of average to marginal revenue; and (c) the behavior of total, average, and marginal revenue as the output of the firm increases.

12. Explain why marginal revenue is always less than average revenue when demand is less than perfectly elastic and how marginal revenue can be computed.

Further Topics in the Theory of Consumer Demand

CHAPTER

In several earlier chapters it was pointed out that consumers typically buy more of a product as its price decreases and less of it as its price increases. Chapter 24 looks behind this law of demand and explains why consumers behave this way. Two explanations are presented. One, developed in terms of the income effect and the substitution effect, is a general and simple explanation. The other, developed in terms of the concept of marginal utility, is a more detailed explanation and is more difficult to understand.

The marginal-utility explanation requires that you first understand the concepts and assumptions upon which this theory of consumer behavior rests, and second, do some rigorous reasoning using these concepts and assumptions. It is an exercise in logic, but be sure that you follow the reasoning. To aid you, several problems are provided so that you can work things out for yourself.

Of course no one believes that consumers actually perform these mental gymnastics before they spend their incomes or make a purchase. But the marginal-utility approach to consumer behavior is studied because consumers behave "as if" they made their purchases on the basis of very fine calculations. Thus, this approach explains what we do in fact observe, and makes it possible for us to predict with a good deal of precision how

consumers will react to changes in their incomes and in the prices of products.

Several criticisms of the marginal-utility theory are found in the text. One of these criticisms is that the consumption of a good or service requires the use of scarce and valuable time and that the theory has neglected this time dimension of consumption. The final section of the chapter will show you how the value of the time required for the consumption of a product can be put into the marginal-utility theory; and what the implications of this modification of the theory are.

■ CHECKLIST

The very least you should be able to do when you have finished this chapter is:

□ Define and distinguish between the income and the substitution effects of a price change; and use the two effects to explain why a consumer will buy more (less) of a commodity when its price falls (rises).

□ Define marginal utility; and state the law of diminishing marginal utility.

□ List the four assumptions made in the theory of consumer behavior.

□ State the utility-maximizing rule.

□ Use the utility-maximizing rule to determine how a consumer would spend his fixed income when you are given the utility and price data.

☐ Derive a consumer's demand for a product from utility, income, and price data.

☐ Explain how the value of time has been incorporated into the theory of consumer behavior; and several of the implications of this modification of the theory.

■ **CHAPTER OUTLINE**

1. The law of consumer demand can be explained by employing either the income-effect and substitution-effect concepts, or the concept of marginal utility.

a. Consumers buy more of a commodity when its price falls because their money income will go further (the income effect) and because the commodity is now less expensive relative to other commodities (the substitution effect).

b. The essential assumption made in the alternative explanation is that the more the consumer buys of any commodity, the smaller becomes the marginal (extra) utility he receives from it.

2. The assumption (or law) of diminishing marginal utility is the basis of the theory that explains how a consumer will spend his income.

a. The typical consumer, it is assumed, is rational, knows his marginal-utility schedules for the various goods available, has a limited money income to spend, and must pay a price to acquire each of the goods which give him utility.

b. Given these assumptions, the consumer maximizes the total utility he receives when the marginal utility of the last dollar spent on a commodity is the same for all commodities.

c. Algebraically, his total utility is a maximum when the marginal utility of the last unit of a commodity purchased divided by its price is the same for all commodities.

3. To find a consumer's demand for a product the utility-maximizing rule is applied to determine the amount of the product he will purchase at different prices, his income and tastes and the prices of other products remaining constant.

4. The marginal-utility theory enables us to predict the way consumers will behave and

explains their reasons for behaving this way; and recently it has been modified to include the fact that consumption takes time and time is a scarce resource.

a. The full price of any consumer good or service is equal to its market price plus the value of the time taken to consume it (the income the consumer could have earned had he used that time for work).

b. The inclusion of the value of consumption time in the theory of consumer behavior has several significant implications.

■ **IMPORTANT TERMS**

Income effect	Rational
Substitution effect	Budget restraint
Utility	Utility-maximizing rule
Marginal utility	
Law of diminishing marginal utility	

■ **FILL-IN QUESTIONS**

1. A fall in the price of a product tends to

_____

the *real* income of a consumer, and a rise in

its price tends to _____

his real income. This is called the _____

_____

effect.

2. When the price of a product increases, the

product becomes relatively (more, less) _____
expensive than it was and the prices of other

products become relatively (higher, lower) ___

_____

than they were; the consumer will, therefore,

buy (less, more) _____

of the product in question and _____

of the other products. This is called the _____

_____

effect.

3. The law of diminishing marginal utility is

that _____ will _____

as the consumer increases his consumption of a particular commodity.

4. The marginal-utility theory of consumer behavior assumes that the consumer is _____ _____

and that he has certain _____ for various goods.

5. A consumer cannot buy all he wishes of every good and service because his income is _____

and goods and services have _____ ; these facts are called the _____ _____

6. When the consumer is maximizing the utility which his income will obtain for him, the _____ is the same for all the products he buys.

7. If the marginal utility of the last dollar spent on one product is greater than the marginal utility of the last dollar spent on another product, the consumer should *increase* his purchases of the first and *decrease* his purchases of the second.

8. Assume there are only two products, X and Y, a consumer can purchase with a fixed income. The consumer is maximizing utility algebraically when:

$$\frac{(a)\ Marg\ Util\ A}{(b)\ price\ A} = \frac{(c)\ Marg\ Util\ B}{(d)\ price\ B}$$

9. The two factors (other than the price of the product and the tastes of the consumer) which determine how much of a particular product a consumer will buy are:

a. _price of other products_

b. _budget restraint_

10. The consumption of any product requires _time_ _____

a. This is a valuable economic resource because it is _scarce_

b. Its value is equal to _the income that can be earned by using time for work_

c. And the full price to the consumer of any product is, therefore, _market price_

plus _value of consumption of tim_

■ **PROBLEMS AND PROJECTS**

1. Suppose that when the price of bread is 50 cents per loaf, the Robertson family buys six loaves of bread in a week.

a. When the price of bread falls to 40 cents, the Robinson family will increase their bread consumption to seven loaves.

(1) Measured in terms of bread, the fall in the price of bread will _increase_

their real income by _one . 4_ loaves. (*Hint:* How many loaves of bread *could* they now buy without changing the amount they spend on bread?)

(2) Is the Robertsons' demand for bread elastic or inelastic? _inelastic_

b. When the price of bread rises from 50 to 60 cents per loaf, the Robertson family will decrease their bread consumption to four loaves.

(1) Measured in terms of bread, this rise in the price of bread will _decrease_

their real income by _one .4_ loaves.

(2) Is the Robertsons' demand for bread elastic or inelastic? _elastic_

2. Assume that Palmer is confronted with three goods, A, B, and C, and that the amounts of utility which their consumption will yield him are as shown in the next table. Compute the marginal utilities for successive units of A, B, and C and enter them in the appropriate columns.

3. Using the marginal-utility data for goods A, B, and C which you obtained in problem 2, assume that the prices of A, B, and C are $5, $1, and $4, respectively, and that Palmer has an income of $37 to spend.

a. Complete the table at the right by computing the *marginal utility per dollar* for successive units of A, B, and C.

b. Palmer would not buy 4 units of A, 1 unit of B, and 4 units of C because _X_
_____

Good A			Good B			Good C		
Quantity	Utility	Marginal utility	Quantity	Utility	Marginal utility	Quantity	Utility	Marginal utility
1	21	21	1	7	7	1	23	23
2	41	20	2	13	6	2	40	13
3	59	18	3	18	5	3	52	12
4	74	15	4	22	4	4	60	8
5	85	9	5	25	3	5	65	5
6	91	6	6	27	2	6	68	3
7	91	0	7	28.2	1.2	7	70	2

c. Palmer would not buy 6 units of A, 7 units of B, and 4 units of C because _____

_____

d. When Palmer is maximizing his utility he will buy: (1) _____ 5 _____ units of A, (2) _____ 0 _____ units of B, (3) _____ 3 _____ units of C; his total utility will be _____

_____and the marginal utility of the last dollar spent on each good will be _____

_____

e. If Palmer's income increased by $1, he would spend it on good _____, assuming he can buy fractions of a unit of a good, because _____

cause _____

4. In the table at the top of page 190 are Thompson's marginal-utility schedules for goods A, B, C, and D and for saving.

a. Assume that the prices of A, B, C, and D are $3, $2, $4, and $5, respectively. Compute the marginal utility per dollar (MU/$) for the four goods and saving. (*Hint:* The price of saving $1 is $1.)

b. If Thompson's income is $69, to maximize his utility he will purchase: (1) _____ units of A, (2) _____ units of B, (3) _____ units of C, (4) _____ units of D, and save $_____. His total utility will be _____

c. Suppose that instead of good A being priced at $3, its price is one of those listed below. How much of good A will Thompson purchase at each of these prices, his income and the prices of other goods remaining constant? (*Hint:* It will be necessary for you to compute marginal utility per dollar spent on A at each of these four prices.) The different prices are: (1) $6: _____ units of A,

Good A		Good B		Good C	
Quantity	Marginal utility per dollar	Quantity	Marginal utility per dollar	Quantity	Marginal utility per dollar
1	_____	1	_____	1	_____
2	_____	2	_____	2	_____
3	_____	3	_____	3	_____
4	_____	4	_____	4	_____
5	_____	5	_____	5	_____
6	_____	6	_____	6	_____
7	_____	7	_____	7	_____

Unit of good or saving	Good A		Good B		Good C		Good D		Saving	
	MU	MU/$	MU	MU/$	MU	MU/$	MU	MU/$	MU	MU/$
1	45	_____	12	_____	40	_____	40	_____	6	_____
2	30	_____	11	_____	36	_____	34	_____	5	_____
3	20	_____	10	_____	32	_____	30	_____	4	_____
4	15	_____	9	_____	28	_____	27	_____	3	_____
5	12	_____	8	_____	24	_____	25	_____	2	_____
6	10	_____	7	_____	20	_____	23	_____	1	_____
7	9	_____	6	_____	16	_____	20	_____	½	_____
8	7½	_____	5	_____	12	_____	15	_____	¼	_____

(2) $4: _____ units of A, (3) $2:

_____ units of A, (4) $1.50: _____

units of A.

d. Put the information you have obtained concerning the amounts of A that Thompson would purchase at various prices in the table below. What is this relationship between price and quantity called? _____

_____

Price of A	Quantity of A demanded
$_____	_____
_____	_____
_____	_____
_____	_____
_____	_____

5. Assume that a consumer can purchase only two goods. These two goods are R (recreation) and M (material goods). The market price of R is $2 and the market price of M is $1. The consumer spends all her income in such a way that the marginal utility of the last unit of R she buys is 12 and the marginal utility of the last unit of M she buys is 6.

a. If we ignore the time it takes to consume R and M, is the consumer maximizing the total utility she obtains from the two goods?

_____

b. Suppose it takes 4 hours to consume each unit of R and 1 hour to consume each unit of M; and the consumer can earn $2 an hour when she works.

(1) The full price of a unit of R is $_____

(2) The full price of a unit of M is $_____

c. If we take into account the full price of each of the commodities, is the consumer maximizing her total utility? _____

How do you know this? _____

d. If the consumer is not maximizing her utility, should she increase her consumption

of R or of M? _____

Why should she do this? _____

e. Will she use more or less of her time for

consuming R? _____

■ SELF-TEST

Circle the T if the statement is true, the F if it is false.

1. An increase in the real income of a consumer will result from an increase in the price of a product which the consumer is buying.
T F

2. Utility and usefulness are not synonymous.
T F

3. All consumers are subject to the budget restraint. **T F**

4. When the consumer is maximizing his total utility, the marginal utilities of the last unit of every product he buys are identical. **T F**

5. Because utility cannot actually be measured, the marginal-utility theory cannot really explain how consumers will behave. **T F**

6. To find a consumer's demand for a product, the price of the product is varied while his tastes and income and the prices of other products remain unchanged. **T F**

7. A consumer can earn $10 an hour when he works. It takes 2 hours to consume a product. The value of the time required for the consumption of the product is $5. **T F**

Underscore the letter that corresponds to the best answer.

1. The reason the substitution effect works to encourage a consumer to buy more of a product when its price decreases is: (*a*) the real income of the consumer has been increased; (*b*) the real income of the consumer has been decreased; (*c*) the product is now relatively less expensive than it was; (*d*) other products are now relatively less expensive than they were.

2. Which of the following best expresses the law of diminishing marginal utility? (*a*) the more a person consumes of a product, the smaller becomes the utility which he receives from its consumption; (*b*) the more a person consumes of a product, the smaller becomes the utility which he receives as a result of consuming an additional unit of the product; (*c*) the less a person consumes of a product, the smaller becomes the utility which he receives from its consumption; (*d*) the less a person consumes of a product, the smaller becomes the utility which he receives as a result of consuming an additional unit of the product.

3. Which of the following is *not* an essential assumption of the marginal-utility theory of consumer behavior? (*a*) the consumer has a small income; (*b*) the consumer is rational; (*c*) goods and services are not free; (*d*) goods and services yield decreasing amounts of marginal utility as the consumer buys more of them.

4. Assume a consumer has the marginal utility schedules for goods X and Y given in the next column, that the prices of X and Y are $1 and $2, respectively, and that the income of the consumer is $9. When the consumer is maximizing the total utility he receives, he will buy (*a*) 7X and 1Y; (*b*) 5X and 2Y; (*c*) 3X and 3Y; (*d*) 1X and 4Y.

5. When the consumer in multiple-choice question 4 above purchases the combination of X and Y that maximizes his total utility, his utility is (*a*) 36; (*b*) 45; (*c*) 48; (*d*) 52.

Good X		Good Y	
Quantity	MU	Quantity	MU
1	8	1	10
2	7	2	8
3	6	3	6
4	5	4	4
5	4	5	3
6	3	6	2
7	2	7	1

6. Suppose that the prices of A and B are $3 and $2, respectively, that the consumer is spending his entire income and buying 4 units of A and 6 units of B, and that the marginal utility of both the 4th unit of A and the 6th unit of B is 6. It can be concluded that: (*a*) the consumer is in equilibrium; (*b*) the consumer should buy more of A and less of B; (*c*) the consumer should buy less of A and more of B; (*d*) the consumer should buy less of both A and B.

7. The full price of a product to a consumer is (*a*) its market price; (*b*) its market price plus the value of its consumption time; (*c*) its market price less the value of its consumption time; (*d*) the value of its consumption time less its market price.

■ **DISCUSSION QUESTIONS**

1. Explain, employing the income-effect and substitution-effect concepts, the reasons consumers buy more of a product at a lower price than at a higher price, and vice versa.

2. Why is utility a "subjective concept"? How does the subjective nature of rationality limit the practical usefulness of the marginal-utility theory of consumer behavior?

3. What essential assumptions are made about consumers and the nature of goods and services in developing the marginal-utility theory of consumer behavior? What is meant by "budget restraint"?

4. When is the consumer in equilibrium and maximizing his total utility? Explain why any deviation from this equilibrium will decrease the consumer's total utility.

5. Using the marginal-utility theory of consumer behavior, explain how an individual's demand schedule for a particular consumer good can be obtained. Why does a demand schedule obtained in this fashion almost invariably result in an inverse or negative relationship between price and quantity demanded?

6. Explain how a consumer might determine the value of his or her time. How does the value of time affect the full price the consumer pays for a good or service?

7. What does the Becker approach to consumer behavior explain that the traditional approach does not explain?

The Costs of Production

In previous chapters the factors which influence the demand for a product purchased by consumers were examined in some detail. Chapter 25 turns to the other side of the market and begins the investigation of the forces which determine the amount of a particular product a business firm will produce and the price it will charge for that product. In addition to the demand for the product, the factors that determine the output of a firm and the price of the product are the costs of producing the product *and* the structure of the market in which the product is sold. Market structures were examined in Chapter 22; and in the next four chapters you will find an explanation of how costs and demand determine price and output in the four different kinds of product markets.

Chapter 25 is an examination of the way in which the costs of the firm change as the output of the firm changes. This chapter is extremely important if the chapters which follow it are to be understood. For this reason it is necessary for you to master the material dealing with the costs of the firm.

You will probably find that you have some difficulty with the new terms and concepts. Particular attention, therefore, should be given to them. These new terms and concepts, which are listed below, are used in the explanation of the costs of the firm and will be used over and over again in later chapters. If you will try to learn them in the order in which you encounter them you will have little difficulty because the later terms build on the earlier ones.

After the new terms and concepts are well fixed in your mind, understanding the generalizations made about the relationships between cost and output will be much simpler. Here the important things to note are (1) that the statements made about the behavior of costs are *generalizations* (they do not apply to any particular firm or enterprise, but are more or less applicable to every business firm); and (2) that the generalizations made about the relationships between particular types of cost and the output of the firm are fairly precise generalizations. When attempting to learn these generalizations, you will find it worthwhile to draw rough graphs (with cost on the vertical and output on the horizontal axis) which describe the cost relationships. Try it especially with the following types of costs. *Short-run* fixed, variable, total, average fixed, average variable, average total, and marginal costs; and *long-term* average cost.

One last cue: In addition to learning *how* the costs of the firm vary as its output varies, be sure to understand *why* the costs vary the way they do. In this connection note that the behavior of short-run costs is the result of the law of diminishing returns and that the behavior of long-run costs is the consequence of economies and diseconomies of scale.

▪ CHECKLIST

The very least you should be able to do when you have finished this chapter is:

□ Define economic cost and distinguish between an explicit and an implicit cost.

□ Explain the difference between normal profit and economic profit and why the former is a cost and the latter is not a cost.

□ State the law of diminishing returns and explain its effect on short-run costs.

□ Explain the difference between a fixed cost and a variable cost; and between average cost and marginal cost.

□ Compute and graph average fixed cost, average variable cost, average total cost, and marginal cost when you are given total cost data.

□ Explain the difference between the short run and the long run; and between short-run costs and long-run costs.

□ State why the long-run average cost curve is expected to be U-shaped; and list the causes of the economies and the diseconomies of scale.

□ Indicate the relationship between the economies and diseconomies of scale and the size and number of firms in an industry.

▪ CHAPTER OUTLINE

1. Because resources are scarce and may be employed to produce many different products, the economic cost of using resources to produce any one of these products is the amount of other products that cannot be produced.

a. In money terms, the costs of employing resources to produce a product are the payments a firm must make to the owners of resources to attract these resources away from their best alternative opportunities for earning incomes; and these costs may be either explicit or implicit.

b. Normal profit is an implicit cost for a firm.

c. Economic or pure profit is any revenue a firm receives in excess of all its economic (explicit plus implicit) costs.

d. The firm's economic costs vary as the firm's output varies; and the way in which costs vary with output depends upon whether the firm is able to make short-run or long-run changes in the amounts of resources it employs.

2. In the short run the firm cannot change the size of its plant and can vary its output only by changing the quantities of the variable resources it employs.

a. The law of diminishing returns is the most important factor influencing the manner in which the costs of the firm change as it changes its output in the short run.

b. The total short-run costs of a firm are partly fixed and partly variable costs; the former are costs which do not change and the latter are costs which do change as the firm's output changes.

c. Average fixed, variable, and total cost are equal, respectively, to the firm's fixed, variable, and total costs divided by the output of the firm.

d. Marginal cost is the extra cost incurred in producing one additional unit of output.

3. In the long run all the resources employed by the firm are variable resources, and all its costs, therefore, are variable costs.

a. As the firm expands its output by increasing the size of its plant, average cost tends to fall at first because of the economies of large-scale production; but as this expansion continues, sooner or later, average cost begins to rise because of the diseconomies of large-scale production.

b. The economies and diseconomies encountered in the production of different goods are important factors influencing the size of firms and the number of firms actually found in various industries.

▪ IMPORTANT TERMS

Economic cost	Short run
Alternative (opportunity) cost doctrine	Long run
Explicit cost	Law of diminishing returns
Implicit cost	
Normal profit	Fixed resource
Economic (pure) profit	Variable resource
	Fixed cost

Variable cost

Total cost

Average fixed cost

Average variable cost

Average (total) cost

Marginal cost

Economies of (large) scale

Diseconomies of (large) scale

■ FILL-IN QUESTIONS

1. The cost of producing a particular product is the quantity of _other products_ that cannot be produced. This way of looking at costs is called the _Opportunity_ of the _Alternative_ cost doctrine.

2. The money cost of producing a product is the amount of money the firm must pay to resource owners to _attract the resources_ from alternative employments. These costs may be either _Explicit_ or _Implicit_ costs.

3. Normal profit is an _Implicit_ cost because it is the payment the firm must make to obtain _Eterprenierial_; but economic profit is the amount by which a firm's total receipts exceed its _Total_ costs, the sum of its _Explicit_ and _Implicit_ costs.

4. In the short run the firm can change its output by changing the _resources_ it employs, but it cannot change _plant capacity_

5. In the long run firms can _enter_ or _leave_ Mumber of firm in an industry, but in the short run the number of firms in an industry is _constant_

6. The law of diminishing returns states that as successive units of a _Variable resource_ are added to a _fixed resourse_, beyond some point the _Marginal Product_ attributable to each additional unit of the _variable resouse_ will _decline_

7. The short-run costs of a firm are either _Fixed_ costs or _Variable_ costs, but in the long run all costs are _Variable_ costs.

8. In the short run, total variable costs at first _increase_ by _decreasing amounts_ amounts, but after some level of output is reached, they _increase_ by _increasing_ amounts.

9. On the graph below sketch the manner in which fixed cost, variable cost, and total cost vary with the output the firm produces in the short run.

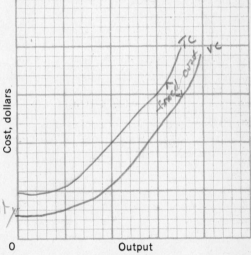

10. The law of diminishing returns causes a firm's _A. Total Cost_ cost, _A VC cost_ cost, and _Marginal_ cost to decrease at first and then to increase as the output of the firm increases. On the next graph sketch these three cost curves in such a way that their proper relationship to each other is shown.

11. Marginal cost is the increase in either _Total_ _Variable_

cost or ___Total Cost_ve___
which occurs when the firm increases its output by one unit.

12. If marginal cost is less than average variable cost, average variable cost will be ___ _decreaseing_ ___,
but if average variable cost is less than marginal cost, average variable cost will be ___ _increaseing_ ___

13. The long-run average cost of producing a product is equal to the lowest of the short-run costs of producing that product after the firm has ___ _expanded_ ___.
Below are the short-run average-cost curves of producing a product with three different sizes of plants, plant 1, plant 2, and plant 3. Draw the firm's long-run average-cost curve.

14. List below four important types of economy of large scale:
a. ___ _Labor Specialization_ ___
b. ___ _Managerial Spe_ ___

c. ___ _Efficient Cap_ ___
d. ___ _By Products_ ___

15. The factor which gives rise to diseconomies of large scale is ___ _Managerial problems_ ___

■ **PROBLEMS AND PROJECTS**

1. Below is a production-possibilities table for an economy. Employing the doctrine of alternative or opportunity cost:

Good X	0	1	2	3	4	5	6	7	8	9	10
Good Y	55	54	52	49	45	40	34	27	19	10	0

a. What is the *total* cost of producing 5 units of X? _____

b. If 2 units of good X are produced, what is the *average* cost of a unit of X? _____

c. Were the economy to increase its output of good X from 6 to 7 units, the *marginal* cost of the additional unit of X would be

_____

2. Assume that a firm has a plant of fixed size and that it can vary its output only by varying the amount of labor it employs. The table at the top of page 197 shows the relationship between the amount of labor employed and the output of the firm.

a. Compute the ten marginal products of labor and enter these figures in the table.

b. Assume each unit of labor costs the firm $10. Compute the total cost of labor for each quantity of labor the firm might employ, and enter these figures in the table.

c. Now determine the marginal cost of the firm's product as the firm increases its output. Divide the *increase* in total labor cost by the *increase in total output* to find the marginal cost. Enter these figures in the table.

d. When the marginal product of labor:

(1) Increases, the marginal cost of the firm's product _____

(2) Decreases, the marginal cost of the firm's product _____

3. In the table at the right you will find a schedule of a firm's fixed cost and variable cost.

a. Complete the table by computing total

Quantity of labor employed	Total output	Marginal product of labor	Total cost of labor	Marginal cost of product
0	0		$_____	
1	5	_____	_____	$_____
2	11	_____	_____	_____
3	18	_____	_____	_____
4	24	_____	_____	_____
5	29	_____	_____	_____
6	33	_____	_____	_____
7	36	_____	_____	_____
8	38	_____	_____	_____
9	39	_____	_____	_____
10	39½	_____	_____	_____

cost, average fixed cost, average variable cost, average total cost, and marginal cost.

b. On the small graph on page 198, plot and label fixed cost, variable cost, and total cost.

c. On the large graph on page 198, plot average fixed cost, average variable cost, average total cost, and marginal cost; label the four curves.

4. To the right are the short-run average-total-cost schedules for three plants of different size which a firm might build to produce its product. Assume that these are the only possible sizes of plants which the firm might build.

Plant size A		Plant size B		Plant size C	
Output	ATC	Output	ATC	Output	ATC
10	$ 7	10	$17	10	$53
20	6	20	13	20	44
30	5	30	9	30	35
40	4	40	6	40	27
50	5	50	4	50	20
60	7	60	3	60	14
70	10	70	4	70	11
80	14	80	5	80	8
90	19	90	7	90	6
100	25	100	10	100	5
110	32	110	16	110	7
120	40	120	25	120	10

Output	Fixed cost	Variable cost	Total cost	Average fixed cost	Average variable cost	Average total cost	Marginal cost
$ 0	$200	$ 0	$_____				
1	200	50	_____	$_____	$_____	$_____	$_____
2	200	90	_____	_____	_____	_____	_____
3	200	120	_____	_____	_____	_____	_____
4	200	160	_____	_____	_____	_____	_____
5	200	220	_____	_____	_____	_____	_____
6	200	300	_____	_____	_____	_____	_____
7	200	400	_____	_____	_____	_____	_____
8	200	520	_____	_____	_____	_____	_____
9	200	670	_____	_____	_____	_____	_____
10	200	900	_____	_____	_____	_____	_____

a. Complete the *long-run* average-cost schedule for the firm below.

Output	Average cost
10	$_____
20	_____
30	_____
40	_____
50	_____
60	_____
70	_____
80	_____
90	_____
100	_____
110	_____
120	_____

b. For outputs between:

(1) _____ and _____, the firm should build plant A.

(2) _____ and _____, the firm should build plant B.

(3) _____ and _____, the firm should build plant C.

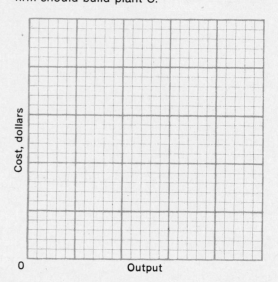

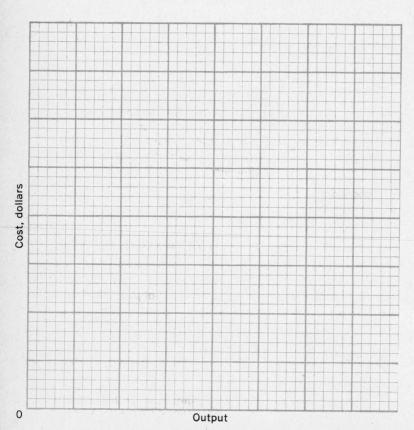

■ **SELF-TEST**

Circle the T if the statement is true, the F if it is false.

1. Economic or pure profit is an explicit cost, while normal profit is an implicit cost.   **T   F**

2. The economic costs of a firm are the payments it must make to resource owners to attract their resources from alternative employments.   **T   F**

3. In the short run, firms are unable to enter an industry or to leave it.   **T   F**

4. The law of diminishing returns states that as successive amounts of a variable resource are added to a fixed resource, beyond some point total output will diminish.   **T   F**

5. The larger the output of a firm, the smaller is the fixed cost of the firm.   **T   F**

6. If the fixed costs of a firm should increase while its variable costs remain unchanged, marginal cost will also remain unchanged.   **T   F**

7. Marginal cost is equal to average variable cost at the output at which average variable cost is a minimum.   **T   F**

8. When the marginal product of a variable resource increases, the marginal cost of producing the product will decrease; and when marginal product decreases, marginal cost will increase.   **T   F**

9. One of the explanations of why the long-run average-cost curve of a firm rises after some level of output has been reached is the law of diminishing returns.   **T   F**

10. A firm can avoid the diseconomies of large scale by becoming a multiplant firm.   **T   F**

Underscore the letter that corresponds to the best answer.

1. In the following production-possibilities table the *average* cost of 5 units of good B is: (*a*) 4 units of A; (*b*) 5 units of A; (*c*) 7 units of A; (*d*) 9 units of A.

Good A	0	11	21	30	38	45	51	56	60	63	65
Good B	10	9	8	7	6	5	4	3	2	1	0

2. Using the same production-possibilities data given in question 1, the *marginal* cost of

the second unit of B is: (*a*) 2 units of A; (*b*) 3 units of A; (*c*) 4 units of A; (*d*) 5 units of A.

3. Which of the following is most likely to be a long-run adjustment for a firm which manufactures jet fighter planes on an assembly-line basis? (*a*) an increase in the amount of steel the firm buys; (*b*) a reduction in the number of "shifts" of workers from three to two; (*c*) a changeover from the production of one type of jet fighter to the production of a later-model jet fighter; (*d*) a changeover from the production of jet fighters to the production of sports cars.

4. Assume that the only variable resource is labor and that as the amount of labor employed by a firm increases, the output of the firm increases in the way shown in the table. The marginal product of the fourth unit of labor is: (*a*) 3 units of output; (*b*) 3¾ units of output; (*c*) 4 units of output; (*d*) 15 units of output.

Amount of labor	Amount of output
1	3
2	8
3	12
4	15
5	17
6	18

5. Because the marginal product of a resource at first increases and then decreases as the output of the firm increases: (*a*) average fixed cost declines as the output of the firm increases; (*b*) average variable cost at first increases and then decreases; (*c*) variable cost at first increases by increasing amounts and then increases by decreasing amounts; (*d*) total cost at first increases by decreasing amounts and then increases by increasing amounts.

For questions 6 and 7 use the data given in the table at the top of page 200. The fixed cost of the firm is $500 and the firm's variable cost is indicated in the table.

6. The average total cost of the firm when 4 units of output are being produced is: (*a*) $175; (*b*) $200; (*c*) $300; (*d*) $700.

7. The marginal cost of the sixth unit of output is: (*a*) $200; (*b*) $300; (*c*) $700; (*d*) $800.

Output	Variable cost
1	$ 200
2	360
3	500
4	700
5	1,000
6	1,800

8. In the table below three short-run cost schedules are given for three plants of different sizes which a firm might build in the long run. What is the *long-run* average cost of producing 40 units of output? (a) $7; (b) $8; (c) $9; (d) $10.

Plant 1		Plant 2		Plant 3	
Output	ATC	Output	ATC	Output	ATC
10	$10	10	$15	10	$20
20	9	20	10	20	15
30	8	30	7	30	10
40	9	40	10	40	8
50	10	50	14	50	9

9. Using the data given for question 8, at what output is long-run average cost a minimum? (a) 20; (b) 30; (c) 40; (d) 50.

10. Which of the following is *not* a factor which results in economies of scale? (a) more efficient utilization of the firm's plant; (b) more efficient utilization of the firm's by-products; (c) greater specialization and division of labor in the management of the firm; (d) utilization of more efficient equipment.

■ **DISCUSSION QUESTIONS**

1. Explain the difference between the opportunity and the money cost of producing a product and the difference between an explicit and an implicit cost. How would you determine the implicit money cost of a resource?

2. What is the difference between normal and economic profit? Why is the former an economic cost?

3. What type of adjustments can a firm make in the long run that it cannot make in the short run? What adjustments can it make in the short run? How long is the short run?

4. Why is the distinction between the short run and the long run important?

5. State precisely the law of diminishing returns. Exactly what is it that diminishes, and why does it diminish?

6. Distinguish between a fixed cost and a variable cost. Why are short-run total costs partly fixed and partly variable costs, and why are long-run costs entirely variable?

7. Why do short-run variable costs increase at first by decreasing amounts and later increase by increasing amounts? How does the behavior of short-run variable costs influence the behavior of short-run total costs?

8. Describe the way in which short-run average fixed cost, average variable cost, average total cost, and marginal cost vary as the output of the firm increases.

9. Why is marginal cost "a very strategic concept"? What is the connection between marginal product and marginal cost? How will marginal cost behave as marginal product decreases and increases?

10. What is the precise relationship between marginal cost and minimum average variable cost and between marginal cost and minimum average total cost? Why are these relationships necessarily true?

11. What does the long-run average-cost curve of a firm show? What relationship is there between long-run average cost and the short-run average total-cost schedules of the different-sized plants which a firm might build?

12. Why is the long-run average-cost curve of a firm U-shaped?

13. What is meant by an economy of large scale? What are some of the more important types of such an economy?

14. What is meant by and what causes diseconomies of large scale?

15. Why are the economies and diseconomies of scale of great significance, and how do they influence the size of firms in an industry and the number of firms in an industry?

Price and Output Determination: Pure Competition

Chapter 26 is the first of four chapters which bring together the demand for a product and the study of production costs found in Chapter 25. Each of the four chapters combines demand and production costs in a *different* market structure; and analyzes and draws conclusions for that particular kind of product market. The questions which are analyzed and for which *both short-run and long-run* answers are sought are the following. Given the costs of the firm, what output will it produce; what will be the market price of the good; what will be the output of the entire industry; what will be the profit received by the firm; and what relationships will exist between price, average total cost, and marginal cost.

In addition to finding the answers to these questions you should learn *why* the questions are answered the way they are in each of the market models and in what way the answers obtained in one model *differ* from those obtained in the other models.

Actually, the answers are obtained by applying logic to different sets of assumptions. It is important, therefore, to note specifically how the assumptions made in one model differ from those of other models. Each model assumes that every firm is guided in making its decisions solely by the desire to maximize

its profits, and that the costs of the firm are not materially affected by the type of market in which it *sells* its output. The important differences in the models which account for the differing answers involve (1) the characteristics of the market, such as the number of sellers, the ease of entry into and exodus from the industry, and the kind of product (standardized or differentiated) being produced; and (2) the way in which the *individual firm* sees the demand for *its* output.

Chapter 26 begins by noting that there are several good reasons for studying pure competition, not the least of which is that in the long run, pure competition—subject to certain exceptions—results in an ideal or perfect allocation of resources. After obtaining the answers to the questions listed in the first paragraph above, the author returns at the end of the chapter to explain in what sense competitive resource allocation is ideal and in what cases it may be less than ideal. In Chapters 27 and 28, which concern monopoly and monopolistic competition, respectively, it will be found that in these market situations resource allocation is less than ideal. You, therefore, should pay special attention in Chapter 26 to what is meant by an ideal allocation of resources and why perfect competition results in this perfect allocation.

■ CHECKLIST

The very least you should be able to do when you have finished this chapter is:

□ List the conditions which must be fulfilled if an industry is to be purely competitive.

□ Use both the total revenue-total cost and the marginal revenue-marginal cost approaches to determine the output the purely competitive firm will produce in the short run; and explain *why* the firm will produce this output.

□ Explain how to find the firm's short-run supply curve; and construct its short-run supply schedule when you are given its short-run cost schedules.

□ Explain how to find the industry's short-run supply curve (or schedule).

□ Determine the price at which the product will sell, the output of the industry, and the output of the individual firm in the short run.

□ Determine the price that will be charged and the output of the individual firm and of the industry when the industry is in long-run equilibrium; and explain how the entry and exit of firms assure this result.

□ Define a constant-cost and an increasing-cost industry; and explain how to obtain the long-run industry supply curve in both of these industries.

□ Explain the significance of $P = AC = MC$ in a purely competitive industry when it is in long-run equilibrium.

□ Identify the several possible shortcomings of a purely competitive price system.

■ CHAPTER OUTLINE

1. Pure competition is a situation in which a large number of independent firms, no one of which is able by itself to influence market price, sell a standardized product in a market which firms are free to enter and to leave in the long run. Although pure competition is rare in practice, there are at least three good reasons for studying this "laboratory case."

2. There are two complementary approaches to the analysis of the output that the purely competitive firm will produce in the short run.

a. Employing the total-revenue–total-cost approach, the firm will produce the output at which total profit is the greatest or total loss is the least, provided that the loss is less than the firm's fixed costs (that is, provided that total revenue is greater than total variable cost). If the firm's loss is greater than its fixed cost, it will lessen its loss by producing no output.

b. Employing the marginal-revenue–marginal-cost approach, the firm will produce the output at which marginal revenue (or price) and marginal cost are equal, provided price is greater than average variable cost. If price is less than average variable cost, the firm will shut down to minimize its loss. The short-run supply curve of the individual firm is that part of its short-run marginal-cost curve which is above average variable cost.

c. Table 26-6 in the text summarizes the principles which the competitive firm follows when it decides what output to produce in the short run.

d. The short-run supply curve of the industry (which is the sum of the supply curves of the individual firms) and the total demand for the product determine the short-run equilibrium price and equilibrium output of the industry; and the firms in the industry may be either prosperous or unprosperous in the short run.

3. In the long run the price of a product produced under conditions of pure competition will equal the minimum average total cost, and firms in the industry will neither receive profits nor suffer losses.

a. If profits are being received in the industry during the short run, firms will enter the industry in the long run (attracted by the profits), increase total supply, and thereby force price down to the minimum average total cost.

b. If losses are being suffered in the industry during the short run, firms will leave the industry in the long run (seeking to avoid losses), reduce total supply, and thereby force price up to the minimum average total cost.

c. If an industry is a constant-cost industry, the entry of new firms will not affect the average-total-cost schedule or curve of firms in the industry. Hence an increase in demand will result in no increase in the long-run equilibrium price, and the industry will be able to supply any quantity of output at a constant price.

d. If an industry is an increasing-cost industry, the entry of new firms will raise the average-total-cost schedule or curve of firms in the industry. Hence an increase in demand will result in an increase in the long-run equilibrium price, and the industry will supply larger quantities only at higher prices.

4. In the long run, each purely competitive firm is compelled by competition to produce that output at which price (or marginal revenue), average total cost, and marginal cost are equal and average total cost is a minimum.

a. An economy in which all industries were purely competitive would tend to result in the most efficient allocation of resources.

(1) Goods are most efficiently produced when the average total cost of producing them is a minimum; and buyers benefit most from this efficiency when they are charged a price just equal to minimum average total cost.

(2) Goods are produced in such quantities that the total satisfaction obtained from the economy's resources is a maximum when the price of every good is equal to its marginal cost.

b. Even in a purely competitive economy, the allocation of resources may not, for at least four reasons, be the most efficient.

■ **IMPORTANT TERMS**

Total-receipts–total-cost approach

Marginal-revenue–marginal-cost approach

The profit-maximizing case

Break-even point

The loss-minimizing case

The close-down case

MR = MC rule

P = MC rule

The firm's short-run supply curve (schedule)

The competitive industry's short-run supply curve (schedule)

Short-run competitive equilibrium

Long-run competitive equilibrium

Constant-cost industry

Increasing-cost industry

Long-run supply

Efficient allocation of resources

■ **FILL-IN QUESTIONS**

1. What are the four specific conditions which characterize pure competition?

a. ___*No Product differentiation*___

b. ___*Universal knowledge*___

c. ___*No control over price*___

d. ___*Many businesses*___

2. Economic profit is equal to ___*TR−TC*___

3. The two approaches which may be used to determine the most profitable output for any firm are the ___*TR−TC*___ approach and the ___*MR = MC*___ approach.

4. A firm should produce in the short run if ___*a Profit is realized*___ ; it should produce the output at which ___*profit is maximized + losses are minimized*___ or, said another way, the output at which ___*MR=MC*___

5. A firm is willing to produce at a loss in the short run if the price which it receives is greater than ___*average variable cost*___

6. In the short run the individual firm's supply curve is ___*fully elastic MC curve that is greater that AVC*___ ; the short-run market supply curve is ___*sum of all*___

7. The short-run equilibrium price for a product produced by a purely competitive industry is the price at which ___*MC = A*___ and _____ are equal; the equilibrium quantity is _____

8. In the short run in a purely competitive industry, the number of firms in the industry and the sizes of their plants are _____, while in the long run they are _____

9. When a purely competitive industry is in long-run equilibrium the price (average revenue) which the firm is paid for its product is equal not only to marginal revenue but to ___*long run avg cost*___

and to _long run Marginal cost_;
and long-run average cost is a _minimum_

10. Firms tend to enter an industry in the long run if _the industry is profitable_ and leave it if _it is not._

11. If the entry of new firms into an industry tends to raise the costs of all firms in the industry, the industry is said to be a(n) _____ _increasing cost_ industry.

12. An industry is apt to be a constant-cost industry if _____

or if _____

13. If resources are efficiently allocated in an economy, _____ is a maximum; this occurs in a purely competitive economy, it is contended, because the goods which the economy produces are those which _____, and these goods are produced in _____ way.

14. The most efficient method of production, it is argued, means that:

a. _modern_ technology is used.

b. _price_ and _cost_ are equal.

c. the only costs involved are those which _are needed in production_

d. each firm produces that output at which its average total cost is a _minimum_

15. The "right" goods (the goods consumers

want most) are produced in an economy if the _MC_ and the _price_ of each good are equal.

16. List four reasons why resource allocation in a purely competitive economy may be less than efficient.

a. _____

b. _____

c. _____

d. _____

■ **PROBLEMS AND PROJECTS**

1. Assume that a purely competitive firm has the schedule of costs given in the table below.
  a. Complete the first table (on page 205) showing the total revenue and total profit of the firm at each level of output the firm might produce, assuming market prices of $55, $120, and $200.
  b. Indicate what output the firm would produce and what its profits would be at a:

(1) Price of $55: output of _____

and profit of _____

(2) Price of $120: output of _____

and profit of _____

(3) Price of $200: output of _____

and profit of _____
  c. Complete the supply schedule of a firm in the next table and indicate what the profit of the firm will be at each price.

Output	TFC	TVC	TC	AFC	AVC	ATC	MC
0	$300	$ 0	$ 300				
1	300	100	400	$300	$100	$400	$100
2	300	150	450	150	75	225	50
3	300	210	510	100	70	170	60
4	300	290	590	75	73	148	80
5	300	400	700	60	80	140	110
6	300	540	840	50	90	140	140
7	300	720	1,020	43	103	146	180
8	300	950	1,250	38	119	156	230
9	300	1,240	1,540	33	138	171	290
10	300	1,600	1,900	30	160	190	360

Output	Market price = $55		Market price = $120		Market price = $200	
	Revenue	Profit	Revenue	Profit	Revenue	Profit
0	$_____	$_____	$_____	$_____	$_____	$_____
1	_____	_____	_____	_____	_____	_____
2	_____	_____	_____	_____	_____	_____
3	_____	_____	_____	_____	_____	_____
4	_____	_____	_____	_____	_____	_____
5	_____	_____	_____	_____	_____	_____
6	_____	_____	_____	_____	_____	_____
7	_____	_____	_____	_____	_____	_____
8	_____	_____	_____	_____	_____	_____
9	_____	_____	_____	_____	_____	_____
10	_____	_____	_____	_____	_____	_____

Price	Quantity supplied	Profit
$360	_____	$_____
290	_____	_____
230	_____	_____
180	_____	_____
140	_____	_____
110	_____	_____
80	_____	_____
60	_____	_____

d. If there are 100 firms in the industry and all have the same cost schedule:

(1) Complete the market supply schedule in the table below.

Quantity demanded	Price	Quantity supplied
400	$360	_____
500	290	_____
600	230	_____
700	180	_____
800	140	_____
900	110	_____
1,000	80	_____

(2) Using the demand schedule given in (1): (*a*) what will the market price of the product be? $_____ ; (*b*) what quantity will the individual firm produce? _____ ; (*c*) how large will the firm's profit be? $_____; (*d*) will firms tend to enter or leave the industry in the long run? _____Why?

_____

2. If the total costs assumed for the individual firm in problem 1 were long-run total costs and if the industry were a constant-cost industry:

a. What would be the market price of the product in the long run? $_____

b. What output would each firm produce when the industry is in long-run equilibrium?

_____

c. Approximately how many firms will there be in the industry in the long run, given the present demand for the product? _____

d. If the following were the market demand schedule for the product, how many firms would there be in the long run in the industry?

Price	Quantity demanded
$360	500
290	600
230	700
180	800
140	900
110	1,000
80	1,100

e. On the graph below draw the long-run supply curve of
(1) a constant-cost industry
(2) an increasing-cost industry

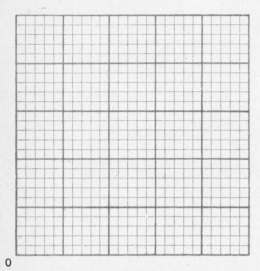

0

■ **SELF-TEST**

Circle the T if the statement is true, the F if it is false.

1. One of the reasons for studying the pure competition model is that many industries are almost purely competitive.　　　　**T　F**

2. A firm will produce in the short run the output at which marginal cost and marginal revenue are equal provided that the price of the product is greater than its average variable cost of production.　　　**T　F**

3. If a firm is producing an output less than its profit-maximizing output, marginal revenue is greater than marginal cost at that output.　　　　　　　　　　　**T　F**

4. The short-run supply curve tends to slope upward from left to right because of the law of diminishing returns.　　　　　**T　F**

5. A firm wishing to maximize its profits will always produce that output at which marginal costs and marginal revenue are equal.　**T　F**

6. Because the individual purely competitive form is unable to influence the market price of the product it produces, the market price will change only if the demand for the product changes.　　　　　　　　　　　**T　F**

7. When firms in an industry are earning profits which are less than normal, the supply of the product will tend to decrease in the long run.　　　　　　　　　　　**T　F**

8. Given the short-run costs of firms in a purely competitive industry, the profits of these firms depend solely upon the level of the total demand for the product.　　**T　F**

9. Pure competition, if it could be achieved in all industries in the economy, would result in the most efficient allocation of resources.　　　　　　　　　　　　　　**T　F**

10. Under conditions of pure competition firms are forced to employ the most efficient production methods available to them if they are to earn no more than normal profits.　　　　　　　　　　　　　**T　F**

11. The marginal costs of a firm in producing a product are society's measure of the marginal worth of alternative products.　**T　F**

12. There is no scientific basis for determining which distribution of total money income results in the greatest satisfaction of wants in the economy.　　　　　　　　**T　F**

Underscore the letter that corresponds to the best answer.

1. In a purely competitive industry: (*a*) each of the firms will engage in various forms of nonprice competition; (*b*) new firms find no obstacles to entering the industry in the short run; (*c*) the individual firms do not have a "price policy"; (*d*) each of the firms produces a differentiated (nonstandardized) product.

2. A firm will be willing to produce at a loss in the short run if: (*a*) the loss is no greater than its total fixed costs; (*b*) the loss is no greater than its average fixed costs; (*c*) the loss is no greater than its total variable costs; (*d*) the loss is no greater than its average variable cost.

3. The MC = *P* rule *cannot* be used to determine the most profitable output of a firm: (*a*) when price and marginal revenue are equal; (*b*) in purely competitive industries; (*c*) when demand is perfectly elastic; (*d*) when average revenue is greater than marginal revenue.

4. The individual firm's short-run supply curve is that part of its marginal-cost curve lying above its: (*a*) average-total-cost curve;

(b) average-variable-cost curve; (c) average-fixed-cost curve; (d) average-revenue curve.

5. If a single purely competitive firm's most profitable output in the short run were an output at which it was neither receiving a profit nor suffering a loss, one of the following would *not* be true. Which one? (a) marginal cost and average total cost are equal; (b) marginal cost and average variable cost are equal; (c) marginal cost and marginal revenue are equal; (d) marginal cost and average revenue are equal.

6. Which one of the following statements is true of a purely competitive industry in short-run equilibrium? (a) price is equal to average total cost; (b) total quantity demanded is equal to total quantity supplied; (c) profits in the industry are equal to zero; (d) output is equal to the output at which average total cost is a minimum.

7. When a purely competitive industry is in long-run equilibrium, one of the following statements is *not* true. Which one? (a) firms in the industry are earning normal profits; (b) price and long-run average total cost are equal to each other; (c) long-run marginal cost is at its minimum level; (d) long-run marginal cost is equal to marginal revenue.

8. Increasing-cost industries find that their costs rise as a consequence of an increased demand for the product because of: (a) the diseconomies of scale; (b) diminishing returns; (c) higher resource prices; (d) a decreased supply of the product.

9. Which one of the following is *most likely* to be a constant-cost industry? (a) agricultural and extractive industries; (b) an industry in the early stages of its development; (c) an industry which employs a significant portion of the total supply of some resource; (d) the steel and oil industries.

10. It is contended that which of the following triple identities results in an ideal allocation of resources? (a) $P = AC = MC$; (b) $P = AR = MR$; (c) $P = MR = MC$; (d) $AC = MC = MR$.

11. An economy is producing the goods most wanted by society when, for each and every good, their: (a) price and average cost are equal; (b) price and marginal cost are equal; (c) marginal revenue and marginal cost are equal; (d) price and marginal revenue are equal.

12. The operation of a competitive price system accurately measures (a) both spillover costs and spillover benefits; (b) spillover costs but not spillover benefits; (c) spillover benefits but not spillover costs; (d) neither spillover costs nor spillover benefits.

■ **DISCUSSION QUESTIONS**

1. Explain exactly what the economist means by pure competition.

2. If pure competition is so rare in practice, why are students of economics asked to study it?

3. Why is a firm willing to produce at a loss in the short run if the loss is no greater than the fixed costs of the firm?

4. Explain how the short-run supply of an individual firm and of the purely competitive industry are determined.

5. What determines the equilibrium price and quantity of a purely competitive industry in the short run? Will economic profits in the industry be positive or negative?

6. Why do the MC = MR rule and the MC = P rule mean the same thing under conditions of pure competition?

7. What are the important distinctions between the short run and the long run and between equilibrium in the short run and in the long run in a competitive industry?

8. When is the purely competitive industry in long-run equilibrium? What forces the purely competitive firm into this position?

9. What is a constant-cost industry? What is an increasing-cost industry? Under what economic conditions is each likely to be found? What will be the nature of the long-run supply curve in each of these industries?

10. What is meant by an ideal or the most efficient allocation of resources? Why is it said that a purely competitive economy results in this type of allocation?

11. What did Adam Smith mean when he said that self-interest and competition bring about results which are in the best interest of the economy as a whole without government regulation or interference?

12. Even if an economy is purely competitive, the allocation of resources may not be ideal. Why?

13. Does pure competition *always* promote both the use of the most efficient technological methods of production and the development of better methods?

Price and Output Determination: Pure Monopoly

Chapter 27 is the second of the four chapters which deal with specific market models and is concerned with what economists call pure monopoly. Like pure competition, pure monopoly is rarely found in the American economy. But there are industries which are very close to being pure monopolies, and an understanding of pure monopoly is helpful in understanding the more realistic situation of oligopoly.

It is only possible for pure monopoly, approximations of pure monopoly, and oligopoly to exist if firms are prevented in some way from entering an industry in the long run. Anything which tends to prevent entry is referred to as a "barrier to entry." The first part of Chapter 27 is devoted to a description of the more important types of barriers to entry. Remember that barriers to entry not only make it possible for monopoly to exist in the economy but also explain why so many markets are oligopolies (which you will study in Chapter 29).

Like the preceding chapter, this chapter tries to answer certain questions about the firm. These are: what output will the firm produce; what price will it charge; what will be the profit received by the firm; and what will be the relationships between price, average cost, and marginal cost? In answering these questions for the monopoly firm and in comparing pure competition and pure monopoly note the following:

1. Both the competitive and monopoly firm try to maximize profits by producing that output at which marginal cost and marginal revenue are equal.

2. The individual competitor sees a perfectly elastic demand for its product at the going market price because it is but one of many firms in the industry; but the monopolist sees the market demand schedule which is less than perfectly elastic because the monopolist *is* the industry. The former, therefore, has *only* an output policy while the latter is able to determine the price at which it will sell its product.

3. When demand is perfectly elastic, price is equal to marginal revenue and is constant; but when demand is less than perfectly elastic, marginal revenue is less than price and both decrease as the output of the firm increases.

4. Because entry is blocked in the long run, firms cannot enter a monopolistic industry to compete away profits as they can under conditions of pure competition.

In addition to determining the price the monopolist will charge, the quantity of its product it will produce, and size of its profits

Chapter 27 has three other goals. It explains what is meant by price discrimination and the conditions which must prevail if a monopolist is to engage in price discrimination and assesses the desirability of price discrimination. Chapter 27 also appraises resource allocation under monopoly conditions by comparing it with resource allocation under purely competitive conditions. The final section of Chapter 27 introduces you to the problem a government agency faces when it must determine the maximum price a public utility, a natural monopoly, will be allowed to charge for its product.

■ **CHECKLIST**

The very least you should be able to do when you have finished this chapter is:

□ Define pure monopoly.

□ List the six barriers to entry and explain how each of them would prevent or deter the entry of new firms into an industry.

□ Describe the demand curve or schedule for the product produced by a pure monopolist.

□ Define marginal revenue and compute marginal revenue when you are given the demand for the monopolist's product.

□ Explain the relationship between the price the monopolist charges and the marginal revenue from the sale of an additional unit of product and between the monopolist's demand and marginal revenue schedule (curve).

□ State the principle which explains what output the monopolist will produce and the price that will be set; and determine this output and price when you are given the demand and cost data.

□ Define price discrimination, list the three conditions which must be found before there can be price discrimination, and explain when such discrimination may be desirable.

□ Describe the effects of pure monopoly on the price of the product, the quantity of the product produced, and the allocation of the economy's resources; on the distribution of income in the economy; and on the rate of technological progress.

□ Identify for the regulated monopoly (a public utility) the socially optimum and the fair-return price; and explain the dilemma which the regulatory agency encounters.

■ **CHAPTER OUTLINE**

1. Pure monopoly is a market situation in which a single firm sells a product for which there are no close substitutes. While it is rare in practice, the study of monopoly provides an understanding of firms which are "almost" monopolies and is useful in understanding monopolistic competition and oligopoly.

2. Pure monopoly (and oligopoly) can exist in the long run only if potential competitors find there are barriers which prevent their entry into the industry. There are at least six types of entry barriers, but they are seldom perfect in preventing the entry of new firms. Efficient production may, in some cases, require that firms be prevented from entering an industry.

3. The pure monopolist employs the cost and demand data to determine the most profitable output and the price to charge.

 a. Unlike the pure competitor, the monopolist has a price policy. Because it is the sole supplier, the price charged will determine the amount of the product sold (or the amount produced and sold will determine the price at which it can be sold). Consequently, marginal revenue is less than price (or average revenue), and both decrease as the output of the monopolist increases.

 b. Monopoly power in the sale of a product does not by itself affect the prices the monopolist pays or the costs of production.

 c. The monopolist produces that output at which marginal cost and marginal revenue are equal; and charges the price at which this profit-maximizing output can be sold.

 d. It is not true that a monopolist charges as high a price as is possible, and it is not true that profit per unit is as large as it might be; a monopoly, in fact, may not be profitable at all.

 e. To avoid public criticism and pressure or to deter the entry of competitors a monopolist may set a price below the one that would maximize profits.

4. To increase profits a pure monopolist may engage in price discrimination by charging different prices to different buyers of the same product (when the price differences do not represent differences in the costs of producing the product).

 a. To discriminate the seller must have

some monopoly power, determine the elasticities of demand of different groups of buyers, and be able to prevent the resale of the product.

b. Price discrimination expands the economic profits of the seller; but may be socially desirable if it redistributes income from high- to low-income groups or enables a public utility to remain in business without a subsidy from the government.

5. Pure monopoly is likely to have the following economic effects:

a. Because it produces smaller outputs and charges higher prices than would result from conditions of pure competition and because price will be greater than both average total and marginal cost, resources are misallocated.

b. Monopoly contributes to income inequality in the economy.

c. Monopolists may or may not use more efficient (less costly) methods of production, and they may or may not inhibit technological progress.

6. The prices charged by monopolists are often regulated by governments to reduce the misallocation of resources.

a. A ceiling price determined by the intersection of the marginal-cost and demand schedules is the socially optimum price and improves the allocation of resources.

b. This ceiling price may force the firm to produce at a loss; and so government may set the ceiling at a level determined by the intersection of the average-cost and demand schedules to allow the monopolist a fair return.

c. The dilemma of regulation is that the socially optimum price may cause losses for the monopolist, and that a fair-return price results in a less efficient allocation of resources.

■ IMPORTANT TERMS

Pure monopoly	Price discrimination
Barrier to entry	Socially optimum price
Natural monopoly	
Tying agreement	Fair-return price
Unfair competition	Dilemma of regulation
The economies of being established	

■ FILL-IN QUESTIONS

1. What are the six most important types of barrier to entry?

a. _the economies of scale_

b. _natural monopolies_

c. _ownership of raw mat'ls_

d. _patents & research_

e. _unfair comp_

f. _the economies being established_

2. If there are substantial economies of scale in the production of a product, a small-scale firm will find it difficult to enter into and survive in such an industry because _barriers to entry_ and a firm will find it difficult to start out on a large scale in the industry because _the size & power of other industries_

3. Public utility companies tend to be _natural_ monopolies, and they receive their franchises from and are _regulated_ by governments.

4. The demand schedule confronting the pure monopolist is _less than_ perfectly elastic; this means that marginal revenue will be _less than_ than average revenue and that both marginal revenue and average revenue _decrease_ as output increases.

5. When the profits of a monopolist are being maximized _MR_ and _MC_ are equal and price (or average revenue) is _more_ than marginal cost.

6. Three common fallacies about the pure monopolist are that:

a. He charges the _most_ price.

b. His average (or per unit) profit is _huge_

_____

c. He always receives a _profit_

7. A monopolist may refuse to set his price and output at the level that would maximize

his profits in order to prevent _competition_

_____

and _public pressure_

8. In the long run the price charged by a monopolist is not forced down to the level of

average cost because there is no _____

competition

to force price downward.

9. There is price discrimination whenever a

product is sold at different _price_
and these differences are not equal to the

differences in the _cost_
of producing the product.

10. Price discrimination is possible only when the following three conditions are found.

a. _seller has monopoly power_

b. _able to segment market_

c. _original buyer cannot resell_

11. The output produced by a monopolist is inefficiently produced because the average

total cost of producing the product is not ____

_____ ,

and resources are not efficiently allocated be-

cause _____

is not equal to _____

12. Resources can be said to be more efficiently allocated by pure competition than by pure monopoly only if the purely competitive

firm and the monopoly have the same _____

_____ and they will not be the same if the monopolist, by virtue of being a

large firm, enjoys _____
not available to the pure competitor.

13. Monopoly seems to result in a greater

inequality of income than there would other-

wise be because _____

14. The misallocation of resources that results from monopoly can be *eliminated* if a ceiling price for the monopolist's product is

set equal to _____;
such a price is, however, usually less than

_____

15. If a regulated monopolist is allowed to earn a fair return, the ceiling price for the

product is set equal to _____;
such a price reduces but does not eliminate

_____

■ **PROBLEMS AND PROJECTS**

1. The demand schedule for the product produced by a monopolist is given in the table below.

Price	Quantity demanded	Total revenue	Marginal revenue
$700	0	$_____	
650	1	_____	$_____
600	2	_____	_____
550	3	_____	_____
500	4	_____	_____
450	5	_____	_____
400	6	_____	_____
350	7	_____	_____
300	8	_____	_____
250	9	_____	_____
200	10	_____	_____

a. Complete the table by computing total revenue at each of the eleven prices and the ten marginal revenue figures.
b. Using the table of costs given in problem 1 of Chapter 26:
(1) What output will the monopolist pro-

duce? _____
(2) What price will the monopolist charge?

$_____

(3) What total profit will the monopolist receive? $_____

c. Assume this monopolist is able to engage in price discrimination and to sell each unit of the product at a price equal to the maximum price the buyer of that unit of the product would be willing to pay.

(1) Complete the table below by computing total revenue at each of the eleven quantities and the marginal revenue this discriminating monopolist obtains from each additional unit sold.

Quantity demanded	Price	Total revenue	Marginal revenue
0	$700	$____	
1	650	____	$____
2	600	____	____
3	550	____	____
4	500	____	____
5	450	____	____
6	400	____	____
7	350	____	____
8	300	____	____
9	250	____	____
10	200	____	____

(2) From the table it can be seen that the marginal revenue which the discriminating monopolist obtains from the sale of an additional unit is equal to the _____

(3) Using the same table of costs, the discriminating monopolist would produce ____ units of the product, charge the buyer of the last unit of product produced a price of $____, and obtain a total economic profit of $_____

(4) If the pure monopolist is able to engage in price discrimination its profits will be (larger, smaller, the same) _____ and it will produce an output that is (larger, smaller, the same) _____

2. Again employing the cost schedule given in problem 1, Chapter 26, and the demand schedules given in the following table, complete the second table below for each set of demand data.

Demand schedule 2		Demand schedule 3	
Price	Quantity demanded	Price	Quantity demanded
$210	0	$80	0
190	1	75	1
170	2	70	2
150	3	65	3
130	4	60	4
110	5	55	5
90	6	50	6
70	7	45	7
50	8	40	8
30	9	35	9
10	10	30	10

	Demand 2	Demand 3
Output of the firm	_____	_____
Price it will charge	_____	_____
Total profit	_____	_____

3. In the table below are cost and demand data for a pure monopolist.

Quantity demanded	Price	Marginal revenue	Average cost	Marginal cost
0	$17.50			
1	16.00	$16.00	$24.00	$24.00
2	14.50	13.00	15.00	6.00
3	13.00	10.00	11.67	5.00
4	11.50	7.00	10.50	7.00
5	10.00	4.00	10.00	8.00
6	8.50	1.00	9.75	8.50
7	7.00	−2.00	9.64	9.00
8	5.50	−5.00	9.34	9.25
9	4.00	−8.00	9.36	9.50

a. An unregulated monopolist would produce _____ units of a product, sell it at a price of _____, and receive a total profit of _____

b. If this monopolist were regulated and the maximum price it could charge were set equal to marginal cost, it would produce _____ units of a product, sell it at a price of _____, and receive a total profit of

_____. Such regulation would either

_____ the firm or require that the regulating government

_____ the firm.

c. If the monopolist were not regulated and were allowed to engage in price discrimination by charging the maximum price it could obtain for each unit sold it would produce 6 units (because the marginal revenue from the 6th unit and the marginal cost of the 6th unit would both be $8.50). Its total revenue

would be $_____, its total costs would

be $_____, and its total profit would

be $_____.

d. If the monopolist were regulated and allowed to charge a fair-return price, it would

produce _____ units of a product, charge

a price of _____, and receive a profit

of _____

e. From which situation—a, b, or d—does the most efficient allocation of resources re-

sult? _____ From which situation does

the least efficient allocation result? _____ In practice, government would probably

select situation _____

■ **SELF-TEST**

Circle the T if the statement is true, the F if it is false.

1. The pure monopolist produces a product for which there are no substitutes. **T** F

2. The weaker the barriers to entry into an industry, the more competition there will be in the industry, other things being equal. **T** F

3. Monopoly is always undesirable unless it is regulated by government. T **F**

4. The monopolist can increase the sale of his product if he charges a lower price. **T** F

5. The monopolist determines his profit-maximizing output by producing that output at which marginal cost and marginal revenue are equal and sets his product price equal to marginal cost and marginal revenue at that output. **T** F

6. When a monopolist is maximizing his total profit he is also producing that output at which his per unit (or average) profit is a maximum. T F

7. A monopolist may refrain from maximizing his total profits in order to discourage the entry of new firms into the industry. **T** F

8. Price discrimination is undesirable. T **F**

9. If a monopolist engages in price discrimination rather than charging all buyers the same price its profits are greater. **T** F

10. Resources are misallocated by a monopoly because price is not equal to marginal cost. T **F**

11. In a society in which technology is not changing and the economies of scale can be employed by both pure competitors and monopolists, the purely competitive firm will use the more efficient methods of production. **T** F

12. The dilemma of monopoly regulation is that the production by a monopolist of an output that causes no misallocation of resources may force the monopolist to suffer an economic loss. **T** F

Underscore the letter that corresponds to the best answer.

1. Which of the following is the *best* example of a pure monopoly? (a) your neighborhood grocer; (b) the telephone company in your community; (c) the manufacturer of a particular brand of toothpaste; (d) the only airline furnishing passenger service between two major cities.

2. Which of the following is *not* an important characteristic of a natural monopoly? (a) substantial economies of scale are available; (b) very heavy fixed costs; (c) it is a public utility; (d) competition is impractical and/or would be very expensive for the consumer.

3. Monopoly can probably exist over a long period of time only if: (a) it is based on the control of raw materials; (b) it controls the patents on the product; (c) cut-throat competition is employed to eliminate rivals; (d) government assists the monopoly and prevents the establishment of rival firms.

4. Which of the following is *not* true with respect to the demand data confronting a monopolist? (a) marginal revenue is greater than average revenue; (b) marginal revenue decreases as average revenue decreases; (c) demand is less than perfectly elastic; (d) average revenue (or price) decreases as the output of the firm increases.

5. Assume the cost and demand data for a pure monopolist as given in the table below. How many units of output will the firm produce? (a) 1; (b) 2; (c) 3; (d) 4.

Output	Total cost	Price
0	$ 500	$1,000
1	520	600
2	580	500
3	700	400
4	1,000	300
5	1,500	200

6. If the monopolist for whom cost and demand data are given in question 5 above were forced to produce the socially optimum output by the imposition of a ceiling price, the ceiling price would have to be: (a) $200; (b) $300; (c) $400; (d) $500.

7. When the monopolist is maximizing total profits *or* minimizing losses: (a) total revenue is greater than total cost; (b) average revenue is greater than average total cost; (c) average revenue is greater than marginal cost; (d) average total cost is less than marginal cost.

8. Which of the following is *not* one of the conditions which must be realized before a seller finds price discrimination is workable? (a) the buyer must be unable to resell the product; (b) the product must be a service; (c) the seller must have some degree of monopoly power; (d) the seller must be able to segment the market.

9. Look at the demand data in question 5 above. If the monopolist could sell each unit of the product at the maximum price the buyer of that unit would be willing to pay for it and if the monopolist sold 4 units, total revenue would be (a) $1200; (b) $1800; (c) $2000; (d) $2800.

10. A monopolist does not *produce* the product as efficiently as is possible because: (a) the average total cost of producing it is not a minimum; (b) the marginal cost of producing the last unit is less than its price; (c) it is earning a profit; (d) average revenue is greater than the cost of producing an extra unit of output.

11. Over time monopoly *may* result in greater technological improvement than would be forthcoming under conditions of pure competition for several reasons. Which of the following is *not* one of these reasons? (a) technological advance will lower the costs and enhance the profits of the monopolist, and these increased profits will not have to be shared with rivals; (b) technological advance will act as a barrier to entry and thus allow the monopolist to continue to be a monopolist; (c) technological advance requires research and experimentation, and the monopolist is in a position to finance them out of his profits; (d) technological advance is apt to make existing capital equipment obsolete, and the monopolist can reduce costs by speeding up the rate at which his capital becomes obsolete.

12. A monopolist who is limited by the imposition of a ceiling price to a fair return sells the product at a price equal to: (a) average total cost; (b) average variable cost; (c) marginal cost; (d) average fixed cost.

■ **DISCUSSION QUESTIONS**

1. What is pure monopoly? Why is it studied if it is so rare in practice?

2. What is meant by a barrier to entry? What kinds of such barriers are there? How important are they in pure competition, pure monopoly, monopolistic competition, and oligopoly?

3. Why are the economies of scale a barrier to entry?

4. Why are most natural monopolies also public utilities? What does government hope to achieve by granting exclusive franchises to and regulating such natural monopolies?

5. What is meant by unfair competition? What kinds of unfair competition are there? How is unfair competition used to create monopolies and to bar the entry of new firms into industries?

6. Why is it said that the "monopoly power achieved through patents may well be cumulative"?

7. What advantage does the going, established firm have over the new, immature firm in an industry?

8. Compare the pure monopolist and the individual pure competitor with respect to: (a) the demand schedule; (b) the marginal-revenue schedule; (c) the relationship between marginal revenue and average revenue; (d) price policy; (e) the ability to administer price.

9. What output will the monopolist produce? What price will he charge?

10. Why does the monopolist not charge the highest possible price for the product? Why does the monopolist not set the price for the product in such a way that average profit is a maximum? Why are some monopolies unprofitable?

11. Why would any monopolist refrain from setting his price and producing an output that would maximize his total profits?

12. What is meant by price discrimination and what conditions must be realized before it is workable? Explain the effect that price discrimination has upon the profits of a monopolist, the distribution of income, and the ability of public utilities to survive without a subsidy from government.

13. In what sense is resource allocation and production more efficient under conditions of pure competition than under monopoly conditions? Does pure competition *always* result in greater efficiency? How does monopoly affect the distribution of income in an economy?

14. Does monopoly, when compared with pure competition, result in more rapid or less rapid technological progress? What are the arguments on *both* sides of this question? What evidence is there to support the two views?

15. Explain under what conditions you would prefer monopoly to pure competition.

16. How do public utility regulatory agencies attempt to eliminate the misallocation of resources that result from monopoly? Explain the dilemma that almost invariably confronts the agency in this endeavor; explain also why a fair-return price only reduces but does not eliminate the misallocation.

Price and Output Determination: Monopolistic Competition

Chapter 28 is the third of the four chapters which deal with specific market situations. As its name implies, monopolistic competition is a blend of pure competition and pure monopoly; and one of the reasons for studying these relatively unrealistic market situations was to prepare you for the more realistic study of monopolistic competition. It must be pointed out that monopolistic competition is not a realistic description of all markets; but the study of it will help you to understand the many markets which are nearly monopolistically competitive. It will also help you to understand why oligopoly is prevalent in the American economy and how oligopoly differs from monopolistic competition.

The first task is to learn exactly what is meant by monopolistic competition. Next you should examine the demand curve which the monopolistically competitive firm sees for its product and note how and why it differs from the demand curves faced by the purely competitive firm and by the monopolist. In this connection it is important to understand that as the individual firm changes the character of the product it produces or changes the extent to which it promotes the sale of its product, both the costs of the firm and the demand for the product will change. A firm confronts a different demand curve every time it alters its product or its promotion of the product.

With the product and promotional campaign of the firm *given,* the price-output analysis of the monopolistic competitor is relatively simple. In the short run this analysis is identical with the analysis of the price-output decision of the pure monopolist in the short run. It is only in the long run that the competitive element makes itself apparent: The entry (or exit) of firms forces the price the firm charges down (up) *toward* the level of average cost. This price is not equal either to *minimum* average cost or to marginal cost; and consequently monopolistic competition, on these two scores, can be said to be less efficient than pure competition.

A relatively large part of Chapter 28 is devoted to a discussion of nonprice competition. This is done for very good reasons. In monopolistically competitive industries a part of the competitive effort of individual firms is given over to product differentiation, product development, and product advertising. Each firm has three things to manipulate—price, product, and advertising—in trying to maximize its profits. While monopolistic competition may not be so economically efficient as pure competition in terms of a *given* product and the promotion of it, when all the economic effects—good and bad—of differentiation, development, and advertising are considered this shortcoming may or may not be offset. Whether it is actually offset is an unanswerable question. If Chapter 28 has one central idea it is this. Monopolistic competition cannot be compared with pure competition solely on the basis of prices charged at any given moment of time; it must also be judged in terms of whether it results in better products, in a wider variety of products, in better-informed consumers, in lower-priced radio and television programs, magazines, and newspapers, and other redeeming features.

In short, the study of monopolistic competition is a realistic study and for that reason it is a difficult study. Many factors have to be considered in explaining how such a group of firms behaves and in appraising the efficiency with which such an industry allocates scarce resources.

■ **CHECKLIST**

The very least you should be able to do when you have finished this chapter is:

□ List the characteristics of monopolistic competition.

□ Determine the output of and the price charged by a monopolistic competitor (producing a given product and engaged in a given amount of sales promotion) in the short run when you are given the cost and demand data.

□ Explain why the price charged by a monopolistic competitor (producing a given product and engaged in a given amount of sales promotion) will in the long run tend to equal average cost.

□ Identify the "wastes of monopolistic competition" and explain why product differentiation may "offset" these wastes.

□ Enumerate the three principal types of nonprice competition.

□ Present the major arguments in the cases for and against advertising.

■ **CHAPTER OUTLINE**

1. A monopolistically competitive industry is one in which a fairly large number of independent firms produce differentiated products, in which both price and various forms of nonprice competition occur, and into which entry is relatively easy in the long run. While there are many industries which approximate monopolistic competition, many more industries are blends of monopolistic competition and oligopoly.

2. Assume that the products the firms in the industry are producing and the amounts of promotional activity in which they are engaged are given.

a. The demand curve confronting each firm will be highly but not perfectly elastic because each firm has many competitors who produce close but not perfect substitutes for the product it produces.

b. In the short run the individual firm will produce that output at which marginal cost and marginal revenue are equal and charge the price at which that output can be sold; either profits or losses may result in the short run.

c. In the long run the entry and exodus of firms will *tend* to change the demand for the product of the individual firm in such a way that profits are eliminated (price and average cost are made equal to each other).

3. Monopolistic competition among firms producing a *given* product and engaged in a *given* amount of promotional activity results in less economic efficiency and more waste than does pure competition. Although average cost and price are equal, the individual firm produces an output smaller than the output at which marginal cost and price are equal and smaller than the output at which average cost is a minimum.

4. In addition to setting its price and output so that its profit is maximized, each individual firm also attempts to differentiate its product and to promote (advertise) it in order to increase the firm's profit; these additional activities give rise to nonprice competition among firms.

a. Product differentiation and product development, as devices which firms employ in the hope of increasing their profit, may offset the wastes of monopolistic competition to the extent that they result in a wider variety and better quality of products for consumers.

b. Whether the advertising of differentiated products results in economic waste or in greater economic efficiency is debatable; there are good arguments on both sides of this question and there is no clear answer to it.

c. The monopolistically competitive firm tries to adjust its price, its product, and the promotion of its product so that the amount by which the firm's total revenue exceeds the total cost of producing and promoting a product is a maximum.

■ **IMPORTANT TERMS**

Monopolistic competition	Informative advertising
Product differentiation	Competitive advertising
Nonprice competition	

■ **FILL-IN QUESTIONS**

1. In a monopolistically competitive market a _____ number of producers sell _____ products; these producers do not _____ _____ and they engage in both _____ and _____ competition. In the long run, entry into the industry is _____

2. The fact that monopolistically competitive firms sell differentiated products results in each firm having _____ control over the price of its product and _____ _____ between the firms.

3. Given the product being produced and the extent to which that product is being promoted, in the *short run:*
  a. The demand curve confronting the monopolistically competitive firm will be _____ _____ elastic than that facing a monopolist and _____ _____ elastic than that facing a pure competitor.
  b. The elasticity of this demand curve will

depend upon _____and _____

  c. The firm will produce that output at which _____ and _____ are equal.

4. In the long run, the *entry* of new firms into a monopolistically competitive industry will _____ the demand for the product being produced by each firm in the industry and _____ _____ the elasticity of that demand.

5. In the long run, *given* the product and the amount of product promotion, the price being charged by the individual firm will tend to _____ , its economic profits will tend to _____ _____ , and its average cost will be _____ than the minimum average cost of producing and promoting the product.

6. Given the product and the extent of product promotion, monopolistic competition is wasteful because _____ and because _____

7. In the long run, the monopolistic competitor cannot protect and increase profits by varying the product's price or output, but it can try to protect and increase profits through _____ and _____

8. Product differentiation and product development tend to result in the consumer being offered _____ at any given moment of time and _____ _____ over a period of time.

9. Advertising that accurately describes the price and qualities of products is called _____ _____ advertising, while that which makes unsubstantiated claims for products is _____ _____ advertising.

10. Those who argue that advertising expenditures are socially desirable contend that advertising (a) increases the _____ _____ of consumers; (b) supports _____; (c) promotes the development of _____ _____; (d) results in lower _____; (e) leads to greater _____ among firms; and (f) induces a higher level of _____, which results in greater total employment.

11. The critics of advertising argue (a) that most advertising is persuasive but not _____ _____; (b) that advertising _____ resources; (c) that it entails significant _____ which are not paid by advertisers; (d) that it does not lower _____; (e) that it leads to more _____ in the economy; (f) that it does not really increase _____ and (g) that advertising expenditures are a significant _____ into many industries.

12. In attempting to maximize his profits the monopolistic competitor will vary the price, the _____, and the _____ of the product until the firm feels no further change in these three variables will result in greater profits.

■ **PROBLEMS AND PROJECTS**

1. Listed below are several industries. Indicate in the space to the right of each whether you believe it is monopolistically competitive (MC) or not monopolistically competitive (N). If you indicate the latter, explain why you think the industry is not a monopolistically competitive one.

a. The production of automobiles in the United States. _____ _____

b. The retail distribution of automobiles in the United States. _____

c. Grocery supermarkets in a city of 500,000 people. _____ _____

d. The retail sale of gasoline in a city of 500,000 people. _____ _____

e. The production of low-priced shoes in the United States. _____ _____

f. The mail-order sale of men's clothes. _____ _____

2. Assume that the short-run cost and demand data given in the table at the top of page 221 confront a monopolistic competitor selling a given product and engaged in a given amount of product promotion.

a. Compute the marginal cost and marginal revenue of each unit of output and enter these figures in the table.

b. In the short run the firm will (1) produce _____ units of output, (2) sell its product at a price of $_____, and (3) have a total profit of $_____

c. In the long run, (1) the demand for the firm's product will _____, (2) until the price of the product equals _____ _____ and (3) the total profits of the firm are _____ _____

■ **SELF-TEST**

Circle the T if the statement is true, the F if it is false.

Output	Total cost	Marginal cost	Quantity demanded	Price	Marginal revenue
0	$ 50		0	$120	
1	80	$_____	1	110	$_____
2	90	_____	2	100	_____
3	110	_____	3	90	_____
4	140	_____	4	80	_____
5	180	_____	5	70	_____
6	230	_____	6	60	_____
7	290	_____	7	50	_____
8	360	_____	8	40	_____
9	440	_____	9	30	_____
10	530	_____	10	20	_____

1. Monopolistic competitors have no control over the price of their products. **T F**

2. The smaller the number of firms in an industry and the greater the extent of product differentiation, the greater will be the elasticity of the individual seller's demand curve. **T F**

3. One reason why monopolistic competition is wasteful, given the products the firms are producing and the extent to which they are promoting them, is that the average cost of producing the product is greater than the minimum average cost at which the product could be produced. **T F**

4. If advertising expenditures fluctuate directly (or positively) with total spending in the economy, they will be countercyclical and lead to greater stability in employment and the price level. **T F**

5. Those who contend that advertising contributes to "social imbalance" argue that there is an overproduction of private goods partly as a result of persuasive advertising. **T F**

6. A firm will improve the quality of its product only if it expects that the additional revenue which it will receive will be greater than the extra costs involved. **T F**

7. There tends to be rather general agreement among both critics and defenders of advertising that advertising increases the average cost of producing and promoting the product. **T F**

8. Empirical evidence clearly indicates that advertising reduces competition and makes entry into an industry more difficult. **T F**

Underscore the letter that corresponds to the best answer.

1. Which of the following is *not* characteristic of monopolistic competition? (*a*) product differentiation; (*b*) a relatively large number of firms; (*c*) a feeling of interdependence among the firms; (*d*) relatively easy entry in the long run.

2. Given the following short-run demand and cost schedules for a monopolistic competitor, what output will the firm produce? (*a*) 2; (*b*) 3; (*c*) 4; (*d*) 5.

Price	Quantity demanded	Total cost	Output
$10	1	$14	1
9	2	17	2
8	3	22	3
7	4	29	4
6	5	38	5
5	6	49	6

3. Assuming the short-run demand and cost data in question 2 above, *in the long run* the number of firms in the industry: (*a*) will be less than in the short run; (*b*) will be the same as in the short run; (c) will be greater than in the short run; (d) cannot be determined from the available information.

4. Given the product the firm is producing and the extent to which the firm is promoting it, *in the long run:* (a) the firm will produce that output at which marginal cost and price are equal; (b) the elasticity of demand for the firm's product will be less than it was in the short run; (c) the number of firms in the industry will be greater than it was in the short run; (d) the profits being earned by the firms in the industry will tend to equal zero.

5. Which of the following is *not* one of the features of monopolistic competition which may offset the wastes associated with such a market structure? (a) a wider variety of products is offered to consumers; (b) advertising tends to be of the competitive type; (c) the quality of products improves over time; (d) consumers are better informed of the availability and prices of products.

6. Which of the following would probably be the best example of "competitive advertising"? (a) a "for sale" ad in the classified section of a newspaper; (b) one of the twice-weekly full-page advertisements of a grocery supermarket in a newspaper; (c) the advertisement for a particular brand of aspirin in a monthly magazine; (d) the national television advertisement of a drugstore chain announcing a "one-cent sale."

7. Which of the following would *not* be characteristic of a monopolistically competitive firm when it is in long-run equilibrium? (a) no further increase in the firm's output will decrease the firm's average revenue more than it decreases average cost; (b) no further decrease in the firm's price will increase the firm's total revenue more than it increases total costs; (c) no further variation in the firm's product will reduce total costs less than it reduces total revenue; (d) no further change in the firm's advertising campaign will increase total revenue more than it increases total costs.

8. Which of the following can be fairly concluded with respect to the economic effects of advertising? (a) advertising helps to maintain a high level of aggregate demand in the economy; (b) consumers benefit less from advertising expenditures than they do from expenditures for product development; (c) advertising in the American economy is more informative than competitive; (d) lower unit costs and lower prices result when a firm advertises because advertising increases the size of the firm's market and promotes economies of scale.

■ **DISCUSSION QUESTIONS**

1. What are the chief characteristics of a monopolistic competitive market? In what sense is there competition and in what sense is there monopoly in such a market?

2. What is meant by product differentiation? By what methods can products be differentiated? How does product differentiation affect the kind of competition in and inject an element of monopoly into markets?

3. Comment on the elasticity of the demand curve faced by the monopolistically competitive firm in the short run, assuming that the firm is producing a given product and is engaged in a given amount of promotional activity. What two factors determine just how elastic that demand curve will be?

4. What output will the monopolistic competitor produce in the short run, and what price will he charge for his product? What determines whether the firm will earn profits or suffer losses in the short run?

5. In the long run what level of profits will the individual monopolistically competitive firm *tend* to receive? Why is this just a tendency? What forces profits toward this level, and why will the firm produce a long-run output which is smaller than the most "efficient" output? (Again assume, in answering this question, that the firm is producing a given product and selling it with a given amount of promotional activity.)

6. In what two senses is monopolistic competition wasteful or a misallocation of resources?

7. What methods, other than price cutting, can an individual monopolistic competitor employ to attempt to protect and increase his profits in the long run?

8. To what extent and how do product differentiation and product development offset the "wastes" associated with monopolistic competition?

9. Does advertising result in a waste of resources, or does it promote a more efficient utilization of resources? What arguments can be presented to support the contention that it is wasteful and detrimental, and what claims are made to support the view that it is beneficial to the economy? What empirical evidence is there?

10. When is a monopolistic competitor in long-run equilibrium not only with respect to the price he is charging but also with respect to the product he is producing and the extent to which he is promoting his product?

Price and Output Determination: Oligopoly

This last of the four chapters dealing with specific market situations is in a way the most difficult. Oligopoly is one of those areas of economic study where economists have found it impossible to reach definite conclusions. Under conditions of pure competition, pure monopoly, and monopolistic competition fairly definite conclusions regarding market prices and the outputs of individual firms are reached; but such conclusions are not easily drawn from an analysis of oligopoly. This is why the study of oligopoly is difficult—the generalizations are few in number—and this is unfortunate but also unavoidable.

Oligopoly is probably the most realistic market situation which the student will examine, and many economists believe it is the type of market most prevalent—or at least, most important—in the American economy. Because it is so realistic its study is all the more difficult. Chapter 29 is little more than an introduction to this very complex market situation. There are, however, certain things you can and should learn about it.

What oligopoly *is* is fairly simple to understand. The *consequences* of "fewness" and the "mutual interdependence" and feeling of uncertainty to which it gives rise are not quite so easy to grasp, but they are of the greatest importance. For these reasons you should make every attempt to learn exactly *what is meant* by mutual interdependence

and uncertainty and *why they exist* in an oligopoly. If you can do this, you will be well on the road to understanding why specific and definite conclusions cannot be reached concerning market prices and the outputs of individual firms. You will also see why oligopolists are loath to engage in price competition and why they frequently resort to collusion to set prices and to nonprice competition to determine market shares.

Chapter 29 employs several devices to explain the two major behavioral characteristics of oligopoly: the tendency for the prices charged by oligopolists to be rigid, and the tendency for oligopolists to determine what price to charge by collusion. The kinked demand curve is one of these devices. It explains why, in the absence of collusion, oligopolists will not raise or lower their prices even when their costs change. But the kinked demand curve does not explain what price oligopolists will set; it explains only why price, once set, will be relatively inflexible. To set price, oligopolists often resort to some form of collusion (such as a cartel, gentlemen's agreement, or price leadership). Collusion reduces the uncertainty each firm has about the prices rivals will charge and enables it to increase its profits. It also enables the industry as a whole to increase its joint profit. The results of collusion are a price and output which are about the same as would prevail if the industry were a pure monopoly. But collusion is seldom perfect because there are so many obstacles to collusion. As a result of these obstacles, price may be somewhat less and output somewhat greater than those which would be set by a monopolist.

Another device used to explain the behavior of oligopolists is the theory of games and the profits-payoff table. Using this table, you will again understand why noncolluding oligopolists tend to keep their price unchanged. The table will also help you see why oligopolists find it more profitable either to set price collusively or to merge their firms.

The final section of the chapter poses the question of whether oligopolists efficiently allocate resources. As with the same question with respect to monopolistic competition, there is only a tentative answer. There are, however, several reasons to believe that over the years oligopoly may have beneficial results for society as a whole, even though it may not appear at any given time to be allocating resources efficiently.

■ **CHECKLIST**

The very least you should be able to do when you have finished this chapter is:

□ Define oligopoly and distinguish between homogeneous and differentiated oligopolies.

□ Identify the two most significant causes of oligopoly and explain how each of these tends to result in oligopolistic industries.

□ Explain why it is difficult to predict what price will be charged and what output will be produced by an oligopolist.

□ Employ the kinked demand curve to explain why oligopoly prices tend to be inflexible (or rigid).

□ Explain the advantages which oligopolists see in collusion, the several forms which collusion may take, and the obstacles which firms that wish to collude will encounter.

□ Use a profits-payoff table to explain mutual interdependence, price rigidity, and the advantages to oligopolists of collusion and merger.

□ Explain the role played by nonprice competition in oligopolistic industries, the principal forms of such competition, and why oligopolists emphasize nonprice competition.

□ Distinguish between restrictive and pro-gressive oligopoly; and between the economic efficiency of the latter in a static and in a dynamic setting.

■ **CHAPTER OUTLINE**

1. An oligopoly is an industry composed of a few mutually interdependent firms selling either a standardized or a differentiated product. The existence of such industries is usually the result of economies of scale and the advantages of merger.

2. The economic analysis of oligopoly is difficult for two reasons: The term "oligopoly" actually covers many different market situations; and the individual oligopolist, because of the uncertainty which accompanies mutual interdependence, is seldom able to estimate his own demand curve. Important characteristics of oligopoly are inflexible prices and simultaneous price changes.

3. An examination of two oligopoly models helps to explain price rigidity and the price-output behavior of oligopolists.

a. Under conditions of noncollusive oligopoly, an oligopolist believes that when he lowers his price his rivals will lower their prices, and that when he increases his price his rivals will not increase their prices. He is therefore reluctant to change his price at all for fear of decreasing his profits.

b. Because of the uncertainties of noncollusive oligopoly, oligopolists may collude to maximize their joint profit by setting their price and joint output at the same levels at which a pure monopolist would set them.

c. Joint-profit maximization by collusive oligopolists is only a tendency because of the several obstacles to collusion.

4. The theory of games and a profits-payoff table help us understand the behavior of oligopolists. A profits-payoff table:

a. Shows the different prices two oligopolists might charge and their profits for every combination of prices.

b. Demonstrates their mutual interdependence: the price one firm should set to maximize its profits depends upon the price charged by the other firm.

c. Illustrates price rigidity and explains why each firm is reluctant either to raise or to lower its price.

d. Indicates how both firms may gain by setting a collusive price or may increase their joint profits by merging.

5. Oligopolistic firms avoid price competition but engage in nonprice competition to determine each firm's market share (sales).

6. Whether oligopoly is economically efficient is almost impossible to determine.

  a. At a given time oligopoly probably results in restricted outputs, economic profits, and higher costs and prices.

  b. Over a period of time, oligopoly may be progressive and result in larger outputs, lower costs, and technological progress.

  (1) Technological competition among firms that have both the means and the incentives to improve their products and production techniques will result in economic progress.

  (2) The evidence suggests that while many oligopolies have been progressive, many others have not engaged in any significant research and have failed to develop better products and processes.

  c. Countervailing power may also limit the restrictive power of oligopolies.

  d. Oligopoly, *if* it results in technological progress or in economies of scale or *if* it is curbed by countervailing power, may be as efficient in allocating resources as competition.

■ IMPORTANT TERMS

Oligopoly	Gentlemen's agreement
Fewness	
Mutual inter-dependence	Price leadership
	Price break
Price rigidity	Theory of games
Noncollusive oligopoly	Profits-payoff (price-profits) table
Collusive oligopoly	
Kinked demand curve	Duopoly
Joint-profit maximization	Restrictive oligopoly
	Progressive oligopoly
Cartel	Countervailing power

■ FILL-IN QUESTIONS

1. In an oligopoly a _____ firms produce either a _____ or a _____

product, and entry into such an industry is _____

2. Because oligopoly consists of a small number of firms, they are necessarily _____ _____ ; this means that when setting the price of its product each firm must consider _____ _____ ; the monopolist does not face this problem because he has _____ rivals, and the pure competitor does not face it because he has _____ rivals.

3. The two major underlying causes of oligopoly are _____ and _____

4. Formal economic analysis cannot be easily used to explain the prices and outputs of oligopolists because _____ and _____

5. Oligopoly prices tend to be _____ and oligopolists tend to change their prices _____ when they change them.

6. There tends to be very little _____ competition and a great deal of _____ _____ competition in oligopolies.

7. The kinked demand curve which the individual oligopolist sees for its product is highly _____ at prices above the current or going price and tends to be only slightly _____ or _____ below that price.

8. The kinked demand curve for an oligopolist is drawn on the assumption that if the oligopolist raises its price its rivals will _____ _____ and if it lowers its price its rivals will _____ _____

9. Because the oligopolist who confronts a kinked demand curve finds that there is a ____ _____ in his marginal-revenue curve, small changes in the marginal-cost curve do not change the _____ _____

10. When oligopolists collude to maximize joint profits, the price they set and their combined output tend to be the same as _____

11. Four obstacles to the tendency of collusive oligopolists to maximize joint profits are:

a. _____

b. _____

c. _____

d. _____

12. A cartel is a written or oral agreement either to _____ or to _____

13. A gentlemen's agreement is a(n) _____ agreement on _____; each firm's share of the market is determined by _____ _____

The firm that sets the price which the other firms in the industry follow is the _____

14. In a profits-payoff (or price-profits) table the _____are along the top and the _____ are along the left side. The two figures in each box (or cell) in the table are the _____ _____

15. The profits-payoff table demonstrates that:
a. The most profitable price for one firm to charge depends upon _____
b. In most cases either a price increase or a decrease by one firm will _____ that firm's profit, because when it raises price its rival will _____

and when it lowers price its rival will _____ _____

c. The two firms can increase their joint profit either by _____ or _____

16. Oligopolists use nonprice competition to determine each firm's share of the market because _____ and _____

17. Oligopolists typically have both the means and the incentives to effect technological advances; the means are _____ _____

and the incentives are:

a. _____

b. _____

c. _____

d. _____

18. Such evidence as is available makes it clear that most oligopolies (have, have not) _____ been progressive in developing new products and techniques; their expenditures for research and development have been _____ and a large percentage of such expenditures by oligopolists has been _____

19. Countervailing power tends to develop for both defensive and offensive reasons. The defensive reason is the desire of _____ and _____ to protect themselves from _____ _____

and the offensive reason is the desire to ____ _____

20. Oligopoly may be more efficient in allocating resources than competition if it has lower _____, produces a _____product, or is curbed by _____; in the absence of these conditions it will produce

_____ outputs and charge
_____ prices than a competitive industry.

■ **PROBLEMS AND PROJECTS**

1. The kinked demand schedule which an oligopolist believes confronts it is given in the table below.
  a. Compute the oligopolist's total revenue at each of the nine prices, and enter these figures in the table.
  b. Also compute marginal revenue and the coefficient of the elasticity of demand between the nine prices, and enter these figures in the table.
  c. What is the current, or going, price for the oligopolist's product? $ _____

How much is it selling? _____
  d. On the graph on page 229 plot the oligopolist's demand curve and marginal-revenue curve. Connect the demand points and the marginal-revenue points with as straight a line as possible. *Be sure* to plot the marginal-revenue figures at the average of the two quantities involved, that is, at 150, 250, 350, 450, 512½, 537½, 562½, and 587½.
  e. Assume that the marginal-cost schedule of the oligopolist is given in columns (1) and (2) of the table on the next column. Plot the marginal-cost curve on the graph on which demand and marginal revenue are plotted.
  (1) Given demand and marginal cost, what price should the oligopolist charge to maxi-

(1) Output	(2) MC	(3) MC′	(4) MC″
150	$1.40	$1.90	$.40
250	1.30	1.80	.30
350	1.40	1.90	.40
450	1.50	2.00	.50
512½	1.60	2.10	.60
537½	1.70	2.20	.70
562½	1.80	2.30	.80
587½	1.90	2.40	.90

mize profits? $ _____
How many units of product will it sell at this

price? _____
  (2) If the marginal-cost schedule changed from that shown in columns (1) and (2) to that shown in columns (1) and (3), what

price should it charge? $_____ What

level of output will it produce? _____
How have profits changed as a result of the

change in costs? _____
Plot the new marginal-cost curve on the graph.
  (3) If the marginal-cost schedule changed from that shown in columns (1) and (2) to that shown in columns (1) and (4), what price

should it charge? $_____ What

level of output will it produce? _____
How have profits changed as a result of the

change in costs? _____
Plot the new marginal-cost curve on the graph.

Price	Quality demanded	Total revenue	Marginal revenue	Elasticity of demand
$2.90	100	$_____		
2.80	200	_____	$_____	$_____
2.70	300	_____	_____	_____
2.60	400	_____	_____	_____
2.50	500	_____	_____	_____
2.40	525	_____	_____	_____
2.30	550	_____	_____	_____
2.20	575	_____	_____	_____
2.10	600	_____	_____	_____

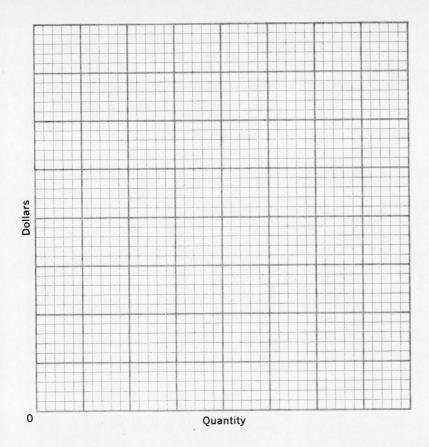

Dollars

0   Quantity

2. An oligopoly producing a homogeneous product is composed of three firms. Assume that these three firms have identical cost schedules. Assume also that if any one of these firms sets a price for the product, the other two firms charge the same price. As long as they all charge the same price they will share the market equally; and the quantity demanded of each will be the same.

Below is the total-cost schedule of one of these firms and the demand schedule that confronts it when the other two firms charge the same price as this firm.

Output	Total cost	Marginal cost	Price	Quantity demanded	Marginal revenue
0	$ 0		$140	0	
1	30	$_____	130	1	$_____
2	50	_____	120	2	_____
3	80	_____	110	3	_____
4	120	_____	100	4	_____
5	170	_____	90	5	_____
6	230	_____	80	6	_____
7	300	_____	70	7	_____
8	380	_____	60	8	_____

a. Complete the marginal-cost and marginal-revenue schedules facing the firm.

b. What price would this firm set if it wished to maximize its profits? $ _____

c. How much would:

(1) It sell at this price? _____

(2) Its profits be at this price? $ _____

d. What would be the industry's:

(1) Total output at this price? _____

(2) Joint profits at this price? $ _____

e. Is there any other price this firm can set, assuming that the other two firms will charge the same price, which would result in a greater joint profit for them? _____

If so, what is that price? $ _____

f. If these three firms colluded (or merged) in order to maximize their joint profit, what price would they charge? $ _____

3. Below is a profits-payoff (or price-profits) table.

Firm Y's prices

Y X	$4	$3	$2
$4	$50 $49	$57 $40	$60 $32
$3	$39 $50	$44 $44	$42 $38
$2	$30 $48	$35 $46	$40 $42

(left label: Firm X's prices)

a. If firm X charges a price of $3, for Y to maximize its profits it should charge a price of $_____. But if firm Y sets a price of $3, the most profitable price for X to charge is $_____. And if X charges $2, the most profitable price for Y is $_____.

b. Assume both firm X and firm Y are initially charging a price of $3.

(1) If X increased its price from $3 to $4, Y (would or would not) _____ increase its price to $4 because _____

_____

(2) Knowing that Y would not follow a price increase from $3 to $4, X (would, would not) _____ increase its price to $4 because _____

_____

(3) If X decreased its price from $3 to $2, Y (would, would not) _____ decrease its price to $2 because _____

(4) Knowing that Y would follow a price decrease from $3 to $2, X (would, would not) _____ decrease its price to $2 because _____

c. If X and Y colluded to maximize their joint profit:

(1) Firm X would set a price of $ _____ and have a profit of $ _____

(2) Firm Y would set a price of $ _____ and have a profit of $ _____

(3) Firms X and Y would have a joint profit of $_____

Circle the T if the statement is true, the F if it is false.

1. The element of "uncertainty" which exists in oligopolies is the uncertainty faced by each firm on how its rivals will react if it changes its price.   **T   F**

2. Price competition between firms is an important characteristic of oligopoly.   **T   F**

3. The kinked demand curve is an economic tool which can be used to explain how the current market price of a product is determined.   **T   F**

4. A cartel is usually a written agreement among firms which sets the price of the product and determines each firm's share of the market.   **T   F**

5. The practice of price leadership is almost always based on a formal written or oral agreement.   **T   F**

6. Whenever oligopoly exists, firms will collude to maximize their joint profit.   **T   F**

7. Nonprice competition is the typical method of determining each oligopolist's share of the total market.   **T   F**

8. It is often argued that oligopolists typically possess both the means and the incentives to technological progress, and that the means are the substantial profits received by them.

T   F

9. Almost all the important technological advances in the United States since 1900 can be attributed to the research and development activities of large business firms.

T   F

10. Oligopoly may be socially desirable if it results in lower production costs or in better products than would be obtainable under more competitive conditions.   **T   F**

Underscore the letter that corresponds to the best answer.

1. "Mutual interdependence" means that: (*a*) each firm produces a product similar but not identical to the products produced by its rivals; (*b*) each firm produces a product identical to the products produced by its rivals; (*c*) each firm must consider the reactions of its rivals when it determines its price policy; (*d*) each firm faces a perfectly elastic demand for its product.

2. The demand curve confronting an oligopolist tends to be: (*a*) elastic; (*b*) of unitary elasticity; (*c*) inelastic; (*d*) one which depends upon the prices charged by his rivals.

3. If an individual oligopolist's demand curve is "kinked," it is necessarily: (*a*) inelastic below the going price; (*b*) inelastic above the going price; (*c*) elastic above the going price; (*d*) of unitary elasticity at the going price.

4. Below is the demand schedule confronting an oligopolist. Which one of the eight prices seems to be the "going" price of the product produced by the firm? (*a*) $4.50; (*b*) $4; (*c*) $3.50; (*d*) $3.

Price	Quantity demanded
$5.00	10
4.50	20
4.00	30
3.50	40
3.00	42
2.50	44
2.00	46
1.00	48

5. When oligopolists collude to maximize their joint profit, the results are generally: (*a*) greater output and higher price; (*b*) greater output and lower price; (*c*) smaller output and lower price; (*d*) smaller output and higher price.

6. Which of the following constitutes an obstacle to collusion among oligopolists? (*a*) a general business recession; (*b*) a small number of firms in the industry; (*c*) a homogeneous product; (*d*) the patent laws.

7. Which of the following is *not* a means of colluding? (*a*) a cartel; (*b*) a price break; (*c*) a gentlemen's agreement; (*d*) price leadership.

8. Which of the following does *not* contribute to the existence of oligopoly? (*a*) the economies of large-scale production; (*b*) the gains in profits that result from mergers; (*c*) low barriers to entry into an industry; (*d*) extensive sales promotion activities by the established firms in an industry.

9. A profits-payoff (or price-profits) table is used to explain all but one of the following: (*a*) mutual interdependence; (*b*) the advantages of collusion; (*c*) price rigidity; (*d*) product differentiation.

10. Countervailing power means that: (*a*) new firms enter oligopolistic industries to compete with and lower the profits of the firms in the industry; (*b*) oligopolists restrict their profits for fear the government will investigate their pricing policy and for fear of adverse public opinion; (*c*) technological advanced results over time in lower prices, improved products, and larger outputs in oligopolies; (*d*) resource suppliers and customers of oligopolists tend to become oligopolists themselves in order to protect themselves and to share in the oligopolists' profits.

■ **DISCUSSION QUESTIONS**

1. What are the essential characteristics of an oligopoly? How does it differ from monopolistic competition?

2. How prevalent is oligopoly in the American economy? Is it more or less prevalent than monopolistic competition?

3. What do "mutual interdependence" and "uncertainty" mean with respect to oligopoly? Why are they special characteristics of oligopoly?

4. What are the underlying causes of oligopoly?

5. Why is it difficult to employ formal economic analysis to explain the prices charged by and the outputs of oligopolists?

6. To what extent are oligopoly prices flexible and to what extent is there price competition among oligopolistic firms?

7. Explain what the kinked demand curve is, its most important characteristics, the assumptions upon which it is based, and the kind of marginal-revenue curve to which it gives rise. How can the kinked demand curve be used to explain why oligopoly prices are relatively inflexible? Under what conditions will oligopolists acting independently raise or lower their prices even though their demand curves may be kinked?

8. Explain the difference between (a) collusive and noncollusive oligopoly, (b) restrictive and progressive oligopoly, and (c) homogeneous and differentiated oligopoly.

9. Why do oligopolists find it advantageous to collude? What are the obstacles to collusion?

10. Explain (a) a cartel, (b) a gentlemen's agreement, and (c) price leadership.

11. Why do oligopolists engage in extensive nonprice competition?

12. Explain what a profits-payoff (or price-profits) table is and how it is used to demonstrate (a) mutual interdependence, (b) price rigidity, and (c) the advantages of collusion and merger.

13. Is oligopoly economically efficient and beneficial to society? Explain why your answer depends upon whether a short-run or a long-run view is taken.

14. What is meant when it is said that oligopolists have both the means and the incentives for technological improvements?

15. Explain precisely what is meant by countervailing power. How does it differ from the more traditional view that the self-interest of firms is regulated by "same-side-of-the-market" competition? What shortcomings does it have as a regulatory force?

Production and the Demand for Economic Resources

Chapter 30 is the first of a group of three chapters which examine the markets for resources. Resource markets are markets in which employers of resources and the owners of these resources determine the prices at which resources will be employed and the quantities of these resources that will be hired. (These resources—you should recall—are labor, land, capital, and entrepreneurial ability. The prices of resources have particular names. The price paid for labor is called a wage, the price paid for the use of land is rent, the price paid for the use of capital is interest, and the price paid for entrepreneurial ability is profit.)

The employers of resources are business firms who use resources to produce their products. When the number of employers *and* the number of owners of a resource are large the market for that resource is a competitive market; and—as you already know—the demand for and the supply of that resource will determine its price and the total quantity of it that will be employed. Chapter 30 begins the examination of resource markets by looking at the business firm and the demand (or employer) side of the resource market. The material in this chapter is *not* an explanation of what determines the demand for a *particular* resource; but it is an explanation of what determines the demand for *any* resource. In Chapters 31 and 32 the other sides of the resource markets and particular resources are examined in detail.

The list of important terms for Chapter 30 is relatively short, but included in the list are two very important concepts—marginal revenue product and marginal resource cost—which you must grasp if you are to understand how much of a resource a firm will hire. These two concepts are similar to but not identical with the marginal-revenue and marginal-cost concepts employed in the study of product markets and in the explanation of how large an output a firm will produce. Marginal revenue and marginal cost are, respectively, the change in the firm's total revenue and the change in the firm's total cost when it produces and sells an additional unit of *output;* marginal revenue product and marginal resource cost are, respectively, the change in the firm's total revenue and the change in the firm's total cost when it hires an additional unit of an *input.* (*Note:* The two new concepts deal with changes in revenue and costs as a consequence of hiring more of a *resource.*)

When a firm wishes to maximize its profits, it produces that *output* at which marginal revenue and marginal cost are equal. But how much of each resource does it hire if it wishes to maximize its profits? It hires that amount of each *resource* at which the marginal revenue product and the marginal resource cost of that resource are equal.

There is still another similarity between the output and the input markets insofar as the firm is concerned. You will recall that the competitive firm's *supply* curve is a portion of its *marginal-cost* curve. The competitive firm's *demand* curve for a resource is a portion of its *marginal-revenue-product* curve. Just as cost is the important determinant of supply, the revenue derived from the use of a resource is the important factor determining the demand for that resource.

■ CHECKLIST

The very least you should be able to do when you have finished this chapter is:

☐ Present three reasons for studying resource pricing.

☐ Define marginal revenue product.

☐ Determine the marginal revenue product schedule of a resource used to produce a product which is sold in a purely competitive market when you are given the relevant data.

☐ Find the marginal revenue product schedule of a resource used to produce a product which is sold in an imperfectly competitive market when you are given the necessary data.

☐ Define marginal resource cost.

☐ State the principle employed by a profit-maximizing firm to determine how much of a resource it will employ; and, when you are given data, apply this principle to find the quantity of a resource a firm will hire.

☐ Explain why the marginal revenue product schedule of a resource is the firm's demand for the resource.

☐ List the three factors which would change a firm's demand for a resource; and predict the effect of an increase or decrease in each of these factors upon the demand of a firm for a resource.

☐ Enumerate the four determinants of the price-elasticity of demand for a resource; and state precisely how a change in each of these four determinants would affect the price-elasticity of demand.

☐ State the principle employed by a profit-maximizing firm to determine how much of each of several resources to employ; and, when you are given the necessary data, apply this principle to find the quantity of each resource the firm will hire.

☐ State the principle employed by a firm to determine the least-cost combination of resources; and utilize this principle to find the least-cost combination when you are given the needed data.

■ CHAPTER OUTLINE

1. The study of what determines the prices of resources is important because resource prices influence the size of individual incomes and the distribution of income; ration scarce resources; affect the way in which firms combine resources to produce their products; and raise ethical questions about the distribution of income.

2. Economists generally agree upon the basic principles of resource pricing, but the complexities of different resources markets make these general principles difficult to apply.

3. The demand for a single resource depends upon (or is derived from) the demand for the goods and services it can produce.

a. Because resource demand is a derived demand, the demand for a single resource depends upon the marginal productivity of the resource and the market price of the good or service it is used to produce.

b. Marginal revenue product combines these two factors—the marginal physical product of a resource and the market value of the product it produces—into a single useful tool.

c. A firm will hire a resource up to the quantity at which the marginal revenue product of the resource is equal to the marginal resource cost.

d. The firm's marginal-revenue-product schedule for a resource is that firm's demand schedule for the resource.

e. If a firm sells its output in an imperfectly competitive market, the more the firm sells the lower becomes the price of the product. This causes the firm's marginal-revenue-product (resource demand) schedule to be less elastic than it would be if the firm sold its output in a purely competitive market.

f. The market (or total) demand for a resource is the sum of the demand schedules of all firms employing the resource.

4. Changes in the demand for the product being produced, changes in the productivity of the resource, and changes in the prices of other resources will tend to change the demand for a resource.

5. The elasticity of the demand for a particular resource depends upon the rate at which the marginal physical product of that resource declines, the extent to which other resources can be substituted for the particular resource, the elasticity of demand for the product being produced, and the ratio of the cost of the resource to the total costs of the firm.

6. Firms typically employ more than one resource in producing a product.

  a. The firm is hiring resources in the most profitable combination, if it hires resources in a competitive market, when the marginal revenue product of each resource is equal to the price of the resource.

  b. The firm employing resources in perfectly competitive markets is hiring resources in the least-cost combination when the ratio of the marginal physical product of a resource to its price is the same for all the resources the firm hires.

  c. If the firm employs resources in imperfectly competitive markets it is hiring resources in the most profitable combination when the marginal revenue product of each resource is equal to its marginal resource cost; and it is hiring resources in the least-cost combination when the ratio of the marginal physical product of a resource to its marginal resource cost is the same for all resources.

■ **IMPORTANT TERMS**

Derived demand	Output effect
Marginal revenue product	Profit-maximizing combination of resources
Marginal resource cost	Least-cost combination of resources
MRP = MRC rule	
Substitution effect	

■ **FILL-IN QUESTIONS**

1. Resource prices ration _____ and are one of the factors that determine the

_____

of households; they are also one of the determinants of the _____
of business firms.

2. The demand for a resource is a _____

demand and depends upon the _____

_____

and the _____

3. A firm will find it profitable to hire additional units of a resource up to the quantity

at which the _____

and the _____
of the resource are equal; if the firm hires the resource in a purely competitive market, the

_____

and the _____
of the resource are necessarily equal.

4. A firm's demand schedule for a resource

is the firm's _____
schedule for that resource because both indi-

cate the _____
of the resource the firm will hire at various

resource _____

5. A producer who sells his product in an imperfectly competitive market finds that the

more of a resource he hires, the _____
becomes the price at which he can sell his product. As a consequence the marginal-revenue-product (or demand) schedule for

the resource is _____
elastic than it would be if the output were sold in a purely competitive market.

6. A firm can hire 4 units of a resource and produce 20 units of a product which sells for $6 per unit; if it were to hire 5 units of the resource, it would be able to produce 27 units of product which would sell for $5 per unit. The marginal revenue product of the 5th unit

of the resource is $_____, which is equal

to _____ × $_____

minus _____ × $_____

7. The market demand curve for a resource

is obtained by _____

_____

8. The demand for a resource will change if

the demand for the _____

changes, if the _____

of the resource changes, or if the _____

_____

of other resources change.

9. In the space to the right of each of the following, indicate whether the change would tend to increase (+), decrease (−), or have no effect (0) upon a firm's demand for a particular resource:

a. An increase in the price of the firm's

product _____

b. A decrease in the amounts of all other

resources the firm employs _____

c. An increase in the productivity of the re-

source _____

d. An increase in the price of a substitute

resource _____

e. A decrease in the price of a complemen-

tary resource _____

10. The output of the firm being constant, a decrease in the price of resource A will in-

duce the firm to hire _____

of resource A and _____ of other

resources; this is called the _____

effect. But if the decrease in the price of A results in lower total costs and an increase in

output, the firm may hire _____

of both resources; this is called the _____

_____ effect.

11. Four determinants of the price-elasticity of demand for a resource are the rate at which

the _____

of the resource decreases, the degree to

which other resources can be _____

for the resource, the _____

for the product which it is used to produce,

and the _____

_____

12. A firm that hires resources in purely competitive markets is employing the combination of resources which will result in maxi-

mum profits for the firm when the _____

of every resource is equal to its _____

13. Suppose a firm employs resources in purely competitive markets. If the firm wishes to produce any given amount of its product in

the least costly way, the ratio of the _____

_____ of each resource to its

_____ must be the same

for all resources.

14. When the marginal revenue product of a resource is equal to the price of that resource, the marginal revenue product of the

resource divided by its price is equal to _____

_____

15. Assume that a firm employs resources in imperfectly competitive markets. The firm is:

a. Employing the combination of resources

that maximizes its profits when the _____

of every resource is equal to its _____

(or when the _____

each resource divided by its _____

is equal to _____).

b. Employing the combination of resources that enables it to produce any given output in

the least costly way when the _____

of every resource divided by its _____

is the same for all resources.

■ **PROBLEMS AND PROJECTS**

1. The table at the top of page 237 shows the total product a firm will be able to obtain if it employs varying amounts of resource A, the amounts of the other resources the firm employs remaining constant.

a. Compute the marginal physical product of each of the seven units of resource A and enter these figures in the table.

b. Assume the product the firm produces sells in the market for $1.50 per unit. Compute the total revenue of the firm at each of the eight levels of output and the marginal revenue product of each of the seven units of resource A. Enter these figures in the table.

c. On the basis of your computations complete the firm's demand schedule for resource A in the next table by indicating how many units of resource A the firm would employ at the given prices.

Quantity of resource A employed	Total product	Marginal physical product of A	Total revenue	Marginal revenue product of A
0	0		$_____	
1	12	_____		$_____
2	22	_____	_____	_____
3	30	_____	_____	_____
4	36	_____	_____	_____
5	40	_____	_____	_____
6	42	_____	_____	_____
7	43	_____	_____	_____

Price of A	Quantity of A demanded
$21	_____
18	_____
15	_____
12	_____
9	_____
6	_____
3	_____
1	_____

a. Compute the total product (output) of the firm for each of the seven quantities of resource B employed and enter these figures in the table.

b. Assume that the firm sells its output in an imperfectly competitive market and that the prices at which it can sell its product are those given in the table. Compute and enter in the table:

(1) Total revenue for each of seven quantities of B employed.

(2) The marginal revenue product of each of the seven units of resource B.

c. How many units of B would the firm employ if the market price of B were:

2. In the table below you will find the marginal-physical-product data for resource B. Assume that the quantities of other resources employed by the firm remain constant.

(1) $25: _____

(2) $20: _____

(3) $15: _____

Quantity of resource B employed	Marginal physical product of B	Total product	Product price	Total revenue	Marginal revenue product of B
0		0		$ 0.00	
1	22	_____	$1.00	_____	$_____
2	21	_____	.90	_____	_____
3	19	_____	.80	_____	_____
4	16	_____	.70	_____	_____
5	12	_____	.60	_____	_____
6	7	_____	.50	_____	_____
7	1	_____	.40	_____	_____

(4) $9: _____

(5) $5: _____

(6) $1: _____

3. In the table below are the marginal-physical- and marginal-revenue-product schedules for resource C and resource D. Both resources are variable and are employed in purely competitive markets. The price of C is $2 and the price of D is $3.

a. The least-cost combination of C and D that would enable the firm to produce:

(1) 64 units of its product is _____ C and _____ D.

(2) 99 units of its product is _____ C and _____ D.

b. The profit-maximizing combination of C and D is _____ C and _____ D.

c. When the firm employs the profit-maximizing combination of C and D, it is also employing C and D in the least-cost combination

because _____

equals _____

d. Examination of the figures in the table reveals that the firm sells its product in a _____ _____ competitive market at a price of $_____

e. Employing the profit-maximizing combination of C and D, the firm's:

(1) Total output is _____

(2) Total revenue is $ _____

(3) Total cost is $ _____

(4) Total profit is $ _____

■ **SELF-TEST**

Circle the T if the statement is true, the F if it is false.

1. The prices of resources are an important factor in the determination of the supply of a product.   T   F

2. A resource which is highly productive will always be in great demand.   T   F

3. A firm's demand schedule for a resource is the firm's marginal-revenue-product schedule for the resource.   T   F

4. A producer's demand schedule for a resource will be more elastic if he sells his product in a purely competitive market than it would be if he sold the product in an imperfectly competitive market.   T   F

5. If two resources are "complementary," an increase in the price of one of them will reduce the demand for the other.   T   F

6. An increase in the price of a resource will cause the demand for the resource to decrease.   T   F

Use the following information as the basis for answering questions 7 and 8. The marginal revenue product and price of resource A are $12 and a constant $2, respectively; and the marginal revenue product and price of resource B are $25 and a constant $5, respectively. The firm sells its product at a constant price of $1.

7. The firm should decrease the amount of A and increase the amount of B it employs if it wishes to decrease its total cost without affecting its total output.   T   F

8. If the firm wishes to maximize its profits, it should increase its employment of both A

Quantity of resource C employed	Marginal physical product of C	Marginal revenue product of C	Quality of resource D employed	Marginal physical product of D	Marginal revenue product of D
1	10	$5.00	1	21	$10.50
2	8	4.00	2	18	9.00
3	6	3.00	3	15	7.50
4	5	2.50	4	12	6.00
5	4	2.00	5	9	4.50
6	3	1.50	6	6	3.00
7	2	1.00	7	3	1.50

and B until their marginal revenue products fall to $2 and $5, respectively. **T F**

Underscore the letter that corresponds to the best answer.

1. The study of the pricing of resources tends to be complex because: (a) supply and demand do not determine resource prices; (b) economists do not agree on the basic principles of resource pricing; (c) the basic principles of resource pricing must be varied and adjusted when applied to particular resource markets; (d) resource pricing is essentially an ethical question.

Use the total-product and marginal-physical-product schedules for a resource found below to answer questions 2, 3, and 4. Assume that the quantities of other resources the firm employs remain constant.

Units of resource	Total product	MPP
1	8	8
2	14	6
3	18	4
4	21	3
5	23	2

2. If the product the firm produces sells for a constant $3 per unit, the marginal revenue product of the 4th unit of the resource is: (a) $3; (b) $6; (c) $9; (d) $12.

3. If the firm's product sells for a constant $3 per unit and the price of the resource is a constant $15, the firm will employ how many units of the resource? (a) 2; (b) 3; (c) 4; (d) 5.

4. If the firm can sell 14 units of output at a price of $1 per unit and 18 units of output at a price of $0.90 per unit, the marginal revenue product of the 3rd unit of the resource is: (a) $4; (b) $3.60; (c) $2.20; (d) $0.40.

5. Which of the following would increase a firm's demand for a particular resource? (a) an increase in the prices of complementary resources used by the firm; (b) a decrease in the demand for the firm's product; (c) an increase in the productivity of the resource; (d) a decrease in the price of the particular resource.

6. Which of the following would result in an increase in the elasticity of demand for a particular resource? (a) an increase in the rate at which the marginal physical product of that resource declines; (b) a decrease in the elasticity of demand for the product which the resource helps to produce; (c) an increase in the percentage of the firm's total costs accounted for by the resource; (d) a decrease in the number of other resources which are good substitutes for the particular resource.

7. A firm is allocating its expenditure for resources in a way that will result in the least total cost of producing any given output when: (a) the amount the firm spends on each resource is the same; (b) the marginal revenue product of each resource is the same; (c) the marginal physical product of each resource is the same; (d) the marginal physical product per dollar spent on the last unit of each resource is the same.

8. A firm that hires resources in competitive markets is *not necessarily* maximizing its profits when: (a) the marginal revenue product of every resource is equal to 1; (b) the marginal revenue product of every resource is equal to its price; (c) the ratio of the marginal revenue product of every resource to its price is equal to 1; (d) the ratio of the price of every resource to its marginal revenue product is equal to 1.

■ **DISCUSSION QUESTIONS**

1. Why is it important to study resource pricing?

2. Why is resource demand a derived demand, and upon what two factors does the strength of this derived demand depend?

3. Explain why firms that wish to maximize their profits follow the MRP = MRC rule.

4. What constitutes a firm's demand schedule for a resource? Why?

5. Why is the demand schedule for a resource less elastic when the firm sells its product in an imperfectly competitive market than when it sells it in a purely competitive market?

6. What determines the total, or market, demand for a resource?

7. Explain what will cause the demand for a resource to increase and what will cause it to decrease.

8. Explain the difference between the "substitution effect" and the "output effect."

9. What determines the elasticity of the demand for a resource? Explain the exact relationship between each of these four determinants and elasticity.

10. Assuming a firm employs resources in purely competitive markets, when is it spending money on resources in such a way that it can produce a given output for the least total cost?

11. When is a firm that employs resources in purely competitive markets utilizing these resources in amounts that will maximize the profits of the firm?

12. Were a firm to employ resources in *imperfectly* competitive markets, what would your answers to questions 10 and 11 be?

The Pricing and Employment of Resources: Wage Determination

The preceding chapter of the text explained marginal revenue product and marginal resource cost. It also explained what determines the demand for *any* resource. Chapter 31 builds upon these explanations and applies them to the study of a particular resource, labor, and the wage rate, the price paid for labor.

But as you learned in Chapters 26 through 29, it requires more than an understanding of supply and demand to explain the price of a product and the output of a firm and an industry. An understanding of the competitiveness of the market in which the product is sold is also required. It was for this reason that purely competitive, monopolistic, monopolistically competitive, and oligopolistic markets were examined in detail. The same is true of labor markets. The competitiveness of labor markets must be examined if the factors which determine wage rates and the quantity of labor employed are to be understood.

Following comments on the meanings of certain terms, the general level of wages, and the reasons for the high and increasing general wage level in the United States, Chapter 31 explains how wage rates are determined in particular types of labor markets. Four kinds of labor markets are studied: (1) the competitive market in which the num-

ber of employers is large and labor is non-unionized; (2) the monopsony market in which a single employer hires labor under competitive (nonunion) conditions; (3) markets in which unions control the supply of labor and the number of employers is large; and (4) bilateral monopoly markets, in which a single employer faces a labor supply controlled by a single union.

It is, of course, important for you to learn the characteristics of and the differences between each of these labor markets. It is also important that you study each of them carefully to see *how* the characteristics of the market affect the wage rate that will be paid in these markets. In the first two types of market the wage rate which will be paid is quite definite, and here you should learn exactly what level of wages and employment will prevail.

When unions control the supply of labor, wage and employment levels are less definite. If the demand for labor is competitive, the wage rate and the amount of employment will depend upon how successful the union is in increasing the demand for labor, in restricting the supply of labor, or in setting a wage rate which employers will accept. If there is but a single employer, wages and employment will fall within certain limits; exactly where they occur within these limits will depend upon the bargaining strength of the union and of the firm. You should, however, know what the limits are.

The sections explaining wages in particular labor markets are the more important parts of the chapter. But the sections which examine the effects of minimum wage laws on employment and wage rates, the effect of unionization upon wage rates in the United States, the reasons why different workers receive different wage rates, and the effect of investment in human capital are also important. You should, therefore, pay attention to (1) the case against, the case for, and the real-world effects of the minimum wage; (2) the two generalizations that emerge from studies of the effects of unions upon wages; (3) the several causes of wage differentials; and (4) the theory of human capital and the criticisms of that theory.

■ **CHECKLIST**

The very least you should be able to do when you have finished this chapter is:

□ Define wages (or the wage rate); and distinguish between money and real wages.

□ List the several factors which have led to the high and rising general level of real wages in the United States.

□ Explain, using graphs, what determines the wage rate and the level of employment in competitive labor markets and in monopsonistic labor markets; and be able, when given numerical data, to find the equilibrium wage rate and employment level in each of these models.

□ Enumerate the devices used by the labor movement and by craft unions to increase wage rates; and explain the effects of each of these devices upon the employment of labor.

□ Explain, using a graph, how the organization of workers by an industrial union in a previously competitive labor market would affect the wage rate and employment level.

□ Use a graph to explain why the equilibrium wage rate and employment level is indeterminate when a labor market is a bilateral monopoly; and to predict the range within which the wage rate will be found.

□ Present the case for and the case against a legally established minimum wage.

□ State the two generalizations that emerge from an examination of the question of whether unions have raised wages in the United States.

□ List the three major factors which explain why wage differentials exist.

□ Define investment in human capital; explain the cause-effect chain in the theory of human capital; and criticize this theory.

■ **CHAPTER OUTLINE**

1. A wage (or wage rate) is the price paid per unit of time for any type of labor and can be measured either in money or in real terms. Earnings are equal to the wage multiplied by the amount of time worked.

2. The general level of wages in the United States is among the highest in the world. This is due to the high productivity of American labor and, therefore, the strong demand for labor relative to the supply of labor.

3. The wage rate received by a specific type of labor depends upon the demand for and the supply of that labor and upon the competitiveness of the market in which labor is hired.

a. In a purely competitive and nonunionized labor market the total demand for and the total supply of labor determine the wage rate; from the point of view of the individual firm the supply of labor is perfectly elastic at this wage rate (that is, the marginal labor cost is equal to the wage rate) and the firm will hire that amount of labor at which the marginal revenue product of labor is equal to the marginal labor cost.

b. In a monopsonistic and nonunionized labor market the firm's marginal labor costs are greater than the wage rates it must pay to obtain various amounts of labor; and it hires that amount of labor at which marginal labor cost and the marginal revenue product of labor are equal. Both the wage rate and the level of employment are less than they would be under purely competitive conditions.

c. In labor markets in which unions control the supply of labor, they attempt to increase wage rates by increasing the demand for labor, by limiting the supply of labor, or by imposing upon employers wage rates in excess of the equilibrium wage rate which would prevail in a purely competitive market.

d. In a labor market characterized by bilateral monopoly, the wage rate depends, within certain limits, on the relative bargaining power of the union and of the employer.

e. Whether minimum wage laws reduce poverty is a debatable question; but the evidence suggests that while they increase the incomes of employed workers they also reduce the number of workers employed.

f. The unionization of workers has increased the wages received by union members slightly above what they would have received in the absence of unionization; but these wage increases have been at the expense of unorganized workers and unionization has not increased the average real wages of all workers.

4. Not all labor receives the same wage. Wage differentials exist because the labor force consists of noncompeting groups, because jobs vary in difficulty and attractiveness, and because laborers are not perfectly mobile.

5. Some economists have argued that differences in the earnings of workers are to a large extent the result of differences in the amounts invested in human capital (the amounts spent to improve the education, health, and mobility of workers) because these investments increase the productivity and, as a consequence, the wage and income of a worker. Recent evidence, however, does not show that the incomes of the poor are increased by greater public expenditures for their education and training.

■ **IMPORTANT TERMS**

Wage (rate)	Inclusive unionism
Earnings	Industrial union
Money wage (rate)	Bilateral monopoly
Real wage (rate)	Minimum wage
Marginal resource (labor) cost	Wage differential
Monopsony	Noncompeting groups
Oligopsony	Equalizing differences
Exclusive unionism	Immobility
Craft union	Investment in human capital

■ **FILL-IN QUESTIONS**

1. A wage rate is the price paid for labor per _____ and the earnings of labor are equal to _____ _____; money wages are an amount of money, while real wages are _____

2. American labor tends to be highly productive, among other reasons, because of the large amounts of _____ and _____ in the economy relative to the size of the labor force, the high _____ of the American labor force, and superior _____

3. In a competitive market the supply curve for a particular type of labor tends to slope upward from left to right because _____ _____; the wage rate in the market will equal the rate at which the _____ and the _____ are equal. Demand here is the sum of the _____ of all firms hiring this type of labor.

4. Insofar as an individual firm hiring labor in a competitive market is concerned, the supply of labor is _____ elastic because _____

5. The individual employer who hires his labor in a competitive market hires that quantity of labor at which the _____ of labor is equal to the _____ or the _____

6. A monopsonist employing labor in a market which is competitive on the supply side will hire that amount of labor at which _____ _____ and _____ are equal. Because _____

is always greater than _____
in such a market, the employer will pay a
wage which is less than _____
and _____

7. When compared with a competitive labor
market, a market dominated by a monopsonist results in _____
wage rates and _____
employment.

8. The basic objective of labor unions is to
_____ ;
they attempt to accomplish this goal either by
_____ ,
by _____ ,
or by _____

9. Craft unions typically try to increase wages
by _____
while industrial unions try to increase wages
by _____ .
If they are successful, employment in the craft
or industry affected is _____

10. In a labor market which is a bilateral
monopoly, the monopsonist will not pay a
wage greater than _____ ;
the union will ask for some wage greater than
the _____ .
Within these limits the wage rate will depend
on _____

11. The imposition of effective minimum
wage rates, ignoring any shock effects, in:

a. competitive labor markets is to _____
the wage rate and to _____ employment.

b. monopsonistic labor markets is to _____
_____ the wage rate and to _____
employment.

c. the economy as a whole seems to have
been to _____ the wage rate and to _____
employment.

12. The effect of the unionization of workers
in the American economy has been to _____

_____ wage rates in the organized industries, to _____ them in the unorganized industries, and to _____
the average level of wages of organized and
unorganized workers.

13. Actual wage rates received by different
workers tend to differ because workers are
not _____ ,
because jobs differ in _____ ,
and because labor markets are _____

14. The total labor force is composed of a
number of _____
groups of workers. Within each of these
groups some workers receive higher wages
than others, and these wage differentials are
called _____
because _____

15. Workers performing identical jobs often
receive different wages; these differences are
due to _____
of three basic types: _____ ,
_____ ,
and _____

16. Investment according to the theory of
human capital:

a. consists of expenditures for _____
_____ , _____ , and _____

b. increases the _____ and
_____ of workers.

c. explains a good part of the increases in
the level of _____ in the United States.

d. and accounts for the existence of _____
_____ groups and _____
in the wages and incomes among groups.

■ **PROBLEMS AND PROJECTS**

1. Suppose a single firm has for a particular
type of labor the marginal revenue product
schedule given in the following table.

Number of units of labor	MRP of labor
1	$15
2	14
3	13
4	12
5	11
6	10
7	9
8	8

a. Assume there are 100 firms with the same marginal-revenue-product schedules for this particular type of labor. Compute the total or market demand for this labor by completing column 1 in the table below.

(1) Quantity of labor demanded	(2) Wage rate	(3) Quantity of labor supplied
_____	$15	850
_____	14	800
_____	13	750
_____	12	700
_____	11	650
_____	10	600
_____	9	550
_____	8	500

b. Using the supply schedule for labor given in columns 2 and 3:
(1) What will be the equilibrium wage rate?

$_____

(2) What will be the total amount of labor

hired in the market? _____

c. The individual firm will:

(1) have a marginal labor cost of $_____

(2) employ _____ units of labor.

(3) pay a wage of $_____
d. On the graph at the right above plot the market demand and supply curves for labor and indicate the equilibrium wage rate and the total quantity of labor employed.

e. On the graph at the right plot the individual firm's demand curve for labor, the supply curve for labor, and the marginal-labor-cost curve which confronts the indi-

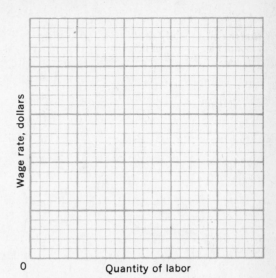

Wage rate, dollars

0   Quantity of labor

vidual firm; indicate the quantity of labor the firm will hire and the wage it will pay.
f. The imposition of a $12 minimum wage rate would change the total amount of labor

hired in this market to _____

2. In the table at the top of page 246, assume a monopsonist has the marginal-revenue-product schedule for a particular type of labor given in columns 1 and 2 and that the supply schedule for labor is that given in columns 1 and 3.

a. Compute the firm's total labor costs at each level of employment and the marginal labor cost of each unit of labor, and enter these figures in columns 4 and 5.
b. The firm will:

(1) hire _____ units of labor.

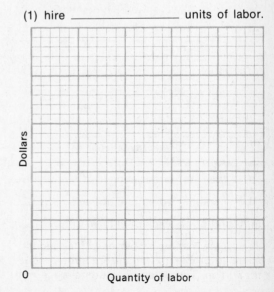

Dollars

0   Quantity of labor

(1) Number of labor units	(2) MRP of labor	(3) Wage rate	(4) Total labor cost	(5) Marginal labor cost
0		$ 2	$_____	
1	$36	4	_____	$_____
2	32	6	_____	_____
3	28	8	_____	_____
4	24	10	_____	_____
5	20	12	_____	_____
6	16	14	_____	_____
7	12	16	_____	_____
8	8	18	_____	_____

(2) pay a wage of $ _____

(3) have a marginal revenue product for

labor of $_____

for the last unit of labor employed.

c. Plot the marginal revenue product of labor, the supply curve for labor, and the marginal-labor-cost curve on the graph below; indicate the quantity of labor the firm will employ and the wage it will pay.

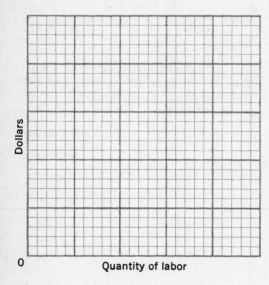

Dollars

0   Quantity of labor

d. If this firm hired labor in a competitive

labor market, it would hire at least _____

units and pay a wage of at least $ _____

3. Assume that the employees of the monopsonist in problem 2 organize a strong industrial union. The union demands a wage rate of $16 for its members, and the monopsonist decides to pay this wage because a strike would be too costly.

a. In the table below compute the supply schedule for labor which now confronts the monopsonist by completing column 2.

(1) Number of labor units	(2) Wage rate	(3) Total labor cost	(4) Marginal labor cost
1	$_____	$_____	$_____
2	_____	_____	_____
3	_____	_____	_____
4	_____	_____	_____
5	_____	_____	_____
6	_____	_____	_____
7	_____	_____	_____
8	_____	_____	_____

b. Compute the total labor cost and the marginal labor cost at each level of employment, and enter these figures in columns 3 and 4.

c. The firm will:

(1) hire _____ units of labor.

(2) pay a wage of $_____

(3) pay total wages of $_____

d. As a result of unionization the wage rate

has _____,

the level of employment has _____,

and the earnings of labor have _____

e. On the graph below plot the firm's marginal revenue product of labor schedule, the labor supply schedule, and the marginal-labor-cost schedule. Indicate also the wage rate the firm will pay and the number of workers it will hire.

Wage rate, dollars

0   Quantity of labor

■ **SELF-TEST**

Circle the T if the statement is true, the F if it is false.

1. The general level of real wages is higher in the United States than in many foreign countries because the supply of labor is great relative to the demand for it.   **T F**

2. If an individual firm employs labor in a competitive market, it finds that its marginal labor cost is equal to the wage rate in that market.   **T F**

3. Both monopsonists and firms hiring labor in competitive markets hire labor up to the quantity at which the marginal revenue product of labor and marginal labor cost are equal.   **T F**

4. A monopsonist is also a monopolist in the product market.   **T F**

5. Restricting the supply of labor is a means of increasing wage rates more commonly used by craft unions than by industrial unions.   **T F**

6. The imposition of an above-equilibrium

wage rate will cause employment to fall off more when the demand for labor is inelastic than it will when the demand is elastic.   **T F**

7. If a labor market is competitive, the imposition of an effective minimum wage will increase the wage rate paid and decrease employment in that market.   **T F**

8. Actual wage rates received in different labor markets tend to differ because the demands for particular types of labor relative to their supplies differ.   **T F**

9. "Ben Robbins is a skilled artisan of a particular type, is unable to obtain membership in the union representing that group of artisans, and is, therefore, unable to practice his trade." This is an example of labor immobility.   **T F**

10. Given a firm's demand for labor the lower the wage it must pay the more workers it will hire.   **T F**

Underscore the letter that corresponds to the best answer.

1. Real wages would decline if the: (a) prices of goods and services rose more rapidly than money wage rates; (b) prices of goods and services rose less rapidly than money wage rates; (c) prices of goods and services and wage rates both rose; (d) prices of goods and services and wage rates both fell.

2. The individual firm which hires labor under competitive conditions faces a supply curve for labor which: (a) is perfectly inelastic; (b) is of unitary elasticity; (c) is perfectly elastic; (d) slopes upward from left to right.

3. A monopsonist pays a wage rate which is: (a) greater than the marginal revenue product of labor; (b) equal to the marginal revenue product of labor; (c) equal to the firm's marginal labor cost; (d) less than the marginal revenue product of labor.

4. Compared with a competitive labor market, a monopsonistic market will result in: (a) higher wage rates and a higher level of employment; (b) higher wage rates and a lower level of employment; (c) lower wage rates and a higher level of employment; (d) lower wage rates and a lower level of employment.

5. Higher wage rates and a higher level of employment are the usual consequences of:

(a) inclusive unionism; (b) exclusive union-ism; (c) an above-equilibrium wage rate; (d) an increase in the productivity of labor.

6. Which of the following has been a conse-quence of unionization? (a) higher wage rates for unionized workers; (b) greater employ-ment of unionized workers; (c) greater em-ployment of the workers in the labor force; (d) a higher level of real wages in the econ-omy.

7. Industrial unions typically attempt to in-crease wage rates by: (a) imposing an above-equilibrium wage rate upon employers; (b) increasing the demand for labor; (c) decreas-ing the supply of labor; (d) forming a bilateral monopoly.

8. The fact that a star baseball player re-ceives a wage of $125,000 a year can *best* be explained in terms of: (a) noncompeting labor groups; (b) equalizing differences; (c) labor immobility; (d) imperfections in the labor market.

9. The fact that unskilled construction work-ers received higher wages than gas-station attendants is *best* explained in terms of: (a) noncompeting labor groups; (b) equalizing differences; (c) labor immobility; (d) imper-fections in the labor market.

10. Which of the following is *not* true? (a) investment in human capital, according to the proponents of the human-capital theory, in-creases the productivity of workers; (b) ex-penditures for health, education, and mo-bility are investments in human capital; (c) whether to invest in real capital is a decision similar to the decision whether to invest in human capital; (d) differences in the amounts invested in human capital, human-capital theorists argue, explain the equalizing dif-ferences in wage rates.

■ **DISCUSSION QUESTIONS**

1. Why is the general level of real wages higher in the United States than in most foreign nations? Why has the level of real wages continued to increase even though the supply of labor has continually increased?

2. Explain why the productivity of the Ameri-can labor force increased in the past to its present high level. What factors may be

working today to slow the rate at which labor-force productivity increases?

3. In the competitive model what determines the market demand for labor and the wage rate? What kind of supply situation do all firms as a group confront? Under what economic conditions would a group of firms in a competitive market not confront such a supply schedule? What kind of supply situation does the individual firm confront? Why?

4. In the monopsony model what determines employment and the wage rate? What kind of supply situation does the monopsonist face? Why? How does the wage rate paid and the level of employment compare with what would result if the market were compe-titive?

5. In what sense is a worker who is hired by a monosponist "exploited" and one who is employed in a competitive labor market "justly" rewarded? *Why* do monopsonists wish to restrict employment?

6. When supply is less than perfectly elastic, marginal labor cost is greater than the wage rate. Why?

7. What basic methods do labor unions em-ploy to try to increase the wages received by their members? If these methods are suc-cessful in raising wages, what effect do they have upon employment?

8. When labor unions attempt to restrict the supply of labor to increase wage rates, what devices do they employ to do this for the economy as a whole and what means do they use to restrict the supply of a given type of worker?

9. How do industrial unions attempt to in-crease wage rates, and what effect does this method of increasing wages have upon em-ployment in the industry affected?

10. What is bilateral monopoly? What deter-mines wage rates in a labor market of this type?

11. What is the effect of minimum wage laws upon wage rates and employment in (a) com-petitive labor markets; (b) monopsony labor markets; (c) the economy as a whole?

12. How has the unionization of workers af-fected the wage rates and the employment of

(a) unionized workers; (b) nonunionized workers; (c) workers in general?

13. Why are the wage rates received by workers in different occupations, by workers in the same occupations, and by workers in different localities different?

14. Explain what is meant by investment in human capital and why the decision to invest in human capital is like the decision to invest in real capital. What, according to the proponents of the human-capital theory, is the effect of investment in human capital upon the productivity, the wage rate, and the income of workers?

15. Using the theory of human capital, explain (a) geographic differences in wage rates; (b) why younger people are more mobile; (c) why a society tends to educate younger rather than older people; and (d) the historic rise in real wages in the American economy.

16. Explain why enthusiasm for the theory of human capital has diminished in recent years.

The Pricing and Employment of Resources: Rent, Interest, and Profits

Chapter 32 concludes the study of the prices of resources by examining rent, interest, and profits. Compared with the study of wage rates in Chapter 31, each of the three major sections in Chapter 32 is considerably briefer and a good deal simpler. You might do well to treat this chapter as if it were actually three very short chapters.

There is nothing especially difficult about Chapter 32. By now you should understand that the marginal revenue product of a resource determines the demand for that resource and that this understanding can be applied to the demand for land and capital. It will be on the supply side of the land market that you will encounter whatever difficulties there are. The supply of land is unique because it is perfectly *inelastic:* changes in rent do not change the quantity of land which will be supplied. Demand, given the quantity of land available, is thus the sole determinant of rent. Of course land varies in productivity and can be used for different purposes, but these are merely the factors which explain why the rent on all land is not the same.

Capital, as the economist defines it, means capital goods. Is the rate of interest, then, the price paid for the use of capital goods? No, not quite. Capital is not one kind of good; it is many different kinds. In order to be able to talk about the price paid for the use of capital goods there must be a common denominator, a simple way of adding up different kinds of capital goods. The common denominator is money. Interest (or the rate of interest) is the price paid for the use of money or for liquidity. It is the demand for and the supply of money that determine the interest rate in the economy. Business firms and households demand—that is, wish to hold—money for at least three reasons. Like the demand for any other good or service, the greater the price of money (the interest rate) the smaller is the amount of money firms and households will wish to hold. And like other *normal* goods and services, the greater the economy's income (NNP) the greater will be the demand for money.

On the supply side, the Federal Reserve Banks, the monetary authority in the American economy, determine how much money or liquidity will be available. At any time the supply of money is a fixed quantity. This means that the quantity of money available does not rise or fall as a result of changes in the interest rate; and the supply of money is said to be perfectly inelastic. It is this perfectly inelastic supply and the demand for money that determine the equilibrium interest rate. Like other commodities a change in either the supply of or the demand for money will cause this equilibrium interest rate to change.

When it comes to profits, supply and demand analysis fails the economist. Profits are not merely a wage for a particular type of labor; rather they are rewards for taking risks and the gains of the monopolist. Such things as "the quantity of risk taken" or "the quantity of effort required to establish a monopoly" simply can't be measured; consequently it is impossible to talk about the demand for or the supply of them. Nevertheless, profits are important in the economy. They are largely rewards for doing things that have to be done if the economy is to allocate resources efficiently and to progress and develop; they are the lure or the bait which makes men willing to take the risks that result in efficiency and progress.

The final section of Chapter 32 answers two questions about the American economy. What part of the national income goes to workers and what part goes to capitalists— those who provide the economy with land, capital goods, and entrepreneurial ability? And have the shares going to workers and to capitalists changed in the past seventy-five or so years? The student may be surprised to learn that the lion's share—about 80%—of the national income goes to workers today and went to workers at the beginning of the century; and that capitalists today and in 1900 got about 20%. There is, in short, no evidence to support the belief that workers get less and capitalists more or the opposite belief that workers obtain a greater part and capitalists a smaller part of the national income today than they did three-quarters of a century ago in the United States.

■ **CHECKLIST**

The very least you should be able to do when you have finished this chapter is:

□ Define economic rent and explain what determines the amount of economic rent paid.

□ Explain why economic rent is a surplus (or unearned income); and state the means Henry George and the socialists would use to recover this surplus.

□ Explain why the owners of land do not all receive the same economic rent; and why, if economic rent is a surplus, a firm must pay rent.

□ Define the interest rate and explain what

determines the level of interest rates (or *the* interest rate) and why interest rates differ.

□ List the three demands for money (or liquidity) and explain what determines the amount of money firms and households will wish to hold for each of these three purposes.

□ Explain what determines the size of the money supply and the equilibrium interest rate.

□ Explain how the equilibrium interest rate affects investment spending and the equilibrium NNP; and the two functions of the interest rate.

□ Define economic profit and distinguish between economic profit, normal profit, and business profit.

□ Explain why profits are received by some firms and the functions of profits in the American economy.

□ State the current relative size of labor's and of capital's share of the national income; and describe what has happened to these shares in the U.S. economy since 1900.

■ **CHAPTER OUTLINE**

1. Economic rent is the price paid for the use of land or natural resources whose supply is perfectly inelastic.

a. Demand is the active determinant of economic rent because changes in the level of economic rent do not change in the quantity of land supplied; and economic rent is, therefore, a payment which in the aggregate need not be paid to ensure that the land will be available.

b. Some people have argued that land rents are unearned incomes and that either land should be nationalized or rents should be taxed away. The single tax advocated by Henry George would have no effect upon resource allocation. While critics have pointed out the disadvantages of such a tax, there is a renewed interest in taxing land values to improve the equity and efficiency of local tax systems.

c. Economic rents on different types of land vary because land differs in its productivity and because land has alternative uses; hence rent is a cost to a firm because it must pay rent to lure land away from alternative employments.

2. The interest rate is the price paid for the

use of money or, said another way, the price of liquidity.

a. While it is convenient to speak as if there were but a single interest rate there are actually a number of different rates of interest.

b. The interest rate is determined by the demand for and the supply of money (liquidity).

c. The transactions and precautionary demands for money are directly related to the level of national income; and the speculative demand is inversely related to the interest rate.

d. The monetary authority (the Federal Reserve Banks) determines the supply of money; and the equilibrium interest rate is the rate at which the quantity of money demanded is equal to the quantity of money supplied.

(1) The equilibrium interest rate determines the level of investment spending; and the level of investment spending affects the equilibrium NNP.

(2) The interest rate performs two important functions: It determines the total amount of investment in the economy, and it rations the investment among different firms and industries.

3. Economic profit is what remains of the firm's revenues after all its explicit and implicit opportunity costs have been deducted.

a. Profit is a payment for entrepreneurial ability, which involves combining and directing the use of resources in an uncertain and innovating world.

b. Profits are rewards for assuming the risks in an economy in which the future is uncertain and subject to change and for assuming the risks and the uncertainties inherent in innovation. They are also surpluses which business firms obtain from the exploitation of monopoly power.

c. The expectation of profits motivates business firms to innovate, and profits (and losses) guide business firms to produce products and to use resources in the way desired by society.

4. National income data for the American economy indicate that:

a. in the period 1971–1976 wages and salaries were 76% of the national income; but, using a broader definition of labor income (wages and salaries plus proprietors' income —which is mostly a payment for labor),

labor's share was 84% and capital's share (rent, interest, and corporate profits) was 16% of national income.

b. since the years 1900–1909 wages and salaries have increased from 55 to 76%; but labor's share, employing the broader definition of labor income, has remained at about 80% and capital's share at about 20% of the national income.

■ IMPORTANT TERMS

Economic rent	Precautionary demand
Incentive function	Speculative demand
Single-tax movement	Economic (pure) profit
Liquidity	
The (*or* pure) rate of interest	Static economy
	Insurable risk
Liquidity preference theory of interest	Uninsurable risk
	Pursuit and escape theory
Transactions demand	

■ FILL-IN QUESTIONS

1. Rent is the price paid for the use of _____

_____

and _____

and their total supply is _____

2. The active determinant of rent is _____

_____ and the passive determinant is

_____. Because rent does not

perform an _____
function economists consider it to be a

_____

3. Socialists argue that land rents are _____

_____

incomes and that land should be _____

_____

so that these incomes can be used for the good of society as a whole. Proponents of

_____

argue that economic rent could be completely taxed away without affecting the amount of land available for productive purposes.

4. Rents on different pieces of land are not the same because _____ _____.
And while rent from the viewpoint of the economy as a whole is a surplus, rent is a cost to _____ users of land which must be paid because land has _____

5. Interest is the price paid for the use of _____
or _____ which is not an economic resource but which business firms are willing to hire because _____

6. Interest rates on different loans tend to differ because of differences in _____, _____ , and _____ , and because of _____

7. There are three components in the demand for liquidity.

a. The _____ and _____ demands are (directly, inversely) _____ related to the _____

b. And the _____ demand is _____ related to the _____

8. If households and business firms may hold their financial wealth in either bonds or money:
a. When the interest rate is expected to be *higher* in the future households and firms will choose to hold _____ rather than _____
b. But when they expect the interest rate will be *lower* in the future they will choose to hold _____ instead of _____

9. In the American economy:
a. At any moment the money supply is an amount determined by _____

b. The equilibrium interest rate is the rate at which the _____ is equal to _____

10. Were the Federal Reserve Banks to increase the money supply:
a. the equilibrium interest rate would _____ _____, investment spending would _____, and the equilibrium NNP would _____ ;
b. but these changes would be partially offset because the change in the NNP would _____ the transactions and precautionary demands for money.

11. In the American economy the interest rate is an "_____ price"; but it performs two important functions. It helps to determine how much _____ will occur in the economy and then _____ _____ it among various firms and industries.

12. Economic profits are a payment for the resource called _____ , which involves combining _____ and making _____ with regard to their use and _____ in an _____ environment.

13. When the future is _____ , businessmen necessarily assume risks, some of which are _____ and some of which are _____. The risks which businessmen cannot avoid arise either because the _____ _____ is changing or because the firm itself deliberately engages in _____

14. Profits:
a. are important in the American economy because the expectation of profits stimulates firms to innovate, and the more innovation there is, the higher will be the levels of _____ ,

_____ ,

and _____
in the economy;

b. and losses promote the efficient _____
of resources in the economy unless the

profits are _____ profits.

15. Defining labor income broadly to include both wages and salaries and proprietors' income:
a. Labor's share of the national income is

today about _____%;
b. The capitalists' share is the sum of

_____, _____, and

_____; and today about _____%
of the national income;
c. Since the beginning of the twentieth century:
(1) Labor's share has (increased, decreased,

remained constant) _____

(2) Capital's share has _____

16. The pursuit and escape theory suggests that:
a. when laborers increase their money

wages they are in pursuit of the _____
of business firms;

b. businesses escape by raising _____

and _____ ;

c. and that as a result _____
remains constant.

■ **PROBLEMS AND PROJECTS**

1. Assume that the quantity of a certain type of land available is 300,000 acres and the demand for this land is that given in the table below.

Pure land rent, per acre	Land demanded, acres
$350	100,000
300	200,000
250	300,000
200	400,000
150	500,000
100	600,000
50	700,000

a. The pure rent on this land will be $_____
b. The total quantity of land rented will be

_____ acres.

c. On the graph below plot the supply and demand curves for this land and indicate the pure rent for land and the quantity of land rented.

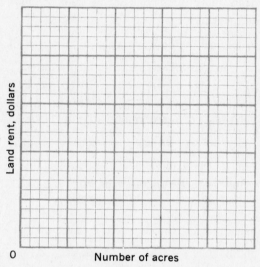

d. If landowners were taxed at a rate of $250 per acre for their land, the pure rent on

this land after taxes would be $ _____

and the number of acres rented would be ____

_____

2. The schedule below shows the speculative demand for money (or liquidity).

Interest rate	Speculative demand for money
8%	$ 60
7%	80
6%	100
5%	120
4%	140
3%	160
2%	180

a. Plot this schedule on the next graph. (The interest rate is measured along the vertical axis and the demand for money is measured along the horizontal axis.)

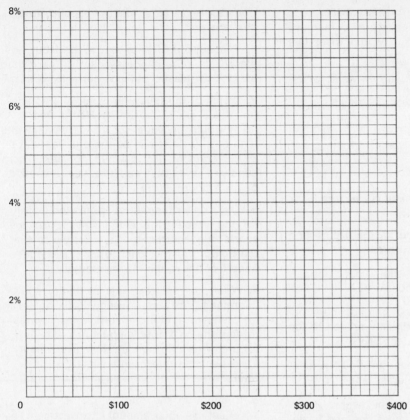

b. Below is a schedule which shows the transactions and precautionary demand for money. Suppose the NNP is $850.

NNP	Transactions and precautionary demand for money
$ 750	$160
800	170
850	180
900	190
950	200
1000	210
1050	220

(1) The transactions and precautionary demand for money is $_____ .

(2) Plot this demand for money on the graph above. (The curve will be a vertical line.)

c. In the table below show the total transactions, precautionary, and speculative demand for money at each of the seven interest rates

when the NNP is $850; and plot this demand for money on the graph above.

Interest rate	Demand for money	Supply of money
8%	$_____	$_____
7%	_____	_____
6%	_____	_____
5%	_____	_____
4%	_____	_____
3%	_____	_____
2%	_____	_____

d. Suppose the money supply is a fixed amount and equal to $280.

(1) Plot the money supply curve on the graph above. (It will be a vertical line.)

(2) Enter the supply of money at each of the seven interest rates in the table above.

(3) Using either the money demand and supply curves or schedules, the equilibrium interest rate when NNP is $850 is _____%.

e. Suppose the NNP remains at $850.

(1) If the money supply were to increase to $300 the interest rate would (rise, fall) _____ to ____%;

(2) and if the money supply were to decrease to $240 the interest rate would _____

_____

■ **SELF-TEST**

Circle the T if the statement is true, the F if it is false.

1. Rent is the price paid for the use of land and other property resources.   **T   F**

2. Rent is a surplus because it does not perform an incentive function.   **T   F**

3. The transactions and precautionary demands for money are directly related to the level of national income (or NNP).   **T   F**

4. The speculative demand for liquidity is inversely related to the interest rate.   **T   F**

5. A decrease in the money supply would tend to increase the interest rate and to decrease investment spending and the equilibrium NNP.   **T   F**

6. If the economists' definition of profits were used, total profits in the economy would be greater than they would be if the businessman's definition were used.   **T   F**

7. The expectation of profits is the basic motive for innovation, while actual profits and losses aid in the efficient allocation of resources.   **T   F**

8. The increasing importance of the corporation in the American economy is a part of the explanation of why wages and salaries have increased and proprietors' incomes have decreased as shares of the national income.   **T   F**

9. The growth of labor unions is the main cause of the expansion of wages and salaries as a share of the national income.   **T   F**

10. Over the past seventy-five years there has been a shift from labor-intensive to capital- and land-intensive production.   **T   F**

Underscore the letter that corresponds to the best answer.

1. The supply of land is: (*a*) perfectly inelastic; (*b*) of unitary elasticity; (*c*) perfectly elastic; (*d*) elastic but not perfectly elastic.

2. Which of the following is *not* characteristic of the tax proposed by Henry George? (*a*) it would be equal to 100 percent of all land rent; (*b*) it would be the only tax levied by government; (*c*) it would not affect the supply of land; (*d*) it would reduce rents paid by the amount of the tax.

3. The smaller the *rate* of interest on a loan: (*a*) the greater the risk involved; (*b*) the shorter the length of the loan; (*c*) the smaller the amount of the loan; (*d*) the greater the imperfections in the money market.

4. When the interest rate is high (above "normal") firms and households on balance (*a*) prefer to hold money rather than bonds; (*b*) find the cost of holding money to be low; (*c*) prefer to hold bonds rather than money; (*d*) expect the rate of interest to rise in the future.

5. Changes in the rate of interest do *not*: (*a*) affect the total amount of investment in the economy; (*b*) affect the amount of investment occurring in particular industries; (*c*) guarantee that the demand for and the supply of liquidity will be equal; (*d*) guarantee that there will be full employment in the economy.

6. Which of the following would *not* be a function of the entrepreneur? (*a*) the introduction of a new product on the market; (*b*) the making of decisions in a static economy; (*c*) the incurring of unavoidable risks; (*d*) the combination and direction of resources in an uncertain environment.

7. The monopolist who earns an economic profit is able to do so because: (*a*) he is an innovator; (*b*) all his risks are insurable; (*c*) uncertainty has been reduced to the minimum; (*d*) most of his decisions are non-routine.

8. Since around 1900: (*a*) capital's share of national income has increased; (*b*) labor's share has increased; (*c*) labor's share has decreased; (*d*) capital's share has been almost constant.

■ DISCUSSION QUESTIONS

1. Explain what determines the economic rent paid for the use of land. What is unique about the supply of land?

2. Why is land rent a "surplus"? What economic difficulties would be encountered if the government adopted Henry George's single-tax proposal as a means of confiscating this surplus? What arguments are used to support the renewed interest in the heavy taxation of land values?

3. Even though land rent is an economic surplus it is also an economic cost for the individual user of land. Why and how can it be both an economic surplus and an economic cost?

4. What is the interest rate?

5. Why are there actually many different rates in the economy at any given time?

6. Explain what determines (a) the amount of money firms and households wish to hold for transaction and precautionary purposes; (b) the amount they wish to have for speculative purposes; (c) the amount of money available for all three of these purposes; and (d) the equilibrium rate of interest.

7. How would a change in the money supply affect (a) the interest rate; (b) investment spending; and (c) the equilibrium NNP? What is the "feedback" problem which complicates monetary policy?

8. What two important functions does the rate of interest perform in the economy? How well does it perform these functions?

9. What are economic profits? For what resource are they a payment, and what tasks does this resource perform?

10. Why would there be no economic profits in a purely competitive static economy?

11. "The risks which an entrepreneur assumes arise because of uncertainties which are external to the firm and because of uncertainties which are developed by the initiative of the firm itself." Explain.

12. What two important functions do profits or the expectation of profits perform in the economy? How does monopoly impede the effective performance of these functions?

13. Monopoly results in profits and reduces uncertainty. Is it possible that monopolists may undertake more innovation as a result? Why?

14. What part of the American national income is wages and salaries and what part is labor income? Why do your answers to these two questions differ? What part of the national income is the income of capitalists? What kinds of income are capitalist income?

15. What have been the historical trends in the shares of national income that are wages and salaries, labor income, and capitalist income? What changes in the American economy can account for these trends?

16. Explain (a) why the growth of labor unions is not a good explanation of the expanding share of the national income going for wages and salaries; (b) the pursuit and escape theory.

General Equilibrium: the Price System and Its Operation

Chapter 33 provides a conclusion to the previous eleven chapters, tying together many of the things you have already learned about microeconomics. By this time you have read a large amount of material concerning the operation of supply and demand in product and resource markets under different market conditions. You may have lost sight of the fact—emphasized in Chapter 5—that the American economy is a *system* of markets and prices. This means that *all* prices and *all* markets are linked together.

The chief purpose of Chapter 33 is to help you understand why and how these markets are linked together, connected, and interrelated. The theory which explains the relationships between different markets and different prices is called *general* equilibrium analysis. (By way of contrast, the theory which explains a single product or resource market and the price of the one good or service bought and sold in that market is called *partial* equilibrium analysis.) An understanding of general equilibrium is necessary in order to understand how the price system as a whole operates to allocate its scarce resources.

The author employs three approaches to enable the student to grasp the essentials and the importance of general equilibrium analysis. He first explains in words the effects of

an increase in the demand for automobiles. Then, using graphs and curves, he explains in more detail the effects of an increase in the demand for a hypothetical product X accompanied by a decrease in the demand for product Y. Both of these explanations include not only the short- and long-run effects upon the products involved but also the effects upon the markets in which the producers employ resources, upon the markets for complementary and substitute products, upon the markets in which the resources used to produce these other products are employed, and upon the distribution of income in the economy. Finally, to help you understand the interrelationships between the different sectors of the economy, the author employs an input-output table.

Having examined these market and price interrelationships, you should next note this. Given the distribution of income among consumers, and subject to several important exceptions, a price system in which all markets are purely competitive will bring about an ideal allocation of the economy's resources. It will maximize the satisfaction of consumer wants and thereby maximize economic welfare in the economy. The American economy, of course, is *not* made up of purely competitive markets. And because of these imperfectly competitive markets, the allocation of resources is actually less than ideal and economic welfare is somewhat less than a maximum.

In addition—and these are important exceptions—even a purely competitive price system does not allocate resources to allow for the spillover costs and the spillover benefits of the products it produces; and it does not produce social goods in sufficient quantities. Hence government seems to be needed (remember the fourth economic function of government in Chapter 6) to adjust output for spillover costs and benefits and to provide society with social goods.

A price system that allocates resources ideally does not necessarily distribute its total output (or income) in accordance with our ethical standards. Economists don't and probably never will know which of the many possible distributions of income is ideal. But according to society's notions of what is right and wrong (just and unjust), it is wrong to have highly unequal distributions of incomes, or incomes below a certain minimum level. Hence the third economic function of government: the redistribution of income and wealth.

Chapter 33 ends by reemphasizing the importance of general equilibrium analysis. Interrelations between markets and prices do exist, and they can be extremely important in tracing through the economy the *total effect* of an economic policy or the *full consequences* of changes in consumers' tastes, the availability of resources, oil, for example, and technology. At the conclusion of this chapter you should be ready to examine several of the trouble spots in the operation of the price system and in the way in which we allocate our scarce resources. These trouble spots are examined in the next seven chapters which make up Part 6 of the text.

■ CHECKLIST

The very least you should be able to do when you have finished this chapter is:

□ Distinguish between partial and general equilibrium analysis.

□ Identify the four concepts which underlie the demand and supply curves in the product and resources markets of the economy.

□ Explain, using graphs if you wish, both the immediate and secondary effects of a change in tastes, technology, or the availability of resources, upon equilibrium prices and quantities in the product and resources markets; and upon the distribution of income in the economy.

□ List the three reasons why a purely competitive price system tends to produce the goods and services which maximize consumer welfare.

□ State the two ways in which the real world differs from a purely competitive price system; and explain the effect of these two imperfections upon allocative efficiency.

□ Give two reasons why, given the distribution of income, even a purely competitive economy would not allocate resources as effectively as possible.

□ Explain why economists are unable to determine which distribution of income is the best.

□ Specify what is shown along the left side, along the top, and in each of the boxes of an input-output table.

□ Find the effects, when you are given an input-output table, of a change in the output of one industry upon the outputs of other industries in the economy.

■ CHAPTER OUTLINE

1. Partial equilibrium analysis is the study of equilibrium prices and quantities in the specific product and resource markets which form the price-market system. General equilibrium analysis is the study of the interrelations between these markets.

2. Any change in tastes, in the supply of resources, or in technology will not only have an immediate effect upon equilibrium price and quantity in a specific market, but will also have secondary effects in other markets and upon other equilibrium prices and quantities.

3. To understand the effects of an increase in consumer demand for product X accompanied by a decrease in consumer demand for product Y, imagine that the industry producing X uses only type A labor and that the industry producing Y uses only type B labor.

a. Assume also that the demand curve for each product has a negative slope because of diminishing marginal utility and the supply curve has a positive slope because of increasing marginal cost; and assume that the demand curve for each type of labor has a negative slope because of diminishing marginal product and the supply curve has a positive slope because of the work-leisure preferences of workers.

b. Beginning with all markets in long-run equilibrium, the short-run effects are an increased (decreased) output and price and economic profits (losses) in industry X (Y), an increased (decreased) derived demand for type A (type B) labor, and increased (decreased) wage rates and employment for type A (type B) labor.

c. The long-run adjustments are the entry (exit) of firms in industry X (Y); an increase (decrease) in the supply of X (Y); a higher (lower) price than existed initially in industry X (Y), assuming increasing-cost industries; an increase (decrease) in the supply of A (B); and higher (lower) wage rates for A (B) than initially existed.

d. In addition to these adjustments there will also be:

(1) An increase (decrease) in the demand for and the prices and outputs of products which are substitutes (complements) for X or complements (substitutes) for Y; and an increased (decreased) demand for the resources used to produce those products whose output increases (decreases).

(2) An increase (decrease) in the demand for the other resources used along with A (B).

(3) A redistribution of income from workers and entrepreneurs in industry Y to those in industry X.

4. Given the distribution of consumer income, purely competitive product and resource markets result in an allocation of an economy's resources and the output of those goods and services which maximize the satisfaction of wants.

5. To the extent that product and resource markets in the real world are imperfectly competitive, the satisfaction of wants will be less than a maximum, and adjustments to changes will be less complete and slower. But this may be offset by more rapid technological progress and greater product variety.

6. For two reasons, even an economy in which all markets are perfectly competitive may not allocate resources efficiently.

a. The price system does not take spillover costs and spillover benefits into account and does not automatically produce social goods.

b. The price system may not distribute the economy's income ideally or optimally.

7. The input-output table indicates the specific relationships that exist between the outputs of the various sectors of the economy.

a. The outputs of each sector are the inputs of the other sectors; and the inputs of each sector are the outputs of the other sectors.

b. Because of this interdependence, any change in the output of one sector will alter the outputs of the other sectors.

8. General equilibrium analysis is important because it provides a wider understanding of the effects of any economic change or policy upon the economy.

a. Real-world examples illustrate the importance of general equilibrium analysis.

b. And input-output analysis is used for economic forecasting and, in underdeveloped nations and the U.S.S.R., for economic planning.

■ **IMPORTANT TERMS**

Price system
Partial equilibrium analysis
General equilibrium analysis

Input-output analysis
Input-output table

■ **FILL-IN QUESTIONS**

1. Partial equilibrium analysis is concerned with prices and outputs in _____ markets in the economy, and general equilibrium analysis is concerned with the _____

_____ between markets and prices.

2. A change in the demand for product Z will affect not only the equilibrium price and quantity of product Z but may also affect the equilibrium price and quantity of:

a. _____

b. _____

c. _____

d. _____

3. General equilibrium exists in an economy

where there is _____

in all the _____ and _____
markets in the economy.

4. The economic changes or disturbances
which may result not only in "big splashes"
but also in little waves and ripples are of three

basic types: changes in _____,

changes in _____,

and changes in _____

5. When studying the markets for products
and for resources, we assume that the de-

mand curves slope _____ and the

supply curves slope _____
  a. The slope of the demand curve for:

  (1) Products is due to _____

  (2) Resources is due to _____
  b. The slope of the supply curve for:

  (1) Products is due to _____

  (2) Labor is due to _____

6. Assume the demand for consumer good P
increases while the demand for consumer
good Q decreases. In the short run:

  a. The price and output of P will _____

_____ and the price and output of

Q will _____

  b. Profits in industry _____ will

increase and profits in industry _____
will decrease.
  c. If the only resource used in industry P is
type C labor and the only resource used in
industry Q is type D labor, the demand for C

will _____ and the demand for

D will _____
  d. Wage rates and the quantity of labor em-

ployed in the market for _____ will

increase while those in the market for _____
will decrease.

7. Using the same assumptions made in 6
above, if the two industries are increasing-
cost industries, the increase in the demand
for P along with the decrease in the demand
for Q will in the long run:

  a. Cause firms to enter industry _____

and to leave industry _____

  b. _____ the supply of P

and _____ the supply of Q.

  c. _____ the price of P and

_____ the price of Q from
what they were originally.

  d. Increase the supply of type _____ labor

and decrease the supply of type _____ labor.

  e. _____ the employment

of type C labor and _____
the employment of type D labor.

8. Still using the assumptions made in 6 and
7 above, the increase in the price of P and
the decrease in the price of Q will:
  a. Increase the demand for products which

are (substitutes, complements) _____

for P and decrease the demand for _____

  b. _____ the demand for
those resources used along with type C labor

and _____ the demand for
those resources used along with type D labor.
  c. Redistribute income from workers and

entrepreneurs in industry _____ to those in

industry _____

9. Given the distribution of income, purely
competitive product and resource markets
bring about the production of a combination

of goods and services which _____
of consumers because:
  a. the price of each good or service is equal

to its _____
  b. the average cost of producing each prod-

uct is a _____
and each firm employs the resources required

to produce its product in the _____
combination.
  c. The utility of the last dollar spent by a

consumer on each good or service is _____

_____

for all goods and services.

10. Product and resource markets in the real

world are actually _____
competitive. As a result the allocation of re-

sources is _____
and adjustments to changes in tastes, technology, and the availability of resources are

_____ and _____

11. Two potential offsets to imperfectly com-

petitive markets are more rapid _____

_____ and greater

_____

12. The ability of a purely competitive price
system to allocate resources efficiently is
open to question for two reasons.

a. It fails to take into account the _____

_____ and the _____
of the goods and services produced and it ne-

glects or ignores the production of _____
b. It does not necessarily result in an ideal

_____ of _____
13. Listed down the left side of an input-

output table are the _____
sectors of the economy and listed across the

top of the table are the _____
sectors. The output of any sector is a(n)

_____ of other sectors; and

the inputs of any sector are the _____
of other sectors.

14. Assuming constant returns to scale, if
industry X sells 30% of its product to industry Y and if industry Y decides to increase its
production by 25%, then industry X will have

to increase its production by _____
%.

15. An understanding of general equilibrium
analysis is important if one is to evaluate

the overall _____,

to understand specific _____,

and to formulate good _____

■ **PROBLEMS AND PROJECTS**

1. Listed below are three types of economic change which can occur in the economy. In the spaces allotted following each
change, indicate what you think the effect
will be—increase (+), decrease (−), no
change (0), or an indeterminate change (?)—
on demand or supply, price, and output or
employment in the markets affected by the
initial change.

No answers to this problem will be found in
the "Answers" section because the answer to
each question depends upon such things as
whether the short run or the long run is considered, whether the industry is an increas-
ing- or constant-cost industry, and whether
you consider only the "immediate-secondary
effect" or consider also the "secondary-
secondary effect" of the initial change. The
purpose of this exercise is simply to get you
to *attempt* to trace through the economy the
full effect of an initial change and to see the
extent and complexity of price-market interrelations.

a. Decrease in the demand for consumer
good X but no *initial* change in the demand
for other consumer goods.

(1) Effect on the price of and the quantity

of good X produced. _____

(2) Effect on the demand for, the price of,
and the output of goods which are substitutes

for good X. _____

(3) Effect on the demand for, the price of,
and the output of goods which are comple-

ments for good X. _____

(4) Effect on the demand for, the price of,
and the employment of resources used in the

production of good X. _____

(5) Effect on the supply of, the price of,
and the output of goods which employ the
same resources used in the production of

good X. _____

(6) Effect on the demand for, the price of,
and the employment of resources which are
substitutes for the resources used to produce

good X. _____

b. Increase in the supply of resource Y.

(1) Effect on the price of and the employ-

ment of resource Y. _____

(2) Effect on the supply of, the price of, and

the output of goods which employ resource

Y in the production process. _____

(3) Effect on the demand for, the price of, and the employment of resources which are

complementary to resource Y. _____

(4) Effect on the demand for, the price of, and the output of those goods which are substitutes for the goods produced with resource

Y. _____

(5) Effect on the demand for, the price of, and the output of those goods which are complements for the goods produced with re-

source Y. _____

(6) Effect on the demand for, the price of, and the employment of resources which are

substitutes for resource Y. _____

c. Improvement in the technology of pro-

ducing good Z. _____

(1) Effect on the supply of, the price of,

and the output of good Z. _____

(2) Effect on the demand for, the price of, and the output of goods which are substi-

tutes for good Z. _____

(3) Effect on the demand for, the price of, and the output of goods which are comple-

ments for good Z. _____

(4) Effect on the demand for, the price of, and the employment of resources used to pro-

duce good Z. _____

(5) Effect on the supply of, the price of, and the output of those goods which also employ the resources used to produce good Z.

_____

2. Below is an incomplete input-output table for an economy with five sectors. All the figures in the table are physical units rather than dollars.

Producing sectors	Using sectors					Total outputs
	A	B	C	D	E	
A	100	150	75	—	25	425
B	30	20	70	80	200	—
C	10	60	—	20	20	110
D	205	35	40	10	—	300
E	—	140	60	35	80	390

a. Complete the table by computing (by addition or subtraction) the missing input-output figures.

b. Assume that sector B wishes to expand its output by 100 units. By what percentage does sector B wish to expand its output?

_____%

c. Assuming constant returns to scale in all sectors of the economy, by how many *units* will each of the following sectors of the economy have to expand their outputs if sector B is to expand its output by 100 units?

(1) Sector A: _____

(2) Sector C: _____

(3) Sector D: _____

(4) Sector E: _____

d. By what *percentage* will each of these sectors have to expand their outputs?

(1) Sector A: _____%

(2) Sector C: _____%

(3) Sector D: _____%

(4) Sector E: _____%

e. What further adjustments in the outputs of the various sectors of the economy will follow those given in (c) and (d) above?

_____

_____

■ SELF-TEST

Circle the T if the statement is true, the F if it is false.

1. General equilibrium analysis is the same thing as macroeconomics.   T F

2. The study of the effect of an increase in the demand for product C, other things remaining equal, upon the price and the output of product C is an example of partial equilibrium analysis.   T F

3. The supply curve for a product slopes upward in the short run because of the diminishing marginal productivity of variable resources.   T F

Use the following data for the three questions below and for multiple choice questions 6 and 7. Initially there is general equilibrium, and then the demand for consumer good W increases and the demand for consumer good Z decreases. Both industries are increasing-cost industries in the long run. Industry W employs only type G labor, and Z employs only type H labor.

4. In the short run, price, output, and profits will increase in industry Z and decrease in industry W. **T F**

5. In the long run, the quantity of type G labor employed will increase and the quantity of type H labor employed will decrease. **T F**

6. Income will be redistributed from workers and entrepreneurs in industry Z to those in industry W. **T F**

7. Given the distribution of income in the economy, purely competitive product and resource markets lead to the production of a collection of products which maximizes the satisfaction of consumer wants. **T F**

8. In the real world, product and resource markets tend to be purely competitive. **T F**

9. A purely competitive price system results in an ideal or optimal distribution of income. **T F**

10. General equilibrium analysis gives a broader picture of the economic consequences of economic changes and economic policies than partial equilibrium analysis even though some of these consequences turn out to be insignificant. **T F**

Underscore the letter that corresponds to the best answer.

1. If the demand for consumer good A increased, which one of the following would *not* be a possible consequence? (a) increase in the price of A; (b) increase in the demand for resources used to produce A; (c) increase in the supply of those goods which are substitutes for A; (d) increase in the prices of other goods which employ the same resources used to produce A.

2. If the supply of resource B increased, which one of the following would *not* be a possible consequence? (a) decrease in the price of B; (b) decrease in the demand for those goods produced from B; (c) decrease in the demand for those resources which are

substitutes for resource B; (d) decrease in the demand for those goods which are substitutes for the goods produced with resource B.

3. The price system produces approximately what percentage of the output and employs about what percentage of the resources of the American economy? (a) 70%; (b) 80%; (c) 90%; (d) 100%.

4. The downward slope of the demand curve for a product is the result of: (a) diminishing marginal utility; (b) diminishing marginal productivity; (c) increasing marginal cost; (d) the work-leisure preferences of workers.

5. The upward slope of the supply curve of labor is the result of: (a) diminishing marginal utility; (b) diminishing marginal productivity; (c) increasing marginal cost; (d) the work-leisure preferences of workers.

Use the data preceding True-False question 4 to answer the following two questions.

6. When the new long-run general equilibrium is reached: (a) the wage rate for type G labor will be higher than it was originally; (b) the wage rate for type G labor will be lower than it was originally; (c) wage rates in both labor markets will be the same as they were originally; (d) it is impossible to tell what will have happened to wage rates.

7. As a result of the changes in the demands for W and Z: (a) the demand for products which are substitutes for Z will have increased; (b) the demand for products which are complements for W will have decreased; (c) the demand for products which are substitutes for Z will have decreased; (d) the demand for products which are complements for Z will have decreased.

8. Which of the following is *not* the result of purely competitive product and resource markets? (a) the distribution of income among consumers maximizes the satisfaction of wants in the economy; (b) the average cost of producing each product is a minimum; (c) the price of each product is equal to its marginal cost; (d) the marginal utility of every product divided by its price is the same for all products purchased by an individual consumer.

9. All but one of the following is the result of imperfectly competitive product and resource markets. Which one? (a) resources are allocated less efficiently than under purely competitive conditions; (b) the price system is less responsive to changes in tastes, technology, and the availability of resources than a purely competitive price system; (c) there is a smaller variety of products than in a purely competitive system; (d) monopoly drives prices above and monopsony drives them below their competitive levels.

10. Which of the following is a disadvantage of a purely competitive price system? (a) underallocates resources to those products whose production entails a spillover cost; (b) overallocates resources to those products whose consumption entails spillover benefits; (c) underallocates resources to the production of social goods and services; (d) fails to distribute income optimally.

Use the following input-output table to answer questions 11 and 12 below.

Producing sectors	Using sectors					Total outputs
	A	B	C	D	E	
A	20	15	35	25	60	155
B	45	55	90	10	20	220
C	40	15	80	10	5	150
D	65	10	25	20	40	160
E	100	75	80	45	10	310

11. If sector C were to decrease its output by 50 units, and assuming constant returns to scale in all sectors, the *initial* impact on sector B would be a decrease in its output of: (a) 5 units; (b) $13^{6}/_{7}$ units; (c) $26^{2}/_{3}$ units; (d) 30 units.

12. If sector C is to increase its output by 20%, and assuming constant returns to scale, sector E's output will have to increase initially by: (a) 5.2%; (b) 19.4%; (c) 20%; (d) 37.5%.

■ **DISCUSSION QUESTIONS**

1. Explain the difference between partial equilibrium and general equilibrium analysis.

2. Why is general equilibrium analysis so important?

3. Suppose the demand for television sets decreases at the same time that the demand for airline travel increases. What would be (a) the short-run effects of these changes in the markets for television sets and airline travel and in the markets for television-set production workers and airline workers; (b) the long-run effects in these markets; (c) the long-run effects in the markets for complementary and substitute products and in the markets for other resources; and (d) the effect upon the distribution of income?

4. Imagine that the availability of iron ore used to produce steel increased or the technology of steel making improved. What would be the short- and long-run effects upon (a) the steel industry; (b) steelworkers; (c) the automobile industry; (d) the aluminum industry; (e) the machine tool industry; and (f) the coal industry?

5. Why is a purely competitive price system "conducive to an efficient allocation of resources"?

6. When a price system is less than purely competitive, what are the economic consequences?

7. What costs, benefits, and goods does even a purely competitive price system neglect or ignore? What are the economic results of this neglect?

8. What is meant by an ideal or optimal distribution of income? Why can't economists determine what the optimal distribution of income is?

9. Explain precisely what an input-output table is and the kind of information it contains.

10. In addition to indicating the interrelationships between the various sectors of the economy, an input-output table can be used for what other purposes?

The Monopoly Problem: the Social Control of Industry

This is the first of seven chapters which deal with specific trouble spots in the American economy and is one of the two chapters which concern the monopoly problem. Chapter 34 examines the monopoly problem in output markets, and Chapter 38 examines the monopoly problem in labor markets. It should be noted that the term "monopoly" as used here does *not* mean pure or absolute monopoly; it means, instead, control of a large percentage of total supply by one or a few suppliers. Actually there is no such thing as pure monopoly.

Whether big business and industrial monopolies are a real threat to efficient resource allocation and technological progress in the United States is certainly a debatable question. It is a question that will be argued from time to time by the American people and their representatives in Congress. Chapter 34 does not attempt to answer the question. It is important, however, for you to see that it is a debatable question, to see that there are good and plausible arguments on both sides of the question, and to see that the empirical evidence is very tentative.

A part of Chapter 34 is devoted to an examination of the ways in which the Federal government has attempted to prevent the formation of business monopolies and to limit the use of monopoly power. In addition, the

chapter examines the ways in which this same government has—either intentionally or unintentionally—promoted and fostered monopoly. In these sections you will find a discussion of a rather large number of Federal laws, and the question which a student almost always raises is, "Am I expected to know all these laws?" The answer is yes, you should have a general knowledge of these laws. If you are to understand how government has restricted and promoted monopoly, you should know (1) what the major pieces of Federal legislation with these aims and/or results have been; (2) what the main provisions of each of these laws were; and (3) how successful each of these laws was in accomplishing its aims.

Another question which students often raise with respect to these laws is, "What good is there in knowing them anyhow?" In examining any important current problem it is important to know how the problem arose, what steps have already been taken to solve it, how successful the attempts were, and why the problem is still not solved. A more general answer to the same question is that an informed citizenry is necessary if a democracy is to solve its problems. And most of these laws continue in force and are enforced; many of you will work for business firms which are subject to their provisions.

Two final points: In studying the ways in which government has promoted business monopoly, you should again note specific laws. In addition, three possible future policies which the government might adopt with respect to business monopoly are listed, and you should learn what arguments proponents of these policies advance to support their proposals.

■ **CHECKLIST**

The very least you should be able to do when you have finished this chapter is:
□ Explain how the term monopoly is used in this chapter.
□ Present the case *for* monopoly.
□ Set forth the case *against* monopoly.
□ Identify the two techniques employed in the United States to control monopoly; and explain when each of them tends to be used.
□ List the five ways in which the Federal government has promoted monopoly; and explain why these exemptions to the antitrust laws were made.
□ Outline the major provisions of each of the following:
    Interstate Commerce Commission Act
    Sherman Act
    Clayton Act
    Federal Trade Commission Act
    Wheeler-Lea Act
    Robinson-Patman Act
    Celler-Kefauver Act
    Webb-Pomerene Act
    Industrial Reorganization Act
□ Enumerate the three policies for dealing with business monopoly that the Federal government might adopt; and present a case for each of these alternatives.

■ **CHAPTER OUTLINE**

1. The term "monopoly," as used in this chapter, means a situation in which a small number of firms control all or a substantial percentage of the total output of a major industry. Business firms may be large in either an absolute or a relative sense, and in many cases they are large in both senses. Chapter 34 is concerned with firms large in both senses.

2. Whether business monopoly is beneficial or detrimental to the American economy is debatable. A case can be made *against* business monopoly and *for* it.

3. Many argue that while competition is not perfect in many industries it is "workable"; that big business is able to realize the economies of mass production; that it is conducive to a rapid rate of technological change; that business investment and pricing policies are a stabilizing influence in the economy; and that socially responsible business leaders do not abuse their monopoly power.

4. Others argue, however, that monopoly power results in restricted outputs, higher prices, misallocation of resources, greater income inequality, a slow rate of technological progress, economic instability, less political freedom, and a society characterized by dehumanization and materialism.

5. Government policies toward business monopoly have not been clear and consistent; legislation and policy have at various times both restricted and promoted monopoly power.
  a. Following the Civil War, the expansion of the American economy brought with it the creation of trusts (or business monopolies) in many industries; and the fear of the trusts resulted in the establishment of regulatory agencies and the enactment of antitrust legislation.
  b. Where natural monopoly existed and competition was not economical (as in the railroad industry) regulatory agencies were empowered to control and limit monopoly power.
  c. Such antitrust legislation as the Sherman Act, the Clayton Act, the Federal Trade Commission Act, and other laws have attempted to restrain the growth and use of monopoly power.
  d. Yet numerous exceptions to and suspensions of the antitrust laws have been made and various pieces of legislation have directly prompted monopoly.

6. There are at least three proposals (with supporting arguments) which have been suggested as future government policies for dealing with business monopoly: maintenance of the present policy, direct government ownership or regulation of business monopoly, and the restoration of effective competition in monopolistic industries.

■ IMPORTANT TERMS

Monopoly

Big business

Workable competition

Regulatory agency

Natural monopoly

Interstate Commerce Act

Sherman Act

Clayton Act

Federal Trade Commission Act

Interlocking directorate

Tying agreement

Cease-and-desist order

Wheeler-Lea Act

Robinson-Patman Act

Celler-Kefauver Act

Conglomerate merger

Reciprocal selling

Webb-Pomerene Act

Technological determinism

Industrial Reorganization Act

■ FILL-IN QUESTIONS

1. As used in this chapter, monopoly means that a _____ firms control _____ of the output of a _____ industry; and this chapter is concerned with firms that are large in both a _____ and an _____ sense.

2. Those who argue the case *for* business monopoly contend that _____ competition regulates big business; that big firms are able to realize the economies of _____ ; that big business leads to a _____ of technological change; that the _____ and _____ policies of large firms contribute to economic stability; and that business leaders have a ___ _____ which prevents abuses of monopoly power.

3. Workable competition includes at least five varieties of competition other than price competition; these are:

a. _____

b. _____

c. _____

d. _____

e. _____

4. Galbraith argues that:
a. the dominant role of the giant corporation is dictated by _____ ; efficient production requires large amounts of _____, highly sophisticated _____, and detailed _____
b. the goals of a mature corporation are _____ and _____; and to achieve these goals the corporation integrates _____, finances its expansion _____, controls consumers by _____ and _____, and allies itself with _____ to manage the economy.

5. Those who argue the case *against* business monopoly assert that monopolists ____ output; _____ prices; _____ resources; contribute to _____ in the distribution of income, to a _____ _____ of technological progress, and to _____ _____ in the economy; pose serious _____ dangers; and fostering dehumanizing _____ _____ arrangements and questionable _____

6. Federal legislation and policies have at times attempted to maintain _____ while at other times they have fostered ____ _____

7. When a single firm is able to supply the entire market at a lower average cost than a number of competing firms, there is a _____ _____ monopoly. In the United States many of these monopolies are controlled by regulatory _____ or _____ whose function is to prevent the abuses of monopoly power.

8. The Sherman Antitrust Act of 1890 made

_____

and _____
illegal.

9. The Clayton Act of 1914 prohibited such

practices as _____ ,

_____ ,

_____ ,

and _____

10. The Federal Trade Commission was set up under the act of that name in 1914; the

commission was given the power to _____

_____ ,

hold _____ ,

and to issue _____ ,
but the power of the commission has been

limited by the ruling of _____

that they hold the final authority to _____

_____

11. The _____
Act banned the acquisition of the assets of

one firm by another, and the _____
Act prohibited the acquisition of the stock of one firm by another when the result would be reduced competition.

12. The _____
Act had the effect of prohibiting false and mis-

leading advertising, and the _____

_____

Act was aimed at eliminating the _____

_____

which large chain stores were able to obtain from their suppliers.

13. Most of the mergers of business firms

within the last ten years have been _____

_____ mergers in which a firm

in one industry merges with firms in _____

_____

14. Government promotes the growth of mo-

nopoly when it _____
certain industries or practices from antitrust

prosecution, when it grants _____ ,

and when it enacts _____

15. Export trade associations were exempted from the provisions of the antitrust laws by

the _____

Act; in addition, _____

and _____
have been made exempt from the antitrust laws by other Federal legislation.

16. The _____
have the effect of granting inventors legal mo-

nopolies on their products, while _____

_____

shelter American producers from foreign competition.

17. Three possible future policy alternatives for dealing with business monopoly are:

a. _____

b. _____

c. _____

18. Effective competition means that the

number of producers is large enough that __

_____ ,

the absence of _____ ,

and _____

■ **PROBLEMS AND PROJECTS**

Below is a list of Federal laws. Following this list is a series of provisions found in Federal laws. Match each of the laws with the appropriate provision by placing the appropriate letter after each of the provisions.
  A. Sherman Act
  B. Clayton Act
  C. Federal Trade Commission Act
  D. Wheeler-Lea Act
  E. Robinson-Patman Act
  F. Celler-Kefauver Act
  G. Webb-Pomerene Act

H. Industrial Reorganization Act
I. Interstate Commerce Act

1. Exempted American exporters from the antitrust laws by permitting them to form export trade associations. _____

2. Established a commission to investigate and prevent unfair methods of competition. _____

3. Established a commission to regulate the railroads, their rates, and their services. _____

4. Made monopoly and restraint of trade illegal and criminal. _____

5. Outlawed quantity discounts and unreasonably low prices where their effect is to eliminate competition. _____

6. Prohibited the acquisition of the assets of a firm by another firm when such an acquisition will lessen competition. _____

7. Had the effect of prohibiting false and misleading advertising and the misrepresentation of products. _____

8. Clarified the Sherman Act and outlawed specific techniques or devices used to create monopolies and restrain trade. _____

9. Would, if enacted, define an illegal monopoly as a firm or group of firms that meet any one of three criteria. _____

■ **SELF-TEST**

Circle the T if the statement is true, the F if it is false.

1. The term "monopoly" in this chapter is taken to mean a situation in which a single firm produces a unique product and entry into the industry is blocked.   **T   F**

2. It is clear that on balance, business monopoly is detrimental to the functioning of the American economy.   **T   F**

3. Those who support the case for business monopoly contend that only big business is able to achieve significant economies of scale.   **T   F**

4. Those who emphasize the importance of workable competition as a device for the regulation of big business contend that the competitiveness of any industry should be judged almost solely on the basis of the number of firms in it and the barriers to entry.   **T   F**

5. The Federal government has consistently passed legislation and pursued policies designed to maintain competition.   **T   F**

6. The Federal courts are the final authority in interpreting the antitrust laws.   **T   F**

7. The Robinson-Patman Act was aimed at preventing firms from acquiring the *assets* of other firms where the effect would be to reduce competition.   **T   F**

8. The doctrine of technological determinism is one of the arguments advanced to support the views of those who advocate the restoration of vigorous and effective competition.   **T   F**

9. Those who propose the maintenance of the *status quo* as a policy for dealing with business monopoly argue that workable competition regulates big business.   **T   F**

10. Proponents of public regulation and ownership as a means of controlling business monopoly point to the success of the antitrust laws in limiting the growth of monopoly power.   **T   F**

Underscore the letter that corresponds to the best answer.

1. "Big business" in this chapter refers to which one of the following? (*a*) firms that are absolutely large; (*b*) firms that are relatively large; (*c*) firms that are either absolutely or relatively large; (*d*) firms that are both absolutely and relatively large.

2. Which of the following is *not* a part of the case *against* business monopoly? (*a*) monopolists charge higher prices than competitive firms would charge; (*b*) monopolists earn economic profits which they use for research and technological development; (*c*) monopoly leads to the misallocation of resources; (*d*) monopoly leads to greater income inequality.

3. An essential part of the case *for* business monopoly is that the operations of big business are regulated by: (*a*) pure competition;

(b) monopolistic competition; (c) workable competition; (d) effective competition.

4. Which one of the following is *not* a part of the case *for* big business? (a) large firms have lower unit costs because they are able to use their power to depress resource prices; (b) large firms are led by socially responsible business executives who refuse to use their economic power in ways detrimental to the public; (c) large firms result in a more rapid rate of technological progress because they have both the resources and the incentives for research; (d) large firms are effectively regulated by interproduct, technological, and potential competition.

5. Which one of the following laws stated that contracts and conspiracies in restraint of trade, monopolies, attempts to monopolize, and conspiracies to monopolize were illegal? (a) Sherman Act; (b) Clayton Act; (c) Federal Trade Commission Act; (d) Robinson-Patman Act.

6. Insofar as its effect upon competition and monopoly is concerned, which one of the following acts has the least in common with the other three acts? (a) Wheeler-Lea Act; (b) Webb-Pomerene Act; (c) Celler-Kefauver Act; (d) Clayton Act.

7. Which one of the following acts specifically outlawed tying contracts and interlocking directorates? (a) Sherman Act; (b) Clayton Act; (c) Federal Trade Commission Act; (d) Wheeler-Lea Act.

8. Which one of the following acts has given the Federal Trade Commission the task of preventing false and misleading advertising and the misrepresentation of products? (a) Clayton Act; (b) Federal Trade Commission Act; (c) Robinson-Patman Act; (d) Wheeler-Lea Act.

9. Which one of the following is *not* characteristic of the Interstate Commerce Act of 1887? (a) it was based on the supposition that competition was unworkable in the railroad industry; (b) transportation was deemed essential to many individuals, firms, and industries; (c) it substituted government management and operation of the railroads for private management and operation; (d) the Interstate Commerce Commission was established to regulate railroad rates and services.

10. If the Industrial Reorganization Act were to become law, an illegal monopoly would be (a) an industry in which the concentration ratio exceeds 50%; (b) an industry in which the firms do not engage in price competition during any three-year period; (c) a firm which has a rate of profit in excess of 15% for five consecutive years; (d) any one of the above.

■ DISCUSSION QUESTIONS

1. Explain the difference between the way the term "monopoly" is used in this chapter and the way it is used in Chapter 27. How can "big business" be defined? How is the expression used in this chapter?

2. What are the chief arguments in the case *for* business monopoly?

3. What are the chief arguments in the case *against* business monopoly? What empirical evidence is there to support this case?

4. Explain what is meant by "workable competition." How does it differ from pure competition, and what forms of competition does it include?

5. Against the argument that big business results in economies of scale (that is, mass-production economies) three counterarguments are often presented. What are they?

6. What are the "technological imperatives" that "have brought the corporate giant to a dominant role in the American economy"? What are the goals of the mature corporation and how does it attempt to achieve these goals, according to Galbraith?

7. In what way is the approach of the Interstate Commerce Act to the problem of monopoly different from the approach of the other antitrust laws? Why were the railroads (and later, other industries) subject to this approach?

8. What are the essential provisions of the Sherman Act?

9. The Clayton Act and the Federal Trade Commission Act amended or elaborated the provisions of the Sherman Act, and both aimed at preventing rather than punishing monopoly. What were the chief provisions of each of these acts, and how did they attempt to prevent monopoly? How has the power of the FTC been subsequently limited by the Federal courts?

10. What are the main provisions of each of the following? (*a*) Wheeler-Lea Act; (*b*) Robinson-Patman Act; (*c*) Celler-Kefauver Act; (*d*) Industrial Reorganization Act.

11. How effective has antitrust legislation been in preventing monopoly *and* in restoring competition? What are the two major criticisms of employing regulatory commissions to control natural monopolies?

12. In what ways has the Federal government fostered the growth of monopoly? How did each of the following acts contribute to such growth? (*a*) Webb-Pomerene Act; (*b*) Robinson-Patman Act; (*c*) the various protective tariffs.

13. How do patent laws contribute to the growth of monopoly power? (In your answer, mention patent pools and tying agreements.)

14. What are the three alternatives which are often suggested as future policies for dealing with business monopoly? What arguments can you present to support each of these policies?

15. Explain the difference between "workable" and "effective" competition.

Rural Economics: the Farm Problem

Probably no economic problem has aroused public interest to the extent and for the number of years that the farm problem has. It has concerned not only those directly engaged in agriculture or living and working in agricultural areas but also every American consumer and taxpayer. Other problems seem to come and go; the farm problem seems always to have been with us.

Chapter 35 is devoted exclusively to an examination of the farm problem—the second of the seven specific trouble spots studied in this part of the book. The chapter opens with a brief history of the experiences of American farmers. The *symptoms* of the farm problem are declining farm prices, declining farm incomes, farm incomes which are low relative to the incomes of nonfarm families, and a highly unequal distribution of farm income among farm families.

The symptoms of the farm problem, however, are not the same thing as the *causes* of the farm problem. If the problem is to be solved, it is necessary to understand what has occasioned the straits in which agriculture finds itself. In fact, as the author points out, the failure to solve the problem has been brought about by the failure to understand and treat its causes. Actually there are two farm problems, a long-term problem and a short-term problem. Each problem has its

own particular causes, and the chapter deals with each of the two problems in turn.

The long-run problem is that farm prices and incomes have tended to decline over the years; and the short-run problem is that farm prices and incomes have fluctuated sharply from year to year. To understand the causes of each of these problems you will have to make use of the concept of inelastic demand and to employ your knowledge of how demand and supply determine price in a competitive market. The effort which you put into the study of these tools in previous chapters will now pay a handsome dividend: understanding the causes of a real-world problem and the policies designed to solve the problem.

The traditional policies of the Federal government were directed at raising farm incomes by supporting farm prices. In connection with the support of farm prices you are introduced to the concept of parity. Once you understand parity and recognize that the parity price has in the past been above what the competitive price would have been you will come to some important conclusions. Consumers paid higher prices for and consumed smaller quantities of the various farm products; and at the prices supported by the Federal government there were surpluses of these products. The Federal government bought these surpluses to keep the price above the competitive market price. The purchases of the surpluses were financed by American taxpayers.

To eliminate these surpluses, government looked for ways to increase the demand for or to decrease the supply of these commodities. Programs to increase demand and decrease supply were put into effect; but they failed to eliminate the annual surpluses. Until the early 1970s agriculture in the United States had a problem which the traditional farm policies, for reasons explained in the text, did not solve.

But in the 1970s an economic boom come to American agriculture. No one can yet say whether this boom is temporary (and agriculture will in the future again face the same old problem) or permanent (and agriculture in the years to come will feature rising prices, increasing farm incomes, and shortages). The causes of the boom are explained and its possible consequences are spelled out. During 1973 Congress also enacted a new farm program designed to increase farm production, reduce the extent of government involvement in agriculture, and decrease the importance of subsidies and price supports. You should be warned that should this boom prove to be permanent the economic welfare of farmers may improve but American households may have to pay higher prices for and consume less food than they have in the years when agriculture was a sick industry.

■ **CHECKLIST**

The very least you should be able to do when you have finished this chapter is:

□ Outline briefly the economic history of American agriculture during the twentieth century.

□ Compare per capita farm and nonfarm income and rural and nonrural poverty; and describe the distribution of income among farmers.

□ Identify both the long-run and the short-run farm problem; and explain the four causes of the former and the cause of the latter problem.

□ Explain why the long-run farm problem is the result of a misallocation of resources in a growing economy.

□ Enumerate the several arguments which

are made in support of Federal assistance to agriculture.

□ Explain how the traditional farm policies of the Federal government tried to increase farm prices and incomes; and the effect and the costs to the consumer and the taxpayer of these policies.

□ Describe the means by which the Federal government attempted to restrict the supply and bolster the demand for farm products.

□ Present two major criticisms of the traditional farm policy.

□ Explain the causes of the increased demand for American agricultural commodities in the 1970s and the three basic features of the new farm program enacted in 1973; and enumerate the possible consequences of these events.

■ **CHAPTER OUTLINE**

1. A history of American agriculture in the twentieth century makes it clear that agricultural prices and farm incomes have fluctuated with changes in demand; and that there has been a general tendency for the prices received by farmers and their incomes to decline relatively.

2. The evidence also makes it clear that farmers are, on the average, poorer than people not engaged in farming; that the distribution of income among farmers is highly unequal; and that rural poverty is exceedingly common.

3. The farm problem is both a long-run and a short-run problem. The symptoms of the former are the relative decreases in farm incomes and prices which have occurred over the years; and the symptoms of the latter are the sharp changes in farmers' incomes from year to year.

 a. The causes of the long-run problem are the inelastic demand for farm products, the large increases in the supply of these products which have taken place relative to modest increases in the demand for them, and the relative immobility of agricultural resources.

 b. The cause of the short-run problem is the inelastic demand for agricultural products: relatively small changes in demand or supply result in relatively large changes in agricultural prices and farm incomes.

 c. The long-run problem is, therefore, the

result of four factors, and the short-run problem is the result of inelastic demand.

d. Another explanation of the long-run problem is that as the American economy grew and improved its agricultural technology, it reallocated too small an amount of its resources away from agriculture and into the nonagricultural sectors of the economy.

4. Those who have represented the farmer have claimed that the farmer has a right to special assistance from the Federal government.

5. Farmers were for over three decades able to obtain various forms of public aid and the traditional policies of the Federal government during this period were designed to raise farm prices and incomes by restricting output; but in the 1970s new policies were designed to reduce government intervention in agricultural markets and to expand the output of farm products.

6. The parity price of an agricultural product would give the farmer year after year the same real income per unit of output.

a. Traditional farm policy supported farm prices at some percentage of the parity price. But because the supported price was almost always above the market price, government had to support the price by purchasing and accumulating surpluses of agricultural products; and while farmers gained from this policy, consumers lost.

b. To reduce the annual and accumulated surpluses, government attempted to reduce output by acreage-allotment and acreage-reserve programs and to expand demand with a variety of programs.

c. The farm program was largely unsuccessful in raising farm prices and incomes because it failed to move resources out of agriculture and because the major benefits were not directed toward the low-income farmers.

7. Economic conditions in American agriculture changed substantially during the 1970s.

a. Outside the United States increased incomes, changed eating habits, poor harvests, the devaluation of the dollar, and the opening of markets in Communist nations and, within the United States, increased incomes worked to expand the total demand for the output of American farmers.

b. New farm legislation was passed in 1973

to lessen government involvement and to make agricultural markets more nearly free markets by replacing price supports with target prices, by encouraging production, and by limiting the size of the subsidy any one farmer might receive.

c. The effects of this new farm policy and the increased demand for agricultural products may be a larger income for farmers, a reduction in excess agricultural capacity, rising food prices in the United States, greater instability in the prices of farm commodities, a smaller balance of payments problem, and fewer barriers to the importation of American farm products abroad.

■ **IMPORTANT TERMS**

Farm problem	**Public Law 480**
Long-run farm problem	**Food for Peace program**
Short-run farm problem	**Acreage-allotment program**
Agricultural Adjustment Act	**Acreage-reserve (soil bank) program**
Parity concept (price)	**Agricultural and Consumer Protection Act**
Price support	**Target price**

■ **FILL-IN QUESTIONS**

1. What was the economic condition—prosperity or depression—of American agriculture in each of the following periods?

a. 1894 to 1914: _____

b. 1914 to 1920: _____

c. 1920 to 1940: _____

d. 1940 to 1950: _____

e. 1950 to 1973: _____

2. The per capita farm income tends to be

(greater, less) _____ than per capita nonfarm income, and the

distribution of farm income is _____

3. The long-run farm problem is one of _____

_____

and the short-run farm problem is one of _____

4. The basic causes of the long-run farm problem are _____,

_____,

and _____

5. The demand for farm products tends to be inelastic because _____

6. The supply of farm products has increased rapidly since about the time of World War I because of _____

7. The demand for agricultural products in the United States has not increased so rapidly as the supply of these products because ____

_____

and _____

8. The price system has failed to reallocate farmers into occupations earning higher incomes because as resources, farmers, their land, and their capital are highly _____

9. The basic cause of the short-run farm problem is the _____ demand for agricultural commodities, and this contributes to unstable farm prices and incomes in two ways. Relatively (large, small) _____ changes in the output of farm products result in relatively _____ changes in farm prices and incomes, and relatively _____ changes in demand result in relatively ____ changes in prices and incomes.

10. As the American economy has grown and improved its agricultural technology, it has failed to reallocate _____ from _____ to _____

11. Two of the reasons advanced to support the farmers' claim to assistance from the Federal government are the contentions that agriculture:

a. Has borne too large a share of the ____ of _____ in the U.S.

b. Sells its products in _____

markets and is unable to control the _____ of these products.

12. Traditional farm policy was largely designed to restrict farm _____ in order to increase farm _____ and farm _____

13. If a farmer were to receive a parity price for his product, he would be guaranteed that year after year a _____ output will enable him to acquire _____

_____

14. If the government supports farm prices at an above-equilibrium level, the result will be _____ which the government must _____ in order to maintain prices at their support levels.

a. Farmers benefit from this price-support program because it increases their _____

b. But consumers are hurt by it because they must pay higher _____ and higher _____

15. To bring the equilibrium level of prices in the market up to their support level, government has attempted to _____ the demand for and to _____ the supply of farm products.

16. Two programs employed by the government to reduce agricultural production are the _____ and the _____ programs. To increase demand it has attempted to find _____ for agricultural commodities, to increase ____

_____,

and to _____ more agricultural products.

17. The traditional farm program was not successful in solving the farm problem because it did not _____ resources and it most benefited those farm-

ers who _____
_____

18. List five causes of the increase in the foreign demand for the products of American farms during the 1970s.

a. _____

b. _____

c. _____

d. _____

e. _____

19. The new farm policy of 1973 tends to (increase, decrease, leave unchanged) _____

_____ the extent of government involvement with agriculture; and resulted in the

_____

Act of 1973 which replaces price supports

with _____ prices, encourages all-out

_____, and limits the total subsidy that may be paid to an individual

farmer to $_____ a year.

20. The increase in the demand for farm products and the new agricultural policy in

the United States will increase the net _____

_____ of farmers and reduce excess

productive _____;

and may increase the prices of _____ in the United States and lead to greater price

_____; will help the economy with

its _____
problem; and may reduce the barriers to

American farm products in _____
markets.

■ **PROBLEMS AND PROJECTS**

1. The following table gives the index of prices farmers paid in three different years. The price farmers received in year 1, the base year, for a certain agricultural product was $.35 per bushel. Complete the table by computing the parity prices of the product in years 2 and 3.

Year	Index of prices farmers paid	Parity price of product
1	100	$.35
2	120	_____
3	200	_____

2. In columns 1 and 2 in the table below is a demand schedule for agricultural product X.

(1) Price	(2) Bushels of X demanded	(3) Bushels of X demanded
$2.00	600	580
1.80	620	600
1.60	640	620
1.40	660	640
1.20	680	660
1.00	700	680
.80	720	700
.60	740	720

a. Is demand elastic or inelastic in the price range given? _____

b. If the amount of X produced should increase from 600 to 700 bushels, the income of producers of X would _____

from $_____ to $_____;

an increase of _____% in the amount of X

produced would cause income to _____

_____ by _____%.

c. If the amount of X produced were 700 bushels and the demand for X decreased from that shown in columns 1 and 2 to that shown in columns 1 and 3, the price of X would

_____

from $_____ to $_____;

the income of farmers would _____

from $_____ to $_____

d. Assume that the government supports a price of $1.80, that the demand for X is that shown in columns 1 and 2, and that farmers grow 720 bushels of X.

(1) At the supported price there will be a

surplus of _____ bushels of X.

(2) If the government buys this surplus at the support price the cost to the taxpayers

of purchasing the surplus is $ _____

(3) The total income of the farmers producing product X when they receive the support price of $1.80 per bushel for their entire crop of 720 bushels is $ _____

(4) Had farmers to sell the crop of 720 bushels at the free-market price, the price of X would be only $_____ per bushel; and the total income of these farmers would be $_____

(5) The gain to farmers producing X from the price-support program is, therefore, $_____

(6) In addition to the cost to taxpayers of purchasing the surplus, consumers pay a price that is $_____ greater than the free-market price and receive a quantity of X that is _____ bushels less than they would have received in a free market.

3. The demand schedule for agriculture product Y is given in columns 1 and 2 of the following table.

(1) Price	(2) Bales of Y demanded	(3) Bales of Y demanded
$5.00	40,000	41,000
4.75	40,200	41,200
4.50	40,400	41,400
4.25	40,600	41,600
4.00	40,800	41,800
3.75	41,000	42,000
3.50	41,200	42,200

a. If farmers were persuaded by the government to reduce the size of their crop from 41,000 to 40,000 bales, the income of farmers would _____ from $_____ to $_____

b. If the crop remained constant at 41,000 bales and the demand for Y increased to that shown in columns 1 and 3, the income of farmers would _____ from $_____ to $ _____

■ **SELF-TEST**

Circle the T if the statement is true, the F if it is false.

1. The distribution of the total farm income among farmers in the American economy can be said to be a highly unequal one.   T   F

2. Per capita nonfarm income is greater than per capita farm income.   T   F

3. Most of the recent technological advances in agriculture have been initiated by farmers.   T   F

4. The supply of agricultural products has tended to increase more rapidly than the demand for these products in the United States.   T   F

5. The size of the farm population of the United States has declined at a more rapid rate than the rate at which agriculture's share of national income has declined.   T   F

6. The size of the farm population in the United States has declined in both relative and absolute terms since about 1935.   T   F

7. The quantities of agricultural commodities produced tend to be fairly *insensitive* to changes in agricultural prices because a large percentage of farmers' total costs are variable.   T   F

8. Application of the parity concept to farm prices causes farm prices to decline and results in agricultural surpluses.   T   F

9. The acreage-allotment and acreage-reserve programs are designed to decrease the supply of farm products.   T   F

10. Restricting the number of acres which farmers employ to grow agricultural products has not been a very successful method of reducing surpluses because farmers tend to cultivate their land more intensively when the acreage is reduced.   T   F

Underscore the letter that corresponds to the best answer.

1. Which one of the following periods has little or nothing in common with the other three insofar as the economic condition of American agriculture in the period is concerned? (a) 1900 to 1914; (b) 1914 to 1920; (c) 1920 to 1940; (d) 1940 to 1950.

2. Which of the following is *not* characteristic of American agriculture? (a) farmers sell their products in highly competitive markets; (b) farmers buy in markets which are largely noncompetitive; (c) the demand for agricultural products tends to be inelastic; (d) agricultural resources tend to be highly mobile.

3. If both the demand for and the supply of a product increase: (a) the quantity of the product bought and sold will increase; (b) the quantity of the product bought and sold will decrease; (c) the price of the product will increase; (d) the price of the product will decrease.

4. Which one of the following is *not* a reason why the increases in the demand for agricultural commodities have been relatively small? (a) the population of the United States has not increased so rapidly as the productivity of agriculture; (b) the increased per capita incomes of American consumers have resulted in less than proportionate increases in their expenditures for farm products; (c) the demand for agricultural products is inelastic; (d) the standard of living in the United States is well above the level of bare subsistence.

5. The price system has failed to solve the problem of low farm incomes because: (a) the demand for agricultural products is relatively inelastic; (b) the supply of agricultural products is relatively elastic; (c) agricultural products have relatively few good substitutes; (d) agricultural resources are relatively immobile.

6. If the demand for agricultural products is inelastic, a relatively small increase in supply will result in: (a) a relatively small increase in farm prices and incomes; (b) a relatively small decrease in farm prices and a relatively large increase in farm incomes; (c) a relatively large decrease in farm prices and incomes; (d) a relatively large increase in farm prices and a relatively small decrease in farm incomes.

7. Farm parity means that: (a) the real income of the farmer remains constant; (b) a given output will furnish the farmer with a constant amount of real income; (c) the purchasing power of the farmer's money income remains constant; (d) the money income of the farmer will buy a constant amount of goods and services.

8. If the price of a certain farm product were $.75 in the base period when the index of prices paid by farmers was 90, and if the present index of prices paid by the farmers is 150, then the parity price of the farm product

today is: (a) $.90; (b) $1.12½; (c) $1.25; (d) $1.50.

9. The necessary consequence of the government's supporting farm prices at an above-equilibrium level is: (a) a surplus of agricultural products; (b) increased consumption of agricultural products; (c) reduced production of agricultural products; (d) the dumping of agricultural products.

10. Which one of the following is *not* a reason why the farm program has been generally unsuccessful in accomplishing its aims? (a) the farm programs have not eliminated the basic cause of the problem; (b) restricting agricultural output increases farm prices but reduces farm income when demand is inelastic; (c) the human and nonhuman resources employed in agriculture have not been reduced and reallocated; (d) the principal beneficiaries of government aid have been farmers with high, not low, incomes.

■ **DISCUSSION QUESTIONS**

1. What was the economic condition of American agriculture: (a) prior to World War I; (b) during World War I; (c) from 1920 to 1940; (d) during World War II; (e) between 1950 and 1970? Explain the fundamental causes of the condition of agriculture in each of these periods.

2. Comment on (a) the size of farm incomes relative to nonfarm incomes; (b) the trend of farm incomes relative to nonfarm incomes; (c) the distribution of total farm income among farmers.

3. What is the long-run farm problem and its specific causes? What is the short-run farm problem and its causes?

4. Why does the demand for agricultural products tend to be inelastic?

5. What have been the specific causes of the large increases in the supply of agricultural products since World War I?

6. Why has the demand for agricultural products failed to increase at the same rate as the supply of these products?

7. Explain why the farm population tends to be relatively immobile. If farmers were more mobile, how would the price system reallocate their labor away from agriculture and into more prosperous occupations?

8. Explain why the inelastic nature of the demand for and the supply of agricultural products results in price and incomes which change by large amounts as a consequence of small changes in either demand or supply.

9. Why do agricultural interests claim that farmers have a special right to aid from the Federal government?

10. What is meant by "the farm program"? What particular aspect of the farm problem has traditionally received the major attention of farmers and their representatives in Congress?

11. Explain the concept of parity.

12. Why is the result of government-supported prices invariably a surplus of farm commodities?

13. What programs has the government used to try to restrict farm production? Why have these programs been relatively unsuccessful in limiting agricultural production?

14. How has the Federal government tried to increase the demand for farm products?

15. Why was the traditional farm policy not successful in preventing falling farm prices and incomes, surpluses, and an unequal distribution of farm income?

16. Explain why American agriculture began to boom in the 1970s.

17. In what ways does the new farm policy initiated in 1973 differ from the previous farm policy?

18. What are the consequences and implications of the new farm policy and of the rise in the demand for American agricultural products during the 1970s?

Urban Economics: the Problems of the Cities

CHAPTER

The farmers whose economic problems were examined in the last chapter have tilled the soil since before the beginning of recorded history. Cities and the problems of city living are nearly as old. Cities have been plagued by crowded conditions, crime, disease, poverty, and pollution for as long as cities have existed. Like the problems of the farmers, the problems of the city are not entirely new. What makes the problems of the cities especially important in the United States today is the simple statistic that nearly three-fourths of the American population now reside in cities. (By way of contrast, only about one-twentieth of the population is engaged in farming.)

While the problems of cities may not be completely new, some of these problems have become more pressing than ever before. Other city problems are new and did not exist in the large cities of early recorded history. It is not possible in a single chapter to examine all the contemporary problems confronting American cities. The author, therefore, focuses his attention on the more crucial of these problems, their causes, and their potential solutions.

Economics is not the only discipline interested in the development of cities and their problems. Other social scientists and natural and physical scientists are concerned and

contribute to the analysis of these problems and to their solutions. This is to say that city problems and solutions go well beyond economics. But economics is an essential part of the explanation of the development of cities, their current plight, and the steps necessary to the improvement of city living. And this is the subject matter of this chapter: the economic aspects of urban problems.

The organization of Chapter 36 is relatively simple. Professor McConnell first explains the economic reasons why cities emerge and grow by examining the economies of agglomeration. But as cities grow larger the disadvantages of agglomeration eventually appear. These deglomerative forces lead firms and families to the suburbs where they can enjoy the benefits of urban life without having to contend with its increasing problems. With this flight to suburbia comes political fragmentation and an economic imbalance between the central city and the suburbs. This historical development is the source of many of our current urban problems. The three problems given special attention by the author are transportation, pollution, and the ghetto. Each is examined in some detail and the possible solutions to each problem are considered. The final section of the chapter looks at the financial and institutional changes which may have to be made before any improvement in city living is possible. These changes include the political consolidation of the fragmented local governments, the employment of new methods of financing metropolitan governments, and the creation of entirely new cities.

The problem of the inadequate income of many of those who live in cities, especially in the ghettos, is not examined in great detail in this chapter. Poverty and the economics of inequality in the American economy is the trouble spot examined in Chapter 37.

■ **CHECKLIST**

The very least you should be able to do when you have finished this chapter is:

□ Define the economies of agglomeration and identify three principal agglomerative economies.

□ Define a deglomerative force and identify the two kinds of deglomerative forces.

□ Explain the advantage firms and households obtain and the disadvantage which they avoid by moving to the suburbs; and identify the two main consequences of this flight to suburbia.

□ Explain what is meant by political fragmentation; and the economic imbalance and the locational mismatch that have resulted from the decline of the central city and suburban growth.

□ Explain why an efficient transportation system is required in the larger cities; why the use of the automobile has increased and mass-transit systems have deteriorated; and the potential short-run and long-run solutions to the urban transportation problem.

□ Describe, using the materials-balance approach, the four causes of the pollution problem and three potential solutions to the problem.

□ Determine, when given the necessary data, the price (emission fee) a government agency should charge for pollution rights.

□ Enumerate the circumstances which have given rise to central-city ghettos; and identify three means by which poverty in the ghettos might be reduced.

□ Present three reasons why the steps taken to eliminate urban blight by stimulating construction have failed to solve the problem.

□ List the institutional and fiscal changes

which are prerequisites to a solution to urban problems; and the three potential solutions to the larger fiscal problem of local governments.

■ **CHAPTER OUTLINE**

1. Today over two-thirds of the American population live in urban areas.

2. Economic forces have lead to the development and expansion of cities.

  a. Firms can lower the cost of transporting resources and products by locating near their markets and other firms.

  b. The increased productivity of agriculture has reduced the number of workers in farming. These excess workers have been drawn to cities where, because of the economies of agglomeration, business firms and jobs are located.

  c. Only the large populations of urban centers have a demand for the amenities of life that is sufficient to warrant their production; and, as a result, consumers in cities find a wider variety of products available.

  d. Deglomerative forces, sooner or later, limit the growth of central cities and the concentration of firms, and lead to the expansion of the suburbs and to business decentralization.

3. To reap the advantages of urban life and to avoid its disadvantages, firms and households have moved to the suburbs. This flight to suburbia and the resulting suburban sprawl have had at least two important consequences.

  a. A large number of separate political units surround the central city.

  b. Wealth and income have increased in the suburbs and decreased in the central city; and the central city has experienced a decline in its tax base while its problems and need for public revenue have expanded.

4. The flight to the suburbs has led to a locational mismatch of jobs and the labor force, automobile congestion and pollution, and the need for a more efficient transportation system.

5. The improvement of urban transportation requires solutions to both a short-run and a long-run problem.

  a. To utilize the existing transport facilities

more effectively entails the adoption of user charges and peak pricing policies.

b. To build a better transport system entails the development of public mass-transit systems.

6. Because of their high concentrations of population and industry, urban areas have a pollution problem.

a. The dimensions of the problem are well known and the long-run consequences are potentially disastrous.

b. The cause of the pollution problem is the material imbalance between the wastes that result from production and consumption and the ability of the environment to reabsorb these wastes.

c. To reduce pollution requires that the costs of pollution be made private instead of social costs (be transferred from society to the polluter); and this may be accomplished by legislating standards, levying special taxes on polluters, or by creating a market for pollution rights.

7. Another problem characteristic of cities is the central city ghetto of low income, non-white, inadequately housed, and poorly educated inhabitants.

a. The poverty of the ghetto can be reduced by providing more and better jobs, income maintenance, and better education and training for those who live there.

b. For a variety of reasons the environment of the ghetto has not yet been improved by subsidized housing and urban renewal.

8. Solutions to the various urban problems require that sufficient financial resources be allocated and that certain institutional changes be made.

a. Consolidation of the many political units would increase the efficiency of decision making and improve equity by putting the needs and the resources within the same governmental unit.

b. To obtain sufficient resources to deal with urban problems may also require Federal revenue sharing, the shifting of some of the burden to the Federal government, and a restructuring of the property tax.

c. Because of the problems currently facing cities and the expected 100 million expansion in the urban population within the next 30 years, entirely new cities may need to be built.

■ IMPORTANT TERMS

Economies of agglomeration	Peak pricing
Internal economies	Materials balance approach
External economies	Emission fees
Infrastructure	Market for pollution rights
Deglomerative forces	
Urban sprawl	Political fragmentation
User charge	Black capitalism

■ FILL-IN QUESTIONS

1. About _____ million people and _____% of the American population live in cities today.

2. Deciding how to produce goods and services includes the decision of _____ to produce them. This latter decision is an important one because there are _____ costs involved in moving _____ to the firm and in moving the finished products to _____.

3. Before cities can develop agriculture must be able to produce _____ food and fiber so that _____ is available to produce nonagricultural goods and services.

4. The economies of agglomeration refer to the lower production and marketing costs which firms realize when they locate _____

_____

The three such principal economies are:

a. _____

b. _____

c. _____

5. The deglomerative forces include all those forces which result in _____ production costs. Some of these are _____ to the firm; and others are _____, are shifted to _____, and are called _____ costs.

6. The flight of people and firms to the suburbs enables them to obtain _____

_____

and to avoid _____.
The chief consequences of this movement
have been political _____ and an
economic _____ between the
central city and the suburbs.

7. The movement of the higher-income families and the wealthier firms to new political
units in suburbia has:

  a. eroded the _____ tax base and
brought about increases in tax _____
in the central city;

  b. left behind a central city of poor families, many of which are _____ and on
_____, living in _____ popu-
lated areas for which the cost of providing
social facilities and services is _____

8. The flight to the suburbs has also resulted
in:

  a. a locational mismatch because the _____
of those who live in suburbia are in the central city and of those who live in the central
city are in suburbia;

  b. the need for a more efficient _____
system;

  c. expanded use of the _____, traffic _____, and air _____

  d. the construction of still more _____
_____, the development of more distant
_____, and still more _____
and _____

  e. the general deterioration of the _____
_____ systems of the cities.

9. It has been suggested that:

  a. to relieve highway congestion there be
_____ on drivers and that _____
_____ policies should be used on highways and mass transit systems;

  b. in the long run it will be necessary to
rebuild the _____
in urban areas.

10. The materials balance approach to pollution is that the weight of the residual _____
_____ produced by society has come to
exceed the ability of _____ to _____
them. This imbalance is the result of increases in the nation's _____
and _____, changes in _____
and the absence of economic _____
to refrain from pollution.

11. The central city ghetto has developed in
major American cities because:

  a. the more prosperous and better _____
_____ whites have moved to the
_____ and left behind obsolete _____

  b. their places have been taken by poorly
_____, unskilled, and _____-income
blacks.

  c. job opportunities for the ghetto inhabitants have shifted from the _____
to the _____; and access to these
opportunities has been limited by the deterioration of the _____ system and
racial _____

12. To alleviate poverty in the ghettos requires that their residents be provided with
more and better _____,
improved _____ and _____; and that
a program of income _____ be instituted.

13. Bringing ghetto residents to the job opportunities in the suburbs will necessitate an
improved _____
One way of creating new job opportunities in
the central city is _____

14. The institutional and financial prerequisites to the solution of urban problems are
political _____ and an increase
in the _____ of urban governments.

15. Political consolidation will result in more
efficient _____ making and reduce

the disparity between _____ and _____ within urban areas.

16. The larger financial problem of urban areas will be reduced by political consolidation, Federal revenue _____, the shifting of some of the financial burden of cities to _____, and by overhauling the property tax so that _____ is taxed more heavily and _____ less heavily.

■ **PROBLEMS AND PROJECTS**

1. Below is a table showing the average number of motor vehicles traveling each mile of highway in a hypothetical metropolitan area and the estimated cost to society of each vehicle-mile traveled during various periods of the day. Compute the total cost per mile of highway in each of the seven periods of the day.

Period of the day	Vehicles per high-way-mile	Cost per vehicle-mile	Total cost
7am–9am	500	$ .60	$_____
9am–12n	150	.10	_____
12n–2pm	200	.15	_____
2pm–4pm	100	.10	_____
4pm–6pm	600	.85	_____
6pm–10pm	200	.15	_____
10pm–7am	50	.10	_____

a. In every twenty-four hour period the total number of vehicles traveling each mile of highway is _____ and the total cost for each mile of highway traveled is $_____.

b. The average cost to society for a vehicle to travel one mile is $_____.

c. Assuming that the number of vehicles per highway-mile is not affected by the imposition of a user charge and that the user charge is the same during all periods, the user charge that would enable society to recover the full

cost of the highway system would be $_____ per vehicle-mile.

d. Imagine now that the imposition of this user charge results in the following change in vehicular traffic during the various periods of the day. The cost per vehicle-mile remains the same in each period; and the total cost in each period is shown in the table below.

Period of the day	Vehicles per high-way-mile	Total cost	Total revenue
7am–9am	450	$270.00	$_____
9am–12n	135	13.50	_____
12n–2pm	180	27.00	_____
2pm–4pm	90	9.00	_____
4pm–6pm	540	459.00	_____
6pm–10pm	180	27.00	_____
10pm–7am	45	4.50	_____

(1) The total cost per day of each mile of highway is $_____

(2) Compute the total revenue in each period when a 50 cents per mile user charge is made. The total revenue per day on each mile of highway is $_____

(3) In what two periods are the revenues received less than the cost in that period?

_____ and _____

e. If it is desired to reduce the number of vehicles per mile of highway in these two periods to 400; and if each 1 cent increase in the user charge decreases the number of vehicles per mile by 10 vehicles, the user charge in the:

(1) 7am–9pm period should be increased to _____ cents per mile

(2) 4pm–6pm period should be increased to _____ cents per mile

2. Assume the atmosphere of Cuyahoga County, Ohio (the Cleveland metropolitan area) is able to reabsorb 1500 tons of pollutants per year. The schedule below shows the price polluters would be willing to pay for the right to dispose of 1 ton of pollutants per year and the total quantity of pollutants they would wish to dispose of at each price.

Price (per ton of pollutant rights)	Total quantity of pollutant rights demanded (tons)
$ 0	4,000
1,000	3,500
2,000	3,000
3,000	2,500
4,000	2,000
5,000	1,500
6,000	1,000
7,000	500

a. If there were no emission fee, polluters would put _____ tons of pollutants in the air each year; and this quantity of pollutants would exceed the ability of nature to reabsorb them by _____ tons.

b. To reduce pollution to the capacity of the atmosphere to recycle pollutants, an emission fee of $_____ per ton should be set.

c. Were this emission fee set, the total emission fees collected would be $_____

d. Were the quantity of pollution rights demanded at each price to increase by 500 tons, the emission fee could be increased by $_____ and total emission fees collected would increase by $_____

3. Describe conditions in the central city ghetto by placing one or more of the adjectives in the list below after each of the following indicators of well-being.

high   crowded
low   grossly inadequate
inadequate   deteriorated
old   deplorable
poor

a. Schools: _____

b. Mortality rates: _____

c. Income levels: _____

d. Medical care: _____

e. Housing: _____

f. Crime rates: _____

g. Sanitation: _____

h. Disease incidence: _____

■ **SELF-TEST**
Circle the T if the statement is true, the F if it is false.

1. Over 150 million Americans live in cities.
T   F

2. External economies of scale shift a firm's average-cost curve downward.   **T   F**

3. A deglomerative force increases the cost of producing a product and may be either internal or external to the firm.   **T   F**

4. Since 1900 the percentage of the American population living in central cities has increased.   **T   F**

5. The flight to the suburbs has involved the migration of families but has not resulted in the movement of business firms.   **T   F**

6. The flight to the suburbs has brought about a general improvement in the public mass-transit systems of cities.   **T   F**

7. Pollution is caused almost exclusively by profit-seeking business firms.   **T   F**

8. An effective antipollution policy requires that the social costs of pollution be turned into private costs.   **T   F**

9. Black capitalism entails the development in ghetto areas of business firms which are owned and operated by blacks.   **T   F**

10. It has been estimated that improved employment opportunities for its residents will eliminate 90% of the ghetto poverty.   **T   F**

Underscore the letter that corresponds to the best answer.

1. About what percentage of the American population lives in cities? (a) 85%; (b) 75%; (c) 55%; (d) 45%.

2. Deciding where to produce a product is a part of the decision a firm makes when it decides (a) what to produce; (b) how much to produce; (c) how to produce; (d) for whom to produce.

3. Which of the following will result in an internal economy of scale for firm A? (a) the growth of the market for firm A's product; (b) the development of other firms who are able to perform specialized services for firm A; (c) the expansion and improvement of the infrastructure; (d) the improvement of the transportation facilities used by firm A.

4. The flight to the suburbs has had all but one of the following consequences. Which one? (a) political consolidation; (b) an economic imbalance between the central city and the suburbs; (c) an erosion of the property tax base in the central city; (d) a mismatch between the location of the labor force and the location of job opportunities.

5. Which of the following is *not* generally considered to be a step that would lead to the solution of the urban transportation problem? (a) the imposition of user charges on the highway system; (b) following a peak pricing policy on the public mass-transit systems; (c) the reconstruction and expansion of the mass-transit systems; (d) the construction of more and the expansion of existing highways to connect the central city with the suburbs.

6. Which of the following would do little or nothing to reduce pollution? (a) create a market for pollution rights; (b) charge polluters an emission fee; (c) enact legislation that prohibits pollution and fines polluters; (d) redesign and reconstruct the infrastructure.

7. Which of the following has probably been the most important cause of the emergence of black ghettos? (a) racial discrimination; (b) the flight to the suburbs; (c) the deterioration of public mass-transit systems; (d) high crime rates in the central cities.

8. The unemployment rate among blacks is (a) less than; (b) about the same as; (c) double; (d) triple the rate for whites.

9. Which of the following would do little by itself to solve the problems of the central city? (a) political consolidation; (b) increased use of local income taxes; (c) Federal revenue sharing with the cities; (d) reduced taxation of buildings.

10. The suggestion to overhaul the property tax system has been made (a) because the property tax is proportional; (b) to reduce land values; (c) as an incentive for the construction and improvement of buildings; (d) to increase the supply of land.

■ DISCUSSION QUESTIONS

1. Explain why firms must decide where to produce and why they tend to agglomerate.

2. What is the difference between an internal and an external economy? What are the principal economies which induce firms to locate near other firms?

3. What is a deglomerative force? What are the principal deglomerative forces internal to the firm? What deglomerative forces are external to the firm?

4. Explain the reasons for the flight of families and business firms to the suburbs. What families and kinds of firms have remained in the central city?

5. Explain in detail the two most important consequences of the flight to suburbia.

6. What are the causes of the urban transportation problem and what might be done to improve urban transportation systems? Include in your answer the user charge and peak pricing concepts.

7. Employing the materials balance approach, explain the causes of the pollution problem. What are the three major policies that might be adopted to reduce pollution and what problems would be encountered in applying these policies?

8. Explain why ghettos developed in central cities and describe living conditions in and the characteristics of the typical ghetto. What can be done to change these conditions?

9. What steps has government taken to stimulate the construction of new housing? Why have these programs failed to help low-income families in the central city?

10. What are the institutional and financial prerequisites to the solution of urban problems? Why are these changes necessary and how might they be accomplished?

The Economics of Income Distribution: Inequality and Poverty

Chapter 37 examines the fourth of the so-called trouble spots in the American economy—the unequal distribution of the total income of the economy among its families and the poverty of many of these families.

The things which you should learn from this chapter are found in the checklist below. In addition, the following ideas have an important bearing on the discussion of inequality and poverty. First, you will recall from Chapter 6 that one of the functions of government in the American economy is to modify the economic results which a *pure* price-market system would yield: it is the price-market system and the institutions of capitalism which bring about an unequal distribution of income, and government in the United States has worked to reduce—but not eliminate—this unequal distribution.

Second, the critics of the price-market system (see Chapter 5) have attacked the system because it has unequally distributed income. But American capitalism has replied by repairing many of its faults. It is for this reason that the Socialist party and other groups advocating drastically different economic systems have met with so little success in the United States.

Third, the single most effective method of reducing the importance of income inequality and the extent of poverty in the United States has been the maintenance of full employment and an expanding average standard of living. Other programs have aided in the achievement of this goal, but the best cure has been the high and ever-increasing output of the American economy.

Fourth, very few people advocate an absolutely equal distribution of income; the question to be decided is not one of inequality or equality, but of how much or how little inequality there should be. The question can be looked at either ethically or economically, and the economist has nothing to offer on the ethical question but his own personal value judgment. From the economic point of view it is the task of the economist to observe that less income inequality may result in a smaller national output and a lower employment rate. This is "the big trade-off" confronting the economy and it requires that the people of the United States make a choice. The pros and cons of the income-inequality issue represent no more than different opinions on the degree to which we should reduce our economic efficiency (total output and employment) in order to reduce income inequality.

Finally, while poverty is caused by many forces, it is essentially an economic problem. Any attack on poverty will have to be basically an economic attack. There are reasons why the problem of poverty may not be solved in the United States; but one of these reasons is not that the American economy cannot afford to abolish poverty. The costs of poverty far outweigh the costs of eliminating it; and surely a rich nation can afford what it costs to provide the necessities of life for all of its citizens.

■ **CHECKLIST**

The very least you should be able to do when you have finished this chapter is:

□ Present data from the textbook to support the conclusion that there is considerable income inequality in the United States.

□ Enumerate five causes of an unequal distribution of income.

□ Report what has happened to the distribution of income in the United States since 1929 and since 1947.

□ Describe the effects of taxes and of in-kind transfers on income distribution.

□ Explain how much mobility between income classes there is in the short run (from one year to the next) and in the long run (from one generation to the next).

□ Make a three-point case against and a three-point case for income inequality.

□ Use current government standards to define poverty and to describe the extent of poverty in the United States; enumerate the groups in which poverty is concentrated; and explain why poverty tends to be invisible.

□ List four kinds of racial discrimination that result in economic discrimination; and explain how much this discrimination costs the United States each year.

□ Contrast the two opposing views on the cause of and remedy for poverty.

□ Enumerate the five components of the American social security system; and four criticisms levied against this system.

□ Describe how the present Federal income tax system might employ a negative income tax to establish a guaranteed minimum income; list the three objectives of such a program; and explain why it is difficult (if not impossible) to devise a program that will achieve all three objectives.

□ Explain why there may be a trade-off between economic efficiency and economic equality.

■ **CHAPTER OUTLINE**

1. The extent of income inequality in the United States can be seen by examining distribution-of-income tables.

a. The impersonal price system does not necessarily result in a distribution of income which society deems just; at least five specific factors explain why income inequality exists.

b. Since 1929 the real incomes received by all income classes have increased; and between 1929 and 1944 the relative distribution of personal income changed to reduce income inequality. But since 1944 the relative distribution has been almost constant; and the income gap between the richest and the poorest families has widened.

c. The relative distribution of income after taxes is about the same as it was before taxes were collected; there is little movement in the short run and more than a little movement in the long run from one income class to another; and Browning has concluded that when in-kind transfers are taken into account inequality in the distribution of income is less than assumed and has lessened in the past two decades to eliminate almost all poverty.

d. Whether income equality is desirable or not is open to debate. Those who attack it contend that it results in reduced consumer satisfaction, lower productivity, and social and political inequality.

e. Income inequality is defended primarily on the grounds that it makes a large volume of saving (and, therefore, investment) possible; that it furnishes incentives to work, produce, and innovate; and that it provides the higher incomes which subsidize the development of new products and cultural progress.

2. Aside from inequality in the distribution of income, there is great concern today with the problem of poverty in the United States.

a. Using the generally accepted definition of poverty, almost 12% of the people in the American economy live in poverty; and these poor tend to be concentrated among certain kinds of families.

b. Poverty in the United States tends to be invisible because it is obscured by the general affluence of the economy as a whole and hidden from the eyes of the remainder of society.

3. The greater incidence of poverty among

nonwhites is in part the result of racial discrimination.

a. This racial discrimination is found in the wage, employment, occupation, human-capital, and other forms of discrimination to which nonwhites are subject.

b. The costs of this discrimination to the economy are estimated at 4% of the GNP.

4. There are two fundamental and opposing philosophies regarding the cause of poverty and the policies to deal with it.

a. One view is that the poor are responsible for their own plight and government should not help them.

b. The opposing view is that poverty is the result of social forces beyond the control of the individual and that society as a whole must assist the poor.

c. The evidence indicates that most of those who are poor are unable to help themselves.

5. The social security system of the United States has five principal programs.

a. OASDI is the national social insurance program financed by taxes levied on employers and employees.

b. The SSI program provides aid for the aged, blind, and disabled; and the AFDC assists families with dependent children.

c. Low-income families are also helped by the food stamp program.

d. Medicare helps the aged and Medicaid helps those who receive aid from the SSI and AFDC programs to obtain medical care.

e. The social security (or welfare) system has been criticized in recent years; and its critics argue that it impairs incentive to work, is abused by those who are not really in need and inequitably distributes benefits, is costly to administer, and is inflationary.

6. A new approach to income maintenance would employ a negative income tax (an income transfer or subsidy) to guarantee a minimum income to all citizens.

a. A negative income tax plan which would retain incentives to work would not raise the incomes of the poor to the minimum level.

b. A plan which raises the incomes of all poor families to the minimum level destroys the incentive to work.

c. And a plan which both retains the incentives to work and raises incomes of the poor to the minimum level results in subsidies to those whose incomes are already above the minimum level.

7. In the American economy there is a trade-off between economic equality and economic efficiency: A more nearly equal distribution of income results in less economic efficiency (a smaller national income) and greater economic efficiency leads to a more unequal distribution of income.

■ **IMPORTANT TERMS**

Income inequality	Aid to families with dependent children (AFDC)
In-kind transfer	
Poverty	Food stamp program
Old age, survivors, and disability insurance (OASDI)	Medicare
	Medicaid
Unemployment insurance (compensation)	Guaranteed minimum income
Supplemental security income (SSI)	Negative income tax

■ **FILL-IN QUESTIONS**

1. It can fairly be said that the extent of income inequality in the United States is _____

_____

2. The important factors which explain income inequality are differences in _____

_____ ,

_____ ,

and _____ ,

the unequal distribution of _____ ,

and the unequal distribution of _____ ,
among the population.

3. The percentage of total personal income received by the highest quintile has since

1929 (increased, decreased) _____
and the percentage received by the lowest

two quintiles has _____ .
These changes can fairly be said to have been

_____ ;

but since the close of World War II the distribution of personal income in the United

States has _____

4. In the United States:

a. There is no noticeable difference in the

_____ and the _____

distributions of income.

b. There is in the short run little _____

of income receiver between income classes.

c. A person's income status (is, is not)

_____ generally inherited.

d. Edgar Browning argues that when _____

_____ transfers are taken into account

the distribution of income has become (more,

less) _____ unequal during the past

twenty years and that poverty, as it is officially

defined, has _____

5. Those who condemn income inequality

contend that it reduces _____

and _____ ;

and that it fosters _____
inequality.

6. The defenders of income inequality argue

that it results in _____ ,

_____ ,

and _____

7. Using the more or less official definition
of poverty,

a. The poor includes any family of four with

less than _____ and any individual with

less than _____
a year to spend.

b. Approximately _____ % of the

population and about _____
million people are poor.

8. Poverty tends to be concentrated:

a. Among the (young, old) _____

b. Among (whites, blacks) _____

c. In families headed by _____

d. Among those who are poorly _____

e. In families in which the working members

do not have _____

and _____ jobs.

9. What four reasons explain why in the
affluent American economy those living in
poverty remain hidden or invisible?

a. _____

b. _____

c. _____

d. _____

10. The median income of nonwhites is only

about _____ % of the median income of
whites.

11. The four principal kinds of economic
discrimination against blacks are:

a. _____

b. _____

c. _____

d. _____

This discrimination costs the economy an

amount equal to _____ % of its present total

output or more than $_____ billion a year.

12. There are two conflicting philosophies
regarding the source of poverty. One philosophy contends that government should not
help the poor because their poverty is due to

_____

_____

and the other argues that the poor must be
helped by government because the causes of

poverty are _____

13. The five parts of the social security sys-

tem are _____

insurance, _____

compensation, the _____

and _____ programs,

the _____ program,

and, to provide medical benefits, the _____

_____ and _____
programs.

14. Despite the success of the social security
(or welfare) system in reducing poverty, its
critics argue that it

a. _____

b. _____

c. _____

d. _____

and some of these critics suggest that it be

replaced by a _____ tax.

15. The so-called "big trade-off" is between

economic _____

and economic _____

■ **PROBLEMS AND PROJECTS**

1. The distribution of personal income among consumer units in a hypothetical economy is shown in the table at the bottom of this page.

a. Complete the table by computing:

(1) The percentage of all consumer units in each income class and all lower classes; enter these figures in column 4.

(2) The percentage of total income received by each income class and all lower classes; enter these figures in column 5.

b. From the distribution of income data in columns 4 and 5 it can be seen that:

(1) Consumer units with less than $3000 a

year income constitute the lowest _____%

of all consumer units and receive _____% of the total personal income.

(2) Consumer units with incomes of $7500

a year or more constitute the highest _____%

of all consumer units and receive _____% of the total personal income.

2. Following is a table containing different possible earned incomes for a family of a certain size.

Earned income	Income deficit	Income subsidy	Total income
$ 0	$_____	$_____	$_____
1,000	_____	_____	_____
2,000	_____	_____	_____
3,000	_____	_____	_____
4,000	_____	_____	_____
5,000	_____	_____	_____

a. Assume that $5000 is the minimum income desirable for a family of this size. Compute the income deficit at each earned income and enter them in the table.

b. Assume the negative income tax rate is 60%. Enter the income subsidy and the total income at each level of earned income in the table.

c. This negative income tax program retains incentives to work because whenever the family earns an additional $1000 the income

subsidy decreases by only $_____ and total

income increases by $_____

d. But this program does not result in a total income of $5000 for the family unless

its earned income is $_____

e. Complete the following table to show the amount of income subsidy the family would

(1) Personal income class	(2) Percentage of all consumer units in this class	(3) Percentage of total income received by this class	(4) Percentage of all consumer units in this and all lower classes	(5) Percentage of total income received by this and all lower classes
Under $2,000	18	4	_____	_____
2,000–2,999	12	6	_____	_____
3,000–3,999	14	12	_____	_____
4,000–4,999	17	14	_____	_____
5,000–7,499	19	15	_____	_____
7,500–9,999	11	20	_____	_____
10,000 and over	9	29	_____	_____

have to receive in order to make its total income $5000. Income subsidies of this size would ensure the family a minimum income of $5000; but would destroy incentives to work because whenever the family earns an additional $1000 its income subsidy would decrease by $_____ and its total income would increase by $_____

Earned income	Income subsidy	Total income
$ 0	$_____	$5,000
1,000	_____	$5,000
2,000	_____	$5,000
3,000	_____	$5,000
4,000	_____	$5,000
5,000	_____	$5,000

f. Below is another table showing the different possible earned income levels for a family of a certain size.

Earned income	Income deficit	Income subsidy	Total income
$ 0	$_____	$_____	$_____
1,000	_____	_____	_____
2,000	_____	_____	_____
3,000	_____	_____	_____
4,000	_____	_____	_____
5,000	_____	_____	_____

(1) Assume that $5000 is still the minimum income desirable for a family of this size; but that the income deficit is found by subtracting earned income from $8333⅓. Compute the income deficit at each level of earned income and enter it in the table.

(2) Assume the negative income tax rate is still 60% of the income deficit. Compute the income subsidy at each earned income level; and the total income. Enter these amounts in the table.

(3) This negative income tax program maintains incentives to work because whenever earned income increases by $1000 the sub-

sidy decreases by $_____ and total income increases by $_____

(4) It also ensures that the family, no matter what its earned income is, receives a total income of $_____ or more; but results in total incomes in excess of $5000 if the family has an earned income greater than $_____

■ **SELF-TEST**

Circle the T if the statement is true, the F if it is false.

1. According to the author of the text, there is considerable income inequality in the United States. **T F**

2. Since 1929 the percentage of total personal income received by consumer units in the highest income quintile has decreased. **T F**

3. In percentage or relative terms the before-tax and after-tax distributions of income in the United States are approximately the same. **T F**

4. There appears to be little mobility between income classes from one generation to the next and considerable mobility between income classes from one year to the next. **T F**

5. Large increases in in-kind transfers during the past fifteen years seem to have decreased income inequality in the United States. **T F**

6. Those who defend income inequality contend that it results in a higher level of consumption spending and thereby promotes a higher level of aggregate demand, output, and employment in the economy. **T F**

7. Using the semiofficial definition of poverty, almost 12% of the population of the United States is poor. **T F**

8. The greater incidence of poverty among nonwhites is, for the most part, attributable to racial discrimination. **T F**

9. The cost of racial discrimination in the United States is equal to approximately 4% of the national output. **T F**

10. Of the two philosophies of poverty, one contends that poverty is caused by social forces beyond the control of the individual and the other believes that poverty is due to government interferences with the price-market system. **T F**

11. Evidence suggests that the vast majority of the poor who obtain public assistance (welfare) are unable to support themselves. **T F**

12. If there is a "big trade-off," a decrease in income inequality will bring about an increase in economic efficiency. **T F**

Underscore the letter that corresponds to the best answer.

1. Approximately what percentage of all American families have personal incomes of over $25,000 annually? (*a*) 5%; (*b*) 10%; (*c*) 15%; (*d*) 20%.

2. Approximately what percentage of all American families have personal incomes of less than $5000 a year? (*a*) 5%; (*b*) 10%; (*c*) 15%; (*d*) 20%.

3. Which of the following is *not* one of the causes of the unequal distribution of income in the United States? (*a*) the unequal distribution of property; (*b*) in-kind transfers; (*c*) the inability of the poor to invest in human capital; (*d*) luck and the unequal distribution of misfortune.

4. Which of the following would be evidence of a decrease in income inequality in the United States? (*a*) a decrease in the percentage of total personal income received by the lowest quintile; (*b*) an increase in the percentage of total personal income received by the highest quintile; (*c*) an increase in the percentage of total personal income received by the four lowest quintiles; (*d*) a decrease in the percentage of total personal income received by the four lowest quintiles.

5. In the post-World War II period there has been: (*a*) a significant decrease in the percentage of total personal income received by the highest quintile; (*b*) a significant increase in the percentage of total personal income received by the lowest quintile; (*c*) a significant increase in the percentage of total personal income received by the middle three quintiles; (*d*) no significant change in the percentage of total personal income received by any of the five quintiles.

6. Which of the following is *not* one of the contentions of those who condemn income inequality? (*a*) it is an obstacle to the maximization of consumer satisfactions; (*b*) it leads to social and political inequality; (*c*) it results in insufficient saving in the economy and thereby causes insufficient investment and an inadequate level of aggregate demand and unemployment; (*d*) it reduces the productivity of the economy's resources.

7. Poverty does not have a precise definition, but the officially accepted definition of "poor" is any family of four and any individual with less to spend annually, respectively, than (approximately): (*a*) $5000 and $2700; (*b*) $6000 and $3000; (*c*) $6000 and $2000; (*d*) $5500 and $2800.

8. Which of the following is *not* a cause of the invisibility of the American poor? (*a*) poverty in the cities is not easily seen from the more common means of transportation; (*b*) poverty in rural areas is not easily seen from the more common means of transportation; (*c*) poverty among the old and sick is not easily seen because these people seldom emerge from their dwelling places; (*d*) poverty among the unemployed is more than offset by unemployment compensation.

9. Which of the following is one of the five parts of the American social security system? (*a*) public housing; (*b*) agricultural subsidies; (*c*) unemployment insurance; (*d*) minimum wage laws.

10. Which of the following is designed to provide a nationwide minimum income for the aged, the blind, and the disabled? (*a*) OASDI; (*b*) SSI; (*c*) AFDC; (*d*) ABD.

11. Which of the following is *not* one of the charges levied against the social security (welfare) system in the United States by its critics? (*a*) it is inflationary; (*b*) it impairs incentives to work; (*c*) it benefits both needy and unneedy families; (*d*) it doesn't reduce poverty.

12. A negative income tax would (*a*) reduce incentives to work; (*b*) fail to guarantee a minimum income to all people; (*c*) subsidize people who are not poor; (*d*) result in at least one but not necessarily all of the above.

■ DISCUSSION QUESTIONS

1. How much income inequality is there in the American economy? Cite figures to support your conclusion. What causes income inequality in American capitalism?

2. Has the distribution of income changed in the United States during the past 45 to 50 years? If it has, in what way, to what extent, and why has it changed? Has income distribution changed in the past 30 or so years?

3. How do taxes affect the relative distribution of income in the United States? Does the passage of time tend to change the income class in which a family is located?

4. Is income inequality desirable? What are the arguments on both sides of this question?

5. What is the currently accepted and more or less official definition of poverty? How many people and what percentage of the American population are poor if we use this definition of poverty?

6. What characteristics—other than the small amounts of money they have to spend—do the greatest concentrations of the poor families of the nation *tend* to have?

7. Why does poverty in the United States tend to be invisible or hidden?

8. In what ways does racial discrimination lead to a greater incidence of poverty among nonwhites than among whites? What is the economic cost to the nation of this discrimination?

9. Is the problem of poverty primarily a problem to be solved by government or by individuals? What are the two opposing philosophies or viewpoints that would underlie the answer to this question? Which view does the evidence support?

10. What are the five programs embodied in the social security system of the United States? Explain why this system has been called a "welfare mess" by its critics.

11. Explain how poverty and the unequal distribution of income would be reduced by a negative income tax. What are the three problems that the use of such a tax would encounter?

12. What would be traded for what in "the big trade-off"?

Unionism, Collective Bargaining, and Women at Work

Another trouble spot in the American economy is in the area of labor-management relations. It is an area that is almost always in the news for one reason or another—strikes, new legislation, wage increases, union demands, and charges and countercharges by both employers and unions.

The labor union has become an important institution in American capitalism. Labor unions did not always occupy the position in the economy that they now do. The first part of Chapter 38 is devoted to a historical review of their development in the United States and is separated into three periods. The important thing for you to see is that the growth and power of unions in each of these periods clearly depended upon the rights and recognition given to them by Federal law. At first the law repressed them, then it encouraged them, and finally it has sought to curb and control their greatly increased power.

In Chapter 31 you learned how unions directly and indirectly seek to influence wage rates. The impact of the union upon its own membership, upon employers, and upon the rest of the economy is more than just a matter of wages, however. The third major section of Chapter 38 examines the contents of a typical contract between a union and an employer. The purpose of this examination is to give you some idea of the goals which unions seek

and other issues over which employers and employees bargain and upon which they must reach an agreement. Another extremely important idea which you will find in the section is this: Labor-management relations mean more than the periodic signing of a contract; they also mean the day-to-day working relations between the union and the employer and the new problems and issues not specifically settled in the contract which must be resolved under the general provisions of that contract.

The final section of this chapter examines the role of women in the labor force and in the labor markets of the American economy. This section explains why the percentage of American women who are members of the labor force is greater today than ever before; and why, therefore, the percentage of the labor force that is female is larger than it has ever been. It also explains why the average working woman earns less than the average working man. Part of this difference in earnings is the result of sexual discrimination; but another part is the consequence of rates of absenteeism and of labor force and job turnover which are higher among women than among men.

A final word of advice. The list of important terms is long, but you will find it worthwhile to master it. An understanding of the terms leads to a better understanding of the history and many of the issues and problems of labor-management relations.

■ **CHECKLIST**

The very least you should be able to do when you have finished this chapter is:

□ Describe the attitudes and behavior of the courts and business toward labor unions during the repression phase.

□ Identify the three fundamental ideas of Samuel Gompers.

□ Explain how the Norris-LaGuardia Act and the Wagner Act contributed to the revival and rapid growth of the labor movement during the encouragement phase.

□ Contrast the beliefs of John L. Lewis and the founders of the CIO with those of the leaders of the AFL during the 1930s.

□ Identify the four headings into which the provisions of the Taft-Hartley Act can be put; outline the provisions of the Landrum-Griffin Act; and explain the principal reasons for the enactment of these laws.

□ Describe the four forces which resulted in the merger of the AFL and CIO; and identify the three internal and the three external obstacles to the growth of the labor movement during the past twenty years.

□ Provide two reasons for the expansion of public-sector collective bargaining and explain the three implications of this expansion.

□ Enumerate and explain the contents of the four basic parts of a collective-bargaining agreement.

□ List five reasons for the increased participation of women in the American labor force since World War II; compare the economic status of female and male workers; and explain the special kind of job segregation to which women are subjected and at least two economically justifiable reasons for segregating women into lower-paying jobs.

■ **CHAPTER OUTLINE**

1. The history of labor unions in the United States can be divided into three periods or phases.

a. During the repression phase, between 1790 and 1930, the growth of unions was severely limited by the judicial application of the criminal conspiracy doctrine and by the refusal of many firms to recognize and bargain with unions; between 1886 and 1930 the AFL, following the union philosophy of Samuel Gompers, was able to organize many crafts and expand its membership.

b. Between 1930 and 1947, the encouragement phase, labor union membership grew rapidly, encouraged by prolabor legislation; and the CIO was formed to unionize industrial workers.

c. In the intervention phase from 1947 onward, government regulation and control of labor-management relations increased with the passage of the Taft-Hartley and Landrum-Griffin Acts.

d. The merger of the AFL and CIO in 1955 reunited the American labor movement.

e. Since the achievement of labor unity, the labor movement, facing both internal and external obstacles, has been unable to increase its membership by any substantial amount; but the number of unionized public employees has increased substantially since 1965.

2. Collective bargaining and the resulting work agreements are more often than not the result of compromise between labor and management; strikes and violence are actually quite rare.

3. The typical agreement between the employer and the union covers four basic areas. But collective bargaining is more than the periodic negotiation of an agreement; it also involves union and workers' security and day-to-day labor-management relations in an economy which is continually changing.

4. Since World War II the participation of women in the labor force has expanded significantly. But both because of discrimination and for sound economic reasons the average income of women is less than the average income of men workers.

■ **IMPORTANT TERMS**

Criminal-conspiracy doctrine	Lockout
Injunction	Yellow-dog contract
Discriminatory discharge	Company union
Blacklisting	Business unionism
	Norris-La Guardia Act

Wagner (National
Labor Relations) Act

National Labor
Relations Board

Taft-Hartley (Labor-
Management
Relations) Act

Jurisdictional strike

Sympathy strike

Secondary boycott

Featherbedding

Closed shop

Union shop

Open shop

Nonunion shop

Right-to-work law

Checkoff

Reopening clause

Landrum-Griffin
(Labor-Management
Reporting and
Disclosure) Act

Preferential hiring

Seniority

Arbitration

American Federation
of Labor

Congress of Indus-
trial Organizations

Female participation
rate

Occupational
discrimination

*Two terms for
review:*

Craft unionism

Industrial
unionism

■ FILL-IN QUESTIONS

1. Over _____ million workers belong to labor unions in the United
States. This is approximately what percent-

age of the nonagricultural labor force? _____

2. During the repression phase of labor union history, union growth was slow because

_____

and _____

3. Unions were limited in their growth between 1790 and 1930 by courts which applied

the _____

doctrine to labor unions and issued _____

_____

to prevent strikes, picketing, and boycotts.

4. Employers used the following nonjudicial
means of retarding the growth of labor unions

in the repression phase: _____

_____ ,

_____ ,

_____ ,

_____ ,

_____ ,

_____ ,

and _____

5. The philosophy of the AFL under the

leadership of Samuel Gompers was _____

_____ ,

_____ ,

and _____

6. In the encouragement phase of labor union history, unions grew as a consequence

of such favorable legislation as the _____

_____

and _____

Acts; and the _____ ,

based on the principle of _____

unionism, was formed to organize the _____

_____

workers.

7. The National Labor Relations Act of 1935
guaranteed the "twin rights" of labor: the

right to _____

and the right to _____ ;

in addition it established the _____

and listed a number of _____

8. Three important events that occurred in
the history of labor unions after 1946 were

the passage of the _____

and _____

Acts and the _____
Some economists contend that in the 1955–
1965 period union membership was almost

_____ and that the labor movement

was characterized by _____ ;

but since 1965 a large number of _____
employees have joined unions.

9. The four principal sections of the Labor-
Management Relations Act of 1947 are:

a. _____

b. _____

c. _____

d. _____

10. The Landrum-Griffin Act of 1959 regulates union _____

and _____

and lists the rights of _____

upon which _____
may not infringe.

11. A typical work agreement between a union and an employer covers four basic areas:

a. _____

b. _____

c. _____

d. _____

12. Labor and management tend to base their arguments for and against higher wages on

four points, namely, _____

_____,

_____,

_____,

and _____

13. Collective bargaining is concerned not

only with wage rates but also with the _____

_____

and _____
of unions and their numbers; and while negotiation of a work agreement is important

_____

and _____
the agreement are equally important.

14. The rate at which women participate in

the labor force has _____ since
World War II because of:

a. _____

b. _____

c. _____

d. _____

e. _____

15. The average earnings of a full-time female

worker is only about _____% of the average
earnings of a full-time male worker because

of _____

and _____

■ **PROBLEMS AND PROJECTS**

1. Below is a list of frequently employed terms, and following the terms is a series of identifying phrases. Match the term with the phrase by placing the appropriate letter after each of the phrases. (*Note:* All the terms will not be needed.)

A. Injunction
B. Blacklisting
C. Lockout
D. Yellow-dog contract
E. Company union
F. Business union
G. Jurisdictional strike
H. Sympathy strike
I. Secondary boycott
J. Featherbedding
K. Closed shop
L. Union shop
M. Open shop
N. Nonunion shop
O. Checkoff
P. Craft union
Q. Industrial union

1. A worker must be a member of the union

before he is eligible for employment. _____

2. A worker agrees when employed not to

join a union. _____

3. A union open to all workers employed by

a given firm or in a given industry. _____

4. A union organized and encouraged by an employer to prevent the formation of a union which might make "unreasonable" demands.

_____

5. The deduction by an employer on behalf of the union of a worker's union dues from

his wages. _____

6. A dispute between two unions over whose members are to perform a certain job.

_____

7. A court order which forbids a person or group of persons to perform some act. _____

8. The closing of the place of employment by the employer as a means of preventing the formation of a union. _____

9. Concern of unions with better pay, hours, and working conditions rather than with plans for social and economic reform. _____

10. Payment of workers for work not actually performed. _____

2. Below is a list of provisions found in four important pieces of labor legislation. Identify the act in which the provision is found by putting either (A) for the Norris-La Guardia Act, (B) for the Wagner Act, (C) for the Taft-Hartley Act, or (D) for the Landrum-Griffin Act in the space following each provision.

a. Specified that contracts between a union and an employer must contain a termination or reopening clause. _____

b. Established a board to investigate unfair labor practices and to conduct elections among workers. _____

c. Guaranteed to workers the right to organize unions and to bargain collectively. _____

d. Declared that yellow-dog contracts were unenforceable and limited the use of injunctions against unions. _____

e. Regulated union elections and finances and guaranteed certain rights to union members in their dealings with the union and its officers. _____

f. Outlawed the closed shop, jurisdictional and certain sympathy strikes, secondary boycotts, and featherbedding. _____

g. Provided a procedure whereby strikes affecting the health and safety of the nation might be delayed. _____

h. Outlawed company unions, antiunion discrimination in hiring and discharging workers and interfering with the rights of workers to form unions. _____

3. Suppose there are only three labor markets in the economy and each of these markets is perfectly competitive. The table below contains the demand (or marginal revenue product) schedule for labot in *each* of these three markets.

Wage rate (marginal revenue product of labor per hour)	Quantity of labor (millions per hour)
$11	4
10	5
9	6
8	7
7	8
6	9
5	10
4	11
3	12

a. Assume there are 24 million homogeneous workers in the economy and that one-half of these workers are male and one-half are female.

(1) If the 12 million female workers can be employed only in labor market Z, for all of them to find employment the hourly wage rate must be $_____.

(2) If of the 12 million male workers, 6 million are employed in labor market X and 6 million are employed in labor market Y, the hourly wage rate in labor markets X and Y will be $_____.

b. Imagine now that the impediment to the employment of females in labor markets X and Y is removed; and that as a result (and because the demand and marginal revenue product of labor is the same in all three markets) 8 million workers find employment in each labor market.

(1) In labor market Z (in which only females had previously been employed):

(a) the hourly wage rate will rise to $_____

(b) the *decrease* in national output that results from the decrease in employment from 12 to 8 million workers is equal to the loss of the marginal revenue products of the workers no longer employed; and it totals $_____ million.

(2) In labor market X and in labor market Y (in each of which only males had previously been employed):

(a) the hourly wage rate will fall to $_____

(b) the *increase* in national output that results from the increase in employment from 6 to 8 million workers is equal to the marginal revenue products of the additional workers employed; and the gain in *each* of these markets is $_____ million and the total gain in the two markets is $_____.

(3) the *net* gain to society from the reallocation of female workers is $_____ million.

■ **SELF-TEST**

Circle the T if the statement is true, the F if it is false.

1. An injunction is a court order which declares that combinations of workmen to raise wages are illegal. **T F**

2. Blacklisting was a device employed by early labor unions to cut off a firm's labor supply. **T F**

3. Union membership has increased in every year since the end of World War II. **T F**

4. The CIO was based on the principle of industrial unionism while the AFL was operated on the craft union philosophy. **T F**

5. The Taft-Hartley Act lists a number of unfair labor practices on the part of management. **T F**

6. Under the provisions of the Labor-Management Relations Act of 1947 the checkoff and featherbedding are prohibited. **T F**

7. The Teamsters and the United Mine Workers are important unions not affiliated with the AFL-CIO. **T F**

8. The four-points criteria employed by unions in arguing for higher wages can also be used by management to resist higher wages and to argue for decreased wages. **T F**

9. Arbitration means the settlement of a dispute by a third party who renders a decision which the parties to the dispute have agreed in advance to accept. **T F**

10. The difference between the average earnings of full-time female and male workers is only partly the result of sexual discrimination. **T F**

Underscore the letter that corresponds to the best answer.

1. About what percentage of all nonagricultural workers are members of unions? (a) 23%; (b) 25%; (c) 27%; (d) 30%.

2. Which of the following would not be used by an employer to prevent the organization of a genuine union among his employees? (a) lockout; (b) featherbedding; (c) company union; (d) yellow-dog contract.

3. Which one of the following was an essential part of Samuel Gompers' union philosophy? (a) industrial unionism; (b) support of the Democratic Party at the polls; (c) establishment of producer cooperatives operated by labor and management; (d) business unionism.

4. The Norris-La Guardia Act outlawed: (a) yellow-dog contracts; (b) the closed shop; (c) company unions; (d) blacklisting.

5. The Wagner Act outlawed: (a) company unions; (b) the closed shop; (c) the checkoff; (d) injunctions against unions.

6. The Taft-Hartley Act outlawed: (a) the nonunion shop; (b) the open shop; (c) the union shop; (d) the closed shop.

7. Which one of the following is *not* a provision of the Landrum-Griffin Act? (a) allows a worker to sue his union if the union denies the member certain rights; (b) unions are prohibited from making political contributions in elections for Federal offices; (c) requires regularly scheduled union elections and the use of secret ballots; (d) guarantees union members the right to attend union meetings, to vote and to participate in the meeting, and to nominate union officers.

8. If workers at the time they are hired have a choice of joining the union and paying dues or of not joining the union and paying no dues, there exists: (a) a union shop; (b) an open shop; (c) a nonunion shop; (d) a closed shop.

9. Which one of the following is not presently an unfair labor practice? (a) the refusal of either unions or companies to bargain in good faith; (b) the coercion of employees by unions to join and by companies not to join unions; (*c*) the practices of company and business unionism; (*d*) both jurisdictional strikes and secondary boycotts.

10. About what percentage of the total labor force are women? (*a*) 44; (*b*) 41; (*c*) 33; (*d*) 28.

■ DISCUSSION QUESTIONS

1. What are the three phases in the history of labor unions in the United States? What was the law with respect to unions, what was the extent of unionization, and what were the principal events in each of these periods?

2. How were the courts able to retard the growth of unions between 1790 and 1930? How did employers attempt to limit union growth?

3. Explain the union philosophy of Samuel Gompers.

4. What were the chief provisions of the Norris-La Guardia Act and the Wagner Act?

5. Explain how the principles of the CIO differed from those on which the AFL was based.

6. Contrast the philosophy and policy embodied in the Wagner Act with that found in the Taft-Hartley Act.

7. What are the four main sections of the Taft-Hartley Act? What specific practices are outlawed by the act and what specific things are required of unions, union officers, and bargaining agreements?

8. Explain the major provisions of the Landrum-Griffin Act.

9. What were the forces which resulted in the merger of the AFL and CIO in 1955?

10. What do economists mean when they talk of stagnation in the labor movement in the United States? What evidence is there of stagnation? What are the probable causes of it?

11. Explain what usually constitute the "prerogatives of management."

12. What are the four arguments employed by labor (management) in demanding (resisting) higher wages? Why are these arguments "two-edged"?

13. What is meant by grievance procedure? Why is such a procedure so important in labor-management relations? In the typical labor-management contract found in the text, what are the four steps which may be used in settling grievances?

14. What is a right-to-work law? What arguments are presented in support of right-to-work laws by those who favor them? What arguments are advanced by labor unions in opposition to them?

15. Explain why the rate at which women participate in the American labor force has increased substantially in the last forty years. How does the economic status of working women compare with that of working men? How do you explain this difference?

16. If labor markets were competitive, what would be the effect of reducing or eliminating sexual discrimination in these labor markets upon the wage rates received by men and women and upon the national output?

The Economics of War and Defense

War and national defense require that scarce resources be used to produce military hardware and to staff the armed forces. Because the employment of scarce resources is the subject matter of economics, war and defense are a part of the study of economics.

This chapter is *not* an examination of the case for and against war. It does not debate the issue of whether the United States employs too large or too small a portion of its resources for national defense. Appraising the *benefits* of American defense is beyond the professional competence of economists and the subject matter of economics. All that economists can do is estimate the cost and examine the effects of defending the nation upon the economy. And this is the purpose of Chapter 39: to look at national defense as a user of scarce resources.

The chapter is divided into six major sections. The first section estimates the dollar size of the American war industry to be equal to the amount spent by the Federal government for national defense; but points out that this figure understates the total cost of defense and past wars to the United States. The real cost of the American defense establishment, it is observed in the second section, is the opportunity cost of defending the nation; and this cost varies inversely with the amount of unemployed resources in the economy: the greater the quantity of resources unemployed the smaller is the real cost of defense.

The third major section of the chapter begins to build the case against the military establishment: wasteful practices, excessive costs, the misuse of labor, the development of a military-industrial complex, and Pentagon capitalism. The case against the military is continued in the fourth section in which the macroeconomic impact of military expenditures is examined; and here you will find it argued that military expenditures are the causes of economic instability, inflation, and unemployment. The defense of the military is in the fifth section and you will find a five-point rebuttal to the case against the military establishment.

The sixth and final section is a brief one. It presents the two sides of the argument over what portions of the economy's resources should be used for civilian and for military purposes; and contains the plea of Charles L. Schultze for the establishment of a national committee to compare the military and nonmilitary requirements of American society and to establishment national priorities.

■ **CHECKLIST**

The very least you should be able to do when you have finished this chapter is:

□ State the size of the American war industry in both dollar and relative terms.

□ Explain the measurement problems associated with determining the cost of the war industry; and the four implications hidden within the overall dollar cost of the war industry.

□ Explain how to determine the economic cost of the military establishment and why this cost depends on the level of unemployment in the economy.

□ Contrast the military establishment with a private business firm.

□ Explain how the Department of Defense procures war goods; what pentagon capitalism is; and why there tend to be cost overruns when war goods are procured.

□ State the case for a volunteer army; the two objections to the volunteer army; and two additional military manpower problems.

□ Explain how military spending may contribute to economic instability and inflation; and why Seymour Melman argues it is the cause of stagflation.

□ State the monetary and fiscal policies the Federal government might follow to obtain a peace dividend if there should be disarmament.

□ Defend the defense establishment.

□ State the proposal suggested by Charles L. Schultze for determining national priorities.

■ **CHAPTER OUTLINE**

1. American military expenditures in 1976 were about $93 billion and 5½% of the GNP.

a. These figures understate the total cost of defense and past wars in the United States.

b. The expenditures made for military purposes have four additional implications for the economy.

2. The opportunity cost of the defense establishment equals the output of civilian goods and services sacrificed in order to produce military goods and services.

a. This cost is zero if the resources used to produce the military goods would have been unemployed in the absence of military expenditures.

b. But if the use of monetary and fiscal policies can maintain full employment the opportunity cost of the military establishment is greater than zero.

c. In terms of a production possibilities curve, the cost of war goods is zero when the military expenditures move the economy from a point inside to a point on the curve without decreasing civilian goods production; and the cost is greater than zero when the military expenditures by moving the economy along the curve increase the production of military and decrease the production of civilian goods.

3. A military establishment and its expenditures affect the allocation of the economy's resources.

a. Unlike a privately owned business firm, the military establishment does not sell its product in the market and is a nonprofit organization whose existence depends upon the existence of hostile military establishments in other nations.

b. The Department of Defense buys military hardware from private firms; but it has been suggested that because the DOD and these firms have a common interest in expanding the size of the defense budget the suppliers of war goods are in fact a part of the military establishment.

c. It is also contended that the DOD acts like a central-management office and military goods producers like its subsidiaries; and that motivated by the desire to expand, they have made unwise decisions.

d. The actual cost of procuring military goods often grossly exceeds the estimated cost because the DOD seems unable to control costs of suppliers and because the DOD employs what are essentially cost-plus contracts.

e. Using conscription to obtain military manpower conflicts with freedom of occupational choice.

f. A volunteer army, it is argued, is a means of distributing military manpower costs equitably, lessening the real cost of the armed forces, and maintaining individual freedom of choice.

g. Critics of the volunteer army contend that it increases the cost of maintaining an army and will produce a professional military force to threaten democracy and political freedom.

h. Critics contend that the armed forces

make poor use of their manpower and have an excess number of commissioned and noncommissioned officers.

4. A military establishment and its expenditures affect the stability of the economy.
  a. Changes in military spending have contributed to economic instability since World War II; and military expenditures have been closely linked historically with inflation.
  b. Should disarmament occur, the economy would realize a peace dividend if it adopted proper fiscal and monetary policies and planned reconversion efficiently.
  c. Seymour Melman argues that the production of a large volume of military goods has led to the current American stagflation (rising prices, falling employment, and a slower rate of economic growth).

5. In defense of the defense establishment it can be argued that:
  a. in a growing economy it is possible to produce both more civilian and more military goods;
  b. military expenditures have significant spillovers on the civilian economy;
  c. inflation accompanies military spending only when government fails to employ monetary and fiscal policies to control it;
  d. cost overruns are also encountered in the procurement of civilian goods and are inevitable in the purchase of modern military goods;
  e. and the military establishment preserves the peace which is necessary to the growth of the economy in a nuclear age.

6. The extensive size of the military establishment and the uses to which the resources it employs could be put in solving domestic social problems has led to the suggestion that a new method is needed to determine national priorities.

■ **IMPORTANT TERMS**

War industry

Military–industrial complex

Pentagon capitalism

Cost-plus contract

Peace dividend

Cost overrun

Volunteer army

■ **FILL-IN QUESTIONS**

1. In 1976 the military expenditures of the United States were about $_____ billion, about _____ percent of the GNP.

2. The opportunity cost of the American defense posture is the _____ the economy forgoes by using resources for military purposes.

3. The military establishment is unlike a private business firm because it:
  a. obtains its revenue from _____ and not from _____
  b. is a _____ organization rather than a _____ seeking organization
  c. depends for its existence upon the existence of _____

4. The methods employed by the Department of Defense to procure military goods from private business firms have been criticized and it is contended that:
  a. the military and weapons suppliers have a common interest in increasing the _____ _____
  b. the military–industrial complex has become a state-management system in which the Pentagon behaves like a _____ office and military goods producers like its _____; and that the goal of this system is to _____
  c. the military is unable to enforce effective _____ controls upon suppliers, extends interest free credit to suppliers in the form of _____, and allows contractors to _____ inventions financed by public money.

5. Those who believe in the volunteer army contend that it more equitably _____ the cost of military manpower, that the cost of this manpower is _____ than the real cost of a conscript army, and that it results in greater freedom of _____

6. The objections to the volunteer army are that it has increased the _____ of maintaining an army and may produce an army of _____.

7. Defense spending during wartime almost always results in inflation because governments fail to increase _____ by enough to prevent _____ inflation, and finance the war by _____ newly created _____.

8. Changes in the amount of military spending since the end of World War II have contributed to the economic _____ of the American economy.

9. A peace dividend is the additional _____ _____ an economy would be able to produce if it decreased its production of ____ _____.

10. To offset a large reduction in military expenditures requires that government do at least one of the following: _____ net taxes, _____ expenditures for nonmilitary goods, or follow a(n) _____ money policy.

11. In defense of the American military establishment it can be argued that:
a. in a growing economy it is possible to produce both more _____ goods and more _____ goods
b. expenditures for space and defense have resulted in significant _____ benefits for the civilian economy
c. cost overruns are found both in the _____ _____ sector of the economy and in the nonmilitary agencies of the public sector; and are probably the _____ consequence of the kinds of products and transactions involved.
d. military spending is inflationary only when government fails to employ the proper _____ and _____ policies

e. military expenditures prevent a major military _____ and that this is a prerequisite for economic _____

12. Charles Schultze has proposed that a committee be formed to assess our _____ _____ and to evaluate our _____ and _____ needs.

■ **PROBLEMS AND PROJECTS**

1. On the graph below is a production possibilities curve showing the different combinations of military and civilian goods and services an economy is capable of producing.

a. If the economy were at point *A* and moved to point *B*, the production of military goods would have increased by _____; and the cost of this increased production of military goods would have been _____ civilian goods.
b. If the economy were at point *B* and moved to point *C*, the production of military goods would have increased by _____; and the cost of this increased production of military goods would have been _____ civilian goods.
c. If the economy were at point *D* and disarmament occurred so that the economy could move to point *E*, the peace dividend would be _____ civilian goods.
d. If the economy were at point *D* and the

economy moved to point *A* as a result of disarmament, the peace dividend would be only

_____ civilian goods.

■ **SELF-TEST**

Circle the T if the statement is true, the F if it is false.

1. Economists are better able to estimate the benefits than the costs of defense spending.
T F

2. If the economy fully employed its resources in the absence of any military expenditures, the opportunity cost of military preparedness is zero. **T F**

3. To prevent a cutback in defense spending from bringing about a recession it would be appropriate to increase taxes and follow a tight money policy. **T F**

4. Most military hardware is not produced in government operated arsenals but by privately operated business firms. **T F**

5. Galbraith argues that the relationship of the Department of Defense to the giant corporate suppliers of war goods is bilateral monopoly; and that the prices paid are approximately competitive. **T F**

6. A volunteer armed force has shifted a part of the cost of military manpower from draftees and reluctant volunteers to taxpayers. **T F**

7. Since the end of World War II changes in military spending have resulted in economic instability in the American economy. **T F**

8. It is not possible for an economy to produce both more military and more civilian goods. **T F**

9. Defenders of the military argue that without a strong military posture peace is impossible and that without peace economic development and progress are impossible.
T F

10. Now that volunteers have replaced conscripts in the armed forces almost all criticism of the manpower policies of the military establishment has ended. **T F**

Underscore the letter that corresponds to the best answer.

1. About what percent of the GNP and labor force of the American economy are used for military purposes? (*a*) 5.5%; (*b*) 7.5%; (*c*) 10%; (*d*) 12%.

2. Which of the following results in an overestimation of the size of the war industry? (*a*) failure to include the spillover benefits of military expenditures to the civilian economy; (*b*) the use of volunteer labor to staff the armed forces; (*c*) the exclusion of veterans' benefits from the Department of Defense budget; (*d*) the inclusion of expenditures for space and atomic energy in the budgets of the NASA and the AEC.

3. The military establishment is like a private business firm because they both (*a*) have a problem in selling their product; (*b*) are monopolists; (*c*) are monopsonists; (*d*) employ labor represented by large labor unions.

4. The notion that the Department of Defense acts like a central-management office and producers of military goods like its subsidiaries is referred to as (*a*) the war industry; (*b*) the military–industrial complex; (*c*) Pentagon capitalism; (*d*) mutual deterrence.

5. Which of the following is *not* a part of the case for the volunteer army? (*a*) the monetary cost of a volunteer army is less; (*b*) military manpower costs are more equitably distributed; (*c*) a volunteer army is more consistent with freedom of occupational choice; (*d*) young people make more rational decisions in choosing an occupation.

6. War almost always results in inflation because (*a*) the production of civilian goods decreases; (*b*) taxes rise; (*c*) governments fail to increase taxes; (*d*) governments borrow newly created money.

7. To prevent unemployment and recession should disarmament take place requires (*a*) a reduction in net taxes; (*b*) an increase in government nondefense expenditures; (*c*) an easy money policy; (*d*) at least one but not necessarily all of the above.

8. If society wishes to take a peace dividend in the form of more private consumption and investment (*a*) government nondefense expenditures should be increased; (*b*) tax rates should be reduced; (*c*) transfer payments should be reduced; (*d*) a tight money policy should be followed.

9. Those who would rebut criticism of the military put forth all but one of the following arguments. Which one? (a) military expenditures are always inflationary; (b) military expenditures result in significant spillover benefits for the civilian economy; (c) cost overruns are not peculiar to the military establishment; (d) more military goods and services do not require fewer civilian goods and services.

10. The proposal to establish a committee to assess national priorities came from (a) John Kenneth Galbraith; (b) Seymour Melman; (c) Charles L. Schultze; (d) Robert McNamara.

■ DISCUSSION QUESTIONS

1. Explain why military expenditures have risen from less than 1 percent of national output in the period prior to World War II to about 5½ percent today.

2. In what three ways may the dollar-and-cents figures for military expenditures in the United States understate the overall cost of the war industry? What effects have military spending had upon consumption, industrial concentration, geographic concentration, and research and development activities?

3. What is meant by the opportunity cost of national security? When will this cost be zero and when will it be greater than zero? What does foreign experience suggest about the opportunity cost of the military establishment?

4. In what ways is the military establishment unlike a private business firm? Are they alike in any way?

5. Explain how the Department of Defense procures war goods and why this procurement method has been subject to severe criticism.

6. Explain: (a) Pentagon capitalism; (b) change order; (c) "buy in, get well later"; and (d) progress payment.

7. What is the case for the volunteer army? What are the objections to the volunteer army?

8. Explain (a) why conscription results in a large and discriminatory tax on draftees and how a volunteer armed force shifts this tax to society as a whole; and (b) why the real cost of a volunteer army is less than a conscripted army of the same size.

9. What are two criticisms of the manpower policies of the armed forces?

10. Does military spending lead to economic instability? Must it also result in inflation?

11. Explain what is meant by a "peace dividend." What fiscal and monetary policies should be followed if a potential peace dividend is to be realized? How does the mix of fiscal and monetary policies chosen determine the form in which this dividend is taken?

12. What are the structural problems that arise as a consequence of demobilization and disarmament?

13. Why does Seymour Melman attribute "American stagflation of the 1970s to the presence of a large military sector"?

14. What arguments can be put forth to defend the war industry and the military establishment against its critics?

15. What is the proposal advanced by Charles Schultze and why did he make this proposal?

The Radical Critique: The Economics of Dissent

Chapter 40 is the last of the seven chapters concerned with the "Current Economic Problems" of the American economy. Unlike the first six chapters in this part of the text, Chapter 40 does not examine a particular trouble spot (such as monopoly, agriculture, the cities, poverty, etc.). Instead it asks if American capitalism is one big trouble spot or problem.

Those who see American capitalism as a giant sore spot are called radical economists, the New Left, or neo-Marxists. Their viewpoint is labeled the radical critique, radical economics, or the economics of dissent. It is their contention that modern capitalism, based on private property, the corporation, and the profit motive, is such a bad system that it ought to be abolished and replaced with a system of socialism. Their contention is essentially an updated or modern version of Marxian economics. Karl Marx argued that capitalism had brought about the tremendous rise in the standard of living in Western Europe; but that capitalism would eventually destroy itself. Its success, he believed, would lead to economic conditions which in turn would lead to the collapse of capitalism, revolution, and the coming of socialism. Chapter 40 begins, therefore, with a detailed examination of the radical economists' Marxian heritage and with an analysis of the New Left's historical predecessor, the Old Left.

From the Old Left the author turns to an explanation of the two fundamental differences between orthodox economics—the kind of economics accepted by almost all economists, including the author of the text— and radical economics. These two differences are differences in approach or methodology. Orthodox economists, the radical economists argue, don't see what is really going on in the world around them. They either have their eyes closed or are rather simpleminded; and see harmony where there is actually conflict. Moreover, orthodox economists, the New Left contends, have too narrow a viewpoint. They look only at economic matters and disregard the other aspects of modern society; and within economics they devote their efforts to nit-picking while ignoring real and important economic problems.

The most important section of Chapter 40 is a summary of the way in which the radical economists view American capitalism. They see the economy dominated by a relatively few large monopoly corporations in league with the state (that is, the Federal government) and out to exploit workers and consumers. This exploitation leads to inequality in the distribution of income and wealth, alienation (which you should be sure to define), an economy which irrationally and wastefully uses its resources, and imperialism which exploits underdeveloped nations.

The radical economists agree that they don't like what they see in the American economy; and that what is needed is socialism. They don't agree at all on just what socialism is— on what a better economic system would be like.

The chapter concludes with a rebuttal by the orthodox economists. Their critique of radical economics has four parts. The first three parts add up to an attack on the objectivity of the radical economists. They are blinded by their preconceptions and ignore any facts that weaken their case. The fourth part is the most devastating in the view of most of their critics. They don't present any of the details of the better economic system which is to replace the capitalism which they detest. Rejecting both the market system and a bureaucratic government, they don't tell us how they are going to allocate scarce resources to satisfy the unlimited wants of society. The histories of France and Russia suggest that revolution and the elimination of an old system do not always bring about the introduction of a better system. And many, like Hamlet, would

. . . rather bear those ills we have
Than fly to others we know not of . . .

■ CHECKLIST

The very least you should be able to do when you have finished this chapter is:

□ Use the following six categories to explain, from the viewpoint of Marx and the Old Left, the development and eventual collapse of capitalism:
the class struggle
private property and the exploitation of labor
capital accumulation and its consequences
the increasing degradation of the working class
monopoly capitalism and imperialism
revolution and socialism
□ Contrast the positions of the orthodox and the radical economists in the "harmony or conflict" controversy.
□ Explain why the radical economists believe orthodox economics is plagued by "disciplinary narrowness."
□ Outline the eight main features in the radical conception of capitalism.

□ Enumerate the three characteristics found in every socialist (radical) vision of a new society.
□ Present the four arguments offered by orthodox economists to rebut the contentions of the radical economists.

■ CHAPTER OUTLINE

1. Radical economists reject the orthodox explanation of the operation of capitalism and the traditional analysis of the problems of a capitalistic society.

2. The radical explanation of capitalism builds upon the work of Karl Marx who examined the development of capitalism and concluded that capitalism would eventually collapse.

a. Marx argued that as capitalist economies expanded the factory system, improved technology, and increased material well-being, one class of people (capitalists) struggled with another class (workers) to take some of the workers' output from them.

b. The capitalists, fortified by the institution of private property, control the machinery and equipment (the capital) needed to produce goods; and driven by their desire for profits (surplus value), they employ their superior bargaining power to exploit workers and pay them a subsistence wage which is less than the value of their production.

c. Competition forces capitalists to reinvest their profits in more and better capital; and this capital accumulation not only expands the national output but also results in technological unemployment, in a growing Industrial Reserve Army, and in a declining rate of profit.

d. These events operate to provide workers with a mere subsistence wage; to ever-increasing unemployment; and, in trying to prevent the profit rate from falling, to still further exploitation of workers.

e. Competition among capitalists in an atmosphere of falling profits and growing unemployment, Marx contended, would lead to the monopolization of industry by a few capitalists; and eventually, searching for cheap foreign labor and foreign markets for their products, to imperialism.

f. The ultimate result of the workings of capitalism is revolution by the workers, the overthrow of capitalism, and the establishment of a socialist state without classes.

3. There are, in the opinion of radical economists, two fundamental shortcomings in orthodox economics.

a. Orthodox economists see a harmony and the reconciliation of opposing interests in capitalism; but radical economists see an irreconcilable conflict between capitalists (and the government which they dominate) and the rest of society.

b. Orthodox economists, according to the radical economists, focus their attention only on the economic aspects of society, ignore the noneconomic aspects of modern capitalism, and fail to understand the real problems of society.

4. The radical economists have a modern version of Marx and see American capitalism in this light.

a. A small group of huge, multiproduct, multinational, monopolistic corporations dominate the American economy.

b. These corporate giants also dominate government and prevent the control of monopoly by government, obtain subsidies from tax revenues, and have government create markets for them.

c. The expansion of capitalism and of the corporate giants requires the expansion of markets and output; and creates new problems while it fails to solve old problems.

d. The first of these problems is the exploitation of laborers and consumers.

e. The second problem is the unequal distribution of income and of wealth.

f. Alienation, or the absence of decision-making power and the inability of individuals to control their lives, is a third problem.

g. A fourth problem is the irrational and wasteful use of resources to produce goods which do not fulfill consumer needs.

h. The last problem is the exploitation of the less developed nations of the world and is the result of imperialism.

i. Radical economists, while agreeing that the socialism which should replace capitalism ought not to be based on private profits and ought to be decent, human, and democratic, cannot agree on the exact nature of the new society.

5. In reply to the radical economists, orthodox economists contend:

a. that this radical conception of capitalism is not consistent with reality;

b. that radical economics is nonobjective because it ignores facts and interprets all events in terms of its conception of capitalism;

c. that the problems of American capitalism cannot all be the result of ideology because other economies with different ideological bases have the same problems;

d. and that the radical economists have not explained the kind of system with which they would replace modern capitalism.

■ **IMPORTANT TERMS**

Radical economics	Monopoly capitalism
Marxian economics	Imperialism
Old Left	Dictatorship of the proletariate
Class struggle	New Left
Bourgeois	
Proletariate	Exploitation
Surplus value	Dual labor market
Law of capitalist accumulation	Alienation
	Participatory socialism
Industrial Reserve Army	

■ **FILL-IN QUESTIONS**

1. Man, according to Marx, is engaged in a perpetual struggle with _____ to obtain material wealth.

a. Simultaneously, some people attempt to improve their own material well-being by wresting output from _____

b. And under the capitalistic system this latter struggle is the struggle of _____ (or the _____) against _____ (or the _____)

2. Because of the institution of _____ _____, capitalists control the _____ and _____ necessary to produce goods and services; workers are dependent upon the capitalists for _____; and the capitalists are driven by their desire for _____ (or _____) to _____ workers by paying them a ____ which is less than the value of their output.

3. The accumulation of capital means that capitalists are forced by _____ to invest their _____ in additional and technologically superior _____ and _____ ; and capital accumulation results in an expansion of the _____, the substitution of _____ for _____, and a decline in the rate of _____

4. In an effort to offset a decline in the profit rate capitalists will increase their _____ _____ of the working class.

5. As capitalism continues to develop:
a. Marx reasoned that unemployment and falling profits would lead to the _____ of industry;
b. Lenin reasoned that the final stage of this development would be _____

6. Exploitation and unemployment would, Marx predicted, eventually result in a _____ by the working class, the establishment of a dictatorship of the _____, the socialization of _____, the abolition of the _____ class, and finally in the formation of a _____ society.

7. The radical economists find two major methodological deficiencies in the orthodox approach to economics and believe:
a. the orthodox economists have an incorrect perception of reality and see _____ where there is actually _____ ;
b. orthodox economics as a discipline is too _____, is too remote from the real _____ of society, and fails to recognize the importance of _____ in capitalistic societies.

8. In the radical conception of capitalism:
a. the economy is dominated by _____

corporations which also dominate the _____ _____, depend upon finding new _____ for their ever-increasing production, and exploit both _____ and _____ ;
b. capitalism brings about income _____ _____, the _____ of individuals, the _____ use of society's resources, and _____ beyond the economy's national boundaries;
c. these evils can be eliminated only by replacing capitalism with _____

9. What are the three ways in which government is alleged by the radical economists to cater to the large corporations?
a. _____
b. _____
c. _____

10. Orthodox economists argue that the wage rate of workers will equal their _____ _____ ; and that all resources will receive a reward (or income) in proportion to their contribution to the production of the _____.
But the radical economists challenge this theory by arguing:
a. that these conclusions are true only when markets in the economy are _____ ;
b. capital goods were created by past _____ ;
c. and while capital goods are productive, the capitalist is not productive and his income from the ownership of capital is _____

11. Radical economists contend that the causes of inequality in the distribution of income and wealth in the United States are:
a. the capitalistic _____ ; and these include private _____, economic _____, and political _____
b. the existence of _____ labor markets and the payment of high wages in the

_____ labor market and the payment
of low wages in the _____
labor market.

12. Alienation:
  a. means that individuals have little control

over their _____ and are remote

from the _____-_____ process;
  b. is primarily the result, in the view of radical economists, of the dominance and size of

_____

13. It is the view of radical economists that capitalism uses its resources irrationally and engages in wasteful production.
  a. The primary cause of this is the capital-

ist's pursuit of _____
  b. And some of the results are the deteriora-

tion of the _____, the creation of

_____, unnecessary _____

spending, and _____ activities throughout the world.

14. The radical economists advocate the replacement of capitalism with some variety of

_____; and agree that the new

society should be _____, _____,

and _____, and that there should be no

private _____

15. The orthodox economists rebut the radical critique of capitalism by arguing that radical economics has an invalid perception

of _____ and is

non _____,
that not all the problems of the American

economy are the result of capitalism's _____

_____, and that the radical economists

offer no viable or attainable _____
for the present economic system.

■ PROBLEMS AND PROJECTS

1. Suppose the subsistence wage for a worker is 4 units of output per day; and that the total daily output that can be produced by from 0 to 7 workers is as shown in the table below.

Number of workers	Output	Marginal product
0	0	—
1	8	___
2	15	___
3	21	___
4	26	___
5	30	___
6	33	___
7	35	___

  a. Compute the daily marginal product of each worker and enter them in the table.
  b. If a capitalist can employ as many workers as he wishes at the subsistence wage, to

maximize his profits he will employ___ workers per day.
  c. The total wages paid to workers each day

will be ___

  d. The daily output of the capitalist is ___

and his daily surplus value is ___
  e. Were the capitalist to employ this number of workers, in order to obtain no surplus value he would have to pay each worker a

daily wage of ___
  f. The daily exploitation of each worker is,

therefore, ___

2. In the table below is a Marxian picture of what happens in a capitalistic economy as it develops.
  a. In addition to the economy's gross national product the table also shows its capital

Year	GNP	CCA	NNP	Wages	Employment	Surplus value	CCA plus wages	Rate of profit
1	500	100	___	280	___	___	___	___
2	504	110	___	276	___	___	___	___
3	509	120.4	___	272	___	___	___	___

consumption allowances (CCA) in each of the three years. Compute and enter into the table the economy's net national product for each year.

b. Workers in this economy always receive a subsistence wage of 4 in each year. Find total employment in each year by dividing the wages paid in that year by the subsistence wage; and enter these employment figures into the table.

c. Marx defined surplus value as all of the NNP not paid to workers as wages. Compute the surplus value in the economy in each year; and enter these surplus values in the table.

d. Marx defined the rate of profit to be equal to surplus value divided by the sum of capital consumption allowances and wages.

(1) Compute capital consumption allowances plus wages in each year. Enter these into the table.

(2) Now compute the rate of profit in each year.

e. As the economy develops:

(1) Employment (increases, decreases, remains constant) _____ ; and,

therefore, unemployment _____

(2) The rate of profit _____

■ **SELF-TEST**

Circle the T if the statement is true, the F if it is false.

1. Among radical economists there is very little difference in their viewpoints.　**T　F**

2. Surplus value equals the value of the daily output of workers less their daily wage.

T　F

3. Capitalists, according to Marx, are able to exploit workers because the capitalists have monopoly control of the machinery and equipment needed to produce goods in an industrial society.　**T　F**

4. In Marx's view the increasing degradation of the working class was the direct result of their tendency to have too many children.

T　F

5. Marx argued that in a capitalistic society the demand for consumer goods would increase more rapidly than the economy's

capacity to produce them and that unemployment would result.　**T　F**

6. Marx's *Capital* contained a clear and detailed picture of the society that would emerge after the overthrow of capitalism by a revolution of the working class.　**T　F**

7. Radical economists contend that the solution to the problems of capitalistic societies require an end to the private ownership of capital goods and the abolition of the market system as the decision-making device for society.　**T　F**

8. The modern and radical conception of capitalism is an extended and updated version of Marx's ideas.　**T　F**

9. Capitalism has reached a stage in the United States in which, according to radical economists, monopoly corporations dominate the economy.　**T　F**

10. Radical economists argue that because labor markets are not competitive workers receive a wage which is greater than their marginal revenue product.　**T　F**

11. Capitalistic institutions, in the opinion of radical economists, create and maintain most of the income inequality found in the United States.　**T　F**

12. Alienation refers to the increase in the proportion of the working class that is either foreign born or from a minority group.

T　F

13. The radical economists argue that capitalism uses its resources to produce little needed goods and services and fails to produce goods and services which are most needed.　**T　F**

14. From the radical viewpoint, two basic causes of the irrational use of resources in capitalistic societies are the pursuit of profits and pollution.　**T　F**

15. The radical economists agree on almost all the particulars of the socialism with which they would replace capitalism.　**T　F**

16. Most radical economists reject both the price-market system and government bureaucracy as a means of allocating scarce resources.　**T　F**

17. The orthodox economists concede that only capitalistic societies are monopolistic, militaristic, and imperialistic; but argue that the abolition of private property and the profit motive will not solve these problems.   **T   F**

18. In their rebuttal of the radical economists' critique of capitalism, orthodox economists argue that radical economists ignore any facts that do not support their conclusions.   **T   F**

Underscore the letter that corresponds to the best answer.

1. In the man-against-man struggle found in capitalistic societies, Marx envisioned the exploitation (*a*) of the bourgeois by capitalists; (*b*) of the proletariate by the bourgeois; (*c*) of workers by the proletariate; (*d*) of the bourgeois by the proletariate.

2. The institution which Marx believed made it possible for one class to exploit another in a capitalistic economy was (*a*) the use of money; (*b*) the use of capital goods; (*c*) the corporation; (*d*) private property.

3. Which of the following was *not* a consequence of capital accumulation in Marx's analysis of capitalism? (*a*) an increase in the profit rate; (*b*) an increase in unemployment; (*c*) an increase in national output; (*d*) an increase in the misery of the working class.

4. Marx argued that the development of capitalism would eventually result in (*a*) imperialism; (*b*) prolonged inflation; (*c*) a decline in the number of capitalists; (*d*) a rise in the real wages of workers.

5. Imperialism, according to Lenin, results from (*a*) the search of capitalists for cheap foreign labor; (*b*) the inability of capitalists to sell all of their output at home; (*c*) higher profit rates in less developed nations; (*d*) all of the above.

6. Which of the following is the process through which Marx predicted capitalism would be replaced by socialism? (*a*) revolution; (*b*) evolution; (*c*) unionization; (*d*) liberalization.

7. The socialism which would replace capitalism would have all but one of the following characteristics. Which one? (*a*) the dictatorship of the proletariate; (*b*) the abolition of the capitalist class; (*c*) the sale of the capitalists' machinery and equipment to the prole-

tariate; (*d*) the establishment of a classless society.

8. The radical economists contend that orthodox economics (*a*) is too broad a discipline to come to grips with real-world problems; (*b*) is overly concerned with the power of large corporations; (*c*) devotes too much of its attention to the study of conflict; (*d*) fails to recognize the political character of the modern corporation.

9. In the radical conception of American capitalism (*a*) the state dominates and controls the large corporations; (*b*) the presence in the economy of a large number of small businesses results in wasteful competition; (*c*) government employs progressive personal and corporate income taxes to subsidize greedy workers; (*d*) military spending by government provides markets for large corporations.

10. Which of the following, in the view of the radical economists, is *not* a consequence of capitalism in the United States? (*a*) alienation; (*b*) anarchism; (*c*) inequality; (*d*) imperialism.

11. Capitalists, the radical economists contend, are able to exploit the working class because of (*a*) their monopsony position in labor markets; (*b*) their monopoly position in product markets; (*c*) the institution of private property; (*d*) all of the above.

12. Which of the following, in the view of radical economists, is *not* a major factor in producing inequality in the distribution of income and in the ownership of wealth in the United States? (*a*) weak inheritance taxes; (*b*) tax loopholes; (*c*) foreign competition; (*d*) the system of higher education.

13. Of the following, which is neither a cause nor a result of alienation? (*a*) the large size of corporate employers; (*b*) the unionization of workers; (*c*) the inability of individuals to influence business decisions; (*d*) assembly-line production.

14. The new society advocated by all radical economists is (*a*) socialism; (*b*) anarchy; (*c*) communism; (*d*) a reformed price-market system.

15. The radical critique of capitalism is, in the opinion of orthodox economists, (*a*) scientific; (*b*) immoral; (*c*) valid; (*d*) ideological.

■ DISCUSSION QUESTIONS

1. Looking back into history Marx saw men engaged in two kinds of struggle. What were these two struggles?

2. Who, according to Marx, were the protagonists of the man-against-man struggle in a capitalistic society?

3. Why, in Marx's explanation of capitalism, are capitalists able to exploit workers? What does "exploit" mean?

4. What does capital accumulation mean? What forced Marx's capitalist to accumulate and what were the consequences of this accumulation?

5. Why did Marx believe that the working class would become increasingly more miserable?

6. What made Marx conclude that capitalistic development would lead to the monopolization of industry by a relatively few capitalists?

7. What is imperialism? Why did Lenin conclude that the development of capitalism would eventually lead to imperialism?

8. What did Marx envision as the causes and the results of the workers' revolution?

9. Explain the two methodological deficiencies which radical economists find in orthodox economics.

10. What evidence is there to suggest that a few large monopolistic corporations dominate the American economy? In what ways does the state allegedly cater to these corporations?

11. What, according to the radical economists, are the major problems that result from corporate capitalism?

12. Explain (a) the orthodox economists' theory of income distribution; and (b) the faults which the radical economists see in this theory.

13. In the view of the radical economists, how does the capitalistic system lead to inequality in the distribution of income and in the ownership of wealth? Why, in their view, are these causes "cumulative and self-reinforcing"?

14. Compare the economic conditions found in the primary labor market with those found in the secondary labor market. What historical reasons can be presented to explain the evolution of these dual labor markets?

15. What is alienation and what do the radical economists see as the causes of alienation in the United States?

16. Why do the radical economists argue that capitalistic production is irrational and its use of resources wasteful?

17. What are the three ways in which imperialism, if one accepts the views of radical economists, serves as an obstacle to the economic development of the poor nations of the world. According to John G. Gurley (quoted in the text), what forms has American imperialism taken in the last thirty years and what has been the aim of these imperialistic activities?

18. "What kind of new society do the radicals envision or advocate?" What are the different economic systems they recommend as replacements for capitalism?

19. How do the orthodox economists rebut the radical economists' critique of American capitalism?

20. What evidence is there to suggest that radical economists (a) have invalid perceptions of reality; (b) are not objective; and (c) overemphasize the significance of ideology?

International Trade and Comparative Advantage

This is the first of four chapters dealing with international trade and finance. International trade is a subject with which most people have little firsthand experience. For this reason many of the terms, concepts, and ideas encountered in these chapters will be unfamiliar and may not be readily grasped. However, most of this material is fairly simple if you will take some pains to examine it. The ideas and concepts employed are new, but they are not especially complex or difficult.

At the beginning it is essential to recognize that international trade is important to the United States. Exports from and imports into the American economy are both close to $120 billion a year. The United States *absolutely* is the greatest exporting and importing nation in the world. In *relative* terms, other nations have exports and imports which are larger percentages of their GNPs. They may export and import more than 40% of GNP, while the United States exports and imports only about 7% of GNP. It is equally important for you to understand from the beginning that international trade differs from the trade that goes on within nations. Different nations use different monies, not just one money; resources are less mobile internationally than they are *intra*nationally; and governments interfere more with foreign than they do with domestic trade.

But while foreign trade differs from domestic trade in these three ways, nations trade for the same basic reason that people within a nation trade: to take advantage of the benefits of specialization. You have already examined the gains that result when there is specialization based on comparative advantage; you are urged to review pages 49 through 52 in Chapter 3. To supplement this review, the author of the text reexamines specialization and trade between two nations.

The international specialization and trade in which the world engages have both microeconomic and macroeconomic effects. The microeconomic effect is a better allocation of the world's resources—a higher standard of living in all nations. And when there are no barriers to international trade there is also a tendency for the prices of products and of resources to be the same in every country.

But the total amount a nation exports and the total amount it imports also have important macroeconomic effects upon that nation's output and income and upon its level of employment. To understand these effects you may have to return to Chapter 13 and review the explanation of what determines the equilibrium levels of income, output, and employment in a closed economy. Once this theory has been reviewed it is not really very difficult to add a new and fourth component

—*net* exports—to aggregate demand and to find the equilibrium in an open economy. Then you should be able to see that the more a nation exports (or the less it imports) the greater will be the levels of income, output, and employment in that nation; and that the less it exports (or the more it imports) the smaller these levels will be. The last things you will learn in this chapter is that a change in net exports—like a change in investment or government expenditures—has a multiplier effect on the equilibrium NNP; and that the value of the multiplier in an open economy depends not only upon the marginal propensity to save but also upon the marginal propensity to import in that economy.

■ CHECKLIST

The very least you should be able to do when you have finished this chapter is:

□ Explain the importance of international trade to the American economy as a whole and to particular industries in the economy; and list the major exports and imports of the United States.

□ Enumerate the three features of international trade which distinguish it from the trade that takes place within a nation.

□ State the two economic circumstances which make it desirable for nations to specialize and trade.

□ Compute, when you are given the necessary figures, the comparative costs of production for two commodities in two countries; determine which nation has the comparative advantage in the production of each commodity; calculate the range in which the terms of trade will be found; and explain the gains to each nation and to the world from specialization and trade.

□ Explain each of the three microeconomic effects of international trade.

□ Identify the major determinant of a nation's exports and the major determinant of its imports; and use the concept of net exports to define aggregate demand in an open economy.

□ Find the equilibrium NNP in an open economy when you are given the appropriate data.

□ Determine the value of the multiplier in an open economy; and explain how a change in

an economy's exports and in its imports would affect the NNP and the level of employment in that nation.

■ CHAPTER OUTLINE

1. Trade between nations is large enough and unique enough to warrant special attention.

a. While the relative importance of international trade to the United States is less than it is to other nations, this country's imports and exports are both about 7% of its GNP and $124 and $120 billion a year, respectively. This trade provides both important raw materials and markets for finished goods; and net exports have a multiplier effect.

b. International trade has three characteristics which distinguish it from domestic trade.

2. Specialization based on comparative advantage and trade between nations is advantageous because the world's resources are not equally distributed and the efficient production of different commodities necessitates different methods and combinations of resources.

3. A simple hypothetical example explains comparative advantage and the gains from trade.

a. Suppose the world is composed of only two nations, each of which is capable of producing two different commodities and in which the production possibilities curves are different straight lines (whose cost ratios are constant but different).

b. With different cost ratios, each nation will have a comparative (cost) advantage in the production of one of the two commodities; and if the world is to use its resources economically each nation must specialize in the commodity in the production of which it has a comparative advantage.

c. Through specialization and trade the world is able to obtain a greater output of both commodities from given quantities of resources than it could produce if nations did not specialize.

d. The ratio at which one product is traded for another—the terms of trade—lies between the cost ratios of the two nations.

e. Each nation gains from this trade because specialization permits a greater total output from the same resources and a better allocation of the world's resources.

f. If costs ratios in the two nations are not constant, specialization may not be complete.

4. The microeconomic effects of international trade and specialization are:

a. A more efficient use of world resources.

b. A tendency toward equal prices for each product throughout the world.

c. A tendency toward equal prices for each resource throughout the world.

d. And a substitution of trade for the international mobility of resources; but only so long as several conditions are realized.

5. International trade and specialization have macroeconomic effects upon aggregate demand and, as a result, upon the total income, output, and employment of a nation.

a. In an open economy aggregate demand is equal to consumption plus net investment plus government spending for goods and services plus net exports. Net exports equal exports minus imports; and a nation's exports depend directly upon the NNPs of foreign nations while its imports depend directly upon its own NNP.

b. The equilibrium NNP in an open economy is the NNP equal to consumption plus net investment plus government spending for goods and services plus net exports; and a change in its net exports has a multiplier effect on a nation's NNP.

c. The value of the multiplier in a open economy is equal to one divided by the sum of the nation's marginal propensity to save and its marginal propensity to import.

■ **IMPORTANT TERMS**

Review

Comparative advantage

Net exports

Specialization

Terms of trade

Production possibilities curve

New

Closed economy

Open economy

Labor-(land-, capital-) intensive commodity

Cost ratio

Trading possibilities line

Open-economy multiplier

Marginal propensity to import

■ **FILL-IN QUESTIONS**

1. Special attention is devoted to international trade because resources are _____ between nations than within a nation, because every nation employs a different _____ _____ and because international trade is subject to more _____ than domestic trade.

2. The imports and exports of the United States amount to about _____% of the economy's GNP or between $_____ and $_____ billion.

3. Ranked in order of their importance the three principal exports of the United States are _____, _____, and _____; the three most important imports are _____ _____, _____, and _____

4. The nations of the world tend to specialize in those goods in the production of which they have a _____, to export these goods, and to import those goods in the production of which they do not have a _____

5. Nations specialize and trade because it is more efficient: it enables each nation to obtain more _____ from the same quantity of _____; and because the distribution of _____ in the world is _____ and the efficient production of different products requires _____

6. If the cost ratio in country X is 4 Panama hats equal 1 pound of bananas, while in country Y, 3 Panama hats equal 1 pound of bananas:

a. Hats are relatively (expensive, inexpensive) _____ in country X and bananas relatively _____

b. Hats are relatively _____ in country Y and bananas relatively _____

c. X has a comparative advantage and should specialize in the production of _____

_____ and Y has a comparative advantage and should specialize in the production of _____

d. When X and Y specialize and trade, the terms of trade will be somewhere between _____ and _____ hats for each pound of bananas; and will depend upon _____

_____

e. When the actual terms of trade turn out to be 3½ hats for 1 pound of bananas, the cost of obtaining:

(1) 1 Panama hat has been decreased from _____ to _____ pounds of bananas in Y

(2) 1 pound of bananas has been decreased from _____ to _____ Panama hats in X

7. International specialization is not complete because the _____ of producing a good _____ as a nation produces more of that good.

8. The microeconomic effects of international trade and specialization are:

a. The more _____ use of the world's resources.

b. A tendency for the _____ of a product to be the same in all nations.

c. A tendency for the price of a _____ to be the same in all nations.

d. The substitution of international trade for the international _____ of resources.

9. When a nation is able to export and import goods and services:

a. Its net exports equal its _____ minus its _____

b. The volume of its total exports depends (directly, indirectly) _____ upon the level of _____ in foreign countries.

c. The volume of its total imports depends (directly, indirectly) _____ upon the level of _____

10. In an open economy:

a. Aggregate demand is equal to consumption plus net investment plus government spending for goods and services plus _____

b. The equilibrium NNP is the NNP which is equal to _____

c. The value of the multiplier is equal to one divided by the sum of the marginal propensities to _____ and to _____

11. An open economy's marginal propensity to import is equal to the fraction (or percentage) of an increase in its _____ which is spent on _____

12. What would be the effect—increase (+) or decrease (−)—of each of the following upon an open economy's equilibrium NNP?

a. An increase in its imports _____

b. An increase in its exports _____

c. A decrease in its imports _____

d. A decrease in its exports _____

■ **PROBLEMS AND PROJECTS**

1. Shown in the next column are the production possibilities curves for two nations: the United States and Chile. Suppose these two nations do not currently engage in international trade or specialization, and suppose that points A and a show the combinations of wheat and copper they now produce and consume.

a. The straightness of the two curves indicates that the cost ratios in the two nations are _____

b. Examination of the two curves reveals that the cost ratio in:

(1) The United States is _____ million

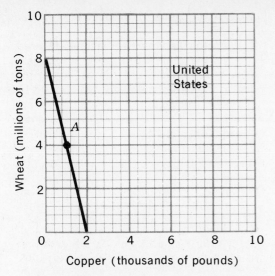

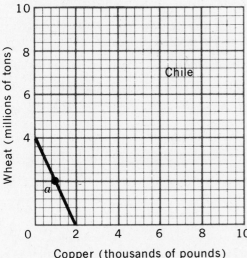

pounds of copper because _____

_____

e. Assume the terms of trade turn out to be 3 million tons of wheat for 1 thousand pounds of copper. Draw in the trading possibilities curve for the United States and Chile.

f. With these trading possibilities curves, suppose the United States decides to consume 5 million tons of wheat and 1 thousand pounds of copper while Chile decides to consume 3 million tons of wheat and 1 thousand pounds of copper. The gains from trade to:

(1) The United States are _____ million

tons of wheat and _____ thousand pounds of copper.

(2) Chile are _____ million tons of wheat

and _____ thousand pounds of copper.

2. Imagine that France and the United States do not specialize or trade. Wine is relatively inexpensive in France and chicken is relatively expensive. In the United States, however, wine is relatively expensive and chicken is relatively inexpensive. This is the result of the relative scarcity and high price of resources used to produce chicken in France and of the relative scarcity and high price of wine-producing resources in the United States.

a. When these two nations begin to specialize and trade, the total demand for:
(1) French-produced wine will (increase, de-

crease) _____ and French-

produced chicken will _____

(2) American-produced wine will _____

and American-produced chicken will _____
b. As a result of these changes in demand,
(1) The price of wine in France will (rise,

fall) _____ and the price of wine

in the United States will _____

until these two prices are _____

(2) The price of chicken in France will ____

_____ and the price of chicken in

the United States will _____

until these two prices are _____
c. Because the demand for resources is a derived demand,

tons of wheat for _____ thousand pounds of copper.

(2) Chile is _____ million tons of wheat

for _____ thousand pounds of copper.
c. If these two nations were to specialize and trade wheat for copper,
(1) The United States would specialize in

the production of wheat because _____

_____

(2) Chile would specialize in the production

of copper because _____

d. The terms of trade, if specialization and trade occur, will be greater than 2 and less than 4 million tons of wheat for 1 thousand

(1) The demand for resources used in France to produce the wine will_____ and the demand for resources used to produce chicken in France will _____

(2) The demand for resources used in the United States to produce wine will _____ and the demand for resources used to produce chicken in the United States will _____

_____

d. These changes in the demands for resources cause the prices paid:

(1) In France for wine-producing resources to _____ and for chicken-producing resources to _____ until they are

_____

(2) In the United States for wine-producing resources to _____ and for chicken-producing resources to _____ until they

are _____

e. The result is that:

(1) France will shift resources from the production of _____ to the production of _____

(2) The United States will shift resources from the production of _____ to the production of _____

3. Below is a schedule showing what aggregate demand (consumption plus net investment plus government spending for goods and services) would be at various levels of net national product in a closed economy.

a. Were this economy to become an open economy the volume of exports would be a constant $90 billion; and the volume of imports at the various levels of NNP would be the amount shown in the table. Compute net exports at each of the seven NNPs and enter them in the table.

b. Compute aggregate demand in this open economy at the seven NNP levels and enter them in the table.

c. The equilibrium NNP in this open economy would be $_____ billion.

d. In this open economy the marginal propensity to save is 0.20 and the marginal propensity to import is _____

e. The value of the multiplier in this open economy is equal to approximately _____

f. A $10 billion increase in:

(1) exports would (increase, decrease) ____ _____ the equilibrium NNP by about $_____ billion.

(2) Imports would (increase, decrease) ____ _____ the equilibrium NNP by about $_____ billion.

■ SELF-TEST

Circle the T if the statement is true, the F if it is false.

1. Nations tend to produce and export those

Aggregate supply or NNP (billions)	Aggregate demand, closed economy (billions)	Exports (billions)	Imports (billions)	Net exports (billions)	Aggregate demand, open economy (billions)
$ 750	$ 776	$90	$74	$_____	$_____
800	816	90	78	_____	_____
850	856	90	82	_____	_____
900	896	90	86	_____	_____
950	936	90	90	_____	_____
1,000	976	90	94	_____	_____
1,050	1,016	90	98	_____	_____

goods in the production of which they have a comparative advantage.　　　　**T　F**

2. The principal import of the United States is nonferrous metals.　　　　**T　F**

3. The principal export of the United States is machinery.　　　　**T　F**

Use the following production possibilities to answer questions 4, 5, and 6 below and to answer multiple-choice questions 4 and 5.

NEPAL PRODUCTION POSSIBILITIES TABLE

| Product | Production alternatives | | | | | |
	A	B	C	D	E	F
Yak fat	0	4	8	12	16	20
Camel hides	40	32	24	16	8	0

KASHMIR PRODUCTION POSSIBILITIES TABLE

| Product | Production alternatives | | | | | |
	A	B	C	D	E	F
Yak fat	0	3	6	9	12	15
Camel hides	60	48	36	24	12	0

4. In Kashmir the cost of 1 camel hide is 3 units of yak fat.　　　　**T　F**

5. Nepal has a comparative advantage in producing camel hides.　　　　**T　F**

6. With specialization and trade, the trading possibilities curves of both nations would move to the right of their production possibilities curves.　　　　**T　F**

7. Increasing production costs tend to prevent specialization among trading nations from being complete.　　　　**T　F**

8. Trade among nations tends to bring about a more efficient use of the world's resources and a greater world output of goods and services.　　　　**T　F**

9. An increase in the volume of a nation's exports, other things being equal, will expand the nation's NNP.　　　　**T　F**

10. The value of the multiplier in an open economy is equal to the reciprocal of the economy's marginal propensity to import.　　　　**T　F**

Underscore the letter that corresponds to the best answer.

1. International trade is a special and separate area of economic study for several reasons. Which one of the following is *not* one of these reasons: (*a*) international trade is based on the principle of comparative advantage; (*b*) resources are less mobile internationally than domestically; (*c*) countries engaged in international trade use different monies; (*d*) international trade is subject to a greater number of political restrictions than domestic trade.

2. In 1976 the imports of the United States amounted to approximately what percentage of the United States's GNP? (*a*) 4%; (*b*) 7%; (*c*) 10%; (*d*) 13%.

3. Nations would not need to engage in trade if: (*a*) all products were produced from the same combinations of resources; (*b*) world resources were evenly distributed among nations; (*c*) world resources were perfectly mobile; (*d*) all of the above.

Use the tables preceding true-false question 4 to answer the following two questions.

4. If Nepal and Kashmir engage in trade, the terms of trade will be: (*a*) between 2 and 4 camel hides for 1 unit of yak fat; (*b*) between ⅓ and ½ units of yak fat for 1 camel hide; (*c*) between 3 and 4 units of yak fat for 1 camel hide; (*d*) between 2 and 4 units of yak fat for 1 camel hide.

5. If Nepal and Kashmir, in the absence of trade between them, both produced combination *C*, the gains from trade would be: (*a*) 6 units of yak fat; (*b*) 8 units of yak fat; (*c*) 6 units of yak fat and 8 camel hides; (*d*) 8 units of yak fat and 6 camel hides.

6. Which of the following is *not* one of the effects when nations begin to specialize and trade? (*a*) a shift of resources away from the production of commodities in which nations have comparative advantages; (*b*) a fall in the prices of resources which were relatively expensive; (*c*) a rise in the prices of products which were relatively inexpensive; (*d*) an increased demand for relatively inexpensive products and resources.

Use the data in the table below to answer questions 7 and 8.

NNP	$C + I + G$	Net exports
$ 900	$ 913	$7
920	929	6
940	945	5
960	961	4
980	977	3
1,000	993	2
1,020	1,009	1

7. If exports in this economy are constant, its marginal propensity to import must be (a) .04; (b) .05; (c) .06; (d) .07.

8. The equilibrium NNP is (a) $960; (b) $980; (c) $1,000; (d) $1,020.

■ **DISCUSSION QUESTIONS**

1. In relative and absolute terms, how important is international trade to the United States? What are the principal exports and imports of the American economy? What commodities used in the economy come almost entirely from abroad, and what American industries sell large percentages of their output abroad?

2. In what ways is international trade different from the trade which takes place within a nation?

3. Why do nations specialize in certain products and export their surplus production of these goods at the same time that they are importing other goods? Why do they not use the resources employed to produce the surpluses which they export to produce the goods which they import?

4. What two facts—one dealing with the distribution of the world's resources and the other related to the technology of producing different products—are the basis for trade among nations?

5. Explain (a) the theory or principle of comparative advantage; (b) what is meant by and what determines the terms of trade; and (c) the gains from trade.

6. What microeconomic effects does the commencement of specialization and trade among nations have upon (a) the allocation of the trading nations' resources, (b) resource prices in the trading nations, and (c) the prices of products in the nations that trade?

7. Explain how exports and how imports affect aggregate demand within a nation. What are the primary determinants of the volume of a nation's exports and imports? How does a change in the volume of exports and in the volume of imports affect income, output, and employment in a nation?

8. What determines the size or value of the multiplier in an open economy? Why is the multiplier larger in a closed then in an open economy?

The Economics
of Free
Trade and
Protection

For well over two hundred years people in America and throughout the world have debated whether free trade or protection was the better policy. Economists took part in this debate and, with few exceptions, argued for free trade and against protection. Those who favor free trade contend that free trade benefits both the nation and the world as a whole. Free trade allows nations to specialize in the production of those goods and services in which they have a comparative advantage; and it increases total production and the standard of living in all countries. "Free traders" argue that tariffs, import quotas, and other barriers to international trade prevent or reduce specialization and decrease both a nation's and the world's production and standard of living.

But nations have and continue to erect barriers to trade with other nations. The questions upon which this chapter focuses attention are (1) what motivates nations to impose tariffs and to limit by quotas the quantities of goods imported from abroad; (2) what effects do such tariffs and quotas have upon a nation's own prosperity and upon the prosperity of the world; and (3) what kinds of arguments do those who favor tariffs and quotas employ to support their position—on what grounds do they base their contention that their nation will benefit from the erection of

barriers which reduce imports from foreign nations.

The chapter's final major section is a brief review of American policy toward trade barriers since 1934. That year began a series of gradual but substantial tariff-rate reductions which have continued almost up to the present year. Despite this progress in decreasing the barriers to trade with other nations, protectionism is not dead. Advocates of tariffs and quotas are alive—though not quite well—and living in the United States.

Whether free trade or protection will be the policy of the United States in the years to come may well depend upon whether you understand that free trade helps everyone and that protection helps no one but the selfish. It is for this reason that Chapter 42 is important.

■ **CHECKLIST**

The very least you should be able to do when you have finished this chapter is:
□ Restate the case for free trade.
□ Identify the two principal types of artificial barriers to international trade and the four motives for erecting these barriers.
□ Explain the economic effects of a protective tariff on resource allocation, the price of

the commodity, the total production of the commodity, and the outputs of foreign and domestic producers of the commodity.

□ Enumerate the six arguments used to support the case for protection and find the weakness in each of these arguments.

□ List the major provisions of the Reciprocal Trade Agreement Act of 1934 and of the General Agreement on Tariffs and Trade of 1947; and explain why the former was a sharp change in the trade policy of the United States.

□ Identify the four major goals of the European Economic Community (the Common Market); present some evidence that shows that the EEC has been successful and explain why it has been successful; and outline the problems this success creates for nonmembers.

□ State the powers which the Trade Expansion Act of 1962 gave to the President and the results of the Kennedy Round of trade negotiations.

□ Explain the timeliness of the Geneva Round of trade negotiations; and state the three problems upon which these negotiations will be centered.

□ List the four reasons why the United States changed its policy toward trade with communist nations; several of the opportunities for trade between the United States and the Soviet Union; and the four problems encountered in East-West trade.

■ **CHAPTER OUTLINE**

1. The argument for free trade is that it leads to a better allocation of resources and a higher standard of living in the world.

2. Nations retard international trade by erecting artificial barriers.

a. Tariffs and import quotas are the principal barriers to trade.

b. Four motives induce nations to erect these barriers.

c. The economic impact of a protective tariff is a misallocation of the world's resources: the price of the good on which the tariff is levied is increased and its total production is reduced; and foreign producers of the good suffer while domestic producers benefit.

3. There are a number of different arguments in the case for protection. Most of these are

fallacious or based on half-truths; but at least two of them warrant the protection of certain industries under certain conditions.

4. Until 1934 the United States steadily increased tariff rates to protect private-interest groups.

a. Since the passage of the Reciprocal Trade Agreements Act, tariff rates have been substantially reduced; many nations, including the United States, have signed the General Agreements on Tariffs and Trade in an attempt to eliminate trade barriers.

b. The European Common Market has sought the economic integration of Western Europe by the abolishment of internal tariffs and quotas, the establishment of common external tariffs, and the eventual free movement of labor and capital within the Common Market area. The Common Market nations have achieved considerable integration, have increased their growth rates, and have expanded trade; but their success has created problems for nonmember nations.

c. The Trade Expansion Act of 1962 permitted closer economic ties between the United States and the Common Market; and the "Kennedy Round" of tariff negotiations, despite some disappointments, did produce substantial tariff-rate reductions.

d. The Trade Reform Act of 1974 made it possible for the United States to enter the new Geneva round of GATT negotiations to reduce the nontariff barriers to trade, to improve the access of nations to raw materials and foodstuffs, and to lower the barriers to American agricultural products in the Common Market.

e. Since 1969 the United States has for several good reasons, reduced the barriers to trade with communist nations. While the potential for increased trade with these nations is considerable, the problems involved in such trade are also considerable; but since 1970 American trade with the U.S.S.R. has grown by almost 1000%.

■ **IMPORTANT TERMS**

Tariff

Revenue tariff

Protective tariff

Import quota

Reciprocal Trade Agreements Act of 1934

Most favored nation clause

General Agreement on Tariffs and Trade

Economic integration

European Common Market (European Economic Community)

Trade Expansion Act of 1962

Kennedy Round

Trade Reform Act of 1974

Geneva Round

Nontariff barriers (NTBs)

■ **FILL-IN QUESTIONS**

1. The basic argument for free trade is that it results in _____ and _____

2. The two most widely employed barriers to international trade are _____ and _____,

which nations establish to _____

_____,

_____,

_____,

and _____

3. When the United States imposes a tariff on a good which is imported from abroad:
a. the price of that good in the United States will (increase, decrease) _____
b. the total purchases of the good in the United States will _____
c. the output of:

(1) American producers of the good will ___

(2) foreign producers of the good will _____
d. the ability of foreigners to buy goods and services in the United States will _____ and, as a result, output and employment in American industries that sell goods and services abroad will _____

4. List the six arguments which protectionists employ to justify trade barriers.

a. _____

b. _____

c. _____

d. _____

e. _____

f. _____

The only two arguments containing any reasonable justification for protection are

the _____

and the _____

arguments.

5. Until 1930 the trend of tariff rates in the United States was _____,

but since the passage of the _____

Act in 1934 the trend has been _____.

This act empowered the President to _____

_____

and incorporated _____ in American trade agreements.

6. The three main principles set down in the General Agreement on Tariff and Trade are:

a. _____

b. _____

c. _____

7. The specific aims of the European Common Market were the abolishment of _____

_____,

the establishment of _____,

the free movement of _____,

and common policies with respect to _____

_____.

Its success, reflected in increased _____

_____

and _____ in the Common Market nations, can be attributed to a better _____

and to the _____ which have resulted from the creation of a mass market.

8. The Trade Expansion Act of 1962 allowed the President to _____

_____

and _____ ;

and resulted in the _____

of trade negotiations which ended in 1967.

9. In 1974 Congress passed the _____

Act; and there followed the _____
Round of trade negotiations which empha-

sized the reduction of the _____
barriers to trade.

10. Until recently the United States restricted

its trade with the _____
nations of the world; but in 1969 its policy
toward these nations began to change for
four reasons:

a. _____

b. _____

c. _____

d. _____

■ **PROBLEMS AND PROJECTS**

1. The table below shows the quantities of
woolen gloves demanded (D) in the United
States at several different prices (P). Also
shown in the table are the quantities of
woolen gloves that would be supplied by
American producers (S_a) and the quantities
that would be supplied by foreign producers
(S_f) at the nine different prices.

P	D	S_a	S_f	S_t	S_f'	S_t'
$2.60	450	275	475	____	____	____
2.40	500	250	450	____	____	____
2.20	550	225	425	____	____	____
2.00	600	200	400	____	____	____
1.80	650	175	375	____	____	____
1.60	700	150	350	____	____	____
1.40	750	125	325	____	____	____
1.20	800	0	300	____	____	____
1.00	850	0	0	____	____	____

a. Compute and enter in the table the total
quantities that would be supplied (S_t) by
American and foreign producers at each of
the prices.

b. If the market for woolen gloves in the
United States is a competitive one the equi-

librium prices for woolen gloves is $_____

and the equilibrium quantity is _____

c. Suppose now that the United States government imposes an 80 cents ($0.80) per
pair of gloves tariff on all gloves imported
into the United States from abroad. Compute
and enter into the table the quantities that
would be supplied (s_f') by foreign producers
at the nine different prices. (*Hint:* If foreign
producers were willing to supply 300 pairs at
a price of $1.20 when there was no tariff
they are now willing to supply 300 pairs at
$2.00, the $0.80 per pair tariff plus the $1.20
they will receive for themselves. The quantities supplied at each of the other prices
may be found in a similar fashion.)

d. Compute and enter into the table the total
quantities that would be supplied (S_t') by
American and foreign producers at each of
the nine prices.

e. As a result of the imposition of the tariff

the equilibrium price has risen to $_____
and the equilibrium quantity has fallen to

_____

f. The number of pairs sold by:
(1) American producers has (increased, de-

creased) _____ by _____
(2) foreign producers has (increased, de-

creased) _____ by _____

g. The total revenues (after the payment of
the tariff) of:
(1) American producers—who do *not* pay

the tariff—have (increased, decreased) _____

by $_____
(2) foreign producers—who *do* pay the tariff

—have (increased, decreased) _____ by

$_____

h. The total amount spent by American buy-

ers of woolen gloves has _____ by

$_____

i. The tariff revenue of the United States

government has _____ by $_____

j. The total number of dollars earned by

foreigners has _____ by $_____ ;
and, as a result, the total foreign demand for

goods and services produced in the United States will _____ by $_____

■ SELF-TEST

Circle the T if the statement is true, the F if it is false.

1. The case for free trade is that it will result in the more efficient use of the world's resources and greater world output.   **T   F**

2. A tariff on coffee in the United States is an example of a protective tariff.   **T   F**

3. The imposition of a tariff on a good imported from abroad will raise the price of the good and lower the quantity of it bought and sold.   **T   F**

4. One crop economies may be able to make themselves more stable and diversified by imposing tariffs on goods imported from abroad; but these tariffs are apt also to lower the standard of living in these economies.   **T   F**

5. Because the General Agreement on Tariffs and Trade committed its signers to eliminate their tariffs on imports, the U.S. Senate refused to ratify the agreement.   **T   F**

6. Since the establishment of the European Common Market its members' share of world trade has increased.   **T   F**

7. Before a firm can enjoy economies of scale it must enjoy a mass market.   **T   F**

8. In order to offset the loss of export markets that will result from the growing strength of the European Common Market, the United States will find it necessary in the future to increase its tariff rates.   **T   F**

9. The Trade Expansion Act of 1962 reversed earlier American economic policy and attempted to expand GNP by restricting imports.   **T   F**

10. The Kennedy Round resulted in fairly substantial reciprocal tariff rate reductions.   **T   F**

Underscore the letter that corresponds to the best answer.

1. Which one of the following is characteristic of tariffs? (a) they prevent the importation of goods from abroad; (b) they specify the maximum amounts of specific commodities which may be imported during a given period of time; (c) they often protect domestic producers from foreign competition; (d) they enable nations to reduce their exports and increase their imports during periods of depression.

2. Which one of the following arguments for protection is the least fallacious and most pertinent in the United States today? (a) the military self-sufficiency argument; (b) the increase-domestic-employment argument; (c) the protect-high-wages argument; (d) the infant-industry argument.

3. When a tariff is imposed on a good imported from abroad (a) the demand for the good increases; (b) the demand for the good decreases; (c) the supply of the good increases; (d) the supply of the good decreases.

4. Tariffs lead to (a) the contraction of relatively efficient industries; (b) an overallocation of resources to relatively efficient industries; (c) an increase in the foreign demand for domestically produced goods; (d) an underallocation of resources to relatively inefficient industries.

5. Which of the following is a likely result of imposing tariffs to increase domestic employment? (a) a short-run increase in domestic employment; (b) retaliatory increases in the tariff rates of foreign nations; (c) a long-run decline in exports; (d) all of the above.

6. Which of the following is the likely result of the United States employing tariffs to protect its high wages and standard of living? (a) an increase in U.S. exports; (b) a rise in the American real NNP; (c) a decrease in the average productivity of American workers; (d) a decrease in the quantities of resources employed by industries producing the goods on which tariffs have been levied.

7. The infant-industry argument for tariffs (a) is especially pertinent to the advanced industrial nations; (b) generally results in tariffs that are removed after the infant industry has matured; (c) makes it rather easy to determine which infant industries will become mature industries with comparative advantages in producing their goods; (d) might better be replaced by an argument for outright subsidies for infant industries.

8. Which one of the following specifically empowered the President of the United States to reduce its tariff rates up to 50% if other nations would reduce their tariffs on American goods? (a) the Underwood Act of 1913; (b) the Hawley-Smoot Act of 1930; (c) the Trade Agreements Act of 1934; (d) the General Agreement on Tariffs and Trade of 1947.

9. Which of the following is *not* characteristic of the General Agreement on Tariffs and Trade? Nations signing the agreement were committed to: (a) the elimination of import quotas; (b) the reciprocal reduction of tariffs by negotiation; (c) the nondiscriminatory treatment of all trading nations; (d) the establishment of a world customs union.

10. The European Common Market: (a) is designed to eliminate import quotas among its members; (b) includes Great Britain, Denmark, France, and Spain among others; (c) aims to abolish tariffs imposed on all goods which member nations import; (d) includes both East and West Germany.

■ **DISCUSSION QUESTIONS**

1. What is the "case for free trade"?

2. How are tariffs and import quotas used to restrict international trade? Why do nations wish to restrict trade?

3. Suppose the United States were to increase the tariff on automobiles imported from West Germany (and other foreign countries). What would be the effect of this tariff-rate increase on (a) the price of automobiles in the United States; (b) the total number of cars sold in the United States during a year; (c) the number of cars produced by and employment in the West German automobile industry; (d) production by and employment in the American automobile industry; (e) West German income obtained by selling cars in the United States; (f) the West German demand for goods produced in the U.S.; (g) the

production of and employment in those American industries which now export goods to West Germany; (h) the standards of living in the U.S. and in West Germany; (i) the allocation of resources in the American economy; and (j) the allocation of the world's resources?

4. What is the "case for protection"? How valid and pertinent to the United States is each of the six basic arguments for protection?

5. What was the tariff policy of the United States: (a) between 1790 and 1930; (b) since 1934? Explain the basic provisions of the Reciprocal Trade Agreements Act. How has the United States cooperated with other nations since 1945 to reduce trade barriers?

6. What is meant by economic integration? What are the four main features of the European Common Market? How successful has it been in achieving its immediate goals and in increasing the economic well-being of its members? Why has it been successful?

7. What problems does the success of the Common Market create for the United States? How might the United States solve these problems?

8. What were the major provisions of the Trade Expansion Act of 1962? What were the accomplishments of the Kennedy Round?

9. Why was the new effort to reduce trade barriers begun in 1973 particularly timely? On what three particular problems has the Geneva Round of negotiations focused its attention? Why will these negotiations be difficult?

10. Why has the American attitude toward trading with the communist nations changed in recent years? Explain why the potential for trade with these nations is apt to be large. What are the problems that will be encountered in trading with the "communist bloc"? By how much have East-West and U.S.S.R.-U.S. trade increased since 1970?

The Balance of Payments and Exchange Rates

In the last two chapters you learned *why* nations engage in international trade and *why* they may erect barriers to trade with other nations. In Chapter 43 you will learn *how* nations using different monies are able to trade among themselves. The means they employ to overcome the difficulties that result from the use of different monies is fairly simple. When a nation wishes to buy a good or service, make a loan, or present a gift in another nation, it *buys* some of the money used in the foreign nation. It pays for the foreign money with some of its own money. In other words, the nation exchanges its own money for foreign money. And when a nation sells a good or service abroad or receives a loan or a gift from abroad and obtains foreign money, it *sells* this foreign money—often called foreign exchange—in return for some of its own money. That is, it exchanges foreign money for its own money. The price a country pays for or is paid for foreign exchange is the foreign exchange rate. And like most prices, the foreign exchange rate is determined by the demand for and the supply of foreign money.

As you know from Chapter 42, nations buy and sell large quantities of goods and services across national boundaries. But nations also make and receive gifts and loans abroad, and own foreign bank accounts and foreign currency. At the end of a year, nations summarize their foreign sales and purchases of goods and services, their gifts and loans, and the changes in the amount of foreign money they own. This summary is a nation's international balance of payments: a record of how it obtained foreign exchange during the year and what it did with that money. Of course, all foreign money obtained was used for some purpose—it did not evaporate—and consequently the balance of payments *always* balances. The international balance of payments is an extremely important and useful device for understanding the amounts and kinds of international transactions in which a nation engages. But it also enables us to understand such things as international equilibrium and disequilibrium, balance of payments surpluses and deficits, and the causes of these problems and how to deal with them.

Probably the most difficult sections of the chapter are concerned with what economists call international disequilibrium and the means by which international disequilibrium can be eliminated. You should pay particular attention to exactly what is meant by international equilibrium and disequilibrium; the three methods which may be employed to correct disequilibrium; and the advantages and disadvantages of each of these three methods.

One last word for you. This chapter is filled with new terms. Some of these are just special words used in international economics to mean things with which you are already familiar. Be very sure you learn what all of the new terms mean. It will simplify your comprehension of this chapter and enable you to understand more readily the international economic and financial problems and policies examined in the next chapter.

■ **CHECKLIST**

The very least you should be able to do when you have finished this chapter is:

□ Explain how American exports create a demand for dollars and a supply of foreign exchange; and how American imports create a demand for foreign exchange and a supply of dollars.

□ Put unarranged data into an organized international balance of payments statement for a nation; and find the amount due to (or from) that nation as a result of its exports and imports of goods and services and its balance of payments surplus (or deficit).

□ Explain how a nation finances a payments deficit and what it does with a payments surplus.

□ Show how a nation can export more goods and services than it imports and still have a balance of payments deficit.

□ Distinguish between and identify autonomous and accommodating transactions; and between international equilibrium and disequilibrium.

□ Identify the three methods that may be employed to restore international equilibrium.

□ Provide an explanation of how freely floating exchange rates function to eliminate international disequilibrium; and enumerate the disadvantages of this method of restoring international equilibrium.

□ Explain how changing price (and income) levels would operate to eliminate a payments deficit or surplus; identify the principal advantage of this method of restoring equilibrium; and enumerate its two main disadvantages.

□ List the two conditions which a nation must fulfill if it is to be on the gold standard; explain how gold flows operate to reduce

payments deficits and surpluses; and identify its two advantages and its basic drawback.

□ Distinguish between foreign exchange and trade controls; explain how a nation with a payments deficit would employ foreign exchange controls to eliminate the deficit; and cite three objections to these controls.

□ List the three kinds of trade controls a nation with a payments deficit might utilize; and state the fundamental objection to trade and foreign exchange controls.

■ **CHAPTER OUTLINE**

1. Trade between two nations differs from domestic trade because the monies of both nations are used.

a. American exports create a demand for dollars and a supply of foreign money. They increase the number of dollars owned by Americans (or decrease the amount of foreign money owned by foreigners). American exports earn the monies to pay for American imports.

b. American imports create a supply of dollars and a demand for foreign money. They decrease the number of dollars owned by Americans (or increase the amount of foreign money owned by foreigners). American imports use up the monies obtained by exporting.

2. The international balance of payments for a nation is a record of its transactions with other nations in the world. It contains eight major sections.

a. The first three sections record a nation's exports of goods and services, its imports of these things, and the difference between exports and imports.

b. The next section records the net remittances (private gifts).

c. The fifth section shows the net governmental transactions (loans and gifts).

d. Net capital movements (loans and investments) are found in the sixth section; and the seventh section records the amount due to or from other nations as a result of the transactions in the first six sections.

e. The last section indicates how the amount due to or from other nations was financed: with foreign monies (international monetary reserves) or with a nation's own money.

f. A nation will lose money to other nations even if it has exported more goods and services than it has imported when the amounts it gives and invests abroad exceed the amount by which its exports are greater than its imports.

3. A nation has a disequilibrium in its international balance of payments when the international monetary reserves it owns less the amount of its own money owned by foreigners increase or decrease. An increase is a balance of payments surplus and a decrease is a deficit.

a. Just like an individual family, a nation has a surplus (or deficit) when it spends, gives, and invests less (or more) than its income.

b. The autonomous transactions are recorded in the first six sections of the international balance of payments and the accommodating transactions in the last section. The latter must make (or accommodate) themselves to the former.

4. When a nation has a payments surplus or deficit there is international disequilibrium and one of three kinds of adjustments may take place to bring about equilibrium.

a. If foreign exchange rates are free to rise and fall, a nation's outpayments will tend to increase (decrease) and its inpayments will tend to decrease (increase) if it began with a payments surplus (deficit).

(1) When a nation has a payments surplus (deficit) foreign exchange rates fall (rise). This makes foreign goods and services less (more) expensive to buy, increases (decreases) imports, makes a nation's goods and services more (less) expensive for foreigners to buy, and decreases (increases) exports.

(2) But freely floating exchange rates increase the risks of exporters, importers, and investors (and reduce international trade); change the terms of trade; destabilize economies (by creating unemploynent or inflation); and may not even correct payments imbalances.

b. Price and income levels in a nation with a payments surplus (deficit) tend to rise (fall), increase (decrease) outpayments, and decrease (increase) inpayments to restore equilibrium.

(1) Such adjustments affect price levels, the level and distribution of real income, and em-

ployment in the nations involved; and these effects may be unwanted by the nations.

(2) The international gold standard was one example of a system which worked in this way and kept exchange rates relatively stable.

c. Public controls are often employed by a nation to eliminate its payments deficit.

(1) The nation may require exporters who earn foreign exchange to sell it to the government; the government will then ration the available foreign exchange among importers and force imports to equal exports.

(2) It may also use tariffs, quotas, and subsidies to expand exports (inpayments) and reduce imports (outpayments).

■ **IMPORTANT TERMS**

Rate of exchange (foreign exchange rate)	**Autonomous transactions**
International balance of payments	**Accommodating transactions**
Remittance	**Freely floating exchange rate**
Net capital movement	**Exchange rate depreciation**
Financing transactions	**Exchange rate appreciation**
(Balance of) payments deficit	**International gold standard**
(Balance of) payments surplus	**Gold export point**
International monetary reserves	**Gold import point**
International equilibrium	**Foreign exchange control**
International disequilibrium	**Trade controls**

■ **FILL-IN QUESTIONS**

1. The rate of exchange for the French franc is the number of _____ which an American must pay to obtain _____

_____

2. When the rate of exchange for the German mark is 40 cents, the rate of exchange for the dollar is _____ marks.

3. American _____ or foreign _____ create a demand for foreign money and a supply of dollars; American _____ or foreign _____ create a demand for dollars and a supply of foreign money.

4. American exports and foreign imports (increase, decrease) _____ the amount of foreign money owned by Americans or _____ the number of dollars owned by foreigners, and _____ the money supply in the United States while it _____ the money supply in foreign nations.

5. The eight principal sections in a nation's international balance of payments are:

a. _____

b. _____

c. _____

d. _____

e. _____

f. _____

g. _____

h. _____

6. When a nation exports more goods and services than it imports, its outpayments are (less, greater) _____ than its inpayments; and a balance is due (to, from) _____ the rest of the world.

7. Net capital movements record the _____ _____ and _____ which one nation makes in other nations. The financing transactions record the changes in a nation's holdings of _____ and in the amount of its money owned by foreigners.

8. A nation has a balance of payments surplus (deficit) when its _____ (_____) exceeds its _____ (_____), and when it gains (loses) _____ or the amount of its money owned by foreigners _____ (_____).

9. A nation is in international disequilibrium

when it has either a payments _____ or payments _____ and is in equilibrium when it has neither.

10. A country can export more than it imports *and* have a payments deficit if it _____, _____, and _____ more abroad than the difference.

11. The accommodating transactions are gains and losses of _____ _____ and _____. Other transactions in the international balance of payments are _____ transactions.

12. The three mechanisms for eliminating international disequilibrium are _____, _____, and _____

13. If foreign exchange rates float freely and a nation has a balance of payments surplus, the price of that nation's money in the foreign exchange market will tend to _____ _____ and the price of foreign exchange in that nation will tend to _____ As these changes take place, the nation's inpayments will _____ and its outpayments will _____ to reduce the surplus.

14. There are four problems which arise when foreign exchange rates float freely: The _____ associated with flexible rates tend to _____ _____ trade, a nation's _____ can be worsened, fluctuating exports and imports can affect _____ and _____ in an economy, and the floating exchange rates may fail to _____

15. A nation is on the gold standard when

it _____

and _____

16. If the nations of the world are on the gold standard, rates of exchange will depend

upon _____

and _____ ;
and the rate will only fluctuate between the

_____

and the _____

17. Assuming exchange rates are stable and a nation has a balance of payments deficit:
a. The money supply and price level in that

nation will _____
b. This will make things bought at home

(more, less) _____ expensive and

things bought abroad _____
expensive.

c. As a result this country will _____

the amount it buys and _____
the amount it sells in the rest of the world.

d. This, in turn, _____ this

country's outpayments and _____
its inpayments, thereby reducing or eliminating its balance of payments deficit.

18. The principal advantage of using changing price and income levels to correct balance

of payments deficits or surpluses is _____

_____ .

The chief disadvantage is that nations must

also accept changes in _____ ,

_____ ,

and _____
in order to have international equilibrium.

19. When a nation with a payments deficit employs exchange controls to obtain international equilibrium, the government of that nation rations foreign exchange among those

who wish to _____ goods and services

and all those who have _____ goods and services are required to sell the foreign

exchange they have earned to _____

20. Nations may also attempt to eliminate a

balance of payments deficit by placing _____

_____ and _____

on imports and by _____
exports.

■ **PROBLEMS AND PROJECTS**

1. Use the hypothetical international balance of payments data for the United States given in the table below.

	Dollars (in billions)
Net remittances	−1.5
Income from U.S. investments abroad	+7.3
Capital outflow	−10.2
Increase in liquid dollar balances held by foreigners	+3.9
Imports of goods	−31.1
Income from foreign investments in the United States	−1.8
Decrease in United States holdings of foreign currencies	+0.7
Imports of services	−6.2
Capital inflow	+3.0
Exports of goods	+32.5
Exports of services	+8.1
Net government transactions	−4.7

a. Compute with the appropriate sign (+ or −):

(1) United States exports: $_____

(2) United States imports: $_____

(3) Net capital movements: $_____

(4) Financing transactions: $_____

b. Using the data and your computations in (*a*), complete the United States balance of international payments below. (Use Table 43–1 in the text as a model and assume that there are no errors or omissions.)

(1) _____ $_____

(1*a*) _____ _____

(1*b*) _____ _____

(1*c*) _____ _____

(2) _____ _____

(2*a*) _____ _____

(2*b*) _____ _____

(2c) _____ _____

(3) _____ _____

(4) _____ _____

(5) _____ _____

(6) _____ _____

(6a) _____ _____

(6b) _____ _____

(7) _____ _____

(8a) _____ _____

(8b) _____ _____

c. The United States had a balance of payments _____ of $_____

d. The autonomous transactions amounted to (use the proper sign) $_____ and the accommodating transactions to $_____

2. Below are a series of foreign exchange rates for the British pound. For each of these rates compute the rate of exchange for the American dollar:

$2.00: £_____ $4.00: £_____

$2.50: £_____ $4.50: £_____

$3.00: £_____ $5.00: £_____

$3.50: £_____

It can be seen that the higher the rate of exchange for the pound, the _____ is the rate of exchange for the dollar.

3. Assume that both the United States and Great Britain are on the gold standard. The United States defines the dollar as being worth $1/35$ of an ounce of gold and Great Britain defines the pound as being worth $1/7$ of an ounce of gold. Assume that the cost of packing, insuring, and shipping *one ounce* of gold between the United States and Great Britain is $0.21.

a. Ignoring the packing, insuring, and shipping charges, £1 is worth $ _____ and $1.00 is worth £ _____

b. In the United States the gold export point will be $ _____ and the gold import point will be $ _____

c. In Great Britain the gold export point will be £ _____ and the gold import point will be £ _____ (Carry your answers to three decimal places.)

4. Below are the demand and supply schedules for the British pound.

Quantity of pounds demanded	Price $	Quantity of pounds supplied
400	5.00	100
360	4.50	200
300	4.00	300
286	3.50	400
267	3.00	500
240	2.50	620
200	2.00	788

a. What will be the rate of exchange for the pound? $_____

b. What will be the rate of exchange for the dollar? £ _____

c. How many pounds will be purchased in the market? _____

d. How many dollars will be purchased in the market? _____

■ **SELF-TEST**

Circle the T if the statement is true, the F if it is false.

1. The importation by Americans of goods from abroad creates a supply of dollars in the foreign exchange market. **T F**

2. If a nation's exports of goods and services are less than its imports of goods and services, the nation's international balance of payments will show a balance is due from other nations. **T F**

3. A nation is in international equilibrium when its exports equal its imports. **T F**

4. The financial transactions are remittances and capital movements. **T F**

5. A nation is in international disequilibrium when the accommodating transactions exceed the autonomous transactions. **T F**

6. If a nation has a balance of payments deficit and exchange rates are freely flexible, the price of that nation's money in the foreign exchange market will tend to fall, and this will reduce its imports and increase its exports. **T F**

7. If country A defines its money as worth 100 grains of gold and country B defines its money as worth 20 grains of gold, then, ignoring packing, insuring, and shipping charges, 5 units of country A's money will be worth 1 unit of country B's money. **T F**

8. When nations are on the gold standard, foreign exchange rates fluctuate only within limits determined by the cost of moving gold from one nation to another. **T F**

9. If exchange rates are stable and a nation has a payments surplus, prices and money incomes in that nation will tend to rise. **T F**

10. A nation using exchange controls to eliminate a payments surplus might depreciate its currency. **T F**

Underscore the letter that corresponds to the best answer.

1. If an American can buy £25,000 for $100,000, the rate of exchange for the pound is: (a) $40; (b) $25; (c) $4; (d) $.25.

2. Which of the following is a financing transaction? (a) gifts of Americans to foreign persons and countries; (b) the transfer of dollars from American to foreign ownership; (c) a loan by an American bank to a foreign firm; (d) the income from United States investments abroad.

3. If a nation's international balance of payments shows that it is losing foreign monies and that foreigners are increasing the amount of money they own, the nation has (a) exported more goods and services than it has imported; (b) imported more goods and services than it has exported; (c) a balance of payments surplus; (d) a balance of payments deficit.

4. When the amount by which its exports of goods and services exceed its imports of goods and services is greater than its net remittances to other nations, its governmental loans and grants, and its capital outflow, a nation has (a) autonomous transactions in excess of accommodating transactions; (b) accommodating transactions in excess of autonomous transactions; (c) a balance of payments surplus; (d) a balance of payments deficit.

5. Which of these is an accommodating transaction? (a) a gift from an American to his uncle in Scotland; (b) an increase in the size of American bank accounts in England; (c) a loan by the United States government to Turkey; (d) the purchase by an American of stock on the French stock exchange.

6. Which of the following would be one of the results associated with the use of freely floating foreign exchange rates to correct a nation's balance of payments surplus? (a) the nation's terms of trade with other nations would be worsened; (b) importers in the nation who had made contracts for the future delivery of goods would find that they had to pay a higher price than expected for the goods; (c) if the nation were at full employment the decrease in exports and the increase in imports would be inflationary; (d) exporters in the nation would find their sales abroad had decreased.

7. If the nations of the world are on the gold standard and one nation has a balance of payments surplus: (a) foreign exchange rates in that nation will rise toward the gold import point; (b) gold will tend to be imported into that country; (c) the level of prices in that country will tend to fall; (d) employment and output in that country will tend to fall.

8. When exchange rates are stable and a nation at full employment has a payments surplus, the result in that nation will be: (a) a declining price level; (b) falling money income; (c) inflation; (d) rising real income.

9. The use of exchange controls to eliminate a nation's balance of payments deficit results in: (a) decreasing the nation's imports; (b) decreasing the nation's exports; (c) decreasing the nation's price level; (d) decreasing the nation's income.

10. A nation with a balance of payments surplus might attempt to eliminate this surplus by employing: (a) import quotas; (b) higher tariffs; (c) subsidies on items which the nation exports; (d) none of the above.

■ **DISCUSSION QUESTIONS**

1. What is foreign exchange and the foreign exchange rate? Who are the demanders and suppliers of a particular foreign exchange, say, the French franc? Why is a buyer (demander) in the foreign exchange markets always a seller (supplier) also?

2. What is meant when it is said that "a nation's exports pay for its imports"? Do nations pay for all their imports with exports?

3. What is an international balance of payments? What are the principal sections of a nation's international balance of payments? What are the three kinds of exports and imports listed in it?

4. What are the two kinds of financing transactions in an international balance of payments?

5. What is meant by international equilibrium and disequilibrium? How does a balance of payments surplus (or deficit) differ from the balance due from (or to) other nations on exports and imports of goods and services?

6. How can a nation have both a balance due it from the export and import of goods and services and a balance of payments deficit? Is it possible for a nation to show a balance due to other nations from the export and import of goods and services and an even larger balance of payments deficit? Or a balance due to other nations and a payments surplus? Explain how.

7. What is the difference between autonomous and accommodating transactions in a nation's international balance of payments? Which transactions are autonomous and which are accommodating?

8. How can freely floating foreign exchange rates restore international equilibrium? What are the problems associated with this method of correcting international disequilibrium?

9. When is a nation on the gold standard? How does the international gold standard correct international disequilibrium? What are the disadvantages of this method of restoring international equilibrium?

10. Why does the operation of the international gold standard ensure relatively stable foreign exchange rates, that is, rates which fluctuate only within very narrow limits? What are the limits and what are the advantages of stable exchange rates?

11. How can foreign exchange controls be used to restore international equilibrium? Why do such exchange controls necessarily involve the rationing of foreign exchange? What effect do these controls have upon prices, output, and employment in nations that use them?

12. What kinds of trade controls may nations with payments deficits employ to eliminate their deficits? Why do these controls often fail to achieve the desired result?

International Trade and Finance: Problems and Policies

The title of this chapter is a brief but clear summary of its contents. Chapter 44 looks at the problems of the United States and of the world that have arisen because they engage in international trade. It also examines the policies that have been used or proposed to solve these problems.

After briefly outlining the history of international trade from the nineteenth century through World War II and explaining how the problem of rebuilding the European economies following World War II was solved, the author turns his attention to an examination of how the Bretton Woods system operated in the twenty-five years following World War II to stabilize foreign exchange rates, to provide a quantity of international monetary reserves sufficient to finance a large and expanding volume of international trade, and to achieve international equilibrium. The Bretton Woods system replaced the gold standard (which you studied in the last chapter) as an international monetary system; relied upon adjustable pegs to stabilize exchange rates and to eliminate payments surpluses and deficits; and utilized gold and such key currencies as the dollar to finance international trade.

But in more recent years it became evident that the Bretton Woods system was unable to provide the increases in international monetary reserves needed to finance continued expansion of world trade unless the United States had balance of payments deficits. These deficits, however, resulted in the reduction of the American gold stock and the increasing unwillingness of foreign governments and central banks to use dollars for their international monetary reserves. This dilemma was one of the two causes of the breakdown of the Bretton Woods system. The other cause was the failure of nations to adjust the levels at which the exchange rates were pegged to eliminate payments deficits and surpluses.

A particular instance of its inability to bring about a balance of payments equilibrium is the American economy's twenty-five year payments deficit which was matched in the rest of the world by a twenty-five year payments surplus. Professor McConnell examines the causes of this deficit; explains the basic measures that must be taken if it is to be eliminated; and considers (and rejects) the use of controls to solve the deficit problem.

Because it could not expand international monetary reserves without U.S. payments deficits and at the same time preserve the status of the dollar and did not bring about international equilibrium, the days of the Bretton Woods system were numbered. The United States administered the *coup de grace* to the system in August 1971 when it ended its thirty-seven year policy of allowing foreign nations and central banks to convert dollars into gold at the rate of $35 dollars for an ounce of gold. Thereafter the value of the dollar was determined by the demand for and the supply of the dollar—the value of the dollar "floated."

The new international monetary system that has emerged since the demise of the Bretton Woods system has three characteristics. Exchange rates are managed for stability in the short term and allowed to float in the long term to eliminate payments deficits and surpluses. A new international money, Special Drawing Rights, has been created by the International Monetary Fund to provide the nations of the world with additional monetary reserves. And the role of gold in international trade has been practically eliminated.

The final brief section of Chapter 44 reaches a most important conclusion: the things a nation must do to promote full employment and stable prices are not always the things it has to do to achieve equilibrium in its balance of payments. The author explains when the policies that will eliminate unemployment and inflation are consistent and when they are inconsistent with the policies that will eliminate a payments surplus or deficit. You must be sure to understand when domestic policies conflict with and when they reinforce a nation's international economic policies.

Again there are a number of new terms in the chapter. But there is really no new theory. The principles and basic notions necessary to understand these problems were developed in Chapters 41, 42, and 43; the same principles and notions should enable you to see how policies have been developed to solve the problems. In fact, the men and governments who designed the policies first had to understand principles, just as you first have to understand principles, in order to understand the problems and develop solutions for them.

■ CHECKLIST

The very least you should be able to do when you have finished this chapter is:

□ Briefly describe international trade during the nineteenth century and the effects of the Great Depression and World War II on world trade.

□ Enumerate the three problems facing the world economy at the end of World War II.

□ Explain how the International Monetary Fund (using the Bretton Woods system) stabilized exchange rates and attempted to provide for orderly changes in exchange rates to eliminate international disequilibria.

□ Define the international monetary reserves of the Bretton Woods system; explain why the United States had to incur balance of payments deficits to expand these reserves; and describe the dilemma this created for the United States.

□ List five causes of the persistent American payments deficits and the four basic steps which might be taken to reduce these deficits (without introducing controls).

□ Describe the two problems which lead to the demise of the Bretton Woods system and how the United States shattered this system in 1971.

□ Explain how the new international monetary system manages exchange rates for stability in the short term and allows them to float to correct disequilibria in the long term.

□ Describe how the new international monetary system has provided the world with a new international money which nations may use as international monetary reserves.

□ State when a nation's policies to reduce unemployment (or to reduce inflationary pressures) are compatible with and when they are in conflict with the policies it might utilize to eliminate balance of payments surpluses or deficits.

■ CHAPTER OUTLINE

1. Prior to 1930 the volume of international trade was large and was based on the principle of comparative advantage, a philosophy of laissez faire, and the automatic operation of the gold standard.

a. The Depression of the 1930s drastically reduced the volume of international trade and lending, and most nations erected trade barriers in a futile attempt to solve their domestic unemployment problems.

b. World War II increased the warring nations' demands for imports, reduced their willingness to export, and resulted in inflation and in the destruction of productive capacity.

c. The world (and especially Europe) at the close of World War II faced the problem of rebuilding its economy. To solve this problem the productive capacity of Europe had to be restored, an international monetary system had to be provided to facilitate and increase trade, and artificial trade barriers had to be reduced.

2. The United States Marshall Plan provided the postwar aid to rebuild Europe.

3. To rebuild the international monetary system and stabilize exchange rates, the International Monetary Fund was formed at the end of World War II.

a. The IMF, using the Bretton Woods (or adjustable-peg) system, stabilized exchange rates by requiring nations to have exchange stabilization funds and by making loans from its own fund to nations with temporary balance of payments deficits.

b. It also provided for orderly changes in exchange rates to correct international disequilibria.

c. An efficient international monetary system requires sufficient international monetary reserves; and gold and key currencies (especially the American dollar) provided these reserves. For these reserves to grow the United States had to incur payments deficits; but the growing number of dollars held abroad made it increasingly difficult for the United States to maintain the convertibility of dollars into gold.

4. Since 1949 the United States has had balance of payments deficits in all but three years.

a. Because of productivity increases in many foreign nations, inflation in the United States, and increased oil prices, the amount by which American exports exceeded its imports has been less than its foreign aid and military expenditures and investments abroad; and the result has been payments deficits.

b. Policies to reduce or eliminate the payments deficits would include having Western Europe assume a larger share of the costs of mutual defense and foreign aid; inducing nations with surpluses to lower their trade barriers and increase their investments in the United States; and increasing productivity and limiting inflation in the United States.

c. To control its payments deficit, the United States temporarily employed various measures or controls which limit and distort world trade.

d. But in the 1970s the international monetary system moved to abandon fixed and to adopt floating exchange rates.

5. Two problems brought to an end the Bretton Woods system of adjustable pegs.

a. To maintain the convertibility of dollars into gold the United States had to reduce its payments deficits; but elimination of these deficits would reduce the growth in reserves needed if world trade is to expand.

b. The elimination of the payments deficits of the United States has been difficult because the exchange rate "pegs" were rarely adjusted and exchange rates were in fact rigid.

c. In August 1971 the United States (faced with another payments deficit) shattered the Bretton Woods system when it suspended the convertibility of dollars into gold. Demand and supply caused the international value of the dollar to float downward; and the dollar was in effect devalued.

6. The Smithsonian Agreement in 1971 realigned exchange rates to correct the overvaluation of the dollar; but early in 1973 the United States abandoned the exchange rates fixed by the Smithsonian Agreement when it again devalued the dollar.

a. Exchange rates are today managed by individual nations to avoid short-term fluctuations and allowed to float in the long term to correct payments disequilibria.

b. The IMF creates Special Drawing Rights (SDRs) which it lends to member nations that wish to increase their international monetary reserves or to cover payments deficits.

c. The use of gold as an international money has been reduced by the employment of SDRs and by other actions of the IMF.

d. This new system of managed floating exchange rates is favored by some and criticized by others; but alternatives to it and to the Bretton Woods system still exist.

7. The domestic economic policies a nation employs to decrease unemployment or to reduce inflation may be either compatible or conflict with the international economic policies it would employ to achieve a balance of payments equilibrium.

a. The policies it would employ to eliminate unemployment conflict with (are compatible with) the policies it would utilize to reduce a payments deficit (surplus).

b. But the policies it would use to combat inflation are compatible with (conflict with) the policies it would invoke to reduce a payments deficit (surplus).

■ IMPORTANT TERMS

European Recovery Program (Marshall Plan)

Bretton Woods system

Adjustable pegs

International Monetary Fund

International monetary reserves

Key currencies

Special Drawing Rights (SDRs)

Smithsonian Agreement

Managed floating exchange rate

Jamaica Agreement

Crawling-peg system

■ FILL-IN QUESTIONS

1. In the last half of the nineteenth century the volume of international trade in the world was _____; and the trade was primarily an exchange of the _____ of the _____ nations for the _____ of the _____ nations. Trade was based on the principle of _____, the ideology of _____, and the automatic operation of the _____ _____

2. In the years following 1929 the amount of international trade was substantially reduced by _____ and _____. The former event gave rise to reduced _____ _____, reduced long-term _____, and _____

3. Nations at war usually want to increase

their _____ and decrease their _____ and this creates a _____ problem for these nations. War also tends to result in _____ and the destruction of _____

4. The postwar programs and institutions to rebuild world trade had three related objectives: to _____, to _____, and to _____

5. The most pressing economic problem facing the world at the end of World War II was to _____. The United States helped to solve this problem by instituting the _____ program.

6. The Bretton Woods system was established to bring about _____ exchange rates. To accomplish this, it employed an _____ system of exchange rates.

7. Under the Bretton Woods system:
a. each member was required to establish a _____ fund which consisted of supplies of _____ and _____ monies and _____
b. the IMF was allowed to make short-term _____ to nations with temporary balance of payments _____
c. a nation with a more deeply rooted payments deficit could, without the permission of the IMF, change the value of its money by up to _____%;
d. it was hoped that exchange rates in the short run would be (stable, flexible) _____ enough to promote trade and in the long run would be _____ enough to correct payments disequilibria.

8. In the Bretton Woods system international monetary reserves included both _____

and "_____," the most important of which was the _____

9. The role of the dollar as a component of international monetary reserves produced a dilemma:
a. For these reserves to grow the United States had to incur balance of payments _____

b. This resulted in an increase in the foreign holdings of American dollars and in a decrease in the American reserves (stock) of _____.

c. The ability of the United States to convert dollars into gold and the willingness of foreigners to hold dollars (because they were "as good as gold"), therefore (increased, decreased) _____

d. For the dollar to remain an acceptable international monetary reserve the U.S. payments deficits had to be (eliminated, continued) _____; but for international monetary reserves to grow the U.S. payments deficits had to be _____

10. The American balance of payments deficits have been caused by increases in the _____ of foreign producers, by _____ in the United States, by substantial American capital _____, by _____ and _____ by the United States in foreign nations, and by the formation of _____

11. Without restricting imports; the United States might reduce its payments deficit by:
a. _____
b. _____
c. _____
d. _____

12. A nation with a balance of payments deficit might introduce controls to reduce its _____ and to expand its _____. But these controls will reduce and distort _____

and are apt to induce other nations to _____

13. Since 1971 the international monetary system has moved from exchange rates which (for all practical purposes) were (fixed, floating) _____ to exchange rates which are _____

14. The problem the Bretton Woods system had with:
a. reserves was that the United States had to eliminate its payments deficit to preserve _____ and if it eliminated this deficit the world's monetary reserves would not _____

b. adjustments was that balance of payments surpluses and deficits persisted because the Bretton Woods system did not in fact adjust the _____

15. The United States completed the destruction of the Bretton Woods system in 1971 when it suspended the convertibility of dollars into _____ and allowed the value of the dollar to be determined by _____

16. The Smithsonian Agreement:
a. corrected the (over-, under-) _____ valuation of the dollar;

b. (did, did not) _____ bring about a reduction in the size of the American payments deficit;

c. was followed in 1973 by a further _____ _____ of the dollar by the United States.

17. The system of exchange rates which has developed since 1973 has been labeled a system of _____ exchange rates. This means that individual nations will:
a. in the short term buy and sell foreign exchange to keep exchange rates _____
b. in the long term allow exchange rates to rise or fall to correct payments _____

18. The IMF is able to create an international money called _____ which it can lend to nations that have pay-

ments _____ or that wish to increase the size of their _____
This new international money had led to the _____ of gold.

19. Those who favor fixed (or stable) foreign exchange rates contend that managed floating exchange rates reinforce _____ and that the managed floating system of exchange rates is actually a _____

20. The domestic policy which would:
a. reduce inflation (conflicts, is compatible) _____ with the policies needed to eliminate a payments surplus;

b. reduce unemployment _____ with the policies required to eliminate a payments deficit.

■ **PROBLEMS AND PROJECTS**

1. Below is a series of identifying phrases followed by a list of acts, programs, institutions, etc. Match the phrase with the act, program, institution, etc., by placing the appropriate letter in the space following each phrase. (*Note:* Not all the items in the list will have an identifying phrase.)
1. Makes short-term loans to member nations temporary balance of payments deficits. _____

2. Bookkeeping entries which may be used to settle payments deficits. _____
3. Corrected the overvaluation of the dollar. _____

4. Legitimized the managed floating system of exchange rates. _____
5. Gold and key currencies in the Bretton Woods system. _____
6. Dollars could no longer be converted into gold and the exchange rate for the dollar depended upon demand and supply. _____
7. Relatively fixed foreign exchange rates managed by the International Monetary Fund. _____

8. Program that would allow nations with chronic balance of payments deficits to increase the par value of their currencies by a small percentage each month. _____
9. Foreign exchange rates stabilized in the short term and changed in the long term to correct balance of payments deficits. _____

10. American program to aid European nations in rebuilding their productive capacities destroyed during World War II. _____
11. Allowing demand and supply to determine exchange rate trends and the smoothing out of day-to-day fluctuations in exchange rates. _____

A. Jamaica Agreement
B. European Recovery Program (Marshall Plan)
C. Adjustment problem
D. Bretton Woods system
E. Adjustable-peg system
F. International Monetary Fund
G. Managed floating exchange rates
H. International monetary reserves
I. Floating the dollar
J. Smithsonian Agreement
K. Crawling-peg system
L. Special Drawing Rights

2. In the schedule below is a hypothetical demand for British pounds in the foreign exchange market.

Price of the pound	Quantity of pounds demanded
$2.40	100
2.20	200
2.00	300
1.80	400
1.60	500
1.40	600

To stabilize the price of the pound at $2.00:
a. When at $2.00 the quantity of pounds supplied (by British demanders of dollars) is 200, the British government would have to (buy, sell) _____ (how many?) _____ pounds and (buy, sell) _____ (how many?) _____ dollars.
b. When at $2.00 the quantity of pounds supplied is 500, the British government would

have to _____ pounds and

_____ dollars.

3. Assume:

a. the American economy has fully employed its labor force, is experiencing inflation, and has a balance of payments *deficit.*

(1) to reduce the inflationary pressures in the economy requires a(n) (expansionary, contractory) _____ fiscal policy and a(n) (tight, easy) _____ monetary policy;

(2) if these measures are successful in curbing inflation without reducing employment, the economy's:

(*a*) exports will tend to (increase, decrease)

_____

(*b*) imports will tend to _____

(*c*) interest rates in the economy will (rise, fall) _____ and this will encourage the flow of capital (into, out of) _____ the United States

(*d*) the payments deficit of the American economy will tend to (increase, decrease)

_____

(3) the measures undertaken to reduce inflation in the United States worked to (reduce, widen) _____ the payments deficit;

(4) but if the economy had begun with a payments *surplus* the fiscal and monetary measures taken to fight inflation would have:

(*a*) increased the economy's (exports, imports) _____

(*b*) reduced its _____

(*c*) driven _____ rates upward and encourage the flow of _____ in the United States

(*d*) and the payments surplus of the economy would have (widened, narrowed) _____

b. the American economy has a relatively large portion (8 to 10%) of its labor force unemployed, is experiencing a depression, and has a balance of payments *surplus.*

(1) to reduce unemployment and increase the economy's real output requires a(n) _____

_____ fiscal policy and a(n) _____ monetary policy;

(2) if these measures are successful in expanding employment and output in the economy:

(*a*) exports will tend to _____

(*b*) imports will tend to _____

(*c*) interest rates will tend to _____ and this will encourage the flow of capital (into, out ot) _____ the United States;

(*d*) the payments surplus of the American economy will tend to _____

(3) the measures undertaken to reduce unemployment in the United States worked to (reduce, widen) _____ the payments surplus;

(4) but if the economy had begun with a payments *deficit* the fiscal and monetary policies employed to fight recession would have (widened, narrowed) _____ the deficit.

c. In summary, policies employed to

(1) combat *inflation* (conflict, are compatible) _____ with the elimination of a payments deficit and

_____ with the reduction of a payments surplus;

(2) reduce *unemployment* _____ with the elimination of a payments deficit and

_____ with the reduction of a payments surplus.

■ **SELF-TEST**

Circle the T if the statement is true, the F if it is false.

1. During the Depression of the 1930s most of the nations of the world lowered barriers to international trade in an attempt to increase domestic employment and output.
                                                                T F

2. Most experts agree that the European Recovery Program was highly successful in restoring the industrial and agricultural capacity of Western Europe.   **T** F

3. In the Bretton Woods system a nation could not devalue its currency by more than 10% without the permission of the International Fund.   **T** F

4. When a nation devalues its currency the goods and services it produces become more inexpensive for foreigners to buy; and goods and services produced abroad become more expensive for its citizens to buy. **T F**

5. Under the Bretton Woods system a nation could not allow the value of its currency to vary. **T F**

6. If a nation maintains an exchange stabilization fund it would purchase its own money with gold or foreign monies when the value of its money falls in foreign exchange markets. **T F**

7. In the Bretton Woods system a nation with persistent balance of payments surpluses had an undervalued currency and should have increased the pegged value of its currency. **T F**

8. The "key currencies" in the Bretton Woods system were the American dollar and—from time to time—the British pound, the German mark, and the Japanese yen. **T F**

9. Because the world's stock of gold did not grow very rapidly it became necessary for the United States to have payments deficits if international monetary reserves were to increase. **T F**

10. American balance of payments deficits in the 1950s and 1960s can be attributed to the economic recovery of Japan and Western Europe and to unemployment in the United States. **T F**

11. One suggested solution for the United States balance of payments problem is an increase in American foreign aid to underdeveloped nations. **T F**

12. One of the basic shortcomings of the Bretton Woods system was its inability to bring about the changes in exchange rates needed to correct persistent balance of payments deficits and surpluses. **T F**

13. Another basic shortcoming of the Bretton Woods system was its failure to maintain stable foreign exchange rates. **T F**

14. Under the Bretton Woods system the American dollar became overvalued. **T F**

15. The United States shattered the Bretton Woods system in August 1971 by raising tariff rates on nearly all the goods it imported by an average of 40%. **T F**

16. Using the managed floating system of exchange rates, a nation with a persistent balance of payments surplus should allow the value of its currency in foreign exchange markets to decrease. **T F**

17. A nation with a balance of payments deficit and without sufficient monetary reserves might transfer SDRs to those nations it owes money. **T F**

18. The creation of SDRs had tended to increase the importance of gold as an international monetary reserve. **T F**

19. The Smithsonian Agreement among IMF members in 1971 legitimized the managed floating system of exchange rates. **T F**

20. The policies used by a country to eliminate unemployment are compatible with the elimination of that country's balance of payments deficit. **T F**

Underscore the letter that corresponds to the best answer.

1. Which one of the following was characteristic of international trade throughout most of the nineteenth century? (*a*) extensive barriers to trade; (*b*) the almost automatic operation of the gold standard; (*c*) a small volume of international trade; (*d*) government regulation of most foreign exchange rates.

2. Which one of the following was *not* characteristic of world trade during World War II? (*a*) trade was based on military objectives rather than on comparative advantages; (*b*) shortages of foreign exchange existed in most countries at war; (*c*) inflation in the warring nations made the exports of these nations more attractive to foreign buyers; (*d*) inflation in the warring nations made foreign goods more attractive to buyers in the warring nations.

3. The *most urgent* of the world's economic problems immediately following World War II was: (*a*) the elimination of trade barriers; (*b*) the development of an international monetary system; (*c*) the economic development of the underdeveloped nations; (*d*) the reconstruction of the European economies.

4. Which of the following has had as its basic objective the restoration of the productive capacity of European industry and agriculture? (*a*) the Jamaica Agreement; (*b*) the

Smithsonian Agreement; (c) the Marshall Plan; (d) the Bretton Woods conference.

5. Which one of the following was *not* characteristic of the International Monetary Fund in the Bretton Woods system? (a) made short-term loans to member nations with balance of payments deficits; (b) tried to maintain relatively stable exchange rates; (c) required member nations to maintain exchange stabilization funds; (d) extended long-term loans to underdeveloped nations for the purpose of increasing their productive capacities.

6. All but one of the following were elements in the adjustable-peg system of foreign exchange rates. Which one? (a) each nation defined its monetary unit in terms of gold or dollars; (b) nations bought and sold their own currencies to stabilize exchange rates; (c) nations were allowed to devalue their currencies when faced with persistent payments deficits; (d) the deposit by all nations of their international reserves with the IMF.

7. The objective of the adjustable-peg system was exchange rates which were (a) adjustable in the short run and fixed in the long run; (b) adjustable in both the short and long run; (c) fixed in both the short and long run; (d) fixed in the short run and adjustable in the long run.

8. Which of the following is the best definition of international monetary reserves in the Bretton Woods system? (a) gold; (b) gold and dollars; (c) gold and key currencies; (d) gold, dollars, British pounds, and Russian rubles.

9. The persistent U.S. balance of payments deficits have resulted in (a) a decrease in the U.S. gold stock; (b) an increase in the foreign holdings of American dollars; (c) the decreased willingness of foreigners to accept dollars in payment of international debts; (d) all of the above.

10. If the United States had eliminated its annual balance of payments deficit in the Bretton Woods system (a) the world's international monetary reserves would have decreased; (b) the annual increases in the world's international monetary reserves would have declined; (c) the number of dollars owned by foreign nations would have expanded; (d) the amount of gold owned by the United States would have increased.

11. The dilemma created by the U.S. payments deficits was that (a) to maintain the status of the dollar as an acceptable international monetary reserve the deficit had to be reduced and to increase these reserves the deficits had to be continued; (b) to maintain the status of the dollar the deficit had to be continued and to increase reserves the deficit had to be eliminated; (c) to maintain the status of the dollar the deficit had to be increased and to expand reserves the deficit had to be reduced; (d) to maintain the status of the dollar the deficit had to be reduced and to expand reserves the deficit had to be reduced.

12. Which of the following has *not* contributed to the persistent American balance of payments deficits? (a) the increased productivity of American workers; (b) inflation in the United States; (c) American military, aid, and capital expenditures abroad; (d) the formation of the Organization of Petroleum Exporting Countries.

13. Which one of the following would *not* tend to reduce a nation's balance of payments deficit? (a) an increase in the productivity of the nation's resources; (b) an increase in the nation's price level; (c) an increase in the flow of private capital into the nation; (d) an increase in the nation's exports.

14. Which of the following would be the *least* desirable method of reducing or eliminating the American balance of payments problem? (a) an increase in American tariff rates; (b) an expansion in the share of the costs of the North American Treaty Alliance borne by the Western European members of the alliance; (c) the restraint of inflation in the United States; (d) the relaxation of foreign restrictions on American goods.

15. "Floating" the dollar means (a) the value of the dollar is determined by the demand for and the supply of the dollar; (b) the dollar price of gold has been increased; (c) the price of the dollar has been allowed to crawl upward at the rate of one-fourth of 1% a month; (d) the IMF decreased the value of the dollar by 10%.

16. A system of managed floating exchange rates (a) allows nations to stabilize exchange rates in the short term; (b) requires nations to stabilize exchange rates in the long term;

(c) entails stable exchange rates in both the short and long term; (d) none of the above.

17. Floating exchange rates (a) tend to correct payments disequilibria; (b) reduce the uncertainties and risks associated with international trade; (c) increase the world's need for international monetary reserves; (d) tend to expand the volume of world trade.

18. Which of the following is *not* true of SDRs? (a) they serve as international reserves; (b) they have no gold backing; (c) they are issued by the United Nations; (d) they are accepted in payment of international debts by the members of the IMF.

19. If the price level in the United States rises and exchange rates are allowed to float (a) the change in the international value of the dollar will be upward; (b) the change in the international value of the dollar will tend to decrease American exports; (c) the change in the international value of the dollar will tend to increase American imports; (d) the change in the international value of the dollar will tend to increase aggregate demand and the price level in the United States.

20. Which of the following policies are compatible? (a) those designed to eliminate inflation and a balance of payments deficit; (b) those utilized to eliminate unemployment and a payment surplus; (c) both of the above; (d) neither of the above.

■ **DISCUSSION QUESTIONS**

1. What were the extent and character of international trade in the nineteenth century?

2. Explain the effects of the Great Depression and of World War II upon the volume and character of world trade and upon the international trade policies of the nations of the world.

3. What was the condition of world trade at the end of World War II? What were the three objectives of the postwar programs used to correct this condition?

4. Which of the economic problems faced by the world at the end of World War II was the most urgent? How did the United States help to solve this problem?

5. Explain (a) why the International Monetary Fund was established and what the objectives of the adjustable-pegs (or Bretton Woods) system were; (b) what the adjustable-peg system was and the basic means it employed to stabilize exchange rates in the short run; and (c) when and how the system was to adjust exchange rates in the long run.

6. Why are international monetary reserves necessary? What is the effect of inadequate monetary reserves upon international trade? What did nations use for an international reserve during the twenty-five years of the Bretton Woods system?

7. Explain the dilemma which the need for expanding international monetary reserves and for maintaining the status of the dollar created.

8. In what way has the international trade position of the United States during the past twenty-five years differed from its position in the years immediately following World War II? What have been the main causes of this change?

9. What are the four basic measures which would help to correct the American balance of payments deficit?

10. Why are controls not generally an economically desirable means of eliminating payments deficits?

11. Explain the two problems which the Bretton Woods system encountered in the early 1970s. How has the new international monetary system resolved each of these problems?

12. Why and how did the United States shatter the Bretton Woods system in 1971? If the international value of the dollar is no longer determined by the amount of gold for which it can be exchanged, what does determine its value?

13. Explain what is meant by a managed floating system of foreign exchange rates. When are exchange rates managed and when are they allowed to float?

14. What are Special Drawing Rights? How are they created, what "backs" them, and for what purposes are they used?

15. Why does a system in which exchange rates float lessen the need for international monetary reserves?

16. What things has the International Monetary Fund done to demonitize gold?

17. Explain the arguments of the defenders and the critics of the managed floating system.

18. Explain when and why the policies employed by a nation to reduce unemployment or inflation conflict and when and why they are compatible with the elimination of a balance of payments disequilibrium.

The Economic System of Soviet Russia

In the past people in the United States were convinced that the economic system of the Soviet Union was totally unworkable and that it would sooner or later break down—proof that Marx, Lenin, and Stalin were unrealistic dreamers—and that the reconversion of their economy to a free enterprise, price-market system would follow. Slowly it dawned upon the American people that the breakdown would not occur and, on the contrary, the Soviet economy was becoming more workable and more productive, and that Soviet Russia was becoming a very strong nation. In part the early American belief that Soviet Russia would collapse was based on prejudice—they wanted it to collapse in order to prove to themselves that the system employed by American capitalism was both the only feasible system of economic organization and an almost perfectly operated system —and in part it was based on ignorance of the institutions and methods employed by Russian communism.

The aim of Chapter 45 is to dispel some of the ignorance surrounding Soviet institutions and methods and by doing so eliminate the basis for much of the unwarranted prejudice against the Soviet economic system. (Chapter 45, of course, does not try to convince you that the United States should adopt the Soviet economic system, nor does it try to

persuade you that the Russian way of life as a whole is morally, politically, or socially preferable.) To accomplish its aim the chapter first examines the two institutions of the Soviet economy which are remarkably different from anything found in American capitalism and which are the framework of the Russian economy. Within this framework the Fundamental Economic Problems are solved through central economic planning. Central economic planning has no counterpart in the United States, and it is to further authoritarian central economic planning that the Soviet institutional framework is maintained. The better part of the chapter is devoted to explaining what central planning is and how it is employed in the U.S.S.R. to obtain answers to the Fundamental Economic Problems.

If you learn anything from this chapter you ought to learn that the Soviet economy is the source of its political and military strength and that the performance and growth of the Soviet and American economic systems (and the social and political institutions that accompany them) are being watched by people throughout the world who will be inclined to adopt the economic and political and social system which promises them the best prospect of improving their own material well-being. In addition, you should be aware that it is not a question of "Will the Soviet system work?" but of how well it works.

There is great strength in the Soviet Union because the government is able to compel the economy to do as it wishes. The large and almost continuous increases in Soviet output are mostly the result of authoritarian central economic planning and the direction of the economy toward the achievement of these plans by central authority. It is both the strength and weakness of the American economy that it lacks central direction. It was once assumed that central planning was too complex to be practical and that only the impersonal price-market system could coordinate the various parts of the economy, just as it was once imagined that only monetary self-interest and private property could provoke increased efficiency, effort, and output. The Soviet experiment suggests the contrary.

Of course, economic and political freedom is lacking in the Soviet Union, but for the underfed, the illiterate, the sick, and those without hope, this would be a small price to pay for even a slightly improved standard of living. Whether the Soviet system will be adopted by underdeveloped nations depends not only upon how successful the Soviet system is in the future, but also upon how well the American system functions in improving its own and others' standards of living, and upon the moral, political, and social costs of this improvement.

Although nondiscussion questions and problems are provided in this study guide, studying these questions is not sufficient to develop and test fully your understanding of the Soviet Union. The nature of the material is such that you should spend considerable time and effort on the discussion questions.

■ **CHECKLIST**

The very least you should be able to do when you have finished this chapter is:

□ Identify the three outstanding institutional characteristics of the economy of the U.S.S.R.

□ List and explain the three techniques used in the Soviet planning system to achieve coordination.

□ Explain how *Gosbank* helps *Gosplan* to achieve the objectives of the economic plan.

□ Describe the incentive system employed in the U.S.S.R.

□ Explain what determines the prices producers pay for inputs and receive for final products in the Soviet Union; and contrast the role of profits and losses and the significance of input prices in the U.S.S.R. and a market economy.

□ Explain how the prices of consumer goods are determined in the Soviet economy and the function these prices perform.

□ Identify three microeconomic problems in the U.S.S.R.

□ Outline the three essential features of the reform proposal called Libermanism.

□ Compare the GNPs and the growth rates of the Soviet and American economies.

□ Enumerate the five factors which have produced rapid growth and five factors which may slow future growth in the U.S.S.R.

□ List the two major accomplishments and the two major shortcomings of the Soviet system.

□ State the convergence hypothesis.

■ **CHAPTER OUTLINE**

1. The major economic characteristics of the U.S.S.R. are:

a. The state ownership of most property resources (as opposed to private ownership).

b. Central and authoritarian economic planning or governmental direction (as opposed to the price-market system).

c. The limited freedom of choice of consumers and workers (as opposed to consumer sovereignty and freedom of occupation).

2. Central planning is used in the Soviet Union to answer the Five Fundamental Economic Questions.

a. Government in the U.S.S.R. sets forth the goals of the economy in its Five-Year and Annual Plans.

b. The basic problem encountered in planning for an entire economy is the difficulty of coordinating the many interdependent segments of the economy and the avoidance of the chain reaction that would result from a bottleneck in any one of these segments.

c. To coordinate the different sectors of the economy, *Gosplan* plans by negotiation, employs the priority principle, and uses inventories to offset bottlenecks.

d. To achieve the objectives of central planning the Soviet government relies upon such control agencies as *Gosplan,* other planning groups, and especially upon *Gosbank.*

e. To motivate economic units to fulfill the plan the U.S.S.R. employs monetary and non-monetary incentives and coercion.

f. Prices in the Soviet economy are established by the state and are used to promote the achievement of the plans.

(1) Producer prices are used to measure the efficiency of production.

(2) Consumer goods prices are employed to ration goods and services.

3. Microeconomic problems have troubled the Soviet economy, and a number of re-forms have been instituted.

a. The three principal problems were the production of unsalable goods, distorted production and poor-quality goods, and resistance to innovation by producing enterprises.

b. At the suggestion of Liberman and others, the government introduced a modified profit motive, less central planning and more planning from below, and greater autonomy for the managers of individual enterprises.

4. The U.S.S.R. has sought the macroeconomic goal of rapid economic growth.

a. The GNP of the U.S.S.R. is little more than one-half that of the United States; but its growth rate has been greater than that of the United States.

b. The sources of growth in the Soviet Union were its large endowment of natural resources, its totalitarian government, its surplus farm labor, its adoption of the superior technologies developed in Western nations, and its virtual elimination of cyclical unemployment.

c. There are at least five factors which slowed Soviet growth in recent years.

d. It is expected that the growth rate of the Soviet economy will decrease in the future.

5. Any evaluation of the Soviet system requires an examination of its principal accomplishments and shortcomings.

a. Its major accomplishments are the great improvements in education and its complete system of social insurance.

b. The shortcomings are the small increases in the consumers' standard of living and the general absence of personal freedom.

6. The hypothesis that the capitalistic and communistic systems are converging and that the differences between the institutions and policies of the two systems are becoming smaller is supported by some evidence; but the differences between the two systems are still great and may not be narrowing at all.

■ **IMPORTANT TERMS**

State ownership	Gosbank
Central economic planning	"Control by the ruble"
Gosplan	Turnover tax
Libermanism	Convergence hypothesis
Priority principle	

■ **FILL-IN QUESTIONS**

1. The two institutions of the U.S.S.R. which are in sharp contrast with private property and the price-market system of the United

States are _____

and _____

2. In the U.S.S.R. the _____ determines the goals or objectives of the economy while in the United States it is the

_____

which sets goals or objectives.

3. The basic planning problem in the Soviet

Union is the _____ of the various sectors of the economy. The failure of any one of these sectors to produce its

planned output results in a _____

which has a _____ throughout the remainder of the economy.

4. To coordinate the various segments of the economy the Soviet government plans by

_____; and when bottlenecks

appear it applies the _____

principle and draws upon _____

5. The agency primarily responsible for the construction of the economic plan in the

Soviet Union is _____ and the agency primarily responsible for ensuring that the provisions of the plan are enforced is _____

6. Production in the Soviet Union is motivated by _____ ,

_____ ,

and _____

7. In the U.S.S.R. prices perform two essential functions, namely, _____ and _____

8. Profits in the Soviet Union are essentially a means of determining _____ while in the United States profits serve to

_____

9. The Soviet economy has had serious microeconomic problems and has had to undertake reform to reduce these problems.
a. Three problems which plagued planners were:

(1) The production of _____ goods and the accumulation of _____ inventories.

(2) A distorted _____ of goods which were of poor _____
(3) The reluctance of enterprise managers to _____
b. The reforms undertaken include:

(1) The introduction of a modified _____

_____

(2) More _____ in the economy and more _____ for enterprise managers.

(3) More planning from _____

c. These reforms were suggested by _____ _____ and others.

10. The gross national product of the U.S.S.R. is slightly more than _____ of the GNP of the United States and grew during the 1970s at a rate of about _____% per year.

11. List five specific reasons why there has been economic growth in the U.S.S.R.

a. _____

b. _____

c. _____

d. _____

e. _____

12. What five factors may retard future economic growth in the Soviet Union?

a. _____

b. _____

c. _____

d. _____

e. _____

13. What have been the two most significant accomplishments of the U.S.S.R. since central planning began?

a. _____

b. _____

14. The two chief shortcomings of the Soviet economy over the past years have been

_____

and _____

■ **PROBLEMS AND PROJECTS**

1. On the left of the table on page 354 are several of the major institutions or characteristics of American capitalism. In the spaces to the right, name the institution or characteristic of the Soviet economy which compares with the American institution or characteristic.

2. On page 354 is a market demand schedule for product X.
a. If Soviet planners decide to produce 50 million units of product X, the price of the product *plus* the turnover tax will be set at

_____ rubles.
b. If the accounting cost of producing product X is 25 rubles, the turnover tax *rate* will

be set at _____%.

American institution or characteristic	Russian institution or characteristic
Private ownership of economic resources	
Consumer freedom to spend income as he sees fit	
Consumer sovereignty	
Worker freedom to select occupation and place of work	
Profit motive	
Entrepreneurial freedom to select product, output, price, etc.	
System of prices and markets	
Self-interest	
Privately owned farms	
Privately owned industrial firms and retail stores	

Price, rubles	Quantity demanded (million)
90	25
80	30
70	35
60	40
50	45
40	50
30	55

■ SELF-TEST

Circle the T if the statement is true, the F if it is false.

1. The Soviet government sets the economic objectives of the economy, directs the resources of the economy toward the achievement of these objectives, and uses the price system as one of the means of achieving these objectives.　　　　**T F**

2. Consumers in the U.S.S.R. are free to spend their incomes on any of the consumer goods provided by the economy's central plan.　　　　**T F**

3. *Gosplan* is the agency in the Soviet Union primarily responsible for preparing the economic plan.　　　　**T F**

4. In the U.S.S.R. individual plants and industries play no part in the formulation of the final economic plan.　　　　**T F**

5. The basic planning problem in the Soviet Union is the determination of the overall goals of the economy.　　　　**T F**

6. Application of the priority principle means that when production bottlenecks develop in the economy, inventories are used to prevent a chain reaction.　　　　**T F**

7. Most workers in the Soviet Union are paid on a piece-rate basis.　　　　**T F**

8. The turnover tax does not affect the price of consumer goods, but it does affect the consumer income available for the purchase of consumer goods.　　　　**T F**

9. The GNP of the U.S.S.R. is slightly more than one-half the size of GNP in the United States, and the rate of growth of the GNP in the Soviet Union has been greater than the rate of growth of GNP in the United States.　　　　**T F**

10. GNP in the U.S.S.R. will undoubtedly expand at a more rapid rate in the future than it has in the past.　　　　**T F**

Underscore the letter that corresponds to the best answer.

1. Which of the following is *not* true? (*a*) the standard of living in the U.S.S.R. is below the standard of living of the U.S.; (*b*) the output of the Russian economy exceeds the output of the American economy; (*c*) the output of the Russian economy is growing at a more rapid rate than the output of the American economy; (d) the Soviet economy devotes a larger percentage of its output to capital accumulation than does the American economy.

2. In the U.S.S.R.: (a) all property is owned by the state or by collective farms and co-operatives; (b) all property except urban housing and farms is owned either by the state or by cooperatives; (c) all property except retail and wholesale enterprises is owned either by the state or by collective farms and cooperatives; (d) all property except small tools, clothing, household furnishings, and rural homes is owned by the state or by collective farms and cooperatives.

3. Which of the following is the most important agency in enforcing and carrying out the central economic plan in the Soviet Union? (a) *Gosplan;* (b) *Gosbank;* (c) the Communist party; (d) the secret police.

4. Prices in the Soviet Union: (a) are used as a device for rationing consumer goods; (b) are determined by the demands for and the supplies of products and resources; (c) are used to allocate resources among different firms and industries; (d) perform a guiding function, but not a rationing function.

5. Profits and losses in the U.S.S.R. are used to determine whether: (a) the production of various consumer goods should be expanded or contracted; (b) various goods are being produced efficiently or inefficiently; (c) more or fewer resources should be devoted to the production of various goods; (d) a product should be taxed or subsidized.

6. Suppose the Soviet government determined that the annual output of a certain quality of wristwatch would be 100,000 and that the accounting cost of producing a watch is 300 rubles. If the demand schedule for these watches were as given in the table below, what turnover tax rate would be placed on watches? (a) 33⅓%) (b) 66⅔%; (c) 100%; (d) 133⅓%.

Price, rubles	Quantity demanded
700	85,000
600	90,000
500	100,000
400	120,000
300	150,000
200	190,000
100	240,000

7. In the late 1960s the Soviet government undertook a number of economic reforms. These include: (a) the abolition of central planning; (b) the introduction of a modified profit motive; (c) the return of public property to private ownership; (d) the reduction of the autonomy of the managers of individual enterprises.

8. In comparing the composition of GNP in the U.S.S.R. and the United States it can be said that: (a) over 25% of the GNP in the United States is devoted to capital goods while less than 20% is so devoted in the U.S.S.R.; (b) government in the U.S.S.R. absorbs over 20% and in the United States absorbs less than 10% of the GNP; (c) over 75% of the GNP in both nations is represented by consumer goods; (d) investment in the U.S.S.R. is over one-half again as large a percentage of the GNP as it is in the United States.

9. Which of the following is *not* a significant factor in explaining the rapid rate of economic growth in the Soviet Union? (a) extensive investment by foreigners in the Soviet economy; (b) high levels of domestic investment in basic industries; (c) adoption of the advanced technological methods employed in Western nations; (d) the reallocation of labor from the agricultural to the industrial sector of the economy.

10. Which of the following is apt to make it difficult for the Soviet Union to sustain its current rate of economic growth? (a) expanded commercial relations with capitalistic nations; (b) conditions in the agricultural sector of the economy; (c) a reduction in its military expenditures; (d) an increase in the size of the labor force.

■ **DISCUSSION QUESTIONS**

1. What are the two principal economic institutions of the U.S.S.R.? How do these institutions compare with the economic institutions of the United States?

2. What is the basic planning problem in the U.S.S.R.? What techniques are used to overcome this problem and make central planning workable?

3. How is an economic plan drawn up in the

Soviet Union? How is such a plan made "realistic and workable"? Why is the process of obtaining the final plan referred to as a "down-and-up evolution"?

4. What means and agencies are used in the Soviet Union to facilitate the achievement of the objectives of the economic plan? What types of incentives and inducements are offered to encourage the achievement of these objectives?

5. What is meant by the priority principle of resource allocation? What sectors of the Soviet economy have received high priorities in the past?

6. Explain the role *Gosbank* plays in the enforcement of the central economic plan in the U.S.S.R.

7. What functions do prices perform in the U.S.S.R.? How does the Russian government use the turnover tax to set the prices of consumer goods?

8. Plants and firms in the U.S.S.R. can earn profits or suffer losses just as plants and firms can in the United States. What role do profits and losses play in the U.S.S.R. and what role do they play in the United States?

9. How is the turnover tax used in the Soviet Union to match the quantities demanded of various consumer goods with the quantities of these goods which *Gosplan* has decided to produce?

10. What microeconomic problems did the Soviet government encounter and what reforms did they introduce in an attempt to resolve these problems? What role did Professor Liberman play in these reforms?

11. Compare the GNP of the Soviet Union and the United States with respect to size, composition, and rate of growth.

12. Why has it been possible for the U.S.S.R. to achieve economic growth? Why is economic growth in the Soviet Union called "forced economic growth"?

13. What have been the major accomplishments of central planning in the U.S.S.R.? What are its chief shortcomings?

14. Explain the convergence hypothesis. What evidence is there in the U.S. and in the U.S.S.R. to support this hypothesis? Why may the tendency toward convergence be more apparent than real?

Answers

CHAPTER 1

Fill-in questions

1. production, exchange, consumption

2. generalizations, abstraction

3. economics is not a laboratory science and economics deals with the behavior of human beings

4. control economic events

5. economic growth, full employment, price stability, economic freedom, equitable distribution of income, economic security

6. *a.* a clear statement of the objectives and goals of the policy; *b.* a statement and analysis of all possible alternative solutions to the problem; *c.* an evaluation of the results of the policy selected after it has been put into operation

7. *a.* failure to distinguish between relevant and irrelevant facts; *b.* failure to recognize economic models for what they are—useful first approximations; *c.* tendency to impute ethical or moral qualities to economic models

8. the economy may be in a different phase of the business cycle

9. employ two different terms to mean the same thing

CHAPTER 2

Fill-in questions

1. *a.* society's material wants are unlimited; *b.* economic resources, which are the ultimate means

10. total, general, individual industry, particular product

Problems and projects

1. An increase in the demand for an economic good will cause the price of that good to rise.

2. All the factors are relevant to some *degree.* However, the degree of relevance of the factors varies; and, depending upon the degree of abstraction and generality desired in the analysis of the production and the price of automobiles, the factors may be included or excluded from consideration. The noneconomic factors are *c* (political), *i* (sociological), *k* (ecological), *l* (psychological), and *m* (political).

5. *a.* The validity of the statement depends upon the phase of the business cycle; *b.* the fallacy of composition; *c.* dual terminology; *d.* the *post hoc, ergo propter hoc* fallacy.

6. *a.* direct, up; *b.* inverse, down; *c.* (1) are, is not, (2) coincidental, incomes (standard of living, or some other such answer).

Self-test

1. F; 2. T; 3. T; 4. T; 5. T; 6. F; 7. F; 8. F; 9. F; 10. F

1. *b;* 2. *c;* 3. *a;* 4. *a;* 5. *d;* 6. *b;* 7. *a;* 8. *d;* 9. *a;* 10. *b*

of satisfying these wants, are scarce in relation to these wants

2. *a.* property resources; (1) land or raw materials,

(2) capital; b. human resources; (1) labor, (2) entrepreneurial ability

3. rental income, interest income, wages, profits

4. the social science concerned with the problem of using or administering scarce resources to attain maximum fulfillment of unlimited wants

5. a. the economy is operating at full employment and full production; b. the available supplies of the factors of production are fixed; c. technology does not change during the course of the analysis; d. the economy produces only two products

6. directly, indirectly

7. a. fewer, more; b. unemployed, underemployed; c. more, more; d. increase resource supplies, improve its technology

8. less

9. economic resources are not completely adaptable between alternate uses

10. a. determination of what is to be produced; b. determination of how the total output should be produced; c. determination of distribution of total output; d. determination of the extent of resource use; e. determination of provisions for flexibility and adaptability to change

11. opportunity cost

12. full employment, full production

13. values (or goals or priorities), nonscientific (or moral or subjective)

14. goals, institutions, organizations, pure (or laissez faire) capitalism, communism

Problems and projects

1. a. land; b. C; c. land; d. C; e. EA; f. land; g. C; h. C; i. labor; j. EA

2. b. 1, 2, 3, 4, 5, 6, 7

4. a. DEP; b. CAP; c. CAP; d. CAP; e. CAP; f. CAP; g. DEP; h. DEP; i. DEP; j. DEP; k. CAP; l. DEP

Self-test

1. T; 2. T; 3. F; 4. F; 5. T; 6. T; 7. F; 8. T; 9. T; 10. F

1. d; 2. b; 3. c; 4. b; 5. b; 6. d; 7. a; 8. c; 9. d; 10. d

CHAPTER 3

Fill-in questions

1. private property

2. enterprise, choice

3. do what is best for itself, competition

4. a. large numbers of independently acting buyers and sellers operating in the markets; b. freedom of those buyers and sellers to enter or leave these markets

5. control price

6. price, market

7. innovators, profit

8. the extensive use of capital, specialization, the use of money

9. interdependent, exchange (trade)

10. medium of exchange

11. coincidence of wants

12. product, resource

13. generally acceptable by sellers in exchange

14. the prices received for resources, the amount of resources sold, the prices received for products, the amounts sold

15. efficient

Problems and projects

1. a. (1) 4, (2) ½; b. (1) 5, (2) ⅓; c. (1) 8, (2) 2; d. (1) 15, (2) 3; e. Brobdingnag, Lilliput; f. bananas, apples; g. 2, 3, ⅓, ½; h. 69, 18, (1) 75, 20, (2) 6, 2

2. a. (1) ⅔, (2) 1½; b. (1) ½, (2) 2; c. (1) Schaffner, ½, ⅔; (2) Hart, 1½, 2; d. 60, 50, 10 pairs of trousers; e. ½, ⅔, 1½, 2

3. a. goods and services; b. expenditures for goods and services; c. money income payments (wages, rent, interest, and profit) d. services of resources (land, labor, capital, and entrepreneurial ability)

Self-test

1. F; 2. T; 3. T; 4. F; 5. T; 6. T; 7. F; 8. T; 9. F; 10. F

1. c; 2. c; 3. c; 4. a; 5. a; 6. d; 7. c.

CHAPTER 4

Fill-in questions

1. business firms, households; demand decisions of households, supply decisions of business firms

2. vertical, horizontal

3. indirect, direct

4. a. the tastes or preferences of consumers; b. the number of consumers in the market; c. the money income of consumers; d. the prices of related goods; e. consumer expectations with respect to future prices and incomes

5. smaller, less

6. inferior, normal (superior)

7. complementary, substitute

8. demand for, a change in the quantity demanded of the product

9. *a.* the technique of production; *b.* resource prices; *c.* prices of other goods; *d.* price expectations; *e.* the number of sellers in the market; *f.* taxes and subsidies

10. increase, decrease

11. quality demanded and quantity supplied are equal

12. below, shortage, rise

13. *a.* +, +; *b.* –, +; *c.* –, –; *d.* +, –; *e.* ?, +; *f.* +, ?; *g.* ?, –; *h.* –, ?

14. rationing

15. other things being equal

16. surplus, shortage

Problems and projects

2. Total: 5, 9, 17, 27, 39

3. Each quantity in column 3 is greater than in column 2, and each quantity in column 4 is less than in column 2.

4. *a.* 30, 4. *b.* (1) 20, 7; (2) inferior; (3) normal (superior)

5. *a.* complementary; *b.* substitute

6. *a.* 6.60; *b.* 25; *d.* surplus, 20

7. 45,000; 33,000; 22,500; 13,500; 6,000; 0

8. *a.* 0.95, 1.00; *b.* 31,000, 33,000; *c.* shortage, 28,500

9. *a.* decrease demand, decrease price; *b.* decrease supply, increase price; *c.* decrease supply, increase price; *d.* increase demand, increase price; *e.* decrease supply, increase price; *f.* increase demand, increase price; *g.* increase supply, decrease price; *h.* decrease demand, decrease price; *i.* increase demand, increase price; *j.* decrease supply, increase price

Self-test

1. F; **2.** F; **3.** F; **4.** F; **5.** T; **6.** F; **7.** F; **8.** F; **9.** F; **10.** T

1. *a;* **2.** *b;* **3.** *b;* **4.** *a;* **5.** *c;* **6.** *d;* **7.** *a;* **8.** *c;* **9.** *d;* **10.** *b*

CHAPTER 5

Fill-in questions

1. communicating, coordinating

2. maximizes the satisfaction received from its income

3. resources are scarce, substitutes

4. it is payment which must be made to a business‑man or entrepreneur to retain his services

5. enter, fall, larger, larger; fall, zero

6. *a.* determination of money incomes; *b.* determination of product prices

7. *a.* is the price system adaptable to change; *b.* is the price system conducive to change

8. artificial barriers

9. profits, borrowed funds

10. private, public (or social), invisible hand

11. it leads to an efficient allocation of resources; it emphasizes personal freedom

12. *a.* it is irksome to individual producers, technological advance contributes to its decline; *b.* (1) unequal; (2) costs, benefits, social; (3) immobile; (4) continuous full employment

Problems and projects

1. $6, –$5; $10; *a.* C; *b.* produce A and have an economic profit of $14; *c.* it would increase

2. *a.* method 2; *b.* 15; *c.* (1) 13, 8; 3, 4, 2, 4; (2) 15, 4

Selt-test

1. T; **2.** T; **3.** T; **4.** T; **5.** T; **6.** T; **7.** T; **8.** F; **9.** T; **10.** T

1. *b;* **2.** *b;* **3.** *c;* **4.** *d;* **5.** *d;* **6.** *c;* **7.** *a;* **8.** *a;* **9.** *c;* **10.** *b*

CHAPTER 6

Fill-in questions

1. market, planned

2. *a.* provide legal foundation and social environment; *b.* maintain competition; *c.* redistribute income and wealth; *d.* reallocate resources; *e.* stabilize the economy

3. *a.* regulate, natural; *b.* ownership of; *c.* antitrust (antimonopoly)

4. inequality; *a.* public assistance (welfare); *b.* direct market; *c.* income

5. *a.* demand; *b.* supply; *c.* benefit, cost

6. spillover costs, spillover benefits

7. people other than the buyers and sellers

8. *a.* over, cost, benefit; *b.* under, marginal benefit, marginal cost

9. *a.* (1) enact legislation, (2) pass special taxes; *b.* (1) subsidize production, (2) take over the production of the product

10. exclusion, spillover

11. taxing, spends the revenue to buy

12. *a.* increases, increasing, decreasing; *b.* decreases, decreasing, increasing

13. stabilizing the economy

14. public goods, private goods

15. *a.* estimate; *b.* output and price level, distribution

16. public sector failure

17. *a.* special interests; *b.* clear, hidden; *c.* select; *d.* incentives, test

18. public choice

19. *a.* private sector; *b.* imperfect; *c.* assigned

20. limited decisions

Problems and projects

1. *a.* reallocates resources; *b.* redistributes in-come; *c.* provides a legal foundation and social environment *and* stabilizes the economy; *d.* reallocates resources; *e.* maintains competition; *f.* provides a legal foundation and social environment *and* maintains competition; *g.* reallocates income; *h.* reallocates resources; *i.* provides a legal foundation and social environment; *j.* reallocates income

2. *a.* p_2, p_1; *b.* p_2, p_1; *c.* optimum, p_e

3. *a.* a supply curve to the left of (or above) the one shown should be drawn in, (1) decreases, increases, (2) greater; *b.* a demand curve to the right of (or above) the one shown should be drawn in, (1) increases, increases, (2) less

4. *a.* marginal cost: $500, $180, $80, $100; marginal benefit: $650, $100, $50, $25; *b.* yes; *c.* (1) 2, (2) $500, (3) $650, (4) $150

Self-test

1. F; **2.** F; **3.** F; **4.** F; **5.** T; **6.** T; **7.** F; **8.** T; **9.** T; **10.** T; **11.** F; **12.** F; **13.** T; **14.** F; **15.** F; **16.** T; **17.** F; **18.** F; **19.** T; **20.** F

1. *a;* **2.** *a;* **3.** *b;* **4.** *a;* **5.** *d;* **6.** *c;* **7.** *b;* **8.** *c;* **9.** *a;* **10.** *d;* **11.** *b;* **12.** *a*

CHAPTER 7

Fill-in questions

1. seventy-four, furnish resources, buy the bulk of the total output of the economy

2. seventy-six

3. composition of national output, level

4. contribution of resources

5. personal consumption, personal saving, personal taxes

6. fourteen, Federal, income

7. services, nondurable goods, durable goods

8. security, speculation

9. 13½, sole proprietorship, corporation

10. unlimited, limited

11. *a.* CORP; *b.* PRO and PART; *c.* PRO; *d.* CORP; *e.* CORP; *f.* CORP; *g.* PART; *h.* PART; *i.* CORP

12. manufacturing

13. few, large, manufacturing, agriculture

14. *a.* desire to achieve greater productive efficiency; *b.* seeking of power and prestige; *c.* se-curity and insurance of long-run survival; *d.* seeking of greater financial rewards

15. internal growth, combination, combination

16. *a.* technology; *b.* efficient, monopoly

Problems and projects

1. 76.3, 6.9, 8.3, 6.8, 1.7

3. *a.* Firms *a, b, c, d,* and *f* are in wholesale and retail trade; firms *b, g, h, i,* and *j* are in manu-facturing; firms *h* and *i* are in mining; firm *e* is in transportation, communications, and public utilities; *b.* the Aluminum Company of America is engaged in the production of primary aluminum and the General Electric Company produces both locomotives (and parts) and electric lamps (bulbs)

Self-test

1. F; **2.** T; **3.** T; **4.** T; **5.** T; **6.** T; **7.** T; **8.** F; **9.** T; **10.** F; **11.** T; **12.** F; **13.** T; **14.** F; **15.** T

1. *c;* **2.** *a;* **3.** *d;* **4.** *b;* **5.** *d;* **6.** *b;* **7.** *a;* **8.** *a;* **9.** *c;* **10.** *b;* **11.** *d;* **12.** *a;* **13.** *a;* **14.** *b;* **15.** *b*

CHAPTER 8

Fill-in questions

1. taxation, expenditures

2. voluntary, compulsory

3. money expenditures for which government currently receives no products or services in return

4. private, social, composition

5. personal income, payroll, income security and health, national defense

6. corporate profits are taxed and then the dividends paid out of these profits are taxed as personal income

7. sales, excise, education, highways

8. property, education

9. tax-exempt securities, the capital gains tax

10. revenue sharing

11. benefits-received, ability-to-pay

12. constant, increasing, decreasing

13. *a.* P; *b.* R; *c.* R; *d.* R; *e.* P

14. *a.* the persons upon whom it is levied; *b.* those who buy the taxed product; *c.* either the firm or its customers; *d.* owners when they occupy their own residences, tenants who rent residences from the owners, consumers who buy the products produced on business property

CHAPTER 9

Fill-in questions

1. level of production in the economy and the long-run course the economy has been following, public policies to improve the performance of the economy

2. market prices

3. the price level changes

4. double counting

5. value added

6. the market value of the final product

7. purely financial

8. nonincome

9. all final purchases of machinery, tools, and equipment by business firms; all construction; changes in inventories; the capital consumption allowance

10. expanding, static

11. supplements; social insurance programs; private pension, health and welfare funds

12. corporation income taxes, dividends, undistributed corporate profits

13. make allowance for that part of this year's output which is necessary to replace the capital goods consumed in the year's production

14. the capital consumption allowance

15. indirect business taxes; earned

16. *a.* old age and survivors' insurance and unemployment compensation insurance payments; *b.* relief payments; *c.* veterans' payments; *d.* private pension and welfare payments; *e.* interest payments made by government and consumers

17. transfer payments, social security contribu-

15. *a.* regressive; *b.* progressive; *c.* proportional; *d.* progressive

Problems and projects

1. tax: $520, $770, $1,060, $1,400, $1,800. $2,270; average tax rate: 20.8%, 22%, 23.6%, 25.5%, 27.7%, 30.3%

2. Tax A: average tax rate: 3, 3, 3, 3, 3, 3, 3; type of tax: proportional. Tax B: average tax rate: 1, 2, 3, 3, 2.5, 2, 2; type of tax: combination. Tax C: average tax rate: 10, 9, 8, 7, 6, 5, 4; type of tax: regressive

3. *a.* $200, $232, $264, $296, $328, $360; *b.* 4%, 3.87%, 3.77%, 3.70%, 3.66%, 3.6%; *c.* regressive

4. *a.* −400, 400, 2400, 4200, 7500; *b.* −20, 10, 24, 28, 30; *c.* progressive, increases

Self-test

1. T; **2.** F; **3.** F; **4.** F; **5.** F; **6.** F; **7.** F; **8.** T; **9.** F; **10.** T

1. *c;* **2.** *a;* **3.** *a;* **4.** *a;* **5.** *d;* **6.** *b;* **7.** *c;* **8.** *a;* **9.** *a;* **10.** *c*

tions, undistributed corporate profits, corporation income taxes; personal consumption expenditures, personal saving, personal taxes

18. personal taxes; personal consumption expenditures, personal saving

19. personal consumption expenditures

20. private business firms, consumers, governments

Problems and projects

1. *a.* (1) price index (1967 = 100): 100, 122, 67, 78, 89; (2) price index (1975 = 100): 113, 138, 75, 88, 100. *b.* (1) adjusted GNP in 1967 dollars (billions): 90, 98.4, 89.6, 83.3, 78.7; (2) adjusted GNP in 1975 dollars (billions): 79.6, 87, 80, 73.9, 70

2. *a.* 23 billion; *b.* 445 billion; *c.* 426 billion; *d.* 361 billion; *e.* 324 billion; *f.* 14 billion

3. See table on page 362. All figures are in billions of dollars.

4. *a.* personal income and disposable income, a public transfer payment; *b.* none; a second-hand sale; *c.* all, represents investment (additions to inventories); *d.* all; *e.* none, a purely financial transaction; *f.* all; *g.* none, a nonmarket transaction; *h.* all; *i.* none, a private transfer payment; *j.* all; *k.* none, a nonmarket transaction; *l.* all; *m.* all, represents additions to the inventory of the retailer; *n.* personal income and disposable income, a public transfer payment; *o.* all; estimate of rental value of owner-occupied homes is included in rents

Self-test

1. F; **2.** F; **3.** T; **4.** T; **5.** F; **6.** T; **7.** F; **8.** F; **9.** T; **10.** T

1. *b;* **2.** *d;* **3.** *d;* **4.** *b;* **5.** *a;* **6.** *c;* **7.** *c;* **8.** *a;* **9.** *a;* **10.** *d*

Income method		Expenditures method	
Gross National Product			
(1) Compensation of employees	$238	(1) Personal consumption expenditures	$217
(2) Rents	9		
(3) Interest	6	(2) Government expenditures for goods and services	71
(4) Proprietors' income	21		
(5) Dividends	13	(3) Gross private domestic investment	56
(6) Corporate income taxes	15		
(7) Undistributed corporate profits	14	(4) Net exports	5
(8) Indirect business taxes	11		$349
(9) Capital consumption allowance	22		
	$349		
Net National Product			
(1) Compensation of employees	$238	(1) Personal consumption expenditures	$217
(2) Rents	9		
(3) Interest	6	(2) Government expenditures for goods and services	71
(4) Proprietors' income	21		
(5) Dividends	13	(3) Net private domestic investment	34
(6) Corporate income taxes	15	(4) Net exports	5
(7) Undistributed corporate profits	14		$327
(8) Indirect business taxes	11		
	$327		
National Income			
(1) Compensation of employees	$238	(1) Net national product	$327
(2) Rents	9	(2) Less: indirect business taxes	11
(3) Interest	6		$316
(4) Proprietors' income	21		
(5) Dividends	13		
(6) Corporate income taxes	15		
(7) Undistributed corporate profits	14		
	$316		
Personal Income			
(1) National income	$316	(1) Personal consumption expenditures	$217
(2) Plus: transfer payments	26		
(3) Less: social security contributions	7	(2) Personal saving	34
(4) Less: corporate income taxes	15	(3) Personal taxes	55
(5) Less: undistributed corporate profits	14		$306
	$306		
Disposable Income			
(1) Personal income	$306	(1) Personal consumption expenditures	$217
(2) Less: personal taxes	55		
	$251	(2) Personal saving	34
			$251

CHAPTER 10

Fill-in questions

1. total spending (demand)
2. larger, more, increases, increase
3. premature, pure
4. 96, cyclical, frictional, structural
5. potential, actual

6. rising general level of prices, falling general level of prices

7. money income, the prices which he must pay for the goods and services he purchases

8. The following is a partial answer. Inflation: hurt—savers, creditors, fixed-income groups; benefit—debtors, some profit receivers, some wage earners. Deflation: hurt—debtors, some profit receivers, wage earners who lose their jobs; benefit—savers, creditors, fixed-income groups

9. 2, 4

10. prosperity, recession, depression, recovery; expansion, contraction, upswing, downswing

11. seasonal variations, secular trends

12. capital and durable, nondurable, low

13. increased, declined, fairly stable, the worst inflation in two decades

14. *a.* inflation, unemployment; *b.* stagflation; *c.* New Economic, decrease, controls

15. *a.* worldwide agricultural shortfalls and rising foreign incomes; *b.* rising crude oil prices; *c.* devaluation of the dollar; *d.* wage- and price-push pressures; *e.* internalization of spillover costs

16. *a.* recession, cost, supply; *b.* a decline in output and a rise in unemployment

17. investment, money, cumulative

18. *a.* the existence of "built-in stabilizers"; *b.* an improved banking and financial system; *c.* the changes in the occupational structure of the labor

force; *d.* the expansion of the public sector; *e.* the increase in economic knowledge

Problems and projects

1. The following figures complete the table. 1974: 5,076, 94.4, 5.6; 1975: 7,830, 91.5, 8.5; 1976: 7,288, 92.3, 7.7; *a.* the labor force increased more than employment increased; *b.* because unemployment and employment in relative terms are percentages of the labor force and *always* add to 100%, if one increases the other must decrease; *c.* no, because unemployment was greater than the 4% considered normal; *d.* because the number of people looking for jobs expands

2. *a.* B, B, B, A; *b.* B, B, B, B; *c.* C, A, A, C

3. *a.* D, B; *b.* I, I; *c.* B, D; *d.* D, B; *e.* D, B; *f.* D, B; *g.* I, I; *h.* D, B

4. *a.* $2,520, $2,646; *b.* $48, $74

5. *a.* 5 years, 10 months; *b.* 7 years, 10 years

6. *a.* equal, the national output demanded and supplied at the equilibrium price level; *b.* (1) increase, (2) demand-pull; *c.* (1) rise, fall, (2) stagflation (inflation that results from cost or supply considerations)

Self-test

1. T; **2.** T; **3.** F; **4.** F; **5.** T; **6.** F; **7.** T; **8.** F; **9.** T; **10.** F; **11.** F; **12.** F

1. *d;* **2.** *c;* **3.** *b;* **4.** *b;* **5.** *d;* **6.** *b;* **7.** *c;* **8.** *a;* **9.** *d;* **10.** *a;* **11.** *d;* **12.** *d*

CHAPTER 11

Fill-in questions

1. closed economy, personal, neither taxes nor spends; *a.* net national product, national income, personal income, disposable income; *b.* consumption, investment

2. Say's Law, price-wage flexibility

3. demand for these goods and services

4. the rate of interest

5. decrease, increase; stabilize

6. decrease; unemployment; down, increase; all who are willing to work at the going wage rate are employed, and total output equals total spending

7. different groups, different reasons, accumulated money balances, commercial banks

8. it does not exist in the degree necessary for ensuring the restoration of full employment in the face of a decline in total spending, lower money incomes, reductions in total spending, lower prices

9. composition

10. *a.* directly, total spending (aggregate demand); *b.* disposable income; *c.* directly

11. consumption

12. increase, decrease

13. *a.* stocks of liquid assets which households have on hand; *b.* the stock of durable goods consumers have on hand; *c.* expectations; *d.* the current volume of consumer credit outstanding; *e.* attitudes toward thrift; *f.* taxation of consumer income

14. the amount consumers will consume (save) will be different at every level of income, the level of income has changed and that consumers will change their consumption (saving) as a result

15. capital goods; *a.* expected, profits; *b.* interest

16. greater

17. inverse; *a.* decrease; *b.* increase

18. *a.* the cost of acquiring, maintaining, and operating the capital goods; *b.* business taxes; *c.* technological change; *d.* the stock of capital goods on hand; *e.* expectations

19. stable, unstable

20. durability, irregularity, variability

Problems and projects

1. saving:−1, 0, 1, 3, 5, 8, 11, 15; APC: 100.3%, 100%, 99.7%, 99.2%, 98.7%, 98%, 97.3%, 96.4%; APS: −0.3%, 0, 0.3%, 0.8%, 1.3%, 2%, 2.7%, 3.6%; MPC: 90%, 90%, 80%, 80%, 70%, 70%, 60%; MPS: 10%, 10%, 20%, 20%, 30%, 30%, 40%

2. *a.* −; *b.* −; *c.* +; *d.* +; *e.* +; *f.* none; *g.* −; *h.* −

3. *a.* 0, 1; *b.* 2, 3; *c.* 3, 6; *d.* 10, 15, 21, 28, 36, 45; *f.* inverse, (1) decrease, (2) increase; *g.* (1) lower, (2) raise; *h.* investment-demand

4. *a.* +; *b.* −; *c.* +; *d.* +; *e.* −; *f.* −; *g.* −; *h.* +; *i.* −

5. *a.* investment; *b.* constant (given); *c.* (1) independent (unrelated), (2) directly

Self-test

1. F; **2.** F; **3.** T; **4.** T; **5.** F; **6.** F; **7.** T; **8.** T; **9.** F; **10.** T

1. *c;* **2.** *a;* **3.** *a;* **4.** *b;* **5.** *b;* **6.** *c;* **7.** *d;* **8.** *d;* **9.** *d;* **10.** *b*

CHAPTER 12

Fill-in questions

1. aggregate demand–aggregate supply, leakages-injections

2. aggregate demand

3. consumption, net investment

4. *a.* saving, net investment; *b.* (1) taxes, imports; (2) government expenditures, exports

5. *a.* less, disinvestment, rise; *b.* greater, investment, fall; *c.* equal to, zero, neither rise nor fall

6. realized (actual), realized (actual): *a.* (1) disinvestment, (2) rise, the multiplier; *b.* (1) investment, (2) fall, $5 times the multiplier

7. greater, increase, remain constant, increase, remain constant, inflation

8. 1/MPS, 1/(1 − MPC); the economy is characterized by repetitive, continuous flows of expenditures and income; any change in income will cause changes in both consumption and saving to vary in the same direction as, and by a fraction of, the change in income

9. decrease, decrease, remain constant, paradox of thrift

10. less, increase, the multiplier

11. inflationary, aggregate demand, the amount by which equilibrium NNP exceeds the full-employment noninflationary NNP

12. *a.* demand-pull (pure); *b.* premature

Problems and projects

1. *a.* 10, 12, 14, 16, 18, 20, 22, 24, 26, 28, 30; *b. I:* 22, 22, 22, 22, 22, 22, 22, 22, 22, 22, 22; *C + I:* 312, 320, 328, 336, 344, 352, 360, 368, 376, 384, 392; *UI:* −12, −10, −8, −6, −4, −2, 0, 2, 4, 6, 8; *c.* 360; *d.* 0.80, 0.20; *e.* 5; *f.* increase, 3, increase, 15; *g.* decrease, 4, decrease, 20

2. change in income: $8.00, $6.40, $5.12, $4.10, $16.38, $50.00; change in consumption: $8.00, $6.40, $5.12, $4.10, $3.28, $13.10, $40.00; change in saving: $2.00, $1.60, $1.28, $1.02, $0.82, $3.28, $10.00

3. *a.* 350, 15; *b.* 0.20, 5; *c.* 10, 20; *d.* 10; *e.* (1) decrease, 340, 15; (2) decrease, 330, 13; (3) decrease, decrease, leave unchanged the amount of, paradox of thrift; (4) multiplier

4. *a.* 2½; *b.* 620, 30, inflationary, 12; *c.* 570, 20, recessionary, 8

Self-test

1. F; **2.** F; **3.** T; **4.** T; **5.** T; **6.** T; **7.** F; **8.** T; **9.** F; **10.** F

1. *c;* **2.** *d;* **3.** *a;* **4.** *c;* **5.** *b;* **6.** *a;* **7.** *b;* **8.** *b;* **9.** *a;* **10.** *b*

CHAPTER 13

Fill-in questions

1. it intensifies both inflation and contraction (tax receipts tend to decrease and expenditures to increase during inflation while taxes tend to increase and expenditures to decrease during depression)

2. recession, inflation, the upswing and downswing of the cycle may not be of equal magnitude and duration

3. full employment without inflation, deficits, public debt

4. Employment, 1946; Council of Economic Advisors, Joint Economic Committee

5. marginal propensity to consume, marginal propensity to save

6. *a.* consumption, investment, government expenditures for goods and services; *b.* saving, taxes, investment, government expenditures for goods and services

7. decrease, the decrease in taxes or in government spending

8. decreased, increased, increased, decreased

9. deficit, surplus

10. *a.* taxes, transfer payments; *b.* increase, decrease

11. built-in; *a.* increase, increase, decrease; *b.* decrease, increase, decrease

12. *a.* assuring full employment without inflation; *b.* fiscal drag; *c.* countercyclical

13. employment, full employment

14. *a.* budget surplus or deficit, full employment; *b.* expansionary, contractionary

15. borrowing from the public, issuing new money; latter, financing in this manner will avoid the crowding-out effect upon investment which borrowing from the public may have

16. 5, 4

17. regressive

18. recognition, administrative, operational

19. internally

20. 37, 2

21. the goods and services that could not be produced because of the production of war goods

22. increases, borrowed, spent

23. government; *a.* decrease; *b.* increase

24. incentives, crowding-out, income inequality, monetary policy

25. highly liquid and virtually riskless securities for small and conservative investors, cyclical downswings, monetary

Problems and projects

1. *a.* *C'*: 316, 325, 334, 343, 352, 361, 370, 379, 388, 397, 406, 415, 424; *S'*: 24, 25, 26, 27, 28, 29, 30, 31, 32, 33, 34, 35, 36; *S' + T*: 34, 35, 36, 37, 38, 39, 40, 41, 42, 43, 44, 45, 46. *b.* *I + G*: 35, 35, 35, 35, 35, 35, 35, 35, 35, 35, 35, 35, 35; *C' + I + G*: 351, 360, 369, 378, 387, 396, 405, 414, 423, 432, 441, 450, 459. *d.* 360. *e.* 100. *f.* 90. *g.* increase, $10

2. *a.* (1) increase, $10, (2) decrease, $20, (3) direct; *b.* (1) $100, (2) increase, (3) less, (4) lessened; *c.* (1) $5, (2) decrease, (3) less, (4) lessened, more; *d.* (1) government expenditures are $200 at all NNPs, governemnt surplus: −40, −30, −20, −10, 0, 10, 20, 30, 40, (2) $30, (3) deficit, $20, (4) expansionary, recession, (5) deficit, $40, (6) deficit, $50

3. *a.* (1) −, −, −; (2) +, +, +; (3) +, +, +; (4) −, −, −; (5) +, +, +. *b.* (1) +, 0, 0; (2) +, 0, 0; (3) +, 0, 0; (4) −, −, −; (5) −, −, −

Self-test

1. T; **2.** T; **3.** T; **4.** T; **5.** F; **6.** T; **7.** F; **8.** T; **9.** F; **10.** F; **11.** T; **12.** F; **13.** T; **14.** F; **15.** T; **16.** F; **17.** T; **18.** T

1. *a;* **2.** *c;* **3.** *b;* **4.** *b;* **5.** *a;* **6.** *b;* **7.** *a;* **8.** *b;* **9.** *c;* **10.** *d;* **11.** *d;* **12.** *d;* **13.** *b;* **14.** *a;* **15.** *b;* **16.** *c;* **17.** *d;* **18.** *b*

CHAPTER 14

Fill-in questions

1. *a.* medium of exchange; *b.* standard of value; *c.* store of value

2. coins, paper money, demand deposits, banks, the Federal government

3. savings, time, thrift, savings bonds

4. M_1

5. *a.* indicates that the definition of money is somewhat arbitrary; *b.* their existence influences consuming-saving habits; *c.* conversion from near-money to money or from money to near-money may affect the stability of the economy; *d.* important when monetary policy is to be employed

6. commercial banks, the Federal Reserve Banks

7. it can be exchanged for goods and services which people desire; inversely, price level

8. *a.* set the discount rate; *b.* set the reserve ratio; *c.* open-market operations

9. Federal Open Market Committee, Federal Advisory Council

10. *a.* they are central banks; *b.* they are quasi-public banks; *c.* they are bankers' banks

11. it accepts deposits of banks, makes loans to banks

12. accept demand deposits, make loans, create money

13. *a.* savings, savings and loan, insurance; *b.* savers, investors; create, destroy

14. *a.* holding the deposits of member banks; *b.* supplying the economy with paper currency; *c.* providing for the collection of checks; *d.* acting as fiscal agents for the Federal government; *e.* supervising member banks; *f.* regulating the money supply; regulating the money supply

15. hold most of the treasury's checking accounts, aid the government in collecting taxes, administer sale and redemption of government bonds

Problems and projects

1. *a.* 79.0 (= 88.6 − 8.3 − 0.5 − 0.8); *b.* 304.4 (= 79.0 + 225.4); *c.* 1189.2 (= 304.4 + 884.8)

2. remained unchanged, changed to include $500 less in currency and $500 more in demand deposits

3. *a.* rise, 25; *b.* fall, 9.1

Self-test

1. F; **2.** F; **3.** T; **4.** F; **5.** T; **6.** T; **7.** F; **8.** T; **9.** T; **10.** T

1. *d;* **2.** *c;* **3.** *d;* **4.** *d;* **5.** *b;* **6.** *b;* **7.** *a;* **8.** *d;* **9.** *a;* **10.** *b*

CHAPTER 15

Fill-in questions

1. assets, liabilities, net worth
2. vault cash, till money
3. demand deposit; time deposit
4. Federal Reserve Bank in its district, deposit liabilities, reserve ratio
5. actual reserves, required reserves
6. fractional
7. not changed
8. decreased, increased; decreased, increased
9. excess reserves
10. increases, 10,000
11. decreases, 2,000
12. profits, liquidity (safety)
13. demand deposit (monetary) multiplier (reciprocal of the reserve ratio), reserves
14. smaller
15. decrease, 36 million

Problems and projects

1.

	(1)	(2)	(3)	(4)
Assets:				
Cash	$100	$100	$100	$100
Reserves	150	150	260	300
Loans	500	500	500	500
Securities	200	200	200	100

Liabilities:				
Demand deposits	850	850	960	900
Capital stock	100	100	100	100

2.

	(1a)	(2a)	(3a)	(4a)	(5a)
A. Required reserve	$35	$40	$30	$36	$44
B. Excess reserve	5	0	−5	4	1
C. New loans	5	0	*	4	1

* If an individual bank is $5 short of reserves it must either obtain additional reserves of $5 by selling loans, securities, or its own IOUs to the reserve bank or contract its loans by $25.

	(1b)	(2b)	(3b)	(4b)	(5b)
Assets:					
Cash	$ 10	$ 20	$20	$ 20	$ 15
Reserves	40	40	25	40	45
Loans	105	100	*	104	151
Securities	50	60	30	70	60
Liabilities:					
Demand deposits	180	200	*	184	221
Capital stock	25	20	25	50	50

* If an individual bank is $5 short of reserves it must either obtain additional reserves of $5 by selling loans, securities, or its own IOUs to the reserve bank or contract its loans by $25.

3. column 2: 8, 6, 5, 4, 3⅓, 3; column 3: 1, 1, 1, 1, 1, 1; column 4: 8, 6, 5, 4, 3⅓, 3

4.

	(1)	(2)	(3)	(4)	(5)	(6)
Assets:						
Cash	$ 50	$ 50	$ 50	$ 50	$ 50	$ 50
Reserves	105	105	108	108	110	110
Loans	200	220	200	240	200	250
Securities	200	200	192	192	200	200
Liabilities:						
Demand deposits	505	525	500	540	500	550
Capital stock	50	50	50	50	50	50
Loans from Federal Reserve	0	0	0	0	50	50
Excess reserves	4	0	8	0	10	10
Maximum possible expansion of the money supply	20	0	40	0	50	0

Self-test

1. F; 2. T; 3. F; 4. F; 5. T; 6. T; 7. F; 8. F; 9. F; 10. F; 11. T; 12. T; 13. T; 14. T; 15. F

1. c; 2. d; 3. b; 4. a; 5. b; 6. b; 7. d; 8. b; 9. b; 10. b

CHAPTER 16

Fill-in questions

1. a full-employment noninflationary level of total output; Board of Governors of the Federal Reserve, the Federal Reserve Banks

2. decrease, contract, rise, decline

3. securities, gold certificates, Federal Reserve Notes, reserves of member banks

4. the reserve ratio, the discount rate, open market operations

5. excess reserves, the multiple by which the banking system can lend

6. influence the ability of commercial banks to create money by lending, influence the rate of interest

7. 10 million, 10 million, 7.5 million; 0, 10 million, 10 million

8. securities held by the Federal Reserve Banks, loans to commercial banks by the Federal Reserve Banks

9. decrease, decrease, buy; increase, increase, sell

10. *a.* −; *b.* +; *c.* +

11. moral suasion, margin requirements, the terms of credit when consumers purchase certain durable goods and real estate

12. open-market operations

13. aggregate demand, consumption, investment, government expenditures for goods and services

14. *a.* net national product (or disposable income), consumption schedule; *b.* expected, profit, interest; *c.* public policy

15. fiscal, monetary

16. employment, the price level, microeconomic, noneconomic, size (quantity), coordinate

Problems and projects

1. Assets: securities, gold certificates, loans to member banks, cash; liabilities: Federal Reserve Notes, member bank reserves, Treasury deposits

2. *a.* (1) reduce, 20; (2) buy, 25; (3) decrease, 1; *b.* (1) increase, 28⁴⁄₇; (2) sell, 12½; (3) increase, 2½

3.

	(2)	(3)	(4)	(5)	(6)
Federal Reserve Banks					
Assets:					
Gold certificates	$ 25	$ 25	$ 25	$ 25	$ 25
Securities	27	34	30	30	30
Loans to commercial banks	10	10	10	10	4
Liabilities:					
Reserve of commercial banks	47	54	50	55	44
Treasury deposits	5	5	5	0	5
Federal Reserve Notes	10	10	10	10	10
Commercial Banks					
Assets:					
Reserves	$ 47	$ 54	$ 50	$ 55	$ 44
Securities	70	66	70	70	70
Loans	90	90	90	90	90
Liabilities:					
Demand deposits	197	200	200	205	200
Loans from Federal Reserve	10	10	10	10	4
A. Required reserves	49.25	50	40	51.25	50
B. Excess reserves	−2.25	4	10	3.75	−6
C. Initial change in the money supply	−3	0	0	+5	0
D. Total potential change in money supply	−12	+16	+50	+20	−24

4. *a.* (2) 850; *b.* 900; *c.* (1) 25, (2) 25, (3) 7; *d.* (1) 0.20, 5, (2) increase, 5, increase, 25

Self-test

1. F; **2.** T; **3.** F; **4.** T; **5.** F; **6.** T; **7.** T; **8.** T; **9.** F; **10.** F; **11.** F; **12.** F

1. *b;* **2.** *b;* **3.** *b;* **4.** *a;* **5.** *c;* **6.** *d;* **7.** *c;* **8.** *a;* **9.** *b;* **11.** *d;* **12.** *a*

CHAPTER 17

Fill-in questions

1. resources, income, stability, fiscal

2. efficiency, freedom, instability, monetary

3. $MV = PQ$; *a.* equation of exchange; *b.* (1) the money supply, (2) the income (circuit) velocity of money, (3) the average price of each unit of physical output, (4) the physical volume of goods and services produced

4. *a.* total spending (aggregate demand), *MV*; *b. PQ*

5. *a.* +, 0; *b.* +, +; *c.* 0, +

6. *a.* (1) fiscal, (2) reallocate, redistribute; *b.* (1) increase, crowding-out, (2) incentives, unneeded, private sector

7. real GNP, 3, 5

8. *a. PQ, M; b.* loose and uncertain

9. 5, 4, inverse

10. *a.* medium of exchange, transactions, money NNP, stable; *b.* store of value, speculative, interest rate, unstable

11. *a.* (1) more, (2) increase, (3) increase, (4) *P, Q*; *b.* (1) decrease, (2) increase, (3) decrease, (4) uncertain

12. *a.* increased; *b.* raises; *c.* reduces; *d.* increases

Problems and projects

1. *a.* (1) 100, 200, 300, 440, 625, 900, 960; *b.* (1) 200; *c.* (1) 200, (2) 1.00, (3) 200; *d.* 300, 300, 1.00, 300; *e.* 900, 1.50, 600; *f.* 960, 1.60, remain at 600

2. *a.* (1) 50, (2) 75, (3) 125, (4) equal to, (5) 4; *b.* (1) 60, 100, (2) 160, equal to, (3) 3.75; *c.* (1) 80, 80, 160, (2) 5; *d.* decrease, increase

Self-test

1. T; 2. T; 3. T; 4. T; 5. F; 6. F; 7. T; 8. T; 9. F; 10. F; 11. T; 12. T; 13. F; 14. T; 15. F

1. *b*; 2. *a*; 3. *b*; 4. *d*; 5. *c*; 6. *d*; 7. *a*; 8. *a*; 9. *d*; 10. *b*; 11. *d*; 12. *c*

CHAPTER 18

Fill-in questions

1. *a.* full employment; *b.* aggregate demand, demand-pull

2. *a.* before full employment is reached; *b.* business firms, labor unions, labor

3. *a.* price level, unemployment; *b.* negative; *c.* premature

4. market power, market power, less than full employment, something extra, higher prices

5. *a.* unit labor cost; *b.* the (money) wage rate; *c.* the productivity of labor; *d.* (1) increase, (2) decrease, (3) remain constant

6. inflation, unemployment

7. market, wage-price, left

8. *a.* manpower, bottlenecks; *b.* pro-competition, market power

9. *a.* antitrust (antimonopoly), tariffs; *b.* antitrust (antimonopoly), bargaining on a centralized nationwide level

10. *a.* incomes, the wages received and the prices paid determine real incomes; *b.* (1) guideposts, voluntary, (2) controls, law

11. productivity, unit labor costs

12. unworkable, enforce, allocation, freedom

13. *a.* shortage, black, ration; *b.* will not, under-

14. *a.* shifted, right; *b.* random, shocks; *c.* exist

15. taxes, military, unemployment, price; *a.* demand-pull; *b.* aggregate, fell, cost-push

16. *a.* a severe worldwide agricultural shortfall; *b.* worldwide shortages of certain strategic raw materials; *c.* devaluation of the dollar; *d.* the formation of OPEC

17. *a.* oil, income, reduce, cost-push; *b.* (1) *P, Q,* (2) *Q*

18. *a.* (1) labor force, (2) expectations, monetary, fiscal, manpower, wage-price; *b.* (1) does not exist, (2) vertical, greater, (3) increases

19. *a.* the U.S. is increasingly linked to the world economy and this growing international interdependence is an added source of macroeconomic instability; *b.* the distinction between demand-pull and cost-push inflation is critical for policy; *c.* management of aggregate demand may not be enough to achieve stability; *d.* structural-institutional changes may require changes in economic theory and policy

20. central (Federal) economic, Humphrey-Hawkins

Problems and projects

1. *a.* 7; *b.* 6; *c.* (it's your choice)

2. *a.* 4; *b.* (1) increase, increase, (2) decrease, decrease, (3) remain constant, remain constant; *c.* (1) remain constant, (2) increase, decrease, remain constant

3. *a.* (1) increase, decrease, (2) increase, decrease, 6, (3) 1, not changed; *b.* (1) profits, real wages, (2) 6, (3) third, inflation, unemployment; *c.* 3, 6; *d.* accelerates

Self-test

1. F; 2. T; 3. T; 4. T; 5. T; 6. F; 7. T; 8. F; 9. T;
10. T; 11. F; 12. F; 13. T; 14. F; 15. F; 16. F;
17. T; 18. T; 19. T; 20. F

1. *a;* 2. *d;* 3. *a;* 4. *c;* 5. *b;* 6. *a;* 7. *a;* 8. *a;* 9. *b;*
10. *d;* 11. *d;* 12. *d;* 13. *d;* 14. *a;* 15. *b;* 16. *b;*
17. *d;* 18. *d*

CHAPTER 19

Fill-in questions

1. fixed, changes (increases)

2. total real output, per capita real output

3. increases, decreases

4. $60, $36, $24

5. quantity and quality of natural resources, quantity and quality of human resources, the supply or stock of capital goods, technology, demand, allocative

6. 8

7. increase, decreasing

8. 10

9. average, decrease

10. optimum population

11. population, decrease

12. productivity

13. aggregate demand (or investment)

14. aggregate demand, productive capacity, capital-output ratio

15. reallocate

Problems and projects

1. *a.* 80, 120, 130, 70, 50, 30, 10, −10; *b.* third, fourth; *c.* positive, negative; *d.* 80, 100, 110, 100, 90, 80, 70, 60; *e.* increasing, decreasing; *f.* 3, average product, a maximum

2. *a.* 100; *b.* 100, 110, 120, 125, 120, 110, 100, 90; *c.* 25; *d.* capital, technology, labor; *e.* increased, 4; *f.* (1) increased, 120; (2) remained constant; (3) decreased to 90

3. *a.* (1) 1100, 1210; (2) consumption: 880, 968; saving: 220, 242; (3) investment: 220, 242; aggregate demand: 1100, 1210; *b.* (1) 10; (2) 10; *c.* (1) 0.8, constant; (2) 0.2, constant; (3) 5; *d.* 1050; (1) 5; (2) less than; (3) unemployment; *e.* 1150; (1) greater than, cannot; (2) inflation; *f.* increases

4. *a.* 270, 270; *b.* 90; *c.* 990, 297, 297, 99; *d.* 1089, 326.7, 326.7, 108.9; *e.* (1) investment; (2) average propensity to save, capital-output ratio; *f.* 2.5

Self-test

1. T; 2. F; 3. T; 4. F; 5. T; 6. T; 7. F; 8. F; 9. T;
10. F; 11. F; 12. T

1. *a;* 2. *d;* 3. *b;* 4. *a;* 5. *b;* 6. *c;* 7. *b;* 8. *c;* 9. *b;*
10. *b*

CHAPTER 20

Fill-in questions

1. *a.* 11; *b.* 2

2. 3.7%, 2.0%

3. quality, leisure, environment, life

4. natural resources

5. size of the population, health, education, training

6. production; investment

7. 30,000, three

8. GNP, slower

9. it must encourage those changes in products, productive techniques, and capital facilities vital to economic growth; it must provide a mechanism which will efficiently reallocate resources in a way appropriate to these changes; price system

10. 45; improved training and education, improved technology, improved resource allocation

11. pollutes, domestic problems, anxiety, insecurity, good life

12. benefits, costs, pollution, equitable, income, a better life

13. *a.* population, natural resources, pollution, food output per capita, industrial output per capita; *b.* 100, population, industrial output (or capacity)

14. zero population growth, zero economic growth

15. unrealistic, technological progress, feedback

Problems and projects

1. *a.* $300, 400, 500, 550, 600, 550, 500; *b.* 150 million; *c.* (1) $15 billion; (2) $100; *d.* (1) 46⅔%; (2) 9.1%

2. *a.* $200.0, 210.0, 242.0, 266.2; *b.* 5%, less, aggregate demand did not increase by enough to induce the economy to produce at capacity; *c.* (1) $10; (2) 4.5%; *d.* (1) $22; (2) $55; (3) more; (4) 15.2%; (5) rise, aggregate demand in constant dollars was greater than the constant dollar productive

capacity; (6) by having idle productive capacity in year 2; *e.* (1) greater, equal to; (2) fall; (3) would

3. *a.* (1) increased, increasing; (2) decreased, increasing; *b.* (1) decrease; (2) pollution, decrease; (3) natural resources; *c.* population, industrial output

CHAPTER 21

Fill-in questions

1. poverty (i.e., a low standard of living)

2. Asia, South America, Africa, ⅔

3. Third World, 50, 12, 1.5

4. supplies of natural resources, human resources, capital goods; technology

5. natural resources

6. *a.* overpopulation; *b.* widespread unemployment; *c.* the poor quality of the labor force

7. consumer goods (food) production ÷ population, aspirations, standard of living

8. capital accumulation increases output and increased output allows a greater volume of saving and more capital accumulation

9. save, invest; low saving potential, investors, incentives to invest

10. agriculture, the improvement of agricultural facilities, the construction of basic social capital

11. the underdeveloped nations may adopt and apply the superior technologies of the advanced nations

12. capital saving

13. institutions and social arrangements

14. income; investment; productivity, output (income)

15. *a.* the existence of widespread banditry and intertribal warfare in many underdeveloped nations; *b.* the absence of a sizable and vigorous entrepreneurial class; *c.* the great need for social goods and services; *d.* government action may

be the only means of promoting saving and investment; *e.* government can more effectively deal with the social-institutional obstacles to growth; *f.* government may be the only mechanism for speeding up the rate of growth

16. by expanding trade with the underdeveloped nations (lowering the barriers to trade), private flows of capital, foreign aid (public loans and grants)

17. exploit, dependent, neocolonialism

18. *a.* population, standard of living; *b.* cartels, the raw materials they produce; *c.* nuclear, redistribution

Problems and projects

1. *a.* low; *b.* short; *c.* widespread; *d.* low; *e.* primitive; *f.* large; *g.* large; *h.* high; *i.* poor; *j.* small; *k.* low; *l.* absent; *m.* small; *n.* small; *o.* small and poor; *p.* small; *q.* low; *r.* common

2. *a.* food supply: 400, 600, 800, 1000, 1200, 1400; population: 40, 80, 160, 320, 640, 1280. *b.* the food supply is just able to support the population. *c.* the inability of the food supply to support a population growing at this rate. *d.* (1) 200, (2) 240, (3) 280. *e.* the population increased as rapidly as the food supply.

Selt-test

1. T; **2.** F; **3.** F; **4.** F; **5.** T; **6.** F; **7.** F; **8.** T; **9.** F; **10.** T; **11.** F; **12.** T

1. *d;* **2.** *a;* **3.** *b;* **4.** *b;* **5.** *c;* **6.** *d;* **7.** *b;* **8.** *d;* **9.** *b;* **10.** *a;* **11.** *c;* **12.** *d*

Selt-test

1. T; **2.** F; **3.** T; **4.** F; **5.** T; **6.** F; **7.** F; **8.** F; **9.** F; **10.** T; **11.** T; **12.** F

1. *d;* **2.** *c;* **3.** *b;* **4.** *a;* **5.** *c;* **6.** *d;* **7.** *b;* **8.** *a;* **9.** *c;* **10.** *d;* **11.** *b;* **12.** *b*

CHAPTER 22

Fill-in questions

1. fully employed, allocated among alternative uses in the most efficient way; latter

2. *a.* a large number of independent sellers in a highly organized market; *b.* the firms produce a standardized or virtually standardized product; *c.* individual firms exert no significant control over product price; *d.* new firms are free to enter and existing firms are free to leave the industry; *e.* there is virtually no room for nonprice competition

3. sellers', buyers'

4. standardized, differentiated; close substitutes

5. there are barriers to entry into the industry

6. public relations, goodwill

7. there are large numbers of sellers, entry into the industry is fairly easy, the firm has some control over the price of its product

8. there is only one firm in the industry; *b.* the firm produces a product for which there are no close substitutes; *c.* the firm exercises considerable control over the price of its product; *d.* there are barriers to entry into the industry; *e.* advertising is limited and of a goodwill or public relations nature.

9. each firm produces a fairly small share of the total industry output

10. *a.* a large number of independent sellers; *b.* the product is differentiated; *c.* the firm has a limited amount of control over the price of its product; *d.* entry into the industry is relatively easy; *e.* there is extensive and vigorous nonprice competition

11. the product is standardized in pure competition and differentiated in monopolistic competition

12. standardized, differentiated

13. raw materials, semifinished goods

14. few, a significant percentage

15. the number of rivals the firm has, the extent to which the products of rival firms are substitutes for the product of the oligopolistic firm

16. (1) pure competition, monopsony, monopsonistic competition, oligopsony; (2) large number of buyers, one buyer, fairly large number of buyers, a few buyers

17. the geographic size of the market, the extent of interindustry competition, the extent of nonprice competition, the rate of technological advance

18. *a.* the legislation and policies of government; *b.* business policies and practices; *c.* technological

development and the role of research in industry; *d.* the permissive characteristic of American capitalism

Problems and projects

1. number of firms: d, a, c, b; type of product: e, e, f, e or f; control over price: m, h, g, g; entry: i, j, k, l; nonprice competition: m, g, h, g or h

2. *a.* oligopoly or monopolistic competition; standardized product, number of firms is fairly large, easy entry; *b.* oligopoly or monopolistic competition; differentiated product, number of firms is fairly large, entry is moderately difficult; *c.* pure competition; large number of firms, standardized product, easy entry; *d.* oligopoly; small number of firms, difficult entry; *e.* oligopoly or monopolistic competition; differentiated product, number of firms is fairly large, easy entry; *f.* oligopoly; small number of firms, entry is fairly difficult

3. *a.* yes; railroads, buses, automobiles; *b.* yes; synthetic fibers (nylon, rayon); *c.* yes; aluminum, steel, wood, copper, glass; *d.* yes; radios, movies, books, records, all forms of entertainment; *e.* yes; aluminum, steel, wood, glass, plastics

Selt-test

1. F; **2.** F; **3.** T; **4.** T; **5.** T; **6.** F; **7.** T; **8.** F; **9.** T; **10.** F; **11.** T; **12.** T; **13.** F; **14.** F; **15.** F

1. *d;* **2.** *c;* **3.** *b;* **4.** *b;* **5.** *a;* **6.** *a;* **7.** *b;* **8.** *b;* **9.** *d;* **10.** *a;* **11.** *b;* **12.** *b*

CHAPTER 23

Fill-in questions

1. inelastic, elastic

2. sensitive, insensitive

3. negatively (inversely), positively (directly)

4. elastic: greater than 1, decrease, increase; inelastic: less than 1, increase, decrease; of unitary elasticity: equal to 1, remain constant, remain constant

5. perfectly inelastic, perfectly elastic, parallel to the vertical axis, parallel to the horizontal axis

6. *a.* greater than; *b.* less than; *c.* equal to

7. *a.* the number of good substitutes for the product which are available; *b.* the relative importance of the product in the total budget of the buyer; *c.* whether the good is a necessity or a luxury; *d.* the period of time in which demand is being considered

8. the amount of time which a producer has to respond to a price change

9. *a.* 7.00, 15,000; *b.* shortage, 4000; *c.* surplus, 2000

10. war, shortages, rationing

11. rationing

12. minimum wages, agricultural price supports

13. surplus, attempt to reduce supply or increase demand, purchase the surplus and store or dispose of it

14. the amount the price of the commodity rises as a result of the tax; *a.* less, more; *b.* more, less

15. remains constant, decreases, equal to, less than

16. elastic, inelastic

Problems and projects

1. total revenue: $300, 360, 400, 420, 420, 400, 360; elasticity coefficient: $2^5/_7$ (2.72), $1^8/_9$ (1.89), $1^4/_{11}$ (1.36), 1, $^{11}/_{15}$ (0.73), $^9/_{17}$ (0.53); character of demand: elastic, elastic, elastic, unitary elasticity, inelastic, inelastic

2. elasticity coefficient: $1^4/_{15}$ (1.27), $1^4/_{13}$ (1.31), $1^4/_{11}$ (1.36), $1^4/_9$ (1.44), $1^4/_7$ (1.57), $1^4/_5$ (1.8); character of supply: elastic, elastic, elastic, elastic, elastic, elastic

3. *a.* (1) S_3; (2) S_2; (3) S_1; *b.* p_1, q_1; *c.* (1) p_4, remain at q_1; (2) p_3, q_2; (3) p_2, q_3; (3) p_2, q_3; *d.* more; *e.* less, greater

4. *a.* $3.60; *b.* (reading down) 600, 500, 400, 300, 200, 100; *c.* $4.00; *d.* (1) $.40, $66^2/_3$; (2) $.20, $33^1/_3$

5. *a.* (2) has not changed; (3) none, all; (4) smaller, larger; (5) larger, smaller; *b.* (2) increased by the amount of the tax; (3) all, none; (4) larger, smaller; (5) smaller, larger

6. *a.* average revenue: $11.00, 10.00, 9.00, 8.00, 7.00, 6.00, 5.00, 4.00, 3.00, 2.00; total revenue: $0, 10.00, 18.00, 24.00, 28.00, 30.00, 30.00, 28.00, 24.00, 18.00; marginal revenue: $10.00, 8.00, 6.00, 4.00, 2.00, 0, −2.00, −4.00, −6.00; elasticity coefficient: 21.0, 6.33, 3.4, 2.14, 1.44, 1.0, 0.7, 0.47, 0.29; *b.* imperfectly competitive; price (average revenue) decreases as the output of the firm increases and is greater than marginal revenue; *d.* (1) elastic, positive; (2) inelastic, negative; (3) of unitary elasticity, equal to 0; *e.* in order to sell a larger quantity, it is necessary for the firm to lower its price not only on the additional units but also on the units which it could have sold at the higher price

7. *a.* average revenue: all are $10.00; total revenue: $0, 10.00, 20.00, 30.00, 40.00, 50.00, 60.00; marginal revenue: all are $10.00; *b.* purely competitive, because price (average revenue) is constant and equal to marginal revenue; *d.* infinity; *e.* they are equal

Self-test

1. F; **2.** T; **3.** F; **4.** T; **5.** T; **6.** F; **7.** F; **8.** T; **9.** F; **10.** T; **11.** T; **12.** T

1. *c;* **2.** *b;* **3.** *a;* **4.** *a;* **5.** *c;* **6.** *b;* **7.** *c;* **8.** *c;* **9.** *a;* **10.** *b;* **11,** *a;* **12.** *b*

CHAPTER 24

Fill-in questions

1. increase, decrease, income

2. more, lower, less, more, substitution

3. marginal utility, decrease

4. rational, preferences

5. limited, prices, budget restraint

6. ratio of the marginal utility of the last unit purchased of a product to its price

7. increase, decrease

8. *a.* MU of product X; *b.* price of X; *c.* MU of product Y; *c.* price of Y

9. *a.* the income of the consumer; *b.* the prices of other products

10. time; *a.* scarce; *b.* the income that can be earned by using the time for work; *c.* market price, value of the consumption time

Problems and projects

1. *a.* (1) increase, 1½; (2) inelastic; *b.* (1) decrease, 1; (2) elastic

2. marginal utility of good A: 21, 20, 18, 15, 11, 6, 0; marginal utility of good B: 7, 6, 5, 4, 3, 2, 1.2; marginal utility of good C: 23, 17, 12, 8, 5, 3, 2

3. *a.* marginal utility per dollar of good A: 4¹/₅, 4, 3³/₅, 3, 2¹/₅, 1¹/₅, 0; marginal utility per dollar of good B: 7, 6, 5, 4, 3, 2, 1¹/₅; marginal utility per dollar of good C: 5¾, 4¼, 3, 2, 1¼, ¾, ½; *b.* the marginal utility per dollar spent on good B (7) is greater than the marginal utility per dollar spent on good A (3), and the latter is greater than the marginal utility per dollar spent on good C (2); he would not be maximizing his utility; *c.* he would be spending more than his $37 income; *d.* (1) 4; (2) 5; (3) 3; 151; 3. *e.* A, he would obtain the greatest marginal utility for his dollar (2¹/₅)

4. *a.* MU/$ of good A: 15, 10, 6²/₃, 5, 4, 3¹/₃, 3, 2½; MU/$ of good B: 6, 5½, 5, 4½, 4, 3½, 3, 2½; MU/$ of good C: 10, 9, 8, 7, 6, 5, 4, 3; MU/$ of good D: 8, 6⁴/₅, 6, 5²/₅, 5, 4³/₅, 4, 3; MU/$ of saving: 6, 5, 4, 3, 2, 1, ½, ¼; *b.* (1) 4; (2) 3; (3) 6; (4) 5, 2, 490; *c.* (1) 2; (2) 3; (3) 6; (4) 8; *d.* price of A: 6.00, 4.00, 3.00, 2.00, 1.50; quantity of A demanded: 2, 3, 4, 6, 8. The relationship between price and quantity is the demand schedule

5. *a.* Yes; *b.* (1) 10, (2) 3; *c.* no, the marginal utility to price ratios are not the same for the two goods; *d.* of *M*, because its MU/P ratio is greater; *e.* less

Self-test

1. F; **2.** T; **3.** T; **4.** F; **5.** F; **6.** T; **7.** F

1. *c;* **2.** *b;* **3.** *a;* **4.** *b;* **5.** *c;* **6.** *c;* **7.** *b*

CHAPTER 25

Fill-in questions

1. other products, opportunity, alternative

2. attract the resources, explicit, implicit

3. implicit, the services of entrepreneurs, total, explicit, implicit

4. amounts of variable resources (labor, raw materials, etc.), the fixed resources (the size of the plant) it employs

5. enter, leave, fixed (constant)

6. variable resource, fixed resource, extra or marginal product, variable resource, decline

7. fixed, variable, variable

8. increase, decreasing, increase, increasing

10. average variable, average total, marginal

11. total variable, total cost

12. decreasing, increasing

13. had time to make all appropriate adjustments in its plant size

14. *a.* increased specialization in the use of labor; *b.* better utilization of and increased specialization in management; *c.* more efficient productive equipment; *d.* greater utilization of by-products

15. managerial complexities (problems)

Problems and projects

1. *a.* 15 units of good Y; *b.* 1½ units of good Y; *c.* 7 units of good Y

2. *a.* 5, 6, 7, 6, 5, 4, 3, 2, 1, ½; *b.* $0, 10, 20, 30, 40, 50, 60, 70, 80, 90, 100; *c.* $2.00, 1.67, 1.43, 1.67, 2.00, 2.50, 3.33, 5.00, 10.00, 20.00; *d.* (1) decreases; (2) increases

3. *a.*

Total cost	Average fixed cost	Average variable cost	Average total cost	Marginal cost
$ 200	—	—	—	—
250	$200.00	$50.00	$250.00	$ 50
290	100.00	45.00	145.00	40
320	66.67	40.00	106.67	30
360	50.00	40.00	90.00	40
420	40.00	44.00	84.00	60
500	33.33	50.00	83.33	80
600	28.57	57.14	85.71	100
720	25.00	65.00	90.00	120
870	22.22	74.44	96.67	150
1,100	20.00	90.00	110.00	230

4. *a.* $7.00, 6.00, 5.00, 4.00, 4.00, 3.00, 4.00, 5.00, 6.00, 5.00, 7.00, 10.00; *b.* (1) 10, 40; (2) 50, 80; (3) 90, 120

Self-test

1. F; **2.** T; **3.** T; **4.** F; **5.** F; **6.** T; **7.** T; **8.** T; **9.** F; **10.** F

1. *a;* **2.** *b;* **3.** *d;* **4.** *a;* **5.** *d;* **6.** *c;* **7.** *d;* **8.** *b;* **9.** *b;* **10.** *a*

CHAPTER 26

Fill-in questions

1. *a.* a large number of independent sellers; *b.* a standardized product; *c.* no single firm supplies enough to influence market price; *d.* no obstacles to the entry of new firms or the exodus of old firms

2. total revenue minus total cost

3. total-receipts–total-cost, marginal-revenue–marginal-cost

4. it can realize a profit or a loss which is less than its fixed costs; its profit is the greatest or its loss the least, marginal revenue equals marginal cost (either order)

5. the minimum average variable cost

6. that portion of the firm's marginal-cost curve which lies above the average-variable-cost curve, the sum of the short-run supply curves of all firms in the industry

7. total quantity demanded, total quantity supplied, the quantity demanded and supplied at the equilibrium price

8. fixed (constant), variable

9. long-run average cost, long-run marginal cost (either order), minimum

10. the firms in the industry are realizing profits in the short run, the firms in the industry are realizing losses in the short run

11. increasing cost

12. the industry's demand for resources is small relative to the total demand for these resources, the industry is using unspecialized resources which are used by other industries

13. total satisfaction of consumers; consumers most want, the most efficient way

14. *a.* the best available (least-cost); *b.* price, cost; *c.* are essential to produce the product; *d.* minimum

15. marginal cost, price

16. *a.* the competitive price system does not necessarily result in an ideal distribution of money income in the economy; *b.* the competitive price system does not accurately measure costs and benefits where spillover costs and benefits are significant; *c.* the competitive price system does not entail the use of the most efficient productive techniques; *d.* the competitive price system may not provide for a sufficient range of consumer choice or for the development of new products

Problems and projects

1. *a.* (see table below); *b.* (1) 0, −$300; (2) 5, −$100; (3) 7, $380;

Market price = $55		Market price = $120		Market price = $200	
Revenue	Profit	Revenue	Profit	Revenue	Profit
$ 0	$ −300	$ 0	$ −300	$ 0	$ −300
55	−345	120	−280	200	−200
110	−340	240	−210	400	−50
165	−345	360	−150	600	90
220	−370	480	−110	800	210
275	−425	600	−100	1,000	300
330	−510	720	−120	1,200	360
385	−635	840	−180	1,400	380
440	−810	960	−290	1,600	350
495	−1,045	1,080	−460	1,800	260
550	−1,350	1,200	−700	2,000	100

c.

Price	Quantity supplied	Profit
$360	10	$1,700
290	9	1,070
230	8	590
180	7	240
140	6	0
110	5	−150
80	4	−270
60	0	−300

d. (1) quantity supplied: 1000, 900, 800, 700, 600, 500, 400; (2) (a) 180; (b) 7; (c) 240; (d) enter, profits in the industry will attract them into the industry

2. a. 140; b. 6; c. 133 = 800 (the total quantity demanded at $140) ÷ 6 (the output of each firm); d. 150 = 900 ÷ 6; e. (1) the curve is a horizontal line, (2) the curve slopes upward

Self-test

1. F; 2. T; 3. T; 4. T; 5. F; 6. F; 7. T; 8. T; 9. F; 10. T; 11. T; 12. T

1. c; 2. a; 3. d; 4. b; 5. b; 6. b; 7. c; 8. c; 9. b; 10. a; 11. b; 12. d

CHAPTER 27

Fill-in questions

1. a. the economies of scale; b. natural monopolies; c. ownership of essential raw materials; d. patents and research; e. unfair competition; f. the economies of being established

2. their costs of production will be greater than those of the large-scale firms, they will find it difficult to obtain the money capital necessary to acquire a large-scale plant

3. natural, regulated

4. less than, less than, will decrease

5. marginal revenue, marginal cost, greater than

6. a. highest possible; b. a maximum; c. profit

7. public criticism or pressure, the entry of new firms into the industry

8. entry of new firms

9. prices, cost

10. a. the seller has some monopoly power; b. the seller is able to segment the market; c. the original buyer cannot resell the product

11. a minimum, price (or average revenue), marginal cost

12. costs (or cost schedule), economies of scale

13. the amount by which price exceeds average cost becomes the income of stockholders who are largely in the upper income groups

14. marginal cost, average (total) cost

15. average (total) cost, the misallocation of resources caused by monopoly

Problems and projects

1. a. total revenue: $0, 650, 1200, 1650, 2000, 2250, 2400, 2450, 2400, 2250, 2000; marginal revenue: $650, 550, 450, 350, 250, 150, 50, −50, −150, −250; b. (1) 6; (2) 400; (3) 1560; c. (1) total revenue: $0, 650, 1250, 1800, 2300, 2750, 3150, 3500, 3800, 4050, 4250; marginal revenue: $650, 600, 550, 500, 450, 400, 350, 300, 250, 200; (2) price; (3) 8, 300, 2550; (4) larger, larger

2. output of the firm: 3, 0; price it will charge: $150, −; total profit: $−60, $−300

3. *a.* 4, 11.50, 4.00; *b.* 6, 8.50, −7.50, bankrupt, subsidize; *c.* 73.50, 58.50, 5.00; *d.* 5, 10.00, zero; *e.* b, a, c

Self-test

1. F; **2.** T; **3.** F; **4.** T; **5.** F; **6.** F; **7.** T; **8.** F; **9.** T; **10.** T; **11.** T; **12.** T

1. *b;* **2.** *c;* **3.** *d;* **4.** *a;* **5.** *c;* **6.** *b;* **7.** *c;* **8.** *b;* **9.** *b;* **10.** *a;* **11.** *d;* **12.** *a*

CHAPTER 28

Fill-in questions

1. relatively large, differentiated, collude, price, nonprice, fairly easy

2. limited, rivalry

3. *a.* more, less; *b.* number of rivals the firm has, the degree of product differentiation; *c.* marginal cost, marginal revenue

4. reduce, increase

5. equal average cost, equal zero, greater

6. average cost is greater than minimum average cost, price is greater than marginal cost

7. product differentiation, product promotion

8. a wider variety of goods, an improved quality of goods

9. informative, competitive

10. (a) information; (b) newspapers, magazines, radio, and television; (c) new products; (d) costs; (e) competition; (f) spending

11. (a) informative; (b) wastes; (c) external costs; (d) costs; (e) monopoly; (f) spending; (g) barrier to entry

12. product, promotion

Problems and projects

2. *a.* marginal cost: $30, 10, 20, 30, 40, 50, 60, 70, 80, 90; marginal revenue: $110, 90, 70, 50, 30, 10, −10, −30, −50, −70; *b.* (1) 4; (2) $80; (3) $180; *c.* (1) decrease; (2) average cost; (3) equal to zero

Self-test

1. F; **2.** F; **3.** T; **4.** F; **5.** T; **6.** T; **7.** F; **8.** F

1. *c;* **2.** *b;* **3.** *c;* **4.** *d;* **5** *b;* **6.** *c;* **7.** *a;* **8.** *b*

CHAPTER 29

Fill-in questions

1. few, standardized, differentiated, difficult

2. mutually interdependent, the reactions of rivals, no, so many

3. the economies of scale, the advantages of merger

4. oligopoly encompasses many specific market situations, the element of mutual interdependence which fewness adds complicates analysis

5. inflexible, simultaneously

6. price, nonprice

7. elastic, elastic, inelastic

8. not raise their prices, lower their prices

9. gap, price the oligopolist will charge in order to maximize his profits

10. would be set by a pure monopolist

11. *a.* legal obstacles (the antitrust laws); *b.* a large number of firms in the industry; *c.* differentiated products; *d.* price breaks

12. set price or output, divide the market

13. informal, prices, the ingenuity of each seller (i.e., nonprice competition), price leader

14. prices one firm might charge, prices the other firm might charge, profits of the two firms

15. *a.* the price charged by the other firm; *b.* decrease, not raise its price, also lower its price; *c.* collusion, merger

16. price cuts can be quickly and easily met by a firm's rivals, oligopolists are typically blessed with substantial financial resources which allow them to support such measures as advertising and product development

17. substantial profits; *a.* technological advance provides an alternative means for enlarging total profits; *b.* technological superiority is a basic means by which survival is ensured; *c.* the presence of strong rivals places the oligopolist under severe pressure to seek maximum productive efficiency; *d.* existence of barriers to entry give the progressive oligopolist some assurance that he will realize some of the profit rewards of research

18. have not, modest, financed from public funds

19. resource suppliers, customers, abuses of original power, share in the profits of original power

20. costs, better, countervailing power, smaller, higher

Problems and projects

1. *a.* total revenue: 290, 560, 810, 1040, 1250, 1260, 1265, 1265, 1260; *b.* marginal revenue: 2.70,

2.50, 2.30, 2.10, 0.40, 0.20, 0, −0.20; elasticity of demand: 19, 11, 7.57, 5.67, 1.2, 1.1, 1.0, 0.9; *c.* 2.50, 500; *e.* (1) 2.50, 500; (2) 2.50, 500, they have decreased; (3) 2.50, 500, they have increased

2. *a.* marginal cost: $30, 20, 30, 40, 50, 60, 70, 80; marginal revenue: $130, 110, 90, 70, 50, 30, 10, −10; *b.* $90; *c.* (1) 5; (2) $280; *d.* (1) 15; (2) $840; *e.* no; *f.* $90

3. *a.* $3, $2, $2; *b.* (1) would not, its profits would decrease; (2) would not, its profits would decrease;

(3) would, this would prevent an even larger decrease in its profits; (4) would not, its profits would decrease; *c.* (1) $4, $49; (2) $4, $50; (3) $99

Self-test

1. T; **2.** F; **3.** F; **4.** T; **5.** F; **6.** F; **7.** T; **8.** T; **9.** F; **10.** T

1. *c;* **2.** *d;* **3.** *c;* **4.** *c;* **5.** *d;* **6.** *a;* **7.** *b;* **8.** *c;* **9.** *d;* **10.** *d*

CHAPTER 30

Fill-in questions

1. resources, incomes, costs

2. derived, productivity of the resource, value of the product produced from the resource

3. marginal revenue product, marginal resource cost; price, marginal resource cost

4. marginal revenue product, quantities, prices

5. lower, less

6. 15, 27, 5, 20, 6

7. adding up the demand curves for the resource of all the firms hiring the resource

8. product, productivity, prices

9. *a.* +; *b.* −; *c.* +; *d.* +; *e.* +

10. more, less, substitution, more, output

11. marginal physical product, substituted, price-elasticity of demand, portion of total production costs accounted for by the resource

12. marginal revenue product, price

13. marginal physical product, price

14. one

15. *a.* marginal revenue product, marginal re-

source cost, marginal revenue product, marginal resource cost, one; *b.* marginal physical product, marginal resource cost

Problems and projects

1. *a.* marginal physical product of A: 12, 10, 8, 6, 4, 2, 1; *b.* total revenue: 0, 18.00, 33.00, 45.00, 54.00, 60.00, 63.00, 64.50; marginal revenue product of A: 18.00, 15.00, 12.00, 9.00, 6.00, 3.00, 1.50; *c.* 0, 1, 2, 3, 4, 5, 6, 7

2. *a.* total product: 22, 43, 62, 78, 90, 97, 98; *b.* (1) total revenue: 22.00, 38.70, 49.60, 54.60, 54.00, 48.50, 39.20; (2) marginal revenue product of B: 22.00, 16.70, 10.90, 5.00, −0.60, −5.50, −9.30; *c.* 0, 1, 2, 3, 4, 4

3. *a.* (1) 1, 3; (2) 3, 5; *b.* 5, 6; *c.* the marginal physical product of C divided by its price, the marginal physical product of D divided by its price; *d.* purely, $.50; *e.* (1) 114; (2) $57; (3) $28; (4) $29

Self-test

1. T; **2.** F; **3.** T; **4.** T; **5.** T; **6.** F; **7.** F; **8.** T

1. *c;* **2.** *c;* **3.** *a;* **4.** *c;* **5.** *c;* **6.** *c;* **7.** *d;* **8.** *a*

CHAPTER 31

Fill-in questions

1. unit of time, the wage rate multiplied by the amount of time worked; the goods and services money wages will purchase

2. capital equipment, natural resources, quality, technology

3. it is necessary for employers to pay higher wages to attract workers from alternative employment; total quantity of labor demanded, total quantity of labor supplied; marginal-revenue-product schedules for labor

4. perfectly, an individual employer is unable to affect the market wage rate

5. marginal revenue product, wage rate, marginal labor cost

6. marginal revenue product, marginal labor cost; marginal labor cost, the wage rate, the marginal revenue product of labor, marginal labor cost

7. lower, less

8. increase wages, increasing the demand for labor, restricting the supply of labor, imposing above-equilibrium wage rates on employers

9. restricting the supply of labor, imposing above-equilibrium wage rates, decreased

10. marginal revenue product of labor, competitive and monopsonistic equilibrium wage, the relative bargaining strength of the union and monopsonist

11. *a.* increase, decrease; *b.* increase, increase; *c.* increase, decrease

12. increase, decrease, leave uneffected

13. homogeneous, attractiveness, imperfect

14. noncompeting, equalizing differences, they must be paid to compensate workers for the non-monetary differences or unattractive aspects of various jobs

15. immobilities, geographical, sociological, institutional

16. *a.* education, health, mobility; *b.* productivity, wage rates (income); *c.* real wages; *d.* noncompeting, differences

Problems and projects

1. *a.* quantity of labor demanded: 100, 200, 300, 400, 500, 600, 700, 800; *b.* (1) 10.00; (2) 600; *c.* (1) 10.00; (2) 6; (3) 10.00; *f.* 400

2. *a.* total labor cost: 0, 4.00, 12.00, 24.00, 40.00, 60.00, 84.00, 112.00, 144.00; marginal labor cost: 4.00, 8.00, 12.00, 16.00, 20.00, 24.00, 28.00, 32.00; *b.* (1) 5; (2) 12.00; (3) 20.00; *d.* 6, 14.00

3. *a.* wage rate: 16.00, 16.00, 16.00, 16.00, 16.00, 16.00, 16.00, 18.00; *b.* total labor cost: 16.00, 32.00, 48.00, 64.00, 80.00, 96.00, 112.00, 144.00; marginal labor cost: 16.00, 16.00, 16.00, 16.00, 16.00, 16.00, 16.00, 32.00; *c.* (1) 6; (2) 16.00; (3) 96.00; *d.* increased, increased, increased

Self-test

1. F; 2. T; 3. T; 4. F; 5. T; 6. F; 7. T; 8. T; 9. T; 10. T

1. *a;* 2. *c;* 3. *d;* 4. *d;* 5. *d;* 6. *a;* 7. *a;* 8. *a;* 9. *b;* 10. *d*

CHAPTER 32

Fill-in questions

1. land, natural resources, fixed (perfectly inelastic)

2. demand, supply, incentive, surplus

3. unearned, nationalized, the single tax

4. land differs in productivity (quality), individual, alternative uses

5. money, liquidity, they can use them to purchase capital goods

6. risk, the length of loan, the amount of the loan, market imperfections

7. *a.* transactions, precautionary, directly, national income (NNP); *b.* speculative, inversely, interest rate

8. *a.* money, bonds; bonds, money

9. *a.* the monetary authority (the Federal Reserve Banks); *b.* quantity of money demanded, the money supply (stock) (either order)

10. *a.* fall, rise, increase; *b.* increase

11. administered, investment, rations

12. entrepreneurial ability, resources, non-routine decisions, innovating, uncertain

13. uncertain, insurable, uninsurable, economy as a whole, innovation

14. *a.* investment, employment, output; *b.* allocation, monopoly

15. *a.* 84; *b.* rent, interest, corporate profit, 16; *c.* (1) remained constant, (2) remained constant

16. *a.* profits; *b.* productivity, the prices of the products they produce; *c.* labor's share of the national income

Problems and projects

1. *a.* 250; *b.* 300,000; *d.* 0, 300,000

2. *b.* (1) 180; *c.* 240, 260, 280, 300, 320, 340, 360; *d.* (2) 280, 280, 280, 280, 280, 280, 280, (3) 6; *e.* (1) fall, 5, (2) rise to 8%

Self-test

1. F; 2. T; 3. T; 4. T; 5. T; 6. F; 7. T; 8. T; 9. F; 10. F

1. *a;* 2. *d;* 3. *b;* 4. *c;* 5. *d;* 6. *b;* 7. *c;* 8. *d*

CHAPTER 33

Fill-in questions

1. particular, interrelationships

2. *a.* the resources used to produce Z; *b.* other products which use these same resources; *c.* products which are substitutes for or complements to product Z; *d.* resources which are substitutes for the resources used to produce Z and other products

3. equilibrium, product, resource

4. tastes, availability of resources, technology

5. downward, upward; *a.* (1) diminishing marginal utility, (2) diminishing marginal productivity; *b.* (1) increasing marginal cost, (2) work-leisure preferences

6. *a.* increase, decrease; *b.* P, Q; *c.* increase, decrease; *d.* C, D

7. *a.* P, Q; *b.* increase, decrease; *c.* increase, decrease; *d.* C, D; *e.* increase, decrease

8. *a.* substitutes, complements; *b.* increase, decrease; *c.* Q, P

9. maximizes the satisfaction of the wants (welfare); *a.* marginal cost; *b.* minimum, least-cost; *c.* the same

10. imperfectly, less than ideal, incomplete, slow

11. technological progress, product variety

12. *a.* spillover costs, spillover benefits, social goods; *b.* distribution, income

13. producing, consuming (using), input, outputs

14. 7.5

15. performance of the economy, economic problems, economic policies

Problems and projects

2. *a.* From left to right: 75, 0, 75, 10, 400; *b.* 25; *c.* (1) 37½; (2) 15; (3) 8¾; (4) 35; *d.* (1) 8.8; (2) 13.6; (3) 2.9; (4) 8.97; *e.* each sector will have to increase its inputs in order to increase its output, and this will require still further increases in the outputs of the various sectors

Self-test

1. F; **2.** T; **3.** T; **4.** F; **5.** T; **6.** T; **7.** T; **8.** F; **9.** F; **10.** T

1. *c;* **2.** *b;* **3.** *b;* **4.** *a;* **5.** *d;* **6.** *d;* **7.** *c;* **8.** *a;* **9.** *c;* **10.** *c;* **11.** *d;* **12.** *a*

CHAPTER 34

Fill-in questions

1. small number of, all or a large portion, major, relative, absolute

2. workable, mass production, high rate, investment, pricing, social responsibility

3. *a.* pervasive competition; *b.* interproduct competition; *c.* innovative competition; *d.* countervailing power; *e.* potential competition

4. *a.* technological imperatives, capital, technology, planning; *b.* security, stability, vertically, internally, advertising, salesmanship, government

5. restrict, charge higher, misallocate, greater inequality, slow rate, instability, political, institutional, values

6. competition, monopoly

7. natural, agencies, commissions

8. monopoly, restraint of trade

9. price discrimination, tying contracts, acquisition of stock of competing corporations to lessen competition, interlocking directorates

10. investigate unfair competitive practices, public hearing on such complaints, "cease and desist" orders, the Federal courts, interpret the meaning of antitrust laws

11. Celler-Kefauver, Clayton

12. Wheeler-Lea, Robinson-Patman, price discounts

13. conglomerate, other industries

14. exempts, patents, protective tariffs

15. Webb-Pomerene; labor unions, agricultural cooperatives

16. patent laws, protective tariffs

17. *a.* maintenance of the status quo; *b.* move toward public regulation and ownership; *c.* restore vigorous competition

18. no individual firm possess considerable market power, collusion, entry into markets is relatively unrestricted.

Problems and projects

1. G; **2.** C; **3.** I; **4.** A; **5.** E; **6.** F; **7.** D; **8.** B; **9.** H

Self-test

1. F; **2.** F; **3.** T; **4.** F; **5.** F; **6.** T; **7.** F; **8.** F; **9.** T; **10.** F

1. *d;* **2.** *b;* **3.** *c;* **4.** *a;* **5.** *a;* **6.** *b;* **7.** *b;* **8.** *d;* **9.** *c;* **10.** *d*

CHAPTER 35

Fill-in questions

1. *a.* prosperity; *b.* prosperity; *c.* depression; *d.* prosperity; *e.* depression

2. less, highly unequal

3. falling farm prices and incomes over the years, extreme year-to-year fluctuations in farm prices and incomes

4. inelastic demand for agricultural products, the

supply of agricultural products has tended to increase more rapidly than the demand for these products, the relative immobility of agricultural resources

5. farm products have few good substitutes

6. technological advances in the production of agricultural products

7. the increase in the size of the American population has not been rapid enough; as the income of Americans has increased, their expenditures for farm products have not increased proportionately

8. immobile

9. inelastic, small, large, small, large

10. resources, agriculture, the nonagricultural sectors of the economy

11. *a.* cost, economic growth; *b.* purely competitive, price

12. output (production), prices, incomes

13. given, a fixed amount of goods and services

14. surplus, purchase; *a.* incomes; *b.* prices for the commodity, taxes to finance the government purchases

15. increase, decrease

16. acreage-allotment, acreage-reserve; new uses, domestic consumption, export

17. reallocate, already had high incomes

18. *a.* increased incomes abroad; *b.* shifts in foreign dietary habits; *c.* poor harvests outside the U.S.; *d.* devaluation of the dollar; *e.* the opening of markets in Communist countries

19. decrease, Agriculture and Consumer Protection, target, production, 20,000

20. incomes, capacity, foodstuffs, instability, balance-of-payments, foreign

Problems and projects

1. .42, .70

2. *a.* inelastic; *b.* decrease, 1,200.00, 700.00, 16⅔, decrease, 41⅔; *c.* fall, 1.00, 0.80, fall, 700.00, 560.00; *d.* (1) 100, (2) 180, (3) 1296, (4) 0.80, 576, (5) 720, (6) 1.00, 100

3. *a.* increase, 153,750.00, 200,000.00; *b.* increase, 153,750.00, 205,000.00

Self-test

1. T; **2.** T; **3.** F; **4.** T; **5.** F; **6.** T; **7.** F; **8.** F; **9.** T; **10.** T

1. *c;* **2.** *d;* **3.** *a;* **4.** *c;* **5.** *d;* **6.** *c;* **7.** *b;* **8.** *c;* **9.** *a;* **10.** *b*

CHAPTER 36

Fill-in questions

1. 150, 75

2. where, transport, resources, buyers

3. surplus, labor

4. near each other and their markets; *a.* internal economies of scale; *b.* locational (transport) economics; *c.* urban economies

5. higher, internal, external, society, spillover

6. the advantages and opportunities of a metropolitan area, the disadvantages, fragmentation, imbalance

7. *a.* property, rates; *b.* large, welfare, densely, high

8. *a.* jobs; *b.* transportation; *c.* highways, congestion, pollution; *d.* highways, suburbs, automobiles, highways; *e.* public mass transit

9. *a.* user charge, peak-pricing; *b.* public mass-transit systems

10. wastes, nature (the ecological system), absorb (reabsorb or recycle), population, per capita income, technology, incentives

11. *a.* trained and educated, suburbs, buildings; *b.* educated, low; *c.* central city, suburbs, mass transit, discrimination

12. jobs, education, training, maintenance

13. public mass-transit system, black capitalism

14. consolidation, revenues

15. decision, needs, means

16. sharing, the Federal government, land, buildings

Problems and projects

1. 300, 15, 30, 10, 510, 30, 5; *a.* 1800, 900; *b.* $.50; *c.* $.50; *d.* (1) 810, (2) Total revenue: 225, 67.50, 90, 45, 270, 90, 22.50; 810, (3) 7am–9am, 4pm–6pm; *e.* (1) 55, (2) 64

2. *a.* 4,000, 2,500; *b.* 5,000; *c.* 7,500,000; *d.* 1,000, 1,500,000

3. *a.* grossly inadequate; *b.* high; *c.* low; *d.* inadequate; *e.* old, deteriorated, crowded; *f.* high; *g.* deplorable; *h.* high

Self-test

1. T; **2.** T; **3.** T; **4.** F; **5.** F; **6.** F; **7.** F; **8.** T; **9.** T; **10.** F

1. *b;* **2.** *c;* **3.** *a;* **4.** *a;* **5.** *d;* **6.** *d;* **7.** *a;* **8.** *c;* **9.** *b;* **10.** *c*

CHAPTER 37

Fill-in questions

1. considerable

2. native abilities; education, training, and opportunity; market power; property resources; misfortune

3. decreased, increased, significant, not changed significantly

4. *a.* before-tax, after-tax; *b.* mobility; *c.* is not; *d.* in-kind, less, virtually been eliminated

5. consumer satisfaction, productivity, social and political

6. a high volume of saving; incentives to work, produce, and innovate; the incomes necessary to bring forth improved products and cultural advances

7. *a.* $5040, $2658; *b.* 12, 24

8. *a.* old; *b.* blacks; *c.* females; *d.* educated; *e.* full-time, year-round

9. *a.* much of it is isolated and unseen in the hearts of large cities; *b.* the sick and old seldom venture onto the streets; *c.* rural poverty is away from the main highways; *d.* the poor have no political voice

10. 64

11. *a.* wage discrimination; *b.* employment discrimination; *c.* occupational discrimination; *d.* human-capital discrimination; 4, 65

12. the faults of the individual, social forces

13. old age, survivors, and disability; unemployment, supplemental security income, aid to families

with dependent children, food stamp; medicare, medicaid

14. *a.* it impairs incentives to work; *b.* it is abused by those who are not needy and results in inequalities; *c.* it is administratively inefficient (too costly); *d.* it is inflationary; negative income

15. equality, efficiency

Problems and projects

1. *a.* (1) column 4: 18, 30, 44, 61, 80, 91, 100; (2) column 5: 4, 10, 22, 36, 51, 71, 100; *b.* (1) 30, 10; (2) 20, 49

2. *a.* 5000, 4000, 3000, 2000, 1000, 0; *b.* Income subsidy: 3000, 2400, 1800, 1200, 600, 0; Total income: 3000, 3400, 3800, 4200, 4600, 5000; *c.* 600, 400; *d.* 5000; *e.* Income subsidy: 5000, 4000, 3000, 2000, 1000, 0; 1000, 0; *f.* (1) 8333⅓, 7333⅓, 6333⅓, 5333⅓, 4333⅓, 3333⅓; (2) Income subsidy: 5000, 4400, 3800, 3200, 2600, 2000; Total income: 5000, 5400, 5800, 6200, 6600, 7000; (3) 600, 400; (4) 5000, 0

Self-test

1. T; **2.** T; **3.** T; **4.** F; **5.** T; **6.** F; **7.** T; **8.** T; **9.** T; **10.** F; **11.** T; **12.** F

1. *b;* **2.** *d;* **3.** *b;* **4.** *c;* **5.** *d;* **6.** *c;* **7.** *a;* **8.** *d;* **9.** *c;* **10.** *b;* **11.** *d;* **12.** *d*

CHAPTER 38

Fill-in questions

1. 20, 25

2. of the attitude of the courts, the resistance of employers to recognizing and bargaining with unions

3. criminal conspiracy, injunctions

4. discriminatory discharge, blacklisting, lockout, strikebreakers, yellow-dog contracts, paternalism, company unions

5. business unionism, political neutrality, craft unionism

6. Norris-La Guardia, Wagner; CIO, industrial, unskilled mass-production

7. organize, bargain collectively; National Labor Relations Board, unfair labor practices of management

8. Taft-Hartley, Landrum-Griffin, merger of the AFL and the CIO, static (constant), stagnation, public

9. *a.* provisions which designate and outlaw certain "unfair union practices"; *b.* provisions which regulate the internal administration of unions; *c.* provisions which specify collective bargaining procedures and regulate the actual contents of bargaining agreements; *d.* provisions for the handling of strikes which threaten to imperil the health and safety of the nation

10. elections, finances, union members, union officers

11. *a.* the degree of recognition and status accorded the union and the prerogatives of management; *b.* wages and hours; *c.* seniority and job opportunities; *d.* a procedure for settling grievances

12. what others are getting, productivity, ability to pay, cost of living

13. status, security, administering, interpreting

14. increased; *a.* greater opportunities; *b.* increased education; *c.* smaller family size; *d.* increased working life; *e.* the substitution of capital for labor at home.

15. 57, discrimination, justifiable disparities

Problems and projects

1. 1. K; 2. D; 3. Q; 4. E; 5. O; 6. G; 7. A; 8. C; 9. F; 10. J

2. *a.* C; *b.* B; *c.* B; *d.* A; *e.* D; *f.* C; *g.* C; *h.* B

3. *a.* (1) 3, (2) 9; *b.* (1) (a) 7, (b) 18, (2) (a) 7, (b) 15, 30, (c) 12

Self-test

1. F; **2.** F; **3.** F; **4.** T; **5.** F; **6.** F; **7.** T; **8.** T; **9.** T; **10.** T

1. *b;* **2.** *b;* **3.** *d;* **4.** *a;* **5.** *a;* **6.** *d;* **7.** *b;* **8.** *b;* **9.** *c;* **10.** *b*

CHAPTER 39

Fill-in questions

1. 93, 5.5

2. civilian goods and services

3. *a.* the Federal government budget, the sale of products in the market; *b.* nonprofit, profit; *c.* rival military establishments in other nations

4. *a.* defense budget; *b.* central-management, subsidiaries, expand its size; *c.* cost, progress payments, patent

5. distributes, less, occupational choice

6. monetary cost, professional mercenaries

7. taxes, demand-pull, borrowing, money

8. instability

9. civilian goods and services, military goods and services

10. decrease, increase, easy

11. *a.* military, civilian; *b.* spillover; *c.* private, inevitable; *d.* fiscal, monetary; *e.* conflict, development

12. national priorities, civilian, military

Problems and projects

1. *a.* 8, 0; *b.* 7, 100; *c.* 300; *d.* 200

Self-test

1. F; 2. F; 3. F; 4. T; 5. F; 6. T; 7. T; 8. F; 9. T; 10. F

1. *a;* 2. *a;* 3. *a;* 4. *c;* 5. *a;* 6. *d;* 7. *d;* 8. *b;* 9. *a;* 10. *c*

CHAPTER 40

Fill-in questions

1. nature; *a.* other people; *b.* capitalists, bourgeois, workers, proletariat

2. private property, machinery, equipment, employment (a livelihood), profit, surplus value, exploit, wage

3. competition, profits (surplus value) machinery, equipment, national output, capital, labor, profits

4. exploitation

5. *a.* monopolization; *b.* imperialism

6. revolution, proletariate, capital, capitalistic, socialist

7. *a.* harmony, conflict; *b.* narrow, problems, political power

8. *a.* large (monopolistic), state (government), markets, workers, consumers; *b.* inequality, alienation, irrational, imperialism; *c.* socialism

9. *a.* It fails to control monopolies; *b.* It uses revenues from regressive taxes to subsidize them; *c.* It provides markets for them

10. marginal product, national income; *a.* competitive; *b.* labor; *c.* unearned

11. *a.* institutions, private property, power, power; *b.* dual, primary, secondary

12. *a.* lives, decision, making; *b.* large corporations

13. *a.* profit; *b.* environment, wants, military, imperialistic

14. socialism, democratic, decent, human, profit

15. reality, objective, ideology, option

Problems and projects

1. *a.* 8, 7, 6, 5, 4, 3, 2; *b.* 5; *c.* 20; *d.* 30, 10; *e.* 6; *f.* 2

2. *a.* 400; 394, 388.6; *b.* 70, 69, 68; *c.* 120, 118, 116.6; *d.* (1) 380, 386, 392.4, (2) .316, .306, .297; *e.* (1) decreases, increases, (2) decreases

Self-test

1. F; 2. T; 3. T; 4. F; 5. F; 6. F; 7. T; 8. T; 9. T; 10. F; 11. T; 12. F; 13. T; 14. F; 15. F; 16. T; 17. F; 18. T

1. *b;* 2. *d;* 3. *a;* 4. *c;* 5. *d;* 6. *a;* 7. *c;* 8. *d;* 9. *d;* 10. *b;* 11. *d;* 12. *c;* 13. *b;* 14. *a;* 15. *d*

CHAPTER 41

Fill-in questions

1. less mobile, money, restrictions

2. 7, 119, 124

3. machinery, transport equipment, grains and cereals; petroleum and products; autos and parts; electrical machinery

4. comparative advantage, comparative advantage

5. output, inputs (resources); resources, uneven, different combination of resources

6. *a.* inexpensive, expensive; *b.* expensive, inexpensive; *c.* hats, bananas; *d.* 3, 4, world demand and supply for hats and bananas; *e.* (1) $1/3$, $2/7$, (2) 4, $3^1/2$

7. cost, increases

8. *a.* efficient; *b.* prices; *c.* resource; *d.* mobility

9. *a.* exports, imports; *b.* directly, total income; *c.* directly, its own total income (or net national product)

10. *a.* net exports; *b.* aggregate demand; *c.* save, import

11. national income (or net national product), imports

12. *a.* −; *b.* +; *c.* +; *d.* −

Problems and projects

1. *a.* constant; *b.* (1) 8, 2, (2) 4, 2; *c.* (1) it has a comparative advantage in producing wheat (its cost of producing wheat is less than Chile's), (2) it has a comparative advantage in producing copper (its cost of producing copper is less than

the United States); *d.* one of the two nations would be unwilling to trade if the terms of trade are outside this range; *f.* (1) 1, 0, (2) 1, 0

2. *a.* (1) increase, decrease, (2) decrease, increase; *b.* (1) rise, fall, equal, (2) fall, rise, equal; *c.* (1) increase, decrease, (2) decrease, increase; *d.* (1) rise, fall, they are the same as the prices for these resources in the United States, (2) fall, rise, they are the same as the prices for these resources in France; *e.* (1) chicken, wine, (2) wine, chicken

3. *a.* $16, 12, 8, 4, 0, −4, −8; *b.* $792, 828, 864, 900, 936, 972, 1,008; *c.* $900; *d.* 0.08; *e.* 3.57; *f.* (1) increase, $35.7, (2) decrease, $35.7

Self-test

1. T; 2. F; 3. T; 4. F; 5. F; 6. T; 7. T; 8 T; 9. T; 10. F

1. *a;* 2. *b;* 3. *d;* 4. *a;* 5. *a;* 6. *a;* 7. *b;* 8. *b*

CHAPTER 42

Fill-in questions

1. a better allocation of resources, a higher standard of living

2. tariffs, import quotas, protect special interest groups, attempt to increase net exports, protect domestic producers of essential war goods, industrialize and diversify their economies

3. *a.* increase; *b.* decrease· *c.* (1) increase, (2) decrease; *d.* decrease, decrease

4. *a.* military self-sufficiency; *b.* infant industry; *c.* increase domestic employment; *d.* diversification for stability; *e.* protect high wages and the high standard of living; *f.* slow down the diffusion of technology; military-self-sufficiency, infant-industry

5. upward, Reciprocal Trade Agreements, downward; lower tariff rates up to 50% in return for a reduction of foreign restrictions on American goods, most-favored-nation clauses

6. *a.* equal, nondiscriminatory treatment of all trading nations; *b.* reduction of tariffs by negotiation; *c.* elimination of import quotas

7. tariffs and import quotas among members, common tariffs on goods imported from nonmembers, capital and labor among member nations, other matters, growth, trade, allocation of resources, economies of scale

8. lower or eliminate tariffs on products where the United States and the Common Market have 80% or more of the world's trade, lower tariffs on other goods up to 50% over five years; Kennedy Round

9. Trade Reform, Geneva, nontariff

10. communist; *a.* the easing of the political climate; *b.* the growing interest of the U.S.S.R. in American products; *c.* persistent Soviet agricultural shortfalls which resulted in agreements to buy American grain; *d.* recognition that the restrictionist American policy was unrealistic and a failure

Problems and projects

a. 750, 700, 650, 600, 550, 500, 450, 300, 0; *b.* $2.00, 600; *c.* 375, 350, 325, 300, 0, 0, 0, 0, 0; *d.* 650, 600, 550, 500, 175, 150, 125, 0, 0; *e.* $2.20, 550; *f.* (1) increased, 25, (2) decreased, 75; *g.* (1) increased, $95, (2) decreased, $345; *h.* increased, $10; *i.* increased, $260; *j.* decreased, $345, decrease, $345

Self-test

1. T; 2. F; 3. T; 4. T; 5. F; 6. T; 7. T; 8. F; 9. F; 10. T

1. *c;* 2. *a;* 3. *d;* 4. *a;* 5. *d;* 6. *c;* 7. *d;* 8. *c;* 9. *d;* 10. *a*

CHAPTER 43

Fill-in questions

1. dollars, one French franc

2. 2½

3. imports, exports, exports, imports

4. increase, decrease, increase, decreases

5. *a.* exports of goods and services; *b.* imports of goods and services; *c.* net balance due on exports and imports; *d.* net remittances; *e.* net government transactions; *f.* net capital move-

ments; *g.* balance due to or from rest of world; *h.* financing (balancing) transactions

6. less, from

7. loans, investments, foreign money

8. inpayments (outpayments), outpayments (inpayments), foreign money, decreases (increases)

9. surplus, deficit

10. gives, loans, invests

11. foreign money, its own money owned by foreigners, autonomous

12. freely floating foreign exchange rates, changing price and income levels, public controls

13. increase, decrease, decrease, increase

14. risks, reduce, terms of trade, prices, output, eliminate balance-of-payments disequilibrium

15. defines its monetary unit in terms of gold and will buy and sell gold at the rate set down in its definition of the monetary unit, allows gold to be exported and imported freely

16. the gold equivalent of monetary units, the cost of transporting gold; gold export point, gold import point

CHAPTER 44

Fill-in questions

1. large, raw materials, underdeveloped, manufactured goods, manufacturing nations, comparative advantage, laissez faire, gold standard

2. depression, war; exports, capital flows, trade barriers

3. imports, exports, balance of payments; inflation, productive capacities

4. assist European recovery, create an international monetary system, reduce trade barriers

5. rebuild the European economy; European Recovery

6. stable, adjustable peg

7. *a.* stabilization, foreign, domestic, gold; *b.* loans, deficits; *c.* 10; *d.* stable, flexible

8. gold, key currencies, the American dollar

9. *a.* deficits; *b.* gold; *c.* decreased; *d.* eliminated, continued

10. productivity, inflation, outflows, military, economic aid expenditures, OPEC

11. *a.* increasing the productivity of American firms; *b.* using monetary and fiscal policies to restrain domestic inflation; *c.* getting Western Europe to assume a larger share of the cost of mutual defense and economic aid to underdeveloped nations; *d.* obtaining the reduction or elimination of the foreign restrictions on the import of American goods

12. imports, exports, international trade, retaliate

17. *a.* decrease; *b.* less, more; *c.* decrease, increase; *d.* decreases, increases

18. stable exchange rates, price levels, outputs, levels of employment

19. import, exported, the government

20. tariffs, quotas, subsidizing

Problems and projects

1. *a.* (1) +47.9, (2) −39.1, (3) −7.2, (4) +4.6; *b.* (reading down) +47.9, +32.5, +8.1, +7.3, −39.1, −31.1, −6.2, −1.8, +8.8, −1.5, −4.7, −7.2, −10.2, +3.0, −4.6, +0.7, +3.9; *c.* deficit, 4.6; *d.* −4.6, +4.6

2. $^1/_2$, $^2/_5$, $^1/_3$, $^2/_7$, $^1/_4$, $^2/_9$, $^1/_5$, lower

3. *a.* 5.00, $^1/_5$; *b.* 5.03, 4.97; *c.* 0.201, 0.199

4. *a.* 4.00; *b.* $^1/_4$; *c.* 300; *d.* 1,200

Self-test

1. T; **2.** F; **3.** F; **4.** F; **5.** F; **6.** T; **7.** F; **8.** T; **9.** T; **10.** F

1. *c;* **2.** *b;* **3.** *d;* **4.** *c;* **5.** *b;* **6.** *d;* **7.** *b;* **8.** *c;* **9.** *a;* **10.** *d*

13. fixed, floating

14. *a.* the status of the dollar, grow; *b.* exchange-rate pegs

15. gold, market forces

16. *a.* over-; *b.* did not; *c.* devaluation

17. managed floating; *a.* stable; *b.* disequilibria

18. Special drawing rights (SDRs), deficits, international monetary reserves, demonitization

19. inflation, nonsystem

20. *a.* conflicts; *b.* conflicts

Problems and projects

1. 1. F; 2. L; 3. J; 4. A; 5. H; 6. I; 7. D; 8. K; 9. E; 10. B; 11. G

2. *a.* sell, 100, buy, 200; *b.* buy 200, sell 400

3. *a.* (1) contractionary, tight, (2) (*a*) increase, (*b*) decrease, (*c*) rise, into, (*d*) decrease, (3) reduce, (4) (*a*) exports, (*b*) imports, (*c*) interest, capital, (*d*) widened; *b.* (1) expansionary, easy, (2) (*a*) decrease, (*b*) increase, (*c*) fall, out of, (*d*) decrease, (3) reduce, (4) widened; *c.* (1) are compatible, conflict, (2) conflict, are compatible

Self-test

1. F; **2.** T; **3.** T; **4.** T; **5.** F; **6.** T; **7.** T; **8.** T; **9.** T; **10.** F; **11.** F; **12.** T; **13.** F; **14.** T; **15.** F; **16.** F; **17.** T; **18.** F; **19.** F; **20.** F

1. *b;* **2.** *c;* **3.** *d;* **4.** *c;* **5.** *d;* **6.** *d;* **7.** *d;* **8.** *c;* **9.** *d;* **10.** *b;* **11.** *a;* **12.** *a;* **13.** *b;* **14.** *a;* **15.** *a;* **16.** *a;* **17.** *a;* **18.** *c;* **19.** *d;* **20.** *c*

CHAPTER 45

Fill-in questions

1. state ownership of property resources, central economic planning

2. Soviet government, many small economic units

3. coordination, bottleneck, chain reaction

4. negotiation, priority, reserve stocks

5. *Gosplan, Gosbank*

6. monetary incentives, nonmonetary incentives, coercive techniques

7. as an accounting device for checking productive efficiency, as a means of rationing products among consumers

8. the efficiency of production, affect the allocation of resources

9. *a.* (1) unsalable, unwanted, (2) production, quality, (3) innovate; *b.* (1) profit motive, (2) decentralized planning, autonomy, (3) below; *c.* Professor E. Liberman

10. one-half, 3½

11. *a.* the large natural resource base; *b.* the totalitarian government has allocated resources to promote growth; *c.* the surplus of farm labor; *d.* the employment of the superior technologies developed in Western nations; *e.* the absence of cyclical unemployment

12. *a.* the diversion of resources to customer goods, foreign aid, and military goods; *b.* increasing replacement investment; *c.* a manpower short-age; *d.* the backwardness of Soviet agriculture; *e.* the increasing complexity of economic planning as the economy grows

13. *a.* the increased quantity and quality of education; *b.* the development of a complete system of social insurance

14. the failure of the consumer's standard of living to increase by as much as is possible; the limited freedom of Soviet citizens

Problems and projects

1. state ownership of property resources; relative consumer freedom to spend income as he sees fit; central economic planning; workers are generally free to choose occupation and place of work; central economic planning and various forms of incentives; central economic planning; central economic planning with prices playing an implemental role; central economic planning and various forms of incentives which appeal to self-interest; state and collective farms; state-owned and co-operative firms and retail stores

2. *a.* 40; *b.* 60

Self-test

1. T; **2.** T; **3.** T; **4.** F; **5.** F; **6.** F; **7.** T; **8.** F; **9.** T; **10.** F

1. *b;* **2.** *d;* **3.** *b;* **4.** *a;* **5.** *b;* **6.** *b;* **7.** *b;* **8.** *d;* **9.** *a;* **10.** *b*

Glossary

Ability-to-pay principle The belief that those who have the greater income (or wealth) should be taxed absolutely and relatively more than those who have less.

Abstraction Elimination of irrelevant and noneconomic facts to obtain an economic principle.

Accelerationist view The contention that the negatively sloped Phillips curve *(see)* does not exist in the long run and that attempts to reduce the Unemployment rate bring about an accelerating rate of Inflation.

Accommodating transactions *(See* Financing transactions.)

Acreage-allotment program The program which determined the total number of acres that was to be used to produce various agricultural products and allocated these acres among individual farmers who were required to limit their plantings to the number of acres alloted to them if they wished to obtain the Support price for their crops.

Acreage-reserve program A program in which the Federal government made payments to farmers who took land away from the production of crops.

Actual investment The amount which business Firms do invest; equal to Planned investment plus unintended (unplanned) investment.

Actual reserve The amount which a Member bank has on deposit at the Federal Reserve Bank of its district (plus its Vault cash).

Actual saving The amount which Households (and business Firms) do save.

Adjustable pegs The device utilized in the Bretton Woods system *(see)* to change Exchange rates in an orderly way to eliminate persistent Payments deficits and surpluses: each nation defined its monetary unit in terms of (pegged it to) gold or the dollar, kept the Rate of exchange for its money stable in the short run, and changed (adjusted) it in the long run when faced with International disequilibrium.

AFDC *(See Aid to families with dependent children.)*

Aggregate demand A schedule which shows the Aggregate quantity demanded *(see)* at different levels of Net national product.

Aggregate demand—aggregate supply approach Determination of the Equilibrium net national product *(see)* by finding the Net national product at which the aggregate quantity of goods and services demanded is equal to the aggregate quantity of goods and services supplied.

Aggregate quantity demanded The total quantity of goods and services which purchasers plan to buy at any level of Net national product.

Aggregate quantity supplied The total

quantity of goods and services producers will offer for sale at any level of Net national product; equal to the Net national product.

Aggregate supply A schedule which shows the Aggregate quantity supplied *(see)* at different levels of Net national product.

Agricultural Adjustment Act The Federal act of 1933 which established the Parity concept *(see)* as the cornerstone of American agricultural policy and provided Price supports for farm products, restriction of agricultural production, and the disposal of surplus output.

Agricultural and Consumer Protection Act The Federal act of 1973 which changed the agricultural policy of the United States toward less government involvement in agriculture and freer markets for farm products; and which provided for Target prices *(see)*, the encouragement of agricultural production, and a limit on the size of the agricultural subsidy that could be received by any one farmer.

Aid to families with dependent children A state-administered and partly Federally funded program in the United States which provides aid to families in which dependent children do not have the support of a parent because of his or her death, disability, or desertion.

Alienation The inability of individuals to take part in the process by which the decisions that affect them are made and to control their own lives and activities.

Allocative factor The ability of an economy to reallocate resources to achieve the Economic growth which the Supply factors *(see)* make possible.

Alternative cost doctrine The cost of producing a particular product is equal to the quantity of other products that cannot be produced (that must be done without, foregone, or sacrificed).

American Federation of Labor The organization of affiliated Craft unions formed in 1886.

Annually balanced budget The equality of government expenditures and tax collections during a year.

Anticipations *(See Expectations.)*

Applied economics *(See Policy economics.)*

Arbitration The designation of a neutral third party to render a decision in a dispute by which both parties (the employer and the labor union) agree in advance to abide.

Asset Anything with a monetary value owned by a firm or an individual.

Authoritarian socialism *(See Communism.)*

Autonomous transactions A nation's Exports of goods and services, Imports of goods and services, Remittances, government transactions, and capital movements; the transactions in the International balance of payments caused by basic economic considerations.

Average fixed cost The total Fixed cost *(see)* of a Firm divided by its output (the quantity of product produced).

Average product Average physical product; the total output produced per unit of a resource employed (total output divided by the quantity of a resource employed).

Average propensity to consume Fraction of Disposable income which households spend for consumer goods and services; consumption divided by Disposable income.

Average propensity to save Fraction of Disposable income which households save; Saving divided by Disposable income.

Average revenue Total revenue from the sale of a product divided by the quantity of the product sold (demanded); equal to the price at which the product is sold so long as all units of the product are sold at the same price.

Average tax rate Total tax paid divided by total (taxable) income; the tax rate on total (taxable) income.

Average (total) cost The Total cost of a Firm divided by its output (the quantity of product produced); equal to Average fixed cost *(see)* plus Average variable cost *(see)*.

Average variable cost The total Variable cost *(see)* of a Firm divided by its output (the quantity of product produced).

Balanced budget multiplier The effect of equal increases (decreases) in government spending for goods and services and in taxes is to increase (decrease) the Equilibrium net national product by the amount of the equal increases (decreases).

Balance of payments deficit *(See Payments deficit.)*

Balance of payments surplus *(See Payments surplus.)*

Balance sheet A statement of the Assets *(see)*, Liabilities *(see)*, and Net worth *(see)* of a Firm or individual at some given time.

Bankers' bank A band which accepts the

deposits of and makes loans to Commercial banks; a Federal Reserve Bank.

Barrier to entry Anything that artificially prevents the entry of Firms into an industry.

Barter The exchange of one good or service for another good or service.

Base year The year with which prices in other years are compared when a Price index *(see)* is constructed.

Basic social capital Public utilities, roads, communication systems, railways, housing, and educational and public health facilities; the Capital goods which must exist before there can be profitable (productive) investments in manufacturing, agriculture, and commerce.

Benefit-cost analysis Deciding whether to employ resources and the quantity of resources to employ for a project or program (for the production of a good or service) by comparing the benefit with the cost.

Benefits-received principle The belief that those who receive the benefits of goods and services provided by government should pay the taxes required to finance them.

Big business A business Firm which either produces a large percentage of the total output of an industry, is large (in terms of number of employees or stockholders, sales, assets, or profits) compared with other Firms in the economy, or both.

Bilateral monopoly A market in which there is a single seller (Monopoly) and a single buyer (Monopsony).

Black capitalism The creation of new business Firms owned and operated by Negroes.

Blacklisting The passing from one employer to another of the names of workers who favor the formation of labor unions and who ought not to be hired.

Board of Governors The seven-member group that supervises and controls the money and banking system of the United States; formally, the Board of Governors of the Federal Reserve System; the Federal Reserve Board.

Bourgeois The capitalists; the capitalistic class; the owners of the machinery and equipment needed for production in an industrial society.

Break-even point Any output which a (competitive) Firm might produce at which its Total cost and Total revenue would be equal; an output at which it has neither profit nor a loss.

Bretton Woods system The international monetary system developed after World War II in which Adjustable pegs *(see)* were employed, the International Monetary Fund *(see)* helped to stabilize Foreign exchange rates, and gold and the Key currencies *(see)* were used as International monetary reserves *(see).*

Budget restraint The limit imposed upon the ability of an individual consumer to obtain goods and services by the size of the consumer's income (and by the prices that must be paid for the goods and services).

Built-in stability The effect of Nondiscretionary fiscal policy *(see)* upon the economy; when Net taxes vary directly with the Net national product the fall (rise) in Net taxes during a recession (inflation) helps to eliminate unemployment (inflationary pressures).

Business cycle Recurrent ups and downs over a period of years in the level of economic activity.

Business unionism The belief that the labor union should concern itself with such practical and short-run objectives as higher wages, shorter hours, and improved working conditions and should not concern itself with long-run and idealistic changes in the capitalistic system.

Capacity-creating aspect of investment The effect of investment spending on the productive capacity (the ability to produce goods and services) of an economy.

Capital Man-made resources used to produce goods and services; goods which do not directly satisfy human wants; Capital goods.

Capital consumption allowances Estimate of the amount of Capital worn out or used up (consumed) in producing the Gross National Product.

Capital gain The gain realized when securities or properties are sold for a price greater than the price paid for them.

Capital goods *(See Capital.)*

Capital-intensive commodity A product in the production of which a relatively large amount of Capital is employed.

Capital-output ratio The ratio of the stock of Capital to the productive (output) capacity of the economy; and the ratio of a change in the stock of Capital (net investment) to the resulting change in productive capacity.

Capital-saving technological advance An improvement in technology that permits a greater quantity of a product to be produced with a given amount of Capital (or the same amount of the product to be produced with a smaller amount of Capital).

Capital-using technological advance An improvement in technology that requires the use of a greater amount of Capital to produce a given quantity of a product.

Cartel A formal written or oral agreement among Firms to set the price of the product and the outputs of the individual firms or to divide the market for the product geographically.

Categorical grant An Intergovernmental grant *(see)* for a specific program and requiring the recipient government to pay a part of the cost of the program.

Causation A cause-and-effect relationship; one or several events bring about or result in another event.

CEA *(See* Council of Economic Advisors.)

Cease-and-desist order An order from a court or government agency (commission or board) to a corporation or individual to stop engaging in a specified practice.

Ceiling price *(See* Price ceiling.)

Celler-Kefauver Act The Federal act of 1950 which amended the Clayton Act *(see)* by prohibiting the acquisition of the assets of one firm by another firm when the effect would be to lessen competition.

Central bank A bank whose chief function is the control of the nation's money supply.

Central economic planning (1) Determination of the objectives of the economy and the direction of its resources to the attainment of these objectives by the national government; (2) the activities of a proposed Federal organization in the United States which would generate information from which economic forecasts can be made, establish macroeconomic targets for the economy, and coordinate policy decisions to achieve these targets.

Change in amount consumed Increase or decrease in consumption spending that results from an increase or decrease in Disposable income, the Consumption schedule (curve) remaining unchanged; movement from one line (point) to another on the same Consumption schedule (curve).

Change in amount saved Increase or decrease in Saving that results from an increase or decrease in Disposable income, the Saving schedule (curve) remaining unchanged; movement from one line (point) to another on the same Saving schedule (curve).

Change in the consumption schedule An increase or decrease in consumption at each level of Disposable income caused by changes in the Nonincome determinants of consumption and saving *(see)*; an upward or downward movement of the Consumption schedule.

Change in the saving schedule An increase or decrease in Saving at each level of Disposable income caused by changes in the Nonincome determinants of consumption and saving *(see)*; an upward or downward movement of the Saving schedule.

Checkoff The deduction by an employer of union dues from the pay of workers and the transfer of the amount deducted to a labor union.

Circuit velocity of money *(See* Income velocity of money.)

Circular flow of income The flow of resources from Households to Firms and of products from Firms to Households accompanied in an economy using money by flows of money from Households to Firms and from Firms to Households.

Classical theory of employment The Macroeconomic generalizations which were accepted by most economists prior to the 1930s and which led to the conclusion that a capitalistic economy would tend to employ its resources fully.

Class struggle The struggle for the output of the economy between the Proletariate *(see)* and the Bourgeois *(see)* in a capitalistic society.

Clayton Act The Federal antitrust act of 1914 which strengthened the Sherman Act *(see)* by making it illegal for business firms to engage in certain specified practices.

Closed economy An economy which neither exports nor imports goods and services.

(The) close-down case The circumstances which would result in a loss greater than its Total fixed cost if a (competitive) Firm were to produce any output greater than zero and which would induce it to cease (close down) production (the plant); when the price at which the Firm can sell its product is less than Average variable cost.

Closed shop A place of employment at which only workers who are already members of a labor union may be hired.

Club of Rome An international group of scientists, businessmen, and academicians which contends that future economic growth in the world is impossible; which bases its predictions on a Doomsday model *(see)*; and which advocates ZEG *(see)* and ZPG *(see)*.

Coincidence of wants The item (good or service) which one trader wishes to obtain is the same item which another trader desires to give up and the item which the second trader wishes to acquire is the same item the first trader desires to surrender.

Collection of checks The process by which funds are transferred from the checking accounts of the writers of checks to the checking accounts of the recipients of the checks; also called the "clearing" of checks.

Collusive oligopoly An Oligopoly in which the Firms act together and in agreement (collude) to set the price of the product and the output each firm will produce or to determine the geographic area in which each firm will sell.

Combination The creation of a new Firm from two or more existing Firms or the purchase by one Firm of the stock or Assets of one or more other Firms.

Combined tax-transfer system The percentage of income collected as taxes less the percentage of income received as transfer payments in different income classes.

Commerical bank A bank which accepts deposits against which checks may be written (which accepts Demand deposits, *see*).

Commercial banking system All Commercial banks as a group.

Communism An economic system (method of organization) in which the public ownership of property resources (Land and Capital) and Central economic planning *(see)* are used to determine how society will employ its scarce resources to satisfy human wants.

Company union An organization of employees which is dominated by the employer (the company) and does not engage in genuine collective bargaining with the employer.

Comparative advantage A lower Comparative cost *(see)* than another producer.

Comparative cost The amount the production of one product must be reduced to increase the production of another product; *(see)* Opportunity cost.

Compensation to employees Wages and salaries paid by employers to workers plus Wage and salary supplements *(see)*.

Competing goods (See Substitute goods.)

Competition The presence in a market of a large number of independent buyers and sellers and the freedom of buyers and sellers to enter and to leave the market.

Competitive advertising Advertising that makes unsubstantiated claims for a product; advertising that is not Informative advertising *(see)*.

(The) competitive industry's short-run supply curve The horizontal summation of the short-run supply curves of the Firms in a purely competitive industry (*see* Pure competition); a curve which shows the total quantities that will be offered for sale at various prices by the Firms in an industry in the Short run *(see)*.

(The) competitive industry's short-run supply schedule The summation of the short-run supply schedules of the Firms in a purely competitive industry (*see* Pure competition); a schedule which shows the total quantities that will be offered for sale at various prices by the Firms in an industry in the Short run *(see)*.

Complementary goods Goods or services such that there is an inverse relationship between the price of one and the demand for the other; when the price of one falls (rises) the demand for the other increases (decreases).

Complex multiplier The Multiplier *(see)* when changes in the Net national product not only change Saving but aslo change Net taxes and Imports.

Conglomerate combination A group of Plants *(see)* owned by a single Firm and engaged at one or more stages in the production of different products (of products which do not compete with each other).

Conglomerate merger The merger of a Firm in one Industry with a Firm in another Industry (with a Firm that is neither supplier, customer, nor competitor).

Congress of Industrial Organizations The organization of affiliated industrial unions formed in 1936.

Constant-cost industry An Industry in which the expansion of the Industry by the entry of new Firms has no effect upon the prices the Firms in the industry pay for resources and no effect, therefore, upon their cost schedules (curves).

Consumer goods Goods and services which satisfy human wants directly.

Consumer sovereignty Determination by consumers of the types and quantities of goods and services that are produced from the scarce resources of the economy.

Consumption schedule Schedule which shows the amounts Households plan to spend for Consumer goods at different levels of Disposable income.

Contractionary fiscal policy A decrease in Aggregate demand brought about by a decrease in Government expenditures for goods and services, an increase in Net taxes, or some combination of the two.

"Control by the ruble" The requirement in the U.S.S.R. that each plant's receipts and expenditures be completed through the use of checks drawn on *Gosbank (see)* which enables *Gosbank* to record the performance and progress of each plant toward the fulfillment of the production targets assigned it by *Gosplan*.

Convergence hypothesis The proposition advanced by some economists that the differences between capitalistic and communistic economic systems will decrease over time.

Corporation A legal entity ("person") chartered by a state or the Federal government, and distinct and separate from the individuals who own it.

Corporation income tax A tax levied on the net income (profit) of Corporations.

Correlation Systematic and dependable association between two sets of data (two kinds of events).

Cost overrun The amount by which the final cost of a project exceeds its initially estimated cost.

Cost-plus contract A contract which provides that the supplier of a product be paid an amount equal to the cost of producing the product plus an additional amount for profit.

Cost-push inflation Inflation which results from an increase in the cost of producing goods and services.

Cost ratio The ratio of the decrease in the production of one product to the increase in the production of another product when resources are shifted from the production of the first to the production of the second product; the amount the production of one product decreases when the production of a second product increases by one unit.

Council of Economic Advisers A group of three persons which advises and assists the President of the United States on economic matters (including the preparation of the economic report of the President to Congress).

Countervailing power The power which (John Kenneth Galbraith believes) arises on the buyers' side of a market to check or restrain the power of a Monopoly or Oligopoly to control price and arises on the sellers' side to limit the power of Monopsony or Oligopsony over price.

Craft union A labor union which limits its membership to workers with a particular skill (craft).

Crawling-peg system A proposed system of Exchange rates that would allow a nation with a Payments deficit to change the defined value of its money by a specified percentage each month.

Creeping inflation A 2 to 4 percent annual rise in the price level.

Criminal-conspiracy doctrine The (now outdated) legal doctrine that combinations of workers (Labor unions) to raise wages were criminal conspiracies and, therefore, illegal.

Crowding-out effect Government borrowing to finance a budget deficit will increase the Interest rate and the higher Interest rate will reduce (crowd out) private investment spending.

Currency Coins and Paper money.

Cyclically balanced budget The equality of Government expenditures for goods and services and Net taxes collections over the course of a Business cycle; deficits incurred during periods of recession are offset by surpluses obtained during periods of prosperity (inflation).

Cyclical unemployment Unemployment caused by insufficient Aggregate demand.

Declining economy An economy in which Net private domestic investment *(see)* is less than zero (Gross private domestic investment is less than Depreciation).

Declining industry An Industry in which Economic profits are negative (losses are incurred) and which will, therefore, decrease its output as Firms leave the industry.

Decrease in demand A decrease in the Quantity demanded of a good or service at every price; a shift of the Demand curve to the left.

Decrease in supply A decrease in the Quantity supplied of a good or service at every price; a shift of the Supply curve to the left.

Deduction Reasoning from assumptions to conclusions; a method of reasoning that tests a hypothesis (an assumption) by comparing the conclusions to which it leads with economic facts.

Deflating   Finding the Real gross national product *(see)* by decreasing the dollar value of the Gross national product produced in a year in which prices were higher than in the Base year *(see)*.

Deflation   A fall in the general (average) level of prices in the economy.

Deglomerative forces   Increases in the cost of producing and marketing that result from the growth of cities and the concentration of firms and industries within a geographic area.

Demand curve   A curve which shows the amounts of a good or service buyers wish to purchase at various prices during some period of time.

Demand deposit   A deposit in a Commercial bank against which checks may be written; bank-created or checking-account money.

Demand-deposit multiplier   The multiple of its Excess reserve *(see)* by which the Commercial banking system *(see)* can expand Demand deposits and the Money supply by making new loans (or buying securities); equal to one divided by the Reserve ratio *(see)*.

Demand factor   The increase in the level of Aggregate demand which brings about the Economic growth made possible by an increase in the productive potential of the economy.

Demand-pull inflation   Inflation which is the result of an increase in Aggregate demand.

Demand schedule   A schedule which shows the amounts of a good or service buyers wish to purchase at various prices during some period of time.

Depreciation   (*See* Capital consumption allowances.)

Derived demand   The demand for a good or service which is dependent upon or related to the demand for some other good or service; the demand for a resource which depends upon the demand for the products it can be used to produce.

Descriptive economics   The gathering or collection of relevant economic facts (data).

DI   (*See* Disposable income.)

Dictatorship of the proletariate   The rule by the working class which is to follow the revolution overthrowing capitalism and the introduction of socialism in the Marxian vision of the future.

Differentiated product   A product which differs physically or in some other way from the similar products produced by other Firms; a product which is similar to but not identical with and, therefore, not a perfect substitute for other products; a product such that buyers are not indifferent to the seller from whom they purchase it so long as the price charged by all sellers is the same.

Dilemma of regulation   When a Regulatory agency *(see)* must establish the maximum legal price a monopolist may charge it finds that if it sets the price at the Socially optimum price *(see)* this price is below Average cost (and either bankrupts the Firm or requires that it be subsidized) and if it sets the price at the Fair-return price *(see)* it has failed to eliminate the underallocation of resources that is the consequence of unregulated monopoly.

Directing function of prices   The ability of price changes to bring about changes in the quantities of products and resources demanded and supplied; (*See* Incentive function of price.)

Directly related   Two sets of economic data that change in the same direction; when one variable increases/(decreases) the other increases/(decreases).

Discount rate   The interest rate which the Federal Reserve Banks charge on the loans they make to Member banks.

Discretionary fiscal policy   Deliberate changes in taxes (tax rates) and government spending (spending for goods and services and transfer payment programs) by Congress for the purpose of achieving a full-employment noninflationary Net national product and economic growth.

Discriminatory discharge   The firing of workers who favor the formation of Labor unions.

Diseconomies of (large) scale   The forces which increases the Average cost of producing a product as the Firm expands the size of its Plant (its output) in the Long run *(see)*.

Disguised unemployment   The inefficient employment (the Underemployment, *see*) of an economic resource, especially Labor.

Disposable income   Personal income *(see)* less Personal taxes *(see)*; income available for Personal consumption expenditures *(see)* and Personal saving *(see)*.

Dissaving   Spending for consumer goods and services in excess of Disposable income; the amount by which Personal consumption expenditures *(see)* exceed Disposable income.

Division of labor Dividing the work required to produce a product into a number of different tasks which are performed by different workers; Specialization *(see)* of workers.

"Divorce" of ownership and control (*See* Separation of ownership and control.)

Domestic capital formation Adding to a nation's stock of Capital by saving a part of its own national output.

Doomsday model An economic model which predicts that within the next one hundred years there will be a sudden collapse in the world's food and industrial output and its population.

Double counting Including the value of Intermediate goods *(see)* in the Gross national product; counting the same good or service more than once.

Double taxation Taxation of both corporate net income (profits) and the dividends paid from this net income when they become the Personal income of households.

Dual labor market A labor market divided into two distinct types of submarkets; a primary labor market in which workers fare well and a secondary labor market in which they fare poorly.

Dual terminology Practice of using two or more terms to mean the same thing.

Dupoly A market in which there are only two sellers; an Industry in which there are two firms.

Durable good A consumer good with an expected life (use) of one year or more.

Earnings The money income received by a worker; equal to the Wage (rate) multiplied by the quantity of labor supplied (the amount of time worked) by the worker.

Easy money policy Expanding the Money supply.

Economic analysis Deriving Economic principles *(see)* from relevant economic facts.

Economic choice A choice which a consumer, resource supplier, or business Firm must make because resources are scarce

Economic cost A payment that must be made to obtain and retain the services of a resource; the income a Firm must provide to a resource supplier to attract the resource away from an alternative use; equal to the quantity of other products that cannot be produced when resources are employed to produce a particular product.

Economic efficiency The relationship between the input of scarce resources and the

resulting output of a good or service; production of an output with a given dollar-and-cents value with the smallest total expenditure for resources; obtaining the largest total production of a good or service with resources of a given dollar-and-cents value.

Economic flexibility Ability of an economy to respond to changes in consumer tastes, in supplies of resources, and in technology to achieve the maximum satisfaction of wants.

Economic growth (1) An increase in the Production possibilities schedule or curve that results from an increase in resource supplies or an improvement in Technology; (2) an increase either in real output (Gross national product) or in real output per capita.

Economic integration Cooperation among and the complete or partial unification of the economies of different nations; the elimination of the barriers to trade among these nations; the bringing together of the markets in each of the separate economies to form one large (a common) market.

Economic law (*See* Economic principle.)

Economic model A simplified picture of reality; an abstract generalization.

Economic policy Course of action that will correct or avoid a problem.

Economic principle Generalization of the economic behavior of individuals and institutions.

Economic profit The total receipts (revenue) of a firm less all its Economic costs; also called "pure profit" and "above normal profit."

Economic rent The price paid for the use of land and other natural resources, the supply of which is fixed (perfectly inelastic).

Economics Social science concerned with using scarce resources to obtain the maximum satisfaction of the unlimited human wants of society.

Economic theory Deriving Economic principles *(see)* from relevant economic facts; an Economic principle *(see)*.

Economies of agglomeration The reduction in the cost of producing or marketing that results from the location of Firms relatively close to each other.

(The) economies of being established Advantages which Firms already producing a product have over potential producers of the product.

Economies of (large) scale The forces which reduce the Average cost of producing a product as the Firm expands the size of its Plant (its output) in the Long run *(see)*; the economies of mass production.

EEC European Economic Community; *(see)* European Common Market.

Efficient allocation of resources The allocation of the resources of an economy among the production of different products that leads to the maximum satisfaction of the wants of consumers.

Elastic demand The Elasticity coefficient *(see)* is greater than one; the percentage change in Quantity demanded is greater than the percentage change in price.

Elasticity coefficient The number obtained when the percentage change in quantity demanded (or supplied) is divided by the percentage change in the price of the commodity.

Elasticity formula The price elasticity of demand (supply) is equal to

$$\frac{\text{percentage change in quantity demanded (supplied)}}{\text{percentage change in price}}$$

which is equal to

$$\frac{\text{change in quantity demanded (supplied)}}{\text{original quantity demanded (supplied)}}$$

$$\text{divided by } \frac{\text{change in price}}{\text{original price}}$$

Elastic supply The Elasticity coefficient *(see)* is greater than one; the percentage change in Quantity supplied is greater than the percentage change in price.

Emission fees Special fees that might be levied against those who discharge pollutants into the environment.

Emotionally loaded terminology Terms which arouse emotions and elicit approval or disapproval.

Employment Act of 1946 Federal legislation which committed the Federal government to the maintenance of economic stability (Full employment, stable prices, and Economic growth); established the Council of Economic Advisers *(see)* and the Joint Economic Committee *(see)*; and provided for the annual economic report of the President to Congress.

Employment rate The percentage of the Labor force *(see)* employed at any time.

Entrepreneurial ability The human re-source which combines the other resources to produce a product, makes nonroutine decisions, innovates, and bears risks.

Equation of exchange MV = PQ; in which *M* is the Money supply *(see)*, *V* is the Income velocity of money *(see)*, *P* is the Price level, and *Q* is the physical volume of final goods and services produced.

Equilibrium level of NNP The Net national product at which Aggregate quantity demanded *(see)* and Aggregate quantity supplied *(see)* are equal; and at which Leakages *(see)* and Injections *(see)* are equal.

Equilbirium price The price in a competitive market at which the Quantity demanded *(see)* and the Quantity supplied *(see)* are equal; at which there is neither a shortage nor a surplus; and at which there is no tendency for price to rise or fall.

Equilibrium quantity The Quantity demanded *(see)* and Quantity supplied *(see)* at the Equilibrium price *(see)* in a competitive market.

Equalizing differences The differences in the Wages received by workers in different jobs which compensate for nonmonetary differences in the jobs.

ERP *(See* European Recovery Program.)

European Common Market The association of nine European nations initiated in 1958 to abolish gradually the Tariffs and Import quotas among them, to establish common Tariffs for goods imported from outside the nine nations, to allow the eventual free movement of labor and capital among them, and to create other common economic policies.

European Economic Community *(See* European Common Market.)

European Recovery Program The American program of grants and loans in and after 1948 to restore the productive capacity of European agriculture and industry and to achieve other objectives; called the "Marshall Plan" after George C. Marshall, the American Secretary of State at the time.

Excess reserve The amount by which a Member bank's Actual reserve *(see)* exceeds its Required reserve *(see)*; Actual reserve minus Required reserve.

Excess wage settlement tax A tax that would be imposed upon business Frims that grant inflationary wages increases to employees.

Exchange rate appreciation An increase in the value of a nation's money in foreign countries; a decrease in the Rates of exchange for foreign monies.

Exchange rate depreciation A decrease in the value of a nation's money in foreign countries; an increase in the Rates of exchange for foreign monies.

Excise tax A tax levied on the expenditure for a specific product or on the quantity of the product purchased.

Exclusion principle The exclusion of those who do pay for a product from the benefits of the product.

Exclusive unionism The policies employed by a Labor union to restrict the supply of labor by excluding potential members in order to increase the Wages received by its members; the policies typically employed by a Craft union *(see)*.

Expanding economy An economy in which Net private domestic investment *(see)* is greater than zero (Gross private domestic investment is greater than Depreciation).

Expanding industry An Industry in which Economic profits are obtained by the firms in the industry and which will, therefore, increase its output as new firms enter the industry.

Expansionary fiscal policy An increase in Aggregate demand brought about by an increase in Government expenditures for goods and services, a decrease in Net taxes, or some combination of the two.

Expectations What consumers, business Firms, and others believe will happen or what conditions will be in the future.

Expected rate of net profits Annual profits which a firm anticipates it will obtain by purchasing Capital (by investing) expressed as a percentage of the price (cost) of the Capital.

Expenditures approach The method which adds all the expenditures made for Final goods and services to measure the Gross national product.

Explicit cost The monetary payment a Firm must make to an outsider to obtain a resource.

Exploitation Paying a worker a Wage which is less than the value of the output produced by the worker; obtaining Surplus value *(see)* or unearned income.

Exports Spending for the goods and services produced in an economy by foreign individuals, firms, and governments.

External benefit (*See* Spillover benefit.)
External cost (*See* Spillover cost.)

External economies The reduction in a Firm's cost of producing and marketing that results from the expansion of (the output of and the number of Firms in) the Industry of which the Firm is a member.

Externality (*See* Spillover.)

Externally held public debt Public debt *(see)* owed to (United States government securities owned by) foreign citizens, firms, and institutions.

Face value The dollar or cents value stamped on a coin.

Factors of production Economic resources: Land, Capital, Labor, and Entrepreneurial ability.

Fair-return price The price of a product which enables its producer to obtain a Normal profit *(see)* and which is equal to the Average cost of producing it.

Fallacy of composition Incorrectly reasoning that what is true for the individual (or part) is therefore necessarily true for the group (or whole).

Farm problem The relatively low income of farmers (compared with incomes in the nonagricultural sectors of the economy) and the tendency for the prices farmers receive and their incomes to fluctuate sharply from year to year.

FDIC (*See* Federal Deposit Insurance Corporation.)

Featherbedding Payment by an employer to a worker for work not actually performed.

Federal Advisory Committee The group of twelve commercial bankers which advises the Board of Governors *(see)* on banking policy.

Federal Deposit Insurance Corporation The federally chartered corporation which insures the deposit liabilities of Commercial banks (Member and qualified nonmember banks).

Federal Open Market Committee The twelve-member group which determines the purchase-and-sale policies of the Federal Reserve Banks in the market for United States government securities.

Federal Reserve Bank Any one of the twelve banks chartered by the United States government to control the Money supply and perform other functions; *(see)* Central bank, Quasi-public bank, and Bankers' bank.

Federal Reserve Note Paper money issued by and the debts of the Federal Reserve Banks.

Federal Trade Commission Act The Federal act of 1914 which established the five-member Federal Trade Commission to investigate unfair competitive practices of business Firms, to hold hearings on the complaints of such practices, and to issue Cease-and-desist orders *(see)* when Firms were found to engage in these practices.

Feedback mechanism A change in human behavior which is the result of an actual or predicted undesirable event and which has the effect of preventing the recurrence or occurrence of the event.

Female participation rate The percentage of the female population of working age in the Labor force *(see)*.

Fewness A relatively small number of sellers (or buyers) of a good or service.

Fiat money Anything that is Money because government has decreed it to be Money.

Final goods Goods which have been purchased for final use and not for resale or further processing or manufacturing (during the year).

Financial capital *(See* Money capital.)

Financial intermediary A Commercial bank or other financial institution (savings bank, savings and loan association, investment bank, insurance company) which uses the funds (savings) deposited with it to make loans (for investment).

Financing transactions The means a nation employs to finance a Payments deficit *(see)* with other nations and the forms in which a Payments surplus *(see)* is obtained from other nations; the changes in the amounts of foreign monies owned by individuals in a nation and in the amounts of its money owned by foreigners.

Firm An organization that employs resources to produce a good or service for profit and owns and operates one or more Plants *(see)*.

(The) firm's short-run supply curve A curve which shows the quantities of a product a Firm in a purely competitive industry *(see* Pure competition) will offer to sell at various prices in the Short run *(see)*; the portion of the Firm's short-run Marginal cost *(see)* curve which lies above its Average variable cost curve.

(The) firm's short-run supply schedule A schedule which shows the quantities of product a Firm in a purely competitive industry *(see* Pure competition) will offer to sell at various prices in the Short run *(see)*; the por-

tion of the firm's short-run marginal cost *(see)* schedule in which Marginal cost is equal to or greater than Average variable cost.

Fiscal drag The difficulty encountered in reaching and maintaining Full employment when the revenues from Net taxes vary directly with the Net national product.

Fiscal policy Changes in government spending and tax collections for the purpose of achieving a full-employment and noninflationary Net national product.

Five fundamental economic questions The five questions which every economy must answer: what to produce, how to produce, how to divide the total output, how to maintain Full employment, and how to assure Economic flexibility *(see)*.

Fixed cost Any cost which in total does not change when the Firm changes its output; the cost of Fixed resources *(see)*.

Fixed resource Any resource employed by a Firm the quantity of which the firm cannot change.

Food for peace program The program established under the provisions of Public Law 480 which permits less developed nations to buy surplus American agricultural products and pay for them with their own monies (instead of dollars).

Food stamp program A program in the United States which permits low-income persons to purchase for less than their retail value, or to obtain without cost, coupons that can be exchanged for food items at retail stores.

Foreign exchange control The control a government may exercise over the quantity of foreign money demanded by its citizens and business firms and over the Rates of exchange in order to limit its outpayments to its inpayments (to eliminate a Payments deficit, *(see.)*

Foreign exchange rate *(See* Rate of exchange.)

Fractional reserve A Reserve ratio *(see)* that is less than 100 percent of the deposit liabilities of a Commercial bank.

Freedom of choice Freedom of owners of property resources and money to employ or dispose of these resources as they see fit, of workers to enter any line of work for which they are qualified, and of consumers to spend their incomes in a manner which they deem to be appropriate (best for them).

Freedom of enterprise Freedom of business Firms to employ economic resources, to use these resources to produce products of the firm's own choosing, and to sell these products in markets of their choice.

Freely floating exchange rates Rates of exchange *(see)* which are not controlled and which may, therefore, rise and fall; and which are determined by the demand for and the supply of foreign monies.

Free trade The absence of artificial (government imposed) barriers to trade among individuals and firms in different nations.

Frictional unemployment Unemployment caused by workers voluntarily changing jobs and by temporary layoffs; unemployed workers between jobs.

Full employment (1) Using all available economic resources to produce goods and services; (2) when 96 percent of the Labor force *(see)* is employed.

Full-employment budget What the government expenditures and revenues and its surplus or deficit would be if the economy were to operate at Full employment throughout the year.

Full-employment rate of growth The rate at which an economy is able to grow when it maintains Full employment; equal to the Average propensity to save *(see)* divided by the Capital-output ratio *(see)*.

Full production The maximum amount of goods and services that can be produced from the employed resources of an economy; the absence of Underemployment *(see)*.

Functional distribution of income The manner in which the economy's (the national) income is divided among those who perform different functions (provide the economy with different kinds of resources); the division of National income *(see)* into wages and salaries, proprietors' income, corporate profits, interest, and rent.

Functional finance Use of Fiscal policy to achieve a full-employment noninflationary Net national product without regard to the effect on the Public debt *(see)*.

Galloping inflation *(See* Hyperinflation.)

GATT *(See* General Agreement on Tariffs and Trade.)

General Agreement on Tariffs and Trade The international agreement reached in 1947 by twenty-three nations (including the United States) in which each nation agreed to give equal and nondiscriminatory treatment to the other nations, to reduce tariff rates by multi-

national negotiations, and to eliminate Import quotas.

General equilibrium analysis A study of the Price system as a whole; of the interrelations among equilibrium prices, outputs, and employments in all the different markets of the economy.

Generalization Statistical or probability statement; statement of the nature of the relation between two or more sets of facts.

Geneva round Negotiations taking place (in 1977) in Geneva, Switzerland, under the provisions of the General Agreement on Tariffs and Trade *(see)* to reduce the Nontariff barriers *(see)* to trade, to improve the accessability of nations to raw materials, and to lower the barriers to the importation of American foodstuffs into the European Common Market *(see)*.

Gentlemen's agreement An informal understanding on the price to be charged among the firms in an Oligopoly.

Given year Any year other than the Base year *(see)* for which a Price index *(see)* is constructed.

GNP *(See* Gross national product.)

GNP gap Potential Real gross national product less actual Real gross national product.

Gold certificate Pieces of paper which are owned by the Federal Reserve Banks and are warehouse receipts for gold held by the United States Treasury.

Gold export point The Rate of exchange for a foreign money above which—(when nations participate in the International gold standard *(see)*—the foreign money will not be purchased and gold will be sent (exported) to the foreign country to make payments there.

Gold import point The Rate of exchange for a foreign money below which—when nations participate in the International gold standard *(see)*—a nation's own money will not be sent (imported) into that country by foreigners to make payments there.

Gold standard *(See* International gold standard.)

Gosbank The state owned and operated (and the only) banking system in the U.S.S.R.

Gosplan The State Planning Commission in the U.S.S.R.

Government purchases of goods and services The expenditures of all governments in the economy for Final goods *(see)* and services.

Government transfer payment Disbursement of money (or goods and services) by government for which government receives no currently produced good or service in return.

Green revolution The major technological advance which created new strains of rice and wheat and increased the output per acre and per man-hour of these crops.

Gross national product The total market value of all Final goods *(see)* and services produced in the economy during a year.

Gross private domestic investment Expenditures for newly produced Capital goods *(see)*—machinery, equipment, tools, and buildings—and for additions to inventories.

Guaranteed minimum income The lowest income any family (or individual) in the economy would receive if any one of several programs designed to reduce or eliminate poverty were enacted.

Guiding function of prices (*See* Directing function of prices.)

Horizontal combination A group of Plants *(see)* in the same stage of production and owned by a single Firm *(see)*.

Household An economic unit (of one or more persons) which provides the economy with resources and uses the money paid to it for these resources to purchase goods and services that satisfy human wants.

Humphrey-Hawkins Bill The Full Employment and Balanced Growth Act introduced in Congress in 1976 which would establish a long-range process designed to achieve a 3 percent rate of adult unemployment within four years and guarantee government jobs for those who cannot find them in the Private sector *(see)*.

Hyperinflation A very rapid rise in the price level.

IMF (*See* International Monetary Fund.)

Immobility The inability or unwillingness of a worker or another resource to move from one geographic area ,or occupation to another or from a lower-paying to a higher-paying job.

Imperfect competition All markets except Pure competition *(see)*; Monopoly, Monopsony, Monopolistic competition, Monopsonistic competition, Oligopoly, and Oligopsony *(see all)*.

Imperialism The Exploitation *(see)* of the less economically developed parts of the world by Capitalists *(see)* in the industrially advanced nations; and characterized by colonialism, the employment of the labor and raw materials of the less developed nations by the capitalistic nations, the sale of manufactured goods to them by the advanced nations, and investment by the developed nations in the underdeveloped ones.

Implicit cost The monetary income a Firm sacrifices when it employs a resource it owns to produce a product rather than supplying the resource in the market; equal to what the resource could have earned in the best-paying alternative employment.

Import quota A limit imposed by a nation on the maximum quantity of a good that may be imported from abroad during some period of time.

Imports Spending by individuals, Firms, and governments of an economy for goods and services produced in foreign nations.

Incentive function The inducement which an increase (a decrease) in the price of a commodity offers to sellers of the commodity to make more (less) of it available; and the inducement which an increase (decrease) in price offers to buyers to purchase smaller (larger) quantities; the Directing (Guiding) function of prices *(see)*.

Inclusive unionism The policies employed by a Labor union that does not limit the number of workers in the union in order to increase the Wage (rate); the policies of an Industrial union *(see)*.

Income approach The method which adds all the incomes generated by the production of Final goods and services to measure the Gross national product.

Income-creating aspect of investment The effect of net investment spending upon Aggregate demand and the resulting effect upon the income (output) of an economy.

Income effect The effect which a change in the price of a product has upon the Real income (purchasing power) of a consumer and the resulting effect upon the quantity of that product the consumer would purchase after the consequences of the Substitution effect *(see)* have been taken into account (eliminated).

Income inequality The unequal distribution of an economy's total income among persons or families in the economy.

Income policy Government policy that affects the Money incomes individuals (the wages workers) receive and the prices they pay for goods and services and thereby affects their Real incomes; *(see)* Wage-price policy.

Income velocity of money (*See* Velocity of money.)

Increase in demand An increase in the Quantity demanded of a good or service at every price; a shift in the Demand curve to the right.

Increase in supply An increase in the Quantity supplied of a good or service at every price; a shift in the Supply curve to the right.

Increasing-cost industry An Industry in which the expansion of the Industry through the entry of new Firms increases the prices the Firms in the Industry must pay for resources and, therefore, increases their cost schedules (moves their cost curves upward).

Increasing returns An increase in the Marginal product *(see)* of a resource as successive units of the resource are employed.

Independent goods Goods or services such that there is no relationship between the price of one and the demand for the other; when the price of one rises or falls the demand for the other remains constant.

Indirect business taxes Such taxes as Sales, Excise, and business Property taxes *(see all)*, license fees, and Tariffs *(see)* which Firms treat as costs of producing a product and pass on (in whole or in part) to buyers of the product by charging them higher prices.

Individual demand The Demand schedule *(see)* or Demand curve *(see)* of a single buyer of a good or service.

Individual supply The Supply schedule *(see)* or Supply curve *(see)* of a single seller of a good or service.

Induction A method of reasoning that proceeds from facts to Generalization *(see)*.

Industrial Reorganization Act Legislation introduced in the United States Congress which would define an illegal monopoly as a Firm (or group of Firms) that satisfies any one of three criteria and would make it unnecessary to show in court that the Firm or Firms had colluded to reduce competition.

Industrial reserve army A Marxian term; those workers who are unemployed as a result of the substitution of Capital for Labor, the growing capacity of the economy to produce goods and services, and the inadequate purchasing power of the working class.

Industrial union A Labor union which accepts as members all workers employed in a particular industry (or by a particular firm) and which contains largely unskilled or semi-skilled workers.

Industry The group of (one or more) Firms that produces identical or similar products.

Inelastic demand The Elasticity coefficient *(see)* is less than one; the percentage change in price is greater than the percentage change in Quantity demanded.

Inelastic supply The Elasticity coefficient *(see)* is less than one; the percentage change in price is greater than the percentage change in Quantity supplied.

Inferior good A good or service of which consumers purchase less (more) at every price when their incomes increase (decrease).

Inflating Finding the Real gross national product *(see)* by increasing the dollar value of the Gross national product produced in a year in which prices are lower than they were in the Base year *(see)*.

Inflation A rise in the general (average) level of prices in the economy.

Inflationary expectations The belief of workers, business Firms, and consumers that there will be substantial inflation in the future.

Inflationary gap The amount by which Aggregate demand must decrease to decrease the money Net national product to the full-employment-without-inflation level.

Inflationary psychosis Tendency of consumers and business Firms to increase their spending before an expected rise in the general level of prices occurs.

Inflationary recession (*See* Stagflation.)

Informative advertising Advertising that accurately describes the qualities and prices of products.

Infrastructure Services and facilities which a Firm must have to produce its product, which would be too costly for the Firm to provide for itself, and which are provided by government or other Firms: water, electricity, waste treatment, transportation, research, engineering, finance, banking, etc.

Injection An addition of spending to the income-expenditure stream: Investment, Government purchases of goods and services, and Exports.

Injunction An order from a court of law that directs a person or organization not to perform a certain act because the act would do irreparable damage to some other person or persons; a restraining order.

In-kind transfer The distribution by government of goods and services to individuals and for which the government receives no currently produced good or service in return; a Government transfer payment *(see)* made in goods or services rather than in money.

Innovation The introduction of a new product, the use of a new method of production, or the employment of a new form of business organization.

Inpayments The receipts of (its own or foreign) money which the individuals, Firms, and governments of one nation obtain from the sale of goods and services, Remittances, government loans and grants, and capital inflows from abroad.

Input-output analysis Using an Input-output table *(see)* to examine interdependencies among different parts (sectors and industries) of the economy and to make economic forecasts and plans.

Input-output table A table which lists (along the left side) the producing sectors and (along the top) the consuming or using sectors of the economy and which shows quantitatively in each of its rows how the output of a producing sector was distributed among consuming sectors and quantitatively in each of its columns the producing sectors from which a consuming sector obtained its inputs during some period of time (a year).

Insurable risk An event, the average occurrence of which can be estimated with considerable accuracy, which would result in a loss that can be avoided by purchasing insurance.

Intended investment (*See* Planned investment.)

Intended saving (*See* Planned saving.)

Intentions *vs.* realizations Difference between what was planned and what was accomplished or done.

Interest income Income of those who supply the economy with Capital *(see)*.

Intergovernmental grant A transfer payment (gift) from the Federal government to a state or local government or from a state to a local government.

Interindustry competition Competition or rivalry between the products produced by Firms in one Industry *(see)* and the products produced by Firms in another Industry (or in other Industries).

Interlocking directorate A situation in which one or more of the members of the board of directors of one Corporation are also on the board of directors of another Corporation; and which is illegal when it tends to reduce competition among the Corporations.

Intermediate goods Goods which are purchased for resale or further processing or manufacturing during the year.

Internal economies The reduction in the cost of producing or marketing a product that results from an increase in output of the Firm; *(see)* Economies of (large) scale.

Internal growth Increase in the size of a Firm accomplished by using the firm's earnings and by selling securities to obtain the funds to construct new Plants.

Internally held public debt Public debt *(see)* owed to (United States government securities owned by) American citizens, Firms, and institutions.

International balance of payments Summary statement of the transactions which took place between the individuals, Firms, and governments of one nation and those in all other nations during a year.

International Bank for Reconstruction and Development (*See* World Bank.)

International disequilibrium The presence of a Payments surplus *(see)* or a Payments deficit *(see)*; an imbalance (inequality) between the Inpayments and Outpayments that result from the Autonomous transactions *(see)*; Financing (Accommodating) transactions *(see)* greater or less than but not equal to zero.

International equilibrium The absence of a Payments surplus *(see)* or a Payments deficit *(see)*; a balance (equality) between the Inpayments and Outpayments that result from the Autonomous transactions *(see)*; Financing (Accommodating) transactions *(see)* equal to zero.

International gold standard An international monetary system employed in the nineteenth and early twentieth centuries in which each nation defined its money in terms of a quantity of gold, converted money into gold and gold into money at the defined rate, and allowed the free importation and exportation of gold.

International Monetary Fund The international association of nations which was formed after World War II to make loans of foreign monies to nations with temporary Payments deficits *(see)* and to administer the Adjustable pegs *(see)*; and which today creates Special drawing rights *(see)*.

International monetary reserves The foreign monies and such other assets as gold and Special drawing rights *(see)* which a nation may use to settle a Payments deficit *(see)*.

Interstate Commerce Act The Federal act of 1887 which established the Interstate Commerce Commission to regulate the rates charged and to monitor the services provided by railroads.

Intrinsic value The value in the market of the metal in a coin.

Inversely related Two sets of economic data that change in opposite directions: when one increases (decreases) the other decreases (increases).

Investment Spending for Capital goods *(see)* and additions to inventories.

Investment curve A curve which shows the amounts firms plan to invest (along the vertical axis) at different income (Net national product) levels (along the horizontal axis).

Investment-demand curve A curve which shows Rates of interest (along the vertical axis) and the amount of Investment (along the horizontal axis) at each Rate of interest.

Investment-demand schedule Schedule which shows Rates of interest and the amount of Investment at each Rate of interest.

Investment in human capital The expenditures which are made to improve the health, education, and mobility (the ability to move) of workers and which increase their productivity.

Investment schedule A schedule which shows the amounts Firms plan to invest at different income (Net national product) levels.

Invisible hand The tendency of Firms and resource suppliers seeking to further their self-interests in competitive markets to further the best interest of society as a whole (the maximum satisfaction of wants).

Jamaica Agreement The agreement in 1976 among members of the International Monetary Fund to allow Managed floating exchange rates *(see)*.

JEC (*See* Joint Economic Committee.)

Joint Economic Committee Committee of Senators and Congressmen which investigates economic problems of national interest.

Joint-profit maximization The behavior of the Firms in a Collusive oligopoly *(see)* which results in the largest combined profit for the firms.

Jurisdictional strike Withholding from an employer the labor services of its members by a Labor union that is engaged in a dispute with another Labor union over which is to perform a specific kind of work for the employer.

Kennedy Round The negotiated reduction in tariff rates which took place under the provisions of the General Agreement on Tariffs and Trade *(see)* at the initiative of President John F. Kennedy and concluded in 1967.

Key currencies The foreign monies which nations universally accept from foreigners in the payment of debts, can always use to make payments to foreigners, and utilize as International monetary reserves *(see)*; the American dollar and, in the immediate post-World War II period, the British pound.

Keynesian economics The macroeconomic generalizations which are today accepted by most (but not all) economists and which lead to the conclusion that a capitalistic economy does not tend to employ its resources fully and that Fiscal policy *(see)* and Monetary policy *(see)* can be used to promote Full employment *(see)*.

Keynesianism The philosophical, ideological, and analytical views of the prevailing majority of American economists; and their employment theory and stabilization policies.

Kinked demand curve The demand curve which a noncollusive oligopolist sees for its output and which is based on the assumption that rivals will follow a price decrease and will not follow a price increase.

Labor The physical and mental talents (efforts) of people which can be used to produce goods and services.

Labor force Persons 16 years of age and older who are not in institutions and who are employed for a wage or a salary, seeking such employment, or self-employed for gain.

Labor-intensive commodity A product in the production of which a relatively large amount of Labor is employed.

Labor-Management Relations Act (*See* Taft-Hartley Act.)

Labor-Management Reporting and Disclosure Act (*See* Landrum-Griffin Act.)

Labor union A group of workers organized to advance the interests of the group (to increase wages, shorten the hours worked, improve working conditions, etc.)

Laissez faire capitalism An economic system (method of organization) in which private property, freedom of choice, and the Price system are used to determine how society will employ its resources to satisfy human wants.

Land Natural resources ("free gifts of nature") which can be used to produce goods and services.

Land-intensive commodity A product in the production of which a relatively large amount of Land is employed.

Landrum-Griffin Act The Federal Act of 1959 which regulates the elections and finances of Labor unions and guarantees certain rights to their members.

Law of capitalist accumulation The tendency seen by Marx for capitalists to react to competition from other capitalists by investing profits (Surplus value) expropriated from workers in additional and technologically superior machinery and equipment (Capital goods).

Law of demand The inverse relationship between the price and the Quantity demanded *(see)* of a good or service during some period of time.

Law of diminishing marginal utility As a consumer increases the consumption of a good or service the Marginal utility *(see)* obtained from each additional unit of the good or service decreases.

Law of diminishing returns When successive equal increments of a Variable resource *(see)* are added to the Fixed resources *(see)*, beyond some level of employment, the Marginal product *(see)* of the Variable resource will decrease.

Law of increasing cost As the amount of a product produced is increased the Opportunity *(see)*—the Marginal cost *(see)*—of producing an additional unit of the product increases.

Law of supply The direct relationship between the price and the Quantity supplied *(see)* of a good or service during some period of time.

Leakage (1) a withdrawal of potential spending from the income-expenditures stream: Saving *(see)*, tax payment and Imports *(see)*; (2) a withdrawal which reduces the lending potential of the Commercial banking system.

Leakages-injections approach Determination of the Equilibrium net national product *(see)* by finding the Net national product at which Leakages *(see)* are equal to Injections *(see)*.

Least-cost combination of resources The quantity of each resource a Firm must employ if it is to produce any output at the lowest total cost; the combination in which the ratio of the Marginal product *(see)* of a resource to its Marginal resource cost *(see)* (to its price if the resource is employed in a competitive market) is the same for all resources employed.

Least-cost technique The most inexpensive method of combining resources to produce a given amount of a product.

Legal reserve (deposit) The minimum amount which a Member bank *(see)* must keep on deposit with the Federal Reserve Bank in its district, or in Vault cash *(see)*.

Legal tender Anything that government has decreed must be accepted in payment of a debt.

(The) lending potential of an individual commercial bank The amount by which a single Commercial bank can safely increase the Money supply by making new loans to (or buying securities from) the public; equal to the Commercial bank's Excess reserve *(see)*.

(The) lending potential of the banking system The amount by which the Commercial banking system *(see)* can increase the Money supply by making new loans to (or buying securities from) the public; equal to the Excess reserve *(see)* of the Commercial banking system multiplied by the Demand deposit multiplier *(see)*.

Liability A debt with a monetary value; an amount owed by a Firm or an individual.

Liberal (democratic) socialism An Economic system (method of organization) in which there is both public and private ownership of property resources; and a mixture of Central economic planning *(see)* and the Price system determine how society will employ its scarce resources to satisfy human wants.

Libermanism The reforms in the economic system of the U.S.S.R. (suggested by Professor Yevsey Liberman) adopted in the late 1960s; the introduction of profitability as a measure of the success of an enterprise, planning from below, greater decentralization of decision making, and more autonomy for enterprise managers.

Limited liability Restriction of the maximum that may be lost to a predetermined amount; the maximum amount that may be lost by the owners (stockholders) of a Corporation is the amount they paid for their shares of stock.

Liquidity Money or things which can be quickly and easily converted into Money with little or no loss of purchasing power.

Liquidity preference theory of interest The theory in which the demand for Liquidity (the quantity of Money firms and households wish to possess) and the supply of Liquidity (the quantity of Money available) determine the equilibrium rate of interest in the economy.

Lockout The temporary closing of a place of employment and the halting of production by an employer in order to discourage the formation of a Labor union or to compel a Labor union to modify its demands.

Long run A period of time long enough to enable producers of a product to change the quantities of all the resources they employ; in which all resources and costs are variable and no resources or costs are fixed.

Long-run competitive equilibrium The price at which the Firms in Pure competition *(see)* neither obtain Economic profit nor suffer losses in the Long run and the total quantity demanded and supplied at that price; a price equal to the minimum long-run average cost of producing the product.

Long-run farm problem The tendency for the prices of agricultural products and the incomes of farmers to decline relative to prices and incomes in the rest of the economy.

Long-run supply A schedule or curve which shows the prices at which a Purely competitive industry will make various quantities of the product available in the Long run.

(The) loss-minimizing case The circumstances which result in a loss which is less than its Total fixed cost when a competitive Firm produces the output at which total profit is a maximum (or total loss is a minimum): when the price at which the firm can sell its product is less than Average total but greater than Average variable cost.

M₁ The narrowly defined Money supply; the Currency (coins and Paper money) and Demand deposits *(see)* not owned by the Federal government or banks.

M₂ The more broadly defined Money supply; equal to M_1 plus the saving and time deposits in Commercial banks and thrift institutions.

Macroeconomics The part of economics concerned with the economy as a whole; with such major aggregates as the household, business, and governmental sectors and with totals for the economy.

Macroeconomic trilogy Economic growth, Full employment *(see both)*, and price stability.

Managed floating exchange rate An Exchange rate that is allowed to change (float) to eliminate persistent Payments deficits and surpluses and is controlled (managed) to eliminate day-to-day fluctuations.

Marginal cost The extra (additional) cost of producing one more unit of output; equal to the change in Total cost divided by the change in output (and in the short run to the change in total Variable cost divided by the change in output).

Marginal labor cost The amount by which the total cost of employing Labor increases when a Firm employs one additional unit of Labor (the quantity of other resources employed remaining constant); equal to the change in the total cost of Labor divided by the change in the quantity of Labor employed.

Marginal product The additional output produced when one additional unit of a resource is employed (the quantity of all other resources employed remaining constant); equal to the change in total output divided by the change in the quantity of a resource employed; Marginal physical product.

Marginal propensity to consume Fraction of any change in Disposable income which is spent for Consumer goods; equal to the change in consumption divided by the change in Disposable income.

Marginal propensity to import The fraction of any change in income (Net national product) spent for imported goods and services; equal to the change in Imports *(see)* divided by the change in income.

Marginal propensity to save Fraction of any change in Disposable income which households save; equal to change in Saving *(see)* divided by the change in Disposable income.

Marginal resource cost The amount by which the total cost of employing a resource increases when a Firm employs one additional unit of the resource (the quantity of all other resources employed remaining constant); equal to the change in the total cost of the resource divided by the change in the quantity of the resource employed.

Marginal revenue The change to the

Total revenue of the Firm that results from the sale of one additional unit of its product; equal to the change in Total revenue divided by the change in the quantity of the product sold (demanded).

Marginal-revenue–marginal-cost approach The method which finds the total output at which Economic profit *(see)* is a maximum (or losses a minimum) by comparing the Marginal revenue *(see)* and the Marginal cost *(see)* of additional units of output.

Marginal revenue product The change in the Total revenue of the Firm when it employs one additional unit of a resource (the quantity of all other resources employed remaining constant); equal to the change in Total revenue divided by the change in the quantity of the resource employed.

Marginal tax rate The fraction of additional (taxable) income that must be paid in taxes.

Marginal utility The extra Utility *(see)* a consumer obtains from the consumption of one additional unit of a good or service; equal to the change in total Utility divided by the change in the quantity consumed.

Margin requirement The minimum percentage down payment which purchasers of shares of stock must make.

Market demand (*See* Total demand.)

Market economy An economy in which only the private decisions of consumers, resource suppliers, and business Firms determine how resources are allocated; Laissez faire capitalism *(see)*; the Price system *(see)*.

Market failure The failure of a market to bring about the allocation of resources that best satisfies the wants of society (that maximizes the satisfaction of wants).

Market for pollution rights A market in which the Perfectly inelastic supply *(see)* of the right to pollute the environment and the demand for the right to pollute would determine the price which a polluter would have to pay for the right.

Market period A period of time in which producers of a product are unable to change the quantity produced in response to a change in its price; in which there is Perfect inelasticity of supply *(see)*; and in which all resources are Fixed resources *(see)*.

Marshall Plan (*See* European Recovery Program.)

Marxian economics The Economic theories and perceptions of Karl Marx (and his followers); an explanation of the forces and contradictions that would cause the breakdown of a capitalistic economy.

Materials balance approach A method of dealing with pollution problems which compares the production of waste materials with the capacity of the environment to absorb these materials.

Medicaid A Federal program in the United States which helps to finance the medical expenses of individuals covered by the Supplemental security income *(see)* and the Aid to families with dependent children *(see)* programs.

Medicare A Federal program in the United States which provides for compulsory hospital insurance for the aged and is financed by Payroll taxes *(see)* and for low-cost voluntary insurance to help the aged pay physicians' fees.

Medium of exchange Money *(see)*; a convenient means of exchanging goods and services without engaging in Barter *(see)*; what sellers generally accept and buyers generally use to pay for a good or service.

Member bank A Commercial bank *(see)* which is a member of the Federal Reserve system; all National banks *(see)* and the State banks *(see)* which have chosen to join the system.

Member bank deposits The deposits which Member banks *(see)* have at the Federal Reserve Banks *(see)*.

Member bank reserves Member bank deposits *(see)* plus their Vault cash *(see)*.

Microeconomics The part of economics concerned with such individual units within the economy as Industries, firms, and Households; and with individual markets, particular prices, and specific goods and services.

Military-industrial complex The loose and informal group of high military officers, defense-oriented Firms, and certain members of Congress and the executive branch of the Federal government that favor the maintenance and expansion of American military power.

Minimum wage The lowest Wage (rate) employers may legally pay for an hour of Labor.

Mixed capitalism An economy in which both government and private decisions determine how resources are allocated.

Monetarism An alternative to Keynesianism *(see)*; the philosophical, ideological, and analytical views of a minority of American economists; and their employment theory and stabilization policy which stress the role of money.

Monetary multiplier (*See* Demand deposit multiplier.)

Monetary policy Changing the Money supply *(see)* in order to assist the economy to achieve a full-employment, noninflationary level of total output.

Monetary rule The rule suggested by the Monetarists *(see)*: the Money supply should be expanded each year at the same annual rate as the potential rate of growth of the Real gross national product; the supply of money should be increased steadily at from 3 to 5 percent per year.

Money Any item which is generally acceptable to sellers in exchange for goods and services.

Money capital Money available to purchase Capital goods *(see)*.

Money income The number of dollars received by an individual during some period of time.

Money market The market in which savers lend and investors borrow Money; (2) the market in which the demand for and the supply of Liquidity *(see)* determine the rate of interest.

Money supply Narrowly defined *(see)* M_1; more broadly defined *(see)* M_2.

Money wage The amount of money received by a worker per unit of time (hour, day, etc.).

Money wage rate (*See* Money wage.)

Monopolistic competition A market in which many Firms sell a Differentiated product *(see)*, into which entry is relatively easy, in which the Firm has some control over the price at which the product it produces is sold, and in which there is considerable Nonprice competition *(see)*.

Monopoly (1) A market in which the number of sellers is so few that each seller is able to influence the total supply and the price of the good or service; (2) a major industry in which a small number of Firms control all or a large portion of its output.

Monopoly capitalism A Marxian term; the ownership and control of the economy's Capital (machinery and equipment) by a small number of capitalists.

Monopsonistic competition A market in which there is a fairly large number of buyers.

Monopsony A market in which there is only one buyer of the good or service.

Moral suasion The statements, pro-nouncements, and appeals made by the Federal Reserve Banks which are intended to influence the lending policies of Commercial banks.

Most favored nation clause A clause in a trade agreement between the United States and another nation which provides that the other nation's Imports into the United States will be subjected to the lowest tariff rates levied then or later on any other nation's Imports into the United States.

MR = MC rule A Firm will maximize its Economic profit (or minimize its losses) by producing the output at which Marginal revenue *(see)* and Marginal cost *(see)* are equal—provided the price at which it can sell its product is equal to or greater than Average variable cost *(see)*.

MRP = MRC rule To maximize Economic profit (or minimize losses) a Firm should employ the quantity of a resource at which its Marginal revenue product *(see)* is equal to its Marginal resource cost *(see)*.

Multinational corporation A business Firm chartered as a Corporation in one nation which employs resources and sells its products (often through subsidiary corporations) in other nations of the world.

Multiplier The ratio of the change in the Equilibrium net national product *(see)* to the change in Investment *(see)*, or to the change in any other component of Aggregate demand or to the change in Net taxes; the number by which a change in any component of Aggregate demand or in Net taxes must be multiplied to find the resulting change in the Equilibrium net national product.

Multiplier effect The effect upon the Equilibrium net national product *(see)* of a change in Aggregate demand caused by a change in the Consumption schedule, Investment, Net taxes, Government expenditures for goods and services, or Exports (see *all*).

Mutual interdependence Situation in which a change in price (or in some other policy) by one Firm will affect the sales and profits of another Firm (or other Firms) and any Firm which makes such a change can expect the other Firm(s) to react in an unpredictable (uncertain) way.

Mutually exclusive goals Goals which conflict and cannot be achieved simultaneously.

National bank A Commercial bank *(see)* chartered by the United States government.

National income Total income earned by

resource suppliers for their contributions to the production of the Gross national product *(see)*; equal to the Gross national product minus the Nonincome charges *(see)*.

National income accounting The techniques employed to measure (estimate) the overall production of the economy and other related totals for the nation as a whole.

National Labor Relations Act *(See* Wagner Act.)

National Labor Relations Board The board established by the Wagner (National Labor Relations) Act *(see)* of 1935 to investigate unfair labor practices, issue Cease-and-desist orders *(see)*, and to conduct elections among employees to determine if they wish to be represented by a Labor union and which union they wish to represent them.

Natural monopoly An industry in which the Economies of scale *(see)* are so great that the product can be produced by one Firm at an average cost which is lower than it would be if it were produced by more than one Firm.

Near-money Financial assets, the most important of which are saving and time deposits in Commercial banks and thrift institutions, that can be readily converted into Money.

Negative income tax The proposed payment of money by the Federal government to families (or individuals) whose incomes fall below some minimum level.

Neocolonialism Domination and exploitation *(see)* of the economies in the Third World by private business Firms and governments in the United States and the industrially developed nations of Europe.

Net capital movement The difference between the real and financial investments and loans made by individuals and Firms of one nation in the other nations of the world and the investments and loans made by individuals and Firms from other nations in a nation.

Net exports Exports *(see)* minus Imports *(see)*.

Net national product Gross national product *(see)* less that part of the output needed to replace the Capital goods worn out in producing the output (Capital consumption allowances, *see*).

Net private domestic investment Gross private domestic investment *(see)* less Capital consumption allowances *(see)*; the addition to the nation's stock of Capital during a year.

Net taxes The taxes collected by govern-

ment less Government transfer payments *(see)*.

Net Worth The total Assets *(see)* less the total Liabilities *(see)* of a Firm or an individual; the claims of the owners of a firm against its total Assets.

New Economic Policy The policy introduced by the Nixon administration in 1971 which included a reduction in taxes and a 90-day freeze on wages, prices, and rents.

New Left The radical economists; those who hold the views called Radical economics *(see)*; the present-day followers of Marx and proponents of Marxian economics *(see)*.

NLRB *(See* National Labor Relations Board.)

NNP *(See* Net national product.)

Noncollusive oligopoly An Oligopoly *(see)* in which the Firms do not act together and in agreement to determine the price of the product and the output each Firm will produce or to determine the geographic area in which each Firm will sell.

Noncompeting groups Groups of workers in the economy that do not compete with each other for employment because the skill and training of the workers in one group are substantially different from those of the workers in other groups.

Nondiscretionary fiscal policy The increases (decreases) in Net taxes *(see)* which occur without Congressional action when the Net national product rises (falls) and which tend to stabilize the economy.

Nondurable good A Consumer good *(see)* with an expected life (use) of less than one year.

Nonfinancial investment An investment which does not require households to save a part of their money incomes; but which uses surplus (unproductive) labor to build Capital goods.

Nonincome charges Capital consumption allowances *(see)* and Indirect business taxes *(see)*.

Nonincome determinants of consumption and saving All influences on consumption spending and saving other than the level of Disposable income.

Noninterest determinants of investment All influences on the level of investment spending other than the rate of interest.

Noninvestment transaction An expenditure for stocks, bonds, or second-hand Capital goods.

Nonmarket transactions The production

of goods and services not included in the measurement of the Gross national product because the goods and services are not bought and sold.

Nonprice competition The means other than decreasing the prices of their products which Firms employ to attempt to increase the sale of their products; and which includes Quality competition (see), advertising, and sales promotion activities.

Nonprice determinant of demand Factors other than its price which determine the quantities demanded of a good or service.

Nonprice determinant of supply Factors other than its price which determine the quantities supplied of a good or service.

Nonproductive transaction The purchase and sale of any item that is not a currently produced good or service.

Nontariff barriers All barriers other than Tariffs (see) which nations erect to impede trade among nations: Import quotas (see), licensing requirements, unreasonable product-quality standards, unnecessary red tape in customs procedures, etc.

Nonunion shop A place of employment at which none of the employees are members of a Labor union (and at which the employer attempts to hire only workers who are not apt to join a union).

Normal good A good or service of which consumers will purchase more (less) at every price when their incomes increase (decrease).

Normal profit Payment that must be made by a Firm to obtain and retain Entrepreneurial ability (see); the minimum payment (income) Entrepreneurial ability must (expect to) receive to induce it to perform the entrepreneurial functions for a Firm; an Implicit cost (see).

Norris-LaGuardia Act The Federal act of 1932 which made it more difficult for employers to obtain Injunctions (see) against Labor unions in Federal courts and which declared that Yellow-dog contracts (see) were unenforceable.

NTBs (See Nontariff barriers.)

OASDI (See Old age, survivors, and disability insurance.)

Occupational discrimination The form of discrimination which excludes women or Blacks from certain occupations and the higher Wages paid workers in these occupations.

Old age, survivors, and disability insur-

ance The social security program in the United States which is financed by Federal payroll taxes (see) on employers and employees and which is designed to replace the Earnings lost when workers retire, die, or become unable to work.

Old Left Karl Marx and his followers during the latter part of the nineteenth and the early part of the twentieth century.

Oligopoly A market in which a few Firms sell either a Standardized or Differentiated product, into which entry is difficult, in which the Firm's control over the price at which it sells its product is limited by Mutual interdependence (see) (except when there is collusion among firms), and in which there is typically a great deal of Nonprice competition (see).

Oligopsony A market in which there are a few buyers.

Open economy An economy which both exports and imports goods and services.

Open-economy multiplier The Multiplier (see) in an economy in which some part of any increase in the income (Net national product) of the economy is used to purchase additional goods and services from abroad.

Open-market operations The buying and selling of United States government securities by the Federal Reserve Banks.

Open shop A place of employment at which the employer may hire either Labor union members or workers who are not (and need not become) members of the union.

Opportunity cost The amount of other products that must be foregone or sacrificed to produce a unit of a product.

Opportunity-cost doctrine (See Alternative-cost doctrine.)

Optimum population The population size at which the real output per person (real output per worker or Average product, see) is a maximum.

"Other things being equal" assumption Assuming that the factors other than those being considered are constant.

Outpayments The expenditures of (its own or foreign) money which the individuals, Firms, and governments of one nation make to purchase goods and services, for Remittances, for government loans and grants, and capital outflows abroad.

Output effect The impact which a change in the price of a resource has upon the output a Firm finds it most profitable to produce and the resulting effect upon the quantity of the resource (and the quantities of other resources) employed by the Firm after the consequences of the Substitution effect *(see)* have been taken into account (eliminated).

Paper money Pieces of paper used as a Medium of exchange *(see)*; in the United States, Federal reserve notes *(see)* and treasury currency.

Paradox of thrift The attempt of society to save more results in the same amount or less Saving.

Parity concept The notion that year after year a given output of a farm product should enable a farmer to acquire a constant amount of nonagricultural goods and services.

Parity price The price at which a given amount of an agricultural product would have to be sold to enable a farmer to obtain year after year the money income needed to purchase a constant total quantity of nonagricultural goods and services.

Partial equilibrium analysis The study of equilibrium prices and equilibrium outputs or employments in a particular market which assumes prices, outputs, and employments in the other markets of the economy remain unchanged.

Participatory socialism A form of socialism in which individuals would take part in the process by which the decisions that affect them are made and would be able to control their own lives and activities.

Partnership An unincorporated business Firm owned and operated by two or more persons.

Payments deficit The Outpayments that result from the Autonomous transactions *(see)* exceeding the Inpayments from these transactions.

Payments surplus The Inpayments that result from the Autonomous transactions *(see)* exceeding the outpayments from these transactions.

Payroll tax A tax levied on employers of Labor equal to a percentage of all or part of the wages and salaries paid by them; and on employees equal to a percentage of all or part of the wages and salaries received by them.

Peace dividend The additional output of nonmilitary goods and services an economy would be able to produce if it were to reduce (or eliminate) its production of military goods and services.

Peak pricing Setting the price charged for the use of a facility (the User charge, *see*) or for a good or service at a higher level when the demand for the use of the facility or for the good or service is greater and at a lower level when the demand for it is less.

Pentagon capitalism The contention of Seymour Melman that the Department of Defense in the United States behaves like the management of a large Corporation and the producers of military goods like its subsidiaries.

Perfect elasticity of demand A change in the Quantity demanded requires no change in the price of the commodity; buyers will purchase as much of a commodity as is available at a constant price.

Perfect elasticity of supply A change in the Quantity supplied requires no change in the price of the commodity; sellers will make available as much of the commodity as buyers will purchase at a constant price.

Perfect inelasticity of demand A change in price results in no change in the Quantity demanded of a commodity; the Quantity demanded is the same at all prices.

Perfect inelasticity of supply A change in price results in no change in the Quantity supplied of a commodity; the Quantity supplied is the same at all prices.

Personal consumption expenditures The expenditures of Households for Durable and Nondurable consumer goods and services.

Personal distribution of income The manner in which the economy's Personal or Disposable income is divided among different income classes or different households.

Personal income The income, part of which is earned and the remainder of which is unearned, available to resource suppliers and others before the payment of Personal taxes *(see)*.

Personal income tax A tax levied on the taxable income of individuals (households and unincorporated firms).

Personal saving The Personal income of households less Personal taxes *(see)* and Personal consumption expenditures *(see)*; Disposable income less Personal consumption expenditures; that part of Disposable income not spent for Consumer goods *(see)*.

Phillips curve A curve which shows the relationship between the Unemployment rate *(see)* (on the horizontal axis) and the annual rate of increase in the price level (on the vertical axis).

Planned economy An economy in which

only government determines how resources are allocated.

Planned investment The amount which business firms plan or intend to invest.

Planned saving The amount which Households plan or intend to save (not spend for Consumer goods).

Plant A physical establishment (Land and Capital) which performs one or more of the functions in the production (fabrication and distribution) of goods and services.

P = **MC rule** A Firm in Pure competition *(see)* will maximize its Economic profit *(see)* or minimize its losses by producing the output at which the price of the product is equal to Marginal cost *(see)*, provided that price is equal to or greater than Average variable cost *(see)* in the short run and equal to or greater than Average (total) cost *(see)* in the long run.

Policy economics The formulation of courses of action to bring about desired results or to prevent undesired occurrences (to control economic events).

Political fragmentation The existence within the larger urban (metropolitan) areas of a great number of separate political entities (states, counties, cities, etc.) which have their own governments.

Post hoc, ergo propter hoc **fallacy** Incorrectly reasoning that when one event precedes another the first event is the cause of the second.

Poverty An existence in which the basic needs of an individual or family exceed the means available to satisfy them.

Precautionary demand for money The amount of money Households and Firms wish to have to protect themselves against unforeseen losses of income and unforeseen expenses; a demand for money that is directly related to the Net national product.

Preferential hiring A practice (often required by the provisions of a contract between a Labor union and an employer) which requires the employer to hire union members so long as they are available and to hire nonunion workers only when union members are not available.

Premature inflation The Inflation *(see)* which results from an increase in Aggregate demand and which occurs before the economy has reached Full employment *(see)*.

Price The quantity of money (or of other goods and services) paid and received for a unit of a good or service.

Price break The termination (breakdown) of the Cartel *(see)* or the informal price-setting arrangement employed by the Firms in an Oligopoly *(see)* and the resulting decline in the price of the product caused by a recession of secret price cutting.

Price ceiling A legally established maximum price for a good or service.

Price-decreasing effect The effect in a competitive market of a decrease in Demand or an increase in Supply upon the Equilibrium price *(see)*.

Price discrimination The selling of a product (at a given time) to different buyers at different prices when the price differences are not justified by differences in the cost of producing the product for the different buyers; and a practice made illegal by the Clayton Act *(see)* and the Robinson-Patman Act *(see)*.

Price elasticity of demand The ratio of the percentage change in Quantity demanded of a commodity to the percentage change in its price; the responsiveness or sensitivity of the quantity of a commodity buyers demand to a change in the price of the commodity.

Price elasticity of supply The ratio of the percentage change in the Quantity supplied of a commodity to the percentage change in its price; the responsiveness or sensitivity of the quantity sellers of a commodity supply to a change in the price of the commodity.

Price guidepost The price charged by an Industry for its product should increase by no more than the increase in the Unit labor cost *(see)* of producing the product.

Price-increasing effect The effect in a competitive market of an increase in Demand or a decrease in Supply upon the Equilibrium price *(see)*.

Price index A ratio (expressed as a percentage) of prices in a Given year *(see)* to prices in the Base year *(see)*.

Price leadership An informal method which the Firms in an Oligopoly *(see)* may employ to set the price of the product they produce: one firm (the leader) is the first to announce a change in price and the other firms (the followers) quickly announce identical (or similar) changes in price.

Price maker A seller (or buyer) of a commodity that is able to affect the price at which the commodity sells by changing the amount it sells (buys).

Price-profits table (*See* Profits-payoff table.)

Price rigidity A tendency for the price of a product to remain unchanged (inflexible) even when the Demand for or the cost of producing the product changes.

Price support The minimum price which government allows sellers to receive for a good or service; a price which is legally established or maintained minimum price.

Price system All the product and resource markets of the economy and the relationships among them; a method which allows the prices determined in these markets to allocate the economy's scarce resources and to communicate and coordinate the decisions made by consumers, business firms, and resource suppliers.

Price taker A seller (or buyer) of a commodity that is unable to affect the price at which a commodity sells by changing the amount it sells (or buys).

Price-wage flexibility Changes in the prices of products and in the Wages paid to workers; the ability of prices and Wages to rise or to fall.

Priority principle The assignment of priorities to the planned outputs of the various sectors and industries in the economy of the U.S.S.R. and the shifting of resources, when bottlenecks develop, from low- to high-priority sectors and industries to assure the fulfillment of the production targets of the latter sectors and industries.

Private good A good or service to which the Exclusion principle *(see)* is applicable; and which is provided by privately owned firms to those who are willing to pay for it.

Private property The right of private persons and Firms to obtain, own, control, employ, dispose of, and bequeath Land, Capital, and other Assets.

Private sector The Households and business Firms of the economy.

Product differentiation Physical or other differences between the products produced by different Firms which result in individual buyers preferring (so long as the price charged by all sellers is the same) the product of one Firm to the products of the other Firms.

Production possibilities curve A curve which shows the different combinations of two goods or services that can be produced in a Full-employment *(see)*, Full-production *(see)* economy in which the available supplies of resources and technology are constant.

Production possibilities table A table which shows the different combinations of two goods or services that can be produced in a Full-employment *(see)*, Full-production *(see)* economy in which the available supplies of resources and technology are constant.

Product market A market in which Households buy and Firms sell the products they have produced.

Profit *(See)* Economic profit and Normal profit; without an adjective preceeding it, the income of those who supply the economy with Entrepreneurial ability *(see)* or Normal profit.

(The) profit-maximizing case The circumstances which result in an Economic profit *(see)* for a (competitive) Firm when it produces the output at which Economic profit is a maximum or losses a minimum: when the price at which the Firm can sell its product is greater than the Average (total) cost of producing it.

Profit-maximizing combination of resources The quantity of each resource a Firm must employ if its Economic profit *(see)* is to be a maximum or its losses a minimum; the combination in which the Marginal revenue product *(see)* of each resource is equal to its Marginal resource cost *(see)* (to its price if the resource is employed in a competitive market).

Profits-payoff table A table which shows along its top the possible prices one oligopolistic Firm might charge for its product, along the left side the possible prices a second oligopolistic Firm might charge for its product, and the resulting profit (payoff) to each of the two firms for every possible combination of prices they might charge.

Profit-push inflation The inflation that results when Firms with market power increase the prices they charge in order to increase their Economic profits *(see)*.

Progressive oligopoly An Oligopoly *(see)* in which the Firms have lowered their costs by making technological advances, increased the Demands for their products by improving them and by their want-creating activities, and, as a result, have expanded their outputs and lowered the prices they charge.

Progressive tax A tax such that the tax rate increases as the taxpayer's income increases and decreases as income decreases.

Proletariate The workers; the working class; those without the machinery and equipment needed to produce goods and services in an industrial society.

Property tax A tax on the value of property (Capital, Land, stocks and bonds, and other Assets) owned by Firms and Households.

Proportional tax A tax such that the tax rate remains constant as the taxpayer's income increases and decreases.

Proprietors' income The net income of the owners of unincorporated Firms (proprietorships and partnerships).

Prosperous industry (See Expanding industry.)

Protective tariff A Tariff (see) designed to protect domestic producers of a good from the competition of foreign producers.

Public debt The amount owed by the Federal government to the owners of United States government securities.

Public Law 480 The Federal law which permits less developed nations to purchase surplus American agricultural products and to pay for them with their own monies (rather than with dollars).

Public sector The part of the economy that contains all its governments; government.

Public utility A Firm which produces an essential good or service, has obtained from a government the right to be the sole supplier of the good or service in an area, and is regulated by that government to prevent the abuse of its monopoly power.

Pure competition (1) A market in which a very large number of Firms sells a Standardized product (see), into which entry is very easy, in which the individual seller has no control over the price at which the product sells, and in which there is no Nonprice competition (see); (2) a market in which there is a very large number of buyers.

Pure inflation The Inflation (see) which results from an increase in Aggregate demand when the economy has reached Full employment (see).

Pure monopoly A market in which one Firm sells a unique product (one for which there are no close substitutes), into which entry is blocked, in which the Firm has considerable control over the price at which the product sells, and in which Nonprice competition (see) may or may not be found.

Pure profit (See Economic profit.)

(The) pure rate of interest (See The rate of interest.)

Pursuit and escape theory An explanation of the stability of labor's relative share of the National income (see) in which Labor tries to obtain (pursues) higher money wages by decreasing the Economic profits of capitalists and capitalists avoid (escape) a reduction in their profits by increasing the productivity of labor or the prices they charge for products.

Qualitative control (See Qualitative credit controls.)

Qualitative credit controls The techniques which the Federal Reserve Banks employ to change the availability of certain specific types of credit (loans).

Quality competition A change in the characteristics (quality) of the product produced by a Firm which is intended to change the quantity of the product the firm can sell.

Quantitative control (See Quantitative credit controls.)

Quantitative credit controls The techniques which the Federal Reserve Banks employ to change the size of the nation's Money supply (see); Open-market operations (see), a change in the Reserve ratio (see), and a change in the Discount rate (see).

Quantity-decreasing effect The effect in a competitive market of a decrease in Demand or a decrease in Supply upon the Equilibrium quantity (see).

Quantity demanded The amount of a good or service buyers wish (or a buyer wishes) to purchase at a particular price during some period of time.

Quantity-increasing effect The effect in a competitive market of an increase in Demand or an increase in Supply upon the Equilibrium quantity (see).

Quantity supplied The amount of a good or service sellers offer (or a seller offers) to sell at a particular price during some period of time.

Quasi-public bank A bank which is privately owned but governmentally (publicly) controlled; each of the Federal Reserve banks.

Quasi-public good A good or service to which the Exclusion principle (see) could be applied, but which has such a large Spillover benefit (see) that government sponsors its production to prevent an underallocation of resources.

Radical economics The modern version of Marxian economics (see) which criticizes the methods of orthodox economists, contends that large monopolistic Corporations dominate American capitalism and government, argues that the expansion of capitalism produces society's major problems, and advocates some form of socialism.

R&D Research and development; activities undertaken to bring about Technological progress.

Rate of exchange The price paid in one's own money to acquire one unit of a foreign money; the rate at which the money of one nation is exchanged for the money of another nation.

Rate of interest Price paid for the use of Money or for the use of Capital; interest rate.

Rational An adjective that describes the behavior of any individual who consistently does those things that will enable him to achieve the declared objective of the individual; and that describes the behavior of a consumer who uses money income to buy the collection of goods and services that yields the maximum amount of Utility *(see)*.

Rationing function of price The ability of price in a competitive market to equalize Quantity demanded and Quantity supplied and to eliminate shortages and surpluses by rising or falling.

Real capital *(See* Capital.)

Real gross national product Gross national product *(see)* adjusted for changes in the price level; Gross national product in a year divided by the Price index *(see)* for that year.

Real income The amount of goods and services which an individual can purchase with his or her Money income *(see)*.

Realized investment *(See* Actual investment.)

Realized saving *(See* Actual saving.)

Real wage The amount of goods and services a worker can purchase with his or her Money wage *(see)*; the purchasing power of the Money wage.

Real wage insurance plan A proposal to exempt workers and employers who voluntarily obey stated wage and price guideposts from some of their social security (payroll) taxes and to prevent the erosion of workers' Real income *(see)* by reimbursing them with tax credits when the cost of living rises by more than some specified amount.

Real wage rate *(See* Real wage.)

Recessionary gap The amount by which Aggregate demand *(see)* must increase to increase the Net national product to the full-employment-without-inflation level.

Reciprocal selling The practice in which

one Firm agrees to buy a product from a second Firm and the second Firm agrees in return to buy another product from the first Firm.

Reciprocal Trade Agreements Act of 1934 The Federal act which gave the President the authority to negotiate agreements with foreign nations and lower American tariff rates by up to 50 percent if the foreign nations would reduce tariff rates on American goods and which incorporated Most favored nation clauses *(see)* in the agreements reached with these nations.

Refinancing the public debt Paying owners of maturing United States government securities with money obtained by selling new securities or with new securities.

Regressive tax A tax such that the tax rate decreases (increases) as the taxpayer's income increases (decreases).

Regulatory agency An agency (commission or board) established by the Federal or a state government to control for the benefit of the public the prices charged and the services offered (output produced) by a Public utility *(see)*.

Remittance A gift or grant; a payment for which no good or service is received in return.

Rental income Income received by those who supply the economy with Land *(see)*.

Reopening clause A clause in an agreement between an employer and a Labor union that requires each to give the other sixty days' notice of its intent to modify or terminate the agreement.

Required reserve (deposit) *(See* Legal reserve (deposit).)

Reserve bank credit The credit which the Federal Reserve Banks extend to the United States government (by buying its securities) and to Member banks *(see)* by making loans to them; equal to the sum of the United States government securities and loans to Member banks appearing as Assets on the Balance sheet *(see)* of the Federal Reserve Banks.

Reserve ratio The specified minimum percentage of its deposit liabilities which a Member bank *(see)* must keep on deposit at the Federal Reserve Bank in its district, or in Vault cash *(see)*.

Resource market A market in which Households sell and Firms buy the services of resources.

Restrictive oligopoly An Oligopoly *(see)* in which Firms (with given demand and cost schedules) restrict (limit) their outputs to be able to charge higher prices and to obtain greater Economic profits *(see).*

Retiring the public debt Reducing the size of the Public debt *(see)* by paying money to owners of maturing United States government securities.

Revenue sharing The distribution by the Federal government of some of its tax revenues to state and local governments.

Revenue tariff A Tariff *(see)* designed to produce income for the (Federal) government.

Right-to-work law A law which has been enacted in twenty states that makes it illegal in those states to require a worker to join a Labor union in order to retain his or her job with an employer.

Robinson-Patman Act The Federal act of 1936 which amended the Clayton Act *(see)*; and which outlawed quantity discounts to large retailers not justified by the actual cost economies of selling to them and prohibited retailers from selling at prices which were intended to eliminate competitors.

Roundabout production The construction and use of Capital *(see)* to aid in the production of Consumer goods *(see).*

Rule of 70 A method by which the number of years it will take for the price level to double can be calculated: divide 70 by the annual rate of inflation.

Sales tax A tax levied on expenditures for a broad group of products.

Saving Disposable income not spent for Consumer goods *(see)*; not spending for consumption; equal to Disposable income minus Personal consumption expenditures *(see).*

Saving schedule Schedule which shows the amounts Households plan to save (plan not to spend for Consumer goods, *see*) at different levels of Disposable income.

Say's Law The (discredited) macroeconomic generalization that the production of goods and services (supply) creates an equal Aggregate demand for these goods and services.

Scarce resources The fixed (limited) quantities of Land, Capital, Labor, and Entrepreneurial ability *(see all)* which are never sufficient to satisfy the wants of humans because their wants are unlimited.

SDRs *(See* Special Drawing Rights.)

Seasonal variation An increase or decrease during a single year in the level of economic activity caused by a change in the season.

Secondary boycott The refusal of a Labor union to buy or to work with the products produced by another union or a group of nonunion workers.

Secular trend The expansion or contraction in the level of economic activity over a long period of years.

Selective credit controls *(See* Qualitative credit controls.)

Self-interest What each Firm, property owner, worker, and consumer believes is best for itself and seeks to obtain.

Self-limiting adjustment A change which eliminates the reason or motive for the change as the change occurs.

Seniority The length of time a worker has been employed by an employer relative to the lengths of time the employer's other workers have been employed; the principle which is used to determine which workers will be laid off when there is insufficient work for them all and which will be rehired when more work becomes available.

Separation of ownership and control Difference between the group that owns the Corporation (the stockholders) and the group that manages it (the directors and officers) and between the interests (goals) of the two groups.

Sherman Act The Federal antitrust act of 1890 which made monopoly, restraint of trade, and attempts, combinations, and conspiracies to monopolize or to restrain trade criminal offenses; and allowed the Federal government or injured parties to take legal action against those committing these offenses.

Short run A period of time in which producers of a product are able to change the quantity of some but not all of the resources they employ; in which some resources—the Plant *(see)*—are Fixed resources *(see)* and some are Variable resources *(see)*; in which some costs are Fixed costs *(see)* and some are Variable costs *(see)*; a period of time too brief to allow a Firm to vary its plant capacity but long enough to permit it to change the level at which the plant capacity is utilized; a period of time not long enough to enable Firms to enter or to leave an Industry *(see).*

Short-run competitive equilibrium The price at which the total quantity of a product supplied in the Short run *(see)* by a purely competitive industry and the total quantity of the product demanded are equal and which is equal to or greater than the Average variable cost *(see)* of producing the product; and the quantity of the product demanded and supplied at this price.

Short-run farm problem The sharp year-to-year changes in the prices of agricultural products and in the incomes of farmers.

Simple multiplier The Multiplier *(see)* in an economy in which government collects no Net taxes *(see)*, there are no Imports *(see)*, and Investment *(see)* is independent of the level of the level of income (Net national product); equal to one divided by the Marginal propensity to save *(see)*

Single-tax movement The attempt of a group which followed the teachings of Henry George to eliminate all taxes except one which would tax all Rental income *(see)* at a rate of 100 percent.

Smithsonian Agreement The agreement reached at a meeting of ten leading trading nations in 1971 at the Smithsonian Institution (in Washington, D.C.) which changed Exchange rates to correct the overvaluation of the American dollar.

Social accounting (*See* National income accounting.)

Social good A good or service to which the Exclusion principle *(see)* is not applicable; and which is provided by government if it yields substantial benefits to society.

Socially optimum price The price of a product which results in the most efficient allocation of an economy's resources and which is equal to the Marginal cost *(see)* of the last unit of the product produced.

Social point of view Looking at the effects of a policy or course of action upon the economy as a whole rather than upon a particular group within the economy.

Soil bank program A program in which the Federal government made payments to farmers who took land away from the production of crops which were sold for cash and used the land either to grow cover crops or for timber.

Sole proprietorship An unincorporated business firm owned and operated by a single person.

Special Drawing Rights Credit created by the International Monetary Fund *(see)* which a member of the IMF may borrow to finance a Payments deficit *(see)* or to increase its International monetary reserves *(see)*; "paper gold."

Special-interest effect Effect on public decision making and the allocation of resources in the economy when government promotes the interests (goals) of small groups to the detriment of society as a whole.

Specialization The use of the resources of an individual, a Firm, a region, or a nation to produce one or a few goods and services.

Speculative demand for money The amount of their wealth Firms and Households wish to hold in Money; the amount of Money they wish to hold as a Store of value *(see)*; the quantity of money demanded at different Rates of interest; the demand for Money that is inversely related to the Rate of interest.

Spillover A benefit or cost associated with the consumption or production of a good or service which is obtained by or inflicted without compensation upon a party other than the buyer or seller of the good or service; *(see)* Spillover benefit and Spillover cost.

Spillover benefit The benefit obtained neither by producers nor by consumers of a product but without compensation by a third party (society as a whole).

Spillover cost The cost of producing a product borne neither by producers nor by consumers of the product but without compensation by a third party (society as a whole).

SSI (*See* Supplemental security income.)

Stabilization policy dilemma The use of monetary and fiscal policy to decrease the Unemployment rate increases the rate of inflation and the use of monetary and fiscal policy to decrease the rate of inflation increases the Unemployment rate.

Stagflation Inflation accompanied by stagnation in the rate of growth of output and a high unemployment rate in the economy; simultaneous increases in both the price level and the Unemployment rate.

Standard of value A means of measuring the relative worth (of stating the prices) of goods and services.

Standardized product A product such that buyers are indifferent to the seller from whom they purchase it so long as the price charged by all sellers is the same; a product such that all units of the product are perfect substitutes for each other (are identical).

State and Local Fiscal Assistance Act

The Federal act of 1972 (extended in 1976), commonly known as the Revenue Sharing Act, which provided for Unrestricted grants from the Federal to state and local governments and a formula for the allocation of funds.

State bank A Commercial bank chartered to engage in the business of banking by a state government.

State ownership The ownership of property (Land and Capital) by government (the state); in the U.S.S.R. by the central government (the nation).

State economy (1) An economy in which Net private domestic investment *(see)* is equal to zero—Gross private domestic investment *(see)* is equal to the Capital consumption allowances *(see)*; (2) an economy in which the supplies of resources, technology, and the tastes of consumers do not change and in which, therefore, the economic future is perfectly predictable and there is no uncertainty.

Store of value Any Asset *(see)* or wealth set aside for future use.

Strike The withholding of their labor services by an organized group of workers (a Labor union).

Strikebreaker A person employed by a Firm when its employees are engaged in a strike against the firm.

Structural unemployment Unemployment caused by changes in the structure of demand for Consumer goods and in technology; workers who are unemployed either because their skills are not demanded by employers or because they lack sufficient skills to obtain employment.

Substitutability The ability of consumers to use one good or service instead of another to satisfy their wants and of Firms to use one resource instead of another to produce products.

Substitute goods Goods or services such that there is a direct relationship between the price of one and the Demand for the other; when the price of one falls (rises) the Demand for the other decreases (increases).

Substitution effect (1) The effect which a change in the price of a Consumer good would have upon the relative expensiveness of that good and the resulting effect upon the quantity of the good a consumer would purchase if the consumer's Real income *(see)* remained constant; (2) the effect which a change in the price of a resource would have upon the quantity of the resource employed by a firm if the firm did not change its output.

Superior good (*See* Normal good.)

Supermultiplier The Multiplier *(see)* when Investment is directly related to the level of income (Net national product); when the Investment curve *(see)* is positively sloped.

Supplemental security income A program Federally financed and administered which provides a uniform nationwide minimum income for the aged, blind, and disabled who do not qualify for benefits under the Old age, survivors, and disability insurance *(see)* and Unemployment insurance *(see)* programs in the United States.

Supply curve A curve which shows the amounts of a good or service sellers (a seller) will offer to sell at various prices during some period of time.

Supply factor An increase in the available quantity of a resource, an improvement in its quality, or an expansion of technological knowledge which makes it possible for an economy to produce a greater output of goods and services.

Supply schedule A schedule which shows the amounts of a good or service sellers (a seller) will offer to sell at various prices during some period of time.

Support price (*See* Price support.)

Surplus value A Marxian term; the amount by which the value of a worker's daily output exceeds his daily Wage; the output of workers appropriated by Capitalists as profit.

Sympathy strike Withholding from an employer the labor services of its members by a Labor union that does not have a disagreement with the employer but wishes to assist another Labor union that does have a disagreement with the employer.

Taft-Hartley Act The Federal act of 1947 which marked the shift from government sponsorship to government regulation of Labor unions and which contained provisions that fall into four major categories.

Target price A minimum price for a basic agricultural product guaranteed to farmers by having the Federal government pay them a subsidy equal to the amount by which the Target price exceeds the market price.

Tariff A tax imposed (only by the Federal government in the United States) on an imported good.

Tax incidence The income or purchasing

power which different persons and groups lose as a result of the imposition of a tax after Tax shifting *(see)* has occurred.

Tax shifting The transfer to others of all or part of a tax by charging them a higher price or by paying them a lower price for a good or service.

Technological determinism The doctrine (or belief) that modern technology requires a small number of large Firms to realize the available productive efficiencies—to obtain all the Economies of scale *(see)*—and to achieve the most rapid rate of technological progress (that comes only from a high level of expenditures for R&D *(see)*.

Technology The body of knowledge that can be used to obtain goods and services from Economic resources.

Terms of trade The rate at which units of one product can be exchanged for units of another product; the Price *(see)* of a good or service; the amount of one good or service that must be given up to obtain one unit of another good or service.

The economizing problem Society's human wants are unlimited but the resources available to produce the goods and services that satisfy wants are limited (scarce); the inability of any economy to produce unlimited quantities of goods and services.

Theory of games An explanation of the behavior of the Firms in an Oligopoly *(see)* which is based upon and similar to the behavior of participants in games that involve moves and countermoves.

Theory of public choice Generalizations that describe how government (the Public sector) makes decisions for the use of economic resources.

The **rate of interest** The Rate of interest *(see)* which is paid solely for the use of Money over an extended period of time and which excludes the charges made for the riskiness of the loan and its administrative costs; and which is approximately equal to the rate of interest paid on the long-term and virtually riskless bonds of the United States government.

Third World The semideveloped and underdeveloped nations; nations other than the industrially advanced market economies and the centrally planned economies.

Tight money policy Contracting the nation's Money supply *(see)*.

Till money (*See* Vault cash.)

Token money Coins which have a Face value *(see)* greater than their Intrinsic value *(see)*.

Total cost The sum of Fixed cost *(see)* and Variable cost *(see)*.

Total demand The Demand schedule *(see)* or the Demand curve *(see)* of all buyers of a good or service.

Total-receipts–total-cost approach The method which finds the output at which Economic profit *(see)* is a maximum or losses a minimum by comparing the total receipts (revenue) and the total costs of a Firm at different outputs.

Total revenue The total number of dollars received by a Firm (or Firms) from the sale of a product; equal to the total expenditures for the product produced by the Firm (or Firms); equal to the quantity sold (demanded) multiplied by the price at which it is sold—by the Average revenue *(see)* from its sale.

Total-revenue test A test to determine whether Demand is Elastic *(see)*, Inelastic *(see)*, or of Unitary elasticity *(see)* between any two prices: demand is elastic (inelastic, unit elastic) if the Total revenue *(see)* of sellers of the commodity increases (decreases, remains constant) when the price of the commodity falls; or Total revenue decreases (increases, remains constant) when its price rises.

Total supply The Supply schedule *(see)* or the Supply curve *(see)* of all sellers of a good or service.

Trade controls Tariffs *(see)*, exports subsidies, Import quotas *(see)*, and other means a nation may employ to reduce Imports *(see)* and expand Exports *(see)* in order to eliminate a Payments deficit *(see)*.

Trade Expansion Act of 1962 The Federal act which gave the President the authority to reduce by reciprocal agreements containing Most favored nation clauses *(see)* with other nations the tariff on certain commodities by up to 50 percent and to eliminate Tariffs *(see)* on certain other commodities.

Trade Reform Act of 1974 The Federal act which enabled the United States to participate in the Geneva round *(see)* of trade negotiations.

Trading possibilities line A line which shows the different combinations of two products an economy is able to obtain (consume) when it specializes in the production of one product and trades (exports) this product to obtain the other product.

Transactions demand for money The amount of Money Households and Firms wish to have to bridge the gap between the receipt of income and the making of expenditures, to use as a Medium of exchange *(see)*; a demand for Money that is directly related to the volume of transactions in the economy (to the Net national product).

Turnover tax The tax added to the accounting price of a good in the U.S.S.R. to determine the price at which the quantity of the good demanded will equal the quantity of the good it has been decided to produce, the rate of taxation being higher on relatively scarce and lower on relatively abundant goods.

Tying agreement A promise made by a buyer when allowed to purchase a patented product from a seller that it will make all of its purchases of certain other (unpatented) products from the same seller; and a practice forbidden by the Clayton act *(see)*.

Underdeveloped nation A nation in which per capita Real income (output) is low.

Underemployment Failure to produce the maximum amount of goods and services that can be produced from the resources employed; failure to achieve Full production *(see)*.

Undistributed corporate profits The after-tax profits of corporations not distributed as dividends to stockholders; corporate or business saving.

Unemployment Failure to use all available Economic resources to produce goods and services; failure of the economy to employ fully its Labor force *(see)*.

Unemployment compensation *(See* Unemployment insurance.)

Unemployment insurance The insurance program which in the United States is financed by state Payroll taxes *(see)* on employers and makes income available to workers who are unable to find jobs.

Unemployment rate The percentage of the Labor force *(see)* unemployed at any time.

Unfair competition Any practice which is employed by a Firm either to eliminate a rival or to block the entry of a new Firm into an Industry and which society (or a rival) believes to be an unacceptable method of achieving these ends.

Uninsurable risk An event, the occurrence of which is uncontrollable and unpredictable, which would result in a loss that cannot be avoided by purchasing insurance and must be assumed by an entrepreneur *(see* Entrepreneurial ability); sometimes called "uncertainty."

Union shop A place of employment at which the employer may hire either Labor union members or workers who are not members of the union but who must become members within a specified period of time or lose their jobs.

Unitary elasticity The Elasticity coefficient *(see)* is equal to one; the percentage change in the quantity (demanded or supplied) is equal to the percentage change in price.

Unit labor cost Labor costs per unit of output; equal to the Money wage rate *(see)* divided by the Average product *(see)* of labor.

Unlimited liability Absence of any limit on the maximum amount that may be lost by an individual and that the individual may become legally required to pay; the maximum amount that may be lost and that a sole proprietor or partner may be required to pay.

Unlimited wants The insatiable desire of consumers (people) for goods and services that will give them pleasure of satisfaction.

Unprosperous industry *(See* Declining industry.)

Unrestricted grants An Intergovernmental grant *(see)* which does not require the government receiving the grant to provide matching funds (to contribute its own funds to pay a part of the cost of the program for which the grant was received); a "block" grant.

Urban sprawl The movement of people and firms from the central city and into the suburbs of a metropolitan area and the resulting expansion of the geographic area of the metropolitan area.

User charge A price paid by those who use a facility which covers the full cost of using the facility.

Utility The want-satisfying power of a good or service; the satisfaction or pleasure a consumer obtains from the consumption of a good or service (or from the consumption of a collection of goods and services).

Utility-maximizing rule To obtain the greatest Utility *(see)* the consumer should allocate his Money income so that the last dollar spent on each good or service yields the same Marginal utility *(see)*; so that the Marginal utility of each good or service divided by its price is the same for all goods and services.

Value added The value of the product sold by a Firm less the value of the goods (materials) purchased and used by the Firm to produce the product; and equal to the revenue which can be used for Wages, rent, interest, and profits.

Value judgment Opinion of what is desirable or undesirable; belief regarding what ought or ought not to be (regarding what is right or just and wrong or unjust).

Variable cost A cost which in total increases (decreases) when the firm increases (decreases) its output; the cost of Variable resources (see).

Variable resource Any resource employed by a firm the quantity of which can be increased or decreased (varied).

Vault cash The Currency (see) a bank has in its safe (vault) and cash drawers.

Velocity of money The number of times per year the average dollar in the Money supply (see) is spent for Final goods (see).

Vertical combination A group of Plants (see) engaged in different stages of the production of a final product and owned by a single Firm (see).

Volunteer army An armed force whose members have enlisted voluntarily and have not been conscripted.

Wage The price paid for Labor (for the use or services of Labor, see) per unit of time (per hour, per day, etc.).

Wage and salary supplements Payments made by employers of Labor into social insurance and private pension, health, and welfare funds for workers; and a part of the employer's cost of obtaining Labor.

Wage differential The difference between the Wage (see) received by one worker or group of workers and that received by another worker or group of workers.

Wage guidepost Wages (see) in all industries in the economy should increase at an annual rate equal to the rate of increase in the Average product (see) of Labor in the economy.

Wage-price controls A Wage-price policy (see) that legally fixes the maximum amounts by which Wages (see) and prices may be increased in any period of time.

Wage-price guideposts A Wage-price policy (see) that depends upon the voluntary cooperation of Labor unions and business firms.

Wage-price policy Government policy that attempts to alter the behavior of Labor unions and business firms in order to make their Wage and price decisions more nearly compatable with the goals of Full employment and stable prices.

Wage-push inflation The inflation that results when Labor unions demand and business firms grant higher Wages to workers.

Wage rate (See Wage.)

Wages The income of those who supply the economy with Labor (see).

Wagner Act The Federal act of 1938 which established the National Labor Relations Board (see), guaranteed the rights of Labor unions to organize and to bargain collectively with employers, and listed and prohibited a number of unfair labor practices by employers.

War industry The group of business Firms and United States government agencies that employ resources to produce national defense.

Webb-Pomerene Act The Federal act of 1918 which permitted American exporters to form export trade associations that would be exempt from the antitrust acts—the Sherman and the Clayton Acts (see).

Wheeler-Lea Act The Federal act of 1938 which amended the Federal Trade Commission Act (see) by prohibiting and giving the commission power to investigate unfair and deceptive acts or practices in commerce (false and misleading advertising and the misrepresentation of products).

(The) "will to develop" Wanting economic growth strongly enough to change from old to new ways of doing things.

Workable competition Competition among Firms which does not require a large number of Firms to regulate their behavior effectively.

World bank A bank supported by 127 nations which lends (and guarantees loans) to underdeveloped nations to assist them to grow; formally, the International Bank for Reconstruction and Development.

Yellow-dog contract The (now illegal) contract in which an employee agrees when he accepts employment with a firm that he will not become a member of a Labor union while employed by the Firm.

ZEG Zero economic growth; no Economic growth (see).

ZPG Zero population growth; no increase in the population of an economy (in the population of the world).